Directions for Use

Part 1 of this Index is in dictionary form with author, title, and subject entries in one alphabet. Part 2 is a list of the collections indexed. Part 3 is a directory of publishers. The following directions apply to Part 1.

Author Entry. This entry gives the full name of the author, years of birth and death, whenever ascertainable, title of story, author and title of collection or collections in which the story is found. It may be recognized by the boldface type, *not* in capital letters.

Sample entry:

> **Faulkner, William,** 1897-
> Spotted horses
> Gordon, C. and Tate, A. eds. House of
> fiction

This means that the short story by William Faulkner "Spotted horses" appears in the collection entitled "House of fiction" edited by C. Gordon and A. Tate. For fuller information about "House of fiction" consult the "List of Collections Indexed," under Gordon, C.

Title Entry. This entry is used primarily to identify the author under whose name the full information will be given. Only the first word of each title entry is in boldface type.

Sample entry:

> **Spotted** horses. Faulkner, W.

Subject Entry. All stories in this Index dealing in whole or in part with a particular subject are listed under that subject. Such entries are in capital letters, in boldface type.

Sample entry:

> **HORSES**
> Faulkner, W. Spotted horses

In some collections all the stories may deal with the same subject. In such cases the entry under that subject indicates the editor or author and title of the collection, followed by the number of stories, rather than the listing of the individual stories.

Sample entry:

> **HORSES**
> Foote, J. T. Hoofbeats; 13 stories

The phrase "13 stories" identifies this type of entry.

SHORT STORY INDEX

Supplement 1950-1954

SHORT STORY INDEX

Supplement 1950-1954

AN INDEX TO 9,575 STORIES TO 549 COLLECTIONS

Compiled by

DOROTHY E. COOK
ESTELLE A. FIDELL

NEW YORK
THE H. W. WILSON COMPANY
1956

Published 1956
Printed in the U.S.A.

Library of Congress Card No. (53-8991)

PREFACE

This supplement to the SHORT STORY INDEX covers the years 1950-1954 and indexes 9,575 stories in 549 collections. In style it basically follows the pattern set up by the compilers for the basic volume of the SHORT STORY INDEX, but with certain changes which the publishers hope will represent improvements.

The innovations in this Supplement are three-fold:

1. **Type:** There has been a substitution of larger 8 point type for the former 6 point type.

2. **Capitalization:** To avoid confusion in distinguishing subjects from authors, the use of all-capital letters in this volume is reserved for subject entries only; authors' names are given in boldface with conventional capitalization.

3. **Directory of Publishers:** A list of the publishers from whom the books indexed may be obtained has been added following the "List of Collections Indexed".

It is hoped that the next supplement covering the years 1955-1959 will be published in the Fall of 1960.

Sincere thanks are extended to various members of the staff who assisted in the work, especially to Mrs. Loretta Devine and Mrs. Agnes Bryceland.

August 1956

DOROTHY E. COOK
ESTELLE A. FIDELL

41432

Directions for Use

Part 1 of this Index is in dictionary form with author, title, and subject entries in one alphabet. Part 2 is a list of the collections indexed. Part 3 is a directory of publishers. The following directions apply to Part 1.

Author Entry. This entry gives the full name of the author, years of birth and death, whenever ascertainable, title of story, author and title of collection or collections in which the story is found. It may be recognized by the boldface type, *not* in capital letters.

Sample entry:

> **Faulkner, William,** 1897-
> Spotted horses
> Gordon, C. and Tate, A. eds. House of
> fiction

This means that the short story by William Faulkner "Spotted horses" appears in the collection entitled "House of fiction" edited by C. Gordon and A. Tate. For fuller information about "House of fiction" consult the "List of Collections Indexed," under Gordon, C.

Title Entry. This entry is used primarily to identify the author under whose name the full information will be given. Only the first word of each title entry is in boldface type.

Sample entry:

> **Spotted** horses. Faulkner, W.

Subject Entry. All stories in this Index dealing in whole or in part with a particular subject are listed under that subject. Such entries are in capital letters, in boldface type.

Sample entry:

> **HORSES**
> Faulkner, W. Spotted horses

In some collections all the stories may deal with the same subject. In such cases the entry under that subject indicates the editor or author and title of the collection, followed by the number of stories, rather than the listing of the individual stories.

Sample entry:

> **HORSES**
> Foote, J. T. Hoofbeats; 13 stories

The phrase "13 stories" identifies this type of entry.

SHORT STORY INDEX

Supplement 1950-1954

PART I

Author, title, subject index to short stories

ABANDONED CHILDREN. See Found-
lings; Orphans
ABANDONED SHIPS. See Ships, Aban-
doned
ABDUCTION. See Disappearances; Kid-
napping
Abduction of Abner Greer. Bond, N. S.
Abdullah, Achmed, 1881-1945
McCarthy hunts peace
American boy (Periodical) American
boy anthology
ABEL (BIBLICAL CHARACTER)
Feild, B. How Abel slew Cain
Abernathy, Robert, 1924-
Heritage
Conklin, G. ed. Omnibus of science fic-
tion
Peril of the blue world
Wollheim, D. A. comp. Flight into space
Able to Zebra. Tucker, W.
ABNORMAL CHILDREN. See Children,
Abnormal and backward
ABOLITION OF SLAVERY. See Slavery
ABORTION
Lowry, R. J. C. For girlhood and for
love
About my sons. Ferrone, J. R.
About Shorty. Gellhorn, M. E.
Above the clouds. Sommerfield, J.
Above the river. Williams, W. C.
Abraham. Kierkegaard, S. A.
ABRAHAM, THE PATRIARCH
Kierkegaard, S. A. Abraham
Abrahams, William
Interpretation of dreams
Story (Periodical) Story; no. 2
Abraham's glory. Davies, R.
Abramovich, Solomon Jacob. See Abramo-
witz, Shalom Jacob
Abramowitz, Shalom Jacob, 1836-1917
The calf
Howe, I. and Greenberg, E. eds. Treas-
ury of Yiddish stories
Same as: Little calf
The exchange
Leftwich, J. ed. Yisröel. 1952 ed.
How the Czar fooled Montefiore
Ausubel, N. ed. Treasury of Jewish
humor
Little calf
Ausubel, N. ed. Treasury of Jewish
humor
Same as: The calf

Absalom. Kuttner, H.
Absence of Mr Glass. Chesterton, G. K.
Absent hat pin. Hitchens, D. B.
ABSENT-MINDEDNESS
Munro, H. H. Louise
Thurber, J. Secret life of Walter Mitty
Absent-mindedness in a parish choir. Hardy,
T.
Absolution. Fitzgerald, F. S. K.
Absolutism. Johnston, N. F.
The academy. Asch, S.
ACADIANS IN LOUISIANA
Jackson, C. T. Horse of Hurricane Reef
Accident. Christie, A. M.
The accident. Williams, W. C.
ACCIDENTAL SHOOTING. See Hunting
—Accidents
ACCIDENTS
Aldrich, T. B. Marjorie Daw
Bennett, P. Fugitive from the mind
Boyle, K. Maiden, maiden
Ervine, St J. G. The mountain
Greene, G. Basement room
Hopkinson, H. T. Mountain madness
Humphrey, W. Man with a family
O'Donovan, M. Vanity
Phillips, A. Presence in the grove
Poe, E. A. Angel of the odd
Young, E. H. The stream
See also Accidents, Industrial Aero-
nautics—Accidents; Automobiles—Ac-
cidents; Hunting—Accidents
ACCIDENTS, AIRPLANE. See Aeronau-
tics—Accidents
ACCIDENTS, INDUSTRIAL
Di Donato, P. Christ in concrete
According to the landmarks. Claudy, C. H.
According to their lights. Porter, W. S.
Account rendered. Harvey, W. F.
ACCOUNTANTS
Collier, J. Midnight blue
Acheson, Edward Goodrich, 1856-1931
Big shot
This week magazine. This week's short-
short stories
Achievement of the cat. Munro, H. H.
Ackerman, Forrest J.
Mute question
Crossen, K. F. ed. Adventures in to-
morrow
ACROBATICS. See Acrobats and acro-
batism

Aegean storm. Cicellis, K.
Æpyornis Island. Wells, H. G.
AERONAUTICS
Jensen, P. ed. Fireside book of flying stories; 19 stories
Marcus, P. Tip the green earth
Verral, C. S. Itch to win
Wells, H. G. Argonauts of the air
Wells, H. G. Filmer
    See also Air pilots

Accidents
Aumonier, S. Source of irritation
La Farge, O. Old century's river
Newhouse, E. Close your eyes
Sansom, W. Small world

Flights
Angell, R. Flight through the dark
Coward, N. P. This time to-morrow
De Vries, P. We don't know
Doyle, Sir A. C. Horror of the heights
Gellhorn, M. E. Miami-New York
Jackson, C. R. The outlander
Litten, F. N. Blackout over Cleveland
AERONAUTICS, MILITARY
Nordhoff, C. B. and Hall, J. N. School for combat
O'Connell, R. B. You'll never mind
    See also European War, 1914-1918—Aerial operations; World War, 1939-1945—Aerial operations
Aesop. Simak, C. D.
AESTHETICS. See Esthetics
Affair at St Albans. Sass, H. R.
Affair at the Victory Ball. Christie, A. M.
Affair of honor. Hutchins, M. P. M.
Affair of the wayward jeep. Mauldin, W. H.
Affair on Jacklight Creek. Hendryx, J. B.
L'affaire foul tip. Brookhouser, F.
AFRICA
Conrad, J. Heart of darkness
Hemingway, E. Snows of Kilimanjaro
Waldeck, T. J. Igongo elephants

Native races
Elliott, G. P. Faq'
Fletcher, I. White leopard
Hughes, L. African morning
Lessing, D. M. Old Chief Mshlanga
AFRICA, NORTH
Bowles, P. F. By the water
Bowles, P. F. Delicate prey
Bowles, P. F. Tea on the mountain
AFRICA, SOUTH
Annixter, P. pseud. The lynching
Cloete, S. Silence of Mr Prendegast
Gordimer, N. Soft voice of the serpent, and other stories; 21 stories
Krige, U. The coffin
Krige, U. The dream
Lessing, D. M. This was the Old Chief's country; 10 stories
Marshall, E. Hill people

African morning. Hughes, L.
AFRICAN TRIBES. See Africa—Native races; also names of individual tribes, e.g. Kafirs (Africa people); Zulus; etc.

After all I did for Israel. Levin, M.

After Holbein. Wharton, E. N. J.
After-hours visitor. Tazewell, C.
After-image. Caldwell, E.
AFTER LIFE. See Future life
After school. Erskine, L. Y.
After the hay-makin'. Schwarz, C. J.
After the storm. Hemingway, E.
After the theatre. Chekhov, A. P.
After twenty years. Porter, W. S.
After you, my dear Alphonse. Jackson, S.
Afternoon. Sansom, W.
Afternoon hunt with the Tantivity hounds. Surtees, R. S.
Afternoon in the life of Father Burrell. Lieberman, R.
Afternoon miracle. Porter, W. S.
Afternoon of a faun. Ferber, E.
Afternoon sun. Willingham, C.
Afterthought. Fyfe, H. B.
Against orders. Claudy, C. H.
Age of love. Kjelgaard, B.
Age of romance. Bentham, J.
AGED. See Old age
Agee, James, 1909-
Mother's tale
    Best American short stories, 1953
Agnon, Samuel Joseph, 1888-
Jack-of-all-trades
    Ausubel, N. ed. Treasury of Jewish humor
Jewish cat
    Ausubel, N. ed. Treasury of Jewish humor
Sabbathai
    Leftwich, J. ed. Yisröel. 1952 ed.
Story of the cantor
    Ausubel, N. ed. Treasury of Jewish humor
AGNOSTICS. See Atheism
AGRICULTURE. See Farm life
Ah the university. Collier, J.
Ah, woe is me. Gordimer, N.
Ah Wong. Travers, P. L.
Ahasuerus. See Xerxes I, King of Persia
The **Aherns.** Corkery, D.
A-hunting of the deer. Warner, C. D.
Aiken, Conrad Potter, 1889-
The anniversary
    Aiken, C. P. Short stories
Bachelor supper
    Aiken, C. P. Short stories
Bow down, Isaac!
    Aiken, C. P. Short stories
Bring! Bring!
    Aiken, C. P. Short stories
By my troth, Nerissa!
    Aiken, C. P. Short stories
Dark city
    Aiken, C. P. Short stories
The disciple
    Aiken, C. P. Short stories
Farewell! Farewell! Farewell!
    Aiken, C. P. Short stories
Field of flowers
    Aiken, C. P. Short stories

Aiken, Conrad P.—*Continued*
Fish supper
Aiken, C. P. Short stories
Gehenna
Aiken, C. P. Short stories
Hello, Tib
Aiken, C. P. Short stories
Hey, Taxi!
Aiken, C. P. Short stories
I love you very dearly
Aiken, C. P. Short stories
Impulse
Aiken, C. P. Short stories
Last visit
Aiken, C. P. Short stories
Life isn't a short story
Aiken, C. P. Short stories
Man alone at lunch
Aiken, C. P. Short stories
Mr Arcularis
Aiken, C. P. Short stories
Fabricant, N. D. and Werner, H. eds.
World's best doctor stories
Night before prohibition
Aiken, C. P. Short stories
Pair of Vikings
Aiken, C. P. Short stories
Round by round
Aiken, C. P. Short stories
Silent snow, secret snow
Aiken, C. P. Short stories
Burrell, J. A. and Cerf, B. A. eds. An-
thology of famous American stories
Schorer, M. ed. The story
Smith and Jones
Aiken, C. P. Short stories
Spider, spider
Aiken, C. P. Short stories
State of mind
Aiken, C. P. Short stories
Strange moonlight
Aiken, C. P. Short stories
Ludwig, J. B. and Poirier, W. R. eds.
Stories, British and American
Thistledown
Aiken, C. P. Short stories
Your obituary, well written
Aiken, C. P. Short stories
Blodgett, H. W. ed. Story survey

AIR PILOTS
Bellah, J. W. Fear
Dodson, D. B. The let-down
Harvey, W. F. Flying out of Mrs Bar-
nard Hollis
Jackson, C. R. The outlander
Jenkins, W. F. Search in the mist
Knapp, S. E. Clipped wings
Litten, F. N. Blackout over Cleveland
Litten, F. N. Winner's money
Mowat, F. Woman he left to die
Redman, B. R. Ground mist
Wells, H. G. Little mother up the
Mörderberg
Woolley, R. The pupil
Youd, C. Christmas tree

AIR RAIDS
Sansom, W. Building alive
Sansom, W. Journey into smoke

AIR TRAVEL. See Aeronautics—Flights

AIRCRAFT CARRIERS. See Airplane carriers

AIRPLANE ACCIDENTS. See Aeronautics—Accidents

AIRPLANE CARRIERS
Beach, E. L. Archerfish
AIRPLANE RACING
Litten, F. N. Winner's money
AIRPLANES
Accidents
See Aeronautics—Accidents
AIRPLANES, HOSPITAL
Bates, H. E. Time expired
AIRPLANES, MILITARY
Moore, W. Flying Dutchman
Stocker, J. S. I rode a tornado
See also Aeronautics, Military
Ajax of Ajax. Pearson, M.
Akeley, Carl Ethan, 1864-1926
Elephant
Andrews, R. C. ed. My favorite stories
of the great outdoors
AKIBA BEN JOSEPH, 50-132
Cohn, E. Legend of Rabbi Akiba

Akutagawa, Ryūnosuke, 1892-1927
The dragon
Akutagawa, R. Rashomon, and other
stories
In a grove
Akutagawa, R. Rashomon, and other
stories
Kesa and Morito
Akutagawa, R. Rashomon, and other
stories
The martyr
Akutagawa, R. Rashomon, and other
stories
Rashomon
Akutagawa, R. Rashomon, and other
stories
Yam gruel
Akutagawa, R. Rashomon, and other
stories

ALABAMA
Bierce, A. Occurrence at Owl Creek
bridge

Alabarce, Arturo Souto. See Souto Alabarce,
Arturo

Alabaster, Mary Ellen
The tide
Stanford short stories, 1951

Alabaster hand. Munby, A. N. L.

Aladdin. Arabian nights

Alarcon, Pedro Antonio de, 1833-1891
Guardian angel
Fremantle, A. J. ed. Mothers
The prophecy
De Onís, H. ed. Spanish stories and
tales

Alas, Leopoldo, 1852-1901
Cock of Socrates
De Onís, H. ed. Spanish stories and
tales

Alas, all thinking! Bates, H.

ALASKA
Annixter, P. pseud. Kadiak
Carrighar, S. Marooned children
Cooke, A. A. One missing
Davis, A. L. The Klondiker
Muir, J. An adventure with a dog and a
glacier

Albee, George Sumner
Pink organdie
Story (Periodical) Story; no. 2
The top
Story (Periodical) Story; no. 3

Albert knows his place. Moore, M.

Albino and Darling Jill. Caldwell, E.

Albrizio, Gene
The bereft
Southern review. Anthology of stories from the Southern review

Alch, Alan Howard
Night to howl
Story (Periodical) Story; no. 3

Alchemist's secret. Gordon, A.

Alcoholic case. Fitzgerald, F. S. K.

ALCOHOLISM
Aswell, J. R. Shadow of evil
Calisher, H. In Greenwich there are many gravelled walks
Felder, D. F. Purple hat
Fitzgerald, F. S. K. Babylon revisited
Maugham, W. S. The pool
Parker, D. R. Big blonde
Russell, J. Jetsam
Walsh, M. Sword of Yung Lo
See also Drunkards

Aldrich, Bess (Streeter) 1881-1954
Another brought gifts
Cooper, A. C. ed. Modern short stories
Bid the tapers twinkle
Lohan, R. and Lohan, M. eds. New Christmas treasury
Day of retaliation
Aldrich, B. S. The Bess Streeter Aldrich reader
The dreams are real
Brentano, F. ed. The word lives on
How far is it to Hollywood?
Aldrich, B. S. The Bess Streeter Aldrich reader
Juno's swans
Aldrich, B. S. The Bess Streeter Aldrich reader
Welcome home, Hal!
Aldrich, B. S. The Bess Streeter Aldrich reader
Will the romance be the same?
Aldrich, B. S. The Bess Streeter Aldrich reader

Aldrich, Thomas Bailey, 1836-1907
How we astonished the Rivermouthians
Davis, C. B. ed. Eyes of boyhood
Marjorie Daw
Burrell, J. A. and Cerf, B. A. eds. Anthology of famous American stories
Cuff, R. P. ed. American short story survey
Fabricant, N. D. and Werner, H. eds. World's best doctor stories
Lamb, L. ed. Family book of best loved short stories
Struggle for life
Christ, H. I. and Shostak, J. eds. Short stories

Aleichem, Sholom, pseud. See Rabinowitz, Shalom

Alex acquires some dust. Hendryx, J. B.

Alexander, Charles, 1897-
As a dog should
Bloch, M. ed. Favorite dog stories

Alexander, David
And on the third day
Mystery Writers of America, inc. Maiden murders

Alexander, Sidney, 1912-
Part of the act
Heilman, R. B. ed. Modern short stories

Alexander, W.
One leg too many
Conklin, G. ed. Big book of science fiction

Alexander Botts goes underground. Upson, W. H.

Alexander Botts vs. the income tax. Upson, W. H.

Alexander the bait. Klass, P.

Alexander to the park. Johnson, J. W.

ALFRED THE GREAT, KING OF ENGLAND, 849-901
Bolton, I. M. Saint for Wessex

Algebra. Yushkevich, S. S.

ALGONQUIAN INDIANS
Garner, H. One, two, three little Indians

Algren, Nelson, 1909-
Captain is impaled
Prize stories of 1950
He swung and he missed
Ribalow, H. U. ed. World's greatest boxing stories
How the devil came down Division Street
Best of the Best American short stories
So help me
Ribalow, H. U. ed. These your children

Ali Baba and the forty horse-power. Bergengruen, W.

Alias All-American. Chute, B. J.

Alibi Ike. Lardner, R. W.

ALIBIS
Fischer, B. Nobody's business

Alice's pint. Davies, R.

Alien. Del Rey, L.

The alien. McConnell, W.

Alien corn. Maugham, W. S.

ALIENS
Boyle, K. Wanderer

Alive—alive oh! Sitwell, Sir O. bart.

All alone again. Cooke, A. A.

All brothers are men. Beck, W.

All gold cañon. London, J.

All good Bems. Brown, F.

All Hallows. De La Mare, W. J.

All horse players die broke. Runyon, D.

All in one day. Florence, G. L.

All kind of pep. Caldwell, E.

All of God's children got shoes. Schoenfeld, H.

All on a winter's night. Strong, A.

All problems are simple. Seager, A.

All roads. Farnsworth, M.

All saints. Bowen, E.

All that glitters. Pratt, F. and De Camp, L. S.
All that glitters. Propes, A.
All the dead pilots. Faulkner, W.
All the little jokers. Parker, J. R.
All the time in the world. Clarke, A. C.
All the town's talking. Schulberg, B. W.
All the way to the moon. Quentin, P. pseud.
All the years of her life. Callaghan, M.
All they do is talk. Newhouse, E.
All things are nothing to me. Farrell, J. T.

Allan, Glenn, 1901-
Kentucky line-up
    Creamer, J. B. comp. Twenty-two stories about horses and men

Allan, Ted, 1916-
Lies my father told me
    Weaver, R. and James, H. eds. Canadian short stories

Allan Franklin. Rossiter, H. D.

Allard, Pat
Lucky star
    Furman, A. L. ed. Teen-age horse stories

Allegheny. Foote, J. T.

ALLEGORIES
Benét, S. V. Johnny Pye and the Fool-killer
Cohn, E. Remains of virtue
Forster, E. M. Other side of the hedge
Gide, A. P. G. Theseus
Hawthorne, N. Celestial railroad
Hawthorne, N. Maypole of Merry Mount
Kafka, F. Hunger-artist
Kafka, F. Hunter Gracchus
Lagerkvist, P. F. Myth of mankind
Peretz, I. L. Pious cat
Quiroga, H. The fatherland
Sansom, W. From the water junction
Simak, C. D. The answers

Allen, Edward, and Kelley, Francis Beverly, 1905-
Public enemies
    Fenner, P. R. comp. Elephants, elephants, elephants

ALLEN, ETHAN, 1737-1789
Allen, M. P. In the name of the Great Jehovah and the Continental Congress

Allen, Grant, 1848-1899
Pausodyne
    Derleth, A. W. ed. Beyond time & space

Allen, Hervey, 1889-1949
Surgery at Aquila
    Fabricant, N. D. and Werner, H. eds. World's best doctor stories

Allen, James Lane, 1849-1925
King Solomon of Kentucky
    Summers, H. S. ed. Kentucky story

Allen, Margaret
Her gift
    Elmquist, R. M. ed. Fifty years of Christmas

Allen, Merritt Parmelee, 1892-1954
Camel into eagle
    Fenner, P. R. comp. Giggle box
Chariots away
    Boy's life (Periodical) Boys' life Adventure stories

In the name of the Great Jehovah and the Continental Congress
    Fenner, P. R. comp. Yankee Doodle
Second race
    Fenner, P. R. comp. Indians, Indians, Indians
Two chests of treasure
    Fenner, P. R. comp. Pirates, pirates, pirates
    Furman, A. L. ed. Teen-age sea stories
Yoo hoo! Mudhen!
    Fenner, P. R. comp. Fun! Fun! Fun!

Allen High's youth problem. Erdman, L. G.

ALLERGY
La Farge, O. No, my darling daughter

ALLIGATORS
Annixter, P. pseud. Dragon rider

Allingham, Margery, 1904-
The Lieabout
    Mystery Writers of America, inc. Crooks' tour
One morning they'll hang him
    Queen, E. pseud. ed. Queen's awards: 5th ser.
Tall story
    Queen, E. pseud. ed. Ellery Queen's awards: 9th ser.

ALMANACS
Bester, A. Of time and Third Avenue

Almond tree. De La Mare, W. J.

Almost like dead. Goldman, A.

Alone in shark waters. Kruse, J.

Alone Men. McHugh, V.

Alone the stranger passes Komroff, M.

Alpert, Hollis
The change
    Seventeen (Periodical) The Seventeen reader

ALPS
Bruhl, E. Great match
Maupassant, G. de. The inn

ALPS, FRENCH
Boyle, K. Wanderer
Knowlton, E. Petite première in the Mont Blanc Massif

ALPS, SWISS
Montague, C. E. Action

ALSACE
Daudet, A. Last class

Alson, Lawrence, 1920-
Lieutenant's laundry
    American vanguard, 1950

The altar. Sheckley, R.

Altar at midnight. Kornbluth, C. M.

Altar cloth. Lyon, K.

Altar of the dead. James, H.

Alte Bobbe. Angoff, C.

Always a bridesmaid. Kober, A.

Always good for a belly laugh. Glen, E.

Always Reddy. Henry, M.

Always trust a cop. Cohen, O. R.

Am I blue? Ullman, J. R.

Amateur night in Harlem. Davis, G.

AMATEUR THEATRICALS
Gordimer, N. The amateurs
Grimson, M. S. When TV came to the backwoods
Munro, H. H. Peace offering
  See also College and school drama

The **amateurs**. Gordimer, N.

Amazing lady. Clark, A. A. G.

The **Amazon**. Leskov, N. S.

The **ambassadors**. White, W. A. P.

Ambassadors from Venus. Crossen, K. F.

The **ambassadress**. Auchincloss, L.

AMBITION
Anderson, S. The egg
Fitzgerald, F. S. K. Winter dreams
Grimson, M. S. Eureca cottage

Ambition. Bade, W. L.

Ambitious guest. Hawthorne, N.

Ambitious violet. Gibran, K.

AMBULANCES
Porter, W. S. Comedy in rubber
Stuart, J. Competition at Slush Creek

AMBULANCES, AIR. See Airplanes, Hospital

American dream girl Farrell, J. T.

American girl looks at Europe. Grimson, M. S.

AMERICAN INDIANS. See Indians of Central America; Indians of Mexico; Indians of North America; Indians of South America; also names of individual tribes or nations

American me. Griffith, B. W.

AMERICAN SOLDIERS. See Soldiers, American

Americanization of Shadrach Cohen. Block, R. E.

Americans all. Foley, M.

AMERICANS IN AFRICA
Ullman, J. R. Between you and I

AMERICANS IN BALI
Benson, T. Funeral feast

AMERICANS IN BRAZIL
Seager, A. Quitandinha

AMERICANS IN ENGLAND
Arlen, M. Gentleman from America
Collins, W. Miss Bertha and the Yankee
James, H. Author of Beltraffio
Montague, M. P. England to America
Salinger, J. D. For Esmé—with love and squalor

AMERICANS IN EUROPE
Auchincloss, L. The ambassadress
Grimson, M. S. American girl looks at Europe
James, H. Daisy Miller
Lawrence, D. H. Things
McCarthy, M. T. The cicerone
Maugham, W. S. Wash-tub

AMERICANS IN FIJI ISLANDS
Michener, J. A. Mynah birds
Vandercook, J. W. Pretending makes it so

AMERICANS IN FRANCE
Boyd, T. A. Responsibility
Brookhouser, F. Not that kind of a deal
Farrell, J. T. Fritz
Farrell, J. T. I want to go home
Farrell, J. T. Love affairs in Paris
Fitzgerald, F. S. K. Babylon revisited
James, H. Bundle of letters
Miller, M. B. Ruth and Irma
Wharton, E. N. J. Madame de Treymes

AMERICANS IN GERMANY
Boyle, K. Soldier ran away
Putnam, C. Old acrobat and the ruined city
Schmidt, C. F. Ancestral voices
Stafford, J. Echo and the nemesis
Stafford, J. The nemesis
Stafford, J. Winter's tale

AMERICANS IN GREAT BRITAIN. See Americans in England

AMERICANS IN HAITI
Rattner, J. Haitian incident

AMERICANS IN ITALY
Bunin, I. A. Gentleman from San Francisco
De La Roche, M. Quartet
Lowry, R. J. Law and order
Maugham, W. S. Woman of fifty
Miller, A. Monte Saint Angelo
Tennyson, H. Home leave

AMERICANS IN JAPAN
Christopher, R. Jishin
Conrad, R. E. Call of the street
Wincelberg, S. The conqueror

AMERICANS IN KOREA
Winter, A. B. Party dress

AMERICANS IN MEXICO
Gordon, E. E. Value of the dollar
Quentin, P. pseud. Love comes to Miss Lucy

AMERICANS·IN NEW GUINEA   .
Ullman, J. R. Am I blue?

AMERICANS IN NEW ZEALAND
Michener, J. A. Until they sail

AMERICANS IN PALESTINE
Lewisohn, L. Holy Land

AMERICANS IN PARIS. See Americans in France

AMERICANS IN PORTUGAL
Saroyan, W. The Assyrian

AMERICANS IN RUSSIA
McKelway, St C. Russian who wanted to be friends
Maugham, W. S. Mr Harrington's washing

AMERICANS IN SHANGHAI
Patterson, R. Babe

AMERICANS IN THE SOUTH SEA ISLANDS
Maugham, W. S. Fall of Edward Barnard
Michener, J. A. Mr Morgan

AMERICANS IN THE WEST INDIES
Goldsmith, G. Tender to the ship

Amethyst cross. Freeman, K.

AMISH MENNONITES. See Mennonites

Anderson, Sherwood—*Continued*
I want to know why
Burrell, J. A. and Cerf, B. A. eds. Anthology of famous American stories
Ludwig, J. B. and Poirier, W. R. eds. Stories, British and American
Shaw, H. and Bement, D. Reading the short story
I'm a fool
Best of the Best American short stories, 1915-1950
Burrell, J. A. and Cerf, B. A. eds. Anthology of famous American stories
Davis, R. G. ed. Ten modern masters
Day, A. G. ed. Greatest American short stories
Millett, F. B. ed. Reading fiction
"Queer"
Forester, N. ed. American poetry and prose. 1952 ed.
Seeds
West, R. B. and Stallman, R. W. eds. Art of modern fiction
Sophistication
Blodgett, H. W. ed. Story survey
Schramm, W. L. ed. Great short stories
Waite, H. O. and Atkinson, B. P. eds. Literature for our time

Andreev, Leonid Nikolaevich, 1871-1919
Love and betrayal
Selden, R. ed. Ways of God and men
On the day of the crucifixion
Brentano, F. ed. The word lives on

Andrews, Mary Raymond (Shipman) 1865?-1936
Counsel assigned
Scribner treasury
Perfect tribute
Scribner treasury

Andrew's father. Krimsky, J.

Andreyev, Leonid. See Andreev, Leonid Nikolaevich

ANDROS, SIR EDMUND, 1637-1714
Hawthorne, N. Gray champion

Andy Munroe's funeral. Davis, S. P.

ANESTHETICS
Harvey, W. F. Account rendered

Angel of the odd. Poe, E. A.

Angel was a Yankee. Benét, S. V.

Angel with purple hair. Paul, H.

Angela. Farrell, J. T.

Angela was eighteen. Wakelee, L.

Angelic angleworm. Brown, F.

Angell, Roger, 1920-
Fight through the dark
Best American short stories, 1951

ANGELS
Benét, S. V. Angel was a Yankee
Collier, J. Fallen star
Collier, J. Hell hath no fury
Connolly, M. Reason for Ann
De La Mare, W. J. The trumpet

Angel's egg. Pangborn, E.

Angels in Chayder. Golding, L.

Angels in the jets. Bixby, J.

Angharad. Ready, W. B.

Angie Lee's fortune. Winslow, T. S.

ANGLING. See Fishing

Angram folly. Bentley, P. E.

Anglo-Saxons of Auxierville. Stuart, J.

Angoff, Charles, 1902-
Alte Bobbe
Ribalow, H. U. ed. This land, these people
Where did yesterday go?
Best American short stories, 1950

Angry lions, lazy lions. Baro, G.

Angus MacAuliffe and the gowden tooch. Tanner, C. R.

Animal-cracker plot. De Camp, L. S.

ANIMAL INTELLIGENCE
Williams, J. H. Elephant intelligence

ANIMAL SOUNDS. See Sound production of animals

ANIMAL TRAINERS. See Animals—Training

ANIMALS
Bottome, P. Man and beast; 5 stories
Harris, J. C. Wonderful Tar-Baby story
Heinlein, R. A. Jerry was a man
Kipling, R. Elephant's child
Lesser, M. Black Eyes and the daily grind
Seton, E. T. Wild animals I have known; 8 stories
Williams, R. Head-hunters
See also names of individual animals

Training
Bottome, P. Caesar's wife's ear
Bottome, P. Henry
Mukerji, D. G. Kari the elephant
Richards, D. Training Alice and Congo
Waldeck, T. J. Evil one

Treatment
Buck, F. Elephant midget
Lang, D. An elephant never forgets

ANIMALS, IMAGINARY. See Animals, Mythical

ANIMALS, MYTHICAL
Cartmill, C. Huge beast
De Camp, L. S. Blue giraffe
Harvey, W. F. Beast with five fingers
Samachson, J. Country doctor
Waldo, E. H. The hurkle is a happy beast
Wellman, M. W. Dhoh
Wells, H. G. Sea raiders
Williams, R. Head hunters
See also Dragons

ANIMALS, PREHISTORIC
De Camp, L. S. Employment

Ann Lee's. Bowen, E.

Anna was bad. Boxer, J.

ANNAM. See Indo-China, French

ANNAPOLIS NAVAL ACADEMY. See United States. Naval Academy, Annapolis

Anne's terrible good nature. Lucas, E. V.

Annett, Ronald Ross, 1895-
Gentle like a cyclone
Creamer, J. B. comp. Twenty-two stories about horses and men
Dennis, W. ed. Palomino and other horses

Annett, William S. 1928-
The relic
Weaver, R. and James, H. eds. Canadian short stories
The **anniversary.** Aiken, C. P.
Annixter, Paul, pseud.
Brought to cover
Annixter, P. pseud. Brought to cover
Dragon rider
Annixter, P. pseud. Brought to cover
First ally
Annixter, P. pseud. Brought to cover
Hunting coat
Annixter, P. pseud. Brought to cover
Kadiak
Annixter, P. pseud. Brought to cover
Ketch dog
Annixter, P. pseud. Brought to cover
Last lobo
Annixter, P. pseud. Brought to cover
Loose tiger
Annixter, P. pseud. Brought to cover
The lynching
Annixter, P. pseud. Brought to cover
Old Hook 'n' Eye
Annixter, P. pseud. Brought to cover
Orchids and crocodiles
Annixter, P. pseud. Brought to cover
Secret of Coon Castle
Annixter, P. pseud. Brought to cover
The swordsman
Annixter, P. pseud. Brought to cover
White possum
Annixter, P. pseud. Brought to cover
With the greatest of ease
Annixter, P. pseud. Brought to cover
Anomaly of the empty man. White, W. A. P.
The **anonymous.** Clark, W. Van T.
Another American tragedy. Collier, J.
Another brought gifts. Aldrich, B. S.
Another part of the sky. Gordimer, N.
Another quiet bye with Mr Jorrocks. Surtees R. S.
Another worry. Cooke, A. A.
Ansky, S. pseud. See Rappoport, Solomon
Answer. Brown, F.
Answer. Stubbs, H. C.
Answer is nothing. Barker, A. L.
The **answers.** Simak, C. D.
Ant and the eye. Oliver, C.
Ant and the grasshopper. Maugham, W. S.
ANTARCTIC REGIONS
Heard, G. Wingless victory
See also Arctic regions
ANTHROPOLOGISTS
Brackett, L. Last days of Shandakor
Gardner, M. Island of five colors
Michener, J. A. The fossickers
ANTI-GRAVITATION. See Gravity
ANTIPATHIES. See Prejudices and antipathies
ANTIQUE DEALERS
De La Mare, W. J. The talisman
ANTISEMITISM. See Jews

ANTS
Beebe, W. Home town of the army ants
Jenkins, W. F. Doomsday deferred
Wells, H. G. Empire of the ants
The **ants.** Snow, W. W.
Any more at home like you? Oliver, C.
Any pain, peril or danger. Claudy, C. H.
Any way race. Person, W. T.
Anything new on the strangler? Ullman, J. M.
APACHE INDIANS
DeVries, M. Stage to Yuma
Apage Satanas. Koestler, A.
APARTMENT HOUSES
Cheever, J. The superintendent
Horwitz, J. The burial
Horwitz, J. The conspirators
Horwitz, J. Generations of man
The **ape.** Pritchett, V. S.
APES
Kafka, F. Report to an academy
Pritchett, V. S. The ape
See also Baboons; Chimpanzees; Gorillas; Monkeys; Orang-utangs
The **apostate.** Milburn, G.
Apostolides, Alex, 1923- See Clifton, M. jt. auth.
Apparition of Mrs Veal. Defoe, D.
APPARITIONS. See Ghosts; Hallucinations and illusions
Appearance and reality. Maugham, W. S.
Appell, George C.
Calculated risk
Argosy (Periodical) Argosy Book of adventure stories
APPENDECTOMY. See Appendicitis
APPENDICITIS
Gray, D. Ting-a-ling
Shaw, I. Faith at sea
Appendicitis. Tennyson, H.
Appet, Nelson, 1910-
The prophet
American vanguard, 1950
Ribalow, H. U. ed. These your children
The test
American vanguard, 1952
Apple for Mom. Pace, J.
Apple seed and apple thorn. Enright, E.
Apple tree. Du Maurier, D.
Apple-tree. Galsworthy, J.
Apple-tree table. Melville, H.
APPLE TREES
Clayton, J. B. White circle
See also Trees
Appleton, Victor, pseud.
Sky ride—a Tom Swift story
Jensen, P. ed. Fireside book of flying stories
Appointment in tomorrow. Leiber, F.
The **appraisal.** Schorr, Z.
Apprentice thief. MacManus, S.
APPRENTICES
Chekhov, A. P. Vanka
Appropriate measures. Chekhov, A. P.

APRIL FOOL'S DAY
Dostoevskiĭ, F. M. Polzunkov

April is the cruelest month. Berger, T. L.

April witch. Bradbury, R.

AQUARIUMS
Clark, W. Van T. Fish who could close his eyes

Arabella, the third. Eggleston, M. W.

ARABIA
Ashkenazi, T. The miserly emir
Graham, R. B. C. Faith

ARABIAN NIGHTS
Aladdin; or the wonderful lamp
Cody, S. ed. Greatest stories and how they were written

Characters from
Poe, E. A. Thousand-and-second tale of Scheherazade

ARABS
Dunsany, E. J. M. D. P. 18th baron. Story of land and sea
Tennyson, H. In the desert

ARABS IN PALESTINE
Stinetorf, L. A. Refugee village

Araby. Joyce, J.

ARAPAHO INDIANS
Cook, K. Ba-ee

Ararat. Henderson, Z.

Arcadia recalled. Johnson, J. W.

ARCHEOLOGISTS
Wharton, E. N. J. A bottle of Perrier

Archerfish. Beach, E. L.

Archibald, J. William, 1918-
Ernestine in Dominica
Story (Periodical) Story no. 3

ARCHITECTS
De Vries, P. Today and today
Porter, W. S. Witches' loaves

ARCTIC REGIONS
Stefánsson, V. Seal hunting
See also Antarctic regions

Are you run-down, tired— Rosmond, B. and Lake, L. M.

Are you too late, or was I too early. Collier, J.

Arena. Brown, F.

Arfon. Davies, R.

ARGENTINE REPUBLIC

19th century
Hudson, W. H. Story of a piebald horse

Buenos Aires
Cancela, A. Life and death of a hero

Argonauts of the air. Wells, H. G.

Argument with death. O'Rourke, F.

Arico, Victor, 1912-
Civil rights
Arico, V. The knight returns, and other stories
Double bliss
Arico, V. The knight returns, and other stories
His great decision
Arico, V. The knight returns, and other stories

Knight returns
Arico, V. The knight returns, and other stories
Merchant's monument
Arico, V. The knight returns, and other stories
Pelican and the lyre bird
Arico, V. The knight returns, and other stories
The promotion
Arico, V. The knight returns, and other stories
The rebel
Arico, V. The knight returns, and other stories
To punish the offender
Arico, V. The knight returns, and other stories
Tomorrow you're sentenced
Arico, V. The knight returns, and other stories
Trusting snakes
Arico, V. The knight returns, and other stories
Water canteen
Arico, V. The knight returns, and other stories

ARISTOCRACY

England
Maugham, W. S. Lord Mountdrago

France
Balzac, H. de. Other Diane

Italy
Gobineau, J. A. comte de. Red handkerchief

Japan
Akutagawa, R. Yam gruel

Russia
Sobol, A. M. Last expedition of Baron Feuhbel-Feuhtzenau

Aristocracy versus hash. Porter, W. S.

The **aristocrat.** Zoshchenko, M. M.

Arkansas. Weeks, R.

Arlen, Michael, 1895-1956
Cavalier of the streets
Cerf, B. A. and Moriarty, H. C. eds. Anthology of famous British stories
Gentleman from America
Davenport, B. ed. Ghostly tales to be told

Arm of Mrs Egan. Harvey, W. F.

Armageddon. Brown, F.

ARMED FORCES. See Soldiers; also names of countries with subdivision Army

ARMENIANS IN THE UNITED STATES
Saroyan, W. My cousin Dikran, the orator
Saroyan, W. Summer of the beautiful white horse
Saroyan, W. Theological student

Armistice. Tennyson, H.

ARMS AND ARMOR
Sheckley, R. Last weapon

Armstrong, Anthony, pseud. See Willis, Anthony Armstrong

Armstrong, Charlotte, 1905-
The enemy
Queen, E. pseud. ed. Queen's awards: 6th ser.
Laugh it off
Queen, E. pseud. ed. The Queen's awards: 8th ser.

Armstrong, Matt
A filly owns a fella!
Furman, A. L. ed. Teen-age horse stories

ARMY AIR FORCES. See United States. Army Air Forces

ARMY ANTS. See Ants

Arnold, Maxwell, 1919-
Cannibal pot
Stanford short stories, 1950

Aronson, Robert
Seaworthy
Furman, A. L. ed. Teen-age dog stories

Arnow, Harriette Louisa (Simpson) 1908-
Washerwoman's day
Southern review. Anthology of stories from the Southern review

Arrhenius horror. Miller, P. S.

The **arrow.** Morley, C. D.

Arrow of heaven. Chesterton, G. K.

ARSON
Collier, J. Great possibilities
Faulkner, W. Barn burning
Waugh, E. Love among the ruins
See also Fires

ARSONISTS. See Arson

Art and the bronco. Porter, W. S.

ART COLLECTORS
Zweig, S. Invisible collection

Art colony. Boyle, K.

ART CRITICS
Werfel, F. Saverio's secret
See also Critics

ART DEALERS
Lawrence, D. H. Lovely lady
Zweig, S. Invisible collection
Zweig, S. Unseen collection

ART GALLERIES AND MUSEUMS
Munro, H. H. Reginald on the Academy

ART OBJECTS

Collectors
See Art collectors

ART SCHOOLS
Brenner, L. Revolt
Salinger, J. D. De Daumier-Smith's blue period

Artful Mr Glencannon. Gilpatric, G.

ARTHUR, KING
Malory, Sir T. Marvellous adventure of the sword

Arthur, Robert
Big money
Mystery Writers of America, inc. Four-&-twenty bloodhounds
Change of address
Mystery Writers of America, inc. Butcher, baker, murder-maker
Evolution's end
Crossen, K. F. ed. Adventures in tomorrow

MWA murder
Mystery Writers of America, inc. Crooks' tour
Man in the morgue
Mystery Writers of America, inc. 20 great tales of murder
Postpaid to Paradise
Magazine of fantasy and science fiction. Best from Fantasy and science fiction; [1st ser]
Wheel of time
Brown, F. and Reynolds, M. eds. Science-fiction carnival

Arthur Aronymus. Lasker-Schüler, E.

ARTIFICIAL LIMBS
Alexander, W. One leg too many
Davies, R. Benefit concert
Wolfe, B. Self portrait

The **artist.** Kaplan, R.

Artist at home. Faulkner, W.

ARTIST LIFE
Boyle, K. Art colony
Humphrey, W.. The fauve
James, H. Tree of knowledge
Porter, W. S. Extradited from Bohemia
Porter, W. S. Last leaf
Porter, W. S. Service of love

ARTISTS
Collier, J. Night! Youth! Paris! And the moon
Hill, M. Y. Sea anchor
See also Architects; Illustrators; Painters; Sculptors

Artist's life. Powell, D.

ARTISTS' MODELS
James, H. Real thing

As a dog should. Alexander, C.

As benefits forgot. Corkery, D.

"As handsome does." Eames, G. T.

As I am, you will be. Friedman, B. H.

As never was. Miller, P. S.

As ye sow— Fisher, D. F. C.

The **ascent.** West, R. B.

Ascent to heaven. Rudnicki, A.

Asch, Nathan, 1902-
Inland, western sea
Best American short stories, 1951
Greene, J. I. and Abell, E. eds. Stories of sudden truth

Asch, Shalom, 1880-
The academy
Ausubel, N. ed. Treasury of Jewish humor
Duty to live
Fremantle, A. J. ed. Mothers
"I will send thee"
Selden, R. ed. Ways of God and men
Into thy hands
Brentano, F. ed. The word lives on
Kola Road
Leftwich, J. ed. Yisröel, 1952 ed.
Same as: Kola Street
Kola Street
Howe, I. and Greenberg, E. eds. Treasury of Yiddish stories
Same as: Kola Road
Mama
Ungar, F. ed. To mother with love

Asch, Shalom—*Continued*
Quiet garden spot
Howe, I. and Greenberg, E. eds. Treasury of Yiddish stories
Sanctification of the Name
Howe, I. and Greenberg, E. eds. Treasury of Yiddish stories
Asch, Sholem. See Asch, Shalom
Asem. Goldsmith, O.
Ashabranner, Brent
Genius of Strap Buckner
Western Writers of America. Holsters and heroes
Ashby, Richard
Master race
Sloane, W. M. ed. Space, space, space
Ashes. Fairbanks, D.
Ashes for the wind. Téllez, H.
Ashes of roses. Coward, N. P.
Ashes of the ages and eternal fire. Gibran, K.
Ashford, Daisy
A proposale
McFarland, W. K. comp. Then it happened
Ashkenazi, Touvia, 1904-
Miserly Emir
Story (Periodical) Story; no. 1
Ashkenazy, Irvin
Pop's boy
Ribalow, H. U. ed. World's greatest boxing stories
Ashley, Elizabeth L. 1926-
Aunt Lil
American vanguard, 1953
In another image
American vanguard, 1952
Asimov, Isaac, 1920-
Belief
Merril, J. ed. Beyond the barriers of space and time
"Breeds there a man. . . ?"
Derleth, A. W. ed. Beachheads in space
Bridle and saddle
Greenberg, M. ed. Men against the stars
C chute
Galaxy science fiction magazine. Second Galaxy reader of science fiction
Catch that rabbit
Asimov, I. I, robot
Christmas on Ganymede
Crossen, K. F. ed. Adventures in tomorrow
Death sentence
Derleth, A. W. ed. The outer reaches
Escape!
Asimov, I. I, robot
Evidence
Asimov, I. I, robot
Evitable conflict
Asimov, I. I, robot
Homo Sol
Conklin, G. ed. Omnibus of science fiction
Hostess
Galaxy science fiction magazine. Galaxy reader of science fiction
"In a good cause—"
Healy, R. J. ed. New tales of space and time

It's such a beautiful day
Star science fiction stories no. 3
Liar!
Asimov, I. I, robot
Little lost robot
Asimov, I. I, robot
Misbegotten missionary
Heinlein, R. A. ed. Tomorrow, the stars
Mother Earth
Greenberg, M. ed. Journey to infinity
Nightfall
Astounding science fiction (Periodical) Astounding science fiction anthology
No connection
Bleiler, E. F. and Dikty, T. E. eds. Science fiction omnibus: The best science fiction stories, 1949, 1950
"Nobody here but. . ."
Star science fiction stories [no. 1]
Not final
Conklin, G. ed. Possible worlds of science fiction
The pause
Derleth, A. W. ed. Time to come
Reason
Asimov, I. I, robot
Robbie
Asimov, I. I, robot
Conklin, G. ed. Science-fiction thinking machines
Red Queen's race
Pratt, F. ed. World of wonder
Runaround
Asimov, I. I, robot
Sally
Abell, E. ed. American accent
Trends
Greenberg, M. ed. Man against the stars
Victory unintentional
Lesser, M. A. ed. Looking forward
What if. . .
Conklin, G. ed. Science-fiction adventures in dimension

Ask me anything. Knight, D.
Ask me no more. Beck, W.
Asleep in Armageddon. Bradbury, R.
Aspern papers. James, H.
Asphodel. Welty, E.
Aspinwall, Marguerite
Night before Christmas
American girl (Periodical) Christmas all year 'round
Secret closet
Furman, A. L. ed. Everygirls mystery stories
Snowbound Christmas
American girl (Periodical) Christmas all year 'round
Thundering Hurd
Furman, A. L. ed. Everygirls career stories
Asquith, Lady Cynthia Mary Evelyn (Charteris) 1887-
One grave too few
Asquith, Lady C. M. E. C. ed. Book of modern ghosts
ASSASSINATION
Gobineau, J. A. comte de. Red handkerchief

August heat. Harvey, W. F.
August tenth. Jones, R. S.
Augustine, Saint, Bp. of Hippo, 354-430
  Monica's son
    Fremantle, A. J. ed. Mothers
Augustus and spring tonic. Henderson, Le G.
Augustus meets his first Indian. Henderson, Le G.
Augustus, pirate. Henderson, Le G.
Aumonier, Stacy, 1887-1928
  Source of irritation
    Cerf, B. A. and Moriarty, H. C. eds. Anthology of famous British stories
Aunt Esther's galoshes. Rosenberg, E. C.
Aunt Lil. Ashley, E. L.
Aunt Rose's ghost story. Yaffe, J.
Aunt Suzanne. McLaverty, M.
Auntie Bissel. Suckow, R.
Auntimay. De La Roche, M.
AUNTS
  Auchincloss, L. Unholy three
  Ballard, J. C. Mountain summer
  Beck, W. Years brought to an end
  De La Mare, W. J. Seaton's aunt
  De La Roche, M. Auntimay
  Macauley, R. The wishbone
  McLaverty, M. Aunt Suzanne
  Miller, C. Gentle season
  Munro, H. H. Way to the dairy
  Rosenberg, E. C. Aunt Esther's galoshes
  Waltari, M. T. Moonscape
  Watson, J. His mother's sermon
  Wesely, D. Week of roses
AURELIUS ANTONINUS, MARCUS, EMPEROR OF ROME, 121-180
  Cohn, E. Rabbi and emperor
Aurevilly, Jules Amédée Barbey d'. See Barbey d' Aurevilly, Jules Amédée
Aurora's Angus. Mannzen, D.
Austin, Mary
  Green bough
    Selden, R. ed. Ways of God and men
AUSTRALIANS IN ENGLAND
  Edginton, H. M. Purple and fine linen
AUSTRIA
  Boyle, K. White horses of Vienna
The **author.** Johnson, J. W.

Author of Beltraffio. James, H.
AUTHORS
  Aiken, C. P. Life isn't a short story
  Aiken, C. P. Your obituary, well written
  Beck, W. Edge of doom
  Benét, S. V. No visitors
  Borges, J. L. Secret miracle
  Brookhouser, F. Young man from yesterday
  Brown, F. All good bems
  Chekhov, A. P. The skit
  Collier, J. Collaboration
  Collier, J. Pictures in the fire
  Collier, J. Variation on a theme
  De La Roche, M. Boy in the house
  Farrell, J. T. John Hitchcock
  Farrell, J. T. The martyr
  Farrell, J. T. Power of literature
  Fitzgerald, F. S. K. Financing Finnegan
  Fletcher, V. Coda to a writers' conference

  Gregutt, H. C. Climb for the big ones
  Gregutt, H. C. The secret
  Harvey, W. F. Habeas Corpus Club
  Hemingway, E. Snows of Kilimanjaro
  Jackson, C. R. The outlander
  James, H. Author of Beltraffio
  James, H. Death of the lion
  James, H. Middle years
  Jarrell, R. Gertrude and Sidney
  Johnson, J. W. The author
  Karchmer, S. N. Fistful of Alamo heroes
  Keller, D. H. Creation unforgivable
  Keller, D. H. Literary corkscrew
  Kipling, R. "Finest story in the world"
  Lawrence, D. H. Two blue birds
  Lewis, S. Post-mortem murder
  Mann, T. Weary hour
  Maugham, W. S. Creature impulse
  Maugham, W. S. Human element
  Maugham, W. S. Round dozen
  Maugham, W. S. Social sense
  Maugham, W. S. Voice of the turtle
  Mitchell, J. Professor Sea Gull
  Munro, H. H. Mark
  Newhouse, E. Irving
  Porter, W. S. Dinner at—
  Porter, W. S. Dog and the playlet
  Porter, W. S. Plutonian fire
  Porter, W. S. Proof of the pudding
  Porter, W. S. Sacrifice hit
  Porter, W. S. Sound and fury
  Porter, W. S. Sparrows in Madison Square
  Saroyan, W. The Assyrian
  Saroyan, W. Cocktail party
  Saroyan, W. Cold day
  Schulberg, B. W. Note on the literary life
  Shultz, W. H. Oreste
  Sutro, A. Bread on the waters
  Tucker, W. "MCMLV"
  Walpole, Sir H. Mr Oddy
  Walsh, M. Thomasheen James and the dictation machine
  Waugh, E. Excursion in reality
  Waugh, E. Work suspended
  West, J. Breach of promise
  Willingham, C. Record of a man
    See also Children as authors; Dramatists; Journalists; Poets; also names of individual authors
AUTOBIOGRAPHICAL STORIES
  Feuchtwanger, L. Balance sheet of my life
  Karchmer, S. N. Fistful of Alamo heroes
  McCarthy, M. T. The blackguard
  McCarthy, M. T. Yonder peasant, who is he?
AUTOMATA
  Asimov, I. I, robot; 9 stories
  Asimov, I. "Nobody here but. . ."
  Asimov, I. Sally
  Asimov, I. Victory unintentional
  Binder, E. I, robot
  Bradbury, R. Marionettes, inc.
  Breuer, M. J. Man with the strange head
  Curtis, B. Peculiar people
  Del Rey, L. Helen O'Loy
  Del Rey, L. Instinct
  Del Rey, L. Into thy hands
  Fyfe, H. B. Manners of the age
  Gallun, R. Z. Old Faithful
  Gault, W. C. Made to measure
  Greenberg, M. ed. Robot and the man
  Highstone, H. A. Frankenstein—unlimited

Babel', Isaak Emmanuilovich, 1894-
  The awakening
    Ausubel, N. ed. Treasury of Jewish
    humor
  In Odessa
    Ausubel, N. ed. Treasury of Jewish
    humor
  The King
    Guerney, B. G. comp. New Russian
    stories
  Rabbi's son
    Leftwich, J. ed. Yisröel. 1952 ed.
Babes in the jungle. Porter, W. S.
Babes in the wood. O'Donovan, M.
Babette. Maupassant, G. de
BABIES. See Children
Babikoff, Vladimir, 1907-
  Day of rest
    American vanguard, 1950
BABOONS
  Annixter, P. pseud. The lynching
Babs and Phill who eloped. Strain, F. B.
Babus of Nayanjore. Tagore, Sir R.
Baby buntings. Squires, R.
Baby killer. Elliott, R. B.
Baby on Neptune. Harris, C. W. and
  Breuer, M. J.
Baby party. Fitzgerald, F. S. K.
Baby sitter for Christmas. Cousins, M.
Baby sitter vs. Ronnie. Johnson, H.
BABY SITTERS
  De Vries, P. They also sit
  Johnson, H. Baby sitter vs. Ronnie
Babylon revisited. Fitzgerald, F. S. K.
Bachelor supper. Aiken, C. P.
BACH, JOHANN SEBASTIAN, 1685-1750
  Brachvogel, A. E. Christmas at the Bachs'
BACHELORS
  Bates, H. E. Little farm
  Bowen, E. The lover
  Bowen, E. New house
  Huysmans, J. K. Monsieur Folantin
  Melville, H. Paradise of bachelors
Bachelor's death. Schnitzler, A.
Back again. Schuyler, W.
Back drawing-room. Bowen, E.
Back for Christmas. Collier, J.
Back of beyond. Maugham, W. S.
Back on the road. Caldwell, E.
Back there in the grass. Morris, G.
Back to Julie. Wilson, R.
Back to school. Doty, W. L.
Back to the beginning. Robertson, J. H.
Back to the land—Oregon, 1907. Davis,
  H. L.
Back to the sea. Pincherle, A.
Back to Treasure Island. Calahan, H. A.
Back where I had never been. McNulty, J.
Backfire. Rocklynne, R.
The background. Munro, H. H.
Backward, turn backward. Davis, D. S.
Backyard ballgame. Farrell, J. T.

Bacon, Francis, viscount St Albans, 1561-
  1626
  New Atlantis
    Derleth, A. W. ed. Beyond time &
    space
BACTERIAL WARFARE
  Jenkins, W. F. Symbiosis
  Robertson, M. Battle of the monsters
BACTERIOLOGISTS
  Wells, H. G. Stolen bacillus
Bad boy from Brooklyn. Seide, M.
Bad corner. Van Doren, M.
Bad day for sales. Leiber, F.
Bad dreams. Taylor, P. H.
Bad man passes on. Hendryx, J. B.
Bad man reaches Halfaday. Hendryx, J. B.
Bad year. Cheshire, G.
Bade, William L.
  Ambition
    Conklin, G. ed. Science-fiction adven-
    tures in dimension
Badge of policeman O'Roon. Porter, W. S.
BADGERS
  Kafka, F. The burrow
Ba-ee. Cook, K.
The bag. Munro, H. H.
Bag of silver. Bentley, P. E.
Bagnold, Enid
  Amorous ghost
    Carrington, H. ed. Week-end book of
    ghost stories
Bailey, Albert Edward, 1871-
  Jimmy finds a plan
    Elmquist, R. M. ed. Fifty years of
    Christmas
Bailiffs at Framley. Trollope, A.
Bair, Tom
  Falcon's nest
    Burnett, W. and Burnett, H. S. eds.
    Sextet
Bait for a tiger. Walker, D. H.
Bait from McGillicudy. Wylie, P.
Baker, Denys Val
  Beautiful house
    Story (Periodical)   Story; no. 1
Baker, Dorothy (Dodds) 1907-
  Little white cat
    Joseph, M. ed. Best cat stories
  Summer
    New writing (Periodical) Best stories
Baker, Frank, 1908-
  Blessed are the clean of heart; they shall
    see God
    Baker, F. Blessed are they
  Blessed are the merciful; they shall obtain
    mercy
    Baker, F. Blessed are they
  Blessed are the patient; they shall inherit
    the land
    Baker, F. Blessed are they
  Blessed are the peace-makers; they shall
    be counted the children of God
    Baker, F. Blessed are they
  Blessed are the poor in spirit; the king-
    dom of heaven is theirs
    Baker, F. Blessed are they

Baker, Frank—*Continued*

Blessed are those who hunger and thirst for holiness; they shall have their fill
Baker, F. Blessed are they
Blessed are those who mourn; they shall be comforted
Baker, F. Blessed are they
Blessed are those who suffer persecution in the cause of right; the kingdom of heaven is theirs
Baker, F. Blessed are they

Baker, Ray Stannard, 1870-1946
A day of pleasant bread
Brentano, F. ed. The word lives on
Lohan, R. and Lohan, M. eds. New Christmas treasury

Baker Street irregulars. Doyle, Sir A. C.

BAKERIES AND BAKERS
Gorky, M. Twenty-six and one
Greene, H. I. Bread and snow
Horwitz, J. The strudel
Porter, W. S. Witches' loaves
Shneur, Z. The girl

Baker's daughter. Bianco, M. W.

BAKING. See Bakeries and bakers

Balance. Christopher, J.

Balance his, swing yours. Stegner, W. E.

Balance sheet of my life. Feuchtwanger, L.

Balch, Glenn, 1902-
Price on Hide-rack
American boy (Periodical) American boy anthology

Balchin, Nigel, 1908-
Now we are broke, my dear
Saturday evening post (Periodical) Saturday evening post stories, 1950

The balcony. Milne, A. A.

Baldwin, Hanson Weightman, 1903-
R. M. S. Titanic
McFee, W. ed. Great sea stories of modern times

Baldwin, James, 1841-1925
Broiefort, the black Arabian
Dennis, W. ed. Palomino and other horses

BALKAN STATES
Munro, H. H. Cupboard of the yesterdays
Munro, H. H. Purple of the Balkan Kings

Ball, Max Waite
Case of the wooden bowls
Bachelor, J. M.; Henry, R. L. and Salisbury, R. eds. Current thinking and writing; 2d ser.

Ball-of-fat. Maupassant, G. de

Ballad of the sad café. McCullers, C. S.

Ballantyne, Thomas A.
Reunion at evening
American vanguard, 1952

Ballard, James Clarence, 1921-
Mountain summer
Best American short stories, 1953

BALLET
Woody, R. L. J. Cue for Connie
Woody, R. L. J. Second chance
See also Dancers; Dancing

BALLET DANCERS. See Ballet

BALLOON ASCENSIONS. See Balloons

Balloon hoax. Poe, E. A.

BALLOONS
Ekbergh, I. D. Up in a balloon
Poe, E. A. Balloon hoax
Poe, E. A. Mellonta Tauta
Poe, E. A. Unparalleled adventure of one Hans Pfaall
Repton, H. From a private mad-house

BALLS (PARTIES) See Parties

Balm of Gilead. Caldwell, E.

Balmer, Edwin, 1883- and Wylie, Philip, 1902-
When worlds collide; excerpts
Kuebler, H. W. ed. Treasury of science fiction classics

Balzac, Honoré de, 1799-1850
Atheist's mass
Fabricant, N. D. and Werner, H. eds. World's best doctor stories
Mother's letter
Ungar, F. ed. To mother with love
Old maid
Dupee, F. W. ed. Great French short novels
Other Diane
Geist, S. ed. French stories and tales
Passion in the desert
Blodgett, H. W. ed. Story survey
Cody, S. ed. Greatest stories and how they were written
Lamb, L. ed. Family book of best loved short stories
Neider, C. ed. Great short stories from the world's literature

Bamberg, Robert Douglas
Cave of warm winds
Hathaway, B. and Sessions, J. A. eds. Writers for tomorrow. 2d ser.

BANANA
Porter, W. S. Day we celebrate

Band concert. Jackson, C. R.

BANDITS. See Brigands and robbers

BANDS (MUSIC)
O'Donovan, M. Orpheus and his lute
See also Musicians

Bandy. Miers, E. S.

Banér, Skulda Vanadis, 1899-
Good dog forward
Cavanna, B. ed. Pick of the litter
Same as: "Good girl—forward!"
"Good girl—forward!"
American girl (Periodical) On my honor
Same as: Good dog forward

Bang on the head. Seager, A.

BANGKOK. See Thailand—Bangkok

Bangs, John Kendrick, 1862-1922
Water ghost of Harrowby Hall
Fenner, P. R. comp. Ghosts, ghosts, ghosts

BANK CLERKS. See Clerks

BANK ROBBERS
Aldrich, B. S. How far is it to Hollywood?
Frazee, S. Fire killer
Muheim, H. Dusty drawer

Bank that broke the man at Monte Carlo. Sansom, W.

BANKERS
  Collins, W. Fauntleroy
  Davis, R. H. Wasted day
  Porter, W. S. Friends in San Rosario
  Porter, W. S. Guardian of the accolade
  Waltari, M. T. Tie from Paris
          See also Banks and banking; Capital-
      ists and financiers
BANKS AND BANKING
  MacDonald, J. D. The miniature
  Nadir, I. M. My first deposit
          See also Bankers
Banquet and a half. Hays, L.
Bantien, Alvin M.
  Emergency
      Oberfirst, R. ed. 1952 anthology of best
      original short-shorts
Baptism of some importance. Becker, S. D.
Baptist hymnal. Miner, M. S.
The **baptizing.** Ingraham, J. H.
Bar-Nothing's happy birthday. Cunning-
  ham, E.
Bar sinister. Davis, R. H.
BARBARIANS. See Man, Prehistoric
BARBARITIES. See War
Barbecue. Runyon, D.
Barbèd rose. Guest, A.
Barber, Alfred, 1922-
  The caught
      American vanguard, 1952
BARBERS
  Lardner, R. W. Haircut
  Schaefer, J. W. Leander Frailey
Barber's clever wife. Steele, F. A.
Barbey d' Aurévilly, Jules Amédée, 1808-1889
  Happiness in crime
      Dupee, F. W. ed. Great French short
      novels
Barbour, Ralph Henry, 1870-1944
  "Hoot!" said the owl
      American boy (Periodical) American boy
      anthology
BARCELONA. See Spain—Barcelona
Bargain in brimstone. Oursler, F.
Barker, A. L. 1919-
  Answer is nothing
      Barker, A. L. Novelette; with other
      stories
  Domini
      Barker, A. L. Novelette; with other
      stories
  The freak
      Barker, A. L. Novelette; with other
      stories
  Heartbreak
      Barker, A. L. Novelette; with other
      stories
  Jane Dore—dear childe
      Barker, A. L. Novelette; with other
      stories
  Novelette
      Barker, A. L. Novelette; with other
      stories
  Pringle
      Barker, A. L. Novelette; with other
      stories

  Romney
      Barker, A. L. Novelette; with other
      stories
  Story of Mathias
      Barker, A. L. Novelette; with other
      stories
  Variations on a theme of rain
      Barker, A. L. Novelette; with other
      stories
  Villain as a young boy
      Barker, A. L. Novelette; with other
      stories
Barker, Squire Omar, 1894-
  Man in the hard hat
      Western Writers of America. Holsters
      and heroes
Barlow, Thomas
  Sudden heart
      Saturday evening post (Periodical) Sat-
      urday evening post stories, 1950
Barn burning. Faulkner, W.
Barnard, Leslie Gordon, 1890-
  Dancing bear
      Pacey, D. ed. Book of Canadian stories
  Four men and a box
      This week magazine. This week's short-
      short stories
Barney. Stanton, W.
Barney whose life was "all work and no
  play." Strain, F. B.
BARNUM, PHINEAS TAYLOR, 1810-1891
  Benét, S. V. Angel was a Yankee
Baro, Gene
  Angry lions, lazy lions
      Story (Periodical) Story no. 2
Baroja y Nessi, Pío, 1872-
  Cabbages of the cemetery
      De Onís, H. ed. Spanish stories and
      tales
BARONS. See Aristocracy
Barr, James, pseud.
  Bottom of the cloud
      Barr, J. pseud. Derricks
  First you take a live goat
      Barr, J. pseud. Derricks
  Good kid
      Barr, J. pseud. Derricks
  Hanging fire
      Barr, J. pseud. Derricks
  Spur piece
      Barr, J. pseud. Derricks
  Success story
      Barr, J. pseud. Derricks
  Tryout
      Barr, J. pseud. Derricks
Barrie, Sir James Matthew, bart. 1860-1937
  Courting of T'nowhead's Bell
      Cerf, B. A. and Moriarty, H. C. eds.
      Anthology of famous British stories
  Farewell Miss Julie Logan
      Scribner treasury
  The last night
      Brentano, F. ed. The word lives on
  Making of a minister
      Neider, C. ed. Men of the high calling
Barrier of dread. Merril, J.
Barring the weight. Ready, W. B.
The **barrister.** Milne. A. A.

Barry, Jerome, 1894-
  Fourth degree
    Mystery Writers of America, inc.
    Maiden murders
BARS. See Hotels, taverns, etc.
Barsetshire. Trollope, A.
Barsetshire worthy—Archdeacon Grantly.
  Trollope, A.
BARTENDERS
  Jenkin, P. A. Cool million
  Saroyan, W. Third day after Christmas
Bartholomew Arnold; or, After the war is
  over. Stein, G.
"Bartimeus," pseud. See Ritchie, Lewis An-
  selm da Costa
Bartleby. Melville, H.
Bartleby the scrivener. Melville, H.
Basch, Monika
  Second act
    Hathaway, B. and Sessions, J. A. eds.
    Writers for tomorrow. 2d ser.
BASEBALL
  Bateman, A. Diamond horseshoes
  Bradbury, R. Big black and white game
  Breslin, H. Bat and a prayer
  Brookhouser, F. L'affaire foul tip
  Brubaker, H. Milk pitcher
  Coombs, C. I. Saga of Sleepy Mugoon
  Cox, W. R. Pinch hitter
  Dailey, J. The rookie
  Erin, B. Don't jinx the pitcher
  Fenner, P. R. Crack of the bat; 10 stories
  Fontaine, R. L. God hit a home run
  Furman, A. L. ed. Teen-age stories of
    the diamond; 13 stories
  Gallery, D. V. Hokey-Pocus McGee
  Gallico, P. W. Summer dream
  Garber, R. S. ed. Baseball reader; 25
    stories
  Hillger, E. H. Lomax pitching
  Holder, W. Storm over second
  Katkov, N. Charlie Baseball
  Lowry, R. Little baseball world
  Miers, E. S. Kid who beat the Dodgers
  Montross, L. Nine ladies vs fate
  Oblinger, M. Jackpot vs Yellowstrike
  O'Rourke, F. Greatest victory, and other
    baseball stories; 12 stories
  O'Rourke, F. The heavenly world series,
    and other baseball stories; 9 stories
  Rutt, E. Canary from Cuba
  Sandberg, H. W. Kid from Shingle Creek
  Schram, W. L. Horse that played third
    base for Brooklyn
  Schramm, W. L. My kingdom for Jones
  Siegel, L. Lay it down, Ziggy!
  Temple, W. H. Most unusual season
  Ullman, J. R. I seen 'em go
  Van Loan, C. E. Mister Conley
  West, C. Smoke ball kid
  Young, S. We won't be needing you, Al
Baseball Hattie. Runyon, D.
The basement. Largerkvist, P. F.
Basement room. Greene, G.
BASKETBALL
  Bee, C. F. Freeze the ball
  Charnley, M. V. Brodie horns in
  Chute, B. J. Five captains
  Chute, B. J. Four-ring circus

Chute, B. J. Kid brother
Coombs, C. I. Hardwood hazard
Coombs, C. I. Part time hoopster
Farrell, J. T. Tournament star
Gartner, J. Left-hand stuff
Jackson, M. W. The hero
Larsen, D. Freeze-out
Miers, E. S. No heroes wanted
Person, W. T. "I play basketball"
Person, W. T. Long-Shot Porter
Peterson, G. M. Sophomore forward
Phillips, J. A. Fast break
Pierrot, G. P. Sheriton turnabout
Roberts, R. M. The fix
Stoakes, H. R. Turtles played the hares
Temple, W. H. Record-breaker
Wilner, H. Whistle and the heroes
BASQUES
  Baroja y Nessi, P. Cabbages of the ceme-
    tery
Bat. Meader, S. W.
Bat and a prayer. Breslin, H.
Bat Eye Cantrill. Hendryx, J. B.
Bateman, Arnold
  Diamond horseshoes
    Boys' life (Periodical) Boys' life Adven-
    ture stories
  Gus the gloom
    Furman, A. L. ed. Teen-age stories of
    the diamond
  Rig ship for diving
    Furman, A. L. ed. Teen-age sea stories
  Submarine jitters
    Furman, A. L. ed. Teen-age sea stories
Bates, Harry
  Alas, all thinking!
    Bleiler, E. F. and Dikty, T. E. eds.
    Imagination unlimited
  Death of a sensitive
    Moskowitz, S. comp. Editor's choice in
    science fiction
Bates, Herbert Ernest, 1905-
  Bedfordshire clanger
    Bates, H. E. Colonel Julian, and other
    stories
  Christmas song
    Bates, H. E. Colonel Julian, and other
    stories
  Colonel Julian
    Bates, H. E. Colonel Julian, and other
    stories
  The flag
    Bates, H. E. Colonel Julian, and other
    stories
  The frontier
    Bates, H. E. Colonel Julian, and other
    stories
  Girl called Peter
    Bates, H. E. Colonel Julian, and other
    stories
  Joe Johnson
    Bates, H. E. Colonel Julian, and other
    stories
  The lighthouse
    Bates, H. E. Colonel Julian, and other
    stories
  Little farm
    Bates, H. E. Colonel Julian, and other
    stories

Bates, Herbert E.—*Continued*
  Major of Hussars
    Bates, H. E. Colonel Julian, and other
     stories
  Mrs Vincent
    Bates, H. E. Colonel Julian, and other
     stories
  No more the nightingales
    Bates, H. E. Colonel Julian, and other
     stories
  The park
    Bates, H. E. Colonel Julian, and other
     stories
  Sugar for the horse
    Bates, H. E. Colonel Julian, and other
     stories
  Time expired
    Bates, H. E. Colonel Julian, and other
     stories

Bates, Ralph, 1899-
  Forty-third division
    Cerf, B. A. and Moriarty, H. C. eds.
     Anthology of famous British stories
  Wailing precipice
    Talbot, D. ed. Treasury of mountaineer-
     ing stories

The **bath.** O'Flaherty, L.

BATHING BEACHES
  Beck, W. Far whistle

BATHS, TURKISH
  Munro, H. H. The Recessional

BATHYSPHERE
  Jenkins, W. F. De profundis

Battle in the moonlight. Ellsberg, E.

Battle of Finney's Ford. West, J.

Battle of life. Dickens, C.

Battle of the marten and the porcupine.
  Reid, M.

Battle of the monsters. Robertson, M.

Battle of the S . . . S. Elliott, B.

Battle royal. O'Rourke, F.

Battle with a whale. Davies, W. M.

Battle with the bees. Stuart, J.

BATTLES
  Coolidge, O. E. Prefect of Jerusalem
     See also names of particular battles

Baudelaire, Charles Pierre, 1821-1867
  Death of a hero
    Geist, S. ed. French stories and tales
  The rope
    Geist, S. ed. French stories and tales

Bauer, Florence Anne (Marvyne)
  The waters of Bethesda
    Brentano, F. ed. The word lives on

Bauer, Gladys V.
  Scared
    Furman, A. L. ed. Everygirls mystery
     stories

Baum, Vicki, 1888-
  Old house
    Leftwich, J. ed. Yisröel. 1952 ed.

Bayou bait. White, L. T.

BAYOUS
  Grau, S. A. Joshua

BAZAARS. See Fairs

Bazán, Emilia Pardo. See Pardo Bazan,
  Emilia, condesa de

Be nice to Mr Campbell. Lowry, R. J. C.

Be present at our table, Lord. Saroyan, W.

Beach, Edward Latimer, 1918-
  Archerfish
    Fenner, P. R. comp. Speed, speed, speed
    McFee, W. ed. Great sea stories of
     modern times
  Wahoo
    Fenner, P. R. comp. Stories of the sea

Beach of Falesá. Stevenson, R. L.

Beach squatter. Davis, H. L.

BEACHCOMBERS
  Russell, J. Jetsam

Beachcroft, Thomas Owen, 1902-
  Erne from the coast
    Certner, S. and Henry, G. H. eds. Short
     stories for our times
    Christ, H. I. and Shostak, J. eds. Short
     stories
  The eyes
    Cerf, B. A. and Moriarty, H. C. eds.
     Anthology of famous British stories
  Old Hard
    Schorer, M. ed. The story

Beachead in Bohemia. Marsh, W. N.

Beachhead. Simak, C. D.

Beaconsfield, Benjamin Disraeli, 1st earl of,
  1804-1881
  Ixion in heaven
    Leftwich, J. ed. Yisröel 1952 ed.

Beal, Forrest
  Bertie the uninvited
    Dachs, D. ed. Treasury of sports humor

Beanstalk. Blish, J.

The **bear.** Faulkner, W.

Bear and the hunter's step-son
  Pacey, D. ed Book of Canadian stories

Bear hunt. Faulkner, W.

Bear that thought he was a dog. Roberts,
  Sir C. G. D.

BEARS
  Annixter, P. pseud. Kadiak
  Barnard, L. C. Dancing bear
  Burke, N. Polar night
  Caldwell, E. Hamrick's polar bear
  Faulkner, W. The bear
  Grimson, M. S. King of the north woods
  Kahanovich, P. From my estates
  Kjelgaard, J. A. Blood on the ice
  Roberts, Sir C. G. D. Thirteen bears;
    13 stories
  Schaefer, J. W. Something lost
  Stuart, J. No hero
  West, R. B. Last of the grizzly bears

Beast from 20,000 fathoms. Bradbury, R.

Beast in the jungle. James, H.

Beast of Bourbon. Pratt, F. and De Camp,
  L. S.

Beast with five fingers. Harvey, W. F.

BEATITUDES
  Baker, F. Blessed are they; 8 stories

Beau: the dog who served two masters.
  Little, G. W.

Beauclerk, Helen De Vere
  Miracle of the vineyard
    Selden, R. ed. Ways of God and men

Beaumont, Charles, 1929-
  Beautiful woman
    Wollheim, D. A. ed. Prize science fiction
  Keeper of the dream
    Derleth, A. W. ed. Time to come
Beaumont, Gerald, 1886-1926
  The crab
    Graber, R. S. ed. Baseball reader
Beautiful, beautiful, beautiful! Freidman, S.
Beautiful house. Baker, D. V.
Beautiful night for Orion. Clay, R.
Beautiful tree. Sangster, M. E.
Beautiful woman. Beaumont, C.
BEAUTY. See Esthetics
BEAUTY, PERSONAL
  Beaumont, C. Beautiful woman
  Brush, K. I. Good Wednesday
Beauty and the diamond ring. Moore, J. P.
BEAUTY SHOPS
  Olds, H. D. Susan steps out
  Pratt, F. and De Camp, L. S. More than skin deep
  Welty, E. Petrified man
  Winslow, T. S. Fur flies
BEAVERS
  Mills, E. A. My beaver pal
Because of little apples. Chekhov, A. P.
Because she was like me. Schweitzer, G.
Beck, V. J.
  Night boat from Barcelona
    Story (Periodical) Story; no. 2
Beck, Warren
  All brothers are men
    Beck, W. Far whistle, and other stories
  Ask me no more
    Beck, W. Far whistle, and other stories
  Blue sash
    Best of the Best American short stories, 1915-1950
  The child is father
    Beck, W. Far whistle, and other stories
  Clean platter
    Beck, W. Far whistle, and other stories
  Detour in the dark
    Beck, W. Far whistle, and other stories
  Edge of doom
    Beck, W. Far whistle, and other stories
    Best American short stories, 1950
  Far whistle
    Beck, W. Far whistle, and other stories
  Felix
    Beck, W. Far whistle, and other stories
  Men working
    Beck, W. Far whistle, and other stories
  No continuing city
    Beck, W. Far whistle, and other stories
  Shadow of turning
    Abell, E. ed. American accent
    Beck, W. Far whistle, and other stories
  Verdict of innocence
    Beck, W. Far whistle, and other stories
  Years brought to an end
    Beck, W. Far whistle, and other stories
Becker, Stephen D. 1927-
  Baptism of some importance
    Story (Periodical) Story; no. 4
  Town mouse
    Best American short stories, 1953

Beckoning sea. Mandel, G.
Becky's Christmas turkey. Skinner, C. L.
Bedford-Jones, Henry, 1887-1949
  Thirteen men
    Bluebook (Periodical) Best sea stories from Bluebook
Bedford-Jones, Henry, 1887-1949 and Williams, L. B.
  Yellow Ship
    Bluebook (Periodical) Best sea stories from Bluebook
Bedfordshire clanger. Bates, H. E.
BEDS
  Collins, W. Terribly strange bed
Bee, Clair Francis, 1900-
  Freeze the ball
    Herzberg, M. J. comp. Treasure chest of sport stories
BEE. See Bees
Beebe, William, 1877-
  Home town of the army ants
    Andrews, R. C. ed. My favorite stories of the great outdoors
Beep. Blish, J.
Beer, Thomas, 1889-1940
  Tact
    Burrell, J. A. and Cerf, B. A. eds. Anthology of famous American stories
BEER
  Rabinowitz, S. My brother Eliyahu's drink
Beerbohm, Sir Max, 1872-1956
  Happy hypocrite
    Cerf, B. A. and Moriarty, H. C. eds. Anthology of famous British stories
BEES
  Gray, W. H. Bees from Borneo
  Stuart, J. Battle with the bees
  Wilson, R. M. Cyprian bees
Bees from Borneo. Gray, W. H.
BEETLES
  Poe, E. A. The gold-bug
Before its time. Dolbier, M.
Before the burning of Rome. Blackburn, E. R.
Before the flood. Milne, A. A.
Before the party. Maugham, W. S.
Before the races. DeJong, D. C.
Before the throne of beauty. Gibran, K.
Before the twilight of the gods. Waltari, M. T.
The beggar. Chekov, A. P.
Beggar-woman of Locarno. Kleist, H. von
BEGGARS
  Benét, S. V. Bishop's beggar
  Bunin, I. A. Evening in spring
  Chekov, A. P. The beggar
  Lagerkvist, P. F. The basement
  Maugham, W. S. The bum
  Munro, H. H. Dusk
  Munro, H. H. The romancers
  Steinberg, Y. Reb Anshel the golden
    See also Tramps
The beggars. O'Flaherty, L.
Begin again. Boyle, K.
Beginning of a story. Taylor, E.

Bennett, Arnold, 1867-1931
  Mary with the high hand
    Cerf, B. A. and Moriarty, H. C. eds.
    Anthology of famous British stories
Bennett, Keith
  Rocketeers have shaggy ears
    Greenberg, M. ed. Travelers of space
Bennett, Kem, 1919-
  Death at attention
    Strang, R. M. and Roberts, R. M. eds.
    Teen-age tales v2
  The soothsayer
    Magazine of fantasy and science fiction.
    Best from Fantasy and science fiction;
    2d ser.
Bennett, Myra E.
  Hornet's nest
    Lantz, J. E. ed. Stories of Christian
    living
Bennett, Peggy, 1925-
  Death under the hawthornes
    Best American short stories, 1950
    Prize stories of 1950
  Fugitive from the mind
    Best American short stories, 1951
Bennett, Richard, 1899-
  Strange little piper
    Story parade (Periodical) Adventure
    stories
Bennett, Russell H. 1896-
  Rancher's horse
    Dennis, W. ed. Palomino and other
    horses
Bennett, Stephen
  Girls are so helpless
    Furman, A. L. ed. Everygirls career
    stories
Benny and the bird-dogs. Rawlings, M. K.
Benny and the Tar-Baby. Watson, J. C.
Benowitz, Elliott, 1930-
  Rush hour
    Wolfe, D. M. ed. Which grain will grow
Benson, Ben
  Killer in the house
    Mystery Writers of America, inc.
    Butcher, baker, murder-maker
Benson, Sally, 1900-
  The overcoat
    Lass, A. H. and Horowitz, A. eds.
    Stories for youth
    Shaw, H. and Bement, D. Reading the
    short story
Benson, Stella, 1892-1933
  Man who missed the bus
    Lynskey, W. C. ed. Reading modern
    fiction
  Story coldly told
    Short, R. W. and Sewall, R. B. eds.
    Short stories for study. 1950 ed.
Benson, Theodora, 1906-
  Bones of A. T. Stewart
    Benson, T. Man from the tunnel, and
    other stories
  Childishness of Mr Mountfort
    Benson, T. Man from the tunnel, and
    other stories
  Door marked exit
    Benson, T. Man from the tunnel, and
    other stories

Frog and the lion
  Benson, T. Man from the tunnel, and
  other stories
Funeral feast
  Benson, T. Man from the tunnel, and
  other stories
Golden fish
  Benson, T. Man from the tunnel, and
  other stories
Harry was good to the girls
  Benson, T. Man from the tunnel, and
  other stories
In the fourth ward
  Benson, T. Man from the tunnel, and
  other stories
Lion and the prey
  Benson, T. Man from the tunnel, and
  other stories
Long time ago
  Benson, T. Man from the tunnel, and
  other stories
Man from the tunnel
  Benson, T. Man from the tunnel, and
  other stories
Man with the phoney tin foot
  Benson, T. Man from the tunnel, and
  other stories
Nice fright
  Benson, T. Man from the tunnel, and
  other stories
Not by bread alone
  Benson, T. Man from the tunnel, and
  other stories
Shakespeare's elderly bore
  Benson, T. Man from the tunnel, and
  other stories
To-morrow is another day
  Benson, T. Man from the tunnel, and
  other stories
White cock
  Benson, T. Man from the tunnel, and
  other stories
White sea monkey
  Benson, T. Man from the tunnel, and
  other stories
Yes-girl
  Benson, T. Man from the tunnel, and
  other stories
Bensusan, Samuel Levy, 1872-
  Death
    Leftwich, J. ed. Yisröel, 1952 ed.
Bent, James F.
  Team man
    Furman, A. L. ed. Teen-age stories of
    the diamond
Bentham, Josephine
  Age of romance
    Stowe, A. comp. It's a date
Bentley, Edmund Clerihew, 1875-1956
  Clever cockatoo
    Bond, R. T. ed. Handbook for poisoners
Bentley, Phyllis Eleanor, 1894-
  Angram folly
    Bentley, P. E. Panorama
  Bag of silver
    Bentley, P. E. Panorama
  Case in Chancery
    Bentley, P. E. Panorama
  Everything under control
    Bentley, P. E. Panorama
  Great lady
    Bentley, P. E. Panorama

Bentley, Phyllis E.—*Continued*
One night in Bradford
Bentley, P. E. Panorama
The sun and the hedge
Bentley, P. E. Panorama

BEQUESTS. See Inheritance and succession; Wills

The **bereaved.** Brookhouser, F.

The **bereft.** Albrizio, G.

Berenice. Poe, E. A.

Berg, Louis, 1900-
Nasty Kupperman and the Ku Klux Klan
Ribalow, H. U. ed. This land, these
people

Berge, B
The lovely green boat
Best American short stories, 1952

Bergelson, David, 1884-
Citizen Woli Brenner
Leftwich, J. ed. Yisröel, 1952 ed.
In a backwoods town
Howe, I. and Greenberg, E. eds. Treasury of Yiddish stories
The squash
Ausubel, N. ed. Treasury of Jewish
humor

Bergengruen, Werner, 1892-
Ali Baba and the forty horse-power
Bergengruen, W. Last Captain of Horse
Concerning muskets
Bergengruen, W. Last Captain of Horse
Easter Greeting
Bergengruen, W. Last Captain of Horse
Eye cure
Bergengruen, W. Last Captain of Horse
Giorgio and Martino
Bergengruen, W. Last Captain of Horse
The knight
Bergengruen, W. Last Captain of Horse
Lykin's sleigh-ride
Bergengruen, W. Last Captain of Horse
Magnanimity contest
Bergengruen, W. Last Captain of Horse
Marshal and his secretary
Bergengruen, W. Last Captain of Horse
Old Hussar
Bergengruen, W. Last Captain of Horse
On presenting arms
Bergengruen, W. Last Captain of Horse
Orban twins
Bergengruen, W. Last Captain of Horse
Pupsik
Bergengruen, W. Last Captain of Horse
Royal game
Bergengruen, W. Last Captain of Horse
Sand doctor
Bergengruen, W. Last Captain of Horse
The sentry
Bergengruen, W. Last Captain of Horse
Shining fools
Bergengruen, W. Last Captain of Horse
Stabenhaüser
Bergengruen, W. Last Captain of Horse
Trivulzio and the King
Bergengruen, W. Last Captain of Horse
When Riga was evacuated
Bergengruen, W. Last Captain of Horse

Berger, T. L.
April is the cruelest month
American vanguard, 1950
Child's play
Wolfe, D. M. ed. Which grain will grow

Berkeley, Anthony, pseud. See Cox, Anthony
Berkeley

Berkshire comedy. Seager, A.

Berman, Hannah, 1890-
Horse thief
Leftwich, J. ed. Yisröel. 1952 ed.

Bernice bobs her hair. Fitzgerald, F. S. K.

Bernstein, David, 1915-
Death of an actor
Ribalow, H. U. ed. This land, these
people

Bernstein, Herman, 1876-1935
Greatest funeral in the world
Leftwich, J. ed. Yisröel. 1952 ed.

Berom. Berryman, J.

Berry, John
New shoes
Prize stories of 1950

Berry patch. Stegner, W. E.

Berryman, John, 1914-
Berom
Bleiler, E. F. and Dikty, T. E. eds.
Imagination unlimited
Imaginary Jew
Swallow, A. ed. Anchor in the sea
Space rating
Conklin, G. ed. Possible worlds of science fiction

Bertie the uninvited. Beal, F.

Bertie's Christmas Eve. Munro, H. H.

Berto, Giuseppe
Lull at Cassino
Berto, G. Works of God, and other
stories
Need to die
Berto, G. Works of God, and other
stories
War passed over us
Berto, G. Works of God, and other
stories
Works of God
Berto, G. Works of God, and other
stories

Beside still waters. Sheckley, R.

Beside the Shalimar. Marshall, E.

Best foot forward. Wright, F. F.

Best of breed. Taber, G. B.

Best of everything. Ellin, S.

Best position. O'Rourke, F.

Best riding and roping. James, W.

Best sea stories from Bluebook. Bluebook
(Periodical)

Best-seller. Porter, W. S.

Bester, Alfred, 1913-
Disappearing act
Star science fiction stories, no. 2
5,271,009
Pohl, F. ed. Assignment in tomorrow
Hobson's choice
Magazine of fantasy and science fiction.
Best from Fantasy and science fiction;
2d ser.

Bester, Alfred—*Continued*
Oddy and Id
Best science fiction stories: 1951
Of time and Third Avenue
Best science fiction stories: 1952
Star light, star bright
Magazine of fantasy and science fiction.
Best from Fantasy and science fiction;
3d ser.
Time is the traitor
Best science-fiction stories: 1954
The **bet** Chekhov, A. P.
Bet the wild queen! Fox, N. A.
Betelgeuse Bridge. Klass, P.
Bethmoora. Dunsany, E. J. M. D. P. 18th
baron
The **betrayers**. Ellin, S.

BETROTHALS
Beer, T. Tact
Hatvany, L. báró. Bondy, jr.
Maugham, W. S. The escape
Maugham, W. S. Fall of Edward Barnard
Newell, V. S. My Julie
O'Donovan, M. Sorcerer's apprentice
O'Donovan, M. Torrent damned
Zangwill, L. Prelude to a pint of bitter

Better mousetrap. Pratt, F. and De Camp,
L. S.

BETTING. See Gambling; Wagers

Betting Scotchman
Cerf, B A. and Moriarty, H. C. eds.
Anthology of famous British stories

Betts, Doris
Child so fair
Betts, D. Gentle insurrection, and other
stories
End of Henry Fribble
Betts, D. Gentle insurrection, and other
stories
Family album
Betts, D. Gentle insurrection, and other
stories
Gentle insurrection
Betts, D. Gentle insurrection, and other
stories
Mark of distinction
Betts, D. Gentle insurrection, and other
stories
Miss Parker possessed
Betts, D. Gentle insurrection, and other
stories
Mr Shawn and Father Scott
Betts, D. Gentle insurrection, and other
stories
Sense of humor
Betts, D. Gentle insurrection, and other
stories
Serpents and doves
Betts, D. Gentle insurrection, and other
stories
The sword
Betts, D. Gentle insurrection, and other
stories
Sympathetic visitor
Betts, D. Gentle insurrection, and other
stories
Very old are beautiful
Betts, D. Gentle insurrection, and other
stories

Bettyann. Neville, K.
Between rounds. Porter, W. S.
Between the acts. Woolf, V. S.
Between the porch and the altar. Stafford, J.
Between you and I. Ullman, J. R.
Bewilderment of Snake McKoy. Spain, N.
Bexar scrip no. 2692. Porter, W. S.
Beyle, Marie Henri, 1783-1842
Mina de Vanghel
Geist, S. ed. French stories and tales
Vanina Vanini
Dupee, F. W. ed. Great French short
novels
Beyond. Faulkner, W.
Beyond Bedlam. Guin, W.
Beyond infinity. Carr, R. S.
Beyond price. Cave, H. B.
Beyond the Black River. Howard, R. E.
Beyond the frontier. Johnson, D. M.
Beyond the glass mountain. Stegner, W. E.
Beyond the grave. Frank, H.
Beyond the Singing Flame. Smith, C. A.
Bezique of death. Johns, V. P.
Bialik, Chaim Nachman. See Bialik, Hayyim
Nahman
Bialik, Elisa
Horse called Pete
Dennis, W. ed. Palomino and other
horses
Bialik, Hayyim Nahman, 1873-1934
King David's cave
Leftwich, J. ed. Yisröel. 1952 ed.
Short Friday
Ausubel, N. ed. Treasury of Jewish
humor
Bianca's hands. Waldo, E. H.
Bianco, Margery (Williams) 1880-1944
Baker's daughter
Fenner, P. R. comp. Fools and funny
fellows
See also Bowman, J. C. jt. auth.

BIBLE IN LITERATURE
Selden, R. ed. Ways of God and man;
24 stories

BIBLICAL CHARACTERS
Frischman, D. Sinai

BIBLICAL STORIES
Hazaz, C. Bridegroom of blood

Bid the tapers twinkle. Aldrich, B. S.

Bierce, Ambrose, 1842-1914?
Boarded window
Burrell, J. A. and Cerf, B. A. eds. An-
thology of famous American stories
Damned thing
Kuebler, H. W. ed. Treasury of sci-
ence fiction classics
Moonlit road
Conklin, G. and Conklin, L. T. eds.
Supernatural reader
Moxon's master
Conklin, G. ed. Science-fiction thinking
machines
Occurrence at Owl Creek bridge
Burrell, J. A. and Cerf, B. A. eds.
Anthology of famous American stories

Bierce, Ambrose—Occurrence at Owl Creek bridge—*Continued*
　Day, A. G. ed. Greatest American short stories
　One of the missing
　　Blodgett, H. W. ed. Story survey. 1953 ed.
Big bed. Monchek, B.
Big black and white game. Bradbury, R.
Big blonde. Parker, D. R.
Big Bones rides alone. Cheley, F. R.
Big Boy Blues. Runyon, D.
Big Buck. Caldwell, E.
Big career. Schlichter, E. W.
Big Chlorinda, happy Chlorinda. Lowrey, P. H.
Big crop of millet. Caldwell, E.
Big Dan Reilly. O'Higgins, H. J.
Big day. Bonner, P. H.
Big Doc's girl. Medearis, M.
Big Ed. Spilo, R.
Big engine. Hayes, W. E.
Big enough for a horse. Van Doren, M.
Big grey picnic. Muheim, H.
Big heart. Vogau, B. A.
Big holiday. Leiber, F.
Big hunger. Miller, W. M.
Big Jack Small. Gally, J. W.
Big Jeff. Farrell, J. T.
Big meeting. Hughes, L.
Big mistake. Caldwell, E.
Big money. Arthur, R.
Big red house on Hope Street. Connolly, M.
Big shot. Acheson, E. G.
Big shot. Chute, B. J.
Big shot. Dresser, D.
Big shoulders. Runyon, D.
The big splash. Miers, E. S.
Big succeh. Reisin, A.
Big train. Foote, J. T.
Big trip up yonder. Vonnegut, K.
Big umbrella. Runyon, D.
BIGAMY
　Maugham, W. S. Round dozen
Bigger they come! Buckingham, N.
Biggest doll in the house. Modell, M.
Biggest flounder. Rendina, L. J. C.
Bigland, Eileen
　Lass with the delicate air
　　Asquith, Lady C. M. E. C. ed. Book of modern ghosts
BILLIARDS
　Munro, H. H. Fate
Billie's fire. Prentice, H.
BILLS, LEGISLATIVE. See Legislation
Bill's eyes. Campbell, W. E. M.
Billy and the gargoyles. Auchincloss, L.
Billy Budd, foretopman. Melville, H.
Billy had a system. Holland, M.
Billy the Bastard. Newhouse, E.

Binder, Eando
　Conquest of life
　　Margulies, L. and Friend, O. J. eds. From off this world
　I, robot
　　Moskowitz, S. comp. Editor's choice in science fiction
Bingo. Seton, E. T.
Bini and Bettine. Kneale, N.
BIOGRAPHERS
　Tarkington, B. Walterson
　　See also Authors
Biography project. Dell, D.
Biological experiment. Keller, K. H.
BIOLOGISTS
　Steinbeck, J. Snake of one's own
Bird, Will Richard, 1891-
　Movies come to Gull Point
　　Pacey, D. ed. Book of Canadian stories
BIRD DEALERS. See Birds
BIRD HUNTERS
　Jewett, S. O. White heron
Bird life. Willingham, C.
Bird of Bagdad. Porter, W. S.
Bird of omen. Marshall, E.
Bird of Paradise. Marshall, E.
Bird of prey. Collier, J.
Bird song. Goss, J. M.
Birdie, come back. Van Doren, M.
BIRDS
　Burroughs, J. Sharp eyes
　De Vries, P. We don't know
　Du Maurier, D. The birds
　Kulbak, M. Munie the bird dealer
　Maugham, W. S. Princess September
　Squires, R. Baby bunting
　　See also names of particular birds: Eagles; Parrots; etc.
BIRDS, EXTINCT
　Wells, H. G. Æpyornis island
The birds. Du Maurier, D.
The birds. Van Doren, M.
Birds of passage Nexø, M. A.
Birds on the western front. Munro, H. H.
Birmingham, Stephen G. 1929-
　Reappearance
　　Story (Periodical) Story; no. 4
Birth. Cronin, A. J.
Birth of a man. Gorky, M.
Birth of a salesman. Wodehouse, P. G.
BIRTH OF CHILDREN. See Childbirth
Birthday of the Infanta. Wilde, O.
BIRTHDAY PARTIES. See Birthdays
BIRTHDAYS
　Clark, W. Van T. Watchful gods
　Cunningham, E. Bar-Nothing's happy birthday
　Grimson, M. S. Happy birthday to you
The birthplace. James, H.
Birthright. Kohn, P. A.

Bishop, Leonard, 1922-
  Crazy Hymie and the nickel
    American vanguard, 1950
  Grass, milk, and children
    Wolfe, D. M. ed. Which grain will grow
Bishop sends his inhibition. Trollope, A.
BISHOPS
  Tolstoĭ, L. N. Graf. Three hermits
BISHOPS, CATHOLIC
  Benét, S. V. Bishop's beggar
  O'Donovan, M. Vanity
    See also Catholic priests
Bishop's beggar. Benét, S. V.
Bishop's fool. Lewis, W.
Bitter dawn. Bonner, P. H.
Bitter farce. Schwartz, D.
Bitter trail. DeRosso, H. A.
Bitter wall. Ferrone, J. R.
Bixby, Jerome, 1923-
  Angels in the jets
    Pohl, F. ed. Assignment in tomorrow
  It's a good life
    Star science fiction stories, no. 2
  Page and player
    Norton, A. M. ed. Space pioneers
Bjørnson, Bjørnstjerne, 1832-1910
  The brothers
    Stauffer, R. M.; Cunningham, W. H.
    and Sullivan, C. J. eds. Adventures
    in modern literature
  How the mountain was clad
    Andrews, R. C. ed. My favorite stories
    of the great outdoors
Black ball. De Camp, L. S. and Pratt, F.
Black ball. Pratt, F. and De Camp, L. S.
Black Bat. Miers, E. S.
Black bile. Rossiter, H. D.
Black brassard. Sheppard, J.
Black bread. Verga, G.
Black cabinet. Carr, J. D.
Black cat. Poe, E. A.
Black devil, mainly. Paterson, N.
Black Eyes and the daily grind. Lesser, M.
Black Falcon. Sperry, A.
Black flag. Powell, F.
Black god's kiss. Moore, C. L.
Black god's shadow. Moore, C. L.
Black horse. Kjelgaard, J. A.
Black John buys a York boat. Hendryx,
  J. B.
Black John chats with Corporal Downey.
  Hendryx, J. B.
Black John delivers a deed. Hendryx, J. B.
Black John departs for Dawson. Hendryx,
  J. B.
Black John does some checking. Hendryx,
  J. B.
Black John gets a tip. Hendryx, J. B.
Black John goes to Dawson. Hendryx, J. B.
Black John goes to Fortymile. Hendryx,
  J. B.
Black John holds a conference. Hendryx,
  J. B.

Black John makes a purchase. Hendryx,
  J. B.
Black John sells his York boat. Hendryx,
  J. B.
Black John talks with the goose. Hendryx,
  J. B.
Black John wins a bet. Hendryx, J. B.
Black Lamars. Mowery, W. B.
Black ledger. Queen, E. pseud.
Black lie. Sandy, S.
Black magician. Coolidge, O. E.
BLACK MARKETS
  Housesold, G. Brandy for the parson
  Putnam, C. Old acrobat and the ruined
    city
BLACK MASS
  Irwin, M. E. F. Earlier service
Black music. Faulkner, W.
Black pits of Luna. Heinlein, R. A.
Black prince. Grau, S. A.
Black road. Steele, W. D.
Black seal. Machen, A.
Black star passes. Campbell, J. W.
Black Storm. Hinkle, T. C.
Black Swamp. Roberts, Sir C. G. D.
Black thirst. Moore, C. L.
Black water blues. Culver, M.
Blackbeard. Malcolmson, A. B.
Blackberry winter. Warren, R. P.
Blackburn, Ernest Richard, 1926-
  Before the burning of Rome
    Blackburn, E. R. The swaying elms, and
    other stories
  Christiane the Huguenot
    Blackburn, E. R. The swaying elms, and
    other stories
  Galatians 2:20
    Blackburn, E. R. The swaying elms, and
    other stories
  Good win
    Blackburn, E. R. The swaying elms, and
    other stories
  Jerome of Prague
    Blackburn, E. R. The swaying elms, and
    other stories
  Last king
    Blackburn, E. R. The swaying elms, and
    other stories
  Missed train
    Blackburn, E. R. The swaying elms, and
    other stories
  Mission door
    Blackburn, E. R. The swaying elms, and
    other stories
  Story of Pompeii
    Blackburn, E. R. The swaying elms, and
    other stories
  Sunrise
    Blackburn, E. R. The swaying elms, and
    other stories
  Swaying elms
    Blackburn, E. R. The swaying elms, and
    other stories
  Walk for me
    Blackburn, E. R. The swaying elms, and
    other stories

Blackburn, Robert Harold, 1919-
Clay dish
Weaver, R. and James, H. eds. Canadian short stories
The **blackguard.** McCarthy, M. T.
Blackjack bargainer. Porter, W. S.
BLACKMAIL
Arlen, M. Cavalier of the streets
Brandon, W. Party to blackmail
Collins, W. Stolen letter
Doyle, Sir A. C. Scandal in Bohemia
Elston, A. V. Blackmail
Munro, H. H. Treasure-ship
Porter, W. S. Remnants of the code
Queen, E. pseud. Money talks
Queen, E. pseud. Sound of blackmail
Blackmail. Elston, A. V.
Blackout over Cleveland. Litten, F. N.
BLACKSMITHS
Cunningham, J. M. Iron rose
Blackwood, Algernon, 1869-1951
Psychical invasion
Carrington, H. ed. Week-end book of ghost stories
Roman remains
Derleth, A. W. ed. Night's yawning peal
Valley of the beasts
Cerf, B. A. and Moriarty, H. C. eds. Anthology of famous British stories
The Wendigo
Davenport, B. ed. Ghostly tales to be told
Bland, Edith (Nesbit) 1858-1924
Digging for treasure
Fenner, P. R. comp. Fun! Fun! Fun!
The pavilion
Conklin, G. and Conklin, L. T. eds. Supernatural reader
The **blanket.** Brooke, J.
The **blanket.** Dell, F.
Blast of the book. Chesterton, G. K.
Bleeding heart. Stafford, J.
Blessed are the clean of heart; they shall see God. Baker, F.
Blessed are the merciful; they shall obtain mercy. Baker, F.
Blessed are the patient; they shall inherit the land. Baker, F.
Blessed are the peace-makers; they shall be counted the children of God. Baker, F.
Blessed are the poor in spirit; the kingdom of heaven is theirs. Baker, F.
Blessed are those who hunger and thirst for holiness; they shall have their fill. Baker, F.
Blessed are those who mourn; they shall be comforted. Baker, F.
Blessed are those who suffer persecution in the cause of right; the kingdom of heaven is theirs. Baker, F.
Blessed event. Sellars, M.
The **blight.** Cox, A. J.
BLIND
Baum, V. Old house
Campbell, W. E. M. Bill's eyes
Corkery, D. Storm struck

Edmonds, W. D. Blind Eve
Kipling, R. 'They'
Lawrence, D. H. Blind man
Schisgall, O. Eyes in the dark
Schnitzler, A. Blind Geronimo and his brother
Taylor, E. Spry old character
Wells, H. G. Country of the blind
Zweig, S. Invisible collection
Zweig, S. Unseen collection
Blind alley. Jameson, M.
Blind Eve. Edmonds, W. D.
Blind Geronimo and his brother. Schnitzler, A.
Blind man. Lawrence, D. H.
Blind man, the deaf man, and the donkey. Frere, M. E. I.
Blind man's buff. Jameson, M.
Blind man's holiday. Porter, W. S.
Blind spot. Munro, H. H.
Blinding of André Maloche. Mowat, F.
Blinding shadows. Wandrei, D.
Blindman's world. Bellamy, E.
BLINDNESS. See Blind
Blish, James
Beanstalk
Crossen, K. F. ed. Future tense
Beep
Sloane, W. M. ed. Stories for tomorrow
The box
Conklin, G. ed. Omnibus of science fiction
FYI
Star science fiction stories, no. 2
Mistake inside
Pratt, F. ed. World of wonder
Okie
Sloane, W. M. ed. Stories for tomorrow
Solar plexus
Merril, J. ed. Beyond human ken
Surface tension
Galaxy science fiction magazine. Second Galaxy reader of science fiction
Year's best science fiction novels, 1953
Bliss. Mansfield, K.
Blister. Foote, J. T.
Blixen, Karen, 1885-
The pearls
Burnett, W. ed. World's best
Bloch, Alan
Men are different
Conklin, G. ed. Science-fiction thinking machines
Bloch, Jean Richard, 1884-1947
Heresy of the water taps
Ausubel, N. ed. Treasury of Jewish humor
Leftwich, J. ed. Yisröel. 1952 ed.
Bloch, Robert, 1914-
Fear planet
Derleth, A. W. ed. Far boundaries
Man who collected Poe
Derleth, A. W. ed. Night's yawning peal
Blochman, Lawrence Goldtree, 1900-
Brood of evil
Best detective stories of the year— 1950
Blochman, L. G. Diagnosis: homicide

Blochman, Lawrence G.—*Continued*
But the patient died
    Blochman, L. G. Diagnosis: homicide
Calendar girl
    Best detective stories of the year—1953
Catfish story
    Blochman, L. G. Diagnosis: homicide
Deadly back-fire
    Blochman, L. G. Diagnosis: homicide
Diagnosis deferred
    Blochman, L. G. Diagnosis: homicide
Fifty-carat jinx
    Mystery Writers of America, inc. Maiden murders
Half-naked truth
    Blochman, L. G. Diagnosis: homicide
Jimat of Dorland
    Mystery Writers of America, inc.
    Crooks' tour
Kiss of Kandahar
    Best detective stories of the year—1952
Phantom cry-baby
    Blochman, L. G. Diagnosis: homicide
Riviera renegade
    Mystery Writers of America, inc.
    20 great tales of murder
Rum for dinner
    Blochman, L. G. Diagnosis: homicide
Zarapore beat
    Mystery Writers of America, inc.
    Four-&-twenty bloodhounds

Block, Rudolph Edgar, 1870-1940
Americanization of Shadrach Cohen
    Ribalow, H. U. ed. These your children

Blockade runner. Jameson, M.

Blond dog. Stoumen, L. C.

Blond mink. Runyon, D.

Blonde nurse. Walsh, T.

Blood-feud of Toad-Water. Munro, H. H.

Blood is a bright shadow. Moseley, H.

Blood of the martyrs. Benét, S. V.

Blood on the ice. Kjelgaard, J. A.

Blood will tell. Marquis, D.

Bloodhound. Boyd, J.

BLOODHOUNDS
Boyd, J. Bloodhound

Bloodstained beach. Marmur, J.

Bloodstock. Irwin, M. E. F.

Bloomfield, Howard, 1900-
Murder tavern
    Argosy (Periodical) Argosy Book of adventure stories
Pirate and the gamecock
    Argosy (Periodical) Argosy Book of sea stories
The trap
    Cuff, R. P. ed. American short story survey

Bloomgarden, Solomon, 1870-
Share of paradise
    Ausubel, N. ed. Treasury of Jewish humor
Zoology
    Ausubel, N. ed. Treasury of Jewish humor

Blossom on the yew. Dawkins, M. L.

"Blow up with the brig!" Collins, W.

Blowing up a train. Lawrence, T. E.

Blowups happen. Heinlein, R. A.

Blue, Edna, 1901-
Nothing overwhelms Giuseppe
    Bachelor, J. M.; Henry, R. L. and Salisbury, R. eds. Current thinking and writing; 2d ser.

Blue Boy. Caldwell, E.

Blue brocade. Hill, M. Y.

Blue carbuncle. Doyle, Sir A. C.

Blue charm. Bonner, P. H.

Blue cross. Chesterton, G. K.

Blue flag. Hill, K.

Blue giraffe. De Camp, L. S.

Blue hat. Elliott, H. S.

Blue Hotel. Crane, S.

Blue hyacinths. Powell, D.

BLUE JAYS
Clemens, S. L. Jim Baker's blue-jay yarn

Blue murder. Steele, W. D.

Blue ribbon. Woolrich, C.

Blue ribbon event. Carter, R. G.

Blue sash. Beck, W.

Blue-winged teal. Stegner, W. E.

Bluff. Adler, J.

Boa constrictor and rabbit. Chekhov, A. P.

Boar-pig. Munro, H. H.

Board of Inland Revenue v. Haddock. Herbert, Sir A. P.

Boarded window. Bierce, A.

BOARDERS. See Boarding houses

BOARDING HOUSES
Barker, A. L. Pringle
Carroll, J. W. At Mrs Farrelly's
Chekhov, A. P. The lodger
De La Roche, M. Widow Cruse
Jackson, C. R. Sleeper awakened
Leiper, G. B. The magnolias
Porter, W. S. Aristocracy versus hash
Porter, W. S. Between rounds
Porter, W. S. Furnished room
Porter, W. S. Skylight room
Porter, W. S. Third ingredient
    See also Hotels, taverns, etc.

BOARDING SCHOOLS. See School life

BOARS
Annixter, P. pseud. Brought to cover

Boat journey. Shackleton, Sir E. H.

BOAT RACES
Coombs, C. I. River challenge
    See also Rowing; Yacht racing

The **boats.** Crawford, C.

BOATS AND BOATING
Clark, W. Van T. The rapids
Loring, S. M. Eel-trap
Michel, E. Moon tide
    See also House boats; Motorboats; River boats; Submarine boats

BOAZ
Fineman, I. In the fields of Boaz

BOB SLEDS. See Tobogganing

Bobo and the Christmas spirit. Price, E. B.

Boccaccio, Giovanni, 1313-1375
  Patient Griselda
    Cody, S. ed. Greatest stories, and how
    they were written
Body of an American. Dos Passos, J. R.
Body-snatcher. Stevenson, R. L.
BODY-SNATCHING
  Harvey, W. F. No body
BODY WEIGHT CONTROL. See Corpu-
  lence
BOERS. See Africa, South
BOHEMIAN LIFE. See Artist life
**BOHEMIANS IN THE UNITED
  STATES.** See Czechoslovakians in
  the United States
Boiler room. Sansom, W.
Bojer, Johan, 1872-
  A letter to Klaus Brock
    Brentano, F. ed. The word lives on
BOLSHEVISM. See Communism—Russia
Bolt from the blue. Broun, H. C.
Bolté, Mary, 1921-
  End of the depression
    Best American short stories, 1951
    Greene, J. I. and Abell, E. eds. Stories
    of sudden truth
Bolton, Isabel, pseud. See Miller, Mary
  Britton
Bolton, Ivy May, 1879-
  Saint for Wessex
    Hazeltine, A. I. comp. Selected stories
    for teen-agers
The **bombardier.** Gallico, P. W.
BOMBARDMENT
  Macfarlan, A. A. Camp at Saint Adrien
Bombers' night. Fabyan, E.
BOMBS. See Projectiles
The **bombshop.** O'Faoláin, S.
Bon-Bon. Poe, E. A.
Bond, Nelson Slade, 1908-
  Abduction of Abner Greer
    Brown, F. and Reynolds, M. eds. Sci-
    ence-fiction carnival
  And lo! The bird
    Derleth, A. W. ed. Far boundaries
  Conquerors' isle
    Pratt, F. ed. World of wonder
  Day we celebrate
    Conklin, G. ed. Possible worlds of sci-
    ence fiction
  The sportsman
    Creamer, J. B. comp. Twenty-two sto-
    ries about horses and men
  Steady like a rock
    Dachs, D. ed. Treasury of sports humor
  This is the land
    Derleth, A. W. ed. The outer reaches
  To people a new world
    Derleth, A. W. ed. Beachheads in space
Bond. Karchmer, S.
Bondarenko, William Carl, 1921-
  Job well done
    American vanguard, 1953
Bondy, jr. Hatvany, L. báró
Bones for Davy Jones. Commings, J.

Bones of A. T. Stewart. Benson, T.
The **bonesetter.** Walsh, M.
Bonham, Frank
  Burn him out
    Argosy (Periodical) Book of adventure
    stories
  I'll take the high road
    Western Writers of America. Holsters
    and heroes
  One ride too many
    Western Writers of America. Bad men
    and good
Bonham, Margaret
  Fine place for the cat
    Joseph, M. ed. Best cat stories
Bonnaffon, Anne
  Quick shoots
    Wolfe, D. M. ed. Which grain will grow
Bonner, Nicholas
  Mr Mitts
    Thinker's digest (Periodical) Spoiled
    priest, and other stories
Bonner, Paul Hyde, 1893-
  Big day
    Bonner, P. H. Glorious mornings
  Bitter dawn
    Bonner, P. H. Glorious mornings
  Blue charm
    Bonner, P. H. Glorious mornings
  Caddis hatch
    Bonner, P. H. Glorious mornings
  Foul is fair
    Bonner, P. H. Glorious mornings
  Made to measure
    Bonner, P. H. Glorious mornings
  Mollie
    Bonner, P. H. Glorious mornings
  Pump house key
    Bonner, P. H. Glorious mornings
  Rajah's Rock
    Bonner, P. H. Glorious mornings
  Stalker & Co.
    Bonner, P. H. Glorious mornings
  The triumph
    Bonner, P. H. Glorious mornings
  Velia
    Bonner, P. H. Glorious mornings
Bontemps. Whitmore, S.
Bontsha the Silent. Peretz, I. L.
The **book.** Irwin, M. E. F.
Book-bag. Maugham, W. S.
BOOK SALESMEN. See Booksellers and
  bookselling
Booker, Adria E.
  Box-car to castle
    Booker, A. E. Was it too late? & other
    stories
  Rancher of the hills
    Booker, A. E. Was it too late? & other
    stories
  Second Christmas
    Booker, A. E. Was it too late? & other
    stories
  That others might live
    Booker, A. E. Was it too late? & other
    stories
  Was it too late?
    Booker, A. E. Was it too late? & other
    stories

Booker, Simeon
She never knew
Ford, N. A. and Faggett, H. L. eds.
Best short stories by Afro-American
writers (1925-1950)

BOOKKEEPERS. See Accountants

BOOKS
Milne, A. A. Rise and fall of Mortimer
Scrivens
Porter, W. S. Best-seller
Tunkel, J. The gift
Yates, E. Enshrined in the heart

BOOKS AND READING
Hall, E. G. Callie of Crooked Creek
P'u Sung-ling. The bookworm

BOOKSELLERS AND BOOKSELLING
Abramowitz, S. J. The exchange
Lagerkvist, P. F. God's little traveling
salesman
Munro, H. H. Mark

BOOKSHOPS. See Booksellers and bookselling

The **bookworm.** P'u Sung-ling

Boomerang. Russell, E. F.

BOONE, DANIEL, 1734-1820
Fast, H. M. Tall hunter

BOOTBLACKS
Brookhouser, F. You aim so high

BOOTH, JOHN WILKES, 1838-1865
Carr, J. D. Black cabinet

Booth, Maud Ballington (Charlesworth)
1865-1948
Christ's tree
Elmquist, R. M. ed. Fifty years to
Christmas

BOOTLEGGING. See Liquor traffic

BOOTS AND SHOES
Porter, W. S. Ships
Porter, W. S. Shoes
See also Shoemakers

Boots, who made the Princess say, "That's
a story." Dasent, Sir G. W.

Borden, Mary, 1886-
In Nazareth
Selden, R. ed. Ways of God and men

BORES (PERSONS)
Cotterell, G. Delicate warning
Munro, H. H. Defensive diamond

BORES (TIDAL PHENOMENA) See
Tidal waves

Borges, Jorge Luis, 1900-
Secret miracle
De Onís, H. ed. Spanish stories and
tales

Born killer. Davis, D. S.

Born of man and woman. Matheson, R.

BORNEO. See Dutch East Indies—Borneo

BORROWING
Jackson, C. R. Money
Maugham, W. S. Ant and the grass-
hopper

Boscombe Valley mystery. Doyle, Sir A. C.

Bosher, E. F.
Too much Hugo
Furman, A. L. ed. Teen-age dog stories

Bosis, Lauro de, 1901-1931?
Story of my death
Jensen, P. ed. Fireside book of flying
stories

BOSTON. See Massachusetts—Boston

Bottle imp. Stevenson, R. L.

Bottle of Perrier. Wharton, E. N. J.

Bottle party. Collier, J.

Bottom of the cloud. Barr, J. pseud.

Bottome, Phyllis, 1884-
Caesar's wife's ear
Bottome, P. Man and beast
Dark Blue
Bottome, P. Man and beast
Henry
Bottome, P. Man and beast
Liqueur glass
Bond, R. T. ed. Handbook for poisoners
A pair
Bottome, P. Man and beast
Pink medicine
Bottome, P. Man and beast
Splendid fellow
Talbot, D. ed. Treasury of mountaineer-
ing stories

Botts and the brink of disaster. Upson,
W. H.

Botts and the jet-propelled tractor. Upson,
W. H.

Botts bogs down. Upson, W. H.

Botts cleans out the parts department. Upson,
W. H.

Botts discovers uranium. Upson, W. H.

Botts gets a new job. Upson, W. H.

Botts makes magic. Upson, W. H.

Boucher, Anthony, pseud. See White, William Anthony Parker

Bound for the bottom. Wallace, J. F.

Bow down, Isaac! Aiken, C. P.

Bowen, Elizabeth, 1899-
All saints
Bowen, E. Early stories
Ann Lee's
Bowen, E. Early stories
Back drawing-room
Bowen, E. Early stories
Breakfast
Bowen, E. Early stories
Cat jumps
Ludwig, J. B. and Poirier, W. R. eds.
Stories, British and American
Charity
Bowen, E. Early stories
Cherry soul
Magazine of fantasy and science fiction.
Best from Fantasy and science fiction;
2d ser.
Coming home
Bowen, E. Early stories
The confidante
Bowen, E. Early stories
The contessina
Bowen, E. Early stories
Daffodils
Bowen, E. Early stories

Bowen, Elizabeth—*Continued*
Demon lover
  Gordon, C. and Tate, A. eds. House of fiction
  Lynskey, W. C. ed. Reading modern fiction
Easter egg party
  Burnett, W. ed. World's best
Evil that men do—
  Bowen, E. Early stories
Hand in glove
  Asquith, Lady C. M. E. C. ed. Book of modern ghosts
Her table spread
  O'Faoláin, S. The short story
Human habitation
  Bowen, E. Early stories
The lover
  Bowen, E. Early stories
Lunch
  Bowen, E. Early stories
Making arrangements
  Bowen, E. Early stories
Mrs Windermere
  Bowen, E. Early stories
Mysterious Kôr
  New writing (Periodical) Best stories
New house
  Bowen, E. Early stories
The parrot
  Bowen, E. Early stories
Recent photograph
  Bowen, E. Early stories
Requiescat
  Bowen, E. Early stories
The return
  Bowen, E. Early stories
The secession
  Bowen, E. Early stories
Shadowy third
  Bowen, E. Early stories
The storm
  Bowen, E. Early stories
Sunday evening
  Bowen, E. Early stories
The visitor
  Bowen, E. Early stories
Bowen, Robert Owen, 1920-
Other river
  Best American short stories, 1952
Bower of roses. Forester, C. S.
Bowes-Lyon, Susannah Sarah, 1920-
Harum Scarum; the life story of a horse
  Dennis, W. ed. Palomino and other horses
The **bowl.** De La Mare, W. J.
The **bowl.** Fitzgerald, F. S. K.
Bowles, Paul Frederic, 1911-
At Paso Rojo
  Bowles, P. F. Delicate prey, and other stories
By the water
  Bowles, P. F. Delicate prey, and other stories
  Lynskey W. C. ed. Reading modern fiction
Call at Corazón
  Bowles, P. F. Delicate prey, and other stories

Circular valley
  Bowles, P. F. Delicate prey, and other stories
Delicate prey
  Bowles, P. F. Delicate prey, and other stories
Distant episode
  Bowles, P. F. Delicate prey, and other stories
The echo
  Bowles, P. F. Delicate prey, and other stories
Fourth day out from Santa Cruz
  Bowles, P. F. Delicate prey, and other stories
How many midnights
  Bowles, P. F. Delicate prey, and other stories
Pages from Cold Point
  Bowles, P. F. Delicate prey, and other stories
  Cory D. W. pseud. comp. 21 variations on a theme
Pastor Dowe at Tacaté
  Best American short stories, 1950
  Bowles, P. F. Delicate prey, and other stories
The scorpion
  Bowles, P. F. Delicate prey, and other stories
Señor Ong and Señor Ha
  Bowles, P. F. Delicate prey, and other stories
Tea on the mountain
  Bowles, P. F. Delicate prey, and other stories
Thousand days for Mokhtar
  Bowles, P. F. Delicate prey, and other stories
Under the sky
  Bowles, P. F. Delicate prey, and other stories
  Ludwig, J. B. and Poirier, W. R. eds. Stories, British and American
You are not I
  Bowles, P. F. Delicate prey, and other stories
Bowman, James Cloyd, 1880-
First war party
  Fenner, P. R. comp. Indians, Indians, Indians
Bowman, James Cloyd, 1880- **and Bianco, Margery (Williams)** 1880-1944
Wise men of Holmola
  Fenner, P. R. comp. Fools and funny fellows
The **box.** Blish, J.
Box-car to castle. Booker, A. E.
Box of ginger. Calisher, H.
Box score battle. Worthington, J.
Boxer, Jack, 1909-
Anna was bad
  Wolfe, D. M. ed. Which grain will grow
Boxer: old. Sylvester, H.
BOXERS. See Boxing
BOXING
  Dachs, D. Speaking of characters
  Fay, W. Lady says murder
  Fay, W. Murder the bum
  Gallico, P. W. Melee of the Mages

BOXING—*Continued*

Griffith, R. Jingle bells
Hemingway, E. Fifty grand
Johnston, N. F. Absolution
Lanham, E. M. Listen to me, boy
Lardner, J. Sudden attack of heartbreak
London, J. Piece of steak
Maxwell, J. A. Fighter
Merson, B. Cross-up
Parker, D. F. Passing of the first floor back
Philips, J. P. Man who had no friends
Porter, W. S. Hygeia at the Solito
Queen, E. pseud. Matter of seconds
Ribalow, H. U. ed. World's greatest boxing stories; 18 stories
Runyon, D. Leopard's spots
Schulberg, B. W. Crowd pleaser
Schulberg, B. W. Meal ticket
Schulberg, B. W. Memory in white
Schulberg, B. W. Pride of Tony Colucci
Switzer, R. Death of a prize fighter
        See also Fighting, Hand-to-hand

Boy and a dog. Singmaster, E.

Boy bites man. Shulman, M.

Boy crazy. De Meyer, J.

Boy in the house. De La Roche, M.

Boy in the mirror. Summers, J. L.

Boy in the summer sun. Schorer, M.

BOY SCOUTS

Long, E. W. Green match
Macfarlan, A. A. Camp at Saint Adrien
Strong, P. N. Shantyboat pirate
Strong, P. N. Trail of the whittle-poof

Boy who drew cats. Hearn, L.

Boy who gave his dog away. Rawlings, C. A.

Boy who ran away. Jackson, C. R.

Boy who went away. Moll, E.

Boy who wrote 'no.' Lord, J.

Boy with a trumpet. Davies, R.

Boy with the innocent eyes. Kandel, L.

BOYCOTTS

Bergelson, D. In a backwoods town

Boyd, James, 1888-1944
Away! Away!
    Boyd, J. Old pines, and other stories
Bloodhound
    Boyd, J. Old pines, and other stories
Civic crisis
    Boyd, J. Old pines, and other stories
Elms and Fair Oaks
    Boyd, J. Old pines, and other stories
    Jones, K. M. ed. New Confederate short stories
Fiesta
    Boyd, J. Old pines, and other stories
Flat town
    Boyd, J. Old pines, and other stories
Gizzard of a scientist
    Boyd, J. Old pines, and other stories
Lookout
    Bachelor, J. M.; Henry, R. L. and Salisbury, R. eds. Current thinking and writing; 2d ser.
Old pines
    Boyd, J. Old pines, and other stories

Shiftless
    Boyd, J. Old pines, and other stories
Verse on the window
    Boyd, J. Old pines, and other stories

Boyd, Thomas Alexander, 1898-1935
Responsibility
    Shaw, H. and Bement, D. Reading the short story

Boyle, Kay, 1903-
Adam's death
    Boyle, K. Smoking mountain
Art colony
    Millett, F. B. Reading fiction
Aufwiedersehen abend
    Boyle, K. Smoking mountain
Begin again
    Boyle, K. Smoking mountain
Bridegroom's body
    Southern review. Anthology of stories from the Southern review
Cabaret
    Boyle, K. Smoking mountain
Crazy hunter
    Ludwig, R. M. and Perry, M. B. eds. Nine short novels
The criminal
    Boyle, K. Smoking mountain
Defeat
    First-prize stories, 1919-1954
Diagnosis of a selfish lady
    Saturday evening post (Periodical) Saturday evening post stories, 1952
Disgrace to the family
    Saturday evening post (Periodical) Saturday evening post stories, 1950
Effigy of war
    Heilman, R. B. ed. Modern short stories
Fife's house
    Boyle, K. Smoking mountain
Frankfurt in our blood
    Boyle, K. Smoking mountain
His idea of a mother
    West, R. B. and Stallman, R. W. eds. Art of modern fiction
Home
    Boyle, K. Smoking mountain
Keep your pity
    Barrows, H. ed. 15 stories
The lost
    Best American short stories, 1952
    Boyle, K. Smoking mountain
Lovers of gain
    Bachelor, J. M.; Henry, R. L. and Salisbury, R. eds. Current thinking and writing; 2d ser.
    Boyle, K. Smoking mountain
Maiden, maiden
    Talbot, D. ed. Treasury of mountaineering stories
Natives don't cry
    Felheim, M.; Newman, F. B. and Steinhoff, W. R. eds. Modern short stories
Nothing ever breaks except the heart
    Best of the Best American short stories, 1915-1950
Soldier ran away
    Saturday evening post (Periodical) Saturday evening post stories, 1953
Summer evening
    Boyle, K. Smoking mountain
    Prize stories of 1950

Boyle, Kay—*Continued*
They weren't going to die
Lynskey, W. C. ed. Reading modern
fiction
Wanderer
Swallow, A. ed. Anchor in the sea
White horses of Vienna
First-prize stories, 1919-1954

Boylston, Helen (Dore) 1895-
Stuff of dreams
Eaton, H. T. ed. Short stories

BOYS

Adler, J. My Pinya
Aiken, C. P. Silent snow, secret snow
Aiken, C. P. Strange moonlight
Allen, M. P. Yoo hoo! Mudhen!
Bennett, P. Death under the hawthornes
Bennett, P. Fugitive from the mind
Boyle, K. His idea of a mother
Casper, L. Sense of direction
Chekhov, A. P. Vanka
Clark, W. Van T. Watchful gods
Clayton, J. B. White circle
Crane, S. The fight
Crane, S. His new mittens
Cuevas, E. Lock the doors, lock the
windows
Davis, R. H. Tree toad
De La Roche, M. Boy in the house
Dostoevskiĭ, F. M. Heavenly Christmas
tree
Doty, W. L. Silver cross
Eisenberg, F. Roof sitter
Ewald, C. My little boy
Fitzgerald, F. S. K. Captured shadow
Fitzgerald, F. S. K. Freshest boy
Fitzgerald, F. S. K. Scandal detectives
Goldman, A. Almost like dead
Goodman, J. C. Kingdom of Gordon
Granberry, E. P. Trip to Czardis
Grau, S. A. Joshua
Greene, G. Basement room
Harte, B. How Santa Claus came to
Simpson's Bar
Heyert, M. New kid
Johnson, D. M. Prairie kid
Kipling, R. Tods' amendment
Krige, U. The dream
Lagerkvist, P. F. Guest of reality
McCourt, E. A. White mustang
Mann, T. Fight between Jappe and Do
Escobar
Miller, C. Gentle season
Modell, J. Day in the sun
Monchek, B. Big bed
Nadir, I. M. My first love
Nuhn, F. Ten
O'Donovan, M. Face of evil
O'Donovan, M. Man of the house
O'Donovan, M. Masculine protest
Paterson, R. Slowpoke
Porter, K. A. Downward path to wisdom
Porter, W. S. Ransom of Red Chief
Rossiter, H. D. How dear to my heart
Salinger, J. D. Down at the dinghy
Sansom, W. From the water junction
Saroyan, W. Parsley garden
Saroyan, W. Pheasant hunter
Saroyan, W. The plot
Saroyan, W. Resurrection of a life
Schweitzer, G. Kid brother

Seide, M. Bad boy from Brooklyn
Stegner, W. E. Butcher bird
Steinbeck, J. Red pony
Street, J. H. Weep no more, My Lady
Tarkington, B. "Little gentleman"
Taylor, P. H. Two ladies in retirement
Ware, L. Phantom of the bridge
Watson, J. C. Benny and the Tar-Baby
Wilbur, R. Game of catch
Wilson, A. Necessity's child
Wolfe, T. Lost boy
See also Adolescence; Children

BOYS' CLUBS
Salinger, J. D. Laughing man

Boy's will. Quentin, P. pseud.

Boys will be boys. Cobb, I. S.

Boz, pseud. See Dickens, Charles

Brace, Gerald Warner, 1901-
Deep water man
Blodgett, H. W. ed. Story survey.
1953 ed.

Brachvogel, Albert Emil, 1824-1878
Christmas at the Bachs'
Lohan, R. and Lohan, M. eds. New
Christmas treasury

Brackett, Leigh
Enchantress of Venus
Margulies, L. and Friend, O. J. eds.
Giant anthology of science fiction
Last days of Shandakor
Wollheim, D. A. ed. Prize science fic-
tion
Retreat to the stars
Crossen, K. F. ed. Adventures in to-
morrow

Bradbury, Ray, 1920-
And the moon be still as bright
Bleiler, E. F. and Dikty, T. E. eds. Sci-
ence fiction omnibus: The best science
fiction stories, 1949, 1950
April witch
Bradbury, R. Golden apples of the sun
Asleep in Armageddon
Conklin, G. ed. Possible worlds of sci-
ence fiction
Beast from 20,000 fathoms
Saturday evening post (Periodical)
Saturday evening post stories, 1951
Big black and white game
Bradbury, R. Golden apples of the sun
The city
Bradbury, R. Illustrated man
Concrete mixer
Bradbury, R. Illustrated man
Dwellers in silence
Best science fiction stories: 1950
Bleiler, E. F. and Dikty, T. E. eds.
Science fiction omnibus: The best
science fiction stories, 1949, 1950
Embroidery
Bradbury, R. Golden apples of the sun
En la noche
Bradbury, R. Golden apples of the sun
The exiles
Bradbury, R. Illustrated man
Derleth, A. W. ed. Beyond time & space
Fire balloons
Bradbury, R. Illustrated man
Flying machine
Bradbury, R. Golden apples of the sun

Bradbury, Ray—*Continued*

Fog horn
  Bradbury, R. Golden apples of the sun
Forever and the earth
  Conklin, G. ed. Big book of science fiction
The fox and the forest
  Bradbury, R. Illustrated man
  Same as: Fox in the forest
Fox in the forest
  Best science fiction stories: 1951
  Same as: The fox and the forest
Fruit at the bottom of the bowl
  Bradbury, R. Golden apples of the sun
Garbage collector
  Bradbury, R. Golden apples of the sun
Golden apples of the sun
  Bradbury, R. Golden apples of the sun
Golden kite, the silver wind
  Bradbury, R. Golden apples of the sun
Great fire
  Bradbury, R. Golden apples of the sun
  Seventeen (Periodical) Nineteen from Seventeen
Great wide world over there
  Bradbury, R. Golden apples of the sun
Hail and farewell
  Bradbury, R. Golden apples of the sun
Here there be tygers
  Healy, R. J. ed. New tales of space and time
The highway
  Bradbury, R. Illustrated man
Holiday
  Derleth, A. W. ed. Far boundaries
I see you never
  Bradbury, R. Golden apples of the sun
The illustrated man
  Bradbury, R. Illustrated man
In this sign
  Leesor, M. A. ed. Looking forward
Invisible boy
  Bradbury, R. Golden apples of the sun
Kaleidoscope
  Bradbury, R. Illustrated man
  Conklin, G. ed. Omnibus of science fiction
King of the gray spaces
  Wollheim, D. A. comp. Every boy's book of science-fiction
Last night of the world
  Bradbury, R. Illustrated world
A little journey
  Galaxy science fiction magazine. Galaxy reader of science fiction
Long rain
  Bradbury, R. Illustrated man
The man
  Best science fiction stories: 1950
  Bleiler, E. F. and Dikty, T. E. eds. Science fiction omnibus: The best science fiction stories, 1949, 1950
  Bradbury, R. Illustrated man
Marionettes, inc.
  Bradbury, R. Illustrated man
Mars is heaven
  Bleiler, E. F. and Dikty, T. E. eds. Science fiction omnibus: The best science fiction stories, 1949, 1950
The meadow
  Bradbury, R. Golden apples of the sun

Million-year picnic
  Pratt, F. ed. World of wonder
The murderer
  Bradbury, R. Golden apples of the sun
Naming of names
  Startling stories (Periodical) Best from Startling stories
Night meeting
  Conklin, G. ed. Science-fiction adventures in dimension
No particular night or morning
  Bradbury, R. Illustrated man
The one who waits
  Derleth, A. W. ed. Far boundaries
Other foot
  Best American short stories, 1952
  Bradbury, R. Illustrated man
The pedestrian
  Best science fiction stories: 1952
  Bradbury, R. Golden apples of the sun
Powerhouse
  Bradbury, R. Golden apples of the sun
Referent
  Bleiler, E. F. and Dikty, T. E. eds. Imagination unlimited
The rocket
  Bradbury, R. Illustrated man
Rocket man
  Bradbury, R. Illustrated man
Scent of sarsaparilla
  Sloane, W. M. ed. Stories for tomorrow
  Star science fiction stories [no. 1]
Shape of things
  Greenberg, M. ed. Travelers of space
The smile
  Derleth, A. W. ed. Worlds of tomorrow
Sound of thunder
  Bradbury, R. Golden apples of the sun
Strawberry window
  Star science fiction stories, no. 3
Subterfuge
  Pohl, F. ed. Assignment in tomorrow
Sun and shadow
  Bradbury, R. Golden apples of the sun
There will come soft rains
  Crossen, K. F. ed. Adventures in tomorrow
Tombling day
  Conklin, G. and Conklin, L. T. eds. Supernatural reader
The veldt
  Bradbury, R. Illustrated man
  Merril, J. ed. Beyond the barriers of space and time
The visitor
  Bradbury, R. Illustrated man
The wilderness
  Bradbury, R. Golden apples of the sun
  Sloane, W. M. ed. Stories for tomorrow
World the children made
  Saturday evening post (Periodical) Saturday evening post stories, 1950
Ylla
  Derleth, A. W. ed. The outer reaches
Zero hour
  Bradbury, R. Illustrated man
Bradford, Roark, 1896-1948
Child of God
  First-prize stories, 1919-1954
Stratagem of Joshua
  Selden, R. ed. Ways of God and men

Bradley, Mary (Hastings)
  Show window
    Stowe, A. comp. It's a date
Brag dog. Bell, V. M.
BRAGGING. See Pride and vanity
BRAHMANS
  Kipling, R. Miracle of Purun Bhagat
Brahmin Beachhead. Hale, N.
BRAHMINS. See Brahmans
BRAIN SURGERY. See Surgery
BRAINS, MECHANICAL. See Automata
Brake happy. Coombs, C. I.
Bramley is so bracing. Wodehouse, P. G.
Brand, Max, pseud.
  Dust storm
    Meredith, S. ed. Bar 2
  The king
    This week magazine. This week's short-
      short stories
  Wine on the desert
    Christ, H. I. and Shostak, J. eds. Short
      stories
Brandel, Marc, 1919-
  Hasty act
    This week magazine. This week's short-
      short stories
BRANDING
  Warren, W. S. The branding
The branding. Warren, W. S.
Brandon, William
  Chiltipiquin
    Creamer, J. B. comp. Twenty-two sto-
      ries about horses and men
  College queen
    This week magazine. This week's short-
      short stories
  Ghost lode
    Meredith, S. ed. Bar 1: roundup of best
      western stories
  Party to blackmail
    This week magazine. This week's short-
      short stories
Brandt, Wolfgang Ernst Langewiesche- See
  Langewiesche-Brandt, Wolfgang Ernst
Brandy for the parson. Household, G.
Brannon, William T.
  Perfect secretary
    Mystery Writers of America, inc. Four-
      &-twenty bloodhounds
Brave new world. Huxley, A. L.
BRAVERY. See Courage
BRAZIL
  Annixter, P. pseud. Orchids and croco-
    diles
  Ullman, J. R. Island of the blue macaws
  Wells, H. G. Empire of the ants

          Rio de Janeiro
  Seager, A. Quitandinha
BREACH OF PROMISE
  Harte, B. Colonel Starbottle for the plain-
    tiff
Breach of promise. West, J.
BREAD
  Porter, W. S. Unknown quantity
Bread and Butter miss. Munro, H. H.

Bread and snow. Greene, H. I.
Bread on the waters. Sutro, A.
Bread upon the waters. Saintsbury, E. B.
The break. Jackson, C. R.
Break in the chain. Doyle, Sir A. C.
Breakdown. Williamson, J.
Breakfast. Bowen, E.
Breakfast in bed. Finney, J.
BREAKFASTS
  Bowen, E. Breakfast
Breaking point. Schulberg, B. W.
Breaking strain. Clarke, A. C.
Brecht, Harold Walton, 1899-
  Vienna roast
    Shaw, H. and Bement, D. Reading the
      short story
Breck, Vivian, pseud. See Breckenfeld,
  Vivian Gurney
Breckenfeld, Vivian Gurney
  Touch of Arab
    American girl (Periodical) Favorite
      stories
Bred for battle. Runyon, D.
"Breeds there a man. . . ?" Asimov, I.
Brement, Marshall, 1932-
  Youth
    American vanguard 1953
Brenner, Leah, 1915-
  Discovery
    Brenner, L. Artist grows up in Mexico
  Drunken lizard
    Brenner, L. Artist grows up in Mexico
  Ghost's shoes
    Brenner, L. Artist grows up in Mexico
  Little general
    Brenner, L. Artist grows up in Mexico
  Merchant of art
    Brenner, L. Artist grows up in Mexico
  Moon magic
    Brenner, L. Artist grows up in Mexico
  Revolt
    Brenner, L. Artist grows up in Mexico
Brentano, Clemens Maria, 1778-1842
  Picnic of Mores the cat
    Pick, R. ed. German stories and tales
  Story of the just Casper and the fair
    Annie
    Lange, V. ed. Great German short
      novels and stories
Breslin, Howard, 1912-
  Bat and a prayer
    Dachs, D. ed. Treasury of sports humor
Bretherton, Vivian Rosamond
  Love me, love my car
    Stowe, A. comp. It's a date
Bretnor, Reginald
  Gnurrs come from the voodvork out
    Best science fiction stories, 1951
  Little Anton
    Healy, R. J. ed. New tales of space and
      time
  Maybe just a little one
    Magazine of fantasy and science fiction.
      Best from Fantasy and science fic-
      tion; 3d ser.

Breuer, Bessie, 1893-
Home is a place
Stegner, W. E.; Scowcroft, R. and Ilyin, B. eds. Writer's art

Breuer, Miles J.
Gostak and the doshes
Conklin, G. ed. Science-fiction adventures in dimension
Man with the strange head
Conklin, G. ed. Big book of science fiction
See also Harris, C. W. jt. auth.

BRIBERY
Dostoevskiĭ, F. M. Polzunkov
Munro, H. H. Boar-pig

Brick, John, 1922-
The captives
Brick, J. They ran for their lives
Message for Uncle Billy
Brick, J. They ran for their lives
Rifleman's run
Brick, J. They ran for their lives

Brick road to glory. Gault, W. C.

Brickdust row. Porter, W. S.

Bridal night. O'Donovan, M.

Bridal party. Fitzgerald, F. S. K.

The **bride.** Wohl, S.

Bride comes to Yellow Sky. Crane, S.

Bride of the man-horse. Dunsany, E. J. M. D. P. 18th baron

Bridegroom of blood. Hazaz, C.

Bridegroom on the scaffold. Cohan, A. E.

Bridegroom's body. Boyle, K.

BRIDES. See Husband and wife

Bride's bed. Gibran, K.

BRIDGE (GAME)
Dahl, R. My ladylove, my dove
Maugham, W. S. Three fat women of Antibes

BRIDGES
Dresser, D. Extradition
Ware, L. Phantom of the bridge

Bridget's burden. Eggleston, M. W.

The **bridle.** Keller, D. H.

Bridle and saddle. Asimov, I.

Brief début of Tildy. Porter, W. S.

Brier, Howard Maxwell, 1903-
Newspaper man
American boy (Periodical) American boy Adventure stories
Sky hook
Boys' life (Periodical) Boys' life Adventure stories
Thoroughbred
Harper, W comp. Dog show
Yogi's dark horse
Strang, R. M. and Roberts, R. M. eds. Teen-age tales; bk 1

BRIGANDS AND ROBBERS
Alarcón, P. A. de. The prophecy
Chekhov, A. P. The dream
Porter, W. S. Hiding of Black Bill
Porter, W. S. Holding up a train
Porter, W. S. Roads we take
See also Bank robbers; Thieves

Brigands in Snuggletop Woods. Weeks, R.

Bright and morning. Parker, G.

Bright day. Grau, S. A.

Brightness falls from the air. Seabright, I.

Brim Beauvais. Stein, G.

Brimstone Bill. Jameson, M.

Bring! Bring! Aiken, C. P.

Brink, Carol (Ryrie) 1895-
Massacree!
Fenner, P. R. comp. Indians, Indians, Indians

Brink of darkness. Winters, Y.

BRITISH. See English

BRITISH COLUMBIA. See Canada—British Columbia

BRITISH NAVY. See Great Britain. Navy

BRITISH SOLDIERS. See Soldiers, British

Bro, Margueritte (Harmon) 1894-
It had to happen
McFarland, W. K. comp. Then it happened

BROADWAY, NEW YORK (CITY) See New York (City)—Manhattan

Broadway incident. Runyon, D.

Broch, Hermann, 1886-1951
Zerline, the old servant girl
Pick, R. ed. German stories and tales

Brod, Max, 1884-
Death is a passing weakness
Leftwich, J. ed. Yisröel. 1952 ed.

Brodie horns in. Charnley, M. V.

The **brogue.** Munro, H. H.

Broiefort, the black Arabian. Baldwin, J.

Broken fan. De La Roche, M.

Broken leg. Stern, J.

BROKERS
Kornbluth, C. M. Dominoes
Porter, W. S. Romance of a busy broker

Bromfield, Louis, 1896-1956
Great façade
Grayson, C. ed. Fourth round
Sugar camp
Andrews, R. C. ed. My favorite stories of the great outdoors
Tabloid news
Queen, E. pseud. ed. Literature of crime

BRONCO-BUSTERS. See Cowboys

Brondfield, Jerome
That's my boy
Herzberg, M. J. comp. Treasure chest of sport stories

Bronson, Wilfred Swancourt, 1894-
Brush with the enemy
Fenner, P. R. comp. Indians, Indians, Indians

Bronx oracle. Kober, A.

BRONX PARK. See New York (City) Zoological Park

Bronze thing. Newhouse, E.

Bronzes of Martel Greer. Winslow, T. S.

The **brooch.** Faulkner, W.

Brood of evil. Blochman, L. G.

Brooke, Jocelyn, 1908-
The blanket
New writing (Periodical) Best stories

Brookhouser, Frank, 1912-
L'affaire foul tip
Brookhouser, F. She made the big town! And other stories
The bereaved
Brookhouser, F. She made the big town! And other stories
Easter egg
Brookhouser, F. She made the big town! And other stories
Certner, S. and Henry, G. H. eds. Short stories for our times
Epilogue in the blues for Joey
Brookhouser, F. She made the big town! And other stories
Grave digger and Biggie Doone
Brookhouser, F. She made the big town! And other stories
Inn was promise
Brookhouser, F. She made the big town! And other stories
Life, going by
Brookhouser, F. She made the big town! And other stories
Little boy blues
Brookhouser, F. She made the big town! And other stories
Love that is lost
Brookhouser, F. She made the big town! And other stories
Mr Timothy and the model
Brookhouser, F. She made the big town! And other stories
My father and the circus
Brookhouser, F. She made the big town! And other stories
Not that kind of a deal
Brookhouser, F. She made the big town! And other stories
Pierre
Brookhouser, F. She made the big town! And other stories
Say that Jimmy kissed me
Brookhouser, F. She made the big town! And other stories
She did not cry at all
Brookhouser, F. She made the big town! And other stories
She made the big town!
Brookhouser, F. She made the big town! And other stories
Snake woman and the preacher's wife
Brookhouser, F. She made the big town! And other stories
Triumph with bells and laughter
Brookhouser, F. She made the big town! And other stories
You aim so high
Brookhouser, F. She made the big town! And other stories
Young man from yesterday
Brookhouser, F. She made the big town! And other stories

BROOKLYN. See New York (City)—Brooklyn

BROOKLYN. BASEBALL CLUB (NATIONAL LEAGUE)
Heuman, W. There are broken hearts in Brooklyn
See also Baseball

BROOKLYN DODGERS. See Brooklyn. Baseball Club (National League)

Brooks, Collin, 1893-
Possession on completion
Asquith, Lady C. M. E. C. ed. Book of modern ghosts
Brooks, Graham
Devil's tail
Story (Periodical) Story; no. 1
Brooks, Walter Rollin, 1886-
Jimmy takes vanishing lessons
Fenner, P. R. comp. Ghosts, ghosts, ghosts
Broomsticks. De La Mare, W. J.
Brophy, Brigid, 1929-
Crown princess
Brophy, B. Crown princess & other stories
Financial world
Brophy, B. Crown princess & other stories
Fordie
Brophy, B. Crown princess & other stories
His wife survived him
Brophy, B. Crown princess & other stories
Late afternoon of a faun
Brophy, B. Crown princess & other stories
Mrs Mandford's drawing-room
Brophy, B. Crown princess & other stories
Broster, Dorothy Kathleen, 1877-1950
Couching at the door
Carrington, H. ed. Week-end book of ghost stories
Davenport, B. ed. Ghostly tales to be told
Brother Bascombe is annoyed. Claudy, C. H.
Brother Boniface. Lavin, M.
Brother Willie. Hendryx, J. B.
A brotherhood. Swinton, A.
BROTHERS
Ballard, J. C. Mountain summer
Barker, A. L. Romney
Bennett, A. Mary with the high hand
Bergengruen, W. The knight
Bjørnson, B. The brothers
Coward, N. P. A richer dust
Farrell, J. T. Two brothers
Fitzgerald, F. S. K. Family in the wind
Garber, G. The gun on the wall
Grinnell, D. pseud. Extending the holdings
Hopkinson, H. T. Mountain madness
Johnson, D. M. War shirt
Lerner, M. The brothers
Maugham, W. S. Ant and the grasshopper
Maupassant, G. de. At sea
Newhouse, E. My brother's second funeral
Parsons, E. Not a soul will come along
Pratt, F. and De Camp, L. S. My brother's keeper
Putman, C. The wounded
Schnitzler, A. Blind Geronimo and his brother
Tucker, W. My brother's wife
Two brothers
Van Doren, M. In what far country

BROTHERS—*Continued*

Walsh, M. Sword of Yung Lo
Waugh, E. Winner takes all
West, J. Shivaree before breakfast
See also Brothers and sisters

The **brothers**. Bjørnson, B.

The **brothers**. Lerner, M.

BROTHERS AND SISTERS

Auchincloss, L. The ambassadress
Benefield, B. Christmas Eve's Day
Cooke, A. A. Four of a kind
Howarth, J. The novitiate
Lamkin, S. Comes a day
Maugham, W. S. Book-bag
Pasinetti, P. M. Family history
Porter, K. A. The grave
Stifter, A. Rock crystal
Tarkington, B. Walterson
Van Doren, M. Four brothers
Williams, T. Resemblance between a violin
case and a coffin

See also Brothers; Children; Sisters

Brothers beyond the void. Fairman, P. W.

BROTHERS-IN-LAW

Maltz, A. Happiest man on earth
Walsh, M. Quiet man

Brother's keeper. Steele, W. D.

Brothers of the yoke. Roberts, Sir C. G. D.

Brought to cover. Annixter, P. pseud.

Broughton, Rhoda, 1840-1920
Behold it was a dream
Merril, J. ed. Beyond the barriers of
space and time

Broun, Heywood Campbell, 1888-1939
Bolt from the blue
Graber, R. S. ed. Baseball reader
Even to Judas
Brentano, F. ed. The word lives on
Fifty-first dragon
Lass, A. H. and Horowitz, A. eds.
Stories for youth
Frankincense and myrrh
Brentano, F. ed. The word lives on
Trials of a ballplayer's wife
Graber, R. S. ed. Baseball reader
We, too, are bidden
Brentano, F. ed. The word lives on

Brown, Bill
Medicine dancer
Merril, J. ed. Beyond the barriers of
space and time
Star ducks
Best science fiction stories: 1951

Brown, E. Leigh, 1877-
Hero
Oberfirst, R. ed. 1954 anthology of best
original short-shorts

Brown, Fredric, 1906-
All good Bems
Brown, F. Space on my hands
Angelic angleworm
Brown, F. Angels and spaceships
Answer
Brown, F. Angels and spaceships
Arena
Conklin, G. ed. Big book of science
fiction
Armageddon
Brown, F. Angels and spaceships

Cain
Brown, F. Mostly murder
Come and go mad
Brown, F. Space on my hands
Crisis, 1999
Best detective stories of the year—1950
Brown, F. Space on my hands
Cry silence
Brown, F. Mostly murder
Daisies
Brown, F. Angels and spaceships
Dangerous people
Brown, F. Mostly murder
Daymare
Brown, F. Space on my hands
Death of Riley
Brown, F. Mostly murder
Don't look behind you
Brown, F. Mostly murder
Etaoin Shrdlu
Brown, F. Angels and spaceships
Pratt, F. ed. World of wonder
Four blind men
Brown, F. Mostly murder
Gateway to darkness
Margulies, L. and Friend, O. J. eds.
Giant anthology of science fiction
Greatest poem ever written
Brown, F. Mostly murder
Hall of mirrors
Pohl, F. ed. Assignment in tomorrow
Hat trick
Brown, F. Angels and spaceships
Honeymoon in hell
Galaxy science fiction magazine. Galaxy
reader of science fiction
I'll cut your throat again, Kathleen
Brown, F. Mostly murder
Knock
Bleiler, E. F. and Dikty, T. E. eds.
Science fiction omnibus: the best
science fiction stories, 1949, 1950
Brown, F. Space on my hands
Last Martian
Best science fiction stories: 1951
Galaxy science fiction magazine. Galaxy
reader of science fiction
Laughing butcher
Brown, F. Mostly murder
Letter to a phoenix
Brown, F. Angels and spaceships
Greenberg, M. ed. Journey to infinity
Little apple hard to peel
Brown, F. Mostly murder
Little white lye
Brown, F. Mostly murder
Miss Darkness
Brown, F. Mostly murder
Mr Smith kicks the bucket
Mystery Writers of America, inc. Four-
&-twenty bloodhounds
Motive goes round and round
Brown, F. Mostly murder
Mouse
Best science fiction stories: 1950
Bleiler, E. F. and Dikty, T. E. eds.
Science fiction omnibus: the best sci-
ence fiction stories, 1949, 1950
Night the world ended
Brown, F. Mostly murder
Nose of Don Aristide
Brown, F. Mostly murder
Nothing Sirius
Brown, F. Space on my hands

Brown, Fredric—*Continued*
Paradox lost
  Brown, F. and Reynolds, M. eds. Science-fiction carnival
Pattern
  Brown, F. Angels and spaceships
Pi in the sky
  Brown, F. Space on my hands
Placet is a crazy place
  Brown, F. Angels and spaceships
  Greenberg, M. ed. Travelers of space
Politeness
  Brown, F. Angels and spaceships
Preposterous
  Brown, F. Angels and spaceships
Reconciliation
  Brown, F. Angels and spaceships
Search
  Brown, F. Angels and spaceships
Sentence
  Brown, F. Angels and spaceships
Solipsist
  Brown, F. Angels and spaceships
Something green
  Brown, F. Space on my hands
Star mouse
  Brown, F. Space on my hands
This way out
  Brown, F. Mostly murder
Town wanted
  Brown, F. Mostly murder
Voice behind him
  Brown, F. Mostly murder
The waveries
  Brown, F. Angels and spaceships
  Conklin, G. ed. Invaders of earth
The weapon
  Conklin, G. ed. Omnibus of science fiction
  Mystery Writers of America, inc. Crooks' tour
Yehudi principle
  Brown, F. Angels and spaceships
    See also Reynolds, M. jt. auth.

Brown, George, 1931-
One in a million
  Oberfirst, R. ed. 1954 anthology of best original short-shorts

Brown, John, 1810-1882
Rab and his friends
  Cerf, B. A. and Moriarty, H. C. eds. Anthology of famous British stories

Brown, Kenneth Irving, 1896-
Christmas guest
  Lohan, R. and Lohan, M. eds. New Christmas treasury

Brown, Margery (Finn) 1913-
Orders for Korea
  Saturday evening post (Periodical) Saturday evening post stories, 1952

Brown, Martha Evelyn
Red hat
  Ford, N. A. and Faggett, H. L. eds. Best short stories by Afro-American writers (1925-1950)

Brown, Will C.
Duel in Captive Valley
  Meredith, S. ed. Bar 2

Brown cap. Van Doren, M.

Brown of Calaveras. Harte, B.

Brown Wolf. London, J.

Browne, John Ross, 1817-1875
Peep at Washoe
  Emrich, D. ed. Comstock bonanza

Browning, John S.
Burning bright
  Greenberg, M. ed. Robot and the man

Brubaker, Howard, 1882-
The milk pitcher
  Cooper, A. C. ed. Modern short stories
  Dachs, D. ed. Treasury of sports humor

Bruce, J. Campbell
Rescuer extraordinary
  McFee, W. ed. Great sea stories of modern times

Bruce, Stanley, 1914-
Farewell to crime
  Oberfirst, R. ed. 1952 anthology of best original short-shorts

Bruggen, Carry (de Haan) van, 1881-1932
Seder night
  Leftwich, J. ed. Yisröel. 1952 ed.

Bruhl, Étienne, 1898-
Great match
  Talbot, D. ed. Treasury of mountaineering stories

Brumbaugh, Florence
Helpful Henry
  Story parade (Periodical) Adventure stories

BRUNN (PREHISTORIC TRIBE) See Man, Prehistoric

Brunner, K. Houston
Thou good and faithful
  Norton, A. M. ed. Space pioneers

Brush, Katharine Ingham, 1902-1952
Football girl
  Dachs, D. ed. Treasury of sports humor
Good Wednesday
  Shaw, H. and Bement, D. Reading the short story
Night club
  Bogorad, S. N. and Tevithick, J. eds. College miscellany
  Burrell, J. A. and Cerf, B. A. eds. Anthology of famous American stories

Brush fire. Cain, J. M.

BRUSH FIRES. See Fires

Brush with the enemy. Bronson, W. S.

Brushwood boy. Kipling, R.

The **brute.** Conrad, J.

Brute's Christmas. Henderson, D.

Bubbles. Steele, W. D.

BUBONIC PLAGUE. See Plague

BUCCANEERS. See Pirates

Buchan, John, 1st baron Tweedsmuir, 1875-1940
An extract from the journal of Father Duplessis
  Brentano, F. ed. The word lives on
Kings of Orion
  Cerf, B. A. and Moriarty, H. C. eds. Anthology of famous British stories
Space
  Derleth, A. W. ed. Beyond time & space

Buck, Frank, 1882-1950
Elephant midget
Fenner, P. R. comp. Elephants, ele-
phants, elephants
Elephants!
Fenner, P. R. comp. Elephants, ele-
phants, elephants
Buck, Pearl (Sydenstricker) 1892-
Good river
Eaton, H. T. ed. Short stories
Man's foes
Certner, S. and Henry, G. H. eds. Short
stories for our times
Old demon
Lass, A. H. and Horowitz, A. eds.
Stories for youth
One named Jesus
Brentano, F. ed. The word lives on
Ransom
Queen, E. pseud. ed. Literature of crime
Buck Fanshaw's funeral. Clemens, S. L.
Buck in the hills. Clark, W. Van T.
Buckingham, Nash, 1880-
Bigger they come!
Buckingham, N. Hallowed years
Carry me back
Buckingham, N. Hallowed years
Comin' twenty-one
Buckingham, N. Hallowed years
Cricket field
Buckingham, N. Hallowed years
Death stalked the spring-stand!
Buckingham, N. Hallowed years
Hallowed years
Buckingham, N. Hallowed years
The high sign
Buckingham, N. Hallowed years
Lady
Buckingham, N. Hallowed years
Remember. . .
Buckingham, N. Hallowed years
Snake-eyes! !
Buckingham, N. Hallowed years
Tight place
Buckingham, N. Hallowed years
"When time who steals our years away!"
Buckingham, N. Hallowed years
The buckpasser. Kahler, H. M.
BUDDHIST PRIESTS
Holland, R. S. Cobra's hood
The buddies. Farrell, J. T.
Budding explorer. Robin, R.
BUDGETS, PERSONAL
Verner, C. Meddlin' Papa
Budrys, Algis J.
Congruent people
Star science fiction stories, no. 2
Frightened tree
Pohl, F. ed. Assignment in tomorrow
BUENOS AIRES. See Argentine Repub-
lic—Buenos Aires
Buffalo and Injuns. Sperry, A.
Buffalo dance. Meigs, C. L.
Buffalo wallow. Jackson, C. T.
The buffalos. Williams, W. C.
Bugles blow retreat. Dowdey, C.
Buglesong. Stegner, W. E.
Building alive. Sansom, W.

Built up logically. Schoenfeld, H.
The bull. Munro, H. H.
Bullard reflects. Jameson, M.
Bulletin board. Canine, W.
Bullets for Bouquet. Doyle, F. C.
BULLFIGHTERS AND BULLFIGHT-
ING
Hemingway, E. Capital of the world
Bullfrog hunt. Macfarlan, A. A.
BULLFROGS. See Frogs
BULLS
Bottome, P. Dark Blue
Munro, H. H. The bull
Munro, H. H. Stalled ox
Stuart, J. To market, to market
See also Cattle
The bully. Reaney, J. C.
Bulwer-Lytton, Edward George Earle
Lytton, 1st baron Lytton. See Lytton,
Edward George Earle Lytton Bulwer-
Lytton, 1st baron
The bum. Maugham, W. S.
Bum: wearer of the Silver Shield. Little,
G. W.
BUMS. See Tramps
Bundle of letters. James, H.
Bunin, Ivan Alekseevich, 1870-1953
Dry valley
Rahv, P. ed. Great Russian short novels
Evening in spring
Neider, C. ed. Great short stories from
the world's literature
Gentleman from San Francisco
Burnett, W. ed. World's best
Schorer, M. ed. The story
West, R. B. and Stallman, R. W. eds.
Art of modern fiction
Bunker Mouse. Greene, F. S.
Bunn, Harriet F.
Sophy's Christmas dinner
American girl (Periodical) Christmas all
year 'round
Bunner, Henry Cuyler, 1855-1896
Infidelity of Zenobia
Fabricant, N. D. and Werner, H. eds.
World's best doctor stories
Love-letters of Smith
Cuff, R. P. ed. American short story
survey
Story of a New York house
Scribner treasury
Two churches of 'Quawket
Blodgett, H. W. ed. Story survey.
1953 ed.
Eaton, H. T. ed. Short stories
Neider, C. ed. Men of the high calling
Bunner sisters. Wharton, E. N. J.
BUNYAN, PAUL
Rounds, G. Knute, the giant bullsnake
Rounds, G. Paul goes hunting
Burden of guilt. Hawkins, J. and Hawkins,
W.
Burden of loveliness. Williams, W. C.
Burdick, Eugene L.
Log the man dead
McFee, W. ed. Great sea stories of
modern times

Burdick's last battle. Thompson, T.

Bureau of slick tricks. Fyfe, H. B.

The **bureaucrat.** Jameson, M.

Burge McCall. Runyon, D.

Burgess, Gelett, 1866-1951
  Ghost-extinguisher
    Carrington, H. ed. Week-end book of
    ghost stories

BURGLARS. See Theft; Thieves

BURIAL. See Burials at sea; Catacombs;
    The dead; Funeral rites and cere-
    monies

BURIAL, PREMATURE
  Aldrich, T. B. Struggle for life
  Irving, C. Buried alive
  Poe, E. A. Fall of the House of Usher
  Poe, E. A. Premature burial

The **burial.** Horwitz, J.

Burial of the guns. Page, T. N.

BURIALS AT SEA
  Conrad, J. The nigger of the Narcissus
  Maugham, W. S. P. & O.

BURIED ALIVE. See Burial, Premature

Buried alive. Irving, C.

Buried treasure. Porter, W. S.

Burke, Norah, 1907-
  Polar night
    Story (Periodical) Story; no. 4

Burke, Thomas, 1887-1945
  Chink and the child
    Cerf, B. A. and Moriarty, H. C. eds.
    Anthology of famous British stories
  Hands of Mr Ottermole
    Lynskey, W. C. ed. Reading modern fic-
    tion
  Johnson looked back
    Davenport, B. ed. Ghostly tales to be
    told

Burks, Arthur J. 1898-
  The captive
    Story (Periodical) Story; no. 1

BURMA
  Marshall, E. Elephant remembers
  Marshall, E. Heart of Little Shikara
  Swinton, A. Courage

Burman, Ben Lucien, 1895-
  Children of Noah
    Summers, H. S. ed. Kentucky story

Burn him out. Bonham, F.

Burned chair. Rinehart, M. R.

Burnet, Dana, 1888-
  Shattered dream
    Saturday evening post (Periodical) Sat-
    urday evening post stories, 1952
  Vision of Henry Whipple
    Saturday evening post (Periodical) Sat-
    urday evening post stories, 1951
  Why did he leave me?
    Saturday evening post (Periodical) Sat-
    urday evening post stories, 1953

Burnett, Hallie Southgate, 1908-
  The burning
    Story (Periodical) Story; no. 3

Burnett, Whit, 1899-
  Suffer the little children
    Story (Periodical) Story; no. 2

Burnett, William Riley, 1899-
  Dressing-up
    First-prize stories, 1919-1954

The **burning.** Burnett, H. S.

The **burning.** Welty, E.

Burning bright. Browning, J. S.

Burning cactus. Spender, S.

Burning of Egliswyl. Wedekind, F.

Burns, John Horne, 1916-1953
  Momma
    Cory, D. W. pseud. comp. 21 variations
    on a theme

BURR, AARON, 1756-1836
  Welty, E. First love

Burrage, Alfred McLelland, 1889-
  The waxwork
    Certner, S. and Henry, G. H. eds. Short
    stories for our times
    Christ, H. I. and Shostak, J. eds. Short
    stories

BURROS
  Clark, W. Van T. Indian well
  Grey, Z. Tappan's burro
    See also Asses and mules

Burroughs, John, 1837-1921
  Sharp eyes
    Andrews, R. C. ed. My favorite stories
    of the great outdoors

The **burrow.** Kafka, F.

Burt, Maxwell Struthers, 1882-1954
  Each in his generation
    First-prize stories, 1919-1954
  Rope and the bulldog
    American boy (Periodical) American
    boy Adventure stories

BURYING GROUNDS. See Cemeteries

BUS DRIVERS
  Lamberton, L. Sleet storm

BUSES. See Motor buses

Bush, Geoffrey, 1929-
  Great reckoning in a little room
    Best American short stories, 1954

Bush medicine. O'Meara, W.

Busher's letters home. Lardner, R. W.

BUSINESS
  De La Mare, W. J. Lispet, Lispett and
    Vaine
  Kahler, H. M. The buckpasser
  Street, J. L. Mr Bisbee's princess
  Thurber, J. Catbird seat
  Van Doren, M. Miss Swallow
    See also Bankers; Capitalists and
    financiers; Merchants; also the names
    of particular businesses, e.g. Real es-
    tate business

      Unscrupulous methods
  Kersh, G. One way of getting a hundred
    pounds

Business, as usual. Reynolds, M.

BUSINESS DEPRESSION, 1929
  Bolté, M. End of the depression

Business of killing. Leiber, F.

Business proposition. Hendryx, J. B.

Busman's holiday. Young, F. B.

But not Jeff. Eicher, E.

But the patient died. Blochman, L. G

But without horns. Page, N. W.

Butch. Anderson, P.

Butch. Bendrodt, J. C.

Butcher bird. Stegner, W. E.

Butcher to the queen, Walsh, M.

The **butcherbirds.** Patt, E.

BUTCHERS
Anderson, E. V. Rib steak
Bergelson, D. In a backwoods town
Caldwell, E. Man who looked like himself
Caldwell, E. Saturday afternoon
Cavanaugh, J. P. The lamb
Suhl, Y. Saved by the sale

Butler, Ellis Parker, 1869-1937
Too much horse
American boy (Periodical) American boy
anthology

Butler, Mabel
Mr Sweeney
Oberfirst, R. ed. 1954 anthology of best
original short-shorts

BUTLERS. See Servants—Butlers

The **butterfly.** Van Doren, M.

Butterworth, Hezekiah, 1839-1905
My grandmother's grandmother's Christ-
mas candle
Lohan, R. and Lohan, M. eds. New
Christmas treasury

Buyer from Cactus City. Porter, W. S.

BUYERS OF DRESSES
Porter, W. S. Buyer from Cactus City

By appointment. Steele, W. D.

By courier. Porter, W. S.

By his bootstraps. Heinlein, R. A.

By Jupiter. Elam, R. M.

By my truth, Nerissa! Aiken, C. P.

By one, by two, and by three. King-Hall, S.

"By the sea."** Jackson, C. R.

By the water. Bowles, P. F.

By the waters of Babylon. Benét, S. V.

By the waters of Babylon. Goudge, E.

By these presents. Kuttner, H.

By virtue of circumference. Van Dresser, P.

By way of a Christmas card. Eggleston,
M. W.

'Bye, 'bye, Bluebeard. Shore, V. B.

Bye-day with Mr Jorrocks. Surtees, R. S.

Byézhin Meadow. Turgenev, I. S.

Byrd, Sigman
Old man's bride
Saturday evening post (Periodical) Sat-
urday evening post stories, 1950

Byrne, Donn, 1889-1928
Rivers of Damascus
Cerf, B. A. and Moriarty, H. C. eds.
Anthology of famous British stories
Tale of James Carabine
Ribalow, H. U. ed. World's greatest
boxing stories

The **bystander.** La Farge, O.

Byzantine omelette. Munro, H. H.

C

C chute. Asimov, I.

C.Y.E. McCarthy, M. T.

CAB DRIVERS
Chekhov, A. P. Grief
Kantor, M. Fabulous cabman
Porter, W. S. From the cabby's seat
Ullman, J. R. White night

CABALA
Peretz, I. L. Cabalists

Cabalists. Peretz, I. L.

Caballero's way. Porter, W. S.

Cabaret. Boyle, K.

CABARETS. See Music halls (Variety
theaters, cabarets, etc.); Night clubs

CABBAGES
Poe, E. A. Devil in the belfry

Cabbages of the cemetery. Baroja y Nessi,
P.

Cabell, James Branch, 1879-
Porcelain cups
Burrell, J. A. and Cerf, B. A. eds. An-
thology of famous American stories

Cabin boy. Knight, D.

Cabin door. Roberts, Sir C. G. D.

Cable, George Washington, 1844-1925
Madame Delphine
Scribner treasury

The **Cabuliwallah.** Tagore, R.

The **cactus.** Porter, W. S.

Caddis hatch. Bonner, P. H.

CAESAR, CAIUS JULIUS
Wilder, T. N. From a journal-letter of
Julius Caesar

Caesar's wife's ear. Bottome, P.

Café in Jaffa. Gellhorn, M. E.

CAFÉS. See Restaurants, lunchrooms, etc.

CAIN (BIBLICAL CHARACTER)
Feild, B. How Abel slew Cain

Cain, James Mallahan, 1892-
Brush fire
Grayson, C. ed. Fourth round

Cain, Jeanette, 1924-
Fantasy
Wolfe, D. M. ed. Which grain will
grow

Cain. Brown, F.

CAJUNS. See Acadians in Louisiana

CAKES. See Food

Calahan, Harold Augustus, 1899-
Back to Treasure Island; excerpt
Fenner, P. R. comp. Pirates, pirates,
pirates

Calculated risk. Appell, G. C.

Calculation of N'bambwe. Kneale, N.

Caldwell, Erskine, 1903-
After-image
Caldwell, E. Complete stories
Albino and Darling Jill
Caldwell, E. Humorous side of Erskine
Caldwell
All kind of pep
Caldwell, E. Humorous side of Erskine
Caldwell

Caldwell, Erskine—*Continued*

Midwinter guest
  Caldwell, E. Complete stories
  Caldwell, E. Courting of Susie Brown
Molly Cotton-Tail
  Caldwell, E. Complete stories
My autumn courtship
  Caldwell, E. Humorous side of Erskine
   Caldwell
My old man
  Caldwell, E. Humorous side of Erskine
   Caldwell
Negro in the well
  Caldwell, E. Complete stories
New cabin
  Caldwell, E. Complete stories
Nine dollars' worth of mumble
  Caldwell, E. Complete stories
Over the Green Mountains
  Caldwell, E. Complete stories
People v. Abe Lathan, colored
  Caldwell, E. Complete stories
  Caldwell, E. Courting of Susie Brown
People's choice
  Caldwell, E. Complete stories
Picking cotton
  Caldwell, E. Complete stories
The picture
  Caldwell, E. Complete stories
Priming the well
  Caldwell, E. Complete stories
Rachel
  Caldwell, E. Complete stories
Return to Lavinia
  Caldwell, E. Complete stories
Romantically inclined
  Caldwell, E. Humorous side of Erskine
   Caldwell
The rumor
  Caldwell, E. Complete stories
Runaway
  Caldwell, E. Complete stories
Sack of turnips
  Caldwell, E. Humorous side of Erskine
   Caldwell
Saturday afternoon
  Caldwell, E. Complete stories
Savannah River payday
  Caldwell, E. Complete stories
The shooting
  Caldwell, E. Complete stories
Sick horse
  Caldwell, E. Complete stories
  Caldwell, E. Courting of Susie Brown
Slow death
  Caldwell, E. Complete stories
Small day
  Caldwell, E. Complete stories
Snacker
  Caldwell, E. Complete stories
Spence cooperates
  Caldwell, E. Humorous side of Erskine
   Caldwell
Squire Dinwiddy
  Caldwell, E. Complete stories
  Caldwell, E. Courting of Susie Brown
Strawberry season
  Caldwell, E. Complete stories
Summer accident
  Caldwell, E. Complete stories
  Caldwell, E. Courting of Susie Brown
The sunfield
  Caldwell, E. Complete stories

Swell-looking girl
  Caldwell, E. Complete stories
Ten thousand blueberry crates
  Caldwell, E. Complete stories
  Caldwell, E. Humorous side of Erskine
   Caldwell
Thunderstorm
  Caldwell, E. Complete stories
  Caldwell, E. Courting of Susie Brown
Uncle Henry's love nest
  Caldwell, E. Complete stories
Uncle Jeff
  Caldwell, E. Complete stories
  Caldwell, E. Courting of Susie Brown
Very late spring
  Caldwell, E. Complete stories
The visitor
  Caldwell, E. Complete stories
Walnut hunt
  Caldwell, E. Complete stories
Warm river
  Caldwell, E. Complete stories
  Greene, J. I. and Abell, E. eds. Stories
   of sudden truth
We are looking at you, Agnes
  Caldwell, E. Complete stories
Where the girls were different
  Caldwell, E. Complete stories
  Caldwell, E. Humorous side of Erskine
   Caldwell
Wild flowers
  Caldwell, E. Complete stories
The windfall
  Caldwell, E. Complete stories
  Caldwell, E. Courting of Susie Brown
Woman in the house
  Caldwell, E. Complete stories
Yellow girl
  Burnett, W. ed. World's best
  Caldwell, E. Complete stories

Caleb Thumble returns to Barchester. Trollope, A.

Caleb's ark. Davies, R.

Calendar girl. Blochman, L. G.

CALF. See Cattle

The **calf.** Abramowitz, S. J.

Calico shoes. Farrell, J. T.

CALIFORNIA

1846-1900

Harte, B. Outcasts of Poker Flat
Harte, B. Tennessee's partner

20th century

Leighton, M. C. Legacy of Canyon John
Steinbeck, J. The chrysanthemums

Fresno

Saroyan, W. Cornet players
Saroyan, W. The foreigner

Hollywood

Brand, M. pseud. The king
Schulberg, B. My Christmas carol

Monterey

Atherton, G. F. H. Pearls of Loreto

CALIFORNIA RANCH LIFE. See Ranch life—California

Caliph and the cad. Porter, W. S.

Caliph, cupid and the clock. Porter, W. S.

Calisher, Hortense, 1911-
  Box of ginger
    Calisher, H. In the absence of angels
  Heartburn
    Calisher, H. In the absence of angels
  In Greenwich there are many gravelled
      walks
    Best American short stories, 1951
    Calisher, H. In the absence of angels
  In the absence of angels
    Calisher, H. In the absence of angels
  Letitia, emeritus
    Calisher, H. In the absence of angels
  Middle drawer
    Calisher, H. In the absence of angels
  Night riders of Northville
    Calisher, H. In the absence of angels
  Old stock
    Calisher, H. In the absence of angels
  One of the chosen
    Calisher, H. In the absence of angels
    Ribalow, H. U. ed. These your children
  Point of departure
    Calisher, H. In the absence of angels
  Pool of narcissus
    Calisher, H. In the absence of angels
  Sound of waiting
    Calisher, H. In the absence of angels
  The watchers
    Calisher, H. In the absence of angels
  Woman who was everybody
    Calisher, H. In the absence of angels
  Wreath for Miss Totten
    Best American short stories, 1952
    Calisher, H. In the absence of angels
The **call.** Laurence, B.
Call at Corazón. Bowles, P. F.
Call it courage. Sperry, A.
Call loan. Porter, W. S.
Call of the blood. Cervantes Saavedra, M. de
Call of the street. Conrad, R. E.
Call of the tame. Porter, W. S.
Call on the President. Runyon, D.
Call this land home. Haycox, E.
Callaghan, Morley Edward, 1903-
  All the years of her life
    Certner, S. and Henry, G. H. eds. Short
      stories for our times
    Lass, A. H. and Horowitz, A. eds.
      Stories for youth
  Father and son
    Pacey, D. ed. Book of Canadian stories
  Luke Baldwin's vow
    Furman, A. L. ed. Teen-age dog stories
  Rigmarole
    Burnett, W. ed. World's best
Callie of Crooked Creek. Hall, E. G.
Calling all cars. Hauser, M. L.
Calling of the lop-horned bull. Roberts, Sir
    C. G. D.
Calloway's code. Porter, W. S.
Calmahain. Wall, J. W.
CALVES. See Cattle
Calvin, the cat. Warner, C. D.
CALVINISM
  De Vries, P. Good boy
  De Vries, P. Tulip
Calvo, Lino Novás. See Novás Calvo, Lino

**CAMBRIDGE, ENGLAND. UNIVER-
SITY**
  Levy, A. Cohen of Trinity
Camel into eagle. Allen, M. P.
The **cameleers.** Curtis, K.
CAMORRA
  Conrad, J. Il conde
Camouflage. Kuttner, H.
Camp, Lyon Sprague de. See De Camp,
    Lyon Sprague
Camp at Saint Adrien. Macfarlan, A. A.
CAMP-MEETINGS
  Hughes, L. Big meeting
  Steele, W. D. Man and boy
The **campaign.** Horwitz, J.
Campaigning cowpoke. Gray, C.
Campanella, Giovanni Domenico. See Cam-
    panella, Tommasi
Campanella, Tommasi
  City of the sun
    Derleth, A. W. ed. Beyond time & space
Campbell, John Wood, 1910-
  Black star passes
    Campbell, J. W. Black star passes
  Cloak of Aesir
    Campbell, J. W. Cloak of Aesir
  The escape
    Campbell, J. W. Cloak of Aesir
  Forgetfulness
    Campbell, J. W. Cloak of Aesir
  The invaders
    Campbell, J. W. Cloak of Aesir
  The machine
    Campbell, J. W. Cloak of Aesir
  Out of the night
    Campbell, J. W. Cloak of Aesir
  Piracy preferred
    Campbell, J. W. Black star passes
  Rebellion
    Campbell, J. W. Cloak of Aesir
  Solarite
    Campbell, J. W. Black star passes
Campbell, Sir Malcolm, 1885-
  Won by inches!
    Fenner, P. R. comp. Speed, speed, speed
Campbell, William Edward March, 1894-1954
  Bill's eyes
    Fabricant, N. D. and Werner, H. eds.
      World's best doctor stories
  I broke my back on a rosebud
    Greene, J. I. and Abell, E. eds. Stories
      of sudden truth
  Personal letter
    Heilman, R. B. ed. Modern short stories
  Sum in addition
    Shaw, H. and Bement, D. Reading the
      short story
CAMPING
  Chute, B. J. Too close to nature
  Macfarlan, A. A. Campfire adventure
    stories; 8 stories
  White, S. E. On lying awake at night
    See also Outdoor life
CAMPS, SUMMER
  Auchincloss, L. Edification of Marianne
Camus, Albert, 1913-
  Sentence of death
    Burnett, W. ed. World's best

Can all this grandeur perish? Farrell, J. T.

Can of paint. Van Vogt, A. E.

CANADA

Pacey, D. ed. Book of Canadian stories; 30 stories

Weaver, R. and James, H. eds. Canadian short stories; 24 stories

British Columbia

McConnell, W. Totem

Mayse, A. Midnight Mike

Montreal

Waddington, P. Street that got mislaid

New Brunswick

Garner, H. One mile of ice

Northwest Territories

Hendryx, J. B. Intrigue on Halfaday Creek; 28 stories

Mowat, F. Woman he left to die

Ontario

Garner, H. One, two, three little Indians

Quebec (Province)

Allan, T. Lies my father told me

Macfarlan, A. A. Moose boy

Marshall, J. Old woman

Thériault, Y. Jeannette

Toronto

Seton, E. T. Silverspot: the story of a crow

CANADA. ROYAL CANADIAN MOUNTED POLICE

Erskine, L. Y. Mystery at Moon Lake

Mowery, W. B. Sagas of the Mounted Police; 8 stories

Canaday, John Edwin, 1907-

Three strips of flesh

Mystery Writers of America, inc. Four-&-twenty bloodhounds

CANADIAN MOUNTED POLICE. See Canada. Royal Canadian Mounted Police

Canary from Cuba. Rutt, E.

Cancel all I said. Collier, J.

Cancela, Arturo, 1892-

Life and death of a hero

De Onís, H. ed. Spanish stories and tales

CANCER (DISEASE)

McCoy, E. The cape

A candle in Vienna. Cronin, A. J.

CANDLEMAKERS. See Candles

CANDLES

Howard, H. Dipping of the candlemaker

Candy from Fairyland. Farrell, J. T.

Candy-man Beechum. Caldwell, E.

Canfield, Dorothy. See Fisher, Dorothea Frances (Canfield)

Canine, William, 1922-

Bulletin board

Story (Periodical) Story; no. 3

The clematis

Story (Periodical) Story; no. 4

Cannibal pot. Arnold, M.

CANNIBALISM

Harris, J. B. Survival

Rabinowitz, S. The pair

Canning, Victor, 1911-

Man who hated time

This week magazine. This week's short-short stories

Mystery of Kela Ouai

Best detective stories of the year—1953

Never trust a lady

This week magazine. This week's short-short stories

The smuggler

Best detective stories of the year—1952

This week magazine. This week's short-short stories

Cannon, James J.

Gambler's sad saga

Dachs, D. ed. Treasury of sports humor

Cannon, Jimmy. See Cannon, James, J.

CANNONS. See Ordnance

Canossa. Munro, H. H.

Can't cross Jordan by myself. Steele, W. D.

Can't slip any drugs to sisters on Fifth Avenue. McNulty, J.

Canticle of the sun. Goudge, E.

CANTORS

Agnon, S. J. Story of the cantor

Dick, I. M. Two strangers came to town

Peretz, I. L. Ne'ilah in Gehenna

Cantrill remains on Halfaday. Hendryx, J. B.

The canyon flowers. Gordon, C. W.

Canzoneri, Robert

Survival

Story (Periodical) Story; no. 2

The cape. McCoy, E.

Cape Race. De La Mare, W. J.

CAPITAL AND LABOR. See Labor and laboring classes

Capital of the world. Hemingway, E.

CAPITAL PUNISHMENT

Chekhov, A. The bet

CAPITALISTS AND FINANCIERS

Brophy, B. Financial world

Porter, W. S. Night in New Arabia

Porter, W. S. Unknown quantity

Cap'n Ezra, privateer. Adams, J. D.

Capote, Truman, 1924-

House of flowers

Greene, J. I. and Abell, E. eds. Stories of sudden truth

Prize stories of 1951

Shut a final door

First-prize stories, 1919-1954

Cappy: the pride of Engine Company 65. Little, G. W.

Capra. Wall, J. W.

CAPRI

Maugham, W. S. Lotus eater

Maugham, W. S. Mayhew

Wells, H. G. Dream of Armageddon

Captain Burle. Zola, E.

Captain Dalgety returns. Whistler, L.

Captain is impaled. Algren, N.

Captain Kidder. Sandberg, H. W.

Captain Kit. Vetter, M. M.

Captain Murderer. Dickens, C.

Captain of the "Ullswater." Roberts, M.

Captain returns. Hill, J. H.

Captain's doll. Lawrence, D. H.

CAPTAINS, ENGLISH. See Great Britain
—Army

CAPTAINS OF SHIPS. See Shipmasters

Captain's prisoner. Clements, C. J.

The captive. Burks, A. J.

The captive. Gordon, C.

Captive audience. Griffith, A. W.

Captive heart. Vance, C.

The captives. Brick, J.

CAPTIVES OF INDIANS. See Indians of
North America—Captivities

Capture of a brig. Meader, S. W.

Captured shadow. Fitzgerald, F. S. K.

CARBONARI
Beyle, M. H. Vanina Vanini

CARBONATED BEVERAGES
Parker, J. R. All the little jokers

Carcassonne. Faulkner, W.

CARD GAMES. See Cards

CARD-SHARPERS. See Gambling

Cardboard box. Doyle, Sir A. C.

Cardiac suture. Weiss, E.

Cardozo, Nancy
Hundred years from now
Seventeen (Periodical) Nineteen from
Seventeen
Unborn ghosts
Best American short stories, 1952

CARDS
Chekhov, A. P. Vint

Career of Augurt Nimrodtk. Willingham, C.

Carelessness. Chekhov, A. P.

Caretaker. Schmitz, J. H.

Carey, Ernestine Moller (Gilbreth) See Gilbreth, F. B. jt. auth.

CARIB INDIANS
Brown, K. I. Christmas guest

Caricature. Rydberg, E.

CARICATURISTS. See Cartoonists

Carlson, Esther, 1921?-
Museum piece
Pratt, F. ed. World of wonder

Carman, Kathleen
The debt
Thinker's digest (Peroidical) Spoiled
priest, and other stories

Carmer, Carl Lamson, 1893-
Mr Sims and Henry
Strang, R. M. and Roberts, R. M. eds.
Teen-age tales v 1
See also Del Rey, L. jt. ed.

Carmi. Karp, D. B.

CARNIVAL
Caldwell, E. Carnival
Collier, J. Sleeping Beauty
Hall, J. B. Spot in history

Carnival. Caldwell, E.

CAROUSEL. See Merry-go-rounds

CARPENTERS
Schaefer, J. W. Hugo Kertchak, builder
Van Doren, M. Three carpenters

Carpenter's daughter. Coolidge, O. E.

Carr, Albert H. Zolotkoff, 1902-
Case of catnapping
Queen, E. pseud. ed. Ellery Queen's
awards: 9th ser.
If a body. . .
Queen, E. pseud, ed. Queen's awards:
8th ser.
Murder at City Hall
Queen, E. pseud. ed. Queen's awards:
6th ser.
Trial of John Nobody
Queen, E. pseud. ed. Queen's awards:
5th ser.
Tyger! Tyger!
Queen, E. pseud. ed. Queen's awards:
7th ser.

Carr, Dickson. See Carr, John Dickson

Carr, John Dickson, 1905-
Black cabinet
Mystery Writers of America inc. 20
great tales of murder
Clue of the red wig
Carr, J. D. The third bullet, and other
stories
Footprint in the sky
Christ, H. I. and Shostak, J. eds. Short
stories
Gentleman from Paris
Best detective stories of the year—1951
Carr, J. D. The third bullet, and other
stories
Queen, E. pseud. ed. Queen's awards:
5th ser.
House in Goblin Wood
Carr, J. D. The third bullet, and other
stories
Locked room
Carr, J. D. The third bullet, and other
stories
Proverbial murder
Carr, J. D. The third bullet, and other
stories
The third bullet
Carr, J. D. The third bullet, and other
stories
Wrong problem
Carr, J. D. The third bullet, and other
stories
Mystery Writers of America, inc. Four-
&-twenty bloodhounds
See also Doyle, A. C. jt. auth.

Carr, Robert Spencer, 1909-
Beyond infinity
Carr, R. S. Beyond infinity
Dictator's double
Saturday evening post (Periodical) Sat-
urday day evening post stories, 1952
Easter eggs
Best science fiction stories: 1950
Bleiler, E. F. and Dikty, T. E. eds. Sci-
ence fiction omnibus: The best science
fiction stories, 1949, 1950
Morning star
Carr, R. S. Beyond infinity

Carr, Robert S.—*Continued*
  Mutation
    Carr, R. S. Beyond infinity
  Those men from Mars
    Carr, R. S. Beyond infinity
Carrighar, Sally
  Marooned children
    Saturday evening post (Periodical) Saturday evening post stories, 1953
Carrington, Hereward, 1880-
  The escape
    Carrington, H. ed. Week-end book of ghost stories
  The miracle
    Carrington, H. ed. Week-end book of ghost stories
rroll, Joseph W. 1911-
  At Mrs Farrelly's
    Best American short stories, 1953
  Matthew and the lace curtain
    Collier's, the national weekly. Collier's best
  Prefect of discipline
    Gable, M. Sister, ed. Many-colored fleece
Carry me back. Buckingham, N.
Carse, Robert, 1903-
  Sailor's pay
    Furman, A. L. ed. Teen-age sea stories
Carson poker incident. Davis, S. P.
Carter, Marjorie
  First car
    Strang, R. M. and Roberts, R. M. eds. Teen-age tales v 1
Carter, Paul
  Ounce of prevention
    Derleth, A. W. ed. Far boundaries
Carter, Russell Gordon, 1892-
  And the Dean was happy
    Lantz, J. E. ed. Stories of Christian living
  Blue ribbon event
    Owen, F. ed. Teen-age victory parade
  Future captain
    Lantz, J. E. ed. Stories of Christian living
  High-pressure stuff
    Strang, R. M. and Roberts, R. M. eds. Teen-age tales v 1
  Parachute warning
    Strang, R. M. and Roberts, R. M. eds. Teen-age tales v 2
  Tea from the brigantine
    Fenner, P. R. comp. Yankee Doodle
Cartmill, Cleve
  Green cat
    Derleth, A. W. ed. The outer reaches
  Huge beast
    Magazine of fantasy and science fiction. Best of Fantasy and science fiction; [1st ser]
  Number nine
    Jenkins, W. F. ed. Great stories of science fiction
  Overthrow
    Greenberg, M. ed. Journey to infinity
  You can't say that
    Healy, R. J. ed. New tales of space and travel
CARTOONISTS
  Ryberg, E. Caricature

Cartur, Peter, pseud.
  The mist
    Conklin, G. ed. Science-fiction adventures in dimension
Carver, Charles, 1915-
  Hanging Hollow
    Peery, W. W. ed. 21 Texas short stories
  Twenty floors up
    This week magazine. This week's short-short stories
CARVING WOOD. See Wood carving
Case in Chancery. Bentley, P. E.
Case of catnapping. Carr, A. H. Z.
Case of Charles Dexter Ward. Lovecraft, H. P.
Case of General Ople and Lady Camper. Meredith, G.
Case of identity. Doyle, Sir A. C.
Case of Karen Smith. Shore, V. B.
Case of myopia. Henderson, S. E.
Case of the irate witness. Gardner, E. S.
Case of the psychoanalyst. Strasser, S.
Case of the southpaw spy. Schneider, G. W.
Case of the wooden bowls. Ball, M. W.
Casey, Marian (Whinery)
  First harpist
    American girl (Periodical) On my honor
Cash, M. L.
  Hangover
    Oberfirst, R. ed. 1954 anthology of best original short-shorts
Cash and carry guy. Holder, W.
Cask of Amontillado. Poe, E. A.
Casper, Leonard, 1923-
  Deep country part
    Stanford short stories, 1953
  Sense of direction
    Best American short stories, 1951
    Prize stories of 1951
Cassill, R. V. 1919-
  Larchmoor is not the world
    Best American short stories, 1951
    Greene, J. I. and Abell, E. eds. Stories of sudden truth
  Life of the sleeping beauty
    Best American short stories, 1953
  War in the air
    Prize stories, 1954
Castaway. Chandler, A. B.
Castaway. Williams, R. M.
CASTAWAYS. See Shipwrecks and castaways
Castle Rackrent. Edgeworth, M.
Casual affair. Maugham, W. S.
Casual incident. Farrell, J. T.
Casualty. Lowry, R. J. C.
The cat. Colette, S. G.
The cat. Freeman, M. E. W.
Cat and Custard-pot day with the Handley Cross. Surtees, R. S.
Cat-eyed woman. Reese, J. H.
Cat jumps. Bowen, E.
Cat nipped. Schaefer, J. W.
Cat that would not die. Marshall, E.

Cat up a tree. Sansom, W.

CATACOMBS
  Poe, E. A. Cask of Amontillado

Catalonian night. Morand, P.

CATASTROPHES. See Accidents

Catbird seat. Thurber, J.

The **catch.** Gordimer, N.

Catch that Martian. Knight, D.

Catch that rabbit. Asimov, I.

Category Phoenix. Ellanby, B.

CATERPILLARS
  Edmonds, W. D. Death of Red Peril

Catfish story. Blochman, L. G.

CATHEDRALS AND CATHEDRAL LIFE
  De La Mare, W. J. All Hallows
  Douglas, L. C. Dean Harcourt

Cather, Willa Sibert, 1873-1947
  Neighbor Rosicky
    Foerster, N. ed. American poetry and prose. 1952 ed.
    Schramm, W. L. ed. Great short stories
    Stauffer, R. M.; Cunningham, W. H. and Sullivan, C. J. eds. Adventures in modern literature
  Paul's case
    Burrell, J. A. and Cerf, B. A. eds. Anthology of famous American stories
    Day, A. G. ed. Greatest American short stories
    Lynskey, W. C. ed. Reading modern fiction
    Queen, E. pseud. ed. Literature of crime

CATHOLIC CHURCH. See Catholic faith

CATHOLIC FAITH
  Balzac, H. de. Atheist's mass
  Daudet, A. Father Gaucher's elixir
  Doty, W. L. Action in Prague
  Doty, W. L. Father Murray's first failure
  Doty, W. L. Rectory parlor
  Doty, W. L. Silver cross
  Fitzgerald, F. S. K. Absolution
  Freemantle, A. J. ed. Mothers; 18 stories
  Gable, M. Sister, ed. Many-colored fleece; 24 stories
  Greene, G. Hint of an explanation
  Lieberman, R. Heaven is so high; 13 stories
  O'Donovan, M. Custom of the country
  O'Donovan, M. Face of evil
  O'Donovan, M. My first Protestant
  Paget, V. Virgin of the Seven Daggers
  Thinker's digest (Periodical)
    Spoiled priest, and other stories; 46 stories

CATHOLIC PRIESTS
  Becker, S. D. Baptism of some importance
  Betts, D. Mr Shawn and Father Scott
  Bloch, J. R. Heresy of the water taps
  Cable, G. W. Madame Delphine
  Chesterton, G. K. Blue cross
  Connolly, M. Seminary Hill
  Doty, W. L. Back to school
  Doty, W. L. The fisherman
  Gautier, T. Clarimonde
  Gordon, A. Devil and Father Francisco
  Goudge, E. Icon on the wall
  Goudge, E. Three gray men
  Harte, B. Knight-errant of the foothills

  Horgan, P. Devil in the desert
  Joyce, J. The sisters
  Lemelin, R. Stations of the Cross
  Lieberman, R. Indiscretions of Father Lawrence
  Lieberman, R. Matter of time
  O'Donovan, M. The frying-pan
  O'Donovan, M. The miracle
  O'Donovan, M. Old faith
  O'Donovan, M. The sentry
  O'Donovan, M. The shepherds
  O'Donovan, M. Vanity
  Powers, J. F. Death of a favorite
  Powers, J. F. The forks
  Powers, J. F. Lions, harts, leaping does
  Powers, J. F. Prince of Darkness
  Pratt, F. and De Camp, L. S. Palimpsest of St Augustine
  Robinson, L. W. Ruin of soul
  Sheehan, P. A. Spoiled priest
  Van Doren, M. Father O'Connell
  Verga, G. His Reverence
  Voorhees, M. B. Robe and the sword
  Werfel, F. V. Third commandment
  Wilde, O. Priest and the acolyte

CATS
  Agnon, S. J. Jewish cat
  Aiken, C. P. Hello, Tib
  Boylston, H. D. Stuff of dreams
  Brentano, C. M. Picnic of Mores the cat
  Carr, A. H. Z. Case of catnapping
  Cartmill, C. Green cat
  Ekbergh, I. D. Lost cat
  Ekbergh, I. D. Toozee the puss
  Fabre, J. H. C. Story of my cats
  Freeman, M. E. W. The cat
  Hearn, L. Boy who drew cats
  Howe, D. White kitten
  Humphrey, W. Sister
  Joseph, M. ed. Best cat stories; 17 stories
  Marmur, J. Mad Island
  Munro, H. H. Achievement of the cat
  Munro, H. H. Tobermory
  Pangborn, E. Mrrrar
  Peretz, I. L. Pious cat
  Phillpotts, E. "Hey diddle diddle, the cat . . ."
  Pirandello, L. House of agony
  Poe, E. A. The black cat
  Runyon, D. Johnny One-Eye
  Steele, W. D. Bubbles
  Steele, W. D. Yellow cat
  Taber, G. B. Never a dull moment
The **cat's**-paw. Ellin, S.

CATSKILL MOUNTAINS
  Irving, W. Rip Van Winkle

CATTLE
  Abramowitz, S. J. The calf
  Abramowitz, S. J. Little calf
  Agee, J. Mother's tale
  Cheshire, G. Bad year
  Davies, R. Conflict in Morfa
  Evans, E. E. The shed
  Herbert, Sir A. P. Board of Inland Revenue v. Haddock
  Mannzen, D. Aurora's Angus
    See also Branding; Bulls

CATTLE DRIVES
  Scott, Sir W. Two drovers

Cattle raid on Cooley. Ready, W. B.

Cattle rustlers. James, W.

CATTLE THIEVES
James, W. Cattle rustlers

Caudill, Rebecca, 1899-
Fern Barrie's new plans
Hazeltine, A. I. comp. Selected stories
for teen-agers

The **caught.** Barber, A.

Caught. Porter, W. S.

Causey, James, 1924-
Teething ring
Galaxy science fiction magazine. Second Galaxy reader of science fiction

Cavalier of the streets. Arlen, M.

Cavalleria rusticana. Verga, G.

Cavanaugh, James Patrick, 1922-
The lamb
American vanguard, 1953
Martha's yesterdays
American vanguard, 1952

Cavanna, Betty, 1909-
Puppy business
American girl (Periodical) Favorite
stories
Furman, A. L. ed. Teen-age dog stories

Cave, Hugh Barnett, 1910-
Beyond price
Certner, S. and Henry, G. H. eds. Short
stories for our times
Peril of the river
This week magazine. This week's short-
short stories
Two were left
Strang, R. M. and Roberts, R. M. eds.
Teen-age tales v2

Cave of warm winds. Bamberg, R. D.

Caveat emptor. Pratt, F. and De Camp,
L. S.

Cawley, Clifford Comer
Belle Monahan
Cawley, C. C. No trip like this, and
other stories
Grunion run
Cawley, C. C. No trip like this, and
other stories
The lost
Cawley, C. C. No trip like this, and
other stories
No trip like this
Cawley, C. C. No trip like this, and
other stories
When day is done
Cawley, C. C. No trip like this, and
other stories

Celebrated jumping frog of Calaveras County. Clemens, S. L.

The **celebration.** De La Roche, M.

CELEBRITIES
Saphir, M. G. A conquest

Celeste. Merochnik, M.

Celestial omnibus. Forster, E. M.

Celestial railroad. Hawthorne, N.

Cellmate. Waldo, E. H.

CEMETERIES
Jackson, C. R. Sunday drive
Johnson, H. It happened to me
Porter, K. A. The grave

Cemetery bait. Runyon, D.

Censored, the goat. Stong, P. D.

CENSUS
Horwitz, J. New York

Census. Simak, C. D.

Centaur in brass. Faulkner, W.

CENTAURS
Dunsany, E. J. M. D. P. 18th baron.
Bride of the man-horse

CEPHALONIA. See Ionian Islands

Cervantes, Miguel de. See Cervantes Saavedra, Miguel de

Cervantes Saavedra, Miguel de, 1547-1616
Call of the blood
De Onís, H. ed. Spanish stories and
tales

CEYLON
Buck, F. Elephants!

Chadwick, Ann
Smith
Joseph, M. ed. Best cat stories

Chaikin, N. G.
Climate of the family
Best American short stories, 1952

Chains. Kneale, N.

Chair of philanthromathematics. Porter,
W. S.

The **challenge.** Newcomb, C.

The **challenge.** O'Flaherty, L.

The **challenge.** Vandercook, J. W.

Chalmers, Bea
The contest
Furman, A. L. ed. Everygirls career
stories

Chamberlain, George Agnew, 1879-
Monarch the bum
Creamer, J. B. comp. Twenty-two stories about horses and men

Chamberlain, William
Chaplain of Company C
Saturday evening post (Periodical)
Saturday evening post stories, 1951

Chambers, Robert William, 1865-1933
Demoiselle d'Ys
Moskowitz, S. comp. Editor's choice
in science fiction

Chambers, Ruth E.
Jinx ship
Furman, A. L. ed. Everygirls mystery
stories

The **Champ.** Ish-Kishor, S.

Champagne for the old lady. Sitwell, Sir O.
bart.

Champion. Lardner, R. W.

The **champion.** Stuart, J.

Champion comes home. Taber, G. B.

Champion of the weather. Porter, W. S.

The **champions.** Hager, M.

CHANCE
Hawthorne, N. David Swan
Johnson, D. M. Warrior's exile
Norris, K. T. What happened to Alanna
Porter, W. S. Phoebe
Pratt, F. and De Camp, L. S. Eve of
St John

Chance for adventure. Shulman, M.

Chandler, A. Bertram
Castaway
Conklin, G. ed. Science-fiction adventures in dimension
False dawn
Greenberg, M. ed. Journey to infinity
Giant killer
Pratt, F. ed. World of wonder
Ship from nowhere
Argosy (Periodical) Argosy Book of sea stories

Chandler, Raymond, 1888-
I'll be waiting
Grayson, C. ed. Fourth round
Mystery Writers of America, inc. Butcher, baker, murder-maker

The **change.** Alpert, H.

Change of address. Arthur, R.

Change of air. Gold, I.

Change of pitchers. Patten, G.

Change of plan. Purdy, K. W.

Change of station. Haycox, E.

CHANNEL ISLANDS
Goudge, E. Doing good
Goudge, E. Midnight in the stable

Channel 10. Hatch, E.

Chaparral Christmas gift. Porter, W. S.

Chaparral prince. Porter, W. S.

Chaplain of Company C. Chamberlain, W.

CHAPLAINS. See Clergy

The **Chaplet.** Munro, H. H.

Chaplin, Sid
Pigeon cree
New writing (Periodical) Best stories

Chapman, Warren, 1917-
Where Teetee Wood lies cold and dead
Stanford short stories, 1951

Chapo—the faker. James, W.

Char on raven's bench. Holwerda, F.

Character of dogs. Stevenson, R. L.

CHARACTERS, LITERARY. See Literary characters

Charcoal burners. Krige, U.

Chariots away. Allen, M. P.

CHARITIES
Crane, S. Men in the storm
Francis, O. Ladies call on Mr Pussick

CHARITY
Benét, S. V. Bishop's beggar
Goudge, E. Doing good
Grebanier, B. D. N. Life began today
Mansfield, K. Cup of tea

Charity. Bowen, E.

Charity ward. Tracy, D.

Charles. Jackson, S.

Charles and Charlemagne. Sitwell, Sir O. bart.

Charles Husson. Verlaine, P. M.

CHARLESTON. See South Carolina— Charleston

Charlie Baseball. Katkov, N.

CHARMS
Jacobs, W. S. Monkey's paw

Charnley, Mitchell Vaughn, 1898-
Brodie horns in
Herzberg, M. J. comp. Treasure chest of sport stories

Chartered rowboat. Millar, B.

Charteris, Leslie, 1907-
Amsterdam: The angel's eye
Charteris, L. The Saint in Europe
Dawn
Charteris, L. Second Saint omnibus
Jeannine
Charteris, L. Second Saint omnibus
Juan-les-pins: the Spanish cow
Charteris, L. The Saint in Europe
Judith
Charteris, L. Second Saint omnibus
Lucerne: The loaded tourist
Charteris, L. The Saint in Europe
Man who liked ants
Charteris, L. Second Saint omnibus
Masked angel
Charteris, L. Second Saint omnibus
Palm Springs
Charteris, L. Second Saint omnibus
Paris: The covetous headsman
Charteris, L. The Saint in Europe
Revolution racket
Best detective stories of the year—1954
The Rhine: The Rhine maiden
Charteris, L. The Saint in Europe
Rome: The Latin touch
Charteris, L. The Saint in Europe
Sizzling saboteur
Charteris, L. Second Saint omnibus
Star producers
Charteris, L. Second Saint omnibus
Teresa
Charteris, L. Second Saint omnibus
Tirol: The golden journey
Charteris, L. The Saint in Europe
Wicked cousin
Charteris, L. Second Saint omnibus

Chase, Francis
General from the Pentagon
Saturday evening post (Periodical) Saturday evening post stories, 1953

Chase, Margaret
I hate a dumpy woman
Collier's the national weekly. Collier's best

Chase, Mary Ellen, 1887-
Reuben's courtship
Brentano, F. ed. The word lives on
Salesmanship
Shaw, H. and Bement, D. Reading the short story

The **chaser.** Collier, J.

Chastity
Lin, Y. ed. Famous Chinese short stories

Château of missing men. Simenon, G.

Chatter-stick sermon. Faggett, H. L.

Chaucer, Geoffrey, 1340?-1400
Pardoner's tale
Cerf, B. A. and Moriarty, H. C. eds. Anthology of famous British stories

CHAUFFEURS. See Servants—Chauffeurs

The **cheapjack.** O'Donovan, M.

The **cheat.** Jackson, C. R.

CHEATING. See Swindlers and swindling

Cheerful tortoise. Hall, J. N.

Cheerio. Powell, D.

Cheery soul. Bowen, E.

Cheever, John, 1912-
The children
  Cheever, J. Enormous radio, and other
  stories
Christmas is a sad season for the poor
  Cheever, J. Enormous radio, and other
  stories
Clancy in the Tower of Babel
  Cheever, J. Enormous radio, and other
  stories
The cure
  Cheever, J. Enormous radio, and other
  stories
Enormous radio
  Best of the Best American short stories,
  1915-1950
  Cheever, J. Enormous radio, and other
  stories
Goodbye, my brother
  Cheever, J. Enormous radio, and other
  stories
The Hartleys
  Cheever, J. Enormous radio, and other
  stories
O city of broken dreams
  Cheever, J. Enormous radio, and other
  stories
Pot of gold
  Cheever, J. Enormous radio, and other
  stories
  Greene, J. I. and Abell, E. eds. Stories
  of sudden truth
  Prize stories 1951
Season of divorce
  Best American short stories, 1951
  Cheever, J. Enormous radio, and other
  stories
Summer farmer
  Cheever, J. Enormous radio, and other
  stories
The superintendent
  Cheever, J. Enormous radio, and other
  stories
Sutton Place story
  Cheever, J. Enormous radio, and other
  stories
Torch song
  Cheever, J. Enormous radio, and other
  stories
Vega
  Prize stories of 1950

CHEFS. See Servants—Cooks

Chekhov, Anton Pavlovich, 1860-1904
Across Siberia
  Chekhov, A. P. Unknown Chekhov
After the theatre
  Davis, R. G. ed. Ten modern masters
Appropriate measures
  Chekhov, A. P. Woman in the case, and
  other stories
Because of little apples
  Chekhov, A. P. Unknown Chekhov
The beggar
  Schramm, W. L. ed. Great short stories
The bet
  Thinker's digest (Periodical) Spoiled
  priest, and other stories

Boa constrictor and rabbit
  Chekhov, A. P. Unknown Chekhov
  Chekhov, A. P. Woman in the case, and
  other stories
Carelessness
  Fabricant, N. D. and Werner, H. eds.
  World's best doctor stories
Chorus girl
  Barrows, H. ed. 15 stories
La Cigale
  West, R. B. and Stallman, R. W. eds.
  Art of modern fiction
De-composition
  Chekhov, A. P. Unknown Chekhov
The diplomat
  Chekhov, A. P. Woman in the case, and
  other stories
Disagreeable experience
  Chekhov, A. P. Woman in the case, and
  other stories
The dream; a Christmas story
  Chekhov, A. P. Woman in the case, and
  other stories
Drowning
  Chekhov, A. P. Unknown Chekhov
Enemies
  Fabricant, N. D. and Werner, H. eds.
  World's best doctor stories
Eve of the the trial; the defendant's story
  Chekhov, A. P. Woman in the case, and
  other stories
A fragment
  Chekhov, A. P. Unknown Chekhov
Good news
  Chekhov, A. P. Unknown Chekhov
Gooseberries
  Felheim, M.; Newman, F. B. and Stein-
  hoff, W. R. eds. Modern short stories
  O'Faoláin, S. The short story
  Schorer, M. ed. The story
  Short, R. W. and Sewall, R. B. eds.
  Short stories for study. 1950 ed.
Grief
  Blodgett, H. W. ed. Story survey.
  1953 ed.
The guest
  Chekhov, A. P. Woman in the case, and
  other stories
His first appearance
  Chekhov, A. P. Woman in the case, and
  other stories
History of a business enterprise
  Chekhov, A. P. Woman in the case, and
  other stories
Holy simplicity
  Chekhov, A. P. Woman in the case,
  and other stories
  Same as: Saintly simplicity
Hydrophobia
  Chekhov, A. P. Unknown Chekhov
In exile
  Stegner, W. E.; Scowcroft, R. and
  Ilyin, B. eds. Writer's art
The lodger
  Chekhov, A. P. Unknown Chekhov
  Chekhov, A. P. Woman in the case,
  and other stories
The mask
  Chekhov, A. P. Woman in the case,
  and other stories
Moscow hypocrites
  Chekhov, A. P. Unknown Chekhov

Chekhov, Anton P.—*Continued*
Mutual superiority
Chekhov, A. P. Woman in the case, and other stories
New villa
Lynskey, W. C. ed. Reading modern fiction
On the harmful effects of tobacco; final version
Chekhov, A. P. Unknown Chekhov
On the harmful effects of tobacco; first version
Chekhov, A. P. Unknown Chekhov
On the road
Gordon, C. and Tate, A. eds. House of fiction
Same as: On the way
On the way
Stegner, W. E.; Scowcroft, R. and Ilyin, B. eds. Writer's art
Same as: On the road
One man's meat
Chekhov, A. P. Woman in the case, and other stories
Other people's misfortune
Chekhov, A. P. Unknown Chekhov
Same as: Other people's trouble
Other people's trouble
Chekhov, A. P. Woman in the case, and other stories
Same as: Other people's misfortune
Out of sheer boredom; a holiday love story
Chekhov, A. P. Woman in the case, and other stories
Peasants
Chekhov, A. P. Unknown Chekhov
Perpetuum mobile
Chekhov, A. P. Unknown Chekhov
Reporter's dream
Chekhov, A. P. Woman in the case, and other stories
Saintly simplicity
Chekhov, A. P. Unknown Chekhov
Same as: Holy simplicity
The schoolmistress
Barrows, H. ed. 15 stories
75,000
Chekhov, A. P. Woman in the case, and other stories
Sinister night
Chekhov, A. P. Woman in the case, and other stories
The skit
Chekhov, A. P. Unknown Chekhov
Tædium vitæ
Chekhov, A. P. Woman in the case, and other stories
Three Annas
Cody, S. ed. Greatest stories and how they were written
Two in one
Chekhov, A. P. Unknown Chekhov
Two of a kind
Chekhov, A. P. Unknown Chekhov
Unpleasant incident
Chekhov, A. P. Woman in the case, and other stories
Same as: An unpleasantness
An unpleasantness
Chekhov, A. P. Unknown Chekhov
Same as: Unpleasant incident

Vanka
Bogorad, S. N. and Trevithick, J. eds. College miscellany
Neider, C. ed. Great short stories
Neider, C. ed. Great short stories from the world's literature
Verotchka
Lamb, L. ed. Family book of best loved short stories
Village Elder
Chekhov, A. P. Unknown Chekhov
Vint
Chekhov, A. P. Unknown Chekhov
Visit to friends
Chekhov, A. P. Unknown Chekhov
Chekhov, A. P. Woman in the case, and other stories
Ward no. 6
Neider, C. ed. Short novels of the masters
Rahv, P. ed. Great Russian short novels
Woman in the case
Chekhov, A. P. Woman in the case, and other stories
Women make trouble
Chekhov, A. P. Unknown Chekhov
Worse and worse
Chekhov, A. P. Unknown Chekhov
Yegor's story; excerpt from "The Island of Sakhalin"
Chekhov, A. P. Unknown Chekhov

Cheley, Frank Hobart, 1889-
Big Bones rides alone
Furman, A. L. ed. Teen-age horse stories

Chelsea cat. Kitchin, C. H. B.

Chemist and druggist. Harvey, W. F.

CHEMISTS
Harvey, W. F. Chemist and druggist
O'Donovan, M. Torrent damned

Ch'en Hsüan-Yu, fl. 8th century
Chienniang
Lin, Y. ed. Famous Chinese short stories

Ch'engshih, T'uan. See T'uan Ch'engshih

Cherchez la femme. Porter, W. S.

Cherchez la frame. Rice, C. and Palmer, S.

Chéri. Colette, S. G.

CHEROKEE INDIANS
Porter, W. S. Atavism of John Tom Little Bear
Porter, W. S. He also serves

Cheshire, Giff
Bad year
Western Writers of America. Holsters and horses
Strangers in the evening
Western Writers of America. Bad men and good

Chesnutt, Charles Waddell, 1856-1932
Wife of his youth
Dreer, H. ed. American literature by Negro authors

CHESS
Aiken, C. P. The disciple
Bergengruen, W. Royal game
Dunsany, E. J. M. D. P. 18th baron. Three sailors' gambit

CHESS—*Continued*

Elin, S. Fool's mate
Nemerov, H. and Johnson, W. R. Exchange of men

Chesterton, Gilbert Keith, 1874-1936

Absence of Mr Glass
Chesterton, G. K. Father Brown omnibus. 1951 ed.
Actor and the alibi
Chesterton, G. K. Father Brown omnibus. 1951 ed.
Arrow of heaven
Chesterton, G. K. Father Brown omnibus. 1951 ed.
Blast of the book
Chesterton, G. K. Father Brown omnibus. 1951 ed.
Blue cross
Chesterton, G. K. Father Brown omnibus. 1951 ed.
Neider, C. ed. Men of the high calling
Chief mourner of Marne
Chesterton, G. K. Father Brown omnibus. 1951 ed.
Crime of the Communist
Chesterton, G. K. Father Brown omnibus. 1951 ed.
Curse of the golden cross
Chesterton, G. K. Father Brown omnibus. 1951 ed.
Dagger with wings
Chesterton, G. K. Father Brown omnibus. 1951 ed.
Doom of the Darnaways
Chesterton, G. K. Father Brown omnibus. 1951 ed.
Duel of Dr Hirsch
Chesterton, G. K. Father Brown omnibus. 1951 ed.
Eye of Apollo
Chesterton, G. K. Father Brown omnibus. 1951 ed.
Fairy tale of Father Brown
Chesterton, G. K. Father Brown omnibus. 1951 ed.
Flying stars
Chesterton, G. K. Father Brown omnibus. 1951 ed.
Ghost of Gideon Wise
Chesterton, G. K. Father Brown omnibus. 1951 ed.
God of the gongs
Chesterton, G. K. Father Brown omnibus. 1951 ed.
Green man
Chesterton, G. K. Father Brown omnibus. 1951 ed.
Hammer of God
Cerf, B. A. and Moriarty, H. C. eds. Anthology of famous British stories
Chesterton, G. K. Father Brown omnibus. 1951 ed.
Head of Cæsar
Chesterton, G. K. Father Brown omnibus. 1951 ed.
Honour of Israel Gow
Chesterton, G. K. Father Brown omnibus. 1951 ed.
Insoluble problem
Chesterton, G. K. Father Brown omnibus. 1951 ed.

Invisible man
Chesterton, G. K. Father Brown omnibus. 1951 ed.
Christ, H. I. and Shostak, J. eds. Short stories
Man in the passage
Chesterton, G. K. Father Brown omnibus. 1951 ed.
Man with two beards
Chesterton, G. K. Father Brown omnibus. 1951 ed.
Miracle of Moon Crescent
Chesterton, G. K. Father Brown omnibus. 1951 ed.
Mirror of the magistrate
Chesterton, G. K. Father Brown omnibus. 1951 ed.
Mistake of the machine
Chesterton, G. K. Father Brown omnibus. 1951 ed.
Oracle of the dog
Chesterton, G. K. Father Brown omnibus. 1951 ed.
Paradise of thieves
Chesterton, G. K. Father Brown omnibus. 1951 ed.
Perishing of the pendragons
Chesterton, G. K. Father Brown omnibus. 1951 ed.
Point of a pin
Chesterton, G. K. Father Brown omnibus. 1951 ed.
Purple wig
Chesterton, G. K. Father Brown omnibus. 1951 ed.
Pursuit of Mr Blue
Chesterton, G. K. Father Brown omnibus. 1951 ed.
Queer feet
Chesterton, G. K. Father Brown omnibus. 1951 ed.
Quick one
Bond, R. T. ed. Handbook for poisoners
Chesterton, G. K. Father Brown omnibus. 1951 ed.
Red moon of Meru
Chesterton, G. K. Father Brown omnibus. 1951 ed.
Resurrection of Father Brown
Chesterton, G. K. Father Brown omnibus. 1951 ed.
Salad of Colonel Cray
Chesterton, G. K. Father Brown omnibus. 1951 ed.
Scandal of Father Brown
Chesterton, G. K. Father Brown omnibus. 1951 ed.
Secret garden
Chesterton, G. K. Father Brown omnibus. 1951 ed.
Secret of Father Brown
Chesterton, G. K. Father Brown omnibus. 1951 ed.
Secret of Flambeau
Chesterton, G. K. Father Brown omnibus. 1951 ed.
Sign of Prince Saradine
Chesterton, G. K. Father Brown omnibus. 1951 ed.
Sign of the broken sword
Chesterton, G. K. Father Brown omnibus. 1951 ed.

Chesterton, Gilbert K.—*Continued*
  Song of the flying fish
    Chesterton, G. K. Father Brown omnibus. 1951 ed.
  Strange crime of John Boulnois
    Chesterton, G. K. Father Brown omnibus. 1951 ed.
  Three tools of death
    Chesterton, G. K. Father Brown omnibus. 1951 ed.
  Vampire of the village
    Chesterton, G. K. Father Brown omnibus. 1951 ed.
  Vanishing of Vaudrey
    Chesterton, G. K. Father Brown omnibus. 1951 ed.
  Worst crime in the world
    Chesterton, G. K. Father Brown omnibus. 1951 ed.
  Wrong shape
    Chesterton, G. K. Father Brown omnibus. 1951 ed.
Chestor, Rui, pseud. See Courtier, Sidney Hobson
CHESTS (FURNITURE)
  De La Mare, W. J. The riddle
CHEYENNE INDIANS
  Johnson, D. M. Scars of honor
  Johnson, D. M. War shirt
  Lane, C. D. River dragon
CHICAGO. See Illinois—Chicago
Chichester, Francis Charles, 1901-
  Palm Island plane factory
    Jensen, P. ed. Fireside book of flying stories
Chicken dinner. Ullman, J. R.
Chicken on the wind. King, M. P.
CHICKENS. See Poultry
Chico and the badman. Thompson, T.
Chidester, Ann, 1919-
  Mrs Ketting and Clark Gable
    Prize stories of 1950
  Wood smoke
    Best American short stories, 1952
Chief mourner of Marne. Chesterton, G. K.
Chief operator. Ward, E. S. P.
Chienniang. Ch'en Hsüan-yu
Child, Charles B.
  Inspector had a habit
    Best detective stories of the year—1950
CHILD AUTHORS. See Children as authors
Child by Chronos. Harness, C. L.
The **child** is father. Beck, W.
CHILD MARRIAGE
  Goodwin, R. V. Going home
Child missing! Queen, E. pseud.
CHILD MURDER. See Infanticide
CHILD MUSICIANS. See Children as musicians
Child of God. Bradford, R.
Child of God. O'Flaherty, L.
Child of void. St Clair, M.
CHILD PRODIGIES. See Children, Gifted
CHILD PSYCHOLOGY. See Children
Child so fair. Betts, D.
Child that walked at night. O'Meara, W.

Child wore a pink sweater. MacDonald, D.
CHILDBIRTH
  Balzac, H. de. Mother's letter
  Becker, S. D. Baptism of some importance
  Cronin, A. J. Birth
  Ferrara, J. Figurine of love
  Gorki, M. Birth of a man
  Irwin, M. E. F. The doctor
  Taylor, E. Light of day
  Vaughn, G. Tornado
Childhood of a leader. Sartre, J. P.
Childish thing. Metcalfe, J.
Childishness of Mr Mountfort. Benson, T.
CHILDREN
  Aiken, C. P. Strange moonlight
  Alexander, S. Part of the act
  Betts, D. Sense of humor
  Birmingham, S. G. Reappearance
  Bolté, M. End of the depression
  Carrighar, S. Marooned children
  Dann, L. One summer afternoon
  Evans, E. E. The shed
  Faulkner, W. That evening sun
  Friedman, S. Adam and Eve
  Goudge, E. Doing good
  Goudge, E. Midnight in the stable
  Horwitz, J. Cup of tea
  Ivanov, V. V. The kid
  Kipling, R. Toomai of the elephants
  Lagerkvist, P. F. Children's campaign
  Mansfield, K. Doll's house
  Munro, H. H. Lumber-room
  Munro, H. H. Morlvera
  Munro, H. H. The penance
  Munro, H. H. The quest
  Rabinowitz, S. Page from the Song of Songs
  Russell, E. F. I am nothing
  Salinger, J. D. For Esmé—with love and squalor
  Schorer, M. What we don't know hurts us
  Seaver, J. Kingdom in the corn
  Stewart, R. The promise
  Taylor, P. H. Bad dreams
  Waldeck, T. J. Evil one
  Wilson, H. L. Wrong twin
  Wolfe, D. M. ed. Which grain will grow; 35 stories
  Yoss, N. Children learn so fast
  Zugsmith, L. Room in the world
    See also Boys; Girls

     Diseases
  Williams, W. C. Use of force
CHILDREN, ABNORMAL AND BACKWARD
  Davies, R. Arfon
  Fitzgerald, F. S. K. Curious case of Benjamin Button
  Kuttner, H. When the bough breaks
  Rosaire, F. Pod of a weed
CHILDREN, CRIPPLED. See Cripples
CHILDREN, DEFORMED. See Children, Abnormal and backward
CHILDREN, GIFTED
  Clifton, M. Star, Bright
  De Vries, P. Tulip
  Humphrey, W. Report cards
  Huxley, A. L. Young Archimedes
  Kuttner, H. Absalom

CHILDREN, GIFTED—*Continued*
Salinger, J. D. Teddy
Shiras, W. H. In hiding
Shiras, W. H. Opening doors

CHILDREN, LOST
Cheever, J. Sutton Place story
Heinlein, R. A. Black pits of Luna
Porter, W. S. Atavism of John Tom Little Bear
Porter, W. S. Church with an overshot-wheel
Saroyan, W. Third day after Christmas
Van Doren, M. Rescue

CHILDREN, SICK
Collette, S. G. Sick child
The **children**. Cheever, J.
Children. Corkery, D.

CHILDREN AND PARENTS. See Parent and child

Children are bored on Sunday. Stafford, J.

CHILDREN AS AUTHORS
Ashford, D. A proposale
Waugh, E. Curse of the horse race

CHILDREN AS MUSICIANS
McCullers, C. S. Wunderkind

Children learn so fast. Yoss, N.

Children of Noah. Burman, B. L.

Children of Old Somebody. Goyen, W.

Children of Ruth. Elliott, G. P.

Children of Set. Coolidge, O. E.

Children of the times. Farrell, J. T.

Children's campaign. Lagerkvist, P. F.

Children's day with Mr Jovey Jessop's hounds. Surtees, R. S.

Children's hour. Keith, E.

CHILDREN'S PARTIES
Bowen, E. Easter egg party
Holland, W. Billy had a system
Munro, H. H. The strategist
See also Birthdays; Parties

Children's room. Jones, R. F.

Child's day. West, J.

Child's dream of a star. Dickens, C.

Child's play. Berger, T. L.

Child's play. Klass, P.

CHILE
Conrad, J. Gaspar Ruiz

Chiltipiquin. Brandon, W.

The **chimes**. Dickens, C.

CHIMES AND CHIMING. See Bells and bell-ringers

CHIMNEYS
Melville, H. I and my chimney

CHIMPANZEES
Leinster, M. Keyhole

Chin, Yuen. See Yuen Chin

CHINA
Dunsany, E. J. M. D. P. 18th baron. East and West
Lin, Y. ed. Famous Chinese short stories; 20 stories

1900-date
Buck, P S. Good river
Buck, P. S. Old demon
Buck, P. S. One named Jesus

Chou, S. Benediction
Shen, T. Little Flute

Hangchow
Mrs White

Hong Kong
Small, S. H. Stalking shadow

Legends and folk tales
See Legends and folk tales—China

Shanghai
Patterson, R. Babe

China run. Paterson, N.

Chinese dagger. Small, S. H.

CHINESE IN AUSTRALIA
Travers, P. L. Ah Wong

CHINESE IN ENGLAND
Burke, T. Chink and the child

CHINESE IN INDO-CHINA
Payne, P. S. R. Red mountain

CHINESE IN MONGOLIA
Vogau, B. A. Big heart

CHINESE IN THE UNITED STATES
Ekbergh, I. D. Mysterious Chinese mandrake
Harte, B. Wan Lee, the pagan
Small, S. H. Chinese dagger

Ching, Ching, Chinaman. Steele, W. D.

The **Chink**. Stegner, W. E.

Chink and the child. Burke, T.

Chinn, Laurene Chambers
Spelling bee
Bachelor, J. M.; Henry, R. L. and Salisbury, R. eds. Current thinking and writing; 2d ser.

Chinoiserie. McCloy, H.

Chip off the old block. Stegner, W. E.

CHIPMUNKS
Van Doren, M. Lady over the wall

CHIPPEWA INDIANS
Macfarlan, A. A. Moose boy

CHIVALRY
Bergengruen, W. Shining fools
See also Knights and knighthood

The **choice**. Wharton, E. N. J.

Choice of the litter. Lull, R.

Choice of weapons. Newhouse, E.

CHOIRMASTERS
Chekhov, A. P. Worse and worse

CHOIRS (MUSIC)
Hardy, T. Absent-mindedness in a parish choir

CHOLERA
Allen, J. L. King Solomon of Kentucky
Kipling, R. Without benefit of clergy
See also Epidemics

Chop-sticks. Chrisman, A. B.

Chore for a spaceman. Sheldon, W.

Chorus girl. Chekhov, A. P.

Chou, Shu-jên, 1881-1936
Benediction
Neider, C. ed. Great short stories from the world's literature

Chowsie. Bendrodt, J. C.

Chrisman, Arthur Bowie, 1889-1953
  Chop-sticks
    Fenner, P. R. comp. Fools and funny
    fellows

Christ in concrete. Di Donato, P.

CHRISTENINGS
  De La Mare, W. J. The bowl
  Hardy, T. Three strangers

CHRISTIAN LIFE
  Blackburn, E. R. Swaying elms
  Lantz, J. E. ed. Stories of Christian liv-
    ing; 18 stories

CHRISTIAN SCIENCE
  Munro, H. H. The quest

Christiane the Huguenot. Blackburn, E. R.

Christie, Agatha (Miller) 1891-
  Accident
    Bond, R. T. ed. Handbook for poisoners.
  Adventure of the Clapham cook
    Christie, A. M. Under dog, and other
    stories
  Affair at the Victory Ball
    Christie, A. M. Under dog, and other
    stories
  Cornish mystery
    Christie, A. M. Under dog, and other
    stories
  King of clubs
    Christie, A. M. Under dog, and other
    stories
  Last séance
    Merril, J. ed. Beyond the barriers of
    space and time
  Lemesurier inheritance
    Christie, A. M. Under dog, and other
    stories
  Market Basing mystery
    Christie, A. M. Under dog, and other
    stories
  Plymouth Express
    Christie, A. M. Under dog, and other
    stories
  Submarine plans
    Christie, A. M. Under dog, and other
    stories
  Under dog
    Christie, A. M. Under dog, and other
    stories

CHRISTMAS
  Aldrich, B. S. Another brought gifts
  American girl (Periodical) Christmas all
    year 'round; 25 stories
  Baker, R. S. A day of pleasant bread
  Broun, H. C. Even to Judas
  Cheever, J. Christmas is a sad season for
    the poor
  Cooke, A. Christmas Eve; 3 stories
  Cousins, M. Christmas gift; 8 stories
  Cousins, M. Uncle Edgar and the reluc-
    tant saint
  Dickens, C. Christmas carol
  Dickens, C. Christmas stories; 3 stories
  Dostoevskiï, F. M. Heavenly Christmas
    tree
  Eggleston, M. W. Red stocking, and
    other Christmas stories; 20 stories
  Elliot, I. Christmas is a time for great
    things

Elmquist, R. M. ed. Fifty years of Christ-
    mas; 16 stories
  Foster, M. Present for Christmas
  Goodman, P. Iddings Clark
  Goudge, E. Reward of faith; 8 stories
  Grimson, M. S. Christmas story
  Grimson, M. S. Gather up the pieces
  Harte, B. How Santa Claus came to
    Simpson's Bar
  Henderson, D. Brute's Christmas
  Hertlein, R. P. G. Christmas
  Irwin, M. E. F. Mistletoe
  Krige, U. Christmas box
  Locke, W. J. Wise men of Trehenna
  Lohan, R. and Lohan, M. eds. New
    Christmas treasury; 27 stories
  Mathews, M. Tough little Christmas
    story
  Miller, A. D. Plum pudding and mince
    pie
  Morley, C. D. Home again
  Munro, H. H. Bertie's Christmas Eve
  Porter, W. S. Chaparral Christmas gift
  Porter, W. S. Christmas by injunction
  Porter, W. S. Compliments of the season
  Porter, W. S. Gift of the magi
  Porter, W. S. Whistling Dick's Christ-
    mas stocking
  Puzo, M. Last Christmas
  Sawyer, R. Fiddler, play fast, play faster
  Schubert, P. White Elk
  Schulberg, B. W. My Christmas carol
  Stifter, A. Rock crystal
  Taber, G. B. Christmas gift
  Van Dyke, H. First Christmas tree
  Van Paassen, P. Uncle Kees protests
  Wall, J. W. Christmas story
  Weber, L. M. Christmas thaw
  Wiggin, K. D. S. The Ruggleses go to
    a Christmas party
          See also Jesus Christ—Nativity

Christmas angel. Eggleston, M. W.

Christmas anyhow. Hill, M. Y.

Christmas at Polly Moran's. Gregutt, H. C.

Christmas at the Bachs'. Brachvogel, A. E.

Christmas at Thunder Gap. Wright, K. O.

Christmas box. Krige, U.

Christmas by injunction. Porter, W. S.

Christmas carol. Davis, S. P.

Christmas carol. Dickens, C.

Christmas cherries. Gray, E. J.

Christmas Day in the workhouse. Wilson,
  A.

Christmas Eve. Cooke, A.

Christmas Eve in a lumber camp. Gordon,
  C. W.

Christmas Eve, one-three. Cooke, A.

Christmas every day. Howells, W. D.

Christmas Eve's Day. Benefield, B.

Christmas game. Munby, A. N. L.

Christmas gift. Powys, T. F.

Christmas gift. Taber, G. B.

A Christmas gift for father. Eggleston,
  M. W.

CHRISTMAS GIFTS. See Christmas;
  Gifts

Christmas guest. Brown, K. I.

Christmas in Carthage. Gilbertson, M. G.

Christmas is a sad season for the poor. Cheever, J.

Christmas is a time for great things. Elliot, I.

Christmas meeting. Timperley, R.

Christmas morning. O'Donovan, M.

Christmas on Ganymede. Asimov, I.

Christmas party. Milne, A. A.

Christmas rose. Fitzsimmons, B. J.

Christmas shadrach. Stockton, F. R.

Christmas skis. Miers, E. S.

Christmas solo. Eggleston, M. W.

Christmas song. Bates, H. E.

CHRISTMAS STORIES. See Christmas

Christmas story. Grimson, M. S.

Christmas story. Wall, J. W.

Christmas thaw. Weber, L. M.

Christmas tree. Youd, C.

Christmas tree and a wedding. Dostoevskiĭ, F. M.

CHRISTMAS TREES
Goudge, E. Legend of the first Christmas tree
Grimson, M. S. Christmas story
Hale, L. P. Peterkins' Christmas tree
Van Dyke, H. First Christmas tree

Christmas visitor. Eggleston, M. W.

Christopher, John, 1922-
Balance
Best science fiction stories: 1952
Man of destiny
Galaxy science fiction magazine. Galaxy reader of science fiction
Lesser, M. A. ed. Looking forward
Socrates
Merril, J. ed. Beyond human ken
Sloane, W. M. ed. Stories for tomorrow

Christopher, Robert, 1924-
Jishin
Best American short stories, 1950

Christowe, Stoyan, 1898-
My grandfather's eyes
Certner, S. and Henry, G. H. eds. Short stories for our times

Christ's tree. Booth, M. B. C.

Chromium helmet. Waldo, E. H.

The chronicler. Van Vogt, A. E.

The chronoclasm. Harris, J. B.

Chronokinesis of Jonathan Hull. White, W. A. P.

The chrysanthemums. Steinbeck, J.

CHURCH ATTENDANCE
Bennett, P. Fugitive from the mind
Hawthorne, N. Sunday at home
Irwin, M. E. F. Earlier service

CHURCH SCHOOLS
Doty, W. L. Parochial school

Church with an overshot-wheel. Porter, W. S.

CHURCHES
Bunner, H. C. Two churches of 'Quawket
Faulkner, W. Shingles for the Lord

Hall, J. B. In the time of demonstration
Lemelin, R. Stations of the Cross
Melville, H. Temple first

Churchyard yew. LeFanu, J. S.

CHURCHYARDS. See Cemeteries

Chute, Beatrice Joy, 1913-
Alias All-American
Chute, B. J. Teen-age sports parade
Bench warmer
Boys' life (Periodical) Boys' life Adventure stories
Big shot
Chute, B. J. Teen-age sports parade
Double fault
Chute, B. J. Teen-age sports parade
Doubles or nothing
Owen, F. ed. Teen-age victory parade
Dumb bunny
Fenner, P. R. comp. Crack of the bat
Fall guy
Owen, F. ed. Teen-age winter sports stories
Five captains
Chute, B. J. Teen-age sports parade
Four-ring circus
Owen, F. ed. Teen-age winter sports stories
Kid brother
Herzberg, M. J. comp. Treasure chest of sport stories
Magnificent merger
Chute, B. J. Teen-age sports parade
Master mind
Chute, B. J. Teen-age sports parade
Really important person
Certner, S. and Henry, G. H. eds. Short stories for our times
Red Pepper
Chute, B. J. Teen-age sports parade
Ski high
Chute, B. J. Teen-age sports parade
Thank you, Dr Russell
Certner, S. and Henry, G. H. eds. Short stories for our times
Too close to nature
Chute, B. J. Teen-age sports parade
Triple threat
Chute, B. J. Teen-age sports parade
The winner
Chute, B. J. Teen-age sports parade

Chute, Verne, 1917-
Never trust the obvious
Mystery Writers of America, inc. Four-&-twenty bloodhounds

Ciancimino, Helen. See Gregutt, Helen Ciancimino

Cicellis, Kay
Aegean storm
Cicellis, K. Easy way
Easy way
Cicellis, K. Easy way
The excursion
Cicellis, K. Easy way
Hungry man
Cicellis, K. Easy way
Miracles of the Saint
Cicellis, K. Easy way
No admittance
Cicellis, K. Easy way
Recovery
Cicellis, K. Easy way

Clark, Walter Van T.—*Continued*
Watchful gods
  Clark, W. Van T. Watchful gods, and
    other stories
Why don't you look where you're going?
  Clark, W. Van T. Watchful gods, and
    other stories
Wind and the snow of winter
  Best of the Best American short sto-
    ries, 1915-1950
  Clark, W. Van T. Watchful gods, and
    other stories
  First-prize stories, 1919-1954
  Ludwig, J. B. and Poirier, W. R. eds.
    Stories, British and American

Clarke, Arthur Charles, 1917-
All the time in the world
  Wollheim, D. A. ed. Prize science fic-
    tion
Breaking strain
  Clarke, A. C. Expedition to earth
Deep range
  Star science fiction stories, no. 3
Exile of the eons
  Clarke, A. C. Expedition to earth
Expedition to earth
  Clarke, A. C. Expedition to earth
Fires within
  Derleth, A. W. ed. Worlds of tomor-
    row
Forgotten enemy
  Sloane, W. M. ed. Stories for tomor-
    row
Hide and seek
  Clarke, A. C. Expedition to earth
  Sloane, W. M. ed. Space, space, space
History lesson
  Clarke, A. C. Expedition to earth
  Conklin, G. ed. Omnibus of science fic-
    tion
"If I forget thee, oh Earth. . ,"
  Clarke, A. C. Expedition to earth
Inheritance
  Clarke, A. C. Expedition to earth
Loophole
  Clarke, A. C. Expedition to earth
Nine billion names of God
  Sloane, W. M. ed. Stories for tomorrow
  Star science fiction stories [no. 1]
No morning after
  Derleth, A. W. ed. Time to come
Second dawn
  Clarke, A. C. Expedition to earth
Seeker of the sphinx
  Year's best science fiction novels, 1952
The sentinel
  Clarke, A. C. Expedition to earth
Superiority
  Clarke, A. C. Expedition to earth
  Derleth, A. W. ed. Worlds of tomorrow
Thirty seconds—thirty days
  Startling stories (Periodical) Best from
    Startling stories
Transience
  Lesser, M. A. ed. Looking forward
Walk in the dark
  Conklin, G. ed. Possible worlds of sci-
    ence fiction
Wall of darkness
  Moskowitz, S. comp. Editor's choice in
    science fiction

Clash by night. Kuttner, H.

Class. Foote, J. T.
CLASS DISTINCTION
  Mansfield, K. Doll's house
Claud's dog. Dahl, R.
Claudy, Carl Harry, 1879-
According to the landmarks
  Claudy, C. H. These were brethren
Against orders
  Claudy, C. H. These were brethren
Any pain, peril or danger
  Claudy, C. H. These were brethren
The atheist
  Claudy, C. H. These were brethren
Brother Bascombe is annoyed
  Claudy, C. H. These were brethren
Diary of a hard-boiled noble
  Claudy, C. H. These were brethren
Due and timely warning
  Claudy, C. H. These were brethren
For a master's wages
  Claudy, C. H. These were brethren
Fourth point
  Claudy, C. H. These were brethren
Gentle Masonic way
  Claudy, C. H. These were brethren
Greater love hath no man than this
  Claudy, C. H. These were brethren
He told it to the judge
  Claudy, C. H. These were brethren
Helmet of Pluto
  American boy (Periodical) American
    boy Adventure stories
Hidden riches of secret places
  Claudy, C. H. These were brethren
High finance
  Claudy, C. H. These were brethren
Land of No Shadow
  Del Rey, L.; Matschat, C. H. and Car-
    mer, C. L. eds. Year after tomorrow
Long arm
  Claudy, C. H. These were brethren
Master minds of Mars
  Del Rey, L.; Matschat, C. H. and Car-
    mer, C. L. eds. Year after tomorrow
Mystery
  Claudy, C. H. These were brethren
Not blotted
  Claudy, C. H. These were brethren
Plumbers
  Claudy, C. H. These were brethren
Three dollars
  Claudy, C. H. These were brethren
To entertain strangers
  Claudy, C. H. These were brethren
Tongue of beast
  Del Rey, L.; Matschat, C. H. and
    Carmer, C. L. eds. Year after tomor-
    row
Two pillars blight
  Claudy, C. H. These were brethren
Was it murder?
  Claudy, C. H. These were brethren
Witnesses
  Claudy, C. H. These were brethren
Yellow streak
  Claudy, C. H. These were brethren
Claustrophobia. Goodloe, A. C.

Clay, Richard, 1915-
Beautiful night for Orion
  Best American short stories, 1954
Very sharp for jagging
  Prize stories 1954

Clay. Joyce, J.

Clay dish. Blackburn, R. H.

Clayton, John Bell, 1906-1955
Ride a pale ghost into night and time
Jones, K. M. New Confederate short stories
White circle
First-prize stories, 1919-1954

Clean platter. Beck, W.

Clean well-lighted place. Hemingway, E.

CLEANING WOMEN. See Servants—Cleaning women

Clearing in the sky. Stuart, J.

The **clematis.** Canine, W.

Clemens, Samuel Langhorne, 1835-1910
Buck Fanshaw's funeral
Emrich, D. ed. Comstock bonanza
Foerster, N. ed. American poetry and prose. 1952 ed.
Celebrated jumping frog of Calaveras County
Burrell, J. A. and Cerf, B. A. eds. Anthology of famous American stories
Day, A. G. ed. Greatest American short stories
Foerster, N. ed. American poetry and prose. 1952 ed.
Lamb, L. ed. Family book of best loved short stories
Concerning notaries
Emrich, D. ed. Comstock bonanza
Dog's tale
Neider, C. ed. Great short stories from the world's literature
Eve's diary
Selden, R. ed. Ways of God and men
Jim Baker's blue-jay yarn
Andrews, R. C. ed. My favorite stories of the great outdoors
Latest sensation (II)
Emrich, D. ed. Comstock bonanza
Man that corrupted Hadleyburg
Burrell, J. A. and Cerf, B. A. eds. Anthology of famous American stories
Foerster, N. ed. American poetry and prose. 1952 ed.
Mr Skae's item
Emrich, D. ed. Comstock bonanza
My bloody massacre (I)
Emrich, D. ed. Comstock bonanza
My late senatorial secretaryship
Emrich, D. ed. Comstock bonanza
My platonic sweetheart
Blodgett, H. W. ed. Story survey. 1953 ed.
Mysterious stranger
Ludwig, R. M. and Perry, M. B. eds. Nine short novels
Petrified man (I-II)
Emrich, D. ed. Comstock bonanza
Stolen white elephant
Queen, E. pseud. ed. Literature of crime
Wings
Brentano, F. ed. The word lives on

Clement, Hal, pseud. See Stubbs, Harry Clement

Clements, Calvin J.
Captain's prisoner
Argosy (Periodical) Argosy Book of **sea stories**

Keep off the rail!
Argosy (Periodical) Argosy Book of sports stories

Cleo. Runyon, D.

CLERGY
Barrie, Sir J. M. bart. Farewell Miss Julie Logan
Betts, D. Family album
Bloch, J. R. Heresy of the water taps
Bowles, P. F. Pastor Dowe at Tacaté
Bunner, M. C. Two churches of 'Quawket
Clemens, S. L. Buck Fanshaw's funeral
Davies, R. Conflict in Morfa
Gally, J. W. Big Jack Small
Galsworthy, J. Manna
Goodman, J. C. Kingdom of Gordon
Hale, E. E. My double, and how he undid me
Harvey, W. F. Vicar's web
Hawthorne, N. Minister's black veil
Munro, H. H. Lost sanjak
Neider, C. ed. Men of the high calling; 14 stories
Russell, B. A. W. R. 3d earl. Benefit of clergy
Schaefer, J. W. Takes a real man. . .
Steele, W. D. Ching, Ching, Chinaman
Street, J. H. The old, old story
Thomason, J. W. Preacher goes to Texas
Watson, J. His mother's sermon
Wolfe, T. Portrait of Bascom Hawke

CLERGY, ANGLICAN AND EPISCOPAL
Queen, E. pseud. Witch of Times Square
Van Paassen, P. The unsaid prayer

CLERGY, CATHOLIC. See Catholic priests

Clerical error. Cozzens, J. G.

CLERKS
Golding, L. Doomington wanderer
Joyce, J. Counterparts
Moore, G. Clerk's quest

Clerk's quest. Moore, G.

CLEVELAND, GROVER, PRESIDENT U.S. 1837-1908
Porter, W. S. Snapshot at the President

Clever cockatoo. Bentley, E. C.

Clever Elsa. Grimm, J. L. K. and Grimm, W. K.

Clever Manka. Fillmore, P. H.

The **cliff.** Sansom, W.

Cliff dance. Thompson, H.

Clifton, Mark, 1906-
The conqueror
Best science-fiction stories: 1953
Conklin, G. ed. Omnibus of science fiction
Star Bright
Galaxy science fiction magazine. Second Galaxy reader of science fiction
Wollheim, D. A. ed. Prize science fiction
What have I done?
Merril, J. ed. Beyond human ken

Clifton, Mark, 1906- **and Apostolides, Alex,** 1923-
Crazy Joey
Merril, J. ed. Beyond the barriers of space and time

Clifton, M. and Apostolides, A.—*Continued*
What thin partitions
Best science-fiction stories: 1954
Moskowitz, S. comp. Editor's choice in
science fiction
Climate of the family. Chaikin, N. G.
Climb for the big ones. Gregutt, H. C.
Climbing for goats. White, S. E.
Clingerman, Mildred
Minister without portfolio
Conklin, G. ed. Invaders of earth
Sloane, W. M. ed. Stories for tomorrow
Stair trick
Magazine of fantasy and science fiction.
Best from Fantasy and science fiction;
2d ser.
The **clinic.** Waldo, E. H.
Clipped wings. Knapp, S. E.
CLIPPER SHIPS. See Sailing vessels
Cloak of Aesir. Campbell, J. W.
Clochette. Maupassant, G. de
CLOCKMAKERS. See Clocks and watches
CLOCKS AND WATCHES
Canning, V. Man who hated time
De La Mare, W. J. The talisman
Farrell, J. T. Willie Collins
Haliburton, T. C. Sam Slick the clock-
maker
Platt, G. Very false alarm
Cloete, Stuart, 1897-
Silence of Mr Prendegast
Esquire (Periodical) Girls from Esquire
Clog dance for a dead farce. Kneale, N.
Close your eyes. Newhouse, E.
Closed cabinet
Davenport, B. ed. Tales to be told in
the dark
Closed door. Guest, A.
Closed shop. Maugham, W. S.
Closed trophy room. Marshall, E.
CLOTHING AND DRESS
Gordimer, N. The talisman
Porter, W. S. From each according to his
ability
Porter, W. S. Purple dress
Woolf, V. S. New dress
Clouds on the Circle-P. Haycox, E.
Clovis on parental responsibilities. Munro,
H. H.
Clovis on the alleged romance of business.
Munro, H. H.
CLUBS
Dunsany, E. J. M. D. P. 18th baron. Ex-
iles' Club
Whitney, P. A. Lucky 'leven
Clue of the red wig. Carr, J. D.
Clues of the tattooed man & the broken leg.
Rawson, C.
Clumpy who was all arms and legs. Strain,
F. B.
Clyde. Farrell, J. T.
COACHING (ATHLETICS)
Scott, V. Don't run, don't pass

COAL MINES AND MINING
Wales
Davies, R. Boy with a trumpet, and other
selected short stories; 20 stories
Coaly-bay the outlaw horse. Seton, E. T.
Coat for St Patrick's Day. Ready, W. B.
Coates, Robert Myron, 1897-
The need
Best American short stories, 1953
Coatsworth, Elizabeth Jane, 1893-
The attack
Fenner, P. R. comp. Indians, Indians,
Indians
Forgotten island
Story parade (Periodical) Adventure
stories
Patchy
Story parade (Periodical) Adventure
stories
Peddler's cart
Fenner, P. R. comp. Yankee Doodle
Race in the wilderness
Fenner, P R. comp. Yankee Doodle
Cobb, Irvin Shrewsbury, 1876-1944
Boys will be boys
Best of the Best American short stories,
1915-1950
Blaustein, A. P ed. Fiction goes to
court
Occurrence up a side street
Bond, R. T. ed. Handbook for poisoners
Snake doctor
First-prize stories, 1919-1954
Summers, H. S. ed. Kentucky story
Cobbler, cobbler, mend my shoe. Maxtone
Graham, J. A.
COBBLERS. See Shoemakers
Coblentz, Catherine (Cate) 1897-1951
Dog who chose a prince
Fenner, P. R. comp. Dogs, dogs, dogs
Montgomery the loyalest
Harper, W. comp. Dog show
Coblentz, Stanton Arthur, 1896-
Sunward
Wollheim, D. A. comp. Flight into space
COBRAS. See Snakes
Cobra's hood. Holland, R. S.
The **cobweb.** Munro, H. H.
COCHISE, APACHE CHIEF, d. 1874
L'Amour, L. Gift of Cochise
Cochran, Ruth Gilbert, 1893-
Present for Elly
American girl (Periodical) Christmas all
year 'round
Sally steps in
Furman, A. L. ed. Everygirls mystery
stories
Cock-a-doodle-doo! Melville, H.
COCK FIGHTING
Benson, T. White cock
Foote, J. T. Fowl disaster
Wolfert, I. The indomitable
See also Roosters
Cock of Socrates. Alas, L.
COCKATOOS
Cottrell, D. M. Pit in the jungle

Cockburn, Claud, 1904-
Total recall
Best detective stories of the year—1952
COCKNEY DIALECT. See Dialect stories—English—Cockney
Cockrell, Eustace Williams
Keyhole artist
This week magazine. This week's short-short stories
COCKROACHES
Babikoff, V. Day of rest
Bates, H. Death of a sensitive
Gilpatric, G. Mr Glencannon and the ailing cockroach
Zamíatin, E. I. God
COCKS. See Cock fighting; Poultry; Roosters
COCKTAIL PARTIES. See Parties
Cocktail party. Saroyan, W.
Coda to a writers' conference. Fletcher, V.
The code. Moore, C. L.
CODES, TELEGRAPH. See Cipher and telegraph codes
Coffin, Robert Peter Tristram, 1892-1955
Seraph in the apple tree
Hazeltine, A. I. comp. Selected stories for teen-agers
The coffin. Krige, U.
COFFINS
Krige, U. The coffin
Pirandello, L. Reserved coffin
Poe, E. A. Oblong box
Coggins, Frank
The killer
Ford, N. A. and Faggett, H. L. eds. Best short stories by Afro-American writers (1925-1950)
Cogswell, Theodore R.
Minimum sentence
Galaxy science fiction magazine. Second Galaxy reader of science fiction
Specter general
Norton, A. M. ed. Space service
Wall around the world
Merril, J. ed. Beyond the barriers of space and time
Cohan, Alfred E. 1920-
Bridegroom on the scaffold
American vanguard, 1950
Cohen, Octavus Roy, 1891-
Always trust a cop
Queen, E. pseud. ed. Queen's awards; 7th ser.
Florian Slappey—private eye
Best detective stories of the year—1951
Law and the profits
Blaustein, A. P. ed. Fiction goes to court
Once upon a crime
Best detective stories of the year—1952
Toot for a toot
Moskowitz, S. ed. Great railroad stories of the world
Cohen of Trinity. Levy, A.
Cohn, Edgar A. 1927-
The present
American vanguard, 1953

Cohn, Emil, 1881-1948
Given years
Cohn, E. Stories and fantasies from the Jewish past
Honi ha-Maeggel
Cohn, E. Stories and fantasies from the Jewish past
It looks like justice
Cohn, E. Stories and fantasies from the Jewish past
Legend of Rabbi Akiba
Cohn, E. Stories and fantasies from the Jewish past
Rabban Gamaliel
Cohn, E. Stories and fantasies from the Jewish past
Rabbi and emperor
Cohn, E. Stories and fantasies from the Jewish past
Rebellious tree
Cohn, E. Stories and fantasies from the Jewish past
Remains of virtue
Cohn, E. Stories and fantasies from the Jewish past
Simha of Worms
Cohn, E. Stories and fantasies from the Jewish past
Waters of Shiloah
Cohn, E. Stories and fantasies from the Jewish past
A coincidence. Farrell, J. T.
Cold day. Saroyan, W.
Cold front. Stubbs, H. C.
Cold money. Queen, E. pseud.
Cold potato. De Vries, P.
Cold war. Neville, K.
Cold water and cherry pie. O'Rourke, F.
Cold winds of Adesta. Flanagan, T.
Cold winter. Caldwell, E.
Cold world. Williams, W. C.
Coleman comes back. Emery, R. G.
Colette, Sidonie Gabrielle, 1873-1954
The cat
Colette, S. G. Short novels of Colette
Chéri
Colette, S. G. Short novels of Colette
Duo
Colette, S. G. Short novels of Colette
Indulgent husband
Colette, S. G. Short novels of Colette
Last of Chéri
Colette, S. G. Short novels of Colette
Other one
Colette, S. G. Short novels of Colette
Sick child
Gordon, C. and Tate, A. eds. House of fiction
Collaboration. Collier, J.
COLLABORATIONISTS. See Treason
Colladay, Morrison M.
Planetoid of doom
Conklin, G. ed. Big book of science fiction
The collar. Irwin, M. E. F.
The collector. Heard, G.
The collectors. Dewey, G. G. and Dancey, M.

COLLEGE ALUMNI
Calisher, H. One of the chosen
Farrell, J. T. Virginians are coming

COLLEGE AND SCHOOL DRAMA
Fitzgerald, F. S. K. Captured shadow
    See also Amateur theatricals

COLLEGE LIFE

United States

Beck, W. Ask me no more
Boyd, J. Elms and Fair Oaks
Brandon, W. College queen
Caldwell, E. Snacker
Fitzgerald, F. S. K. Woman with a past
Milburn, G. Student in economics
Parker, J. R. Domino method
Porter, W. S. Chair of philanthro-
    mathematics
Rydberg, E. Little genius
Seager, A. All problems are simple
Seager, A. Bang on the head
Shulman, M. The many loves of Dobie
    Gillis; 11 stories
Willingham, C. Wilby spirit

College marriage. Woodward, G. B.

COLLEGE SPORTS. See Sports

College queen. Brandon, W.

College star. Doty, W. L.

Collier, John, 1901-
Ah the university
    Collier, J. Fancies and goodnights
Another American tragedy
    Collier, J. Fancies and goodnights
    Fabricant, N. D. and Werner, H. eds.
      World's best doctor stories
Are you too late or was I too early
    Collier, J. Fancies and goodnights
Back for Christmas
    Collier, J. Fancies and goodnights
Bird of prey
    Collier, J. Fancies and goodnights
    Conklin, G. and Conklin, L. T. eds.
      Supernatural reader
Bottle party
    Carrington, H. ed. Week-end book of
      ghost stories
    Collier, J. Fancies and goodnights
Cancel all I said
    Collier, J. Fancies and goodnights
The chaser
    Collier, J. Fancies and goodnights
Collaboration
    Collier, J. Fancies and goodnights
De mortuis
    Collier, J. Fancies and goodnights
The Devil, George and Rosie
    Collier, J. Fancies and goodnights
Evening primrose
    Collier, J. Fancies and goodnights
Fallen star
    Collier, J. Fancies and goodnights
Frog prince
    Collier, J. Fancies and goodnights
Gavin O'Leary
    Collier, J. Fancies and goodnights
Great possibilities
    Collier, J. Fancies and goodnights
Green thoughts
    Collier, J. Fancies and goodnights

Halfway to Hell
    Collier, J. Fancies and goodnights
Hell hath no fury
    Collier, J. Fancies and goodnights
If youth knew if age could
    Collier, J. Fancies and goodnights
In the cards
    Collier, J. Fancies and goodnights
Incident on a lake
    Collier, J. Fancies and goodnights
Interpretation of a dream
    Collier, J. Fancies and goodnights
    Merril J. ed. Beyond the barriers of
      space and time
Invisible dove dancer of Strathpheen Is-
    land
    Collier, J. Fancies and goodnights
Lady on the grey
    Collier, J. Fancies and goodnights
Little memento
    Collier, J. Fancies and goodnights
Mary
    Collier, J. Fancies and goodnights
Midnight blue
    Collier, J. Fancies and goodnights
Night! Youth! Paris! And the moon
    Collier, J. Fancies and goodnights
Old acquaintance
    Collier, J. Fancies and goodnights
Over insurance
    Collier, J. Fancies and goodnights
Pictures in the fire
    Collier, J. Fancies and goodnights
Possession of Angela Bradshaw
    Collier, J. Fancies and goodnights
Right side
    Collier, J. Fancies and goodnights
Romance lingers, adventure lives
    Collier, J. Fancies and goodnights
Rope enough
    Collier, J. Fancies and goodnights
Season of mists
    Collier, J. Fancies and goodnights
Sleeping Beauty
    Collier, J. Fancies and goodnights
Special delivery
    Collier, J. Fancies and goodnights
Spring fever
    Collier, J. Fancies and goodnights
Squirrels have bright eyes
    Collier, J. Fancies and goodnights
Steel cat
    Collier, J. Fancies and goodnights
Three Bears Cottage
    Collier, J. Fancies and goodnights
Thus I refute Beelzy
    Collier, J. Fancies and goodnights
    Davenport, B. ed. Tales to be told in
      the dark
    Millett, F. B. ed. Reading fiction
Touch of nutmeg makes it
    Collier, J. Fancies and goodnights
Variation on a theme
    Collier, J. Fancies and goodnights
Wet Saturday
    Collier, J. Fancies and goodnights
Witch's money
    Collier, J. Fancies and goodnights
Without benefit of Galsworthy
    Collier, J. Fancies and goodnights
Youth from Vienna
    Collier, J. Fancies and goodnights

Collins, Wilkie, 1824-1889
  'Blow up with the brig!'
    Collins, W. Tales of suspense
    Eaton, H. T. ed. Short stories
  Dead hand
    Collins, W. Tales of suspense
  Dream-woman
    Collins, W. Tales of suspense
  Fauntleroy
    Collins, W. Tales of suspense
  Lady of Glenwith Grange
    Collins, W. Tales of suspense
  Miss Bertha and the Yankee
    Collins, W. Tales of suspense
  Mr Lepel and the housekeeper
    Collins, W. Tales of suspense
  Mr Policeman and the cook
    Collins, W. Tales of suspense
  Stolen letter
    Collins, W. Tales of suspense
  Terribly strange bed
    Blodgett, H. W. ed. Story survey.
      1953 ed.
    Collins, W. Tales of suspense
COLLISIONS, RAILROAD. See Railroads
    —Accidents
Colloquy of Monos and Una. Poe, E. A.
COLOMBIA
  Tablanca, L. Country girl
The colonel. Doty, W. L.
Colonel Julian. Bates, H. E.
Colonel Starbottle for the plaintiff. Harte, B.
Colonel's lady. Maugham, W. S.
Color out of space Lovecraft, H. P.
COLORADO
  Gardiner, D. Not a lick of sense
Colored girls of Passenack—old and new.
    Williams, W. C.
COLORED PEOPLE. See Negroes
Colossus. Wandrei, D.
The colt. Stegner, W. E.
COLUMBUS, CHRISTOPHER, 1446?-1506
  Walsh, M. Mission sermon
Columbus was a dope. Heinlein, R. A.
Combat with the octopus. Hugo, V. M.
    comte
The combination. Van Doren, M.
Come again another day. Newhouse, E.
Come and go mad. Brown, F.
Come back, my love. Walsh, M.
Come fly with me. De La Roche, M.
Come on, Wagon! Henderson, Z.
The comeback. Powell, D.
Comedy cop. Farrell, J. T.
Comedy entombed: 1930. Williams, W. C.
Comedy in rubber. Porter, W. S.
Comes a day. Lamkin, S.
The Comet. Derieux, S. A.
Comfort, Alexander, 1920-
  Martyrdom of the house
    Felheim, M.; Newman, F. B. and Stein-
      hoff, W. R. eds. Modern short stories
Comfort and joy. Glen, M. A.
Comfort and joy. Hill, J. H.

Comin' twenty-one. Buckingham, N.
Coming attraction. Leiber, F.
Coming down the mountain. Stuart, J.
Coming home. Bowen, E.
Coming of Lad. Terhune, A. P.
Coming of the white man
  Pacey, D. ed. Book of Canadian stories
Coming-out of Maggie. Porter, W. S.
Command. Kahn, B. I.
Command performance. Miller, W. M.
COMMANDMENTS, TEN
  Hurston, Z. N. The tablets of the law
COMMENCEMENTS
  Toole, K. Short space
  Van Doren, M. Truth about Sylvanus
Comments of Moung Ka. Munro, H. H.
COMMERCIAL TRAVELERS
  Campbell, W. E. M. Sum in addition
  Harte, B. Dick Boyle's business card
  Munro, H. H. The background
    See also Salesmen and salesmanship
Commings, Joseph
  Bones for Davy Jones
    Mystery Writers of America, inc.
      Crooks' tour
  Death by black magic
    Mystery Writers of America, inc. Four-
      &-twenty bloodhounds
Common confusion. Kafka, F.
Common denominator. MacDonald, J. D.
Common meter. Fisher, R.
Commonplace story. Gordimer, N.
COMMUNION. See Lord's Supper
COMMUNISM
  Shaw, I. Sailor off the Bremen
      Czechoslovak Republic
  Doty, W. L. Action in Prague
          Russia
  Fraerman, R. I. The expedition
  Frank, P. Those wily Americans
  Yakovlev, A. S. The wizard
        United States
  Cheever, J. Vega
  Farrell, J. T. The martyr
  Farrell, J. T. The renegade
  Fiedler, L. A. Fear of innocence
  Greenfield, R. Way of a traitor
  Lowry, R. J. C. Defense in University
    City
  Wallace, R. Secret weapon of Joe Smith
COMMUTERS
  Dahl, R. Galloping Foxley
  Humphrey, W. Last husband
COMPANIONS. See Servants—Companions
COMPETITION
  Ball, M. W. Case of the wooden bowls
Competition. Hull, E. M.
Competition at Slush Creek. Stuart, J.
Competitors. Rosenfeld, J.
Compleat werewolf. White, W. A. P.
Complete life of John Hopkins. Porter, W. S.
Completely automatic. Waldo, E. H.
Compliments of the author. Kuttner, H.

Conquest of life. Binder, E.

Conquest of two worlds. Hamilton, E.

El conquistador. Doyle, T. L.

Conrad, Joseph, 1857-1924
Amy Foster
Schorer, M. ed. The story
The brute
Conrad, J. Tales of land and sea
Il Conde
Conrad, J. Tales of land and sea
The duel
Conrad, J. Tales of land and sea
End of the tether
Conrad, J. Tales of land and sea
Freya of the Seven Isles
Conrad, J. Tales of land and sea
Gaspar Ruiz
Conrad, J. Tales of land and sea
Heart of darkness
Conrad, J. Tales of land and sea
Ludwig, J. B. and Poirier, W. R. eds.
Stories, British and American
Ludwig, R. M. and Perry, M. B. eds.
Nine short novels
Short, R. W. and Sewall, R. B. eds.
Short stories for study. 1950 ed.
Initiation
Andrews, R. C. ed. My favorite stories
of the great outdoors
The lagoon
Millett, F. B. ed. Reading fiction
Nigger of the Narcissus
Conrad, J. Tales of land and sea
Secret sharer
Connolly, C. ed. Great English short
novels
Conrad, J. Tales of land and sea
Davis, R. G. ed. Ten modern masters
Lamb, L. ed. Family book of best loved
short stories
Lynskey, W. C. ed. Reading modern
fiction
McFee, W. ed. Great sea stories of
modern times
Schramm, W. L. ed. Great short stories
Waite, H. O. and Atkinson, B. P. eds.
Literature for our time
West, R. B. and Stallman, R. W. eds.
Art of modern fiction
The shadow-line
Conrad, J. Tales of land and sea
Typhoon
Conrad, J. Tales of land and sea
Youth
Cerf, B. A. and Moriarty, H. C. eds.
Anthology of famous British stories
Conrad, J. Tales of land and sea
Davis, R. G. ed. Ten modern masters

Conrad, Robert E. 1928-
Call of the street
Oberfirst, R. ed. 1952 anthology of best
original short-shorts

CONSCIENCE
Kuttner, H. Private eye
Maugham, W. S. Lord Mountdrago
Nordau, M. S. Share in the hereafter
Poe, E. A. William Wilson
Stevenson, R. L. Markheim
Villiers de l'Isle-Adam, J. M. M. P. A.
comte de. Desire to be a man

Conscience in art. Porter, W. S.

Conscience of the court. Hurston, Z. N.

CONSCIENTIOUS OBJECTORS
Ullman, J. R. Presumed lost

CONSCRIPTION. See Military service,
Compulsory

Consider courage. Van Doren, M.

Considine, Bob. See Considine, Robert Bernard

Considine, Robert Bernard, 1906-
How Babe got his name
Fenner, P. R. comp. Crack of the bat

CONSPIRACIES
Porter, W. S. Ruler of men

The conspirators. Horwitz, J.

Constable of Lone Sioux. Mowery, W. B.

CONSTANTINOPLE. See Turkey—Constantinople

Constiner, Merle
Lady and the tumblers
Argosy (Periodical) Argosy Book of
adventure stories

The consul. Davis, R. H.

The consul. Maugham, W. S.

CONSULS
Davis, R. H. The consul
Maugham, W. S. The consul
Porter, W. S. Cupid's exile number two
Porter, W. S. Lotus and the bottle
Porter, W. S. Phonograph and the graft
Porter, W. S. Remnants of the code
Porter, W. S. Ships
Porter, W. S. Shoes
See also Diplomatic life

CONSUMPTION (DISEASE) See Tuberculosis

Contact, incorporated. Osborne, R.

Contagion. MacLean, K.

The contessina. Bowen, E.

The contest. Chalmers, B.

Continent makers. De Camp, L. S.

Continuation of the reminiscences of John
Watson, M. D. Doyle, Sir A. C.

Contradictory case. Philips, J. P.

Contraption. Simak, C. D.

CONVALESCENT HOMES. See Hospitals, Convalescent

CONVENT LIFE
Lieberman, R. Heaven is so high; 13
stories

CONVENT SCHOOLS
Connolly, M. Big red house on Hope
Street
MacMahon, B. Corn was springing

CONVENTIONS. See Congresses and conventions

Conversation in Prague. Stern, D.

Conversation of Eiros and Charmion. Poe,
E. A.

CONVERSION
Blackburn, E. R. Good win
Bradbury, R. Powerhouse
De La Roche, M. Word for Coffey
Maupassant, G. de. My uncle Sosthenes
Oursler, F. Bargain in brimstone

Conversion of Willie Heaps. Garner, H.

The **convert**. Shaw, I.

CONVERTS, CATHOLIC
O'Donovan, M. Custom of the country
O'Donovan, M. My first Protestant

CONVICT SHIPS. See Prison ships

CONVICTS
Chekhov, A. P. Yegor's story
Faulkner, W. Old man
  See also Convicts, Escaped; Prison-
ers and prisons

CONVICTS, ESCAPED
Arico, V. His great decision
Collins, W. Lady of Glenwith Grange
Ekbergh, I. D. Lady's maid
Hardy, T. Three strangers
Jackson, C. R. The break
Moreau, L. The face
Paul, L. No more trouble for Jedwick
Rader, P. Tabby cat
Russell, J. Fourth man

Coo-Cullen. Ready, W. B.

Coo-Cullen growing up. Ready, W. B.

Cook, Kathryn
Ba-ee
 Furman, A. L. ed. Teen-age horse
  stories

Cook-runner. Household, G.

Cooke, Alistair, 1908-
Christmas Eve
 Lohan, R. and Lohan, M. eds. New
  Christmas treasury
Christmas Eve, one-three
 Cooke, A. Christmas Eve

Cooke, Arthur A.
All alone again
 Cooke, A. A. Beguile
Another worry
 Cooke, A. A. Beguile
Disappointed, but
 Cooke, A. A. Beguile
For the love of a race horse
 Cooke, A. A. Beguile
Four of a kind
 Cooke, A. A. Beguile
Goose and the gander
 Cooke, A. A. Beguile
The Grace Mansion
 Cooke, A. A. Beguile
In exchange for poverty
 Cooke, A. A. Beguile
My own brother
 Cooke, A. A. Beguile
My own son
 Cooke, A. A. Beguile
N.R.A. for a dollar
 Cooke, A. A. Beguile
One missing
 Cooke, A. A. Beguile
The prey
 Cooke, A. A. Beguile
Returning good for evil
 Cooke, A. A. Beguile
Scum of the earth
 Cooke, A. A. Beguile
Three links
 Cooke, A. A. Beguile

Two peas in a pod
 Cooke, A. A. Beguile
A wasted life
 Cooke, A. A. Beguile

Cooke, Charles, 1904-
Nothing can change it
 Fabricant, N. D. and Werner, H. eds.
  World's best doctor stories

COOKERY
Porter, W. S. Third ingredient
Pratt, F. and De Camp, L. S. Green thumb
Rogow, L. That certain flavor
Saphir, M. G. Gastronomy of the Jews
  See also Bakeries and bakers

Cookie. Taylor, P. H.

COOKS. See Servants—Cooks

Cooky: the heroic dog who wasn't brave.
 Little, G. W.

Cool million. Jenkin, P. A.

Coolidge, Olivia E.
Black magician
 Coolidge, O. E. Egyptian adventures
Carpenter's daughter
 Coolidge, O. E. Egyptian adventures
Children of Set
 Coolidge, O. E. Egyptian adventures
Escape from Kosseir
 Coolidge, O. E. Egyptian adventures
Feast of Cats
 Coolidge, O. E. Egyptian adventures
First-born
 Coolidge, O. E. Egyptian adventures
Judgment of the gods
 Coolidge, O. E. Egyptian adventures
Little Pharaoh
 Coolidge, O. E. Egyptian adventures
Luck charm
 Coolidge, O. E. Egyptian adventures
Prefect of Jerusalem
 Coolidge, O. E. Egyptian adventures
The tree
 Coolidge, O. E. Egyptian adventures
Unquiet spirit
 Coolidge, O. E. Egyptian adventures

Coombs, Charles Ira, 1914-
Brake happy
 Coombs, C. I. Teen-age champion sports
  stories
Downhill dilemma
 Coombs, C. I. Teen-age champion sports
  stories
Fielder's choice
 Furman, A. L. ed. Teen-age stories of
  the diamond
Four fathom fury
 Coombs, C. I. Teen-age champion sports
  stories
Freeze out
 Coombs, C. I. Teen-age champion sports
  stories
Hardwood hazard
 Coombs, C. I. Teen-age champion sports
  stories
Headline halfback
 Coombs, C. I. Teen-age champion sports
  stories
Hillbilly halfback
 Coombs, C. I. Teen-age champion sports
  stories

Coombs, Charles I.—*Continued*
  Ice ostrich
    Coombs, C. I. Teen-age champion sports
      stories
  Lucky stick
    Coombs, C. I. Teen-age champion sports
      stories
  Millie's big story
    Furman, A. L. ed. Everygirls career
      stories
  Net nemesis
    Coombs, C. I. Teen-age champion sports
      stories
  Newton man
    Coombs, C. I. Teen-age champion sports
      stories
  Nose for news
    Furman, A. L. ed. Everygirls career
      stories
  Part time hoopster
    Coombs, C. I. Teen-age champion sports
      stories
  River challenge
    Coombs, C. I. Teen-age champion sports
      stories
  Saga of Sleepy Mugoon
    Coombs, C. I. Teen-age champion sports
      stories
  Silent wings
    Coombs, C. I. Teen-age champion sports
      stories
  Strictly big league
    Furman A. L. ed. Teen-age stories of
      the diamond
  Unlucky number
    Coombs, C. I. Teen-age champion sports
      stories
  Varsity vaulter
    Coombs, C. I. Teen-age champion sports
      stories
  Water bug
    Coombs, C. I. Teen-age champion sports
      stories

Co-operate—or else. Van Vogt, A. E.

Cooter James. Schaefer, J. W.

Cop and the anthem. Porter, W. S.

Cop-killer. Stout, R.

Coppard, Alfred Edgar, 1878-
  Fifty pounds
    Heilman, R. B. ed. Modern short stories
  Handsome lady
    Blodgett, H. W. ed. Story survey.
      1953 ed.
  The higgler
    Cerf, B. A. and Moriarty, H. C. eds.
      Anthology of famous British stories
  Piffingcap
    Conklin, G. and Conklin, L. T. eds.
      Supernatural reader

Coppel, Alfred, 1921-
  The dreamer
    Best science-fiction stories: 1953
  The exile
    Sloane, W. M. ed. Stories for tomorrow
  The Peacemaker
    Wollheim D. A. ed. Prize science fiction

Coppock, Charles, 1906-
  Pirate gold
    Fenner, P. R. comp. Pirates, pirates,
      pirates

Cop's gift. Stout, R.

Copy girl. Hillman, G. M.

Coquette. Horwitz, M.

Corazón. Pattullo, G.

Corduroy pants. Caldwell, E.

Corkery, Daniel, 1878-
  The Aherns
    Corkery, D. The wager, and other
      stories
  As benefits forgot
    Corkery, D. The wager, and other
      stories
  The awakening
    Corkery, D. The wager, and other
      stories
  Children
    Corkery, D. The wager, and other
      stories
  Emptied sack
    Corkery, D. The wager, and other
      stories
  Lilac tree
    Corkery, D. The wager, and other
      stories
  On the heights
    Corkery, D. The wager, and other
      stories
  Ploughing of the leaca
    Corkery, D. The wager, and other
      stories
  The return
    Corkery, D. The wager, and other
      stories
  Rock-of-the-mass
    Corkery, D. The wager, and other
      stories
  The stones
    Corkery, D. The wager, and other
      stories
  Storm struck
    Corkery, D. The wager, and other
      stories
  Unfinished symphony
    Corkery, D. The wager, and other
      stories
  Vanity
    Corkery, D. The wager, and other
      stories
  Vision
    Corkery, D. The wager, and other
      stories
  The wager
    Corkery, D. The wager, and other sto-
      ries

CORN
  Giono, J. Corn dies

Corn dies. Giono, J.

Corn was springing. MacMahon, B.

CORNET PLAYERS. See Musicians—
    Cornet players

Cornet players. Saroyan, W.

CORNETISTS. See Musicians—Cornet
    players

Cornier, Vincent
  O time in your flight
    Queen, E. pseud. ed. Queen's awards:
      6th ser.

Cornish mystery. Christie, A. M.

CORNWALL. See England, Provincial and
    rural—Cornwall

Coroner de luxe. McDaniel, R.

Coroner's inquest. Connelly, M. C.

Coroner's inquest. Hendryx, J. B.

Corporal Downey appears on Halfaday. Hendryx, J. B.

Corporal Downey gets a tip. Hendryx, J. B.

Corporal Downey makes an arrest. Hendryx, J. B.

Corporal Downey states his case. Hendryx, J. B.

Corporal Downey visits Halfaday. Hendryx, J. B.

Corporal Hardy. Danielson, R. E.

Corporal Nat. Mowery, W. B.

CORPSES. See The dead

CORPULENCE
Maugham, W. S. Three fat women of Antibes
Stafford, J. The nemesis
Wells, H. G. Truth about Pyecraft

Corpus delectable. Pratt, F. and De Camp, L. S.

Corpus delicti. Post, M. D.

CORRESPONDENCE. See Letters, Stories about

CORRUPTION (IN POLITICS)
Brookhouser, F. A life, going by
Faulkner, W. Monk

CORSICA
Mérimée, P. Mateo Falcone
Russell, B. A. W. R. 3d earl. Corsican ordeal of Miss X
Sansom, W. My little robins

Corsican ordeal of Miss X. Russell, B. A. W. R. 3d earl

CORSICANS
Maugham, W. S. French Joe

Corwin, Cecil. See Pearson, M. jt. auth.

Cosmic jackpot. Smith, G. O.

COSMOGONY, BIBLICAL. See Creation

Cosmopolite in a café. Porter, W. S.

COSSACKS
Porter, W. S. Foreign policy of company 99

Cost of living. Sheckley, R.

Costa Rican counterpoint. Stettner, S.

Costly outing. Maupassant, G. de

COTTAGES, SUMMER. See Summer homes

Cotterell, Geoffrey, 1919-
Delicate warning
This week magazine. This week's short-short stories

COTTON
Kidd, H. L. Low road go down

Cottrell, Dorothy (Wilkinson) 1902-
Pit in the jungle
Saturday evening post (Periodical) Saturday evening post stories, 1951
Sharks were hungry
Argosy (Periodical) Argosy Book of adventure stories

Couch, Sir Arthur Thomas Quiller. See Quiller-Couch, Sir Arthur Thomas

Couching at the door. Broster, D. K.

COUGARS. See Pumas

Counsel assigned. Andrews, M. R. S.

Counsel for Œdipus. O'Donovan, M.

Counselman, Mary Elizabeth
Tree's wife
Conklin, G. and Conklin, L. T. eds. Supernatural reader

COUNSELS. See Law and lawyers

Count and the wedding guest. Porter, W. S.

Count Magnus. James, M. R.

Counter charm. Phillips, P.

Counter-transference. Temple, W. F.

COUNTERFEITERS
Agnon, S. J. Sabbathai
Porter, W. S. One dollar's worth

Counterparts. Joyce, J.

Country doctor. Kafka, F.

Country doctor. Marquis, D.

Country doctor. Samachson, J.

Country excursion. Maupassant, G. de

Country full of Swedes. Caldwell, E.

Country gentleman. Irwin, M. E. F.

Country girl. Tablanca, L.

COUNTRY LIFE

New England
Cheever, J. Summer farmer

Poland
Bergelson, D. In a backwoods town
Singer, I. J. Sand

United States
Baker, R. S. Day of pleasant bread
Steele, W. D. Black road

Country love story. Stafford, J.

Country of elusion. Porter, W. S.

Country of the blind. Wells, H. G.

Country rain. Williams, W. C.

COUNTY KERRY. See Ireland—County Kerry

Couple next door. Millar, M.

Couple of old-timers. Newhouse, E.

Coupling, J. J. pseud.
Mr Kincaid's pasts
Merril, J. ed. Beyond the barriers of space and time
Period piece
Bleiler, E. F. and Dikty, T. E. eds. Science fiction omnibus: The best science fiction stories, 1949, 1950

COURAGE
Faulkner, W. Turnabout
Humphrey, W. The shell
Kirtland, A. Trial by fire
Munro, H. H. Easter egg
Porter, W. S. Afternoon miracle
See also Cowardice; Heroes

Courage. Carrington, H. ed.

Courage. Irwin, M. E. F.

Courage. Swinton, A.

Courage and the power. Van Doren, M.

Cournos, John, 1881-
The samovar
Leftwich, J. ed. Yisröel. 1952 ed.
Course of true love. Kober, A.
COURT MARTIAL. See Courts martial and courts of inquiry
COURT-ROOM SCENES. See Trials
Courtesy. Simak, C. D.
Courtesy of the road. Morriss, M.
The courthouse. Faulkner, W.
Courtier, Sidney Hobson
Run for your life
Argosy (Periodical) Argosy Book of adventure stories
Courtin' on Cutshin. Fox, J.
Courting of Miss Darlie Blanche. Knox, J.
Courting of Sister Wisby. Jewett, S. O.
Courting of Susie Brown. Caldwell, E.
Courting of T'nowhead's Bell. Barrie, Sir J. M. bart.

COURTS AND COURTIERS

England

Cabell, J. B. Porcelain cups

France

Bergengruen, W. Trivulzio and the King

Italy

Paget, V. Amour dure
Paget, V. Prince Alberic and the Snake Lady

Russia

Tynîanov, I. N. Second Lieutenant Likewise

COURTS MARTIAL AND COURTS OF INQUIRY
Hale, E. E. Man without a country
Kipling, R. 'Love-o'-women'
Melville, H. Billy Budd, foretopman
Voorhees, M. B. Robe and the sword

COURTSHIP
Barrie, Sir J. M. bart. Courting of T'nowhead's Bell
Caldwell, E. Autumn courtship
Collins, W. Miss Bertha and the Yankee
Ekbergh, I. D. Courtship of Lydia
Faulkner, W. A courtship
Fox, J. Courtin' on Cutshin
Irwin, M. E. F. Mistletoe
Irwin, M. E. F. Where beauty lies
Miller, C. Gentle season
O'Donovan, M. Lady of the sagas
Upson, W. H. Quiet wedding
A courtship. Faulkner, W.
Courtship deferred. Kober, A.
Courtship of Lydia. Ekbergh, I. D.
Cousin Phillis. Gaskell, E. C. S.
Cousin Teresa. Munro, H. H.
Cousins, Margaret, 1905-
Baby sitter for Christmas
Cousins, M. Christmas gift
Fifty-dollar bottle
Cousins, M. Christmas gift
Homemade miracle
Cousins, M. Christmas gift
Inconstant star
Cousins, M. Christmas gift

Poor black sheep
Cousins, M. Christmas gift
Santa Claus and the Tenth Avenue kid
Cousins, M. Christmas gift
She didn't like people
Furman, A. L. ed. Teen-age dog stories
Small world
Cousins, M. Christmas gift
Uncle Edgar and the reluctant saint
Peery, W. W. ed. 21 Texas short stories
White kid gloves
Cousins, M. Christmas gift
Lohan, R. and Lohan, M. eds. New Christmas treasury

COUSINS
Davies, R. Pleasures of the table
Lawrence, D. H. Lovely lady
Livesay, D. Glass house
Saroyan, W. Summer of the beautiful white horse
Schorr, Z. Her rich American cousin
Wharton, E. N. J. The old maid

Coventry. Heinlein, R. A.

Coward, Noël Pierce, 1899-
Ashes of roses
Coward, N. P. Star quality
Mr and Mrs Edgehill
Coward, N. P. Star quality
Richer dust
Coward, N. P. Star quality
Star quality
Coward, N. P. Star quality
Stop me if you've heard it
Coward, N. P. Star quality
This time to-morrow
Coward, N. P. Star quality

COWARDICE
Crane, S. Red badge of courage
Hemingway, E. Short happy life of Francis Macomber
Jackson, C. R. Boy who ran away
Maugham, W. S. Door of opportunity
Maugham, W. S. Yellow streak

COWBOYS
Bonham, F. One ride too many
Burtis, T. Rope and the bulldog
Erskine, L. Y. Horses and men
Fenner, P. R. comp. Cowboys, cowboys, cowboys; 17 stories
Fleming, J. S. Ride 'im Chick Norris!
James, W. Will James' Book of cowboy stories; 15 stories
Pattullo, G. Corazón
Payne, S. With an O X herd
Porter, W. S. Art and the bronco
Porter, W. S. Last of the troubadours
Porter, W. S. The Marquis and Miss Sally
Souto Alabarce, A. Coyote 13
Wister, O. Journey in search of Christmas
Wood, K. Workaday cowboy
See also Ranch life; The West; Western stories

Cowpony's prize. Davis, L. R.

COWRIE ISLAND
Coward, N. P. Mr and Mrs Edgehill

COWS. See Cattle

Cox, Anthony Berkeley, 1893-
  Avenging chance
    Bond, R. T. ed. Handbook for poison-
    ers
Cox, Arthur Jean, 1929-
  The blight
    Derleth, A. W. ed. Time to come
Cox, Irving
  Hole in the sky
    Derleth, A. W. ed. Time to come
  Like gods they came
    Sloane, W. M. ed. Space, space, space
Cox, William R.
  Pinch hitter
    Argosy (Periodical) Argosy Book of
    sports stories
Coxe, George Harmon, 1901-
  Death certificate
    Mystery Writers of America, inc. Four-
    &-twenty bloodhounds
  Doctor takes a case
    Mystery Writers of America, inc. 20
    great tales of murder
Coyote 13. Souto Alabarce, A.
COYOTES
  Clark, W. Van T. The pretender
  Souto Alabarce, A. Coyote 13
Cozzens, James Gould, 1903-
  Clerical error
    Queen, E. pseud. ed. Literature of crime
  Men running
    Grayson, C. ed. Fourth round
    Jones, K. M. ed. New Confederate short
    stories
  Total stranger
    First-prize stories, 1919-1954
The crab. Beaumont, G.
CRAB FISHERIES. See Shell-fish fisheries
Crabfroth. Sansom, W.
Crane, Robert, pseud. See Glemser, Bernard
Crane, Stephen, 1871-1900
  Blue Hotel
    Crane, S. Stephen Crane: an omnibus
    Foerster, N. ed. American poetry and
    prose. 1952 ed.
    Lynskey, W. C. ed. Reading modern
    fiction
  Bride comes to Yellow Sky
    Crane, S. Stephen Crane: an omnibus
    Schorer, M. ed. The story
  Episode of war
    Crane, S. Stephen Crane: an omnibus
  Experiment in misery
    Crane, S. Stephen Crane: an omnibus
  The fight
    Davis, C. B. ed. Eyes of boyhood
  George's mother
    Crane, S. Stephen Crane: an omnibus
  Gray sleeve
    Lamb, L. ed. Family book of best loved
    short stories
  His new mittens
    Crane, S. Stephen Crane: an omnibus
  The knife
    Crane, S. Stephen Crane: an omnibus
  Maggie: a girl of the streets
    Crane, S. Stephen Crane: an omnibus
  Men in the storm
    Crane, S. Stephen Crane: an omnibus

  Mystery of heroism
    Crane, S. Stephen Crane: an omnibus
  Open boat
    Barrows, H. ed. 15 stories
    Burrell, J. A. and Cerf, B. A. eds. An-
    thology of famous American stories
    Crane, S. Stephen Crane: an omnibus
    Day, A. G. ed. Greatest American short
    stories
    Gordon, C. and Tate, A. eds. House of
    fiction
    Schramm, W. L. ed. Great short stories
    West, R. B. and Stallman, R. W. eds.
    Art of modern fiction
  Red badge of courage
    Ludwig, R. M. and Perry, M. B. eds.
    Nine short novels
  Upturned face
    Crane, S. Stephen Crane: an omnibus
    Short, R. W. and Sewall, R. B. eds.
    Short stories for study. 1950 ed.
CRATES, OF THEBES
  Schwob, M. Crates
Crawford, Constance
  The boats
    Stanford short stories, 1952
Crawford, Elizabeth, and Dalmas, Herbert
  Rush-hour romance
    This week magazine. This week's short-
    short stories
Crawford, Francis Marion, 1854-1909
  For the blood is the life
    Conklin, G. and Conklin, L. T. eds.
    Supernatural reader
  Screaming skull
    Davenport, B. ed. Ghostly tales to be
    told
Crawford's consistency. James, H.
Crazy hunter. Boyle, K.
Crazy Hymie and the nickel. Bishop, L.
Crazy Joey. Clifton, M. and Apostolides, A.
Crazy over horse mackerel. Wylie, P.
Crazy Sunday. Fitzgerald, F. S. K.
CREATION
  Del Rey, L. Into thy hands
Creation unforgivable. Keller, D. H.
Creative impulse. Maugham, W. S.
The creatures. De La Mare, W. J.
Credle, Ellis, 1902-
  Mary Lou's Christmas
    Story parade (Periodical) Adventure
    stories
  Pudding that broke up the preaching
    Fenner, P. R. comp. Fun! Fun! Fun!
  Tall tale from the high hills
    Fenner, P. R. comp. Fun! Fun! Fun!
CREMATION
  Fairbanks, D. Ashes
Crémieux, Benjamin, 1888-
  The traveller
    Leftwich, J. ed. Yisröel. 1952 ed.
Cremona violin. Hoffmann, E. T. A.
Crevasse. Faulkner, W.
Cricket boy. P'u Sung-ling
Cricket field. Buckingham, N.
Cricket on the hearth. Dickens, C.

CRICKETS (INSECTS)
P'u Sung-ling. Cricket boy
CRIME AND CRIMINALS
Aiken, C. P. Smith and Jones
Buckingham, N. Death stalked the spring-stand!
Chekhov, A. P. Yegor's story
Connolly, M. Big red house on Hope Street
Frazee, S. Graveyard shift
Maugham, W. S. Episode
Milton, M. E. Favor granted
Moore, G. M. Two for a ride
Peacock, W. S. Night in the warehouse
Porter, W. S. Clarion call
Pratt, F. and De Camp, L. S. Ancestral amethyst
Queen, E. pseud. ed. Literature of crime; 26 stories
Rath, I. E. Longest day I live
Sheehan, D. V. Get-away boy
Sinclair, J. L. Killer and the pit
Taubes, F. Trouble on 98th Street
Zoshchenko, M. M. Sleuth-hound
    See also Convicts; Murder stories; Mystery and detective stories; and names of particular crimes, e.g. Embezzlement; Theft; Treason; etc.
Crime of the Communist. Chesterton, G. K.
CRIMEAN WAR, 1853-1856
Rappoport, S. Moses Montefiore
The criminal. Boyle, K.
The criminal. Gibran, K.
CRIMINALS. See Crime and criminals
Crip, come home! Thomas, R.
CRIPPLES
Blackburn, E. R. Walk for me
Butler, M. Mr Sweeney
Campbell, W. E. M. I broke my back on a rosebud
Jones, J. Two legs for the two of us
Lagerkvist, P. F. The basement
Lowry, R. Little baseball world
Schulberg, B. W. Road to recovery
Upshaw, N. Love smelled of vanilla
Crisis. Grendon, E.
Crisis in Utopia. Knight, N. L.
Crisis, 1999. Brown, F.
Crispin's way. Downey, H.
Critchell, Laurence Sanford, 1918-
Loyalty check
    Best Army short stories, 1950
Critical factor. Stubbs, H. C.
The "critter." Terhune, A. P.
The critters. Long, F. B.
Crockett, Samuel Rutherford, 1860-1914
Reverend John Smith prepares his sermon
    Neider, C. ed. Men of the high calling
Stickit minister
    Neider, C. ed. Men of the high calling
Crocodile tears. Gilpatric, G.
CROCODILES
Annixter, P. pseud. Orchids and crocodiles
Kipling, R. Elephant's child
    See also Alligators
CRO-MAGNON. See Man, Prehistoric

CROMWELL, ELIZABETH (BOUR-CHIER) fl. 17th century
Irwin, M. E. F. Mrs Oliver Cromwell
Cronin, Archibald Joseph, 1896-
Birth
    Burnett, W. ed. World's best
A candle in Vienna
    Brentano, F. ed. The word lives on
Crooked arm. Meader, S. W.
Crooked man. Doyle, Sir A. C.
CROQUET
Williams, T. Three players of a summer game
Crosbie starts his honeymoon. Trollope, A.
Cross, John A.
Hunch that clicked
    Oberfirst, R. ed. 1952 anthology of best original short-shorts
Railroad tangle
    Oberfirst, R. ed. 1954 anthology of best original short-shorts
Cross, Joseph, pseud. See Nemerov, Howard, and Johnson, William R.
Cross, Mary Ann (Evans) See Eliot, George, pseud.
Cross buns for Friday. Johnson, R.
Cross currents. Munro, H. H.
CROSS-EXAMINATION. See Trials
The cross-up. Merson, B.
Crossen, Kendell Foster, 1910-
Ambassadors from Venus
    Derleth, A. W. ed. Beachheads in space
Assignment to Aldebaran
    Year's best science fiction novels, 1954
Restricted clientele
    Crossen, K. F. ed. Adventures in tomorrow
Things of distinction
    Crossen, K. F. ed. Future tense
Too late for murder
    Mystery Writers of America, inc. Four-&-twenty bloodhounds
CROW INDIANS
Gulick, G. C. Rendezvous romance
Johnson, D. M. Man called Horse
Johnson, D. M. The unbeliever
Crowbar Captain. Patrick, J.
Crowd pleaser. Schulberg, B. W.
Crowell, Chester Theodore, 1888-1941
The stoic
    Peery, W. W. ed. 21 Texas short stories
Crown-fire. Caldwell, E.
Crown princess. Brophy, B.
Crowning glory. Newby, P. H.
Crowning glory. Paterson, N.
CROWS
Seton, E. T. Silverspot
Crucible of power. Williamson, J.
Crucifixus Etiam. Miller, W. M.
"Cruel and barbarous treatment." McCarthy, M. T.
CRUELTY
Grimson, M. S. At the crossroads
Sergîeev-Tsenskiĭ, S. N. Man you couldn't kill
Shneur, Z. The girl

CRUELTY TO ANIMALS. See Animals—
Treatment

Cruise. Waugh, E.

Cruises in the sun. Curtis, K.

Crump, Irving, 1887-
Dead men on parade
Fenner, P. R. comp. Ghosts, ghosts,
ghosts
Little guy
Boys' life (Periodical) Boys' life Adven-
ture stories
Pirate island
Furman, A. L. ed. Teen-age sea stories
Two-bits of traffic C
Furman, A. L. ed. Teen-age horse
stories

Crunch catches one. Wylie, P.

Crushed orchid. Hanlon, B.

Cry deep, cry still. Haycox, E.

Cry of the graves. Gibran, K.

Cry silence. Brown F.

CRYPTOGRAPHY
Poe, E. A. Gold bug
See also Ciphers and telegraph codes

Crystal egg. Wells, H. G.

CRYSTAL GAZING. See Clairvoyance

Crystal stream. Rudnicki, A.

Cub-hunting with Mr Neville's hounds. Surtees, R. S.

Cubic city. Tucker, L.

Cue for Connie. Woody, R. L. J.

Cuevas, Ernesto, 1923-
Lock the doors, lock the windows
Weaver, R. and James, H. eds. Cana-
dian short stories

Culture. Household, G.

Culture. Shelton, J.

Culver, Monty, 1929-
Black water blues
Prize stories of 1951

CUMBERLAND MOUNTAINS. See Kentucky—Cumberland Mountains

Cummings, Ray
Girl in the golden atom
Margulies, L. and Friend, O. J. eds.
Giant anthology of science fiction
Gravity professor
Wollheim, D. A. comp. Every boy's
book of science-fiction

Cunningham, Eugene, 1896-
Bar-Nothing's happy birthday
Peery, W. W. ed. 21 Texas short stories

Cunningham, John M.
Iron rose
Western Writers of America. Holsters
and heroes
Tin star
Western Writers of America. Bad men
and good

Cunninghame Graham, Robert Bontine. See
Graham, Robert Bontine Cunninghame

Cup of tea. Horwitz, J.

Cup of tea. Mansfield, K.

Cupboard of the yesterdays. Munro, H. H.

Cupid à la carte. Porter, W. S.

Cupid wags his tail. Faggett, H. L.

Cupid's exile number two. Porter, W. S.

Curates. See Clergy

Curate's friend. Forster, E. M.

Curbstone philosophy. Farrell, J. T.

The cure. Cheever, J.

The cure. Kuttner, H.

Cure for lumbago. Van Loan, C.

Curious case of Benjamin Button. Fitzgerald,
F. S. K.

Curle, Richard, 1883-
Suppressed edition
Derleth, A. W. ed. Night's yawning
peal

Curling, Jonathan
Restless rest-house
Asquith, Lady C. M. E. C. ed. Book of
modern ghosts

Curly-beard. Tu Kwang-t'ing

Curly maple. Knox, J.

Curphey's follower. Kneale, N.

Curry, Peggy (Simpson)
Osage Girl
Creamer, J. B. comp. Twenty-two stor-
ies about horses and men

Curse of the golden cross. Chesterton, G. K.

Curse of the horse race. Waugh, E.

CURSES
Harvey, W. F. Arm of Mrs Egan
Peretz, I. L. Devotion without end

CURSES, FAMILY
Closed cabinet

Curtain of green. Welty, E.

Curtis, Betsy, 1917-
Peculiar people
Best science fiction stories: 1952

Curtis, Kent
The cameleers
Curtis, K. Cruises in the sun
Cruises in the sun
Curtis, K. Cruises in the sun
Drumbeaters Island
Curtis, K. Cruises in the sun

Curtis, Maxine
Navy blue and bold
Seventeen (Periodical) The Seventeen
reader
Sleek sixteen
Seventeen (Periodical) Nineteen from
Seventeen
Stowe, A. comp. It's a date

Curtiss, Philip Everett, 1885-
Eight-dollar pup
Cavanna, B. ed. Pick of the litter

Curwood, James Oliver, 1878-1927
Kazan
Bloch, M. ed. Favorite dog stories

Cush gets a toothache. Hendryx, J. B.

Cush takes inventory. Hendryx, J. B.

Custom of the country. Haycox, E.

Custom of the country. O'Donovan, M.

Cut yourself a slice of show. Kaufman, W.

Cuter Malone turns down a deal. Hendryx,
J. B.

Cuthbert, Chester D.
  Sublime vigil
    Moskowitz, S. comp. Editor's choice in
    science fiction
Cutler, J. Linwood
  Fire-boy of Dunsoon
    Story parade (Periodical) Adventure
    stories
CYBERNETICS. See Automata
Cycle of Manhattan. Winslow, T. S.
Cyclists' raid. Rooney, F.
Cyclops, Heard, G.
Cynthia who was afraid not to pet. Strain,
  F. B.
Cyprian bees. Wilson, R. M.
Czech dog. Hardy, W. G.
CZECHOSLOVAKIANS IN TAHITI
  Hall, J. N. Haunted island
CZECHOSLOVAKIANS IN THE
  UNITED STATES
  Cather, W. S. Neighbour Rosicky

D

DP! Kuttner, H.
Dachs, David, 1922-
  Speaking of characters
    Dachs, D. ed. Treasury of sports humor
Daffodils. Bowen, E.
Dagger with wings. Chesterton, G. K.
Daggle-Tail. Lavin, M.
Daguio, Amador T. 1912-
  Wedding dance
    Stanford short stories, 1953
Dahl, Roald, 1916-
  Claud's dog
    Dahl, R. Someone like you
  Death of an old man
    Jensen, P. ed. Fireside book of flying
    stories
  Dip in the pool
    Dahl, R. Someone like you
  Galloping Foxley
    Dahl, R. Someone like you
  Great automatic grammatisator
    Dahl, R. Someone like you
  Lamb to the slaughter
    Dahl, R. Someone like you
  Man from the south
    Dahl, R. Someone like you
  My lady love, my dove
    Dahl, R. Someone like you
  Neck
    Dahl, R. Someone like you
  Nunc dimittis
    Dahl, R. Someone like you
  Poison
    Dahl, R. Someone like you
  Skin
    Dahl, R. Someone like you
  The soldier
    Dahl, R. Someone like you
  Someone like you
    Jensen, P. ed. Fireside book of flying
    stories

Sound machine
    Dahl, R. Someone like you
Taste
    Dahl, R. Someone like you
    Grayson, C. ed. Fourth round
The wish
    Dahl, R. Someone like you
DAHLIAS
  Clifton, M. The conqueror
Dailey, Jim
  The rookie
    Herzberg, M. J. comp. Treasure chest
    of sport stories
DAIRYING
  Brubaker, H. Milk pitcher
    See also Farm life
Daisies. Brown, F.
Daisy Miller. James, H.
DAKOTA INDIANS
  Johnson, D. M. Flame on the frontier
  Johnson, D. M. Journey to the fort
  Meigs, C. L. Buffalo dance
Dalmas, Herbert. See Crawford, E. jt. auth.
Daly, Maureen, 1921-
  Sixteen
    Lass, A. H. and Horowitz, A. eds.
    Stories for youth
    Thinker's digest (Periodical) Spoiled
    priest, and other stories
Dames and ethics. Kaufman, W.
Damned thing. Bierce, A.
Damsel with a dulcimer. Ferguson, M.
Dance for the devil. McCourt, E. A.
DANCE HALLS
  Benson, T. Harry was good to the girls
DANCE MARATHONS
  McCoy, H. They shoot horses, don't they?
Dance of a new world. MacDonald, J. D.
Dance of the dead. Matheson, R.
DANCE ORCHESTRA. See Orchestra
Dance with the devil. Emmons, B.
DANCES. See Dancing
DANCES (PARTIES) See Parties
Dancey, Max, 1916-. See Dewey, G. G. jt.
  auth.
DANCING
  Ekbergh, I. D. Pink Ballerina
  Fitzgerald, F. S. K. Woman with a past
  Galsworthy, J. Salta pro nobis
  Lansing, E. C. H. There's something
    about you
  Maupassant, G. de. Minuet
  Porter, W. S. Unprofitable servant
  Ullman, J. R. White night
  Willingham, C. Career of Augurt Nim-
    rodtk
    See also Ballet
Dancing bear. Barnard, L. G.
Dandy: the funny-looking dog. Little, G. W.
Danger by candlelight. Macfarlan, A. A.
Danger wears two faces. Kaplan, A. H.
Dangerous ice. Young, S.
Dangerous people. Brown, F.
Daniel, Hawthorne, 1890-
  Shores of Tripoli
    Furman, A. L. ed. Teen-age sea stories

Danielson, Richard Ely, 1885-
  Corporal Hardy
    Cooper, A. C. ed. Modern short stories
  The quid pro quo
    Bachelor, J. M.; Henry, R. L. and
    Salisbury, R. eds. Current thinking
    and writing; 2d ser.
Dann, Lois, 1922-
  One summer afternoon
    American vanguard, 1950
Dannay, Frederic, 1905- and Lee, Manfred
  Bennington, 1905- See Queen, Ellery,
  pseud.
Danny Hagan's blind spot. Gilmour, W.
Danse Macabre. Strong, L. A. G.
Danse pseudomacabre. Williams, W. C.
Darcy in the Land of Youth. O'Donovan, M.
The dare. Schulberg, B. W.
Daring young man on the flying trapeze.
  Saroyan, W.
Dark Blue. Bottome, P.
Dark city. Aiken, C. P.
Dark horses. Harvey, W. F.
Dark interlude. McClure, J.
Dark interlude. Reynolds, M. and Brown,
  F.
Dark knight. Doty, W. L.
Dark night of Ramón Yendía. Novás Calvo,
  L.
Dark nuptial. Locke, R. D.
Dark red chrysanthemum. Thorne, A.
Dark walk. Taylor, P. H.
Darkness in Paris. Remarque, E. M.
Darling, Frederick
  The drag
    Story (Periodical) Story; no. 3
Darwick, Richard, 1928-
  Mother and son
    American vanguard, 1950
DARWINISM. See Evolution
Dasent, Sir George Webbe, 1817-1896
  Boots, who made the Princess say, "That's
  a story"
    Fenner, P. R. comp. Fools and funny
    stories
Date to remember. Temple, W. F.
Date with Dora. McLaren, F. C.
Date with Janie. Roberts, R. M.
Date with Ricky. Emery, A.
Daudet, Alphonse, 1840-1897
  Death of the Dauphin
    Schramm, W. L. ed. Great short stories
  Father Gaucher's elixir
    O'Faoláin, S. The short story
  Last class
    Eaton, H. T. ed. Short stories
  M. Seguin's goat
    Blodgett, H. W. ed. Story survey.
    1953 ed.
Daughter. Caldwell, E.
DAUGHTERS. See Fathers and daughters;
  Mothers and daughters; Parent and
  child
Daughters of earth. Merril, J.
Daughters of the late colonel. Mansfield, K.

Dauphin, Death of the. Daudet, A.
DAVID, KING OF ISRAEL
  Schmitt, G. David and Bathsheba
David and Bathsheba. Schmitt, G.
David Swan. Hawthorne, N.
Davidson, Sue
  City of the angels
    Stanford short stories, 1951
  The rivals
    Stanford short stories, 1951
Davies, Rhys, 1903-
  Abraham's glory
    Davies, R. Boy with a trumpet, and
    other selected short stories
  Alice's pint
    Davies, R. Boy with a trumpet, and
    other selected short stories
  Arfon
    Davies, R. Boy with a trumpet, and
    other selected short stories
  Benefit concert
    Davies, R. Boy with a trumpet, and
    other selected short stories
  Boy with a trumpet
    Davies, R. Boy with a trumpet, and
    other selected short stories
  Caleb's ark
    Davies, R. Boy with a trumpet, and
    other selected short stories
  Conflict in Morfa
    Davies, R. Boy with a trumpet, and
    other selected short stories
  Dilemma of Catherine Fuchsias
    Davies, R. Boy with a trumpet, and
    other selected short stories
  The farm
    Davies, R. Boy with a trumpet, and
    other selected short stories
  Fashion plate
    Davies, R. Boy with a trumpet, and
    other selected short stories
  Foolish one
    Davies, R. Boy with a trumpet, and
    other selected short stories
  Gents only
    Davies, R. Boy with a trumpet, and
    other selected short stories
  Human condition
    Davies, R. Boy with a trumpet, and
    other selected short stories
  Mourning for Ianto
    Davies, R. Boy with a trumpet, and
    other selected short stories
  Nightgown
    Davies, R. Boy with a trumpet, and
    other selected short stories
  Pleasures of the table
    Davies, R. Boy with a trumpet, and
    other selected short stories
  Resurrection
    Davies, R. Boy with a trumpet, and
    other selected short stories
  River, flow gently
    Davies, R. Boy with a trumpet, and
    other selected short stories
  The sisters
    Davies, R. Boy with a trumpet, and
    other selected short stories
  Two friends
    Davies, R. Boy with a trumpet, and
    other selected short stories

Davies, Valentine, 1905-
  Great King Kelly
    Graber, R. S. ed. Baseball reader
Davies, William Morris, 1814?-1890
  Battle with a whale
    Andrews, R. C. ed. My favorite stories
    of the great outdoors
Davis, Alice Lee
  First disciple
    Elmquist, R. M. ed.   Fifty years to
    Christmas
  The Klondiker
    Oberfirst, R. ed. 1954 anthology of best
    original short-shorts
Davis, Chan
  Letter to Ellen
    Conklin, G. ed. Science-fiction thinking
    machines
Davis, Dorothy Salisbury
  Backward, turn backward
    Queen, E. pseud. ed. Ellery Queen's
    awards: 9th ser.
  Born killer
    Queen, E. pseud. ed. The Queen's
    awards: 8th ser.
  Spring fever
    Queen, E. pseud. ed. Queen's awards:
    7th ser.
Davis, Franklin Milton, 1918-
  Five Alls
    Best Army short stories, 1950
Davis, Gene
  Amateur night in Harlem
    Ford, N. A. and Faggett, H. L. eds.
    Best short stories by Afro-American
    writers (1925-1950)
Davis, Harold Lenoir, 1896-
  Back to the land—Oregon, 1907
    Davis, H. L. Team bells woke me, and
    other stories
  Beach squatter
    Davis, H. L. Team bells woke me, and
    other stories
  Extra gang
    Davis, H. L. Team bells woke me, and
    other stories
  Flying switch
    Davis, H. L. Team bells woke me, and
    other stories
  Homestead orchard
    Davis, H. L. Team bells woke me, and
    other stories
  Old man Isbell's wife
    Davis, H. L. Team bells woke me, and
    other stories
  Open winter
    Davis, H. L. Team bells woke me, and
    other stories
  Shiloh's water's
    Davis, H. L. Team bells woke me, and
    other stories
  Stubborn spearmen
    Davis, H. L. Team bells woke me, and
    other stories
  Team bells woke me
    Davis, H. L. Team bells woke me, and
    other stories
  Town in eastern Oregon
    Davis, H. L. Team bells woke me, and
    other stories

Vanishing wolf
  Davis, H. L. Team bells woke me, and
  other stories
World of little doves
  Davis, H. L. Team bells woke me, and
  other stories
Davis, Lavinia (Riker) 1909-
  Cowpony's prize
    Fenner, P. R. comp. Cowboys, cowboys,
    cowboys
  Feeling for human interest
    Furman, A. L. ed. Everygirls career
    stories
Davis, Richard Harding, 1864-1916
  Bar sinister
    Burrell, J. A. and Cerf, B. A. eds. An-
    thology of famous American stories
    Scribner treasury
  The consul
    Scribner treasury
  The deserter
    Scribner treasury
  In the fog
    Lamb, L. ed. Family book of best loved
    short stories
  Wasted day
    Blaustein, A. P. ed. Fiction goes to
    court
Davis, Robert, 1881-1949
  Ne-nu-ka
    Fenner, P. R. comp. Dogs, dogs, dogs
Davis, Robert Hobart, 1869-1942
  Tree toad
    Davis, C. B. ed. Eyes of boyhood
Davis, Samuel Post, 1850-1918
  Andy Munroe's funeral
    Emrich, D. ed. Comstock bonanza
  Carson poker incident
    Emrich, D. ed. Comstock bonanza
  Christmas carol
    Emrich, D. ed. Comstock bonanza
  Mystery of the Savage sump
    Emrich, D. ed. Comstock bonanza
  Sage-brush chief
    Emrich, D. ed. Comstock bonanza
  Stock chapter
    Emrich, D. ed. Comstock bonanza
Dawkins, Mary Lucile, 1927-
  Blossom on the yew
    Stanford short stories, 1953
Dawn. Charteris, L.
Dawn of another day. Williams, W. C.
Dawn of remembered spring. Stuart, J.
Daxbr baxbr. Smith, E. E.
Day, Clarence Shepard, 1874-1935
  Noblest instrument
    Lass, A. H. and Horowitz, A. eds.
    Stories for youth
Day after tomorrow. Powell, D.
Day at the zoo. Farrell, J. T.
Day before. Newhouse, E.
Day he got fired. Lowry, R. J. C.
Day in a woman's life. Kaye-Smith, S.
Day in Hit-im-and Hold-im-shire. Surtees,
  R. S.
Day in New York. Montross, L. S.
Day in the sun. Modell, J.
Day in town. Haycox, E.

Death of Iván Ilých. Tolstoĭ, L. N. Graf
Death of Judas. Komroff, M.
Death of Pierce. Fay, S.
Death of Red Peril. Edmonds, W. D.
Death of Riley. Brown, F.
Death of the Dauphin. Daudet, A.
Death of the glen. Stewart, G. R.
Death of the lion. James, H.
Death of the moon. Phillips, A. M.
Death of the Zulu. Krige, U.
Death of Uncle Andy. Knox, J.
Death sentence. Asimov, I.
Death stalked the spring-stand! Bucking-
    ham, N.
Death under the hawthornes. Bennett, P.

DEATHBED SCENES
    Bennett, A. Mary with the high hand
    Daudet, A. Death of the Dauphin
    Eliot, G. pseud. Lifted veil
    Lytle, A. N. Jericho, Jericho, Jericho
    Poe, E. A. Facts in the case of M.
        Valdemar
    Poe, E. A. Ligeia
    Porter, W. S. Lord Oakhurst's curse
    Turgenev, I. S. District doctor
    Watson, J. Story of Dr MacLure
    Whitmore, S. Bontemps
    Zangwill, I. Sabbath breaker
Death's eye view. MacDonald, J. D.
The debt. Carman, K.
Debt of honor. Household, G.

DEBTS
    Shaw, I. Triumph of justice
    Thomson, E. W. Privilege of the limits

DECALOGUE. See Commandments, Ten

De Camp, Lyon Sprague, 1907-
    Animal-cracker plot
        De Camp, L. S. Continent makers, and
            other tales of the Viagens
    Blue giraffe
        Pratt, F. ed. World of wonder
    Continent makers
        De Camp, L. S. Continent makers, and
            other tales of the Viagens
    Employment
        Bleiler, E. F. and Dikty, T. E. eds.
            Imagination unlimited
    The exalted
        Astounding science fiction (Periodical)
            Astounding science fiction anthology
    Finished
        De Camp, L. S. Continent makers, and
            other tales of the Viagens
    Galton whistle
        De Camp, L. S. Continent makers, and
            other tales of the Viagens
    Git along
        De Camp, L. S. Continent makers, and
            other tales of the Viagens
        Derleth, A. W. ed. The outer reaches
    Hyperpilosity
        Conklin, G. ed. Omnibus of science
            fiction
    Inspector's teeth
        De Camp, L. S. Continent makers, and
            other tales of the Viagens
    Ordeal of Professor Klein
        Derleth, A. W. ed. Beachheads in space

Perpetual motion
    De Camp, L. S. Continent makers, and
        other tales of the Viagens
Summer wear
    Best science fiction stories: 1951
    De Camp, L. S. Continent makers, and
        other tales of the Viagens

De Camp, Lyon Sprague, 1907- **and Pratt,
    Fletcher,** 1897-1956
    Black ball
        Magazine of fantasy and science fiction.
            Best from Fantasy and science fiction;
            2d ser.
    Gavagan's bar
        Magazine of fantasy and science fiction.
            Best from Fantasy and science fiction;
            [1st ser.]
    Untimely toper
        Magazine of fantasy and science fiction.
            Best from Fantasy and science fiction;
            3d ser.
        See also Pratt, F. jt. auth.

DECATUR, STEPHEN, 1779-1820
    Daniel, H. Shores of Tripoli

DECEIT. See Truthfulness and falsehood

DECEPTION. See Hoaxes

Decision. O'Rourke, F.

Decision for spring. Summers, J. L.

Declaration of independence. Wright, F. F.

De-composition. Chekhov, A. P.

De Courcy, Dorothy, and De Courcy, John
    Rat race
        Conklin, G. ed. Big book of science
            fiction

De Courcy, John. See De Courcy, D. jt.
    auth.

De Daumier-Smith's blue period. Salinger,
    J. D.

Dee, Roger, pseud. See Aycock, Roger D.

Deed of entail. Hoffmann, E. T. A.

Deenie. Powell, D.

Deep country part. Casper, L.

Deep range. Clarke, A. C.

Deep water man. Brace, G. W.

DEER
    Rawlings, C. A. Flash of lightning
    Schulberg, B. W. Our white deer
    Seton, E. T. Trail of the Sandhill Stag

DEER HUNTING
    Bonner, P. H. Stalker & Co.
    Clark, W. Van T. Buck in the hills
    Warner, C. D. A-hunting of the deer

Defeat. Boyle, K.

Defeat. Sitwell, Sir O. bart

Defeat of the city. Porter, W. S.

The defeated. Gordimer, N.

DEFECTIVES AND DELINQUENTS
    Cather, W. S. Paul's case

Defender of the faith. Doty, W. L.

Defense. Van Vogt, A. E.

Defense in University City. Lowry, R. J. C.

Defense mechanism. MacLean, K.

Defensive diamond. Munro, H. H.

Defoe, Daniel, 1661?-1731
All Hollows
Apparition of Mrs Veal
Cerf, B. A. and Moriarty H. C. eds.
Anthology of famous British stories
Same as: True relation of the apparition
of one Mrs Veal
Friendly demon
Magazine of fantasy and science fiction.
Best from Fantasy and science fiction;
[1st ser.]
True relation of the apparition of one
Mrs Veal
Neider, C. ed. Great short stories from
the world's literature
Same as: Apparition of Mrs Veal

DeFord, Miriam Allen, 1888-
The oleander
Bond, R. T. ed. Handbook for poisoners
Throwback
Crossen, K. F. ed. Future tense

DEFORMITIES
Chandler, A. B. Giant killer
Fitzgerald, F. S. K. Curious case of
Benjamin Button
Merril, J. That only a mother
Sayres, W. C. Olaf the magnificent
Welty, E. Petrified man
See also Face—Abnormities and
deformities

DeJong, David Cornel, 1905-
Before the races
Oberfirst, R. ed. 1954 anthology of best
original short-shorts
Preparations for the night
Swallow, A. ed. Anchor in the sea

De La Mare, Walter John, 1873-1956
All Hollows
De La Mare, W. J. Collected tales
Almond tree
De La Mare, W. J. Collected tales
The bowl
De La Mare, W. J. Collected tales
Broomsticks
Joseph, M. ed. Best cat stories
Cape Race
De La Mare, W. J. Collected tales
The connoisseur
De La Mare, W. J. Collected tales
The creature
De La Mare, W. J. Collected tales
The guardian
Asquith, Lady C. M. E. C. ed. Book of
modern ghosts
Ideal craftsman
De La Mare, W. J. Collected tales
Queen, E. pseud. ed. Literature of crime
In the forest
De La Mare, W. J. Collected tales
Lispet, Lispett and Vaine
De La Mare, W. J. Collected tales
Miss Duveen
De La Mare, W. J. Collected tales
Missing
De La Mare, W. J. Collected tales
The nap
Blodgett, H. W. ed. Story survey.
1953 ed.
De La Mare, W. J. Collected tales
The orgy: an idyll
De La Mare, W. J. Collected tales

Physic
De La Mare, W. J. Collected tales
The riddle
De La Mare, W. J. Collected tales
Seaton's aunt
De La Mare, W. J. Collected tales
Strangers and pilgrims
De La Mare, W. J. Collected tales
The talisman
De La Mare, W. J. Collected tales
Three friends
De La Mare, W. J. Collected tales
The tree
De La Mare, W. J. Collected tales
The trumpet
De La Mare, W. J. Collected tales
The vats
De La Mare, W. J. Collected tales
The wharf
De La Mare, W. J. Collected tales
Willows
De La Mare, W. J. Collected tales

De La Roche, Mazo, 1885-
Auntimay
De La Roche, M. Boy in the house, and
other stories
Boy in the house
De La Roche, M. Boy in the house, and
other stories
Broken fan
De La Roche, M. Boy in the house, and
other stories
The celebration
De La Roche, M. Boy in the house, and
other stories
Come fly with me
Pacey, D. ed. Book of Canadian stories
Death of a centenarian
Burnett, W. ed. World's best
Patient Miss Peel
De La Roche, M. Boy in the house, and
other stories
Quartet
De La Roche, M. Boy in the house, and
other stories
Submissive wife
De La Roche, M. Boy in the house, and
other stories
"Twa kings"
De La Roche, M. Boy in the house, and
other stories
Widow Cruse
De La Roche, M. Boy in the house, and
other stories
Word for Coffey
De La Roche, M. Boy in the house, and
other stories

De La Torre, Lillian, 1902-
Disappearing servant wench
Mystery Writers of America, inc. Four-
&-twenty bloodhounds
Second sight of Dr Sam: Johnson
Mystery Writers of America, inc.
Maiden murders
Stroke of thirteen
Queen, E. pseud, ed. Queen's awards:
8th ser.

Delavigne, Jean François Casimir, 1792-1843
Up the garret stairs
Carrington, H. ed. Week-end book of
ghost stories

Delayed decision. O'Rourke, F.

Deledda, Grazia, 1871-1936
Two miracles
Fremantle, A. J. ed. Mothers
Delicate female. Whitney, P. A.
Delicate prey. Bowles, P. F.
Delicate warning. Cotterell, G.
DELICATESSEN STORES. See Food stores
Delilah and the space-rigger. Heinlein, R. A.
Dell, Dudley
Biography project
Galaxy science fiction magazine. Galaxy reader of science fiction
Dell, Floyd, 1887-
The blanket
Christ, H. I. and Shostak, J. eds. Short stories
Dell'archiprete, Ruby
Good girl
American vanguard, 1950
Del Rey, Lester, 1915-
Alien
Star science fiction stories, no. 3
And it comes out here
Conklin, G. ed. Science-fiction adventures in dimension
Helen O'Loy
Merril, J. ed. Beyond human ken
Pohl, F. ed. Assignment in tomorrow
Idealist
Star science fiction stories [no. 1]
Instinct
Conklin, G. ed. Omnibus of science fiction
Into thy hands
Greenberg, M. ed. Robot and the man
Lesser, M. A. ed. Looking forward
Kindness
Del Rey, L.; Matschat, C. H. and Carmer, C. L. eds. Year after tomorrow
Luck of Ignatz
Del Rey, L.; Matschat, C. H. and Carmer, C. L. eds. Year after tomorrow
The monster
Heinlein, R. A. ed. Tomorrow, the stars
Over the top
Astounding science fiction (Periodical) Astounding science fiction anthology
Pound of cure
Star science fiction stories, no. 2
Though dreamers die
Greenberg, M. ed. Robot and the man
Wings of night
Conklin, G. ed. Big book of science fiction
"The years draw nigh"
Derleth, A. W. ed. Beachheads in space
Delta interlude. Newman, R. S.
DeLynn, Leslie, 1922-
How I came to love the smell of a barroom
Wolfe, D. M. ed. Which grain will grow
De Maupassant, Guy. See Maupassant, Guy de
De Meyer, John
Boy crazy
Saturday evening post (Periodical) Saturday evening post stories, 1953

Deming, Richard
For value received
Best detective stories of the year—1953
Hanging fire
Meredith, S. ed. Bar 2
Mugger murder
Best detective stories of the year—1953
DEMOCRACY
Munro, H. H. Comments of Moung Ka
Porter, W. S. Sociology in serge and straw
Rinehart, M. R. One hour of glory
Saroyan, W. Ancient history and low hurdles
Demoiselle d'Ys. Chambers, R. W.
Demon lover. Bowen, E.
DEMONOLOGY. See Devil
DEMONS. See Devil
The **demons.** Sheckley, R.
Demotion. Locke, R. D.
DeMott, Benjamin Haile
Sense that in the scene delights
Best American short stories, 1954
Dempsey, David K. 1914-
Hope chest
Story (Periodical) Story; no. 3
Denicoff Marvin
Winter detail
Story (Periodical) Story; no. 3
DENMARK
Nexø, M. A. Birds of passage
DENTISTS
Benchley, R. C. The tooth, the whole tooth, and nothing but the tooth
Lewis, S. Land
Vickers, R. Man with the sneer
DEPARTMENT STORES
Calisher, H. Woman who was everybody
Collier, J. Evening primrose
Porter, W. S. Lickpenny lover
Porter, W. S. Trimmed lamp
Departmental case. Porter, W. S.
DEPRESSION. See Business depression, 1929
De profundis. Jenkins, W. F.
De Quille, Dan, pseud. See Wright, William
De Quincey, Thomas, 1785-1859
Savannah-al-mar
Neider, C. ed. Great short stories from the world's literature
The **derelict.** Tomlinson, H. M.
Derieux, Samuel Arthur, 1881-1922
The Comet
Bloch, M. ed. Favorite dog stories
Derleth August William, 1909-
Adventure of Ricoletti of the club foot
Derleth, A. W. Memoirs of Solar Pons
Adventure of the Black Narcissus
Mystery Writers of America, inc. Maiden murders
Adventure of the broken chessman
Derleth, A. W. Memoirs of Solar Pons
Adventure of the Camberwell beauty
Derleth, A. W. Three problems for Solar Pons
Adventure of the circular room
Derleth, A. W. Memoirs of Solar Pons

Derleth, August W.—*Continued*

Adventure of the dog in the manger
  Derleth, A. W. Memoirs of Solar Pons
Adventure of the five royal coachmen
  Derleth, A. W. Memoirs of Solar Pons
Adventure of the lost locomotive
  Derleth, A. W. Memoirs of Solar Pons
Adventure of the paralytic mendicant
  Derleth, A. W. Memoirs of Solar Pons
Adventure of the perfect husband
  Derleth, A. W. Memoirs of Solar Pons
Adventure of the proper comma
  Derleth, A. W. Memoirs of Solar Pons
Adventure of the purloined periapt
  Mystery Writers of America, inc. Four-
  & twenty bloodhounds
Adventure of the remarkable worm
  Derleth, A. W. Three problems for
  Solar Pons
Adventure of the Rydberg numbers
  Derleth, A. W. Three problems for
  Solar Pons
Adventure of the six silver spiders
  Derleth, A. W. Memoirs of Solar Pons
Adventure of the Tottenham werewolf
  Derleth, A. W. Memoirs of Solar Pons
The lonesome place
  Derleth, A. W. ed. Night's yawning
  peal
McIlvaine's star
  Derleth, A. W. ed. Worlds of tomorrow
  Wollheim, D. A. ed. Prize science
  fiction
Sheraton mirror
  Cuff, R. P. ed. American short story
  survey
The telescope
  Story (Periodical) Story; no. 2

DeRosso, H. A.

Bitter trail
  Meredith, S. ed. Bar 3

Des takes a holiday. Wylie, P.

Descendant of kings. Williams, W. C.

Descent into the maelström. Poe, E. A.

Desert fire. O'Meara, W.

DESERT ISLANDS
  Wells, H. G. Æpyornis Island

Desert orchid. Reese, J. H.

DESERTED HOUSES. See Houses, Deserted

Deserted mine. Sawyer, R.

The **deserter.** Davis, R. H.

The **deserter.** Klass, P.

Desertion. Simak, C. D.

DESERTION, MILITARY
  Davis, R. H. The deserter

DESERTION AND NON-SUPPORT
  Hawthorne, N. Wakefield
  Winslow, T. S. Mrs Wilson's husband
  goes for a swim

DESERTS
  Brand, M. pseud. Wine on the desert
  Clark, W. Van T. Indian well
  Grey, Z. Tappan's burro
  Prado, P. Laugh in the desert

Desire to be a man. Villiers de l'Isle-Adam,
  J. M. M. P. A. comte de

De Soto, Hernando. See Soto, Hernando
  de

DESPERADOES. See Outlaws

Desperate journey. Gunn, N. M.

DESPOTISM
  Hawthorne, N. Gray champion

Desrick on Yandro. Wellman, M. W.

De Stendhal, pseud. See Beyle, Marie Henri

Destiny strikes back. Whitley, C. M.

Destiny times three. Leiber, F.

DESTRUCTION OF EARTH. See Earth,
  Destruction of

**DETECTIVE AND MYSTERY STO-
  RIES.** See Mystery and detective
  stories

Detective detector. Porter, W. S.

DETECTIVES
  Alcazar, Doctor. See stories by Mac-
  Donald, P.
  Arnold, Shadrack. See stories by Chute, V.
  Banner, Brooks Urban. See stories by
  Commings, J.
  Bell, Adam. See stories by Carr, J. D.
  Brown, Father. See stories by Chesterton,
  G. K.
  Burgess, James. See stories by Brannon,
  W. T.
  Campion, Albert. See stories by Alling-
  ham, M.
  Chafik, Chafik J. See stories by Child,
  C. B.
  Coffee, Dr Daniel Webster. See stories
  by Blochman, L. G.
  Death, Mortimer, See stories by Crossen,
  K. F.
  Duffy, Detective Henry. See stories by
  Hayward, J. L.
  Dupin, C. Auguste. See stories by Poe,
  E. A.
  Fell, Gideon. See stories by Carr, J. D.
  Finney, Mary. See stories by Canaday,
  J. E.
  Forsythe, Wade II. See stories by Rine-
  hart, M. R.
  Gryce, Ebenezer. See stories by Green,
  A. K.
  Gurney, Cap. See stories by Brown, F.
  Hazlerigg, Chief Inspector. See stories by
  Gilbert, M. F.
  Holmes, Sherlock. See stories by Doyle.
  Sir A. C.
  Holmes, Sherlock. See stories by Doyle,
  A. C. and Carr, J. D.
  Joad, Bela. See stories by Brown, F.
  Johnson, Dr Samuel. See stories by De
  La Torre, L.
  Jolnes, Shamrock. See stories by Porter,
  W. S.
  Jordan, Scott. See stories by Masur,
  H. Q.
  Liddell, Johnny. See stories by Kane, F.
  Luke, Charley. See stories by Alling-
  ham, M.
  Lupin, Arsène. See stories by LeBlanc, M.
  MacDonald, Lieutenant. See stories by
  White, W. A. P.
  McGarry, Dan. See stories by Taylor, M.
  Magruder, Inspector John Bankhead. See
  stories by Prince, J. and Prince, H.

Devries, Marvin
Stage to Yuma
Saturday evening post (Periodical)
Saturday evening post stories, 1953

De Vries, Peter
Cold potato
De Vries, P. No but I saw the movie
Different cultural levels eat here
De Vries, P. No but I saw the movie
Double or nothing
De Vries, P. No but I saw the movie
Every leave that falls
De Vries, P. No but I saw the movie
Flesh and the devil
De Vries, P. No but I saw the movie
From there to infinity
De Vries, P. No but I saw the movie
Good boy
De Vries, P. No but I saw the movie
Household words
De Vries, P. No but I saw the movie
How can I leave thee?
De Vries, P. No but I saw the movie
I don't want to go
De Vries, P. No but I saw the movie
If he hollers let him holler
De Vries, P. No but I saw the movie
If the shoe hurts
De Vries, P. No but I saw the movie
Jam today
De Vries, P. No but I saw the movie
Let 'em eat cook
De Vries, P. No but I saw the movie
Life among the winesaps
De Vries, P. No but I saw the movie
One
De Vries, P. No but I saw the movie
Open house
De Vries, P. No but I saw the movie
Overture
De Vries, P. No but I saw the movie
Pygmalion
De Vries, P. No but I saw the movie
Requiem for a noun
De Vries, P. No but I saw the movie
Scene
De Vries, P. No but I saw the movie
They also sit
De Vries, P. No but I saw the movie
Through a glass darkly
De Vries, P. No but I saw the movie
Today and today
De Vries, P. No but I saw the movie
Touch and go
De Vries, P. No but I saw the movie
Tulip
De Vries, P. No but I saw the movie
We don't know
De Vries, P. No but I saw the movie
You and who else?
De Vries, P. No but I saw the movie

De Wets come to Kloof Grange. Lessing, D. M.

Dewey, G. Gordon, 1916-
The tooth
Magazine of fantasy and science fiction.
Best from Fantasy and science fiction;
2d ser.

Dewey, G. Gordon, 1916- and **Dancey, Max,** 1916-
The collectors
Best science-fiction stories: 1954

Dhoh. Wellman, M. W.

DIABETES
Shapiro, L. Journeying through the milky way

DIABETICS. See Diabetes

Diagnosis deferred. Blochman, L. G.

Diagnosis of a selfish lady. Boyle, K.

DIALECT STORIES

Cockney
See Dialect stories—English—Cockney

English—Cockney
Kipling, R. On Greenhow Hill
Munro, H. H. Morlvera

English—Devonshire
Phillpotts, E. "Hey diddle diddle, the cat. . ."

English—Yorkshire
Knight, E. M. Flying Yorkshireman

Irish
Kipling, R. Incarnation of Krishna Mulvaney
Lover, S. The gridiron
Walsh, M. Thomasheen James and the dictation machine

Jewish
Kober, A. Bella, Bella kissed a fella; 15 stories

Middle West
Clemens, S. E. Celebrated jumping frog of Calaveras County
Garland, H. Under the lion's paw

Mountain whites (Southern States)
Hall, E. G. Callie of Crooked Creek
Harris, G. W. Sut Lovingood; 8 stories
Porter, W. S. Whirligig of life
Still, J. Master time

Negro
Cohen, O. R. Law and the profits
Harris, J. C. Wonderful Tar-Baby story
Paul, L. No more trouble for Jedwick
Rice, A. C. H. Hoodooed

New England
Benét, S. V. Devil and Daniel Webster
Freeman, M. E. W. Revolt of "Mother"
Jewett, S. O. Courting of Sister Wisby
Slosson, A. T. Fishin' Jimmy

Scotch
Barrie, Sir J. M. bart. Courting of T'nowhead's Bell
Crockett, S. R. Reverend John Smith prepares his sermon
Crockett, S. R. Stickit minister
Gilpatric, G. Last Glencannon omnibus; 10 stories
Watson, J. Story of Dr MacLure

DIALECT STORIES—*Continued*

Southern

Dowdey, C. Bugles blow Retreat
Fox, J. Courtin' on Cutshin
Furman, L. Experience on the dress line
Granberry, E. P. Trip to Czardis
Kidd, H. L. Low road go down
Pratt, F. and De Camp, L. S. Stone of the sages
Rawlings, M. K. Benny and the bird-dogs
Rawlings, M. K. Gal young un
Smith, E. V. Prelude

Southwestern

Cunningham, E. Bar-Nothing's happy birthday
Watson, J. C. Benny and the Tar-Baby

Texas

See Dialect stories—Southwestern

Western

Clemens, S. L. Buck Fanshaw's funeral
Harte, B. Mrs Skaggs's husbands
Meredith, S. ed. Bar 2; 12 stories

Yiddish

See Dialect stories—Jewish

A dialogue. Walsh, M.

Diamant, Gertrude, 1901-
Snows of Bardonechhia
Queen, E. pseud. ed. Queen's awards: 7th ser.

Diamond as big as the Ritz. Fitzgerald, F. S. K.

Diamond horseshoes. Bateman, A.

Diamond lens. O'Brien, F.-J.

Diamond necklace. Maupassant, G. de

Diamond of Kali. Porter, W. S.

DIAMONDS
Fitzgerald, F. S. K. Diamond as big as the Ritz
Porter, W. S. Diamond of Kali

DIARIES (STORIES IN DIARY FORM)
Barrie, Sir J. M. bart. Farewell Miss Julie Logan
Clifton, M. Star, Bright
Collier, J. Evening primrose
Maupassant, G. de. Diary of a madman
Maupassant, G. de. The Horla
Paget, V. Amour dure
Shute, H. A. "Sequil" - or, Things whitch aint finished in the first
Wolfe, B. Self portrait

DIARIES, STORIES ABOUT
Chekhov, A. P. A fragment
Elston, A. V. Last day of my life
Willingham, C. Secret journal

Diary of a hard-boiled noble. Claudy, C. H.

Diary of a madman. Maupassant, G. de

DICE, See Gambling

Dick, Isaac Meier, 1807?-1893
Two strangers came to town
Ausubel, N. ed. Treasury of Jewish humor

Dick, Philip K. 1928-
Foster, you're dead
Star science fiction stories, no. 3

Golden man
Merril, J. ed. Beyond the barriers of space and time
Jon's world
Derleth, A. W. ed. Time to come
Second variety
Year's best science fiction novels, 1954

Dick Boyle's busines card. Harte, B.

Dickens, Charles, 1812-1870
Battle of life
Dickens, C. Christmas books
Captain Murderer
Davenport, B. ed. Ghostly tales to be told
Child's dream of a star
Cody, S. ed. Greatest stories and how they were written
The chimes
Dickens, C. Christmas books
Dickens, C. Christmas stories
Christmas carol
Cerf, B. A. and Moriarty, H. C. eds. Anthology of famous British stories
Cody, S. ed. Greatest stories and how they were written
Dickens, C. Christmas books
Dickens, C. Christmas stories
Lamb, L. ed. Family book of best loved short stories
Cricket on the hearth
Dickens, C. Christmas books
Dickens, C. Christmas stories
Haunted man
Dickens, C. Christmas books
Hunted down
Queen, E. pseud. ed. Literature of crime
Rat that could speak
Magazine of fantasy and science fiction. Best from Fantasy and science fiction; [1st ser.]
The signal-man
Blodgett, H. W. ed. Story survey. 1953 ed.
Moskowitz, S. ed. Great railroad stories of the world

About

Walpole, Sir H. Mr Huffam

Dickinson, Hugh
Reluctant hangman
Gable, M. Sister, ed. Many-colored fleece

Dickson, Carter, pseud. See Carr, John Dickson

Dickson, Gordon R.
Listen
Wollheim, D. A. ed. Prize science fiction
Lulungomeena
Lesser, M. A. ed. Looking forward
Steel brother
Norton, A. M. ed. Space service
See also Anderson, P. jt. auth.

Dickson, Helen, pseud. See Reynolds, Helen Mary Greenwood (Campbell)

Dicky. Porter, W. S.

DICTAPHONES
Walsh, M. Thomasheen James and the dictation machine

DICTATION MACHINES. See Dictaphones

DICTATORS
Benét, S. V. Blood of the martyrs
Kohnbluth, C. M. Marching morons
Dictator's double. Carr, R. S.
Did he touch you? Gatty, L.

Diderot, Denis, 1713-1784
Rameau's nephew
Dupee, F. W. ed. Great French short
novels

Di Donato, Pietro, 1911-
Christ in concrete
Best of the Best American short stories,
1915-1950

Die, Maestro, die! Waldo, E. H.
Different cultural levels eat here. De
Vries, P.
Difficult man. Williams, W. C.
Digging for treasure. Bland, E. N.
Digging our own graves. Farrell, J. T.
Dignity, a springer spaniel. Meek, S. St P.
Dilemma of Catherine Fuchsias. Davies, R.
Dilemma of Grampa Dubois. Lipman, C.
and Lipman, M.
Dill pickle. Mansfield, K.
Dime brings you success. Pratt, F. and De
Camp, L. S.
Diminishing draft. Kaempffert, W. B.
DINERS. See Restaurants, lunch rooms,
etc.
Dinesen, Isak, pseud. See Blixen, Karen

Dingle, Aylward Edward, 1874-
Owner's interest
Bluebook (Periodical) Best sea stories
from Bluebook

Dingle, Captain. See Dingle, Aylward Ed-
ward
DINING. See Dinners
Dinner at—. Porter, W. S.

DINNERS
Aiken, C. P. Fish supper
Bowen, E. Her table spread
Ekbergh, I. D. Katherine the clown
Farrell, J. T. Romantic interlude in the
life of Willie Collins
Humphrey, W. Quail for Mr Forester
Huysmans, J. K. Monsieur Folantin
Mallea, E. Pillars of society
Maugham, W. S. The luncheon
Munro, H. H. Phantom luncheon
Runyon, D. Piece of pie
Seager, A. Second wedding

Dinnis, Enid Maud, 1873-1942
The intervener
Thinker's digest (Periodical) Spoiled
priest, and other stories
No-man's Danny
Thinker's digest (Periodical) Spoiled
priest, and other stories
The peacemaker
Thinker's digest (Periodical) Spoiled
priest, and other stories

Dionea. Paget, V.
Dip in the pool. Dahl, R.
Diplomacy in Hollywood. Kaufman, W.
The diplomat. Chekhov, A. P.

DIPLOMATIC LIFE
Maugham, W. S. His Excellency
Piper, H. B. He walked around the
horses
See also Consuls
DIPLOMATS. See Diplomatic life
Dipping of the candlemaker. Howard, H.
Dirt-track thunder. Gault, W. C.
DISABLED. See Cripples
Disabled soldier. Goldsmith, O.
Disagreeable experience. Chekhov, A. P.
Disappearance of Crispina Umberleigh.
Munro, H. H.

DISAPPEARANCES
Cuthbert, C. D. Sublime vigil
De La Mare, W. J. Missing
Hawthorne, N. Wakefield
Huckabay, M. B. Ghost of Sam Bates
Kaempffert, W. B. Diminishing draft
MacDonald, P. Private—keep out
Munro, H. H. Disappearance of Crispina
Umberleigh
Porter, W. S. Renaissance at Charleroi
Porter, W. S. Strange story
Richter, C. Sinister journey
Sherwood, R. E. "Extra! Extra!"
Wells, H. G. The Plattner story
Winslow, T. S. Bronzes of Martel Greer
Woolrich, C. Wait for me downstairs
See also Invisibility
Disappearing act. Bester, A.
Disappearing act. Matheson, R.
Disappearing servant wench. De La
Torre, L.
Disappointed, but. Cooke, A. A.

DISASTERS
Colladay, M. M. Planetoid of doom
McMorrow, T. Mr Murphy of New York
See also Accidents; Fires; Floods;
Shipwrecks and castaways; Storms
The **disciple.** Aiken, C. P.

DISCIPLINE
Doty, W. L. Back to school
Discord makers. Reynolds, M.
Discounters of money. Porter, W. S.
Discovery. Brenner, L.

DISEASES
MacLean, K. Contagion
See also names of diseases, e.g.
Malaria
DISFIGUREMENTS. See Face—Abnormi-
ties and deformities
Disgrace to the family. Boyle, K.
Disguise. Wollheim, D. A.
DISGUISES. See Impersonations
DISHONESTY. See Honesty
The **disinherited.** Pagano, J.
DISMISSAL OF EMPLOYEES. See Em-
ployees, Dismissal of
Disorder and early sorrow. Mann, T.
DISORDERS OF PERSONALITY. See
Personality, Disorders of
Dispatch to the general. Haycox, E.
"Disperse, ye rebels!" Forbes, E.
Displaced persons. Sansom, W.

The **dispossessed**. Sullivan, R.

Disraeli, Benjamin. See Beaconsfield, Benjamin Disraeli, 1st earl of

Distant episode. Bowles, P. F.

DISTILLING, ILLICIT
Rawlings, M. K. Gal young un

DISTINCTION, CLASS. See Class distinction

Distressing tale of Thangobrind the jeweller. Dunsany, E. J. M. D. P. 18th baron

District doctor. Turgenev, I. S.

Ditzen, Rudolf, 1893-1947
Fifty marks
Lohan, R. and Lohan, M. eds. New Christmas treasury

Diversion. Ullman, J. R.

Divine, Arthur Durham, 1904-
Thirty minutes to zero
Saturday evening post (Periodical) Saturday evening post stories, 1953

Divine, David, pseud. See Divine, Arthur Durham

DIVINE HEALING. See Christian science; Faith cure; Miracles

DIVING
Coombs, C. I. Water bug
Maugham, W. S. Gigolo and gigolette
Miers, E. S. Big splash
Reck, F. M. Diving fool

DIVING, SUBMARINE
Crump. I. Dead men on parade
Doyle, Sir A. C. Maracot Deep
Hemingway, E. After the storm
Rieseberg, H. E. I dive for treasure
Wells, H. G. In the abyss
See also Skin diving

Diving fool. Reck, F. M.

DIVORCE
Connolly, M. Natural causes
Doty, W. L. Rectory parlor
Grau, S. A. Fever flower
McCarthy, M. T. "Cruel and barbarous treatment"
McCullers, C. S. The sojourner
Maugham, W. S. Closed shop
Munro, H. H. Unkindest blow
O'Donovan, M. Father and son
Patterson, E. G. Homecoming
Porter, W. S. Hypotheses of failure
Porter, W. S. Whirligig of life
Stewart, R. The promise
Stranger's note
Tarkington, B. Rennie Peddigoe
Wharton, E. N. J. Autres temps
Wharton, E. N. J. Madame De Treymes
Wharton, E. N. J. The other two
Winslow, T. S. Hotel dog
See also Marriage problems

Divorce in Naples. Faulkner, W.

DIVORCÉES. See Divorce

Dixon, Edwina Streeter
Pa sees again
Ford, N. A. and Faggett, H. L. eds. Best short stories by Afro-American writers (1925-1950)

Do-gooder. Benjamin, I. E.

Do you like it here? O'Hara, J.

Do you remember Mary? Kutner, N.

Doar, Graham
Outer limit
Conklin, G. ed. Big book of science fiction

Dobie, James Frank, 1888-
Midas on a goatskin
Peery, W. W. ed. 21 Texas short stories

The **doctor**. Irwin, M. E. F.

Dr Fillgrave refuses a fee. Trollope, A.

Doctor Hanray's second chance. Richter, C.

Dr Heidegger's experiment. Hawthorne, N.

The **doctor**, his wife, and the clock. Green, A. K.

Doctor-know-it-all. Gág, W.

Dr Lu-Mie. Kruse, C. B.

Doctor Mallory. Hart, A.

Dr Martino. Faulkner, W.

Dr Ox's experiment. Verne, J.

Doctor takes a case. Coxe, G. H.

DOCTORS. See Dentists; Physicians

Doctors of death. Thompson, T.

Dodge, John Everett
Headwall tempo
Owen, F. ed. Teen-age winter sports stories

DODGERS. See Brooklyn. Baseball club (National League)

Dodson, Daniel B. 1918-
The let-down
Story (Periodical) Story; no. 1

Doestoevsky, Feodor. See Dostoevskiĭ, Feodor Mikhailovich

Dog and the playlet. Porter, W. S.

Dog Andrew. Train, A. C.

Dog days. Jones, M. P. jr.

Dog died first. Fischer, B.

Dog for Miss Boo. Runbeck, M. L.

Dog in the double bottoms. White, R.

Dog man. Bell, V. M.

DOG SHOWS
Davis, R. H. Bar sinister
Taber, G. B. Best of breed
Taber, G. B. Top Hat goes to town
Taber, G. B. You can't buy a dog

Dog that sounded like a fire siren. Lull, R.

Dog who chose a prince. Coblentz, C. C.

Doggone Douthits. Caldwell, E.

DOGS
Anderson, E. V. Old Tom O'Grady of Shay Ranch
Annixter, P. pseud. First ally
Annixter, P. pseud. Hunting cost
Annixter, P. pseud. Ketch dog
Balch, G. Price on Hide-rack
Bell, V. M. Dog man
Bendrodt, J. C. Butch
Bendrodt, J. C. Chowsie
Blish, J. Beanstalk
Bloch, M. ed. Favorite dog stories; 14 stories
Bottome, P. Pink medicine
Brown, J. Rab and his friends
Buckingham, N. Cricket field
Buckingham, N. Hallowed years

Doremus, John, 1920-
The whistle
Wolfe, D. M. ed. Which grain will grow

Dormant. Van Vogt, A. E.

Dorothy. Caldwell, E.

Dorrance, Ward Allison, 1904-
Stop on the way to Texas
Best American short stories, 1954

Dos Passos, John Roderigo, 1896-
Body of an American
Burrell, J. A. and Cerf, B. A. eds.
Anthology of famous American stories

Dostoevskiĭ, Fedor Mikhaĭlovich, 1821-1881
Christmas tree and a wedding
Dostoevskiĭ, F. M. White nights, and
other stories
Eternal husband
Rahv, P. ed. Great Russian short novels
Faint heart
Dostoevskiĭ, F. M. White nights, and
other stories
Father Zossima's duel
Hazeltine, A. I. comp. Selected stories
for teen-agers
Heavenly Christmas tree
Neider, C. ed. Great short stories from
the world's literature
Little hero
Dostoevskiĭ, F. M. White nights, and
other stories
Mr Prohartchin
Dostoevskiĭ, F. M. White nights, and
other stories
Notes from underground
Dostoevskiĭ, F. M. White nights, and
other stories
Neider, C. ed. Short novels of the
masters
Peasant Marey
Short, R. W. and Benson, R. B. eds.
Short stories for study. 1950 ed.
Polzunkov
Dostoevskiĭ, F. M. White nights, and
other stories
White nights
Dostoevskiĭ, F. M. White nights, and
other stories

Doty, William Lodewick, 1919-
Action in Prague
Doty, W. L. Stories for discussion
Back to school
Doty, W. L. Stories for discussion
College star
Doty, W. L. Stories for discussion
The colonel
Doty, W. L. Stories for discussion
Dark knight
Doty, W. L. Stories for discussion
Defender of the faith
Doty, W. L. Stories for discussion
Father Murray's first failure
Doty, W. L. Stories for discussion
The fisherman
Doty, W. L. Stories for discussion
Greatest of these
Doty, W. L. Stories for discussion
Maggie Winthrop
Doty, W. L. Stories for discussion
Man with the monocle
Doty, W. L. Stories for discussion

Mr Dee and the middle-man
Doty, W. L. Stories for discussion
Parochial school
Doty, W. L. Stories for discussion
Pittsburgh special
Doty, W. L. Stories for discussion
Rectory parlor
Doty, W. L. Stories for discussion
Silver cross
Doty, W. L. Stories for discussion
Welcome home
Doty, W. L. Stories for discussion

Double bliss. Arico, V.

Double corner, Stegner, W. E.

Double cross. Marshall, E.

Double-dyed deceiver. Porter, W. S.

Double-dyed villains. Anderson, P.

Double exposure. Hecht, B.

Double fault. Chute, B. J.

Double image. Vickers, R.

Double or nothing. De Vries, P.

Double your money. Queen, E. pseud.

Doubles or nothing. Chute, B. J.

Doubles or nothing. Reeve, J.

Dougherty's eye-opener. Porter, W. S.

Doughnut jockey. Fennel, E.

DOUGHNUTS
McCloskey, R. The doughnuts

The **doughnuts.** McCloskey, R.

Doughty, LeGarde S.
The firebird
Best American short stories, 1954

Douglas, John Scott, 1905-
Water broncs
Fenner, P. R. comp. Speed, speed, speed

Douglas, Lloyd Cassel, 1877-1951
Dean Harcourt
Neider, C. ed. Men of the high calling
Pentecost
Brentano, F. ed. The word lives on

Dovbish, Bella, 1898-
White light
American vanguard, 1952

Dove of God. Schneider, G. W.

DOVES. See Pigeons

Dowdey, Clifford, 1904-
Bugles blow retreat
Jones, K. M. ed. New Confederate
short stories

Down at the dinghy. Salinger, J. D.

Down from the mountains. Parker, J. R.

"Down pens" Munro, H. H.

Downey, Fairfax Davis, 1893-
Stand to horse
Furman, A. L. ed. Teen-age horse
stories

Downey, Harris
Crispin's way
Best American short stories, 1953
The hunters
Best American short stories, 1951
First-prize stories, 1919-1954
Greene, J. I. and Abell, E. ed. Stories
of sudden truth
Prize stories of 1951

Downhill dilemma. Coombs, C. I.

Downing, J. Hyatt, 1888-
Man needs a horse
Dennis, W. ed. Palomino and other horses

Downward path to wisdom. Porter, K. A.

Doyle, Adrian Conan, 1910-1955
Adventure of Foulkes Rath
Doyle, A. C. and Carr, J. D. Exploits of Sherlock Holmes
Adventure of the Abbas ruby
Doyle, A. C. and Carr, J. D. Exploits of Sherlock Holmes
Adventure of the Dark Angels
Doyle, A. C. and Carr, J. D. Exploits of Sherlock Holmes
Adventure of the Deptford horror
Doyle, A. C. and Carr, J. D. Exploits of Sherlock Holmes
Adventure of the red widow
Doyle, A. C. and Carr, J. D. Exploits of Sherlock Holmes
Adventure of the two women
Doyle, A. C. and Carr, J. D. Exploits of Sherlock Holmes

Doyle, Adrian Conan, 1910-1955, **and Carr, John Dickson,** 1905-
Adventure of the black baronet
Doyle, A. C. and Carr, J. D. Exploits of Sherlock Holmes
Adventure of the gold hunter
Doyle, A. C. and Carr, J. D. Exploits of Sherlock Holmes
Adventure of the Highgate miracle
Doyle, A. C. and Carr, J. D. Exploits of Sherlock Holmes
Adventure of the sealed room
Doyle, A. C. and Carr, J. D. Exploits of Sherlock Holmes
Adventure of the seven clocks
Doyle, A. C. and Carr, J. D. Exploits of Sherlock Holmes
Adventure of the wax gamblers
Doyle, A. C. and Carr, J. D. Exploits of Sherlock Holmes

Doyle, Sir Arthur Conan, 1859-1930
Adventure of the Beryl Coronet
Doyle, Sir A. C. Adventures of Sherlock Holmes
Adventure of the blue carbuncle
Doyle, Sir A. C. Adventures of Sherlock Holmes
Same as: Blue carbuncle
Adventure of the Copper Beeches
Doyle, Sir A. C. Adventures of Sherlock Holmes
Adventure of the engineer's thumb
Doyle, Sir A. C. Adventures of Sherlock Holmes
Adventure of the noble bachelor
Doyle, Sir A. C. Adventures of Sherlock Holmes
Adventure of the speckled band
Doyle, Sir A. C. Adventures of Sherlock Holmes
Cerf, B. A. and Moriarty, H. C. eds. Anthology of famous British stories
Christ, H. I. and Shostak, J. eds. Short stories
Lamb, L. ed. Family book of best loved short stories
Same as: Speckled band

Avenging angels
Doyle, Sir A. C. Adventures of Sherlock Holmes
Baker Street irregulars
Doyle, Sir A. C. Adventures of Sherlock Holmes
Blue carbuncle
Doyle, Sir A. C. Sherlock Holmes
Same as: Adventures of the blue carbuncle
Boscombe Valley mystery
Doyle, Sir A. C. Adventures of Sherlock Holmes
Doyle, Sir A. C. Book of Sherlock Holmes
Break in the chain
Doyle, Sir A. C. Adventures of Sherlock Holmes
Cardboard box
Doyle, Sir A. C. Adventures of Sherlock Holmes
Case of identity
Doyle, Sir A. C. Adventures of Sherlock Holmes
Doyle, Sir A. C. Book of Sherlock Holmes
The conclusion
Doyle, Sir A. C. Adventures of Sherlock Holmes
Continuation of the reminiscences of John Watson, M. D.
Doyle, Sir A. C. Adventures of Sherlock Holmes
Crooked man
Doyle, Sir A. C. Adventures of Sherlock Holmes
Empty house
Doyle, Sir A. C. Sherlock Holmes
End of the Islander
Doyle, Sir A. C. Adventures of Sherlock Holmes
Episode of the barrel
Doyle, Sir A. C. Adventures of Sherlock Holmes
Final problem
Doyle, Sir A. C. Adventures of Sherlock Holmes
Five orange pips
Doyle, Sir A. C. Adventures of Sherlock Holmes
Flight for life
Doyle, Sir A. C. Adventures of Sherlock Holmes
Flower of Utah
Doyle, Sir A. C. Adventures of Sherlock Holmes
The "Gloria Scott"
Doyle, Sir A. C. Adventures of Sherlock Holmes
Great Agra treasure
Doyle, Sir A. C. Adventures of Sherlock Holmes
Greek interpreter
Doyle, Sir A. C. Adventures of Sherlock Holmes
Doyle, Sir A. C. Sherlock Holmes
His last bow
Doyle, Sir A. C. Sherlock Holmes
Horror of the heights
Jensen, P. ed. Fireside book of flying stories

Doyle, Sir Arthur C.—*Continued*
In quest of a solution
  Doyle, Sir A. C. Adventures of Sherlock
    Holmes
John Ferrier talks with the prophet
  Doyle, Sir A. C. Adventures of Sherlock
    Holmes
Lauriston Gardens mystery
  Doyle, Sir A. C. Adventures of Sherlock
    Holmes
Light in the darkness
  Doyle, Sir A. C. Adventures of Sherlock
    Holmes
Man with the twisted lip
  Doyle, Sir A. C. Adventures of Sherlock
    Holmes
Maracot Deep
  Kuebler, H. W. ed. Treasury of science
    fiction classics
Missing three-quarter
  Doyle, Sir A. C. Sherlock Holmes
Mr Sherlock Holmes
  Doyle, Sir A. C. Adventures of Sherlock
    Holmes
Musgrave ritual
  Doyle, Sir A. C. Adventures of Sherlock
    Holmes
Naval treaty
  Doyle, Sir A. C. Adventures of Sherlock
    Holmes
  Doyle, Sir A. C. Sherlock Holmes
On the great alkali plain
  Doyle, Sir A. C. Adventures of Sherlock
    Holmes
Our advertisement brings a visitor
  Doyle, Sir A. C. Adventures of Sherlock
    Holmes
Red-Headed League
  Doyle, Sir A. C. Adventures of Sherlock
    Holmes
  Doyle, Sir A. C. Book of Sherlock
    Holmes
  Doyle, Sir A. C. Sherlock Holmes
  Schramm, W. L. ed. Great short stories
Reigate squires
  Doyle, Sir A. C. Adventures of Sherlock
    Holmes
Resident patient
  Doyle, Sir A. C. Adventures of Sherlock
    Holmes
Scandal in Bohemia
  Doyle, Sir A. C. Adventures of Sherlock
    Holmes
  Doyle, Sir A. C. Book of Sherlock
    Holmes
  Doyle, Sir A. C. Sherlock Holmes
Science of deduction
  Doyle, Sir A. C. Adventures of Sherlock
    Holmes
Sherlock Holmes gives a demonstration
  Doyle, Sir A. C. Adventures of Sherlock
    Holmes
Sign of the four
  Doyle, Sir A. C. Book of Sherlock
    Holmes
  Doyle, Sir A. C. Sherlock Holmes
Silver Blaze
  Doyle, Sir A. C. Adventures of Sherlock
    Holmes
  Doyle, Sir A. C. Sherlock Holmes

Speckled band
  Doyle, Sir A. C. Sherlock Holmes
  Same as: Adventure of the speckled
    band
Statement of the case
  Doyle, Sir A. C. Adventures of Sherlock
    Holmes
Stockbroker's clerk
  Doyle, Sir A. C. Adventures of Sherlock
    Holmes
Story of the bald-headed man
  Doyle, Sir A. C. Adventures of Sherlock
    Holmes
Strange story of Jonathan Small
  Doyle, Sir A. C. Adventures of Sherlock
    Holmes
A study in scarlet
  Doyle, Sir A. C. Book of Sherlock
    Holmes
Tobias Gregson shows what he can do
  Doyle, Sir A. C. Adventures of Sherlock
    Holmes
Tragedy of Pondicherry Lodge
  Doyle, Sir A. C. Adventures of Sherlock
    Holmes
What John Rance had to tell
  Doyle, Sir A. C. Adventures of Sher-
    lock Holmes
Yellow face
  Doyle, Sir A. C. Adventures of Sherlock
    Holmes
Doyle, Fredric Clyde
Bullets for Bouquet
  Hazeltine, A. I. comp. Selected stories
    for teen-agers
Doyle, Louis, 1920-
Go to the ant
  Wolfe, D. M. ed. Which grain will grow
Doyle, Thomas L.
El conquistador
  Stanford short stories, 1950
DRAFT, MILITARY. See Military service,
  Compulsory
The **drag.** Darling, F.
Drago, Harry Sinclair, 1888-
Long winter
  Western Writers of America. Bad men
    and good
Sagebrush champion
  Furman, A. L. ed. Teen-age horse stories
The **dragon.** Akutagawa, R.
Dragon! Everett, E. W.
Dragon rider. Annixter, P. pseud.
DRAGONS
  Akutagawa, R. The dragon
  Grahame, K. Reluctant dragon
DRAMATISTS
  Cheever, J. O city of broken dreams
  Saroyan, W. Poet at home
  Winslow, T. S. Technique
The **dream.** Caldwell, E.
The **dream.** Chekhov, A. P.
The **dream.** Krige, U.
The **dream.** Maugham, W. S.
The **dream.** Porter, W. S.
The **dream.** Van Doren, M.
Dream of Armageddon. Wells, H. G.
Dream of drums. Sullivan, R.

Dream-woman. Collins, W.

The **dreamer.** Coppel, A.

The **dreamer.** Munro, H. H.

DREAMS
Aikens, C. P. Mr Arcularis
Benét, S. V. End to dreams
Bowles, P. F Thousand days for Mokhtar
Caldwell, E. The dream
Chekhov, A. P. Reporter's dream
Clemens, S. L. My platonic sweetheart
Clemens, S. L. Mysterious stranger
Collier, J. Interpretation of a dream
Collier, J. Midnight blue
Collins, W. Dream-woman
Curry, P. S. Osage Girl
De La Mare, W. J. Three friends
De La Mare, W. J. The wharf
Ekbergh, I. D. Astral plane—land of dreams
Fitzgerald, F. S. K. Winter dreams
Hawthorne, N. Celestial railroad
James, H. Great good place
Johnson, D. M. Warrior's exile
Kipling, R. Brushwood Boy
Maugham, W. S. The dream
Maugham, W. S. Lord Mountdrago
Moore, C. L. Scarlet dream
Myers, H. Pale sergeant
Nourse, A. E. Nightmare brother
Poe, E. A. Angel of the odd
Poe, E. A. Domain of Arnheim
Poe, E. A. Tale of the Ragged Mountains
Porter, W. S. The dream
Robin, R. Pleasant dreams
Schoenfeld, B. C. Eagle and the cheetah
Schwartz, D. In dreams begin responsibilities
Van Doren, M. The dream
Van Doren, M. Grandison and son
Waldo, E. H. Chromium helmet
Wells, H. G. Dream of Armageddon
Wilson, L. Not quite Martin

The **dreams** are real. Aldrich, B. S.

Dreams are sacred. Phillips, P.

Dream's end. Kuttner, H.

Dreiser, Theodore, 1871-1945
Lost Phoebe
Burrell, J. A. and Cerf, B. A. eds. Anthology of famous American stories
Day, A. G. ed. Greatest American short stories
Foerster, N. ed. American poetry and prose. 1952 ed.
Schramm, W. L. ed. Great short stories

Dress for Kitty. Grove, E.

Dress of white silk. Matheson, R.

Dresser, Daniel
White army
Wollheim, D. A. comp. Every boy's book of science-fiction

Dresser, Davis, 1904-
Big shot
Mystery writers of America, inc. Crooks' tour
Extradition
Mystery Writers of America, inc. Butcher, baker, murder-maker

Michael Shayne as I know him
Mystery Writers of America, inc. Four-&-twenty bloodhounds
You killed Elizabeth
Mystery Writers of America, inc. 20 great tales of murder

Dresser, Peter van. See Van Dresser, Peter

DRESSES. See Clothing and dress

Dressing-up. Burnett, W. R.

DRESSMAKERS
Furman, L. Experience on the dress line

DREYFUS, ALFRED, 1859-1935
Rabinowitz, S. Dreyfus in Kasrilevke

Dreyfus in Kasrilevke. Rabinowitz, S.

Drezmal Grace I.
Little Mohammed and Egypt's king
Best Army short stories, 1950

Drink. Anderson, S.

Drinkard, Ivey Noah
Mission for baby
Oberfirst, R. ed. 1952 anthology of best original short-shorts

DRIVERS. See Teamsters

DRIVERS, AUTOMOBILE. See Automobile drivers

Driver's seat. Queen, E. pseud.

Drop in the bucket. Fisher, D. F. C.

Drop of pure liquid. Willingham, C.

Droste-Hülshoff, Annette Elizabeth, Freiin von, 1797-1848
Jews' beech tree
Lange, V. ed. Great German short novels and stories

DROUGHTS
Güiraldes, R. Old ranch
Wilson, J. W. Grass grown again

DROWNING
Welty, E. Wide net
Wharton, E. N. J. The choice

Drowning. Chekhov, A. P.

DRUGS
Smith, C. A. Plutonian drug
Wells, H. G. New accelerator

Drumbeaters Island. Curtis, K.

DRUMMERS. See Commercial travelers

Drums in the fog. Holland, R. S.

Drums of the fore and aft. Kipling, R.

The **drunkard.** O'Donovan, M.

DRUNKARDS
Algren, N. How the devil came down Division Street
Benjamin, I. E. Do-gooder
Bunin, I. A. Evening in spring
De Vries, P. Every leave that falls
Fitzgerald, F. S. K. Alcoholic case
Hughes, L. On the way home
Li Kung-tso. Drunkard's dream
Maugham, W. S. Before the party
Porter, K. A. Day's work
Porter, W. S. Blackjack bargainer
Porter, W. S. Rubaiyat of a Scotch highball
Stuart, J. Woman in the house
Van Doren, M. Birdie, come back
See also Alcoholism

Drunkard's dream. Li Kung-tso

Drunken lizard. Brenner, L.
DRUNKENNESS. See Alcoholism; Drunkards

Dry September. Faulkner, W.

Dry valley. Bunin, I. A.

DUAL PERSONALITY
Dostoevskiĭ, F. M. Notes from underground
Guin, W. Beyond Bedlam
Lincoln, V. E. No evidence
Stevenson, R. L. Strange case of Dr Jekyll and Mr Hyde
Wharton, E. N. J. After Holbein

DUBLIN. See Ireland—Dublin

Du Bose, Virginia G.
Full cycle
Oberfirst, R. ed. 1954 anthology of best original short-shorts

Duc de L'Omelette. Poe, E. A.

Duchess and the jeweller. Woolf, V. S.

DUCK SHOOTING
Bonner, P. H. Bitter dawn
Buckingham, N. Comin' twenty-one
Buckingham, N. High sign
Lowrey, P. H. Too young to have a gun
Lytle, A. N. The guide
Stegner, W. E. Blue-winged teal
    See also Game and game birds

DUCKS
McLaverty, M. Wild duck's nest

Due and timely warning. Claudy, C. H.

Due process. Miner, H.

The duel. Conrad, J.

The duel. Maupassant, G. de

The duel. Porter, W. S.

Duel at 70 miles an hour. Floherty, J. J.

Duel in Captive Valley. Brown, W. C.

Duel of Dr Hirsch. Chesterton, G. K.

DUELING
Collins, W. Miss Bertha and the Yankee
Dostoevskiĭ, F. M. Father Zossima's duel
Harte, B. Passage in the life of Mr John Oakhurst
Maupassant, G. de. The duel
Verga, G. Cavalleria rusticana

DUELS. See Dueling

Dueña for a day. Von Hagen, C. I. B.

Duke, Osborn
Struttin' with some barbecue
Best American short stories, 1953

The Duke entertains. Trollope, A.

Duke: the gun-shy watchdog. Little, G. W.

Dumas in Hollywood. Kaufman, W.

Du Maurier, Daphne, 1907-
Apple tree
Du Maurier, D. Kiss me again, stranger
The birds
Du Maurier, D. Kiss me again, stranger
Kiss me again, stranger
Du Maurier, D. Kiss me again, stranger
Little photographer
Du Maurier, D. Kiss me again, stranger
Monte Verità
Du Maurier, D. Kiss me again, stranger

No motive
Du Maurier, D. Kiss me again, stranger
Old man
Du Maurier, D. Kiss me again, stranger
Split second
Du Maurier, D. Kiss me again, stranger

DUMB. See Deaf and dumb

Dumb-animal. Sitwell, Sir O. bart.

Dumb bunny. Chute, B. J.

Dumb waiter. Miller, W. M.

Dumbest man in the army. Sneider, V. J.

DUMMIES. See Models, Fashion

Dunbar, Olivia Howard, 1873-1953
Shell of sense
Carrington, H. ed. Week-end book of ghost stories

Dunbar, Paul Laurence, 1872-1906
Strength of Gideon
Dreer, H. ed. American literature by Negro authors

Duncan, Norman, 1871-1916
Fruits of toil
Pacey, D. ed. Book of Canadian stories

Dune roller. May, J.

DUNGEONS. See Prisoners and prisons

Dunkerley, Arthur Charles. See Oxenham, John

Dunne, Finley Peter, 1867-1936
Mr Dooley on athletics
Dachs, D. ed. Treasury of sports humor

Dunsany, Edward John Moreton Drax Plunkett, 18th baron, 1878-
Autumn cricket
Asquith, Lady C. M. E. C. ed. Book of modern ghosts
Bethmoora
Dunsany, E. J. M. D. P. 18th baron. Sword of Welleran, and other tales of enchantment
Bride of the man-horse
Dunsany, E. J. M. D. P. 18th baron. Sword of Welleran, and other tales of enchantment
Distressing tale of Thangobrind the jeweller
Dunsany, E. J. M. D. P. 18th baron. Sword of Welleran, and other tales of enchantment
East and West
Dunsany, E. J. M. D. P. 18th baron. Sword of Welleran, and other tales of enchantment
Exiles' club
Dunsany, E. J. M. D. P. 18th baron. Sword of Welleran, and other tales of enchantment
The hen
Dunsany, E. J. M. D. P. 18th baron. Sword of Welleran, and other tales of enchantment
Idle days on the Yan
Dunsany, E. J. M. D. P. 18th baron. Sword of Welleran, and other tales of enchantment
Kith of the Elf-folk
Dunsany, E. J. M. D. P. 18th baron. Sword of Welleran, and other tales of enchantment

Dunsany, Edward J. M. D. P. 18th baron
—Continued
Memory machine
  This week magazine. This week's short-short stories
Most dangerous man in the world
  Queen, E. pseud. ed. Queen's awards: 6th ser.
Poltarnees, Beholder of Ocean
  Dunsany, E. J. M. D. P. 18th baron. Sword of Welleran, and other tales of enchantment
The return
  Dunsany, E. J. M. D. P. 18th baron. Sword of Welleran, and other tales of enchantment
The sign
  Derleth, A. W. ed. Night's yawning peal
Story of land and sea
  Dunsany, E. J. M. D. P. 18th baron. Sword of Welleran, and other tales of enchantment
Sword of Welleran
  Cerf, B. A. and Moriarty, H. C. eds. Anthology of famous British stories
  Dunsany, E. J. M. D. P. 18th baron. Sword of Welleran, and other tales of enchantment
Thirteen at table
  Conklin, G. and Conklin, L. T. eds. Supernatural reader
Three sailors' gambit
  Dunsany, E. J. M. D. P. 18th baron. Sword of Welleran, and other tales of enchantment
Two bottles of relish
  Davenport, B. ed. Tales to be told in the dark
Widow Flynn's apple tree
  Dunsany, E. J. M. D. P. 18th baron. Sword of Welleran, and other tales of enchantment
Wonderful window
  Dunsany, E. J. M. D. P. 18th baron. Sword of Welleran, and other tales of enchantment

Dunsing, Dee May
Vireo's song
  Fenner, P. R. comp. Yankee Doodle

Duo. Colette, S. G.

Duplicity of Hargraves. Porter, W. S.

Duranty, Walter, 1884-
The parrot
  First-prize stories, 1919-1954

Dusk. Munro, H. H.

Dust storm. Brand, M. pseud.

Dusty drawer. Muheim, H.

DUTCH EAST INDIES
Annixter, P. pseud. Loose tiger
Benson, T. Golden fish
Benson, T. Yes-girl
Maugham, W. S. Vessel of wrath

Borneo
Blochman, L. G. Jimat of Dorland
Maugham, W. S. Before the party
Maugham, W. S. Force of circumstance
Maugham, W. S. Neil MacAdam

Maugham, W. S. The outstation
Maugham, W. S. Yellow streak

Java
Benson, T. White sea monkey
DUTCH IN BORNEO
Maugham, W. S. End of the flight
DUTCH IN SOUTH AFRICA. See Africa, South
DUTCH IN THE EAST INDIES
Maugham, W. S. Four Dutchmen
DUTCH IN THE UNITED STATES
Irving, W. Legend of Sleepy Hollow
Irving, W. Rip Van Winkle
Duty to live. Asch, S.
Duvoisin, Roger Antoine, 1904-
Three sneezes
  Fenner, P. R. comp. Fools and funny fellows
DWARFS
Connelly, M. C. Coroner's inquest
Newhouse, E. Gorgeous number
Wilde, O. Birthday of the Infanta
Dwellers in silence. Bradbury, R.
DWELLINGS. See Houses
Dworzan, Helene L. 1925-
Husband for Bluma
  American vanguard, 1953
Dyalhis, Nictzin
When the green star waned
  Derleth, A. W. ed. Beyond time & space
Dye, Charles
Syndrome Johnny
  Galaxy science fiction magazine. Galaxy reader of science fiction
Dyer, Walter Alden, 1878-1943
Gulliver the Great
  Fenner, P. R. comp. Dogs, dogs, dogs
  Harper, W. comp. Dog show
DYING. See Death
Dying man. Rudnicki, A.
DYING SCENES. See Deathbed scenes

E

E for effort. Sherred, T. L.
E pluribus unicorn. Waldo, E. H.
E S P. See Thought-transference
Each in his generation. Burt, M. S.
The **eagle.** Newhouse, E.
Eagle and the cheetah. Schoenfeld, B. C.
EAGLES
Beachcroft, T. O. Erne from the coast
Roberts, Sir C. G. D. "The young ravens that call upon him"
Sass, H. R. Gray Eagle
Eames, Genevieve Torrey
"... as handsome does"
  Fenner, P. R. comp. Dogs, dogs, dogs
Earley, Stephen B.
Baa-baa, black sheep
  Gable, M. Sister, ed. Many-colored fleece
Earlier service. Irwin, M. E. F.

EARTH
Clarke, A. C. Fires within
EARTH, DESTRUCTION OF
Balmer, E. and Wylie, P. When worlds collide
Carr, R. S. Mutation
Cox, I. Like gods they came
Dyalhis, N. When the green star waned
Hubbard, L. R. When shadows fall
Keller, D. H. The Star
Kornbluth, C. M. Silly season
Page, N. W. But without horns
Russell, E. F. Dear Devil
Van Vogt, A. E. The monster
Wandrei, D. Infinity zero
   See also End of the world

Earth-bound. Grimson, M. S.

Earthquake in Chile. Kleist, H. von

East and West. Dunsany, E. J. M. D. P. 18th baron

EAST SIDE. See New York (City)—East Side

EASTER
Connolly, M. Pigeon from St Bartholomew's
Munro, H. H. Easter egg
Porter, W. S. Day resurgent
Taber, G. B. Man at the gate
Taylor, M. McGarry joins the Easter parade

Easter egg. Brookhouser, F.

Easter egg. Munro, H. H.

Easter egg party. Bowen, E.

Easter eggs. Carr, R. S.

Easter Greeting. Bergengruen, W.

Easter of the soul. Porter, W. S.

Easy day for a lady. Ullman, J. R.

Easy going man. O'Rourke, F.

Easy way. Cicellis, K.

EATING CONTESTS. See Dinners

Eating days. Shapiro, L.

Eaton, C. E.
Motion of forgetfulness is slow
   Best American short stories, 1952

Ebbie. Guthrie, A. B.

Eberhart, Mignon (Good) 1899-
Wagstaff pearls
   Best detective stories of the year—1953

Ebner-Eschenbach, Marie von. See Ebner von Eschenbach, Marie, Freifrau

Ebner von Eschenbach, Marie, Freifrau, 1830-1916
Krambambuli
   Pick, R. ed. German stories and tales

Ebony elephant. Lawson, E.

Eça de Queiroz, José Maria, 1845-1900
Woman taken in adultery
   Selden, R. ed. Ways of God and men

The echo. Bowles, P. F.

Echo and the nemesis. Stafford, J.

ECUADOR
Wells, H. G. Country of the blind

Ed Walsh pitches a no-hit game. Farrell, J. T.

Eddy, C. M.
Loved dead
   Derleth, A. W. ed. Night's yawning peal

EDEN
Clemens, S. L. Eve's diary
Lagerkvist, P. F. Paradise

Edge of doom. Beck, W.

Edgeworth, Maria, 1767-1849
Castle Rackrent
   Connolly, C. ed. Great English short novels

Edginton, Helen Marion, 1883-
Purple and fine linen
   Cerf, B. A. and Moriarty, H. C. eds. Anthology of famous British stories

Edginton, May. See Edginton, Helen Marion

Edification of Marianne. Auchincloss, L.

EDISON, THOMAS ALVA, 1847-1931
Serviss, G. P. Edison's conquest of Mars

Edison's conquest of Mars. Serviss, G. P.

Editha. Howells, W. D.

EDITORS. See Journalists

Edmée. Zhabotinskiĭ, V. E.

Edmonds, Walter Dumaux, 1903-
Blind Eve
   Blodgett, H. W. ed. Story survey. 1953 ed.
Death of Red Peril
   Christ, H. I. and Shostak, J. eds. Short stories
Honor of the county
   Grayson, C. ed. Fourth round
Judge
   Cuff, R. P. ed. American short story survey

EDUCATION
Asch, S. The academy
Higbee, A. R. Words for John Willie
Rabinowitz, S. Gy-ma-na-si-a
   See also School life; Teachers

Education in the world state. Huxley, A. L.

Edwards, Dolton
Meihem in ce klasrum
   Astounding science fiction (Periodical)
   Astounding science fiction anthology

Eel by the tail. Lang, A. K.

The eel-trap. Loring, S. M.

EELS
Loring, S. M. The eel-trap
Millay, E. St V. Murder in the Fishing Cat

Effie Whittlesy. Ade, G.

Effigy of war. Boyle, K.

The egg. Anderson, S.

Egg farm. Lee, U.

Egg from the sky. Hunt, F. C.

Eggleston, Margaret (White) 1878-
Arabella, the third
   Eggleston, M. W. Red stocking, and other Christmas stories
Bridget's burden
   Eggleston, M. W. Red stocking, and other Christmas stories
By way of a Christmas card
   Eggleston, M. W. Red stocking, and other Christmas stories

Eggleston, Margaret W.—*Continued*

Christmas angel
  Eggleston, M. W. Red stocking, and other Christmas stories
A Christmas gift for father
  Eggleston, M. W. Red stocking, and other Christmas stories
Christmas solo
  Eggleston, M. W. Red stocking, and other Christmas stories
Christmas visitor
  Eggleston, M. W. Red stocking, and other Christmas stories
Gift of the wise man
  Eggleston, M. W. Red stocking, and other Christmas stories
In the patchwork quilt
  Eggleston, M. W. Red stocking, and other Christmas stories
Indian's Christmas gift
  Eggleston, M. W. Red stocking, and other Christmas stories
Love gift
  Eggleston, M. W. Red stocking, and other Christmas stories
Mother's Christmas present
  Eggleston, M. W. Red stocking, and other Christmas stories
On Christmas Day
  Eggleston, M. W. Red stocking, and other Christmas stories
Peter's Christmas present
  Eggleston, M. W. Red stocking, and other Christmas stories
Red stocking
  Eggleston, M. W. Red stocking, and other Christmas stories
Smile box
  Eggleston, M. W. Red stocking, and other Christmas stories
Smiling lady
  Eggleston, M. W. Red stocking, and other Christmas stories
The thief
  Eggleston, M. W. Red stocking, and other Christmas stories
Uncle David's Christmas
  Eggleston, M. W. Red stocking, and other Christmas stories
When Santa helped
  Eggleston, M. W. Red stocking, and other Christmas stories

EGGS

Anderson, S. The egg

Ego machine. Kuttner, H.

EGOISM

Aleksander, I. The Landrath
Auchincloss, L. Romantic egoists; 8 stories
Mansfield, K. Dill pickle
Maugham, W. S. Door of opportunity

EGYPT

To 640

Coolidge, O. E. Egyptian adventures; 12 stories

1882-date

Shaw, I. Walking wounded
Wall, J. W. Capra

Cairo

Tennyson, H. Appendicitis

Kings and rulers

Drezmal, G. I. Little Mohammed and Egypt's king

EGYPTIAN SLAVES. See Slavery—Egypt

Ehrenburg, Il'íA Grigor'evich, 1891-
The storm; excerpts
  Burnett, W. ed. World's best

Eichelberger, Rosa (Kohler)
On Christmas Eve
  Furman, A. L. ed. Everygirls career stories

Eicher, Elizabeth
But not Jeff
  American girl (Periodical) Favorite stories

Eichrodt, John
Nadia Devereux
  Burnett, W. and Burnett, H. S. eds. Sextet

Eight-dollar pup. Curtiss, P. E.

Eighty-yard run. Shaw, I.

Eighty years old. Grimson, M. S.

EIRE. See Ireland

Eisenberg, Frances, 1912-
Roof sitter
  Eaton, H. T. ed. Short stories

Ekbergh, Ida Diana
Astral plane—land of dreams
  Ekbergh, I. D. Mysterious Chinese mandrake, and other stories
Courtship of Lydia
  Ekbergh, I. D. Mysterious Chinese mandrake, and other stories
Gentleman from India
  Ekbergh, I. D. Mysterious Chinese mandrake, and other stories
Hindu Yogi science of breath
  Ekbergh, I. D. Mysterious Chinese mandrake, and other stories
Katherine the clown
  Ekbergh, I. D. Mysterious Chinese mandrake, and other stories
Lady's maid
  Ekbergh, I. D. Mysterious Chinese mandrake, and other stories
Lost cat
  Ekbergh, I. D. Mysterious Chinese mandrake, and other stories
Lure of perfume
  Ekbergh, I. D. Mysterious Chinese mandrake, and other stories
Matron in distress
  Ekbergh, I. D. Mysterious Chinese mandrake, and other stories
Mysterious Chinese mandrake
  Ekbergh, I. D. Mysterious Chinese mandrake, and other stories
Pink ballerina
  Ekbergh, I. D. Mysterious Chinese mandrake, and other stories
Strange story
  Ekbergh, I. D. Mysterious Chinese mandrake, and other stories
Toozee the puss
  Ekbergh, I. D. Mysterious Chinese mandrake, and other stories

Ekbergh, Ida D.—*Continued*
Up in a balloon
  Ekbergh, I. D. Mysterious Chinese
    mandrake, and other stories
White silk gloves
  Ekbergh, I. D. Mysterious Chinese
    mandrake, and other stories
Ekrem, Selma
Bekir and his dog, Aslan
  Furman, A. L. ed. Teen-age dog stories
Elaine's hope. Levine, T. M.
Elam, Richard M.
By Jupiter
  Elam, R. M. Teen-age science fiction
    stories
Day the flag fell
  Elam, R. M. Teen-age science fiction
    stories
Hands across the deep
  Elam, R. M. Teen-age science fiction
    stories
Iron moon
  Elam, R. M. Teen-age science fiction
    stories
Lunar trap
  Elam, R. M. Teen-age science fiction
    stories
Project ocean floor
  Elam, R. M. Teen-age science fiction
    stories
Red sands
  Elam, R. M. Teen-age science fiction
    stories
Sol's little brother
  Elam, R. M. Teen-age science fiction
    stories
Strange men
  Elam, R. M. Teen-age science fiction
    stories
Venusway
  Elam, R. M. Teen-age science fiction
    stories
What time is it?
  Elam, R. M. Teen-age science fiction
    stories
ELECTIONS
Munro, H. H. Hyacinth

Corrupt practices

Stuart, J. Thirty-two votes before breakfast
Elegy for Alma's Aunt Amy. Suckow, R.
Eleonora. Poe, E. A.
Elephant. Akeley, C. E.
Elephant adventure. Mukerji, D. G.
ELEPHANT DRIVERS. See Mahouts
Elephant intelligence. Williams, J. H.
Elephant midget. Buck, F.
Elephant never forgets. Lang, D.
Elephant remembers. Marshall, E.
ELEPHANTS
Akeley, C. E. Elephant
Bunner, H. C. Infidelity of Zenobia
Clemens, W. L. Stolen white elephant
Fenner, P. R. comp. Elephants, elephants,
  elephants; 14 stories
Kipling, R. Moti Guj—mutineer
Marshall, E. Elephant remembers

Elephants. Buck, F.
Elephant's child. Kipling, R.
Elephas frumenti. Pratt, F. and De Camp,
  L. S.
ELEVATOR OPERATORS
Cheever, J. Christmas is a sad season for
  the poor
Lanning, G. Old Turkey Neck
ELEVATORS
Carver, C. Twenty floors up
Elias, Alice, 1925-
Jarka
  American vanguard, 1950
Eliot, George, pseud.
In the prison
  Brentano, F. ed. The word lives on
Lifted veil
  Connolly, C. ed. Great English short
    novels
Eliot, George Fielding, 1894-
Uncertain weapon
  Bluebook (Periodical) Best sea stories
    from Bluebook
ELK
Munro, H. H. The elk
Poe, E. A. The elk
  See also Deer
The **elk.** Munro, H. H.
The **elk.** Poe, E. A.
Elkins, Evelyn
The no-counts
  Furman, A. L. ed. Teen-age dog stories
Ellanby, Boyd
Category Phoenix
  Year's best science fiction novels, 1953
Ellin, Stanley, 1917?-
Best of everything
  Queen, E. pseud. ed. Queen's awards:
    7th ser.
The betrayers
  Mystery Writers of America, inc.
    Butcher, baker, murder-maker
  Queen, E. pseud. ed. Queen's awards:
    8th ser.
The cat's-paw
  Best detective stories of the year—1950
Fool's mate
  Queen, E. pseud. ed. Queen's awards:
    6th ser.
House party
  Queen, E. pseud. ed. Ellery Queen's
    awards: 9th ser.
Orderly world of Mr Appleby
  Best detective stories of the year—1951
  Queen, E. pseud. ed. Queen's awards:
    5th ser.
Specialty of the house
  Mystery Writers of America, inc.
    Maiden murders
Elliot, Ian
Christmas is a time for great things
  Hathaway, B. and Sessions, J. A. eds.
    Writers for tomorrow. 2d ser.
Elliott, Bruce, 1914-
Battle of the S . . . S
  Crossen, K. F. ed. Future tense
Devil was sick
  Crossen, K. F. ed. Adventures in tomorrow

England, George Allan, 1877-1936
  Prize cargo
    Bluebook (Periodical) Best sea stories
    from Bluebook

ENGLAND
16th century
Evans, T. M. Gentlemen of valor
19th century
Dickens, C. See all stories by this author
James, H. Great good place
Invasions
Hardy, T. Tradition of 1804
London
Morley, C. D. The arrow
London—16th century
Irwin, I. H. Spring flight
London—19th century
Melville, H. Rich man's crumbs
Melville, H. Temple second
London—20th century
Lewis, W. Rotting Hill; 9 stories
Maugham, W. S. Jane
Maugham, W. S. Virtue
Smith, L. P. 'Ivanhoe'
Waugh, E. Work suspended

ENGLAND, PROVINCIAL AND RURAL
Aiken, C. P. Pair of Vikings
Boyle, K. Bridegroom's body
Irwin, M. E. F. Courage
Kipling, R. 'They'
Kipling, R. Village that voted the earth
  was flat
Lawrence, D. H. Shades of spring
Maugham, W. S. Home
Maugham, W. S. Round dozen
Surtees, R. S. Hunting scenes; 26 stories
Taylor, E. I live in a world of make-
  believe
Taylor, E. Shadows of the world
Taylor, E. Swan-moving
Trollope, A. Bedside Barsetshire; 26
  stories
Waugh, E. Englishman's home
Waugh, E. Period piece
Waugh, E. Winner takes all
Cornwall
Tregarthen, J. C. Great run
Trollope, A. Malachi's Cove
Devonshire
Galsworthy, J. The apple tree
Essex
Harvey, W. F. Euphemia witchmaid
Yorkshire
Bentley, P. E. Panorama; 7 stories
Knight, E. M. Lassie Come-Home

England to America. Montague, M. P.

English, Thelma
  Troubled water
    Wolfe, D. M. ed. Which grain will grow

ENGLISH DIALECT STORIES. See
  Dialect stories—English

ENGLISH IN AFRICA
Conrad, J. Heart of darkness

De Camp, L. S. Blue giraffe
Laurence, M. Uncertain flowering
Stern, J. Man who was loved

ENGLISH IN AFRICA, EAST
Buchan, J. 1st baron Tweedsmuir. Kings
  of Orion

ENGLISH IN ASIA MINOR
Maugham, W. S. In a strange land

ENGLISH IN BORNEO
Maugham, W. S. Before the party
Maugham, W. S. Flotsam and jetsam
Maugham, W. S. Force of circumstance
Maugham, W. S. The outstation
Maugham, W. S. Virtue
Maugham, W. S. Yellow streak

ENGLISH IN BURMA
Maugham, W. S. Mabel
Maugham, W. S. Masterson

ENGLISH IN CAPRI
Maugham, W. S. Lotus eater

ENGLISH IN CHINA
Maugham, W. S. The consul
Maugham, W. S. The taipan

ENGLISH IN DUTCH EAST INDIES
Benson, T. Yes-girl

ENGLISH IN EGYPT
Shaw, I. Walking wounded

ENGLISH IN GERMANY
Piper, H. B. He walked around the horses

ENGLISH IN INDIA
Forster, E. M. The trial
Kipling, R. At the end of the passage
Kipling, R. Man who was
Kipling, R. Mark of the beast
Kipling, R. On Greenhow Hill
Kipling, R. Tods' amendment
Kipling, R. Tomb of his ancestors
Kipling, R. William the Conqueror
Kipling, R. Without benefit of clergy
Weston, C. Forest of the night

ENGLISH IN INDO-CHINA, FRENCH
Maugham, W. S. Mirage

ENGLISH IN IRELAND
Irwin, M. E. F. Bloodstock
Irwin, M. E. F. Country gentleman
O'Donovan, M. Custom of the country

ENGLISH IN MALAY ARCHIPELAGO
Maugham, W. S. Back of beyond
Maugham, W. S. Casual affair

ENGLISH IN MALAY PENINSULA
Maugham, W. S. Door of opportunity
Maugham, W. S. Footprints in the jungle

ENGLISH IN MONGOLIA
Vogau, B. A. Big heart

ENGLISH IN OCEANICA
Coward, N. P. Mr and Mrs Edgehill

ENGLISH IN RUSSIA
Munro, H. H. Reginald in Russia

ENGLISH IN SAMOA
Maugham, W. S. Mackintosh
Maugham, W. S. The pool

ENGLISH IN SPAIN
Maugham, W. S. Happy man

ENGLISH IN SWITZERLAND
Ervine, St J. G. The mountain
Maugham, W. S. Miss King

ENGLISH IN THE RIVIERA
Maugham, W. S. Lion's skin

ENGLISH IN THE UNITED STATES
Evans, T. M. Transients
McCall, M. C. Fraternity
ENGLISH NAVY. See Great Britain. Navy
ENGLISH POLITICS. See Politics—England
ENGLISH SOLDIERS. See Soldiers—British
Englishman's home. Waugh, E.
ENOCH ARDEN STORIES
Morrison, A. That brute Simmons
Porter, W. S. Thing's the play
Sherwood, R. E. "Extra! Extra!"
    See also Disappearances
Enormous radio. Cheever, J.
Enormous room. Gold, H. L. and Krepps, R. W.
Enormous window. Styron, W.
Enough. Schulberg, B. W.
Enright, Elizabeth, 1909-
Apple seed and apple thorn
  Best American short stories, 1954
First face
  Best American short stories, 1952
The sardillion
  Prize stories of 1950
Temperate zone
  Best American short stories, 1951
Enshrined in the heart. Yates, E.
Ensign Carson, USCGR. Lane, G. C.
Ensign Weasel. Schulberg, B. W.
ENTOMBMENT. See Burial, Premature
The envelope. Taylor, C. L.
Environment. Geier, C. S.
Envy. Olyesha, I. K.
EPIDEMICS
Simak, C. D. Courtesy
EPIGRAMS
De Vries, P. One
EPILEPTICS
Poe, E. A. Berenice
Epilogue in the blues for Joey. Brookhouser, F.
Episode. Maugham, W. S.
Episode at the Honeypot. Van Doren, M.
Episode—1880. Haycox, E.
Episode in the life of the Marshal de Bassompieere. Hofmannsthal, H. H. Edler von
Episode of the barrel. Doyle, Sir A. C.
Episode of war. Crane, S.
Episode on Dhee Minor. Walton, H.
Erdman, Loula Grace
Allen High's youth problem
  Strang, R. M. and Roberts, R. M. eds. Teen-age tales v 1
Medal for Becky
  American girl (Periodical) On my honor
There was a star
  Elmquist, R. M. ed. Fifty years to Christmas
ERIE CANAL
Edmonds, W. D. Blind Eve

Erin, Bill, 1918-
Don't jinx the pitcher
  Argosy (Periodical) Argosy Book of sports stories
Quiet morning
  Meredith, S. ed. Bar 3
Ermine, Will, pseud. See Drago, Harry Sinclair
Erne from the coast. Beachcroft, T. O.
Ernenwein, Leslie Charles, 1900-
Trail hand
  Western Writers of America. Bad men and good
ERNES. See Eagles
Ernestine in Dominica. Archibald, J. W.
Ernst, Paul, 1866-1933
Microscopic giants
  Margulies, L. and Friend, O. J. eds. From off this world
"Nothing happens on the moon"
  Conklin, G. ed. Omnibus of science fiction
Thing in the pond
  Stauffer, R. M.; Cunningham, W. H. and Sullivan, C. J. eds. Adventures in modern literature
Erostratus. Sartre, J. P.
ERRORS
Brandel, M. Hasty act
Erskine, Laurie York, 1894-
After school
  American boy (Periodical) American boy anthology
Horses and men
  American boy (Periodical) American boy Adventure stories
Mystery at Moon Lake
  Strang, R. M. and Roberts, R. M. eds. Teen-age tales v 1
Mystery of Mike
  Boys' life (Periodical) Boys' life Adventure stories
Ervine, St John Greer, 1883-
The mountain
  Talbot, D. ed. Treasury of mountaineering stories
Escape! Asimov, I.
The escape. Campbell, J. W.
The escape. Carrington, H.
The escape. Hendryx, J. B.
The escape. Maugham, W. S.
Escape from Kosseir. Coolidge, O. E.
Escape from Pharaoh. Hurston, Z. N.
ESCAPED CONVICTS. See Convicts, Escaped
ESCAPES
Brick, J. Message for Uncle Billy
Brick, J. Rifleman's run
Carrington, H. The escape
Conrad, J. Secret sharer
Coolidge, O. E. Escape from Kosseir
Corkery, D. On the heights
Futrelle, J. Problem of Cell 13
Hardy, T. Three strangers
Hilton, J. Twilight of the wise
Martyr, W. Sleeping draft
Wassermann, J. Lukardis
Woods, W. Free man

ESKIMOS
Carrighar, S. Marooned children
Cave, H. B. Two were left
Mowat, F. Lost in the barren lands
Mowat, F. Woman he left to die
Mowery, W. B. Mannikin talk
Porter, W. S. Ferry of unfulfilment
Roberts, Sir C. G. D. On the roof of the world
Stefánsson, V. Seal hunting
Sullivan, A. Salving of Pyack
Esmé. Munro, H. H.
ESPIONAGE. See Spies
ESPRITU SANTO
Michener, J. A. The good life
Essence of strawberry. Kneale, N.
ESSEX, ENGLAND. See England, Provincial and rural—Essex
The **essrig.** Ogus, A. D.
Estate and trespass. Hall, J. B.
Estate of Alice V. Gregg. Parker, J. R.
ESTATES. See Houses; Real property
Estes, Eleanor, 1906-
Trainload of soldiers; excerpt from "Rufus M"
Fenner, P. R. comp. Giggle box
ESTHETICS
Lieberman, E. Thing of beauty
Etaoin Shrdlu. Brown, F.
Eternal husband. Dostoevskiĭ, F. M.
ETERNAL LIFE. See Immortality; Longevity
Eternal life. Rabinowitz, S.
Eternal man. Sharp, D. D.
Eternal rectangle. Willingham, C.
Eternal smile. Lagerkvist, P. F.
Eternal triangle. O'Donovan, M.
Eternal wedding gown. Opatoshu, J.
Eternity lost. Simak, C. D.
Ethan Brand. Hawthorne, N.
Ethics of pig. Porter, W. S.
ETHROG
Ogus, A. D. The essrig
Etnier, Elizabeth (Jax) 1911-
The willow
Aswell, M. L. W. ed. New short novels
Eupepsia. Willingham, C.
Euphemia witchmaid. Harvey, W. F.
Eureca cottage. Grimson, M. S.
EUROPEAN WAR, 1914-1918
Auchincloss, L. Maud
Aumonier, S. Source of irritation
Hemingway, E. Now I lay me
Munro, H. H. Birds on the western front
Munro, H. H. Square egg

Aerial operations
Bellah, J. W. Fear
Nordhoff, C. B. and Hall, J. N. In pyjamas

France
Boyd, T. A. Responsibility

Italy
Hemingway, E. In another country
Hemingway, E. Way you'll never be

Medical and sanitary affairs
Scott, H. S. Sister

Russia
Bergengruen, W. When Riga was evacuated

Secret service
Maugham, W. S. Giulia Lazzari
Maugham, W. S. Hairless Mexican
Maugham, W. S. The traitor
Noyes, A. Uncle Hyacinth
Eustis, Helen, 1916-
Rider on the pale horse
Saturday evening post (Periodical) Saturday evening post stories, 1950
Evans, Edward Everett, 1893-
The shed
Sloane, W. M. ed. Stories for tomorrow
Evans, Hubert Reginald, 1892-
Ghost-town dog
Harper, W. comp. Dog show
Evans, Thomas M. 1881-
Gentlemen of valor
Evans, T. M. Gentlemen of valor, and other stories
The salesman
Evans, T. M. Gentlemen of valor, and other stories
Transients
Evans, T. M. Gentlemen of valor, and other stories
Eve and the sea serpent. Wylie, P.
Eve enters. Van de Water, F. F.
Eve of St John. Pratt, F. and De Camp, L. S.
Eve of the trial. Chekhov, A. P.
Evelyn and the rest of us. Caldwell, E.
Even to Judas. Brown, H. C.
EVENING AND CONTINUATION SCHOOLS
Rosten, L. C. Mr K*A*P*L*A*N the Magnificent
Evening in Nuevo Leon. Caldwell, E.
Evening in spring. Bunin, I. A.
Evening primrose. Collier, J.
EVENING SCHOOLS. See Evening and continuation schools
Evenings at home. Hardwick, E.
An evening's entertainment. Haycox, E.
Evensong. Waldron, D.
Eventide of the feast. Gibran, K.
Ever been to Brooklyn? Newhouse, E.
EVEREST, MOUNT
Jenks, A. No way down
Everett, Ethel Walton
Dragon!
Story parade (Periodical) Adventure stories
Every day is ladies' day. Powell, D.
Every leave that falls. De Vries, P.
Everybody loves my baby. Shulman, M.
Everything under control. Bentley, P. E.
Eve's diary. Clemens, S. L.
EVICTION
Thompson, T. Shore for the sinking

FACE
Abnormities and deformities
Donahoe, E. Head by Scopas
Grimson, M. S. Story of Paula
Maugham, W. S. Man with the scar
The **face.** Moreau, L.
Face behind the bar. Stern, J.
Face is familiar but— Shulman, M.
Face of evil. O'Donovan, M.
Face of Hollywood. Schulberg, B. W.
Face of stone. Williams, W. C.
Face of the poor. Graham, M. C.
FACTORIES
Kaplan, R. The artist
O'Donovan, M. Darcy in the Land of Youth
O'Donovan, M. Jerome
FACTORY WORKERS. See Factories
Facts about the hyacinthes. Van Doren, M.
Facts in the case of M. Valdemar. Poe, E. A.
Facts of life. Maugham, W. S.
Faggett, Harry Lee, 1911-
Chatter-stick sermon
Ford, N. A. and Faggett, H. L. eds. Best short stories by Afro-American writers (1925-1950)
Cupid wags his tail
Ford, N. A. and Faggett, H. L. eds. Best short stories by Afro-American writers (1925-1950)
Goldfish bowl
Ford, N. A. and Faggett, H. L. eds. Best short stories by Afro-American writers (1925-1950)
The **failure.** Taylor, K. H.
Faint heart. Dostoevskiĭ, F. M.
Fairbanks, Douglas, 1909-
Ashes
Grayson, C. ed. Fourth round
FAIRIES
Collier, J. Bottle party
Kuttner, H. Gnome there was
Munro, H. H. Saint and the Goblin
Walsh, M. Come back, my love
See also Fantasies; Legends and folk tales; Supernatural phenomena
Fairman, Paul W.
Brothers beyond the void
Derleth, A. W. ed. Worlds of tomorrow
FAIRS
Grimson, M. S. Grandma goes to the Fair
Joyce, J. Araby
Van Doren, M. Dollar bill
Fairy tale of Father Brown. Chesterton, G. K.
FAIRY TALES. See Fairies; Fantasies; Legends and folk tales
FAITH
Cronin, A. J. A candle in Vienna
Eliot, G. pseud. In the prison
Grimson, M. S. Gather up the pieces
Llewellyn, R. Faith to be healed
Melville, H. The sermon
Faith. Graham, R. B. C.

Faith at sea. Shaw, I.
FAITH CURE
Hughes, L. Tain't so
FAITH HEALING. See Faith cure
Faith, hope and charity. Grimson, M. S.
Faith to be healed. Llewellyn, R.
FAITHFULNESS
Hurston, Z. N. Conscience of the court
FAKES. See Swindlers and swindling
FALCONRY
Chambers, R. W. Demoiselle d'Ys
FALCONS
Bair, T. Falcon's nest
Falcon's nest. Bair, T.
Fall guy. Chute, B. J.
Fall of a sparrow. Auchincloss, L.
Fall of Edward Barnard. Maugham, W. S.
Fall of the House of Usher. Poe, E. A.
Fallada, Hans, pseud. See Ditzen, Rudolf
Fallen star. Collier, J.
FALLS. See Accidents
FALSE ACCUSATION
Maupassant, G. de. The string
Stoumen, L. C. The blond dog
False dawn. Chandler, A. B.
False gems. Maupassant, G. de
FALSEHOOD. See Truthfulness and falsehood
FAMILY. See Family life
Family affair. Maupassant, G. de
Family album. Betts, D.
FAMILY CHRONICLES
Bunner, H. C. Story of a New York house
Van Doren, M. One of the Garretsons
See also Family life
Family history. Pasinetti, P. M.
Family in the wind. Fitzgerald, F. S. K.
FAMILY LIFE
Aiken, C. P. Dark city
Aldrich, B. S. Will the romance be the same?
Allan, T. Lies my father told me
Asch, S. The academy
Barrie, Sir J. M. bart. The last night
Betts, D. Family album
Bolté, M. End of the depression
Cheever, J. Goodbye, my brother
Chekhov, A. P. Two of a kind
De La Roche, M. The celebration
Elliott, G. P. Family matter
Enright, E. Temperate zone
Freedman, D. Mendel Marantz—genius
Gilbreth, F. B. and Carey, E. M. C. Pygmalion
Grau, S. A. Miss Yellow Eyes
Grimson, M. S. Eureca cottage
Hauser, M. L. Calling all cars
Hayes, H. M. Jenny takes a holiday
Hertlein, R. P. G. Christmas
Hill, M. Y. Sea anchor
Humphrey, W. Sister
Jones, R. F. Farthest horizon
Krige, U. The dream
Lagerkvist, P. F. Guest of reality
Lamkin, S. Comes a day
Lloyd, B. B. Forgotten greeting cards

Farley, Walter, 1915-
The storm
   Strang, R. M. and Roberts, R. M. eds.
   Teen-age tales v 1
The **farm.** Davies, R.
FARM LIFE
Bates, H. E. Little farm
Glaspell, S. Jury of her peers
Graham, M. C. Face of the poor
Grimson, M. S. When Dan came home
Humphrey, W. Man with a family
Love, P. H. Jersey heifer
Porter, W. S. Defeat of the city
Stull, P. Growing pains

Arkansas
Weeks, R. Arkansas

Ireland
Corkery, D. Rock-of-the-mass
O'Donovan, M. Uprooted

Kansas
Le Sueur, M. Persephone

Middle West
Cather, W. S. Neighbour Rosicky
Garland, H. Under the lion's paw
Johnson, J. W. Arcadia recalled

Nebraska
Aldrich, B. S. Day of retaliation

New England
Aiken, C. P. Bow down, Isaac!
Freeman, M. E. W. Revolt of "Mother"

Russia
Chekhov, A. P. Gooseberries

Sicily
Verga, G. The gentry

Tennessee
Warren, R. P. Blackberry winter

Vermont
Lewis, S. Land

Wales
Davies, R. The farm

The West
Babb, S. Wild flower

FARM TENANCY. See Tenant farming

Farmer, Philip José
Attitudes
   Magazine of fantasy and science fiction.
   Best from Fantasy and science fiction;
   3d ser.
Mother
   Pohl, F. ed. Assignment in tomorrow

FARMERS. See Farm life

Farmer's wife. Maupassant, G. de

Farnsworth, Mona
All roads
   Moskowitz, S. comp. Editor's choice in
   science fiction

Farrell, James Thomas, 1904-
All things are nothing to me
   Farrell, J. T. Short stories
American dream girl
   Farrell, J. T. American dream girl

Angela
   Farrell, J. T. Short stories
Backyard ballgame
   Graber, R. S. ed. Baseball reader
Benefits of American life
   Farrell, J. T. Short stories
Big Jeff
   Farrell, J. T. Short stories
The buddies
   Farrell, J. T. Short stories
Calico shoes
   Farrell, J. T. Short stories
Can all this grandeur perish?
   Farrell, J. T. Short stories
Candy from Fairyland
   Farrell, J. T. American dream girl
Casual incident
   Cory, D. W. pseud. comp. 21 variations
   on a theme
   Farrell, J. T. Short stories
Children of the times
   Farrell, J. T. Short stories
Clyde
   Farrell, J. T. Short stories
A coincidence
   Farrell, J. T. American dream girl
Comedy cop
   Farrell, J. T. Short stories
Curbstone philosophy
   Farrell, J. T. Short stories
Day at the zoo
   Farrell, J. T. American dream girl
Digging our own graves
   Farrell, J. T. American dream girl
Ed Walsh pitches a no-hit game
   Graber, R. S. ed. Baseball reader
Fastest runner on Sixty-first Street
   Farrell, J. T. American dream girl
Footnote
   Farrell, J. T. Short stories
For white men only
   Farrell, J. T. Short stories
Fritz
   Farrell, J. T. Further short stories
Front-page story
   Farrell, J. T. Short stories
Game in the park
   Graber, R. S. ed. Baseball reader
Girls at the Sphinx
   Farrell, J. T. American dream girl
Guillotine party
   Farrell, J. T. Short stories
Have I got sun in my eyes?
   Farrell, J. T. American dream girl
Helen I love you
   Farrell, J. T. Short stories
Hell of a good time
   Farrell, J. T. Short stories
Honey, we'll be brave
   Farrell, J. T. Short stories
I want to go home
   Farrell, J. T. American dream girl
In accents of death!
   Farrell, J. T. Short stories
In City Hall Square
   Farrell, J. T. Short stories
Jim O'Neill
   Farrell, J. T. Short stories
John Hitchcock
   Farrell, J. T. Further short stories
Johnny's old man
   Farrell, J. T. American dream girl

FATE AND FATALISM
   Harvey, W. F. August heat
Father and I. Lagerkvist, P. F.
Father and son. Callaghan, M.
Father and son. O'Donovan, M.
Father and the boys. Weissenberg, I. M.
Father Christmas. McLaverty, M.
Father comes home. Welshimer, H.
Father Gaucher's elixir. Daudet, A.
Father Murray's first failure. Doty, W. L.
Father O'Connell. Van Doren, M.
Father Zossima's duel. Dostoevskiĭ, F. M.
The **fatherland**. Quiroga, H.

FATHERS
   Caldwell, E. First autumn
   Corkery, D. Emptied sack
   Davies, R. Abraham's glory
   De La Mare, W. J. The nap
   Elliott, G. P. Family matter
   Marquand, J. P. Yoicks—and away
   Mathews, M. Tough little Christmas story
   Michener, J. A. The story
   Newhouse, E. Seventy thousand dollars
   Putman, C. News from Troy
   Stuart, J. Clearing in the sky
   Verner, C. Meddlin' Papa
         See also Fathers and daughters;
         Fathers and sons

FATHERS AND DAUGHTERS
   Aiken, C. P. I love you very dearly
   Brown, G. One in a million
   Cancela, A. Life and death of a hero
   Cheever, J. The Hartleys
   Dell'Archiprete, R. Good girl
   Donahoe, E. Madness in the heart
   Dovbish, B. White light
   Fitzgerald, F. S. K. Babylon revisited
   Hawthorne, N. Rappaccini's daughter
   Miner, M. S. Jocelyn
   Newhouse, E. The eagle
   Newhouse, E. New Year's Day
   Newhouse, E. The wolf
   Rabinowitz, S. Hodel
   Robinson, R. S. Mango tree
   Schulberg, B. W. Short digest of a long
      novel
   Thériault, Y. Jeannette
   Trilling, L. Other Margaret
   Unamuno y Jugo, M. de. Solitude
   Winn, J. Hungry sister

FATHERS AND SONS
   Anderson, S. "Queer"
   Appet, N. The test
   Auchincloss, L. The miracle
   Beachcroft, T. O. Erne from the coast
   Beck, W. Detour in the dark
   Beck, W. Far whistle
   Betts, D. The sword
   Block, R. E. Americanization of Shadrach
      Cohen
   Bowles, P. F. Pages from Cold Point
   Boyle, K. Soldier ran away
   Bradbury, R. Rocket man
   Burnett, W. Suffer the children
   Callagan, M. Father and son
   Casper, L. Sense of direction
   Chekhov, A. P. Holy simplicity
   Chekhov, A. P. Saintly simplicity
   Collier, J. Ah the university

Collier, J. Thus I refute Beelzy
Connolly, M. Love, Tomi
Corkery, D. Vision
Cozzens, J. G. Total stranger
De La Mare, W. J. Almond tree
Ewald, C. My little boy
Faulkner, W. Barn burning
Goodman, J. C. Kingdom of Gordon
Goudsmit, S. Romantic boy
Hemingway, E. My old man
Horwitz, M. Coquette
Horwitz, J. Generations of man
Kafka, F. The judgment
Lagerkvist, P. F. Father and I
Lanham, E. M. Listen to me, boy
Levine, S. Gift for a birthday
Loveridge, G. Latter end
Mabry, T. D. Indian feather
Maupassant, G. de. Hautot, father and son
Mérimée, P. Mateo Falcone
Milburn, G. The apostate
Newhouse, E. War for Tony
O'Donovan, M. Father and son
Reisin, A. Tuition for the rebbe
Saroyan, W. Pheasant hunter
Schaefer, J. W. Harvey Kendall
Schoenfeld, B. C. Eagle and the cheetah
Scott, W. R. My father doesn't like me
Sherman, R. Now there is peace
Stafford, J. A reunion
Stegner, W. E. Blue-winged teal
Stull, P. Growing pains
Taylor, K. Pale green fishes
Taylor, P. H. Porte-cochere
Thibaudeau, C. City underground
Thurber, J. More alarms at night
Ullman, J. R. Visitation
Van Doren, M. Grandison and son
Van Doren, M. Rich, poor, and indifferent
         See also Parent and child

FATHERS-IN-LAW
Goyen, W. White rooster
Waltari, M. T. Tie from Paris

Faulkner, William, 1897-
Ad Astra
   Faulkner, W. Collected stories
All the dead pilots
   Faulkner, W. Collected stories
Artist at home
   Faulkner, W. Collected stories
Barn burning
   Faulkner, W. Collected stories
   Faulkner, W. Faulkner reader
   First-prize stories, 1919-1954
The bear
   Day, A. G. ed. Greatest American short
      stories
   Faulkner, W. Faulkner reader
   Ludwig, R. M. and Perry, M. B. eds.
      Nine short novels
   Schramm, W. L. ed. Great short stories
   Short, R. W. and Sewall, R. B. eds.
      Short stories for study. 1950 ed.
   Waite, H. O. and Atkinson, B. P. eds.
      Literature for our time
Bear hunt
   Faulkner, W. Collected stories
Beyond
   Faulkner, W. Collected stories
Black music
   Faulkner, W. Collected stories
The brooch
   Faulkner, W. Collected stories

Faulkner, William—*Continued*

Carcassonne
  Faulkner, W. Collected stories
Centaur in brass
  Faulkner, W. Collected stories
The courthouse
  Faulkner, W. Faulkner reader
A courtship
  Faulkner, W. Collected stories
  First-prize stories, 1919-1954
Crevasse
  Faulkner, W. Collected stories
Death drag
  Faulkner, W. Collected stories
Divorce in Naples
  Faulkner, W. Collected stories
Dr Martino
  Faulkner, W. Collected stories
Dry September
  Davis, R. G. ed. Ten modern masters
  Faulkner, W. Collected stories
  Faulkner, W. Faulkner reader
  Lynskey, W. C. ed. Reading modern
    fiction
Elly
  Faulkner, W. Collected stories
Fox hunt
  Faulkner, W. Collected stories
Golden land
  Faulkner, W. Collected stories
Hair
  Faulkner, W. Collected stories
Hand upon the waters
  Best of the Best American short stories,
    1915-1950
Honor
  Faulkner, W. Collected stories
The hound
  Bogorad, S. N. and Trevithick, J. eds.
    College miscellany
A justice
  Faulkner, W. Collected stories
  Faulkner, W. Faulkner reader
The leg
  Faulkner, W. Collected stories
Lo!
  Faulkner, W. Collected stories
Mistral
  Faulkner, W. Collected stories
Monk
  Queen, E. pseud. ed. Literature of crime
Mountain victory
  Faulkner, W. Collected stories
Mule in the yard
  Faulkner, W. Collected stories
My Grandmother Millard and General Bed-
    ford Forrest and the Battle of Harry-
    kin Creek
  Faulkner, W. Collected stories
Name for the city
  Prize stories of 1951
Odor of verbena
  Faulkner, W. Faulkner reader
Old man
  Faulkner, W. Faulkner reader
Old people
  Davis, R. G. ed. Ten modern masters
  Schorer, M. ed. The story
Pennsylvania Station
  Faulkner, W. Collected stories
Percy Grimm
  Faulkner, W. Faulkner reader

Red leaves
  Faulkner, W. Collected stories
Rose for Emily
  Burrell, J. A. and Cerf, B. A. eds. An-
    thology of famous American stories
  Faulkner, W. Collected stories
  Faulkner, W. Faulkner reader
  Foerster, N. ed. American poetry and
    prose. 1952 ed.
  West, R. B. and Stallman, R. W. eds.
    Art of modern fiction
Shall not perish
  Faulkner, W. Collected stories
Shingles for the Lord
  Faulkner, W. Collected stories
  Faulkner, W. Faulkner reader
Slouch
  Farrell, J. T. American dream girl
Spotted horses
  Faulkner, W. Faulkner reader
  Felheim, M.; Newman, F. B. and Stein-
    hoff, W. R. eds. Modern short stories
  Gordon, C. and Tate, A. eds. House of
    fiction
  Ludwig, J. B. and Poirier, W. R. eds.
    Stories, British and American
Sunday morning at the Compsons
  Burnett, W. ed. World's best
Tall men
  Faulkner, W. Collected stories
That evening sun
  Blodgett, H. W. ed. Story survey.
    1953 ed.
  Faulkner, W. Collected stories
  Faulkner, W. Faulkner reader
  Heilman, R. B. ed. Modern short stories
  Same as: That evening sun go down
That evening sun go down
  Neider, C. ed. Great short stories from
    the world's literature
  Same as: That evening sun
That will be fine
  Faulkner, W. Collected stories
There was a queen
  Faulkner, W. Collected stories
Tomorrow
  Blaustein, A. P. ed. Fiction goes to
    court
Turnabout
  Faulkner, W. Collected stories
  Faulkner, W. Faulkner reader
  Jensen, P. ed. Fireside book of flying
    stories
Two soldiers
  Faulkner, W. Collected stories
Uncle Willy
  Faulkner, W. Collected stories
Victory
  Faulkner, W. Collected stories
Was
  Davis, R. G. ed. Ten modern masters
  Millett, F. B. ed. Reading fiction
Wash
  Faulkner, W. Collected stories
  Faulkner, W. Faulkner reader

Fauntleroy. Collins, W.

Faust, Frederick, 1892-1944. See Brand, M.
  pseud.

The **fauve.** Humphrey, W.

Favicchio, John
Three buttonholes
Oberfirst, R. ed. 1954 anthology of best
original short-shorts
Favor granted. Milton, M. E.
Fay, Sarah, 1924-
Death of Pierce
Stanford short stories, 1952
Fay, William, 1872-1947
Lady says murder
Argosy (Periodical) Argosy Book of
sports stories
Murder the bum!
Herzberg, M. J. comp. Treasure chest
of sport stories
A nice, clean job
Best detective stories of the year—1950
Touchdown crazy
Herzberg, M. J. comp. Treasure chest
of sport stories
Fe-fi-fo-fum. Steele, W. D.
FEAR
Clark, W. Van T. The pretender
Faulkner, W. That evening sun
Hergesheimer, J. Wild oranges
Keller, D. H. Thing in the cellar
Kipling, R. At the end of the passage
Maugham, W. S. End of the flight
Maupassant, G. de. The duel
Maupassant, G. de. The Horla
Poe, E. A. Fall of the House of Usher
Rath, I. E. Longest day I live
Sansom, W. Little fears
Sansom, W. Vertical ladder
See also Cowardice
Fear. Bellah, J. W.
Fear of innocence. Fiedler, L. A.
Fear planet. Bloch, R.
Fearsome fable. Elliott, B.
Feast of Cats. Coolidge, O. E.
Feast of Nemesis. Munro, H. H.
FEAST OF TABERNACLES. See Sukkoth
Feathers. Sullivan, R.
Feathers. Van Vechten, C.
FEBRUARY
Grimson, M. S. Leap year
FEEBLE-MINDED
Hall, J. B. In the time of demonstrations
Kuehn, S. The hunt
Lardner, R. W. Haircut
Welty, E. Lily Daw and the three ladies
See also Idiocy
Feeling for human interest. Davis, L. R.
Feeney, Thomas Butler
Whiter than snow
Thinker's digest (Periodical) Spoiled
priest, and other stories
Feet of clay. Wodehouse, P. G.
Feet on the ground. Powell, D.
Feild, Bruce
How Abel slew Cain
Dachs, D. ed. Treasury of sports humor
Felder, Dora Fishman, 1917-
Purple hat
American vanguard, 1953
Time for silence
American vanguard, 1953

Felix. Beck, W.
Felsen, Gregor, 1916-
Horatio
Seventeen (Periodical) Nineteen from
Seventeen
Hot rod; condensation
Strang, R. M. and Roberts, R. M. eds.
Teen-age tales v2
Trenton in thirty minutes
Fenner, P. R. comp. Speed, speed, speed
Felsen, Henry Gregor. See Felsen, Gregor
Feminine wiles. Williams, R. E.
FENCES
Betts, D. Mark of distinction
FENCING
Lewis, R. Roman holiday
Fennel, Erik
Doughnut jockey
Bleiler, E. F. and Dikty, T. E. eds. Sci-
ence fiction omnibus: The best science
fiction stories, 1949, 1950
Fenton, Edward, 1917-
Gun shy
Fenner, P. R. comp. Dogs, dogs, dogs
Fenton, Frank, 1904- and **Petracca, Joseph**
Tolliver's travels
Healy, R. J. ed. New tales of space and
time
Ferber, Edna, 1887-
Afternoon of a faun
Burrell, J. A. and Cerf, B. A. eds. An-
thology of famous American stories
Old lady Mandle
Ungar, F. ed. To mother with love
Old man Minick
Leftwich, J. ed. Yisröel. 1952 ed.
Ferguson, Malcolm
Damsel with a dulcimer
Derleth, A. W. ed. Night's yawning peal
Fern Barrie's new plans. Caudill, R.
Ferrara, Jackie, 1930?-
Figurine of love
American vanguard, 1953
FERRETS
Munro, H. H. Sredni Vashtar
Ferrone, John R.
About my sons
Stanford short stories, 1952
Bitter wall
Stanford short stories, 1951
Her own people
Stanford short stories, 1952
Rise of Lorenzo Villari
Stanford short stories, 1953
Ferry of fulfilment. Porter, W. S.
Fessenden's worlds. Hamilton, E.
Fessier, Michael, 1903-
Fascinating stranger
Jenkins, W. F. ed. Great stories of sci-
ence fiction
Man-taming woman
Meredith, S. ed. Bar 2
That's what happened to me
Christ, H. I. and Shostak, J. eds. Short
stories
FESTIVALS
Boyd, J. Fiesta
Buck, F. Elephants!

FESTIVALS—*Continued*
  Coolidge, O. E. Feast of Cats
  Hawthorne, N. Maypole of Merry Mount
Feuchtwanger, Lion, 1884-
  Balance sheet of my life
    Ausubel, N. ed. Treasury of Jewish
    humor
  Mendel Hirsch
    Leftwich, J. ed. Yisröel. 1952 ed.
FEUDS
  Bergengruen, W. Magnanimity contest
  Drinkard, I. N. Mission for baby
  Kantor, M. Life in her hands
  Munro, H. H. The interlopers
  Porter, W. S. Blackjack bargainer
  Porter, W. S. Squaring the circle
  Porter, W. S. Technical error
  Stuart, J. Land of our enemies
  Stuart, J. When mountain men make
    peace
  Trollope, A. Malachi's Cove
  Van Doren, M. Not a natural man
Fever flower. Grau, S. A.
Fickle fortune. Porter, W. S.
FICTITIOUS ANIMALS. See Animals,
  Mythical
The **fiddler.** Melville, H.
Fiddler, play fast, play faster. Sawyer, R.
Fiedler, Leslie A. 1917-
  Fear of innocence
  Best American short stories, 1950
Field, Rachel Lyman, 1894-1942
  A woman of virtue
  Brentano, F. ed. The word lives on
Field, S. S. 1906-
  Good-by to Cap'm John
    Southern review. Anthology of stories
    from the Southern review
Field of flowers. Aiken, C. P.
FIELD SPORTS. See Hunting; Track
  athletics
Field study. Phillips, P.
FIELD TRIALS. See Dogs
Fielder's choice. Coombs, C. I.
Fielding, Edward
  Fountain of youth
    This week magazine. This week's short-
    short stories
Fields of wheat. Lynch, J. A.
FIENDS. See Crime and criminals
Fiesta. Boyd, J.
FIESTAS. See Festivals
Fife's house. Boyle, K.
Fifteen. Sherman, D.
Fifth commandment. Hutchins, M. P. M.
Fifth friend. Kjelgaard, J. A.
Fifth wheel. Porter, W. S.
Fifty-carat jinx. Blochman, L. G.
Fifty-dollar bottle. Cousins, M.
Fifty-first dragon. Broun, H. C.
Fifty-four, forty and fight. Wylie, P.
Fifty grand. Hemingway, E.
Fifty marks. Ditzen, R.
Fifty pounds. Coppard, A. E.
Fifty yard dash. Saroyan, W.

FIG
  Sultan, S. Fugue of the fig tree
The **fight.** Crane, S.
Fight between Jappe and Do Escobar,
  Mann, T.
Fight number twenty-five. Stuart, J.
Fighter. Maxwell, J. A.
FIGHTING. See Boxing; Dueling; Fight-
  ing, Hand-to-hand
FIGHTING, HAND-TO-HAND
  Crane, S. Blue Hotel
  Crane, S. The fight
  Mahoney, W. B. Wrong guy
  Mann, T. Fight between Jappe and Do
    Escobar
  Modell, J. Day in the sun
  O'Flaherty, L. The challenge
  Sansom, W. Boiler room
  Walsh, M. Quiet man
Fighting finish. Lacy, M.
Figurine of love. Ferrara, J.
FIJI ISLANDS
  Michener, J. A. Mynah birds
Filboid Studge, the story of a mouse that
  helped. Munro, H. H.
Filial sentiments of a parracide. Proust, M.
Fillmore, Parker Hoysted, 1878-1944
  Clever Manka
    Fenner, P. R. comp. Fools and funny
    fellows
  Mary, Mary, so contrary
    Fenner, P. R. comp. Fools and funny
    fellows
A **filly** owns a fella! Armstrong, M.
Film library. Van Vogt, A. E.
Filmer. Wells, H. G.
Final command. Van Vogt, A. E.
Final embarrassment. Williams, W. C.
Final problem. Doyle, Sir A. C.
Finality unlimited. Wandrei, D.
Financial world. Brophy, B.
FINANCIERS. See Capitalists and finan-
  ciers
Financing Finnegan. Fitzgerald, F. S. K.
Find the woman. Millar, K.
Findlay, D. K.
  Suicide on skis
    Herzberg, M. J. comp. Treasure chest
    of sport stories
Fine place for the cat. Bonham, M.
Fineman, Irving, 1893-
  In the fields of Boaz
    Selden, R. ed. Ways of God and men
  Interview with Ahashuerus
    Ausubel, N. ed. Treasury of Jewish
    humor
Finest story in the world. Kipling, R.
Finger, Charles Joseph, 1871-1941
  Na-Ha the fighter
    Hazeltine, A. I. comp. Selected stories
    for teen-agers
  Yankee captain in Patagonia
    Fenner, P. R. comp. Pirates, pirates pi-
    rates
Finger man. Prince, J. and Prince, H.
Fingers of fear. MacDonald, P.

Finish, good lady. Auchincloss, L.

Finished. De Camp, L. S.

FINLAND

20th century

Sillanpää, F. E. Night of the harvest festival

Waltari, M. T. Moonscape

Finney, Jack, 1912?-
Breakfast in bed
Collier's, the national weekly. Collier's best
I'm scared
Heinlein, R. A. ed. Tomorrow, the stars
Third level
Magazine of fantasy and science fiction
Best from Fantasy and science fiction; 2d ser.

FIRE
London, J. To build a fire

Fire and the sword. Robinson, F. M.

Fire balloons. Bradbury, R.

Fire-boy of Dunsoon. Cutler, J. L.

FIRE EXTINCTION. See Firemen

Fire in the bush. Warwick, J.

Fire killer. Frazee, S.

FIREARMS
Bonner, P. H. Made to measure

The **firebird.** Doughty, LeG. S.

Fireboat style. Gallister, M. pseud.

FIREMEN
Brier, H. M. Sky hook
Gallister, M. pseud. Fireboat style
Porter, W. S. Foreign policy of Company 99
Sansom, W. In the morning
Sansom, W. Journey into smoke
See also Fire extinction; Fires

FIREMEN, RAILROAD. See Railroads—Employees

FIRES
Caldwell, E. Grass fire
Kirtland, A. Trial by fire
Newell, A. S. Grandpop comes home
Strong, J. Hired man
Vickers, R. Man with the sneer
Walton, H. Episode on Dhee Minor
Warwick, J. Fire in the bush
Welty, E. The burning

FIRES (AT SEA)
Conrad, J. Youth
Floherty, J. J. Sea afire

FIRES, FOREST. See Forest fires

Fires within. Clarke, A. C.

Firewater. Klass, P.

First ally. Annixter, P. pseud.

First autumn. Caldwell, E.

First blood. Household, G.

First-born. Coolidge, O. E.

First car. Carter, M.

First Christmas tree. Van Dyke, H.

First confession. O'Donovan, M.

First contact. Jenkins, W. F.

First death of her life. Taylor, E.

First disciple. Davis, A. L.

First face. Enright, E.

First Fourth in White Pine. Hart, F.

First harpist. Casey, M. W.

First love. Kaufman, A.

First love. O'Donovan, M.

First love. Turgenev, I. S.

First love. Welty, E.

First sad facts. Stein, M.

First stone. Mason, G. S.

First war party. Bowman, J. C.

First you take a live goat. Barr, J. pseud.

Fischer, Bruno, 1908-
Dog died first
Best detective stories of the year—1950
My Aunt Celia
Mystery Writers of America, inc. Butcher, baker, murder-maker
Nobody's business
Mystery Writers of America, inc. Crooks' tour

Fish, Horace, 1885-
Wrists on the door
Thinker's digest (Periodical) Spoiled priest, and other stories

FISH. See Fishes

Fish are such liars. Pertwee, R.

Fish bites man. Wylie, P.

Fish supper. Aiken, C. P.

Fish wagon. Comstock, H. B.

Fish who could close his eyes. Clark, W. Van T.

Fisher, Dorothea Frances (Canfield) 1879-
As ye sow—
Brentano, F. ed. The word lives on
Lohan, R. and Lohan, M. eds. New Christmas treasury
Drop in the bucket
Burnett, W. ed. World's best
Flint and fire
Stegner, W. E.; Scowcroft, R. and Ilyin, B. eds. Writer's art
Forgotten mother
Ungar, F. ed. To mother with love
Sex education
Best of the Best American short stories, 1915-1950
Sunset at sixteen
Hazeltine, A. I. comp. Selected stories for teen-agers
Witch doctor
McFarland, W. K. comp. Then it happened

Fisher, Philip M.
Lights
Conklin, G. and Conklin, L. T. eds. Supernatural reader

Fisher, Rudolph, 1897-1934
Common meter
Ford, N. A. and Fagget, H. L. eds. Best short stories by Afro-American writers (1925-1950)

The **fisherman.** Doty, W. L.

Fisherman's luck. Matthews, R. D.

FISHERMEN
  Canning, V. The smuggler
  Connolly, J. B. The trawler
  Maugham, W. S. Salvatore
  Maupassant, G. de. At sea
  Mayse, A. Midnight Mike
  Peretz, I. L. Miracle on the sea
  Poe, E. A. Descent into the maelström
  Thériault, Y. Jeannette
  Ullman, J. R. Pau
  Watkins, R. H. Offshore
  Welty, E. At the landing
    See also Fishing

Fishers of the air. Roberts, Sir C. G. D.

FISHES
  Conner, R. The long pike
  Gordimer, N. The catch
  Li Fu-yen. Man who became a fish
  Pertwee, R. Fish are such liars
  Walsh, M. Honest fisherman

Fishin' Jimmy. Slosson, A. T.

FISHING
  Beal, F. Bertie, the uninvited
  Bonner, P. H. Blue charm
  Bonner, P. H. Caddis hatch
  Bonner, P. H. Foul is fair
  Bonner, P. H. Rajah's Rock
  Bonner, P. H. Velia
  Ford, C. Trout widows
  Gordon, A. Sea devil
  Gordon, C. Old Red
  Grau, S. A. Joshua
  Keith, S. Siren of hope
  Macfarlan, A. A. Tackle buster
  Perrault, E. G. Silver King
  Person, W. T. Monster of Blue-Hole Lake
  Person, W. T. Won by a tail
  Sherman, H. M. Porky, the outboarder
  Slosson, A. T. Fishin' Jimmy
  Spiller, B. L. Net profit
  Verga, G. Ugly weather
  Walsh, M. Honest fisherman
  Watkins, R. H. Offshore
  Welty, E. Wide net
  Wylie, P. Best of Crunch and Des; 21
    stories
  Wylie, P. Sporting blood
  Wylie, P. Way of all fish
    See also Fishermen

Fishing excursion. Maupassant, G. de

Fishman, Joseph Fulling
  Old Calamity tries a bluff
    Mystery Writers of America, inc.
    Maiden murders

Fisk Fogle. Van Doren, M.

FIST FIGHTING. See Fighting, Hand-to-hand

Fistful of Alamo heroes. Karchmer, S.

Fitt, Mary, pseud. See Freeman, Kathleen

The **fittest.** MacLean, K.

Fitts, Henry K.
  Rattlesnake Trail
    Owen, F. ed. Teen-age winter sports
    stories

Fitzgerald, Bill
  Iron maiden
    Best Army short stories, 1950

Fitzgerald, Francis Scott Key, 1896-1940
  Absolution
    Fitzgerald, F. S. K. Stories
  Alcoholic case
    Fitzgerald, F. S. K. Stories
  Baby party
    Fitzgerald, F. S. K. Stories
  Babylon revisited
    Bogorad, S. N. and Trevithick, J. eds.
      College miscellany
    Fitzgerald, F. S. K. Stories
    Foerster, N. ed. American poetry and
      prose. 1952 ed.
    Ludwig, J. B. and Poirier, W. R. eds.
      Stories, British and American
  Bernice bobs her hair
    Fitzgerald, F. S. K. Stories
  The bowl
    Grayson, C. ed. Fourth round
  Bridal party
    Fitzgerald, F. S. K. Stories
  Captured shadow
    Fitzgerald, F. S. K. Stories
  Crazy Sunday
    Fitzgerald, F. S. K. Stories
  Curious case of Benjamin Button
    Kuebler, H. W. ed. Treasury of science
      fiction classics
  Diamond as big as the Ritz
    Fitzgerald, F. S. K. Stories
  Family in the wind
    Fitzgerald, F. S. K. Stories
  Financing Finnegan
    Fitzgerald, F. S. K. Stories
  Freshest boy
    Blodgett, H. W. ed. Story survey.
      1953 ed.
    Fitzgerald, F. S. K. Stories
    Schorer, M. ed. The story
  Ice palace
    Fitzgerald, F. S. K. Stories
  Jelly-bean
    Shaw, H. and Bement, D. Reading the
      short story
  Last of the belles
    Fitzgerald, F. S. K. Stories
    Lynskey, W. C. ed. Reading modern
      fiction
  Long way out
    Fitzgerald, F. S. K. Stories
  Lost decade
    Fitzgerald, F. S. K. Stories
  Magnetism
    Fitzgerald, F. S. K. Stories
  May Day
    Fitzgerald, F. S. K. Stories
  Pat Hobby himself: a patriotic short
    Fitzgerald, F. S. K. Stories
  Pat Hobby himself: two old-timers
    Fitzgerald, F. S. K. Stories
  Rich boy
    Burrell, J. A. and Cerf, B. A. eds.
      Anthology of famous American stories
    Fitzgerald, F. S. K. Stories
    Waite, H. O. and Atkinson, B. P. eds.
      Literature for our time
  Rough crossing
    Fitzgerald, F. S. K. Stories
  Scandal detectives
    Fitzgerald, F. S. K. Stories

Fitzgerald, Francis S. K.—*Continued*
  "The sensible thing"
    Fitzgerald, F. S. K. Stories
  Three hours between planes
    Fitzgerald, F. S. K. Stories
  Two wrongs
    Fitzgerald, F. S. K. Stories
  Winter dreams
    Fitzgerald, F. S. K. Stories
  Woman from Twenty-One
    Esquire (Periodical) Girls from Esquire
  Woman with a past
    Fitzgerald, F. S. K. Stories

Fitzsimmons, Betty Jung
  Christmas rose
    Elmquist, R. M. ed. Fifty years to
      Christmas

Five Alls. Davis, F. M.

Five captains. Chute, B. J.

5,271,009. Bester, A.

Five orange pips. Doyle, Sir A. C.

Five parts of summer. Littledale, H. A.

Five wives of Fergus O'Malley. Maguire,
  R. A.

Five years in the Marmalade. Krepps, R. W.

The fix. Roberts, R. M.

The flag. Bates, H. E.

Flag paramount. Porter, W. S.

Flagman Thiel. Hauptmann, G. J. R.

FLAGMEN. See Railroads—Employees

FLAGS
  Hart, F. First Fourth in White Pine
  Porter, W. S. Flag paramount

Flame on the frontier. Johnson, D. M.

Flanagan, Thomas
  Cold winds of Adesta
    Queen, E. pseud. ed. Queen's awards:
      7th ser.

Flash of lightning. Rawlings, C. A.

FLASHBACKS. See Retrospective stories

Flashing spikes. O'Rourke, F.

Flat town. Boyd, J.

Flaubert, Gustave, 1821-1880
  Legend of St Julian the Hospitaller
    Dupee, F. W. ed. Great French short
      novels
    Neider, C. ed. Great short stories from
      the world's literature
  Simple heart
    Geist, S. ed. French stories and tales
    Gordon, C. and Tate, A. eds. House of
      fiction
    Neider, C. ed. Short novels of the
      masters

Flaw. MacDonald, J. D.

The flea. Sawyer, R.

FLEAS
  Collier, J. Gavin O'Leary

Fleg, Edmond, 1874-
  The adulteress
    Leftwich, J. ed. Yisröel. 1952 ed.
  Solomon the King
    Selden, R. ed. Ways of God and men

Fleming, Joseph S.
  Ride 'im Chick Norris
    Furman, A. L. ed. Teen-age horse
      stories

Flesh and the devil. De Vries, P.

Fletcher, Grace Nies
  Texas Christmas 1872
    Elmquist, R. M. ed. Fifty years of
      Christmas

Fletcher, Inglis (Clark) 1888-
  White leopard
    American boy (Periodical) American
      boy Adventure stories

Fletcher, Vivian, 1913-
  Coda to a writers' conference
    Story (Periodical) Story; no. 4

FLIERS. See Air pilots

FLIES
  Pirandello, L. The fly
  Porges, A. The flies

FLIGHT
  Bradbury, R. Flying machine
  Jenkins, W. F. Historical note
  Keller, D. H. Flying fool
  Knight, E. M. Flying Yorkshireman
  Lieberman, R. Sister Innocent and the
    useful miracle
  Stapledon, W. O. Flying men
  Tale of a chemist

Flight for life. Doyle, Sir A. C.

Flight into Egypt. Rosegger, P.

Flight south. Seager, A.

Flight that failed. Hull, E. M.

Flight through the dark. Angell, R.

Flight to forever. Anderson, P.

Flimsy walls. Parker, C. W.

Flint and fire. Fisher, D. F. C.

Flo. Kneale, N.

Floherty, John Joseph, 1882-
  Duel at 70 miles an hour
    Fenner, P. R. comp. Speed, speed, speed
  Sea afire
    Fenner, J. J. comp. Stories of the sea

The flood. Parker, Sir G. bart.

FLOODS
  Becker, S. D. Baptism of some importance
  Brace, G. W. Deep water man
  Burman, B. L. Children of Noah
  Cave, H. B. Peril of the river
  Harte, B. High-water mark
  Kantor, M. Life in her hands
  MacDonald, P. Man out of the rain
  Marquis, D. Country doctor
  Munro, H. H. The guests
  Welty, E. At the landing

Flora, Fletcher
  Torrid zone
    Queen, E. pseud. ed. Queen's awards:
      7th ser.

Florence, Gordon Louis, 1915-
  All in one day
    Oberfirst, R. ed. 1954 anthology of best
      original short-shorts

FLORENCE. See Italy—Florence

Florian Slappey—private eye. Cohen, O. R.

FLORICULTURE. See Gardens and gardening

FLORIDA
   Curtis, K. Cruises in the sun; 3 stories
   Granberry, E. Trip to Czardis
   Rawlings, M. K. Benny and the bird-dogs
   Rawlings, M. K. Gal young un
   Rinehart, M. R. Murder and the south wind

St. Petersburg
   Lardner, R. W. Golden honeymoon

Flotsam and jetsam. Maugham, W. S.

The flower. Rugel, M.

FLOWER GARDENING. See Gardens and gardening

Flower of Utah. Doyle, Sir A. C.

Flowering Judas. Porter, K. A.

Flowering of the strange orchid. See Wells, H. G. Strange orchid

FLOWERS. See Gardens and gardening; also names of particular flowers, e.g. Orchids

Flowers for an angel. Morland, N.

Flowers for Marjorie. Welty, E.

Fluffy. Waldo, E. H.

Flute-player. O'Flaherty, L.

FLUTE PLAYERS. See Musicians—Flute players

Fluted arrow. Mowery, W. B.

The fly. Pirandello, L.

The fly. Porges, A.

Fly away home. Jackson, R. B.

Fly chaser. Sherman, H. M.

Fly in the coffin. Caldwell, E.

FLYERS. See Air pilots

Flying Cloud in the Roaring Forties. Sperry, A.

Flying Dutchman. Moore, W.

Flying fool. Keller, D. H.

Flying machine. Bradbury, R.

Flying men. Stapledon, W. O.

Flying out of Mrs Barnard Hollis. Harvey, W. F.

FLYING SAUCERS
   Doar, G. Outer limit
   Holmes, K. Man who rode the saucer

Flying stars. Chesterton, G. K.

Flying switch. Davis, H. L.

Flying Yorkshireman. Knight, E. M.

Flynn, Thomas Theodore, 1902-
   Congo cargo
      Argosy (Periodical) Argosy Book of sea stories

FOG
   Heard, G. Great fog
   Porter, W. S. Fog in Santone

Fog and the saints. Anderson, M.

Fog horn. Bradbury, R.

FOG HORNS
   Bradbury, R. Fog horn

Fog in Santone. Porter, W. S.

Foggy. Hall, D.

Foley, Martha
   Americans all
      Lantz, J. E. ed. Stories of Christian living
   Glory, glory, hallelujah
      Ribalow, H. U. ed. World's greatest boxing stories

Foley, Teresa
   Sam and the dean
      Story (Periodical) Story; no. 1

FOLK TALES. See Legends and folk tales

FOLKLORE. See Legends and folk tales

Follow that car. Roberts, R. M.

Fonger, Hilary
   Ripeness of the time
      Seventeen (Periodical) Nineteen from Seventeen

Fontaine, Robert Louis, 1912?-
   God hit a home run
      Dachs, D. ed. Treasury of sports humor
   How do you say good-bye?
      McFarland, W. K. comp. Then it happened

FOOD
   Hays, L. Banquet and a half
   Huysmans, J. K. Monsieur Folantin
   Maugham, W. S. The luncheon
   Munro, H. H. Blind spot
   Munro, H. H. The Chaplet
   Munro, H. H. Quail seed
   Nadir, I. M. Nuttose and protose
   Nadir, I. M. Ruined by success
   Renard, J. Spoiled cake

      See also Bread; Breakfasts; Dinners and Dining

Fool about a horse. Santee, R.

Fool dog. Vetter, M. M.

The fool-killer. Porter, W. S.

Foolish one. Davies, R.

Foolproof frame-up. Klingsberg, H. M.

FOOLS AND JESTERS
   Baudelaire, C. P. Death of a hero
   Benét, S. V. Johnny Pye and the fool killer
   Poe, E. A. Hop-Frog

Fool's mate. Ellin, S.

FOOTBALL
   Brondfield, J. That's my boy
   Brush, K. I. Football girl
   Chute, B. J. Alias All-American
   Chute, B. J. Bench warmer
   Chute, B. J. Big shot
   Chute, B. J. Master mind
   Coombs, C. I. Headline halfback
   Coombs, C. I. Hillbilly halfback
   Coombs, C. I. Newton man
   Coombs, C. I. Unlucky number
   Fay, W. Touchdown crazy
   Fitzgerald, F. S. K. The bowl
   Heinz, W. C. Man's game
   Heyliger, W. Man who wouldn't break
   Herndon, B. Run, iron man
   Holder, W. Cash and carry guy
   Johnson, H. She'll be sorry
   Miers, E. S. Scrub cure
   Platt, G. Touchdown for Rex
   Runyon, D. Hold 'em Yale

FOOTBALL—*Continued*
Shaw, I. Eighty-yard run
Sylvester, H. Return of the hero
Tunis, J. R. Ronald leaves the Academy
Young, S. Maloney's last stand

Football girl. Brush, K. I.

Foote, John Taintor, 1881-1950
Allegheny
Bloch, M. ed. Favorite dog stories
Big train
Foote, J. T. Hoofbeats
Blister
Foote, J. T. Hoofbeats
Class
Creamer, J. B. comp. Twenty-two
stories about horses and men
Foote, J. T. Hoofbeats
Fowl disaster
Foote, J. T. Hoofbeats
Look of eagles
Foote, J. T. Hoofbeats
Herzberg, M. J. comp. Treasure chest of
sport stories
Old pastures
Foote, J. T. Hoofbeats
Ole man Sanford
Foote, J. T. Hoofbeats
Salvation
Foote, J. T. Hoofbeats
Shame on you
Foote, J. T. Hoofbeats
Spirit dope
Foote, J. T. Hoofbeats
Tip in time
Foote, J. T. Hoofbeats
Très Jolie
Foote, J. T. Hoofbeats
Two ringers
Creamer, J. B. comp. Twenty-two
stories about horses and men
Foote, J. T. Hoofbeats

Foote, Shelby, 1916-
Ride out
Aswell, M. L. W. ed. New short novels

Footnote. Farrell, J. T.

Footprint in the sky. Carr, J. D.

Footprints in the jungle. Maugham, W. S.

For a horse. James, W.

For a master's wages. Claudy, C. H.

For Esmé—with love and squalor. Salinger,
J. D.

For girlhood and for love. Lowry, R. J. C.

For love of a man. London, J.

For men only. Wilsey, R. G.

For military merit. Lukert, E. P.

For the blood is the life. Crawford, F. M.

For the duration of the war. Munro, H. H.

For the honor of XDY. Kahmann, M. C.

For the last time. Jordan, G.

For the love of a race horse. Cooke, A. A.

For the public. Kahn, B. I.

For the sake of freedom. James, W.

For the want of a cigarette. Schneider,
G. W.

For they know not what they do. Steele,
W. D.

For this is Christmas Day. Sangster, M. E.

For value received. Deming, R.

For white men only. Farrell, J. T.

Foran, John P.
The kiss-off
Best detective stories of the year—1952

Forbes, Esther, 1894-
"Disperse, ye rebels!"
Fenner, P. R. comp. Yankee Doodle

Forbidden buzzards. Munro, H. H.

Force of circumstance. Maugham, W. S.

Ford, Corey, 1902-
Man of his own
This week magazine. This week's short-
short stories
Slipstream
Bloch, M. ed. Favorite dog stories
Snake dance
Lass, A. H. and Horowitz, A. eds.
Stories for youth
Trout widows
Dachs, D. ed. Treasury of sports humor

Ford, James Lauren, 1854-1928
Spiritualist's tale
Carrington, H. ed. Week-end book of
ghost stories

Ford, Nick Aaron, 1904-
Let the church roll on
Ford, N. A. and Faggett, H. L. eds.
Best short stories by Afro-American
writers (1925-1950)
Majesty of the law
Ford, N. A. and Faggett, H. L. eds.
Best short stories by Afro-American
writers (1925-1950)
No room in the inn
Ford, N. A. and Faggett, H. L. eds.
Best short stories by Afro-American
writers (1925-1950)
One way to victory
Ford, N. A. and Faggett, H. L. eds.
Best short stories by Afro-American
writers (1925-1950)

Fordie. Brophy, B.

Forecast. Jones. R. F.

FOREIGN CORRESPONDENTS. See
Journalists

FOREIGN LEGION (FRENCH ARMY)
Miller, W. H. Message to the Camel Corps

Foreign policy of Company 99. Porter, W. S.

FOREIGN SERVICE. See Civil service

The foreigner. Adams, B. M.

The foreigner. Saroyan, W.

Forest of the night. Weston, C. G.

FOREST FIRES
Anderson, E. V. Smell of smoke
Cain, J. M. Brush fire
Carter, R. G. Parachute warning
Roberts, Sir C. G. D. Gauntlet of fire
Stewart, G. R. Death of the glen

Forest of the South. Gordon, C.

Forester, Cecil Scott, 1899-
Bower of roses
Forester, C. S. The nightmare

Forester, Cecil S.—*Continued*

Evidence
  Forester, C. S. The nightmare
Head and the feet
  Forester, C. S. The nightmare
Hornblower and Noah's ark
  Forester, C. S. Mr Midshipman Hornblower
Hornblower and the cargo of rice
  Forester, C. S. Mr Midshipman Hornblower
Hornblower and the even chance
  Forester, C. S. Mr Midshipman Hornblower
Hornblower and the examination for lieutenant
  Forester, C. S. Mr Midshipman Hornblower
Hornblower and the man who felt queer
  Forester, C. S. Mr Midshipman Hornblower
Hornblower and the man who saw God
  Forester, C. S. Mr Midshipman Hornblower
Hornblower and the penalty of failure
  Forester, C. S. Mr Midshipman Hornblower
Hornblower and the Spanish galleys
  Forester, C. S. Mr Midshipman Hornblower
Hornblower, the Duchess, and the Devil
  Forester, C. S. Mr Midshipman Hornblower
Hornblower, the frogs, and the lobsters
  Forester, C. S. Mr Midshipman Hornblower
The hostage
  Forester, C. S. The nightmare
Indecision
  Forester, C. S. The nightmare
Letters in evidence
  Queen, E. pseud. ed. Literature of crime
Man whose wishes came true
  Queen, E. pseud. ed. Queen's awards: 6th ser.
Miriam's miracle
  Forester, C. S. The nightmare
Physiology of fear
  Forester, C. S. The nightmare
To be given to God
  Forester, C. S. The nightmare
The unbelievable
  Forester, C. S. The nightmare
Wandering Gentile
  Forester, C. S. The nightmare

FORESTERS
Munro, H. H. The interlopers

FORESTS AND FORESTRY
Hudson, W. H. Mysterious forest
Van Vogt, A. E. Process

Forever and the earth. Bradbury, R.

Forever Florida. Gizycka, F.

Forewarned. Munro, H. H.

FORGERY
Collins, W. Fauntleroy

FORGERY OF WORKS OF ART
Harvey, W. F. Old masters

Forget-me-not. Temple, W. F.

Forgetfulness. Campbell, J. W.

FORGIVENESS
Goudge, E. Canticle of the sun

Forgiveness of Tenchu Taen. Kummer, F. A.

Forgotten. Miller, P. S.

Forgotten enemy. Clarke, A. C.

Forgotten greeting cards. Lloyd, B. B.

Forgotten island. Coatsworth, E. J.

Forgotten mother. Fisher, D. F. C.

Forgotten world. Hamilton, E.

The forks. Powers, J. F.

Forster, Edward Morgan, 1879-
Celestial omnibus
  Cerf, B. A. and Moriarty, H. C. eds. Anthology of famous British stories
  Ludwig, J. B. and Poirier, W. R. eds. Stories, British and American
  Shaw, H. and Bement, D. Reading the short story
Curate's friend
  Conklin, G. and Conklin, L. T. eds. Supernatural reader
Machine stops
  Felheim, M.; Newman, F. B. and Steinhoff, W. R. eds. Modern short stories
  Kuebler, H. W. ed. Treasury of science fiction classics
  Waite, H. O. and Atkinson, B. P. eds. Literature for our time
Mr Andrews
  Heilman, R. B. ed. Modern short stories
Other side of the hedge
  Ludwig, J. B. and Poirier, W. R. eds. Stories, British and American
  Lynskey, W. C. ed. Reading modern fiction
The trial
  Burnett, W. ed. World's best

Fortune of Arcus Kane. Auchincloss, L.

FORTUNE-TELLING
Collier, J. In the cards
Porter, W. S. Tobin's palm
Van Doren, M. Consider courage
Winslow, T. S. Angie Lee's fortune

Forty-third division. Bates, R.

Forty years of firewood. Anderson, D.

The fossickers. Michener, J. A.

Foster, Bennett
Outlaws are in town
  Meredith, S. ed. Bar 2

Foster, Constance Jackson, 1899-
It's a man's world
  Stowe, A. comp. It's a date

Foster, Michael, 1904-
Later
  Thinker's digest (Periodical) Spoiled priest, and other stories
Present for Christmas
  Saturday evening post (Periodical) Saturday evening post stories, 1951

FOSTER CHILDREN
Annett, W. S. The relic
Cooke, A. A. Returning good for evil
Devin, B. The rattle
Ringwood, G. P. Little ghost

FOSTER CHILDREN—*Continued*
Rosenberg, E. Happy one
Stevenson, R. L. Treasure of Franchard
Wharton, E. N. J. Mission of Jane
See also Foundlings; Orphans
Foster, you're dead. Dick, P. K.
Foul is fair. Bonner, P. H.
Found out. Haycox, E.
FOUNDLINGS
Goyen, W. Pore Perrie
FOUNTAIN OF YOUTH. See Rejuvenation
Fountain of youth. Fielding, E.
Four blind men. Brown, F.
Four bottles of beer. Williams, W. C.
Four brothers. Van Doren, M.
Four-dimensional roller-press. Olsen, B.
Four Dutchmen. Maugham, W. S.
Four fathom fury. Coombs, C. I.
Four freedoms. Newhouse, E.
Four in one. Knight, D.
Four meetings. James, H.
Four men and a box. Barnard, L. G.
Four-minute mile. Rackowe, A.
Four of a kind. Cooke, A. A.
Four-poster. Munby, A. N. L.
Four-ring circus. Chute, B. J.
The fourflusher. Perry, G. S.
Fournier, Alain, 1886-1914
Miracle of the farmer's wife
Fremantle, A. J. ed. Mothers
Fourth day out from Santa Cruz. Bowles, P. F.
Fourth degree. Barry, J.
FOURTH DIMENSION
Jenkins, W. F. Sidewise in time
Kuttner, H. Time locker
Olsen, B. Four-dimensional roller-press
Fourth-dimensional demonstrator. Jenkins, W. F.
Fourth dynasty. Winterbotham, R. R.
Fourth in Salvador. Porter, W. S.
Fourth man. Russell, J.
FOURTH OF JULY CELEBRATIONS
Hart, F. First Fourth in White Pine
Porter, W. S. Fourth in Salvador
Fourth point. Claudy, C. H.
Fowl disaster. Foote, J. T.
Fowler, Bertram Baynes, 1893-
Some can't take it
Eaton, H. T. ed. Short stories
Fox, James M. pseud. See Knipscheer, James M. W.
Fox, John, 1862-1919
Courtin' on Cutshin
Summers, H. S. ed. Kentucky story
Knight of the Cumberland
Scribner treasury
Fox, Monroe L. 1914?-
Seeing eye dog
Bloch, M. ed. Favorite dog stories

Fox, Norman Arnold, 1911-
Bet the wild queen!
Western Writers of America. Bad men and good
Only the dead ride proudly
Western Writers of America. Holsters and heroes
The fox. Lawrence, D. H.
The fox and the forest. Bradbury, R.
Fox hunt. Faulkner, W.
FOX HUNTING
Boyd, J. Away! Away!
Caldwell, E. Negro in the well
Faulkner, W. Fox hunt
Kantor, M. Voice of Bugle Ann
McCauley, M. C. Li'l Reynard
Munro, H. H. The bag
Munro, H. H. Esmé
Somerville, E. A. O. and Martin, V. F. Philippa's fox-hunt
Surtees, R. S. Hunting scenes; 26 stories
Tregarthen, J. C. Great run
Williamson, H. Trapper's mates
Fox in the forest. Bradbury, R.
"Fox-in-the-morning." Porter, W. S.
Fox in the Pennine Hills. Proctor, M.
FOXES
Kjelgaard, J. A. Blood on the ice
Lawrence, D. H. The fox
Seton, E. T. Springfield fox
Tregarthen, J. C. Great run
Foxhole in Washington. Schulberg, B. W.
Foxholes of Mars. Leiber, E.
Fraerman, Ruvim Isaevich
The expedition
Guerney, B. G. comp. New Russian stories
A fragment. Chekhov, A. P.
France, Anatole, 1844-1924
Manuscript of a village doctor
Blodgett, H. W. ed. Story survey. 1953 ed.
Our lady's juggler
Lamb, L. ed. Family book of best loved stories
Procurator of Judæa
Selden, R. ed. Ways of God and men
FRANCE
15th century
Stevenson, R. L. Sire de Malétroit's door
16th century
Chambers, R. W. Demoiselle d'Ys
Lewis, J. Wife of Martin Guerre
17th century
Blackburn, E. R. Christiane the Huguenot
18th century—1789-1799
Irving, W. Adventure of the German student
1870-1940
Macfarlan, A. A. Camp at Saint Adrien
1940-1945
Macfarlan, A. A. Danger by candlelight
Avignon
See France, Provincial and rural—Avignon

FRANCE—*Continued*

Marseilles

Collier, J. If youth knew if age could

Paris

Charteris, L. Paris: The covetous headsman

Paris—15th century

Stevenson, R. L. Lodging for the night

Paris—20th century

Collier, J. Old acquaintance
Crémieux, B. The traveller
Farrell, J. T. Paris scene: 1931
Fitzgerald, F. S. K. Babylon revisited
Maugham, W. S. Appearance and reality

Provence

See France, Provincial and rural—Provence

Pyrénees-Orientales

See France, Provincial and rural—

FRANCE, PROVINCIAL AND RURAL
Becker, S. D. Baptism of some importance
Maugham, W. S. The unconquered

Avignon

Fabre, J. H. C. Story of my cats

Provence

Daudet, A. M. Seguin's goat

Pyrénees-Orientales

Collier, J. Witch's money
Franchise. Neville, K.

FRANCIS I, KING OF FRANCE, 1494-1547
Bergengruen, W. Trivulzio and the King

FRANCIS OF ASSISI, SAINT, 1182-1226
Untermeyer, L. Donkey of God

Francis, Owen, 1898-
Ladies call on Mr Pussick
    Blodgett, H. W. ed. Story survey. 1953 ed.
Francis cures the leper. White, H. C.

FRANCISCANS
Powers, J. F. Lions, harts, leaping does

FRANCO-GERMAN WAR, 1870-1871
Maupassant, G. de. La Mère Sauvage

FRANCO-PRUSSIAN WAR. See Franco-German War, 1870-1871

Frank, Hans
Beyond the grave
    Ungar, F. ed. To mother with love

Frank, Pat, 1908-
The madman
    Argosy (Periodical) Argosy Book of adventure stories
Those wily Americans
    This week magazine. This week's short-short stories

Frank, Waldo David, 1889-
Under the dome
    Leftwich, J. ed. Yisröel. 1952 ed.
    Same as: Under the dome: Aleph
Under the dome: Aleph
    Ribalow, H. U. ed. This land, these people
    Same as: Under the dome

Frank and honest. Upson, W. H.
Frank takes a brother's privilege. Trollope, A.

Frankau, Gilbert, 1884-1952
An outlier from his tribe
    Leftwich, J. ed. Yisröel. 1952 ed.

Frankau, Pamela, 1908-
Jezebel covets a vineyard
    Selden, R. ed. Ways of God and men
Frankenstein—unlimited. Highstone, H. A.
Frankfurt in our blood. Boyle, K.
Frankie the newspaperman. Williams, W. C.
Frankincense and myrrh. Broun, H. C.

Franklin, George Cory, 1872-
Snip; the dog that became a coyote
    Harper, W. comp. Dog show

Franzos, Karl Emil, 1848-1904
Saviour of the people
    Leftwich, J. ed. Yisröel. 1952 ed.
Shylock in Czernowitz
    Ausubel, N. ed. Treasury of Jewish humor

FRATERNITIES. See Greek letter societies

Fraternity. McCall, M. C.
A fratricide. Kafka, F.

FRAUD
Annett, W. S. The relic
Collier, J. Sleeping Beauty
Russell, B. A. W. R. 3d earl. Infraredioscope
Stout, R. Cop's gift
    See also Swindlers and swindling

Fraudulent skunk. Guthrie, A. B.

Frazee, Steve
Fire killer
    Meredith, S. ed. Bar 2
Graveyard shift
    Best detective stories of the year—1954
Great medicine
    Meredith, S. ed. Bar 3
Luck of Riley
    Western Writers of America. Holsters and heroes
Man at Gantt's Place
    Meredith, S. ed. Bar 1 roundup of best western stories
My brother down there
    Best American short stories, 1954
    Queen, E. pseud. ed. Queen's awards: 8th ser.

The freak. Barker, A. L.

FREAKS. See Deformities

Free as the air. Keller, D. H.

Free Joe and the rest of the world. Harris, J. C.

Free man. Woods, W.

Freedman, David, 1898-1936
Mendel Marantz—genius
    Ausubel, N. ed. Treasury of Jewish humor

FREEDOM. See Liberty

Freedom. O'Donovan, M.

Freedom. Sabin, E. L.

Freedom's a hard-bought thing. Benét, S. V.

Freeman, Kathleen, 1897-
Amethyst cross
  Asquith, Lady C. M. E. C. ed. Book of
  modern ghosts
Freeman, Mary Eleanor (Wilkins) 1852-1930
The cat
  Andrews, R. C. ed. My favorite stories
  of the great outdoors
New England nun
  Burrell, J. A. and Cerf, B. A. eds. An-
  thology of famous American stories
Revolt of "Mother"
  Cuff, R. P. ed. American short story
  survey
  Ungar, F. ed. To mother with love
Freeman, Richard Austin, 1862-1943
Rex v. Burnaby
  Bond, R. T. ed. Handbook for poisoners
FREEMASONS
  Claudy, C. H. These were brethren; 24
  stories
  Maupassant, G. de. My uncle Sosthenes
FREETHINKERS. See Atheism
Freeze out. Coombs, C. I.
Freeze-out. Larsen, D.
Freeze the ball. Bee, C. F.
Freighted hour. Lieberman, R.
FREIGHTS AND FREIGHTERS
  Stevens, J. Jerkline
French, Frank C.
Stick up
  Oberfirst, R. ed. 1952 anthology of best
  original short-shorts
FRENCH ACADIANS. See Acadians in
  Louisiana
FRENCH ALPS. See Alps, French
FRENCH ARISTOCRACY. See Aristoc-
  racy—France
FRENCH COURTIERS. See Courts and
  courtiers—France
FRENCH GUIANA
  Maugham, W. S. Man with a conscience
  Maugham, W. S. Official position
FRENCH IN AFRICA
  Balzac, H. de. Passion in the desert
FRENCH IN THE SOUTH SEAS
  Michener, J. A. The good life
FRENCH IN THE UNITED STATES
  Field, R. L. A woman of virtue
  Horwitz, M. Coquette
  Whitney, P. A. Lucky 'leven
FRENCH INDO-CHINA. See Indo-China,
  French
French Joe. Maugham, W. S.
Frere, Marie. See Frere, Mary Eliza Isa-
  bella
Frere, Mary Eliza Isabella, 1845-1911
Blind man, the deaf man, and the donkey
  Fenner, P. R. comp. Fools and funny
  fellows
The jackal and the alligator
  Fenner, P. R. comp. Fools and funny
  fellows
Fresh and open sky. Sullivan, R.
Fresh snow. Humphrey, W.
Freshest boy. Fitzgerald, F. S. K.

FRESNO. See California—Fresno
Freya of the Seven Isles. Conrad, J.
Friedman, Bernard Harper
As I am, you will be
  Hathaway, B. and Sessions, J. A. eds.
  Writers for tomorrow. 2d ser.
Friedman, Stuart, 1913-
Beautiful, beautiful, beautiful!
  Derleth, A. W. ed. Worlds of tomorrow
Friedman, Sylvia
Adam and Eve
  American vanguard, 1950
Friend, Oscar Jerome, 1897-
Impossible highway
  Jenkins, W. F. ed. Great stories of sci-
  ence fiction
Friend in need. Maugham, W. S.
Friend in the closet. Kesten, H.
Friend of Buck Hollister. Raine, W. M.
Friend of the family. McCarthy, M. T.
Friend of the family. Wilson, R.
Friend to man. Kornbluth, C. M.
Friendly call. Porter, W. S.
Friendly demon. Defoe, D.
FRIENDS. See Friendship
FRIENDS, SOCIETY OF
  Lewis, M. Well of anger
  West, J. The illumination
  West, J. Shivaree before breakfast
Friends in San Rosario. Porter, W. S.
FRIENDSHIP
  Aldrich, B. S. Juno's swans
  Beck, W. No continuing city
  Davies, R. Two friends
  Galbraith, N. F. To have and to lose
  Gomberg, V. G. Glaciers
  Harte, B. Left out on Lone Star Mountain
  Harte, B. Tennessee's partner
  London, J. Shadow and the flash
  Maupassant, G. de. Two friends
  O'Donovan, M. A romantic
  Patton, F. G. The game
  Porter, W. S. After twenty years
  Porter, W. S. Friendly call
  Porter, W. S. Telemachus, friend
  Porter, W. S. Trimmed lamp
  Young, E. H. The stream
Friendship's due. Sitwell, Sir O. bart.
FRIGHT. See Fear
Frightened tree. Budrys, A. J.
Frightened wife. Rinehart, M. R.
Frischman, David, 1865?-1922
Sinai
  Leftwich, J. ed. Yisröel. 1952 ed.
Frishman, David. See Frischman, David
Frison-Roche, Roger, 1906-
Their kingdom
  Talbot, D. ed. Treasury of mountaineer-
  ing stories
Fritz. Farrell, J. T.
Frog and the lion. Benson, T.
Frog prince. Collier, J.
FROGS
  Clemens, S. L. Celebrated jumping frog of
  Calaveras County
  Macfarlan, A. A. Bullfrog hunt

From a journal-letter of Julius Caesar. Wilder, T. N.

From a private mad-house. Repton, H.

From beyond. Lovecraft, H. P.

From each according to his ability. Porter, W. S.

From morning till night. Hutchins, M. P. M.

From my estates. Kahanovich, P.

From the cabby's seat. Porter, W. S.

From the water junction. Sansom, W.

From there to infinity. De Vries, P.

From what a Litvak makes a living. Tunkel, J.

Front-page story. Farrell, J. T.

The frontier. Bates, H. E.

FRONTIER AND PIONEER LIFE
Johnson, D. M. Indian country; 11 stories

Alabama
Vines, H. Ginsing gatherers

Illinois
Wellman, M. W. Tall Bram of Little Pigeon

Kentucky
Webber, E. M. Passage to Kentucky

Nevada
Clemens, S. L. My bloody massacre (I)

Emrich, D. ed. Comstock bonanza; 21 stories

New England
Hawthorne, N. Roger Malvin's burial

North Dakota
Wood, F. G. Turkey-red

Ohio
Bierce, A. Boarded window

The West
Schaefer, J. W. The pioneers; 11 stories

Froscher, Wingate
Death in the family
Best American short stories, 1953

Frost, Frances Mary, 1905-
Heart being perished
Certner, S. and Henry, G. H. eds. Short stories for our times

Frost, Lesley
Very mischief
Fenner, P. R. comp. Giggle box

Frost-giant's daughter. Howard, R. E.

Frozen truth. Gally, J. W.

Fru Holm. Karmel, I.

Frug, Simon Samuel, 1860-1917
Last kopeck
Ausubel, N. ed. Treasury of Jewish humor
Leftwich, J. ed. Yisröel. 1952 ed.

Fruit at the bottom of the bowl. Bradbury, R.

Fruits of toil. Duncan, N.

Frying-pan. O'Donovan, M.

Fuchs, Abraham Moses, 1890-
Among the trees
Leftwich, J. ed. Yisröel. 1952 ed.

Fugitive from the mind. Bennett, P.

FUGITIVE SLAVES. See Slavery—Fugitive slaves

FUGITIVES
Novás Calvo, L. Dark night of Ramón Yendía
Procter, M. Fox in the Pennine Hills
See also Convicts, Escaped

Fugue for harmonicas. Seager, A.

Fugue of the fig tree. Sultan, S.

Fulfillment. Van Vogt, A. E.

Full circle. Matheson, R.

Full cycle. Du Bose, V. G.

Fultz, Dessa M.
Snowshoe Thompson
Story parade (Periodical) Adventure stories

Fulvous yellow. Kauffmann, S.

FUND RAISING
Cohen, O. R. Law and the profits

Funeral feast. Benson, T.

FUNERAL RITES AND CEREMONIES
Arnow, H. L. S. Washerwoman's day
Bernstein, H. Greatest funeral in the world
Betts, D. Sense of humor
Bunner, H. C. Two churches of 'Quawket
Caldwell, E. Fly in the coffin
Clemens, S. L. Buck Fanshaw's funeral
Coolidge, O. E. Unquiet spirit
Crane, S. Upturned face
Davies, R. Human condition
Davies, R. Mourning for Ianto
Davis, S. P. Andy Munroe's funeral
Farrell, J. T. Wake of Patsy McLaughlin
Johnson, D. M. Man who shot Liberty Valance
Newhouse, E. My brother's second funeral
Sheppard, J. Black brassard
Spettigue, D. Asters for Teddie
Watson, J. Story of Dr. MacLure
Weissenberg, I. M. Mazel tov
See also Funeral orations

Jewish
Gordimer, N. Watcher of the dead
Klein, J. M. Yisgadel

FUNGI
Pratt, F. and Ruby, B. F. Thing in the woods

Fur. Munro, H. H.

Fur flies. Winslow, T. S.

FUR TRAPPERS. See Trappers

FURLOUGHS. See Soldiers—Furloughs

Furman, Lucy, 1870-
Experience on the dress line
Summers, H. S. ed. Kentucky story

FURNACES
De Vries, P. I don't want to go

Furnas, Joseph Chamberlain, 1905-
Laocoön complex
Merril, J. ed. Beyond the barriers of space and time

Furnished room. Porter, W. S.

FURNITURE. See specific articles of furniture, e.g. Sofas

Fusty Devil. Tolstoi, A. N.

Futrelle, Jacques, 1875-1912
Problem of Cell 13
Christ, H. I. and Shostak, J. eds. Short stories

FUTURE, STORIES OF THE
Asimov, I. "In a good cause—"
Best science fiction stories: 1950; 13 stories
Bradbury, R. Forever and the earth
Bradbury, R. King of the gray spaces
Bradbury, R. The pedestrian
Bradbury, R. Referent
Bradbury, R. The wilderness
Brown, F. Crisis, 1999
Campbell, J. W. Cloak of Aesir; 7 stories
Cartmill, C. You can't say that
Clarke, A. C. Expedition to earth; 11 stories
Conklin, G. ed. Omnibus of science fiction; 42 stories
Crossen, K. F. ed. Adventures in tomorrow; 15 stories
De Camp, L. S. Continent makers, and other tales of the Viagens; 8 stories
Derleth, A. W. ed. Beachheads in space; 14 stories
Derleth, A. W. ed. Far boundaries; 20 stories
Derleth, A. W. ed. The outer reaches; 17 stories
Derleth, A. W. ed. Worlds of tomorrow; 19 stories
Fenton, F. and Petracca, J. Tolliver's travels
Frank, P. The madman
Galaxy science fiction magazine. Galaxy reader of science fiction; 33 stories
Gallery, D. V. Enemy planet
Greenberg, M. comp. Five science fiction novels; 5 stories
Greenberg, M. ed. Journey to infinity; 12 stories
Greenberg, M. ed. Men against the stars; 12 stories
Grendon, E. Crisis
Heinlein, R. A. Green hills of earth
Heinlein, R. A. Man who sold the moon; 6 stories
Huxley, A. L. Brave new world
Huxley, A. L. Education in the world state
Jameson, M. Bullard of the space patrol; 7 stories
Keller, D. H. Biological experiment
Keller, D. H. Free as the air
Kornbluth, C. M. Marching morons
Leiber, F. Moon is green
Lesser, M. A. ed. Looking forward; 20 stories
MacDonald, J. D. The miniature
Margulies, L. and Friend, O. J. eds. From off this world; 18 stories
Merril, J. Barrier of dread
Van Vogt, A. E. The seesaw
Verne, J. In the year 2889

Waugh, E. Love among the ruins
Wells, H. G. Story of the days to come
White, W. A. P. Quest for Saint Aquin
See also Science fiction

Future captain. Carter, R. G.

FUTURE LIFE
Clemens, S. L. Wings
Milne, A. A. The balcony
Stephens, J. The threepenny-piece
See also Heaven

FUTURE TIME. See Time

Fu-yen, Li. See Li Fu-Yen

Fuzzy things. Hitchens, D. B.

Fyfe, H. B.
Afterthought
Merril, J. ed. Beyond human ken
Bureau of slick tricks
Greenberg, M. ed. Travelers of space
Implode and peddle
Norton, A. M. ed. Space service
In value deceived
Conklin, G. ed. Possible worlds of science fiction
Sloane, W. M. ed. Stories for tomorrow
Locked out
Greenberg, M. ed. Men against the stars
Manners of the age
Conklin, G. ed. Omnibus of science fiction
Moonwalk
Norton, A. M. ed. Space pioneers
Protected species
Astounding science fiction (Periodical)
Astounding science fiction anthology
Ransom
Magazine of fantasy and science fiction. Best from Fantasy and science fiction; 2d ser.
Star-linked
Norton, A. M. ed. Space service
Well-oiled machine
Brown, F. and Reynolds, M. eds. Science-fiction carnival

G

Gable type. Herbert, F. H.

Gabriel-Ernest. Munro, H. H.

Gabrielle de Bergerac. James, H.

Gadget had a ghost. Jenkins, W. F.

Gág, Wanda, 1893-1946
Doctor-know-it-all
Fenner, P. R. comp. Fools and funny fellows
Gone is gone
Fenner, P. R. comp. Fools and funny fellows

Gainfort, Phyllis, 1924-
The pact
Wolfe, D. M. ed. Which grain will grow

Gal young un. Rawlings, M. K.

Gala programme. Munro, H. H.

Galahad, Sir
Malory, Sir T. Marvellous adventure of the sword

GALAPAGOS ISLANDS
Melville, H. The encantadas or enchanted isles

Galatians 2:20. Blackburn, E. R.

Galbraith, N. F.
To have and to lose
Oberfirst, R. ed. 1954 anthology of best original short-shorts

Gale, Zona, 1874-1938
Human
Lohan, R. and Lohan, M. eds. New Christmas treasury

GALICIA. See Poland

Gallegher plus. Kuttner, H.

Gallegos, Rómulo, 1884-
Man of character
De Onís, H. ed. Spanish stories and tales

Gallery, David Vincent, 1901-
Enemy planet
Grayson, C. ed. Fourth round
Hokey-Pocus McGee
Argosy (Periodical) Argosy Book of sports stories

Gallery-shy. Gault, W. C.

Gallico, Paul William, 1897-
The bombardier
Eaton, H. T. ed. Short stories
McKabe
Grayson, C. ed Fourth round
Man who hated people
Saturday evening post (Periodical) Saturday evening post stories, 1950
Melee of the Mages
Dachs, D. ed. Treasury of sports humor
Secret ingredient
Saturday evening post (Periodical) Saturday evening post stories, 1952
Summer dream
Bachelor, J. M.; Henry, R. L. and Salisbury, R. eds. Current thinking and writing; 2d ser.
"When in doubt—wash"
Joseph, M. ed. Best cat stories

Gallister, Michael, pseud.
Fireboat style
Bluebook (Periodical) Best sea stories from Bluebook

Galloping Foxley. Dahl, R.

Gallun, Raymond Z.
Asteroid of fear
Norton, A. M. ed. Space pioneers
Old Faithful
Bleiler, E. F. and Dikty, T. E. eds. Imagination unlimited
Operation pumice
Conklin, G. ed. Possible worlds of science fiction
Return of a legend
Norton, A. M. ed. Space service
The scarab
Conklin, G. ed. Science-fiction thinking machines
Trail blazer
Norton, A. M. ed. Space pioneers

Gally, James W. 1828-1891
Big Jack Small
Emrich, D. ed. Comstock bonanza
Frozen truth
Emrich, D. ed. Comstock bonanza

Hualapi
Emrich, D. ed. Comstock bonanza
Spirits
Emrich, D. ed. Comstock bonanza

Galsworthy, John, 1867-1933
Apple-tree
Cerf, B. A. and Moriarty, H. C. eds. Anthology of famous British stories
Scribner treasury
The juryman
Blaustein, A. P. ed. Fiction goes to court
Queen, E. pseud. ed. Literature of crime
Manna
Short, R. W. and Sewall, R. B. eds. Short stories for study. 1950 ed.
Quality
Lass, A. H. and Horowitz, A. eds. Stories for youth
Shaw, H. and Bement, D. Reading the short story
Salta pro nobis
Blodgett, H. W. ed. Story survey. 1953 ed.
Timber
Schramm, W. L. ed. Great short stories
Ultima Thule
Cooper, A. C. ed. Modern short stories

Galton whistle. De Camp, L. S.

Galway Bay. O'Flaherty, L.

GAMALIEL I
Cohn, E. Rabban Gamaliel

Gambler, the nun, and the radio, Hemingway, E.

GAMBLERS. See Gambling

Gambler's Club. Queen, E. pseud.

Gambler's sad saga. Cannon, J. J.

GAMBLING
Blackburn, E. R. Last king
Cannon, J. J. Gambler's sad saga
Collier, J. Ah the university
Collins, W. Terribly strange bed
Cooke, A. A. The Grace Mansion
Crane, S. Blue Hotel
Doty, W. L. Pittsburgh special
Fitzgerald, B. Iron maiden
Fitzgerald, F. S. K. Jelly-bean
Fox, N. A. Bet the wild queen!
Frazee, S. Luck of Riley
Harte, B. Brown of Calaveras
Harte, B. Outcasts of Poker Flat
Harte, B. Passage in the life of Mr John Oakhurst
Harte, B. Protégée of Jack Hamlin's
Lawrence, D. H. Rocking-horse winner
Maugham, W. S. Facts of life
Maugham, W. S. Raw material
Munro, H. H. The stake
Munro, H. H. Way to the dairy
Nordau, M. S. Share in the hereafter
Porter, W. S. Suite homes and their romance
Queen, E. pseud. Gambler's Club
Saroyan, W. The Assyrian
Taylor, E. Oasis of gaiety
Woodward, G. B. College marriage
See also Lotteries; Wagers

The game. Patton, F. G.

GAME AND GAME BIRDS
  Buckingham, N. Remember. . .
  Gordon, C. Last day in the field
      See also Birds; Duck shooting;
      Grouse hunting; Hunting
GAME BIRDS. See Game and game birds
Game chickens. Seager, A.
Game cock. McLaverty, M.
GAME COCKS. See Roosters; Cock fight-
  ing
Game for blondes. MacDonald, J. D.
Game grows hotter. Patten, G.
GAME HUNTING. See Hunting
Game in the park. Farrell, J. T.
Game of catch. Wilbur, R.
GAME PROTECTION
  Buckingham, N. Bigger they come!
  Buckingham, N. High sign
  Buckingham, N. Tight place
  Ebner von Eschenbach, M. Freifrau. Kram-
  bambuli
GAMEKEEPERS. See Game protection
GAMES
  Harvey, W. F. Vicar's web
  Munro, H. H. Reginald's Christmas revel
  Munro, H. H. The strategist
  Munro, H. H. Touch of realism
GANGS
  Newhouse, E. The Mentocrats
GANGSTERS
  Babel', I. E. In Odessa
  Babel', I. E. The King
  Burnett, W. R. Dressing-up
  Hemingway, E. The killers
  Kirch, J. A. Murder for two
  La Farge, O. The bystander
  Porter, W. S. Vanity and some sables
  Runyon, D. Sense of humor
Gannett, Ruth Stiles, 1923-
  Some of father's adventures
    Fenner, P. R. comp. Giggle box
Gannon, S. Anna
  Me and Joe
    Oberfirst, R. ed. 1954 anthology of best
    original short-shorts
GARAGE WORKERS
  Ferber, E. Afternoon of a faun
  Fowler, B. B. Some can't take it
  Jones, R. F. Tools of the trade
Garbage collector. Bradbury, R.
Garber, Gladys, 1919-
  Gun on the wall
    Story (Periodical) Story; no. 2
GARDEN PARTIES
  Mansfield, K. Garden-party
  Munro, H. H. Boar-pig
  Munro, H. H. Reginald
Garden-party. Mansfield, K.
The **gardener.** St Clair, M.
GARDENING. See Gardens and garden-
  ing
GARDENS AND GARDENING
  Hawthorne, N. Rappaccini's daughter
  Livesay, D. Glass house
  Munro, H. H. Occasional garden

Parker, J. R. Monks revel at Winkton
Steinbeck, J. The chrysanthemums
Welty, E. Curtain of green
Gardiner, Dorothy, 1894-
  Not a lick of sense
    Mystery Writers of America, inc.
    Crooks' tour
Gardner, Erle Stanley, 1889-
  Case of the irate witness
    Best detective stories of the year—1954
    Blaustein, A. P. ed. Fiction goes to
    court
Gardner, Martin, 1914-
  Island of five colors
    Crossen, K. F. ed. Future tense
  No-sided professor
    Magazine of fantasy and science fiction.
    Best from Fantasy and science fiction;
    ₁1st ser.₁
  Thang
    Bleiler, E. F. and Dikty, T. E. eds. Sci-
    ence fiction omnibus: The best science
    fiction stories, 1949, 1950
Gardner, Thomas S.
  Last woman
    Margulies, L. and Friend, O. J. eds.
    From off this world
Gardner, W. W.
  Many are the brave
    Lantz, J. E. ed. Stories of Christian
    living
Garland, Hamlin, 1860-1940
  Mrs Ripley's trip
    Blodgett, H. W. ed. Story survey.
    1953 ed.
  Return of a private
    Burrell, J. A. and Cerf, B. A. eds. An-
    thology of famous American stories
  Under the lion's paw
    Foerster, N. ed. American poetry and
    prose. 1952 ed.
Garner, Hugh, 1913-
  Conversion of Willie Heaps
    Best American short stories, 1952
  One mile of ice
    Weaver, R. and James, H. eds. Canadian
    short stories
  One, two, three little Indians
    Weaver, R. and James, H. eds. Canadian
    short stories
Garrigue, Jean
  The snowfall
    Swallow, A. ed. Anchor in the sea
Garrold, Richard Philip, 1874-1920
  Man's hand
    Thinker's digest (Periodical) Spoiled
    priest, and other stories
Garthwaite, Marion (Hook) 1893-
  Riding the Pony Express
    Fenner, P. R. comp. Yankee Doodle
Gartner, John
  Jug Leg Kelley
    Owen, F. ed. Teen-age winter sports
    stories
  Left-hand stuff
    Owen, F. ed. Teen-age winter sports
    stories

Gaskell, Elizabeth Cleghorn (Stevenson) 1810-1865
Cousin Phillis
Connolly, C. ed. Great English short novels
The half-brothers
Cerf, B. A. and Moriarty, H. C. eds. Anthology of famous British stories
Ungar, F. ed. To mother with love

Gaspar Ruiz. Conrad, J.

Gastronomy of the Jews. Saphir, M. G.

Gates, Doris, 1901-
Seventh pup
Harper, W. comp. Dog show

Gateway to darkness. Brown, F.

Gather up the pieces. Grimson, M. S.

Gatty, Lin
Did he touch you?
Hathaway, B. and Sessions, J. A. eds. Writers for tomorrow. 2d ser.

Gault, William Campbell
Brick road to glory
Argosy (Periodical) Argosy Book of sports stories
Dirt-track thunder
Argosy (Periodical) Argosy Book of sports stories
Gallery-shy
Argosy (Periodical) Argosy Book of sports stories
Made to measure
Galaxy science fiction magazine. Galaxy reader of science fiction
Marksman
Mystery Writers of America, inc. Maiden murders
Thunder Road
Fenner, P. R. comp. Speed, speed, speed

Gauntlet of fire. Roberts, Sir C. G. D.

Gautier, Théophile, 1811-1872
Clarimonde
Carrington, H. ed. Week-end book of ghost stories

Gavagan's bar. De Camp, L. S. and Pratt, F.

Gavin O'Leary. Collier, J.

Geer, Elizabeth, 1927-
Genoese street song
American vanguard, 1952

GEESE
Dunsany, E. J. M. D. P. 18th baron. Widow Flynn's apple tree
Rosenfeld, J. Sick goose

GEHENNA. See Hell

Gehenna. Aiken, C. P.

Gehrig, Henry Louis, 1903-1941
Graham, F. Joining the Yankees

Geier, Chester S.
Environment
Conklin, G. ed. Omnibus of science fiction

Gellhorn, Martha Ellis, 1908-
About Shorty
Esquire (Periodical) Girls from Esquire
Gellhorn, M. E. Honeyed peace
Café in Jaffa
Gellhorn, M. E. Honeyed peace
Exile
Gellhorn, M. E. Honeyed peace

The German
Gellhorn, M. E. Honeyed peace
Honeyed peace
Gellhorn, M. E. Honeyed peace
Miami-New York
Gellhorn, M. E. Honeyed peace
Psychiatrist of one's own
Gellhorn, M. E. Honeyed peace
Venus ascendant
Gellhorn, M. E. Honeyed peace
Voyage forme la jeunesse
Gellhorn, M. E. Honeyed peace
Weekend at Grimsby
Best American short stories, 1952
Gellhorn, M. E. Honeyed peace

Gemlike flame. Auchincloss, L.

General from the Pentagon. Chase, F.

General Pingley. Schaefer, J. W.

General Washington's pig. Hale, E. E.

GENERALS
Chase, F. General from the Pentagon

Generation of Noah. Klass, P.

Generations of man. Horwitz, J.

GENEROSITY
Goudge, E. Doing good

Generous wine. Schmitz, E.

GENETICS. See Evolution

Genial check-capped ghosts. Gilpatric, G.

GENII. See Jinn

GENIUS
Babel', I. E. Awakening
Christopher, J. Balance
France, A. Manuscript of a village doctor
Mann, T. Death in Venice
See also Children, Gifted

Genius. Anderson, P.

Genius of Strap Buckner. Ashabranner, B.

Genoese street song. Geer, E.

Gentle insurrection. Betts, D.

Gentle like a cyclone. Annett, R. R.

Gentle Masonic way. Claudy, C. H.

Gentle season. Miller, C.

Gentleman and the tiger. Marshall, E.

Gentleman from America. Arlen, M.

Gentleman from India. Ekbergh, I. D.

Gentleman from Paris. Carr, J. D.

Gentleman from San Francisco. Bunin, I. A.

Gentleman is an Epwa. Jacobi, C.

Gentlemen, be seated. Heinlein, R. A.

Gentlemen of valor. Evans, T. M.

Gentlemen—the Queen! Tucker, W.

The gentry. Verga, G.

Gents only. Davies, R.

GEORGE, SAINT
Grahame, K. Reluctant dragon

GEORGE V, KING OF GREAT BRITAIN, 1865-1936
Jubilee
De La Roche, M. "Twa kings"

George, Walter Lionel, 1882-1926
Ave, amor, morituri te salutant
Leftwich, J. ed. Yisröel. 1952 ed.

George Ingram pays his debt. Hendryx, J. B.

George's mother. Crane, S.

GEORGETOWN, MARYLAND. See Maryland—Georgetown

GEORGIA
Fitzgerald, F. S. K. Jelly-bean
Fitzgerald, F. S. K. Last of the belles
Harris, J. C. Free Joe and the rest of the world

Georgia's ruling. Porter, W. S.

Gerahty, Digby George
Six months more to live
Saturday evening post (Periodical) Saturday evening post stories, 1952

The **German**. Gellhorn, M. E.

German Harry. Maugham, W. S.

GERMAN LEGENDS. See Legends and folk tales—Germany

GERMAN OFFICERS. See Germany—Army

GERMAN SOLDIERS. See Soldiers, German

GERMANS IN FRANCE
Boyle, K. Defeat
Farrell, J. T. Fritz

GERMANS IN ITALY
Mann, T. Death in Venice
Paget, V. Amour dure

GERMANS IN NETHERLANDS
Hebel, J. P. Kannitverstan

GERMANS IN NORWAY
Lyon, K. Altar cloth

GERMANS IN SWITZERLAND
Ullman, J. R. Mountains of the Axis

GERMANS IN THE UNITED STATES
Aldrich, B. S. Day of retaliation
Gellhorn, M. E. Exile

GERMANY
8th century
Van Dyke, H. First Christmas tree
14th century
Roth, C. The martyr
18th century
Auerbach, B. Hansjorg and his pipe
1918-date
Boyle, K. Smoking mountain; 11 stories
Ditzen, R. Fifty marks
Forester, C. S. The nightmare; 10 stories
Putnam, C. Old acrobat and the ruined city
Stafford, J. Winter's tale
Van Vogt, A. E. Secret unattainable
Army
Forester, C. S. Indecision
Lawrence, D. H. Prussian officer
Waltari, M. T. Before the twilight of the gods
Heidelberg
Stafford, J. The nemesis
Nuremberg
Saphir, M. G. A conquest

Gertrude and Sidney. Jarrell, R.

"**Get** a horse, comrade." Petrov, V.

Get-away boy. Sheehan, D. V.

Getting quick rich. Papashvily, G. and Papashvily, H. W.

Ghetto dog. Spiegel, I.

Ghost. Kuttner, H.

Ghost and flesh, water and dirt. Goyen, W.

Ghost-extinguisher. Burgess, G.

Ghost lode. Brandon, W.

Ghost of a chance. Porter, W. S.

Ghost of General Jackson. Moody, M. H.

Ghost of Gideon Wise. Chesterton, G. K.

Ghost of Gillin Run. Mowery, W. B.

Ghost of me. White, W. A. P.

Ghost of Sam Bates. Huckabay, M. B.

Ghost runner. Miers, E. S.

GHOST SHIPS
Poe, E. A. Ms. found in a bottle
Steele, W. D. Yellow cat
Wetjen, A. R. Ship of silence
See also Ships

GHOST STORIES. See Ghosts

Ghost-town dog. Evans, H. R.

GHOST WRITING. See Writing, Automatic

Ghostly rental. James, H.

GHOSTS
Addison, J. Vision of Mirzah
Anderson, E. V. Phantom Hall
Asquith, Lady C. M. E. C. Book of modern ghosts; 20 stories
Bergengruen, W. Pupsik
Bierce, A. Damned thing
Bowen, E. Cat jumps
Bowen, E. Demon lover
Boyd, J. Verse on the window
Buckingham, N. Cricket field
Carrington, H. ed. Week-end book of ghost stories; 20 stories
Collier, J. Are you too late or was I too early
Conklin, G. and Conklin, L. T. eds. Supernatural reader; 27 stories
Coolidge, O. E. Unquiet spirit
Davenport, B. ed. Ghostly tales to be told; 16 stories
Davenport, B. ed. Tales to be told in the dark; 13 stories
Defoe, D. Apparition of Mrs Veal
Defoe, D. True relation of the apparition of one Mrs Veal
De La Mare, W. J. All Hallows
De La Mare, W. J. Seaton's aunt
De La Mare, W. J. Strangers and pilgrims
Derleth, A. W. ed. Night's yawning peal; 15 stories
Derleth, A. W. Sheraton mirror
Dickens, C. Christmas carol
Dickens, C. The signal-man
Dunsany, E. J. M. D. P. 18th baron. The return
Fenner, P. R. comp. Ghosts, ghosts, ghosts; 15 stories
Goyen, W. Ghost and flesh; 8 stories
Hawthorne, N. Gray champion
Irving, W. Legend of Sleepy Hollow
James, H. Ghostly rental
James, H. Jolly corner
Jealousy
Kipling, R. 'They'

GHOSTS—*Continued*

Kleist, H. von. Beggar-woman of Locarno
Kuttner, H. Ghost
Lytton, E. G. E. L. B-L. 1st baron. House and the brain
Maugham, W. S. Man from Glasgow
Merochnik, M. Influence
Miers, E. S. Ghost runner
Munby, A. N. L. Alabaster hand and other stories; 14 stories
Munro, H. H. The hedgehog
Munro, H. H. Laura
Paget, V. Wicked voice
Poe, E. A. King Pest
Porter, W. S. Ghost of a chance
Priestley, J. B. Uncle Phil on TV
P'u Sung-ling. Jojo
Quiller-Couch, Sir A. T. Roll-call of the reef
Sansom, W. Saving grace
Steele, W. D. Can't cross Jordan by myself
Stevenson, R. L. Thrawn Janet
Tucker, W. Tourist trade
Van Doren, M. The key
Van Doren, M. No thunder, no lightning
Van Doren, M. Twentieth floor
Van Doren, M. Witch of Ramoth
Wells, H. G. Inexperienced ghost
Weston, C. G. Man in gray
Wharton, E. N. J. The lady's maid's bell
Winslow, T. S. Rudolph
    See also Hallucinations and illusions; Supernatural phenomena

Ghost's shoes. Brenner, L.

GI story. Queen, E. pseud.

Giant Finn MacCool. Ready, W. B.

Giant killer. Chandler, A. B.

GIANTS
Blish, J. Beanstalk
Chandler, A. B. Giant killer

GIBBONS
Annixter, P. pseud. With the greatest of ease

Gibbs, Angelica
The test
    Lass, A. H. and Horowitz, A. eds. Stories for youth

Gibbs, Sir Philip Hamilton, 1877-
Stranger in the village
    Cerf, B. A. and Moriarty, H. C. eds. Anthology of famous British stories

Gibran, Kahlil, 1886-1931
Ambitious violet
    Gibran, K. Treasury of Kahlil Gibran
Ashes of the ages and eternal fire
    Gibran, K. Treasury of Kahlil Gibran
Before the throne of beauty
    Gibran, K. Treasury of Kahlil Gibran
Behind the garment
    Gibran, K. Treasury of Kahlil Gibran
Bride's bed
    Gibran, K. Treasury of Kahlil Gibran
City of the dead
    Gibran, K. Treasury of Kahlil Gibran
The criminal
    Gibran, K. Treasury of Kahlil Gibran
Cry of the graves
    Gibran, K. Treasury of Kahlil Gibran

Eventide of the feast
    Gibran, K. Treasury of Kahlil Gibran
Grave digger
    Gibran, K. Treasury of Kahlil Gibran
Honeyed poison
    Gibran, K. Treasury of Kahlil Gibran
John the madman
    Gibran, K. Treasury of Kahlil Gibran
Khalil the heretic
    Gibran, K. Treasury of Kahlil Gibran
Last supper
    Selden, R. ed. Ways of God and men
Lonely poet
    Gibran, K. Treasury of Kahlil Gibran
Madame Rose Hanie
    Gibran, K. Treasury of Kahlil Gibran
The mermaids
    Gibran, K. Treasury of Kahlil Gibran
Rafca, the bride of Cana
    Brentano, F. ed. The word lives on
Satan
    Gibran, K. Treasury of Kahlil Gibran
Secrets of the heart
    Gibran, K. Treasury of Kahlil Gibran
The tempest
    Gibran, K. Treasury of Kahlil Gibran
Two infants
    Gibran, K. Treasury of Kahlil Gibran
Two wishes
    Gibran, K. Treasury of Kahlil Gibran
Widow and her son
    Gibran, K. Treasury of Kahlil Gibran
Yesterday and today
    Gibran, K. Treasury of Kahlil Gibran

Gidé, Andre Paul Guillaume, 1869-1951
My mother
    Neider, C. ed. Great short stories from the world's literature
Theseus
    Geist, S. ed. French stories and tales
The gift
    Ausubel, N. ed. Treasury of Jewish humor

The gift. Steinbeck, J.

The gift. Tunkel, J.

Gift for a birthday. Levine, S.

Gift of Cochise. L'Amour, L.

Gift of God. Pratt, F. and De Camp, L. S.

Gift of love. Jackson, D. V. S.

Gift of the emperor. Katz, L.

Gift of the Magi. Porter, W. S.

Gift of the wise man. Eggleston, M. W.

GIFTED CHILDREN. See Children, Gifted

GIFTS
Clemens, S. L. Man that corrupted Hadleyburg
Gordimer, N. Present for a good girl
Munro, H. H. "Down pens"
Munro, H. H. Fur
Munro, H. H. Reginald on Christmas presents
Robinson, F. M. Santa Claus planet

Gigolo and gigolette. Maugham, W. S.

Gilbert, Kenneth, 1889-
Jungle brothers
    American boy (Periodical) American boy Adventure stories

Gilbert, Kenneth—*Continued*
Old man of the mountains
American boy (Periodical) American boy
Adventure stories
. Pool of adventure
American boy (Periodical) American boy
Anthology
Gilbert, Michael Frances, 1912-
Modus operandi
Mystery Writers of America, inc.
Butcher, baker, murder-maker
Source seven
Mystery Writers of America, inc.
Crooks' tour
Gilbert, Nan, pseud. See Gilbertson, Mildred
Geiger
Gilbertson, Mildred Geiger
Christmas in Carthage
American girl (Periodical) Christmas all
year 'round
American girl (Periodical) On my honor
Gilbreth, Frank Bunker, 1911- and **Carey,**
Ernestine Moller (Gilbreth) 1908-
Orphans in uniform
Fenner, P. R. comp. Fun! Fun! Fun!
Pygmalion
McFarland, W. K. comp. Then it hap-
pened
Gilford, C. B.
Heaven can wait
Queen, E. pseud, ed. Queen's awards:
8th ser.
Gill, Brendan, 1914-
The knife
Gable, M. Sister, ed. Many-colored fleece
Night bus to Atlanta
Esquire (Periodical) Girls from Esquire
Gill, Tom, 1891-
Jungle war
Fremantle, A. J. ed. Mothers
Gilman, Charlotte (Perkins) Stetson, 1860-
1935
Yellow wall-paper
Davenport, B. ed. Ghostly tales to be
told
Gilmour, William, 1924?-
Danny Hagan's blind spot
American vanguard, 1950
Gilpatric, Guy, 1896-1950
Artful Mr Glencannon
Gilpatric, G. Last Glencannon omnibus
Crocodile tears
Gilpatric, G. Last Glencannon omnibus
Genial check-capped ghosts
Jensen, P. ed. Fireside book of flying
stories
Glasgow fantom
Gilpatric, G. Last Glencannon omnibus
Glencannon collection
Gilpatric, G. Last Glencannon omnibus
Home stretch
Gilpatric, G. Last Glencannon omnibus
Masked monster
Gilpatric, G. Last Glencannon omnibus
Mr Glencannon and the ailing cockroach
Gilpatric, G. Last Glencannon omnibus
Monkey business at Gibraltar
Gilpatric, G. Last Glencannon omnibus
Souse of the border
Gilpatric, G. Last Glencannon omnibus

Where early fa's the dew
Gilpatric, G. Last Glencannon omnibus
Wing walker
Jensen, P. ed. Fireside book of flying
stories
Gilpatrick, Elsie
Concrete experience
Oberfirst, R. ed. 1952 anthology of best
original short-shorts
Gimpel the fool. Singer, I. B.
Gin comes in bottles. Pratt, F. and De
Camp, L. S.
Gingerbread. Wahl, B.
Ginsing gatherers. Vines, H.
Gioconda smile. Huxley, A. L.
Giono, Jean, 1895-
Corn dies
Short, R. W. and Sewall, R. B. eds.
Short stories for study. 1950 ed.
Giorgio and Martino. Bergengruen, W.
GIPSIES
Alarcón, P. A. de. The prophecy
Mulhoffer, D. B. Last year
Gipson, Fred Benjamin, 1908-
My kind of a man
Peery, W. W. ed. 21 Texas short sto-
ries
"**Girl.**" Porter, W. S.
The **girl.** Shneur, Z.
Girl and the graft. Porter, W. S.
Girl and the habit. Porter, W. S.
Girl called Peter. Bates, H. E.
Girl Ellen. Caldwell, E.
Girl in the golden atom. Cummings, R.
Girl next door. Sullivan, R.
Girl on horseback. Ullman, J. R.
Girl on the bus. Sansom, W.
Girl on the lake. Roberts, D.
Girl overboard. Quentin, P. pseud.
Girl who had to get married. Newhouse, E.
Girl who married a monster. White,
W. A. P.
Girl who wasn't wanted. McNeil, S.
Girl with a pimply face. Williams, W. C.
Girl with the flaxen hair. Grau, S. A.
GIRLS
Aldrich, B. S. How far is it to Hollywood?
Aldrich, B. S. Juno's swans
American girl (Periodical) Favorite sto-
ries; 21 stories
American girl (Periodical) On my honor;
20 stories
Gustafson, R. The pigeon
Harte, B. M'liss
McFarland, W. K. comp. Then it hap-
pened; 21 stories
Parker, J. R. Katrina
Quentin, P. pseud. Witness for the pros-
ecution
Sansom, W. Something terrible, some-
thing lovely
Schwartz, R. A. Shoes of bright green
leather
Stowe, A. comp. It's a date; 10 stories
See also Brothers and sisters; Chil-
dren; Parent and child

Girls are so helpless. Bennett, S.

Girls at the Sphinx. Farrell, J. T.

GIRLS' CLUBS
Doty, W. L. Father Murray's first failure

Girls from Earth. Robinson, F. M.

Girls in black. Winslow, T. S.

Gissing, George, 1857-1903
Pig and whistle
Blodgett, H. W. ed. Story survey. 1953 ed.

Git along. De Camp, L. S.

'Git or git got.' Wolfert, I.

Giulia Lazzari. Maugham, W. S.

Give my love to Maggie. Van Ness, L.

Given years. Cohn, E.

Gizycka, Felicia, 1905-
Forever Florida
Story (Periodical) Story; no. 3

Gizzard of a scientist. Boyd, J.

GLACIERS
Muir, J. An adventure with a dog and a glacier

Glaciers. Gomberg, V. G.

GLADNESS. See Happiness

The glads. Powell, D.

GLANDERS (DISEASE)
Pirandello, L. The fly

Glasgow fantom. Gilpatric, G.

Glaspell, Susan, 1882-1948
Jury of her peers
Burrell, J. A. and Cerf, B. A. eds. Anthology of famous American stories

Glass boy. Summers, J. L.

Glass eye. Russell, E. F.

Glass house. Livesay, D.

Glass of milk. Rojas, M.

Glass of orange juice. Reynolds, Q. J.

Glass of tea. Tunkel, J.

Glass wall. Lincoln, V. E.

Glassman, Baruch, 1893-
Tarnished gold
Leftwich, J. ed. Yisröel. 1952 ed.

Glatstein, Jacob, 1896-
The return
Howe, I. and Greenberg, E. eds. Treasury of Yiddish stories

Gleeb for earth. Schafhauser, C.

Gleeps. Miller, P. S.

Glemser, Bernard, 1908-
Purple fields
Star science fiction stories, no. 2

Glen, Enid
Always good for a belly laugh
Best American short stories, 1952

Glen, Mary Avery
Comfort and joy
American girl (Periodical) Christmas all year 'round

GLIDERS (AERONAUTICS)
Coombs, C. I. Silent wings
Hallstead, W. F. Thunder and the wise guy

Gliding gulfs and going people. Sansom, W.

The "Gloria Scott." Doyle, Sir A. C.

Glory, glory, hallelujah. Foley, M.

GLOVES
Ekbergh, I. D. White silk gloves

Glow-worm. Sitwell, Sir O. bart.

Glückel of Hamelin. See Hameln, Glückel of

Gnome there was. Kuttner, H.

GNOMES. See Fairies

Gnurrs come from the voodvork out. Bretnor, R.

Go to the ant. Doyle, L.

GOATS
Caldwell, E. My old man
Daudet, A. M. Seguin's goat
Hinton, J. Mediators to the goatherd
Kilcrin, I. Star buck
O'Flaherty, L. Wild goat's kid
Stong, P. D. Censored, the goat
Tolstoĭ, A. N. Graf. Fusty Devil
See also Rocky Mountain goats

Gobineau, Joseph Arthur, comte de, 1816-1882
Red handkerchief
Geist, S. ed. French stories and tales

GOBLINS. See Fairies

GOD
Brown, F. Search
De Quincey, T. Savannah-la-mar
Horowitz, E. God's agents have beards
Lagerkvist, P. F. Paradise
Rilke, R. M. The stranger
Temple, W. F. Forget-me-not

God. Zamiatin, E. I.

God and Daphne. Kneale, N.

God and the angry men. Johnston, N. F.

God and the little cat. Jepson, S.

God has no wife. Van Doren, M.

God hit a home run. Fontaine, R. L.

God in the bowl. Howard, R. E.

God is good to a Jew. Hecht, B.

God of the gongs. Chesterton, G. K.

God wheel. Keller, D. H.

Godchaux, Elma, d. 1941
Horn that called Bambine
Southern review. Anthology of stories from the Southern review

Godfrey, Peter
Lady and the dragon
Queen, E. pseud. ed. Queen's awards: 5th ser.

GODS
Beaconsfield, B. D. 1st earl of. Ixion in heaven

God's agents have beards. Horowitz, E.

Gods in exile. Heine, H.

God's little traveling salesman. Lagerkvist, P. F.

Godwin, Francis, Bp. of Hereford, 1562-1633
Man in the moone
Derleth, A. W. ed. Beyond time & space

Goethe, Johann Wolfgang von, 1749-1832
Sorrows of Young Werther
Lange, V. ed. Great German short novels and stories

About
Bergengruen, W. On presenting arms

Gogol', Nikolaĭ Vasil'evich, 1809-1852
Old-world landowners
Gordon, C. and Tate, A. eds. House of fiction
The overcoat
Rahv, P. ed. Great Russian short novels
Goin' to town. Stegner, W. E.
Going home. Goodwin, R. V.
Gold, Herbert, 1924-
Mirror and Mr Sneeves
Story (Periodical) Story; no. 3
The witch
Prize stories, 1954
Gold, Horace L.
Man with English
Star science fiction stories ₍no. 1₎
Matter of form
Conklin, G. ed. Big book of science fiction
Pohl, F. ed. Assignment in tomorrow
Perfect murder
Conklin, G. ed. Science-fiction adventures in dimension
Gold, Horace L. and Krepps, Robert Wilson, 1919-
Enormous room
Year's best science fiction novels, 1954
Gold, Ivan, 1932-
Change of air
Best American short stories, 1954
Gold, Michael, 1894-
Mushrooms in Bronx Park
Ausubel, N. ed. Treasury of Jewish humor
Sam Kravitz, that thief
Ausubel, N. ed. Treasury of Jewish humor
Gold, Zachary
Spring over Brooklyn
Stauffer, R. M.; Cunningham, W. H. and Sullivan, C. J. eds. Adventures in modern literature
The gold bug. Poe, E. A.
Gold-fever. Caldwell, E.
Gold mine in the sky. Williams, H. L.
GOLD MINES AND MINING
Davis, A. L. The Klondiker
London, J. All-gold cañon
London, J. Too much gold
Mowery, W. B. Long shadow
See also Mines and mining
Gold of Caxamalca. Wassermann, J.
Gold that glittered. Porter, W. S.
Golden apples of the sun. Bradbury, R.
Golden arm. Jacobs, J.
Golden bough. Keller, D. H.
Golden egg. Waldo, E. H.
Golden fish. Benson, T.
Golden honeymoon. Lardner, R. W.
Golden kite, the silver wind. Bradbury, R.
Golden land. Faulkner, W.
Golden man. Dick, P. K.
Golden pitcher. Gunterman, B. L.
Golden pot. Hoffmann, E. T. A.
Golden wedding. Suckow, R.
Goldfish bowl. Faggett, H. L.

Goldilocks. Waltari, M. T.
Golding, Louis, 1895-
Angels in Chayder
Ausubel, N. ed. Treasury of Jewish humor
Doomington wanderer
Leftwich, J, ed. Yisröel. 1952 ed.
Goldman, Alvin, 1927-
Almost like dead
Weaver, R. and James, H. eds. Canadian short stories
Goldsmith, Gloria, 1925-
Tender to the ship
American vanguard, 1953
Goldsmith, Oliver, 1728-1774
Asem
Cerf, B. A. and Moriarty, H. C. eds. Anthology of famous British stories
Disabled soldier
Ludwig, J. B. and Poirier, W. R. eds. Stories, British and American
Neider, C. ed. Great short stories from the world's literature
Goldsmith, Ruth M. 1919-
Yankee exodus
Best science-fiction stories: 1954
Goldstone, H.
Virtuoso
Conklin, G. ed. Science-fiction thinking machines
The golem. Peretz, I. L.
GOLF
Bond, N. S. Steady like a rock
Field, S. S. Good-by to Cap'm John
Gault, W. C. Gallery-shy
Miers, E. S. Skeedunk Special
Person, W. T. Pony Porter swing
Train, A. Mr Tutt collects a bet
Van Loan, C. Cure for lumbago
Gomberg, Vladimïr Germanovich, 1894-
Glaciers
Talbot, D. ed. Treasury of mountaineering stories
Gomez. Kornbluth, C. M.
GONDOLIERS
Sansom, W. Miss Haines and the gondolier
Gone is gone. Gág, W.
Gonzalez, N. V. M.
Morning star
Stanford short stories, 1950
Warm hand
Stanford short stories, 1950
Good, Edward, 1885-
Salt for the soul
Leftwich, J. ed. Yisröel. 1952 ed.
GOOD AND EVIL
Hawthorne, N. Great Stone Face
Hawthorne, N. Young Goodman Brown
Maugham, W. S. Judgment seat
O'Donovan, M. Face of evil
Russell, B. A. W. R. 3d earl. Satan in the suburbs
Stevenson, R. L. Markheim
Good Anna. Stein, G.
Good boy. De Vries, P.
Good-by, Debbie. McDowell, D.
Good-by to Cap'm John. Field, S. S.

Good-by to Miss Stoddard's. Pultz, C.

Good dog forward. Banér, S. V.

Good girl. Dell'Archiprete, R.

"Good girl—forward!" Banér, S. V.

Good kid. Barr, J. pseud.

The good life. Michener, J. A.

Good marriage. Haycox, E.

Good-natured slob. Williams, W. C.

Good news. Chekhov, A. P.

Good night, Mr James. Simak, C. D.

Good old days. Williams, W. C.

Good people of Milton. Schwartz, R. H.

Good provider. Gross, M.

Good river. Buck, P. S.

GOOD SAMARITAN (PARABLE)
  Goudge, E. Doing good

Good thing to know. Van Doren, M.

Good Wednesday. Brush, K. I. ·

Good-willer. Plumb, B.

Good win. Blackburn, E. R.

Goodbye forever. Rice, C.

Good-bye, Ilha! Manning, L.

Goodbye, my brother. Cheever, J.

Goodloe, Abbie Carter, 1867-
  Claustrophobia
    Thinker's digest (Periodical) Spoiled
    priest, and other stories

Goodly creatures. Kornbluth, C. M.

Goodman, J. Carol
  Kingdom of Gordon
    Best American short stories, 1951

Goodman, Joseph T. 1838-1917
  "Trumpet" comes to Pickeye!
    Emrich, D. ed. Comstock bonanza

Goodman, Paul, 1916-
  Iddings Clark
    Horizon (Periodical) Golden Horizon
  Memorial synagogue
    Ribalow, H. U. ed. This land, these
    people

Goodridge Roberts, Theodore, 1877-1953
  White wolf
    Pacey, D. ed. Book of Canadian stories

Goodwin, Ruth V.
  Going home
    Abell, E. ed. American accent

GOOSE. See Geese

Goose and the gander. Cooke, A. A.

Gooseberries. Chekhov, A. P.

GOPHERS
  Howarth, J. The novitiate

Gordimer, Nadine
  Ah, woe is me
    Gordimer, N. Soft voice of the serpent,
    and other stories
  The amateurs
    Gordimer, N. Soft voice of the serpent,
    and other stories
  Another part of the sky
    Gordimer, N. Soft voice of the serpent,
    and other stories
  The catch
    Gordimer, N. Soft voice of the serpent,
    and other stories

Commonplace story
    Gordimer, N. Soft voice of the serpent,
    and other stories
The defeated
    Gordimer, N. Soft voice of the serpent,
    and other stories
End of the tunnel
    Gordimer, N. Soft voice of the serpent,
    and other stories
Hour and the years
    Gordimer, N. Soft voice of the serpent,
    and other stories
In the beginning
    Gordimer, N. Soft voice of the serpent,
    and other stories
Is there nowhere else where we can meet?
    Gordimer, N. Soft voice of the serpent,
    and other stories
Kindest thing to do
    Gordimer, N. Soft voice of the serpent,
    and other stories
Monday is better than Sunday
    Gordimer, N. Soft voice of the serpent,
    and other stories
Present for a good girl
    Gordimer, N. Soft voice of the serpent,
    and other stories
The prisoner
    Gordimer, N. Soft voice of the serpent,
    and other stories
Soft voice of the serpent
    Gordimer, N. Soft voice of the serpent,
    and other stories
The talisman
    Gordimer, N. Soft voice of the serpent,
    and other stories
Train from Rhodesia
    Gordimer, N. Soft voice of the serpent,
    and other stories
Treasures of the sea
    Gordimer, N. Soft voice of the serpent,
    and other stories
Umbilical cord
    Gordimer, N. Soft voice of the serpent,
    and other stories
La vie Bohème
    Gordimer, N. Soft voice of the serpent,
    and other stories
Watcher of the dead
    Gordimer, N. Soft voice of the serpent,
    and other stories

Gordon, Arthur, 1912-
Alchemist's secret
    This week magazine. This week's short-
    short stories
Devil and Father Francisco
    This week magazine. This week's short-
    short stories
Kiss for the Lieutenant
    This week magazine. This week's short-
    short stories
Old Ironpuss
    Saturday evening post (Periodical)
    Saturday evening post stories, 1951
Sea devil
    Saturday evening post (Periodical)
    Saturday evening post stories, 1953

Gordon, Caroline, 1895-
The captive
    Lynskey, W. C. ed. Reading modern
    fiction

Gordan, Caroline—*Continued*
Forest of the South
Jones, K. M. ed. New Confederate short
stories
Her quaint honour
West, R. B. and Stallman, R. W. eds.
Art of modern fiction
Last day in the field
Heilman, R. B. ed. Modern short sto-
ries
Old Red
Summers, H. S. ed. Kentucky story

Gordon, Charles Monroe, 1857-1946
Christmas Eve in a lumber camp
Elmquist, R. M. ed. Fifty years of
Christmas

Gordon, Charles William, 1860-1937
The canyon flowers
Brentano, F. ed. The word lives on

Gordon, Ethel (Edison)
Value of the dollar
Best American short stories, 1951

Gorge of the Churels. Wakefield, H. R.

Gorgeous number. Newhouse, E.

GORILLAS
Collier, J. Variation on a theme

Gorki, Maxim, pseud. See Gorky, Maxim

Gorky, Maxim, 1868-1936
Birth of a man
Fremantle, A. J. ed. Mothers
Might of motherhood
Ungar, F. ed. To mother with love
On the way
Guerney, B. G. comp. New Russian
stories
One autumn night
Blodgett, H. W. ed. Story survey.
1953 ed.
Short, R. W. and Sewall, R. B. eds.
Short stories for study. 1950 ed.
Twenty-six and one
Cody, S. ed. Greatest stories and how
they were written

Gorska, Halina, d. 1943
Prince Godfrey frees mountain dwellers
and little shepherds from a savage
werewolf and from witches
Fenner, P. R. comp. Ghosts, ghosts,
ghosts

Goss, John Mayo, 1892-
Bird song
First-prize stories, 1919-1954

GOSSIP
Brush, K. I. Good Wednesday
Hawthorne, N. Mr Higginbotham's catas-
trophe
Welty, E. Petrified man

Gostak and the doshes. Breuer, M. J.

Goudge, Elizabeth, 1900-
By the waters of Babylon
Goudge, E. Reward of faith
Canticle of the sun
Goudge, E. Reward of faith
Doing good
Brentano, F. ed. The word lives on
Icon on the wall
Goudge, E. Reward of faith
Legend of the first Christmas tree
Goudge, E. Reward of faith

Midnight in the stable
Lohan, R. and Lohan, M. eds. New
Christmas treasury
Reward of faith
Goudge, E. Reward of faith
Son-of-David
Goudge, E. Reward of faith
Three gray men
Goudge, E. Reward of faith
Well of the star
Goudge, E. Reward of faith

Goudsmit, Samuel, 1884-
Romantic boy
Leftwich, J. ed. Yisröel. 1952 ed.

GOVERNESSES
Birmingham, S. G. Reappearance
Maugham, W. S. String of beads

GOVERNMENT EMPLOYEES. See Civil
service

Governor Warburton's right-hand man.
Stuart, J.

Goyen, William, 1918-
Children of Old Somebody
Goyen, W. Ghost and flesh
Ghost and flesh, water and dirt
Goyen, W. Ghost and flesh
Grasshopper's burden
Goyen, W. Ghost and flesh
Her breath upon the windowpane
Best American short stories, 1951
Peery, W. W. ed. 21 Texas short stories
Letter in the cedarchest
Goyen, W. Ghost and flesh
Nests in a stone image
Goyen, W. Ghost and flesh
Pore Perrie
Goyen, W. Ghost and flesh
Shape of light
Goyen, W. Ghost and flesh
White rooster
Goyen, W. Ghost and flesh
Ludwig, J. B. and Poirier, W. R. eds.
Stories, British and American

Grace, Skinner, 1922-
Nice little girl
Wolfe, D. M. ed. Which grain will grow

Grace Crawley and the Archdeacon. Trollope, A.

The **Grace** Mansion. Cooke, A. A.

GRACES. See Prayers

Grade, Chaim, 1910-
My quarrel with Hersh Rasseyner
Howe, I. and Greenberg, E. eds. Treas-
ury of Yiddish stories

GRADUATIONS. See Commencements

Graham, Frank, 1893-
Joining the Yankees
Fenner, P. R. comp. Crack of the bat

Graham, Margaret (Collier) 1850-1910
Face of the poor
Cooper, A. C. ed. Modern short stories

Graham, Robert Bontine Cunninghame,
1852-1936
Faith
Cerf, B. A. and Moriarty, H. C. eds.
Anthology of famous British stories

Grahame, Kenneth, 1859-1932
Reluctant dragon
Fenner, P. R. comp. Fun! Fun! Fun!

GRAMOPHONE. See Phonograph

The gramophone. Wendroff, Z.

GRANADA. See Spain—Granada

Granberg, Bill
  Hi, sailor!
    Fenner, P. R. comp. Stories of the sea

Granberry, Edwin Phillips, 1897-
  Trip to Czardis
    Blodgett, H. W. ed. Story survey.
      1953 ed.
    Shaw, H. and Bement, D. Reading the
      short story

Grand march. Powell, D.

Grand prize. Newcomb, C.

GRANDCHILDREN
  Betts, D. Child so fair

GRANDFATHERS
  Beck, W. Verdict of innocence
  Clay, R. Very sharp for jagging
  Cohn, E. A. The present
  Dell, F. The blanket
  Goyen, W. White rooster
  Jenkins, W. F. Little terror
  Newell, A. S. Grandpop comes home
  Overholser, W. D. Patriarch of Gunsight
    Flat
  Rinehart, M. R. One hour of glory
  Steinbeck, J. Leader of the people
  Van Doren, M. The pair
  Van Doren, M. Wild wet place

Grandfather's tale. Schneider, G. W.

Grandison and son. Van Doren, M.

Grandma. Winslow, T. S.

Grandma goes to the Fair. Grimson, M. S.

GRANDMOTHERS
  Aiken, C. P. Last visit
  Grimson, M. S. Grandma goes to the Fair
  Kensinger, F. R. Sense of destination
  O'Donovan, M. First confession
  Pendergast, C. The picnic
  Poe, E. A. The spectacles
  Riter, F. Sense of destination
  Somerville, E. A. Œ. and Martin, V. F.
    Trinket's colt
  Van Doren, M. Wild wet place
  Winslow, T. S. Grandma
  Winslow, T. S. Odd old lady

GRANDPARENTS. See Grandfathers;
  Grandmothers

Grandpop comes home. Newell, A. S.

Grant, George Hook, 1896-
  The hurricane
    Bluebook (Periodical) Best sea stories
      from Bluebook

Grass fire. Caldwell, E.

Grass grow again. Wilson, J. W.

Grass, milk, and children. Bishop, L.

Grass on the other side. Smith, L.

Grasshopper a burden. Thompson, L.

Grasshopper's burden. Goyen, W.

GRATITUDE
  Schwarz, F. C. Serpent's tooth
  Shaw, I. Faith at sea

Grau, Shirley Ann
  Black prince
    Grau, S. A. Black prince, and other
      stories

Bright day
  Grau, S. A. Black prince, and other
    stories

Fever flower
  Grau, S. A. Black prince, and other
    stories

Girl with the flaxen hair
  Grau, S. A. Black prince, and other
    stories

Joshua
  Grau, S. A. Black prince, and other
    stories

Miss Yellow Eyes
  Grau, S. A. Black prince, and other
    stories

One summer
  Grau, S. A. Black prince, and other
    stories

Way of a man
  Grau, S. A. Black prince, and other
    stories

White girl, fine girl
  Grau, S. A. Black prince, and other
    stories

The grave. Porter, K. A.

Grave digger. Gibran, K.

Grave digger and Biggie Doone. Brookhouser, F.

GRAVE ROBBERS
  Coolidge, O. E. Black magician

GRAVEDIGGERS
  Farrell, J. T. Digging our own graves

Graves, Robert, 1895-
  The shout
    Magazine of fantasy and science fiction.
      Best from Fantasy and science fiction;
      2d ser.

GRAVES. See Cemeteries; Funeral rites
  and ceremonies

Graveyard shift. Frazee, S.

GRAVEYARDS. See Cemeteries

GRAVITY
  Clifton, M. and Apostolides, A. What thin
    partitions
  Cummings, R. Gravity professor
  Jones, R. F. Noise level

Gravity professor. Cummings, R.

Gray, Clark
  Campaigning cowpoke
    Meredith, S. ed. Bar 1 roundup of best
      western stories

Gray, David, 1870-
  His first race
    Creamer, J. B. comp. Twenty-two
      stories about horses and men
  Ting-a-ling
    Creamer, J. B. comp. Twenty-two
      stories about horses and men

Gray, Elizabeth Janet, 1902-
  Christmas cherries
    Story parade (Periodical) Adventure
      stories

Gray, Will H.
  Bees from Borneo
    Conklin, G. ed. Omnibus of science fic-
      tion

Gray champion. Hawthorne, N.

Gray goose. Steele, W. D.

Greenfield, Robert, 1911-
Jonathan Harrow
American vanguard, 1953
Way of a traitor
American vanguard, 1950
GREENWICH VILLAGE. See New York
(City)—Greenwich Village
The greeting. Sitwell, Sir O. bart.
Gregory, Vahan Krikorian, 1927-
Athens, Greece, 1942
Best American short stories, 1953
Greg's peg. Auchincloss, L.
Gregutt, Helen Ciancimino
Christmas at Polly Moran's
American girl (Periodical) Christmas
all year 'round
Climb for the big ones
Furman, A. L. ed Everygirls career
stories
Jam session at Abby's
American girl (Periodical) Favorite sto-
ries
The secret
Furman, A. L. ed Everygirls career
stories
There isn't time now
McFarland, W. K. comp. Then it hap-
pened
Victory
American girl (Periodical) On my honor
GRENADA. See Spain—Granada
Grendon, Edward
Crisis
Conklin, G. ed. Invaders of earth
Trip one
Sloane, W. M. ed. Space, space, space
Grendon, Stephen, 1909-
Mr George
Derleth, A W. ed. Night's yawning peal
Mrs. Manifold
Conklin, G. and Conklin, L. T. eds.
Supernatural reader
Open, sesame!
Derleth, A. W. ed. Far boundaries
Song of the pewee
Derleth, A. W. ed. Far boundaries
Gresham, William Lindsay
Star gypsies
Magazine of fantasy and science fiction.
Best from Fantasy and science fiction;
3d ser.
Grey, Zane, 1872-1939
Old Well-Well
Graber, R. S. ed. Baseball reader
The rube
Graber, R. S. ed. Baseball reader
Tappan's burro
Andrews, R. C. ed. My favorite stories
of the great outdoors
Grey eagle. Sass, H. R.
Grey ones. Priestley, J. B.
Grey seagull. O'Flaherty, L.
GRIDDLE CAKES
Porter, W. S. Pimienta pancakes
The gridiron. Lover, S.
GRIEF. See Joy and sorrow
Grief. Chekhov, A. P.

Griffin, John Howard, 1920-
Miss Henrietta Briggs and her metamor-
phosis
Story (Periodical) Story; no. 3
Griffith, Ann Warren
Captive audience
Magazine of fantasy and science fiction.
Best from Fantasy and science fiction;
3d ser.
Zeritsky's law
Conklin, G. ed. Omnibus of science fic-
tion
Griffith, Beatrice Winston
American me
Seventeen (Periodical) Nineteen from
Seventeen
Griffith, Robert
Jingle bells
Dachs, D. ed. Treasury of sports humor
Grimm, Jakob Ludwig Karl, 1785-1863, and
Grimm, Wilhelm Karl, 1786-1859
Clever Elsa
Fenner, P. R. comp. Fools and funny
fellows
Grimm, Wilhelm Karl, 1786-1859. See
Grimm, J. L. K. jt. auth.
Grimson, Marie S.
American girl looks at Europe
Grimson, M. S. At the crossroads, and
other stories and sketches
At the crossroads
Grimson, M. S. At the crossroads, and
other stories and sketches
Christmas story
Grimson, M. S. At the crossroads, and
other stories and sketches
Concerning discoveries
Grimson, M. S. At the crossroads, and
other stories and sketches
Earth-bound
Grimson, M. S. At the crossroads, and
other stories and sketches
Eighty years old
Grimson, M. S. At the crossroads, and
other stories and sketches
Eureca cottage
Grimson, M. S. At the crossroads, and
other stories and sketches
Faith, hope and charity
Grimson, M. S. At the crossroads, and
other stories and sketches
Gather up the pieces
Grimson, M. S. At the crossroads, and
other stories and sketches
Grandma goes to the Fair
Grimson, M. S. At the crossroads, and
other stories and sketches
Happy birthday to you
Grimson, M. S. At the crossroads, and
other stories and sketches
It never fails
Grimson, M. S. At the crossroads, and
other stories and sketches
King of the north woods
Grimson, M. S. At the crossroads, and
other stories and sketches
Leap year
Grimson, M. S. At the crossroads, and
other stories and sketches

Grimson, Marie S.—*Continued*
Leif goes west
Grimson, M. S. At the crossroads, and other stories and sketches
Norway
Grimson, M. S. At the crossroads, and other stories and sketches
Regarding monuments
Grimson, M. S. At the crossroads, and other stories and sketches
Story of Paula
Grimson, M. S. At the crossroads, and other stories and sketches
When Dan came home
Grimson, M. S. At the crossroads, and other stories and sketches
When TV came to the backwoods
Grimson, M. S. At the crossroads, and other stories and sketches
Who is my neighbor?
Grimson, M. S. At the crossroads, and other stories and sketches
Will and a way
Grimson, M. S. At the crossroads, and other stories and sketches
Won and lost
Grimson, M. S. At the crossroads, and other stories and sketches

Grinevskii, Aleksandr Stepanovich, 1880-1932
The ratcatcher
Guerney, B. G. comp. New Russian stories

Grinnell, David, pseud.
Extending the holdings
Best science fiction stories: 1952
Malice aforethought
Merril, J. ed. Beyond the barriers of space and time
Rag thing
Conklin, G. ed. Omnibus of science fiction
Top secret
Conklin, G. ed. Invaders of earth

Gronowicz, Antoni, 1913-
Mania-head-in-the-clouds
Hazeltine, A. I. comp. Selected stories for teen-agers

Groseclose, Elgin Earl, 1899-
The healing of the lepers
Brentano, F. ed. The word lives on

Gross, Marion
Good provider
Conklin, G. ed. Science-fiction adventures in dimension

Grosskopf, Edward K. 1920-
Tea for Tamahara
Oberfirst, R. ed. 1952 anthology of best original short-shorts

Ground mist. Redman, B. R.

GROUSE HUNTING
Bonner, P. H. Big day

Grove, Edgar
Dress for Kitty
Story (Periodical) Story; no. 2

Grove, Frederick Philip, 1872-1948
Snow
Pacey, D. ed. Book of Canadian stories

Grove, Walt, 1921-
Man who flew into a rage
Collier's, the national weekly. Collier's best

Growing pains. Stull, P.

Growing season. Caldwell, E.

Grunert, Karl, 1865-1907
Enemies in space
Conklin, G. ed. Invaders of space

Grunion run. Cawley, C. C.

GUADALCANAL
Michener, J. A. The story

GUADALUPE, OUR LADY OF
Steinbeck, J. Miracle of Tepayac

GUARD DUTY
Bergengruen, W. The sentry
O'Donovan, M. The sentry

The guardian. De La Mare, W. J.

The guardian. Robertson, F. C.

Guardian angel. Alarcon, P. A. de.

Guardian angel. Willingham, C.

Guardian of the accolade. Porter, W. S.

GUARDIANS
Harte, B. Protégé of Jack Hamlin's
Harte, B. Ward of Colonel Starbottle's

Guardians of Parnassus. Russell, B. A. W. R. 3d earl

GUAYANA INDIANS
Hudson, W. H. Mysterious forest

Guest, Anna, 1913?-
Barbèd rose
American vanguard, 1953
Closed door
American vanguard, 1952

The guest. Chekhov, A. P.

Guest of honour. Priestley, J. B.

Guest of reality. Lagerkvist, P. F.

GUESTS
Bowen, E. The visitor
Hawthorne, N. Ambitious guest
Munro, H. H. The hen
Parker, J. R. Joy, joy, joy!
Parker, J. R. Lower Mississippi
Parker, J. R. Red carpet
Rabinowitz, S. Passover guest

The guests. Munro, H. H.

Guests of the nation. O'Donovan, M.

The guide. Lytle, A. N.

GUIDES (HUNTING)
La Farge, O. Old century's river
Mowery, W. B. Man-killer

Guillotine party. Farrell, J. T.

Guilty. Hurst, F.

"Guilty party." Porter, W. S.

Guilty witness. Hershman, M.

Guin, Wyman
Beyond Bedlam
Galaxy science fiction magazine. Galaxy reader of science fiction
Trigger tide
Conklin, G. ed. Omnibus of science fiction

Guinea pig. McKenney, R.

Guinevere for everybody. Williamson, J.

Guiney, Louise Imogen, 1861-1920
  The provider
    Fremantle, A. J. ed. Mothers
Guinness, Alec
  Money for jam
    New writing (Periodical) Best stories
Güiraldes, Ricardo, 1886-1927
  Old ranch
    De Onís, H. ed. Spanish stories and tales
Gulf. Heinlein, R. A.
Gulick, Bill. See Gulick, Grover C.
Gulick, Grover C. 1916-
  Rendezvous romance
    Western Writers of America. Bad men
    and good
  Squaw fever
    Meredith, S. ed. Bar 2
  Two-faced promise
    Meredith, S. ed. Bar 1 roundup of best
    western stories
  Waters of Manitou
    Western Writers of America. Holsters
    and heroes
Gulliver the Great. Dyer, W. A.
Gun job. Thompson, T.
Gun on the wall. Garber, G.
Gun shy. Fenton, E.
Gunn, James E.
  The misogynist
    Galaxy science fiction magazine. Sec-
    ond Galaxy reader of science fiction
Gunn, Neil Miller, 1891-
  Desperate journey
    Saturday evening post (Periodical) Sat-
    urday evening post stories, 1952
Gunnarson, Gunnar, 1889-
  Advent
    Brentano, F. ed. The word lives on
The gunny. Turner, R.
GUNS. See Firearms
Gunterman, Bertha L.
  Golden pitcher
    Fenner, P. R. comp. Ghosts, ghosts,
    ghosts
Gurnard, Joseph
  Poets' excursion
    New Writing (Periodical) Best stories
Gus the gloom. Bateman, A.
Gust of wind. Hill, J. H.
Gustafson, Ralph, 1909-
  The pigeon
    Best American short stories, 1950
Guthrie, Alfred Bertram, 1901-
  Ebbie
    Abell, E. ed. American accent
    Summers, H. S. ed. Kentucky story
  Fraudulent skunk
    Meredith, S. ed. Bar I roundup of best
    western stories
Gutman, Chaim, 1887-
  No enemy of his
    Ausubel, N. ed. Treasury of Jewish
    humor
  Real customers
    Ausubel, N. ed. Treasury of Jewish
    humor

Gy-ma-na-si-a. Rabinowitz, S.
GYMNASTS. See Acrobats and acrobatism
GYPSIES. See Gipsies

H

Haardt, Sara Powell, 1898-1935
  Little white girl
    Thinker's digest (Periodical) Spoiled
    priest, and other stories
Habeas Corpus Club. Harvey, W. F.
Hadji Murad. Tolstoĭ, L. N. Graf
Hagedorn, Herman, 1882-
  Hour of stars
    Elmquist, R. M. ed. Fifty years of
    Christmas
Hager, Mark
  The champions
    Fenner, P. R. comp. Dogs, dogs, dogs
Hail, Steve
  Taste of command
    Argosy (Periodical) Argosy Book of
    sea stories
Hail and farewell. Bradbury, R.
"Hail, brother and farewell." Karchmer, S.
Hail fellow well met. Herron, E.
HAIR
  De Camp, L. S. Hyperpilosity
  Fitzgerald, F. S. K. Bernice bobs her hair
  Hauser, M. The mouse
  Maupassant, G. de. One phase of love
  Porter, W. S. Gift of the Magi
Hair. Faulkner, W.
HAIR DRESSERS. See Barbers; Beauty,
  Personal
Hair shirt. Vickers, R.
Haircut. Lardner, R. W.
Hairless Mexican. Maugham, W. S.
HAITI
  Capote, T. House of flowers
  Litten, F. N. Tell it to the Marines
    Port-Au-Prince
  Rattner, J. Haitian incident
Haitian incident. Rattner, J.
Halberdier of the Little Rheinschloss. Por-
  ter, W. S.
Hale, Edward Everett, 1822-1909
  General Washington's pig
    Eaton, H. T. ed. Short stories
  Man without a country
    Burrell, J. A. and Cerf, B. A. eds. An-
    thology of famous American stories
  My double, and how he undid me
    Cuff, R. P. ed. American short story
    survey
Hale, Lucretia Peabody, 1820-1900
  Peterkins' Christmas tree
    Fenner, P. R. comp. Fools and funny
    fellows
Hale, Nancy, 1908-
  No one my grief can tell
    Blodgett, H. W. ed. Story survey.
    1953 ed.

Hale, Nathan
Brahmin Beachhead
Best American short stories, 1952

Half-brothers. Gaskell, E. C. S.

HALF-CASTES
Maugham, W. S. Yellow streak

Half-naked truth. Blochman, L. G.

HALF-SISTERS
Rinehart, M. R. If only it were yesterday

Halfway to Hell. Collier, J.

Haliburton, Thomas Chandler, 1796-1865
Sam Slick the clockmaker
Pacey, D. ed. Book of Canadian stories

Hall, Desmond
Pickles and pearls
Argosy (Periodical) Argosy Book of
adventure stories

Hall, Douglass
Foggy
Ford, N. A. and Faggett, H. L. eds.
Best short stories by Afro-American
writers (1925-1950)

Hall, Esther Greenacre
Callie of Crooked Creek
American girl (Periodical) Favorite sto-
ries

Hall, James B.
Estate and trespass: a Gothic story
Prize stories, 1954
In the time of demonstrations
Prize stories of 1951
Spot in history
Best American short stories, 1953

Hall, James Norman, 1887-1951
Cheerful tortoise
McFee, W. ed. Great sea stories of
modern times
Haunted island
Saturday evening post (Periodical)
Saturday evening post stories, 1950
See also Nordhoff, C. B. jt. auth.

Hall, Stephen. See King-Hall, Stephen

Hall of mirrors. Brown, F.

Hallack, Cecily, 1898-1938
Wretched old capitalist
Thinker's digest (Periodical) Spoiled
priest, and other stories

Halladay, Velma, 1919?-
One-beautiful Ellie
Oberfirst, R. ed. 1952 anthology of best
original short-shorts

Halliday, Brett, pseud. See Dresser, Davis

Hallinan, Nancy, 1921-
Limbo
American vanguard, 1950

Hallowed years. Buckingham, N.

Hallstead, William F.
Space Lane cadet
Fenner, P. R. comp. Speed, speed, speed
Thunder and the wise guy
Fenner, P. R. comp. Speed, speed, speed

Hallucination orbit. Macgregor, J. M.

HALLUCINATIONS AND ILLUSIONS
Dreiser, T. Lost Phoebe
Gellhorn, M. E. Psychiatrist of one's own
Hurst, F. Guilty
Maugham, W. S. The taipan

Miller, W. M. Little creeps
Munro, H. H. Soul of Laploshka
Nelson, A. Narapoia
Poe, E. A. Ligeia
Poe, E. A. The sphinx
Priestley, J. B. Grey ones
Richter, C. Doctor Hanray's second
chance
Thurber, J. The whip-poor-will
Wells, H. G. Remarkable case of David-
son's eyes
See also Ghosts

Halper, Albert, 1904-
My mother's love story
Ribalow, H. U. ed. These your children

Hameiri, Avigdor, 1890-
Three Halutzot
Leftwich, J. ed. Yisröel. 1952 ed.

Hamelyn, Glückel of, 1646-1724
A story
Leftwich, J. ed. Yisröel. 1952 ed.

Hamilton, Edmond, 1904-
Conquest of two worlds
Wollheim, D. A. comp. Every boy's
book of science-fiction
Dead planet
Derleth, A. W. ed. Worlds of tomorrow
Exile
Lesser, M. A. ed. Looking forward
Fessenden's worlds
Derleth, A. W. ed. Beyond time & space
Forgotten world
Margulies, L. and Friend, O. J. eds.
Giant anthology of science fiction
Man who evolved
Margulies, L. and Friend, O. J. eds.
From off this world
What's it like out there?
Startling stories (Periodical) Best from
Startling stories

Hamilton, Roland T.
Symbol of courage
Ford, N. A. Faggett, H. L. eds. Best
short stories by Afro-American writers
(1925-1950)

Hammer of God. Chesterton, G. K.

Hammett, Dashiell, 1894-
His brother's keeper
Ribalow, H. U. ed. World's greatest
boxing stories

Hammond, Keith, pseud. See Kuttner,
Henry

Hamos, George
The conjurer
Story (Periodical) Story; no. 3

Hamrick's polar bear. Caldwell, E.

Hamsun, Knut, 1859-1952
Wonderful new machine
Burnett, W. ed. World's best

HAND
Maupassant, G. de. The hand

Hand in glove. Bowen, E.

Hand of God. Keeler, H. S.

The hand that riles the world. Porter, W. S.

HAND-TO-HAND-FIGHTING. See Fighting, Hand-to-hand

Hand upon the waters. Faulkner, W.

Handbook of Hymen. Porter, W. S.

Hands. Anderson, S.

Hands across the deep. Elam, R. M.

Hands across the sea. Williams, W. C.

Hands of Mr Ottermole. Burke, T.

Handsome lady. Coppard, A. E.

Handy. Caldwell, E.

HANGCHOW. See China—Hangchow

HANGING
Baudelaire, C. P. The rope
Bierce, A. Occurrence at Owl Creek
bridge
Bradford, R. Child of God
Carver, C. Hanging Hollow
Harte, B. Tennessee's partner
Lagerkvist, P. F. The hangman

Hanging fire. Barr, J. pseud.

Hanging fire. Deming, R.

Hanging Hollow. Carver, C.

HANGINGS (EXECUTIONS). See Hanging

The hangman. Lagerkvist, P. F.

HANGMEN. See Hanging

Hangover. Cash, M. L.

Hanlon, Brooke
Crushed orchid
Saturday evening post (Periodical)
Saturday evening post stories, 1950

Hannibal's elephants. Powers, A.

HANSEN'S DISEASE. See Leprosy

Hansjorg and his pipe. Auerbach, B.

HANUKKAH (FEAST OF LIGHTS)
Peretz, I. L. Little Hanukkah lamp

Happiest creature. Williamson, J.

Happiest man on earth. Maltz, A.

HAPPINESS
Maugham, W. S. Happy man
Maupassant, G. de. Happiness

Happiness in crime. Barbey d'Aurevilly,
J. A.

Happy birthday to you. Grimson, M. S.

Happy couple. Maugham, W. S.

Happy ending. Kuttner, H.

Happy failure. Melville, H.

Happy hypocrite. Beerbohm, Sir M.

Happy man. Maugham, W. S.

Happy New Year. Sansom, W.

Happy New Year, kamerades! Lowry,
R. J. C.

Happy one. Rosenberg, E.

The harbinger. Porter, W. S.

Hard day. Parker, J. R.

Hard-luck diggings. Kuttner, H.

HARDWARE STORES
De Vries, P. Household words

Hardwick, Elizabeth, 1916-
Evenings at home
Summers, H. S. ed. Kentucky story

Hardwood hazard. Coombs, C. I.

Hardy, Thomas, 1840-1928
Absent-mindedness in a parish choir
Ludwig, J. B. and Poirier, W. R. eds.
Stories, British and American

Son's veto
Fremantle, A. J. ed. Mothers
Three strangers
Bogorad, S. N. and Trevithick, J. eds.
College miscellany
Cerf, B. A. and Moriarty, H. C. eds.
Anthology of famous British stories
Short, R. W. and Sewall, R. B. eds.
Short stories for study. 1950 ed.
Tony Kytes, the arch-deceiver
Blodgett, H. W. ed. Story survey.
1953 ed.
Tradition of 1804
Barrows, H. ed. 15 stories
Tragedy of two ambitions
Felheim, M.; Newman, F. B. and Stein-
hoff, W. R. eds. Modern short stories

Hardy, William George, 1896-
Czech dog
Pacey, D. ed. Book of Canadian stories

The Hardys. Humphrey, W.

Hare, Cyril, pseud. See Clark, Alfred Alexander Gordon

Harlem tragedy. Porter, W. S.

The harmonizer. Van Vogt, A. E.

Harmony. Lardner, R. W.

Harnden, Ruth Peabody
Rebellion
Prize stories, 1954

Harness, Charles L.
Child by Chronos
Magazine of fantasy and science fiction.
Best from Fantasy and science fiction;
3d ser.
New reality
Best science fiction stories: 1951

HARNESS RACING. See Horse racing

Harrington, Dennis
Trouble with the union
Gable, M. Sister, ed. Many-colored fleece

Harris, Clare Winger, 1891- and Breuer,
Miles, J.
Baby on Neptune
Wollheim, D. A. comp. Flight into space

Harris, George Washington, 1814-1869
In the family bosom
Harris, G. W. Sut lovingood
Second view of the family bosom
Harris, G. W. Sut Lovingood
Sut and the Burns family
Harris, G. W. Sut Lovingood
Sut as a boy
Harris, G. W. Sut Lovingood
Sut meets the law
Harris, G. W. Sut Lovingood
Sut on the national scene
Harris, G. W. Sut Lovingood
Sut sets certain individuals right
Harris, G. W. Sut Lovingood
Sut takes on the whole world
Harris, G. W. Sut Lovingood

Harris, Joel Chandler, 1848-1908
Free Joe and the rest of the world
Scribner treasury
Wonderful Tar-Baby story
Day, A. G. ed. Greatest American short
stories

Harvey, William F.—*Continued*
Atmospherics
Harvey, W. F. Arm of Mrs Egan, and other strange stories
August heat
Carrington, H. ed. Week-end book of ghost stories
Christ, H. I. and Shostak, J. eds. Short stories
Davenport, B. ed. Ghostly tales to be told
Beast with five fingers
Davenport, B. ed. Tales to be told in the dark
Chemist and druggist
Harvey, W. F. Arm of Mrs Egan, and other strange stories
Dark horses
Harvey, W. F. Arm of Mrs Egan, and other strange stories
Dead of night
Harvey, W. F. Arm of Mrs Egan, and other strange stories
Euphemia witchmaid
Harvey, W. F. Arm of Mrs Egan, and other strange stories
Flying out of Mrs Barnard Hollis
Harvey, W. F. Arm of Mrs Egan, and other strange stories
Habeas Corpus Club
Harvey, W. F. Arm of Mrs Egan, and other strange stories
The lake
Harvey, W. F. Arm of Mrs Egan, and other strange stories
Long road
Harvey, W. F. Arm of Mrs Egan, and other strange stories
Mishandled
Harvey, W. F. Arm of Mrs Egan, and other strange stories
No body
Harvey, W. F. Arm of Mrs Egan, and other strange stories
Old masters
Harvey, W. F. Arm of Mrs Egan, and other strange stories
Ripe for development
Harvey, W. F. Arm of Mrs Egan, and other strange stories
Vicar's web
Harvey, W. F. Arm of Mrs Egan, and other strange stories
Harvey Kendall. Schaefer, J. W.
Harwood, Kitty
Papa's going bye-bye
Queen, E. pseud. ed. Queen's awards: 7th ser.
Hasas, Haïm, 1897-
Bridegroom of blood
Leftwich, J. ed. Yisröel. 1952 ed.
Hasley, Lucile
Little girls
Gable, M. Sister, ed. Many-colored fleece
Hasty act. Brandel, M.
Hat trick. Brown, F.
Hat trick. Muller, C. G.
Hatch, Eric, 1901-
Channel 10
This week magazine. This week's short-short stories

HATS
Crossen, K. F. Things of distinction
Porter, W. S. Red roses of Tonia
Rabinowitz, S. On account of a hat
Taylor, M. McGarry joins the Easter parade
Welty, E. Purple hat
Hatvany, Lajos, báró, 1880-
Bondy, jr.
Ausubel, N. ed. Treasury of Jewish humor
Haunted hollow. Mowery, W. B.
HAUNTED HOUSES. See Ghosts
Haunted island. Hall, J. N.
Haunted man. Dickens, C.
Haunted wreck. Henderson, Le G.
Hauptmann, Gerhart Johann Robert, 1862-1946
Flagman Thiel
Lange, V. ed. Great German short novels and stories
Moskowitz, S. ed. Great railroad stories of the world
Hause, Mary
Turn off the moon
Oberfirst, R. ed. 1952 anthology of best original short-shorts
Hauser, Margaret Louise, 1909-
Calling all cars
Strang, R. M. and Roberts, R. M. eds. Teen-age tales v2
Hauser, Marianne, 1920-
The mouse
Best American short stories, 1950
Hautot, father and son. Maupassant, G. de
Hautot Senior & Hautot Junior. Maupassant, G. de
Have a heart, lady! Lamson, R. R.
Have I got sun in my eyes? Farrell, J. T.
HAWAIIAN ISLANDS
Marquand, J. P. You can't do that
Maugham, W. S. Honolulu
Stern, J. Travellers' tears
Stevenson, R. L. Bottle imp
Stevenson, R. L. Isle of voices
Ullman, J. R. Pau
Ullman, J. R. Silver sword
Hawkins, John, 1910- and Hawkins, Ward, 1912-
Burden of guilt
Best detective stories of the year—1951
End of the line
Saturday evening post (Periodical) Saturday evening post stories, 1952
Killer is loose
Best detective stories of the year—1954
Love song in a honky-tonk
Saturday evening post (Periodical) Saturday evening post stories, 1951
Hawkins, Ward, 1912- See Hawkins, J. jt. auth.
HAWKS
Clark, W. Van T. Hook
Hawthorne, Nathaniel, 1804-1864
Ambitious guest
Day, A. G. ed. Greatest American short stories
Hawthorne, N. Best of Hawthorne

Haycox, Ernest—*Continued*
Weight of command
Haycox, E. By rope and lead
Wild Jack Rhett
Haycox, E. Rough justice
HAYDEN PLANETARIUM (NEW YORK CITY)
Beck, W. Shadow of turning
Hayes, Hazel M.
Jenny takes a holiday
Oberfirst, R. ed. 1952 anthology of best original short-shorts
Hayes, Nelson
Weaning of Laura Wade
Story (Periodical) Story; no. 2
Hayes, William Edward
Big engine
Moskowitz, S. ed. Great railroad stories of the world
HAY-FEVER
Canine, W. The clematis
Hays, Lee
Banquet and a half
Queen, E. pseud. ed. Ellery Queen's awards: 9th ser.
Haywood, Carolyn, 1898-
Little Eddie goes to town
Fenner, P. R. comp. Giggle box
Prize corn chowder
Fenner, P. R. comp. Giggle box
Haywood, John L.
Heat spell
Queen, E. pseud. ed. Ellery Queen's awards: 9th ser.
Hazaz, Hayyim. See Hasas, Haïm
Hazlitt, William, 1778-1830
Liber amoris
Connolly, C. ed. Great English short novels
He also serves. Porter, W. S.
He don't plant cotton. Powers, J. F.
He sought to know God. Hobart, A. T. N.
He swung and he missed. Algren, N.
He told it to the judge. Claudy, C. H.
He walked around the horses. Piper, H. B.
He who laughs last. Miers, E. S.
He who woos and runs away. Kober, A.
He wouldn't be a Jew, by an Elder of Zion
Ausubel, N. ed. Treasury of Jewish humor
Head, Gay, pseud. See Hauser, Margaret Louise
Head, Matthew, pseud. See Canaday, John Edwin
Head and the feet. Forester, C. S.
Head by Scopas. Donahoe, E.
The **head**-hunter. Porter, W. S.
Head-hunters. Williams, R.
Head of Cæsar. Chesterton, G. K.
Headley, Elizabeth (Cavanna) See Cavanna, Betty
Headline halfback. Coombs, C. I.
Headwall tempo. Dodge, J. E.
Heagney, Harold Jerome, 1890-
Madame Jeanne De Chantal
Fremantle, A. J. ed. Mothers

Healing of the lepers. Groseclose, E. E.
HEALTH RESORTS, WATERING-PLACES, ETC.
Hearn, L. The storm
Healthiest girl in town. Stafford, J.
Heard, Gerald, 1889-
B+M—planet 4
Healy, R. J. ed. New tales of space and time
The collector
Magazine of fantasy and science fiction. Best from Fantasy and science fiction, 1952
Cyclops
Crossen, K. F. ed. Future tense
Great fog
Heilman, R. B. ed. Modern short stories
The swap
Conklin, G. and Conklin, L. T. eds. Supernatural reader
Wingless victory
Derleth, A. W. ed. Beyond time & space
Heard, Henry Fitzgerald. See Heard, Gerald
Hearn, Lafcadio, 1850-1904
Boy who drew cats
Burrell, J. A. and Cerf, B. A. eds. Anthology of famous American stories
Mujina
Davenport, B. ed. Tales to be told in the dark
The storm
Andrews, R. C. ed. My favorite stories of the great outdoors
HEART
Diseases
Cather, W. S. Neighbour Rosicky
Maugham, W. S. Louise
Heart being perished. Frost, F. M.
Heart in the mouth. Household, G
Heart of darkness. Conrad, J.
Heart of elm. Wilson, A.
Heart of Lily Long. Marshall, E.
Heart of Little Shikara. Marshall, E.
Heartbreak. Barker, A. L.
Heartburn. Calisher, H.
Hearts and crosses. Porter, W. S.
Hearts and hands. Porter, W. S.
Heart's reason. Mallea, E.
Heat spell. Hayward, J. L.
Heath, Priscilla
Farewell, sweet love
Best American short stories, 1954
Heathcott, Mary
Neil's girl
Story (Periodical) Story; no. 4
Heather wine. Walsh, M.
Heatter, Basil, 1918-
Island happy
Saturday evening post (Periodical) Saturday evening post stories, 1950
HEAVEN
Bradford, R. Child of God
Clemens, S. L. Wings
Forster, E. M. Mr Andrews
Temple, W. F. Forget-me-not
See also Future life

Heaven can wait. Gilford, C. B.

Heaven in my hand. Humphreys, A. L.

Heaven to hell. Hughes, L.

Heavenly Christmas tree. Dostoevskiĭ, F. M.

Heavenly world series. O'Rourke, F.

Heavyside Hunt: The new Master's first day. Surtees, R. S.

Heavyside Hunt again: The lady whipper-in. Surtees, R. S.

Hebel, Johann Peter, 1760-1826
  The hussar
    Pick, R. ed. German stories and tales
  Kannitverstan
    Pick, R. ed. German stories and tales
  Unexpected reunion
    Pick, R. ed. German stories and tales

Hébert, Anne
  House on the esplanade
    Best American short stories, 1954

HEBREWS. See Jews

Hecht, Ben, 1893-
  Double exposure
    Best detective stories of the year—1950
  God is good to a Jew
    Ribalow, H. U. ed. These your children
  Miracle of the fifteen murderers
    Fabricant, N. D. and Werner, H. eds. World's best doctor stories
  Swindler's luck
    Grayson, C. ed. Fourth round

Hector. West, M. P.

Hedenstjerna, Alfred von
  A mother
    Ungar, F. ed. To mother with love

The **hedgehog.** Munro, H. H.

Heggen, Thomas, 1919-1949
  Night watch
    Stegner, W. E.; Scowcroft, R. and Ilyin, B. eds. Writer's art

Heide, Helen J.
  End of her rope
    Oberfirst, R. ed. 1952 anthology of best original short-shorts

HEIDELBERG. See Germany—Heidelberg

Heijermans, Herman, 1864-1924
  Shabbes-soup
    Ausubel, N. ed. Treasury of Jewish humor

Heimann, Moritz, 1868-1925
  Message that failed
    Pick, R. ed. German stories and tales

Heine, Heinrich, 1797-1856
  Gods in exile
    Lange, V. ed. Great German short novels and stories
  Seder night
    Leftwich, J. ed. Yisröel. 1952 ed.
    Same as: Tale of olden time
  Tale of olden time
    Neider, C. ed. Great short stories from the world's literature
    Same as: Seder night

Heinlein, Robert Anson, 1907-
  Black pits of Luna
    Conklin, G. ed. Possible worlds of science fiction
    Heinlein, R. A. Green hills of earth

Blowups happen
  Astounding science fiction (Periodical)
    Astounding science fiction anthology
  Heinlein, R. A. Man who sold the moon
By his bootstraps
  Margulies, L. and Friend, O. J. eds.
    Giant anthology of science fiction
Columbus was a dope
  Greenberg, M. ed. Travelers of space
Coventry
  Heinlein, R. A. Revolt in 2100
Delilah and the space-rigger
  Heinlein, R. A. Green hills of earth
Elsewhen
  Heinlein, R. A. Assignment in eternity
Gentlemen, be seated
  Heinlein, R. A. Green hills of earth
Green hills of earth
  Heinlein, R. A. Green hills of earth
Gulf
  Heinlein, R. A. Assignment in eternity
"If this goes on-"
  Heinlein, R. A. Revolt in 2100
"It's great to be back"
  Heinlein, R. A. Green hills of earth
Jerry was a man
  Heinlein, R. A. Assignment in eternity
"Let there be light"
  Heinlein, R. A. Man who sold the moon
Life-line
  Heinlein, R. A. Man who sold the moon
Logic of empire
  Heinlein, R. A. Green hills of earth
Long watch
  Derleth, A. W. ed. Beyond time & space
  Heinlein, R. A. Green hills of earth
Lost legacy
  Heinlein, R. A. Assignment in eternity
Man who sold the moon
  Heinlein, R. A. Man who sold the moon
Misfit
  Heinlein, R. A. Revolt in 2100
Ordeal in space
  Heinlein, R. A. Green hills of earth
Our fair city
  Merril, J. ed. Beyond human ken
Requiem
  Heinlein, R. A. Man who sold the moon
Roads must roll
  Heinlein, R. A. Man who sold the moon
Space jockey
  Heinlein, R. A. Green hills of earth
They
  Pratt, F. ed. World of wonder
Water is for washing
  Argosy (Periodical) Argosy Book of adventure stories
"—We also walk dogs"
  Heinlein, R. A. Green hills of earth
Year of the jackpot
  Galaxy science fiction magazine. Second Galaxy reader of science fiction

Heinz, W. C.
  Man's game
    Herzberg, M. J. comp. Treasure chest of sport stories

Heir apparent. Moore, C. L.

Heir unapparent. Van Vogt, A. E.

HEIRS. See Inheritance and succession

Helen, I love you. Farrell, J. T.

Helen O'Loy. Del Rey, L.

Helfer, Harold
Sea serpent of Spoonville Beach
Story (Periodical) Story; no. 4
Strange notion
Story (Periodical) Story; no. 1
HELL
Collier, J. Devil, George and Rosie
Lagerkvist, P. F. Lift that went down
into hell
Munro, H. H. Infernal Parliament
Peretz, I. L. Ne'ilah in Gehenna
Hell hath no fury. Collier, J.
Hell of a good time. Farrell, J. T.
Hello darling. Ullman, J. R.
Hello, Tib. Aiken, C. P.
Helmet of Pluto. Claudy, C. H.
Help gets the legs. Hutchins, M. P. M.
Helpful Henry. Brumbaugh, F.
Helping hand. Anderson, P.
Helping the other fellow. Porter, W. S.
Helvick, James, pseud. See Cockburn, Claud
Hemingway, Ernest, 1898-
After the storm
Blodgett, H. W. ed. Story survey.
1953 ed.
Grayson, C. ed. Fourth round
Hemingway, E. Hemingway reader
Capital of the world
Hemingway, E. Hemingway reader
Clean, well-lighted place
Heilman, R. B. ed. Modern short stories
Hemingway, E. Hemingway reader
Schorer, M. ed. The story
Day's wait
Davis, C. B. ed. Eyes of boyhood
Fable of the good lion
Hemingway, E. Hemingway reader
Fifty grand
Hemingway, E. Hemingway reader
Ribalow, H. U. ed. World's greatest
boxing stories
Gambler, the nun, and the radio
Burrell, J. A. and Cerf, B. A. eds.
Anthology of famous American stories
In another country
Davis, R. G. ed. Ten modern masters
Ludwig, J. B. and Poirier, W. R. eds.
Stories, British and American
Shaw, H. and Bement, D. Reading the
short story
Short, R. W. and Sewall, R. B. eds.
Short stories for study. 1950 ed.
The killers
Burrell, J. A. and Cerf, B. A. eds.
Anthology of famous American stories
Foerster, N. ed. American poetry and
prose. 1952 ed.
Lamb, L. ed. Family book of best loved
short stories
Queen, E. pseud. ed. Literature of
crime
Short, R. W. and Sewall, R. B. eds.
Short stories for study. 1950 ed.
Light of the world
Hemingway, E. Hemingway reader
O'Faoláin, S. The short story
My old man
Best of the Best American short stories,
1915-1950
Davis, R. G. ed. Ten modern masters

Now I lay me
Barrows, H. ed. 15 stories
Schramm, W. L. ed. Great short stories
Old man at the bridge
Hemingway, E. Hemingway reader
Short happy life of Francis Macomber
Davis, R. G. ed. Ten modern masters
Hemingway, E. Hemingway reader
West, R. B. and Stallman, R. W. eds.
Art of modern fiction
Snows of Kilimanjaro
Burnett, W. ed. World's best
Foerster, N. ed. American poetry and
prose. 1952 ed.
Gordon, C. and Tate, A. eds. House of
fiction
Hemingway, E. Hemingway reader
Lynskey, W. C. ed. Reading modern fic-
tion
Neider, C. ed. Great short stories from
the world's literature
Waite, H. O. and Atkinson, B. P. eds.
Literature for our time
Three-day blow
Millett, F. B. ed. Reading fiction
Way you'll never be
Hemingway, E. Hemingway reader
The hen. Dunsany, E. J. M. D. P. 18th
baron
The hen. Munro, H. H.
Henderson, Dion, 1921-
Brute's Christmas
Strang, R. M. and Roberts, R. M. eds.
Teen-age tales v 1
Henderson, Le Grand, 1901-
Augustus and spring tonic
Fenner, P. R. comp. Giggle box
Augustus meets his first Indian
Fenner, P. R. comp. Indians, Indians,
Indians
Augustus, pirate
Fenner, P. R. comp. Pirates, pirates,
pirates
Haunted wreck
Story parade (Periodical) Adventure
stories
Henderson, Stephen E.
Case of myopia
Lantz, J. E. ed. Stories of Christian
living
Henderson, Zenna, 1917-
Ararat
Best science-fiction stories: 1953
Come on, Wagon!
Magazine of fantasy and science fiction.
Best from Fantasy and science fiction;
2d ser.
You know what, teacher?
Queen, E. pseud. ed. Ellery Queen's
awards: 9th ser.
Hendryx, James Beardsley, 1880-
Affair on Jacklight Creek
American boy (Periodical) American
boy anthology
Alex acquires some dust
Hendryx, J. B. Intrigue on Halfaday
Creek
"And the goose hangs high"
Hendryx, J. B. Intrigue on Halfaday
Creek

Herzl, Theodor, 1860-1904
Thumbling and Sapling
Leftwich, J. ed. Yisröel. 1952 ed.
Heseltine, Nigel, 1916-
Day's pleasure
Felheim, M.; Newman, F. B. and Stein-
hoff, W. R. eds. Modern short stories
Hesse, Hermann, 1877-
Within and without
Burnett, W. ed. World's best
Youth, beautiful youth
Pick, R. ed. German stories and tales
Hester Lilly. Taylor, E.
Heuman, William
There are broken hearts in Brooklyn
Saturday evening post (Periodical) Sat-
urday evening post stories, 1953
"Hey diddle diddle, the cat. . ." Phillpotts, E.
Hey, taxi! Aiken, C. P.
Hey wait for me. Williams, B.
Heyerdahl, Thor, 1914-
Kon-Tiki reaches the South Sea Islands
Fenner, P. R. comp. Stories of the sea
Heyert, Murray
New kid
Christ, H. I. and Shostak, J. eds. Short
stories
Heyliger, William, 1884-
Man who wouldn't break
American boy (Periodical) American
boy anthology
Steelman's nerve
Boys' life (Periodical) Boys life Adven-
ture stories
Too many crooks
Furman, A. L. ed. Teen-age stories of
the diamond
Hi, sailor! Granberg, B.
Hickey, H. B.
Like a bird, like a fish
Derleth, A. W. ed. Worlds of tomorrow
Hicks, Michael Allen
The wake
Story (Periodical) Story; no. 3
Hidden riches of secret places. Claudy,
C. H.
Hide and seek. Clarke, A. C.
Hiding of Black Bill. Porter, W. S.
Higbee, Alma Robison
Words for John Willie
Hazeltine, A. I. comp. Selected stories
for teen-agers
The higgler. Coppard, A. E.
High court. Kyd, T. pseud.
High finance. Claudy, C. H.
HIGH SCHOOL LIFE. See School life
HIGH SCHOOLS. See School life
The high sign. Buckingham, N.
High threshold. Nourse, A. E.
High victory. Lavender, D. S.
High-water mark. Harte, B.
Higher abdication. Porter, W. S.
Higher and higher. Marcus, P.
Higher pragmatism. Porter, W. S.

Highstone, Harold Alfred, 1901-
Frankenstein—unlimited
Derleth, A. W. ed. Far boundaries
The highway. Bradbury, R.
Highway. Lowndes, R. W.
HIGHWAYMEN. See Brigands and rob-
bers
HIGHWAYS. See Roads
Hill, James H.
Captain returns
Ford, N. A. and Faggett, H. L. eds.
Best short stories by Afro-American
writers (1925-1950)
Comfort and joy
Ford, N. A. and Faggett, H. L. eds.
Best short stories by Afro-American
writers (1925-1950)
Gust of wind
Ford, N. A. and Faggett, H. L. eds.
Best short stories by Afro-American
writers (1925-1950)
Hill, Kay
Blue flag
Joseph, M. ed. Best cat stories
Hill, Marjorie (Yourd)
Blue brocade
American girl (Periodical) On my honor
Christmas anyhow
American girl (Periodical) Christmas
all year 'round
Sea anchor
American girl (Periodical) Christmas
all year 'round
American girl (Periodical) Favorite
stories
Hill people. Marshall, E.
Hillbilly halfback. Coombs, C. I.
Hillger, Elwood H.
Lomax pitching
Owen, F. ed. Teen-age victory parade
Hilliard, Alec Rowley, 1908-
Green torture
Margulies, L. and Friend, O. J. eds.
From off this world
Hillman, Gordon Malherbe
Copy girl
McFarland, W. K. comp. Then it hap-
pened
Hills of Donegal. Murtagh, L. D.
Hilton, James, 1900-1954
Twilight of the wise
Lohan, R. and Lohan, M. eds. New
Christmas treasury
The war years
Brentano, F. ed. The word lives on
HIMALAYA MOUNTAINS
Bottome, P. Splendid fellow
Ullman, J. R. Top man
Hindsight. Williamson, J.
Hindu Yogi science of breath. Ekbergh,
I. D.
HINDUS IN THE UNITED STATES
Ekbergh, I. D. Gentleman from India
Hine, Alfred Blakelee, 1915-
Kissing kind
Collier's, the national weekly. Collier's
best

Hines and Heatherly explain the deal. Hendryx, J. B.

Hinkle, Thomas Clark, 1876-1949
Black Storm
Dennis, W. ed. Palomino and other horses

Hint of an explanation. Greene, G.

Hinternhoff, John F.
Mutineers be hanged
Fenner, P. R. comp. Pirates, pirates, pirates
Furman, A. L. ed. Teen-age sea stories

Hinton, James, 1915-
Mediators to the goatherd
Southern review. Anthology of stories from the Southern review

HIRED GIRLS. See Servants—Hired girls

Hired man. Strong, J.

HIRED MEN. See Servants—Hired men

Hirshbein, Peretz, 1880-
Leftwich, J. ed. Yisröel. 1952 ed.

His brother's keeper. Hammett, D.

His Excellency. Maugham, W. S.

His first appearance. Chekhov, A. P.

His first race. Gray, D.

His great decision. Arico, V.

His idea of a mother. Boyle, K.

His last bow. Doyle, Sir A. C.

His mother. O'Higgins, H. J.

His mother's sermon. Watson, J.

His new mittens. Crane, S.

His Reverence. Verga, G.

His ship comes home. Sitwell, Sir O. bart.

His spurs. James, W.

His wife survived him. Brophy, B.

HISTORIANS
Auchincloss, L. Greg's peg
Maugham, W. S. Mayhew

Historical note. Jenkins, W. F.

History lesson. Clarke, A. C.

History of a business enterprise. Chekhov, A. P.

History of Krakatuk. Hoffmann, E. T. A.

The hitch-hikers. Welty, E.

Hitchens, Dolores (Birk) 1907-
Absent hat pin
Mystery Writers of America, inc. 20 great tales of murder
Fuzzy things
Mystery Writers of America, inc. Four-&-twenty bloodhounds

HITCHHIKERS
Barker, A. L. Villain as a young boy
Welty, E. Hitch-hikers

HITLER, ADOLF, 1889-1945
Forester, C. S. Wandering Gentile

Hoar, Roger Sherman
Liquid life
Jenkins, W. F. ed. Great stories of science fiction

HOAXES
Clemens, S. L. My bloody massacre (I)
Clemens, S. L. Petrified man (I-II)
Davis, R. H. In the fog

Dick, I. M. Two strangers came to town
Maugham, W. S. Winter cruise
Munro, H. H. Phantom luncheon
Poe, E. A. Balloon hoax
Poe, E. A. The spectacles
Poe, E. A. Unparalleled adventure of one Hans Pfaall
Porter, W. S. Double-dyed deceiver
Queen, E. pseud. Emperor's dice
Steinberg, Y. Reb Anshel the golden
See also Humor—Practical jokes

Hobart, Alice Tisdale (Nourse) 1882-
He sought to know God
Brentano, F. ed. The word lives on

Hobbies. Simak, C. D.

Hobbs, Augusta Kent
River pirates
American girl (Periodical) Favorite stories

Hobbyist. Russell, E. F.

HOBOES. See Tramps

Hobson's choice. Bester, A.

HOCKEY
Bendrodt, J. C. Spike
Coombs, C. I. Freeze out
Coombs, C. I. Ice ostrich
Coombs, C. I. Lucky stick
Kempton, K. P. Puck-eater
Muller, C. G. Hat trick
Sandberg, H. W. Captain Kidder
Sherman, H. M. Reeder, left defense
Young, S. Dangerous ice

Hodel. Rabinowitz, S.

Hodgson, William Hope, 1878-1918
Noise in the night
Derleth, A. W. ed. Beyond time & space

Hodkin, Ruth E.
Tomboy
Wolfe, D. M. ed. Which grain will grow

Hoffmann, Eleanor, 1895-
On trial
American girl (Periodical) On my honor
Polonaise
American girl (Periodical) Christmas all year 'round

Hoffmann, Ernst Theodor Amadeus, 1776-1822
Cremona violin
Lange, V. ed. Great German short novels and stories
Deed of entail
Hoffmann, E. T. A. Tales from Hoffmann
Golden pot
Hoffmann, E. T. A. Tales from Hoffmann
History of Krakatuk
Neider, C. ed. Great short stories from the world's literature
Mlle de Scudéri
Hoffmann, E. T. A. Tales from Hoffmann
The sandman
Hoffmann, E. T. A. Tales from Hoffmann
Story of Krespel
Hoffmann, E. T. A. Tales from Hoffmann

Hofmannsthal, Hugo Hofmann, Edler von, 1874-1929
Episode in the life of the Marshal de Bassompierre
Pick, R. ed. German stories and tales

Hogan, Alice
Sorority
American girl (Periodical) On my honor

HOGS. See Swine

Hokey-Pocus McGee. Gallery, D. V.

Holberg, Lewis. See Holberg, Ludvig, baron

Holberg, Ludvig, baron, 1684-1754
Tree men of Potu
Derleth, A. W. ed. Beyond time & space

Hold back tomorrow. Neville, K.

Hold 'em Yale. Runyon, D.

Holder, William
Cash and carry guy
Argosy (Periodical) Argosy Book of sports stories
Nitro ship
Argosy (Periodical) Argosy Book of sea stories
One guy, one gal, one island
Argosy (Periodical) Argosy Book of adventure stories
Storm over second
Argosy (Periodical) Argosy Book of sports stories

Holding up a train. Porter W. S.

HOLDUPS. See Robbery

Hole, Lucy Ellen
Prowler on the hill
Oberfirst, R. ed. 1954 anthology of best original short-shorts

Hole in the moon. Seabright, I.

Hole in the sky. Cox, I.

Holenia, Alexander Maria Lernet- See Lernet-Holenia, Alexander Maria

Holiday. Bradbury, R.

Holiday house party. Vetter, M. M.

Holiday task. Munro, H. H.

HOLIDAYS. See names of particular holidays; also Vacations

Holland, Marion
Billy had a system
Fenner, P. R. comp. Giggle box

Holland, Rupert Sargent, 1878-1952
Cobra's hood
Fenner, P. R. comp. Ghosts, ghosts, ghosts
Drums in the fog
Fenner, P. R. comp. Indians, Indians, Indians
Pirates of Charles Town harbor
Fenner, P. R. comp. Pirates, pirates, pirates
Turn and turn about
Fenner, P. R. comp. Pirates, pirates, pirates

HOLLYWOOD, CALIFORNIA. See California—Hollywood

Holmes, H. H. pseud. See White, William Anthony Parker

Holmes, Kenyon
Man who rode the saucer
Derleth, A. W. ed. Far boundaries

Holmes, Wilfred Jay, 1900-
Action off Formosa
Saturday evening post (Periodical) Saturday evening post stories, 1950

Holohan's hoist. McNamara, E.

Holt, Stephen, pseud. See Thompson, Harlan

Holtman, Alice, 1914-
Min's God
Wolfe, D. M. ed. Which grain will grow

Holwerda, Frank, 1908-
Char on raven's bench
Best American short stories, 1954

Holy door. O'Donovan, M.

HOLY LAND. See Palestine

Holy Land. Lewisohn, L.

Holy simplicity. Chekhov, A. P.

Home. Boyle, K.

Home. Hughes, L.

Home. Maugham, W. S.

Home again. Morley, C. D.

HOME COMING
Arico, V. The knight returns
Brookhouser, F. Young man from yesterday
Garland, H. Return of a private
Hesse, H. Youth, beautiful youth
Markewich, R. Return to the Bronx
Maugham, W. S. Home
Newhouse, E. Pro and con
Van Doren, M. Night at the Notch

HOME ECONOMICS
Hope, M. R. Secret recipe
See also Cookery

Home fires. Sullivan, R.

Home front. Stafford, J.

Home game. O'Rourke, F.

Home is a place. Breuer, B.

Home is in the heart. Nathan, R.

Home is the hunter. Kuttner, H.

Home is where the wreck is. Tucker, W.

Home stretch. Gilpatric, G.

Home to roost. Stout, R.

Home town of the army ants. Beebe, W.

Home tragedy. Verga, G.

HOMECOMING. See Home coming

Homecoming. Johns, V. P.

Homecoming. Nye, N. C.

Homecoming. Patterson, E. G.

Homeland. Wolf, M.

Homemade miracle. Cousins, M.

Homer and the lilies. West, J.

HOMES. See Houses

Homesick Buick. MacDonald, J. D.

Homesickness night. Kinau, R.

Homestead orchard. Davis, H. L.

Homicide House. Keene, D.

Homo Sol. Asimov, I.

HOMOSEXUALITY
Barr, J. pseud. Derricks; 7 stories
Cory, D. W. ed. 21 variations on a theme; 20 stories
Lowry, R. J. C. The victim
Maupassant, G. de. Paul's mistress
Honest fisherman. Walsh, M.

HONESTY
Lipman, C. and Lipman, M. Dilemma of Grampa Dubois
Marquand, J. P. You can't do that
Porter, W. S. Masters of arts
Stern, R. G. Present for Minna
Honey and the home front. Taber, G. B.
Honey house. King, M. P.
Honey, we'll be brave. Farrell, J. T.
Honeyed peace. Gellhorn, M. E.
Honeyed poison. Gibran, K.
Honeymoon. Caldwell, E.
Honeymoon. Sullivan, R.
Honeymoon. Van Doren, M.
Honeymoon. Wincelberg, S.
Honeymoon in hell. Brown, F.
HONG KONG. See China—Hong Kong
Honi ha-Maeggel. Cohn, E.
HONOLULU. See Hawaiian Islands
Honolulu. Maugham, W. S.
Honor. Faulkner, W.
Honor of his house. Wyld Ospina, C.
Honor of the county. Edmonds, W. D.
Honour of Israel Gow. Chesterton, G. K.
Hoodooed. Rice, A. C. H.
Hook. Clark, W. Van T.
HOOKED RUGS. See Rugs, Hooked
Hooky line and sinker. Wylie, P.
"Hoot!" said the owl. Barbour, R. H.
Hop-Frog. Poe, E. A.

Hope, M. Russell
Secret recipe
Oberfirst, R. ed. 1951 anthology of best original short-shorts
Hope chest. Dempsey, D. K.

HOPE CHESTS
Paget, V. Wedding chest

Hopkinson, Henry Thomas, 1905-
I have been drowned
New writing (Periodical) Best stories
Mountain madness
Talbot, D. ed. Treasury of mountaineering stories
Hopkinson, Tom. See Hopkinson, Henry Thomas
Horace Chooney, M.D. West, J.
Horatio. Felsen, G.

Horgan, Paul, 1903-
Devil in the desert
Gable, M Sister, ed. Many-colored fleece
Saturday evening post (Periodical) Saturday evening post stories, 1950
National honeymoon
Collier's, the national weekly. Collier's best
Peach stone
Best of the Best American short stories, 1915-1950

The **Horla.** Maupassant, G. de
Hormones. Pratt, F.
Horn that called Bambine. Godchaux, E.
Hornblower and Noah's ark. Forester, C. S.
Hornblower and the cargo of rice. Forester, C. S.
Hornblower and the even chance. Forester, C. S.
Hornblower and the examination for lieutenant. Forester, C. S.
Hornblower and the man who felt queer. Forester, C. S.
Hornblower and the man who saw God. Forester, C. S.
Hornblower and the penalty of failure. Forester, C. S.
Hornblower and the Spanish galleys. Forester, C. S.
Hornblower, the Duchess, and the Devil. Forester, C. S.
Hornblower, the frogs, and the lobsters. Forester, C. S.

HORNED TOADS
Porter, W. S. Jimmy Hayes and Muriel
Hornet's nest. Bennett, M. E.
Hornets of space. Starzl, R. F.

HOROSCOPES. See Astrologers

Horowitz, Emmanuel, 1910-
God's agents have beards
Ribalow, H. U. ed. These your children
Horror of the heights. Doyle, Sir A. C.

HORROR STORIES
Bierce, A. Boarded window
Blackwood, A. The Wendigo
Bowles, P. F. Distant episode
Bradbury, R. World the children made
Collier, J. Evening primrose
Collier, J. Green thoughts
Coppel, A. The exile
Crawford, F. M. Screaming skull
Davenport, B. ed. Tales to be told in the dark; 13 stories
Doyle, Sir A. C. Adventure of the speckled band
Eliot, G. pseud. Lifted veil
Faulkner, W. Rose for Emily
Gilman, C. P. S. Yellow wall-paper
Harris, J. B. Survival
Jacobs, W. S. Monkey's paw
James, H. Turn of the screw
Keller, D. H. Tiger cat
Keller, D. H. The worm
Kipling, R. Mark of the beast
Machen, A. White powder
Moore, C. L. Scarlet dream
Mudford, W. Iron shroud
Munby, A. N. L. Herodes redivivus
Parker, Sir G. bart. The flood
Poe, E. A. Berenice
Poe, E. A. Descent into the maelström
Poe, E. A. Fall of the house of Usher
Poe, E. A. Ligeia
Poe, E. A. Ms. found in a bottle
Poe, E. A. Morella
Poe, E. A. Pit and the pendulum
Poe, E. A. Tell-tale heart
Poe, E. A. William Wilson
Wakefield, H. W. Red Lodge

HORSE. See Horses
Horse called Pete. Bialk, E.
Horse dealer's daughter. Lawrence, D. H.
Horse drive. Martin, C. M.
Horse in the moon. Pirandello, L.
Horse of her own. Payne, S.
Horse of Hurricane Reef. Jackson, C. T.
HORSE RACING
  Anderson, S. I want to know why
  Anderson, S. I'm a fool
  Bendrodt, J. C. Irish lad
  Bendrodt, J. C. Valiant lady
  Byrne, D. Rivers of Damascus
  Chamberlain, G. A. Monarch the bum
  Clements, C. J. Keep off the rail!
  Cooke, A. A. For the love of a race horse
  Curry, P. S. Osage Girl
  DeJong, D. C. Before the races
  Foote, J. T. Class
  Foote, J. T. Hoofbeats; 13 stories
  Foote, J. T. Look of eagles
  Foote, J. T. Two ringers
  Gray, D. His first race
  Harvey, W. F. Dark horses
  Hemingway, E. My old man
  Irwin, M. E. F. Bloodstock
  Lawrence, D. H. Rocking-horse winner
  McKenney, J. Skycaptain
  Munro, H. H. Bread and Butter miss
  Munro, H. H. The Brogue
  Runyon, D. All horse players die broke
  Runyon, D. Snatching of Bookie Bob
  Sharp, M. Winning sequence
  Thompson, M. My brother who talked
    with horses
  Van Loan, C. E. Levelling with Elisha
  Van Loan, C. E. Playing even for
    Obadiah
  Winchell, P. Devil on wheels
HORSE SHOWS
  Allan, G. Kentucky line-up
  Newcomb, C. Grand prize
  Newcomb, E. Two for the show
Horse that played third base for Brooklyn.
    Schramm, W. L.
Horse thief. Berman, H.
Horse thief. Caldwell, E.
Horse thief. Opatovsky, J.
HORSE THIEVES
  Caldwell, E. Horse thief
  Loomis, N. M. Mustang trail to glory
  Opatovsky, J. Horse thief
  Somerville, E. A. Œ. and Martin, V. F.
    Trinket's colt
HORSE-TRADING
  Annett, R. R. Gentle like a cyclone
  Benefield, B. Incident at Boiling Springs
  Faulkner, W. Spotted horses
  Stuart, J. Horse trading Trembles
Horse-trading Trembles. Stuart, J.
HORSE TRAINING. See Horses
HORSEBACK RIDING. See Horseman-
    ship
HORSEMANSHIP
  Bond, N. S. The sportsman
  Bottome, P. A pair
  Erskine, L. Y. Horses and men

  Harnden, R. P. Rebellion
  James, W. Best riding and roping
  Lambert, J. Tall as the stars
HORSES
  Bates, H. E. Sugar for the horse
  Bendrodt, J. C. Irish lad
  Bendrodt, J. C. Valiant lady
  Bendrodt, J. C. Zaimis
  Bergengruen, W. Ali Baba and the forty
    horse-power
  Berman, H. Horse thief
  Bonham, F. I'll take the high road
  Bottome, P. A pair
  Breckenfeld, V. G. Touch of Arab
  Butler, E. P. Too much horse
  Caldwell, E. Sick horse
  Creamer, J. B. comp. Twenty-two stories
    about horses and men; 17 stories
  Davis, H. L. Open winter
  Dennis, W. Palomino and other horses
  Doyle, Sir A. C. Silver Blaze
  Drinkard, I. N. Mission for baby
  Farley, W. The storm
  Faulkner, W. Spotted horses
  Fenner, P. R. comp. Cowboys, cowboys,
    cowboys; 17 stories
  Foote, J. T. Hoofbeats; 13 stories
  Furman, A. L. ed. Teen-age horse sto-
    ries; 13 stories
  Hudson, W. H. Story of a piebald horse
  Jackson, C. T. Horse of Hurricane Reef
  James, W. Will James' Book of cowboy
    stories; 15 stories
  McCourt, E. A. White mustang
  McNulty, J. Where the grass, they say,
    is blue
  Miers, E. S. Bandy
  Miers, E. S. Black Bat
  Nason, L. H. Rodney
  O'Flaherty, L. Old hunter
  Pattullo, G. Corazón
  Reymont, W. S. Twilight
  Ross, S. The outlaw
  Runyon, D. Old Em's Kentucky home
  Saroyan, W. Summer of the beautiful
    white horse
  Schaefer, J. W. That Mark horse
  Seton, E. T. Pacing mustang
  Steele, W. D. Blue murder
  Steinbeck, J. The gift
  Steinbeck, J. Red pony
  Sture-Vasa, M. A. My friend Flicka
  Watson, J. C. Benny and the Tar-Baby
The **horses.** Stephens, J.
Horses and men. Erskine, L. Y.
Horseshoe nails. Benét, L.
Horseshoes. Lardner, R. W.
Horsie. Parker, D. R.
Horton, Philip
  What's in a corner
    Best American short stories, 1952
Horwitz, Julius, 1920-
  The burial
    Horwitz, J. The city
  The campaign
    Horwitz, J. The city
  The city
    Horwitz, J. The city
  The conspirators
    Horwitz, J. The city

Household, Geoffrey, 1900-
  Brandy for the parson
    Household, G. Tales of adventurers
  Cook-runner
    Household, G. Tales of adventurers
  Culture
    Household, G. Tales of adventurers
  Debt of honor
    Household, G. Tales of adventurers
  First blood
    Household, G. Tales of adventurers
  Heart in the mouth
    Household, G. Tales of adventurers
  The hut
    Household, G. Tales of adventurers
  Low water
    Household, G. Tales of adventurers
  The pejemuller
    Household, G. Tales of adventurers
  Picket lines of Marton Hevessy
    Household, G. Tales of adventurers
  Railroad harvest
    Household, G. Tales of adventurers
  Three kings
    Household, G. Tales of adventurers
  Woman in love
    Household, G. Tales of adventurers

HOUSEHOLD APPLIANCES
  Jakes, J. W. Machine

Household words. De Vries, P.

HOUSEKEEPERS. See Servants—Housekeepers

HOUSEKEEPING. See Home economics

HOUSEMAIDS. See Servants—Maids

HOUSES
  Arthur, R. Change of address
  Baker, D. V. The beautiful house
  Bunner, H. C. Story of a New York
    house
  Chekhov, A. P. New villa
  Chekhov, A. P. Other people's misfor-
    tune
  De Vries, P. Today and today
  Grimson, M. S. Will and a way
  Humphrey, W. The Hardys
  Melville, H. The piazza
  Smith, L. P. 'Ivanhoe'
  Stettner, S. Summer place

HOUSES, APARTMENT. See Apartment
houses

HOUSES, DESERTED
  Grinevskiĭ, A. S. The ratcatcher

HOUSES, HAUNTED. See Ghosts

HOUSTON. See Texas—Houston

How Abel slew Cain. Feild, B.

How Babe got his name. Considine, R. B.

How bad? How long? Van Doren, M.

How beautiful with shoes. Steele, W. D.

How Brother Aaron was saved. Knox, J.

How can I leave thee? De Vries, P.

How Claeys died. Sansom, W.

How dear to my heart. Rossiter, H. D.

How do you say good-bye? Fontaine, R. L.

How far is it to Hollywood? Aldrich, B. S.

How I came to love the smell of a bar-room.
  DeLynn, L.

How many midnights. Bowles, P. F.

How Old Stormalong captured Mocha Dick.
  Shapiro, I.

How old Timofei died singing. Rilke, R. M.

How Rezi baked motzas. Oesterreicher, A.

How Santa Claus came to Simpson's Bar.
  Harte, B.

How the Czar fooled Montefiore. Sforim,
  M. M.

How the devil came down Division Street.
  Algren, N.

How the good gifts were used by two.
  Pyle, H.

How the mountain was clad. Bjørnson, B.

How war came to Arcadia, N. Y. Jackson,
  C. R.

How we astonished the Rivermouthians.
  Aldrich, T. B.

Howard, Hayden
  Dipping of the candlemaker
    Queen, E. pseud. ed. Ellery Queen's
    awards: 9th ser.

Howard, Quentin R.
  Time for a change
    Oberfirst, R. ed. 1952 anthology of best
    original short-shorts

Howard, Robert Ervin, 1906-1936
  Beyond the Black River
    Howard, R. E. King Conan
  Frost-giant's daughter
    Howard, R. E. Coming of Conan
  God in the bowl
    Howard, R. E. Coming of Conan
  Jewels of Gwahlur
    Howard, R. E. King Conan
  Mirrors of Tuzun Thune
    Howard, R. E. Coming of Conan
  People of the black circle
    Howard, R. E. The sword of Conan
  Phoenix on the sword
    Howard, R. E. King Conan
  Pool of the black one
    Howard, R. E. The sword of Conan
  Queen of the Black Coast
    Howard, R. E. Coming of Conan
  Red nails
    Howard, R. E. The sword of Conan
  Rogues in the house
    Howard, R. E. Coming of Conan
  Scarlet citadel
    Howard, R. E. King Conan
  Shadow kingdom
    Howard, R. E. Coming of Conan
  Slithering shadow
    Howard, R. E. Sword of Conan
  Tower of the Elephant
    Howard, R. E. Coming of Conan
  Treasure of Tranicos
    Howard, R. E. King Conan

Howard, Wendell, 1891?-
  Last refuge of a scoundrel
    Howard, W. Last refuge of a scoundrel,
    and other stories
  The masterstroke
    Howard, W. Last refuge of a scoundrel,
    and other stories
  Put on the spot
    Howard, W. Last refuge of a scoundrel,
    and other stories

Howard, Wendell—*Continued*
The rainbow
Howard, W. Last refuge of a scoundrel,
and other stories
Rude awakening
Howard, W. Last refuge of a scoundrel,
and other stories

Howarth, Jean
The novitiate
Weaver, R. and James, H. eds. Canadian
short stories

Howe, Diana, 1931-
White kitten
American vanguard, 1952

Howe, Joseph, 1804-1873
Locksmith of Philadelphia
Pacey, D. ed. Book of Canadian stories

Howells, William Dean, 1837-1920
Christmas every day
Lohan, R. and Lohan, M. eds. New
Christmas treasury
Editha
Burrell, J. A. and Cerf, B. A. eds.
Anthology of famous American stories
Ungar, F. ed. To mother with love

Howland, Rosemary
Magic night
McFarland, W. K. comp. Then it hap-
pened
Tonight will be different
Certner, S. and Henry, G. H. eds. Short
stories for our times

How's that umpire? Wodehouse, P. G.

Hsieh Liang
Wolf of Chungshan
Lin, Y. ed. Famous Chinese short
stories

Hsüan-Yu, Ch'en. See Ch'en Hsüan-yu

Hsün, Lu, pseud. See Chou, Shu-Jên

Hualapi. Gally, J. W.

The **hub.** MacDonald, P.

Hubbard, Lafayette Ronald, 1911-
When shadows fall
Greenberg, M. ed. Men against the stars

Hubbard, P. M.
Manuscript found in a vacuum
Magazine of fantasy and science fiction.
Best from Fantasy and science fiction;
3d ser.

Huckabay, Mary Barrow
Ghost of Sam Bates
Oberfirst, R. ed. 1952 anthology of best
original short-shorts

Huckabuck family and how they raised popcorn in Nebraska and quit and came
back. Sandburg, C.

HUCKSTERS. See Peddlers and peddling

Huddling place. Simak, C. D.

Hudson, Alec, pseud. See Holmes, Wilfred
Jay

Hudson, William Henry, 1841-1922
Mysterious forest
Andrews, R. C. ed. My favorite stories
of the great outdoors
Story of a piebald horse
Cerf, B. A. and Moriarty, H. C. eds.
Anthology of famous British stories

HUDSON RIVER
Irving, W. Legend of Sleepy Hollow

Huge beast. Cartmill, C.

Hughes, Langston, 1902-
African morning
Hughes, L. Laughing to keep from
crying
Big meeting
Hughes, L. Laughing to keep from
crying
Heaven to hell
Hughes, L. Laughing to keep from
crying
Home
Gable, M. Sister, ed. Many-colored fleece
Little old spy
Hughes, L. Laughing to keep from
crying
Mysterious Madame Shanghai
Hughes, L. Laughing to keep from
crying
Name in the papers
Hughes, L. Laughing to keep from
crying
Never room with a couple
Hughes, L. Laughing to keep from
crying
On the road
Hughes, L. Laughing to keep from
crying
On the way home
Hughes, L. Laughing to keep from
crying
One Friday morning
Certner, S. and Henry, G. H. eds. Short
stories for our times
Hughes, L. Laughing to keep from
crying
Powder-white faces
Hughes, L. Laughing to keep from
crying
Professor
Hughes, L. Laughing to keep from
crying
Pushcart man
Hughes, L. Laughing to keep from
crying
Rouge high
Hughes, L. Laughing to keep from
crying
Sailor ashore
Hughes, L. Laughing to keep from
crying
Saratoga rain
Hughes, L. Laughing to keep from
crying
Slice him down
Hughes, L. Laughing to keep from
crying
Something in common
Hughes, L. Laughing to keep from
crying
Spanish blood
Hughes, L. Laughing to keep from
crying
Tain't so
Hughes, L. Laughing to keep from
crying
Tragedy at the Baths
Hughes, L. Laughing to keep from
crying

Hughes, Langston—*Continued*
Trouble with the angels
  Hughes, L. Laughing to keep from crying
Who's passing for who?
  Hughes, L. Laughing to keep from crying
Why, you reckon?
  Hughes, L. Laughing to keep from crying

Hughes, Richard Arthur Warren, 1900-
The stranger
  Conklin, G. and Conklin, L. T. eds. Supernatural reader

Hugo, Victor Marie, comte, 1802-1885
Combat with the octopus
  Andrews, R. C. ed. My favorite stories of the great outdoors

Hugo Kertchak, builder. Schaefer, J. W.

HUGUENOTS
Blackburn, E. R. Christiane the Huguenot

Hull, Edith Maude
Competition
  Greenberg, M. ed. Men against the stars

Hull, Edna Mayne
Flight that failed
  Conklin, G. ed. Science-fiction adventures in dimension

Hull down. Wylie, P.

Human. Gale, Z.

Human condition. Davies, R.

Human element. Maugham, W. S.

Human habitation. Bowen, E.

HUMAN RACE. See Man

Hume, Sue Tempest, 1915-
Shake hands with a murderer
  Oberfirst, R. ed. 1954 anthology of best original short-shorts

Humiliation. Maupassant, G. de

HUMOR
Ausubel, N. ed. Treasury of Jewish humor; 82 stories
Chekhov, A. P. Woman in the case
Clemens, S. L. Celebrated jumping frog of Calaveras County
Cockrell, E. W. Keyhole artist
Dachs, D. ed. Treasury of sports humor; 36 stories
De Vries, P. Overture
Fenner, P. R. ed. Fools and funny fellows; 21 stories
Fenner, P. R. comp. Fun! Fun! Fun! 20 stories
Fenner, P. R. comp. Giggle box; 15 stories
Fessier, M. Man-taming woman
Hale, E. E. My double, and how he undid me
Hardy, T. Tony Kytes, the arch-deceiver
Harris, G. W. Sut Lovingood; 8 stories
Hersey, J. R. Peggety's parcel of shortcomings
Jackson, S. Charles
Kober, A. Bella, Bella kissed a fella; 15 stories
Mauldin, W. H. Affair of the wayward jeep
Mowery, W. B. Lamb and some slaughtering

Munro, H. H. Short stories of Saki; 134 stories
Munro, H. H. The storyteller
Pagano, J. Signor Santa
Porter, W. S. Confessions of a humorist
Porter, W. S. O. Henry's best stories; 25 stories
Rogow, L. Laziest man in Texas
Runyon, D. More guys and dolls; 34 stories
Schaefer, J. W. Leander Frailey
Stockton, F. R. Christmas shadrach
Surtees, R. S. Hunting scenes; 26 stories
Tarkington, B. "Little gentleman"
Thurber, J. More alarms at night
Thurber, J. Secret life of Walter Mitty
Tucker, W. Home is where the wreck is
Wodehouse, P. G. Jeeves and the song of songs
Wodehouse, P. G. Nothing serious; 10 stories

  See also Improbable stories; Satire

Practical jokes
Betts, D. Sense of humor
Munro, H. H. Adrian
Munro, H. H. Bertie's Christmas Eve
Munro, H. H. The lull
Munro, H. H. Open window
Munro, H. H. She-wolf
Munro, H. H. Unrest-cure
Noyes, A. Uncle Hyacinth
Perry, G. S. The fourflusher
Porter, W. S. The Marquis and Miss Sally
Simpson, M. E. Practical joker

HUMOROUS STORIES. See Humor

Humphrey, William, 1924-
The fauve
  Humphrey, W. Last husband, and other stories
Fresh snow
  Humphrey, W. Last husband, and other stories
The Hardys
  Humphrey, W. Last husband, and other stories
Prize stories of 1950
In sickness and health
  Humphrey, W. Last husband, and other stories
Last husband
  Humphrey, W. Last husband, and other stories
Man with a family
  Humphrey, W. Last husband, and other stories
Quail for Mr Forester
  Humphrey, W. Last husband, and other stories
Report cards
  Humphrey, W. Last husband, and other stories
The shell
  Humphrey, W. Last husband, and other stories
Sister
  Humphrey, W. Last husband, and other stories

Humpty Dumpty had a great fall. Long, F. B.

Hunch that clicked. Cross, J. A.

HUNCHBACKS
Mann, T. Little Herr Friedemann
West, J. Breach of promise
Hundred years from now. Cardozo, N.
HUNGARIAN SOLDIERS. See Soldiers, Hungarian
HUNGARIANS IN THE UNITED STATES
Sinclair, J. pseud. Red necktie
Walden, A. E. So I'm home again
HUNGER
Maupassant, G. de. A vagabond
Rojas, M. Glass of milk
See also Famines
Hunger. Yezierska, A.
Hunger-artist. Kafka, F.
The hungry. Mann, T.
Hungry man. Cicellis, K.
Hungry sister. Winn, J.
Hungry stones. Tagore, Sir R.
Hunt, Finley C.
Egg from the sky
Hathaway, B. and Sessions, J. A. eds. Writers for tomorrow. 2d ser.
The hunt. Kuehn, S.
Hunted down. Dickens, C.
Hunter, Evan, 1926-
Small homicide
Best detective stories of the year—1954
Hunter Gracchus. Kafka, F.
The hunters. Downey, H.
HUNTING
Akeley, C. E. Elephant
Annixter, P. pseud. Dragon rider
Annixter, P. pseud. Hunting coat
Annixter, P. pseud. Kadiak
Annixter, P. pseud. Secret of Coon Castle
Blackwood, A. Valley of the beasts
Bond, N. S. The sportsman
Buck, F. Elephants!
Buckingham, N. Hallowed years; 12 stories
Caldwell, E. Molly-Cotton-Tail
Carrighar, S. Marooned childern
Faulkner, W. The bear
Faulkner, W. Old people
Flaubert, G. Legend of St Julian the Hospitaller
Gipson, F. B. My kind of a man
Gordon, C. Last day in the field
Hemingway, E. Short happy life of Francis Macomber
Humphrey, W. The shell
Marshall, E. Elephant remembers
Marshall, E. Heart of Little Shikara
Seton, E. T. Trail of the Sandhill stag
Stefánsson, V. Seal hunting
Stuart, J. Thanksgiving hunting
Waldeck, T. J. Igongo elephants
Williams, R. Head-hunters
See also Bird hunters; Deer hunting; Duck shooting; Fox hunting; Guides (Hunting); Shooting; Trappers

Accidents
Gray, D. His first race
Hunting coat. Annixter, P. pseud.

HUNTING DOGS. See Dogs
HUNTING GUIDES. See Guides (Hunting)
Hunting season. Robinson, F. M.
The huntress. Kaula, D.
The hurkle is a happy beast. Waldo, E. H.
The hurricane. Grant, G. H.
HURRICANES
Carse, R. Sailor's pay
Grant, G. H. The hurricane
Jackson, C. T. Horse of Hurricane Reef
Powell, F. Black flag
See also Storms
Hurry, hurry! Wilson, E.
Hurst, Fannie, 1889-
Guilty
Queen, E. pseud. ed. Literature of crime
Hurston, Zora Neale, 1901-
Conscience of the court
Saturday evening post (Periodical) Saturday evening post stories, 1950
Escape from Pharaoh
Seldon, R. ed. Ways of God and men
The tablets of the law
Brentano, F. ed. The word lives on
HUSBAND AND WIFE
Adler, J. Yente Telebende
Beck, W. The child is father
Benchley, N. Mrs Crocker's mutiny
Benson, S. The overcoat
Bergelson, D. The squash
Bottome, P. Pink medicine
Bowen, E. Evil that men do—
Bowen, E. Shadowy third
Bowles, P. F. Call at Corazón
Brookhouser, F. She did not cry at all
Caldwell, E. Here and today
Caldwell, E. Uncle Jeff
Callaghan, M. E. Rigmarole
Cave, H. B. Peril of the river
Cheever, J. Season of divorce
Chekhov, A. P. Three Annas
Cicellis, K. Aegean storm
Collier, J. Incident on a lake
Collier, J. Over insurance
Collier, J. Romance lingers, adventure lives
Collier, J. Three Bears Cottage
Collier, J. Youth from Vienna
Coward, N. P. Stop me if you've heard this
Davies, R. Foolish one
De La Roche, M. Submissive wife
De Vries, P. Cold potato
De Vries, P. Flesh and the devil
De Vries, P. Overture
De Vries, P. Scene
Howard, Q. R. Time for a change
Humphrey, W. The Hardys
Humphrey, W. In sickness and health
James, H. The liar
Juan Manuel, Infante of Castille. Man who married an ill-tempered wife
King, M. P. Chicken on the wind
Lagerkvist, P. F. Masquerade of souls
McCarthy, M. T. The weeds
MacDonald, J. D. I love you (occasionally)
Michener, J. A. The jungle
Munro, H. H. Reticence of Lady Anne

HUSBAND AND WIFE—*Continued*

Newhouse, E. Magic hour
Norris, H. Take her up tenderly
Parker, J. R. Tenth Street idyll
Pincherle, A. Back to the sea
Porter, W. S. Dougherty's eye-opener
Porter, W. S. The harbinger
Porter, W. S. Harlem tragedy
Porter, W. S. The pendulum
Prichard, R. Men and babies
Priestley, J. B. Night sequence
Pultz, C. Good-by to Miss Stoddard's
Rabinowitz, S. Menachem-Mendel, fortune hunter
Schaefer, J. W. Prudence by name
Schulberg, B. W. Breaking point
Seager, A. Second wedding
Shapiro, L. Rebbe and the rebbetsin
Strindberg, A. Autumn
Taylor, P. H. Cookie
Thompson, L. Grasshopper a burden
Van Dyke, H. Wedding ring
Walsh, M. Come back, my love
Waugh, E. Tactical exercise
Welty, E. The key
Welty, E. The whistle
White, A. Moment of truth
Williams, R. E. Feminine wiles
Willingham, C. Guardian angel
Winslow, T. S. Mrs Wilson's husband goes for a swim
Winslow, T. S. Other woman

Husband for Bluma. Dworzan, H. L.

HUSBANDS AND WIVES. See Husband and wife

The **hussar**. Hebel, J. P.

Hussar who loved three Jews. Molnar, F.

HUSSARS. See Soldiers, German

The **hut**. Household, G.

Hutchins, Maude Phelps (McVeigh)
Affair of honor
  Hutchins, M. P. M. Love is a pie
Fifth commandment
  Hutchins, M. P. M. Love is a pie
From morning till night
  Hutchins, M. P. M. Love is a pie
Help gets the legs
  Hutchins, M. P. M. Love is a pie
Innocents
  Hutchins, M. P. M. Love is a pie
Les malheurs des mannequins
  Hutchins, M. P. M. Love is a pie
Soliloquy at dinner
  Hutchins, M. P. M. Love is a pie
Sweet girl graduate
  Hutchins, M. P. M. Love is a pie
A tale
  Hutchins, M. P. M. Love is a pie
What's in two names
  Hutchins, M. P. M. Love is a pie

Huxley, Aldous Leonard, 1894-
Brave new world; excerpts
  Kuebler, H. W. ed. Treasury of science fiction classics
Education in the world state
  Waite, H. O. and Atkinson, B. P. eds. Literature for our time
Farcical history of Richard Greenow
  Connolly, C. ed. Great English short novels

Gioconda smile
  Cerf, B. A. and Moriarty, H. C. eds. Anthology of famous British stories
  Heilman, R. B. ed. Modern short stories
  Queen, E. pseud. ed. Literature of crime
Nuns at luncheon
  Stegner, W. E.; Scowcroft, R. and Ilyin, B. eds. Writer's art
Tillotson banquet
  Burnett, W. ed. World's best
Young Archimedes
  Short, R. W. and Sewall, R. B. eds. Short stories for study. 1950 ed.
  Waite, H. O. and Atkinson, B. P. eds. Literature for our time

Huysmans, Joris Karl, 1848-1907
Monsieur Folantin
  Geist, S. ed. French stories and tales

Hyacinth. Munro, H. H.

HYDROPHOBIA
Chekhov, A. P. Hydrophobia
Kipling, R. Mark of the beast

Hydrophobia. Chekhov, A. P.

HYENAS
Munro, H. H. Esmé

Hygeia at the Solito. Porter, W. S.

Hyman, Mark
The shepherd
  Ford, N. A. and Faggett, H. L. eds. Best short stories by Afro-American writers (1925-1950)

Hyperpilosity. De Camp, L. S.

Hyperspherical basketball. Nearing, H.

HYPNOTISM
Harvey, W. F. Long road
Lytton, E. G. E. L. B.-L. 1st baron. House and the brain
Mann, T. Mario and the magician
Poe, E. A. Facts in the case of M. Valdemar
Poe, E. A. Mesmeric revelation
Poe, E. A. Tales of the ragged mountains

Hypotheses of failure. Porter, W. S.

I

I am Edgar. Wexler, J.
I am not a stranger. Street, J. H.
I am nothing. Russell, E. F.
I and my chimney. Melville, H.
I broke my back on a rosebud. Campbell, W. E. M.
I came from yonder mountain. Connell, E. S.
I dive for treasure. Rieseberg, H. E.
I don't want to go. De Vries, P.
I hate a dumpy woman. Chase, M.
I have been drowned. Hopkinson, H. T.
I hope you'll understand. Newhouse, E.
I live in a world of make-believe. Taylor, E.
I love you (occasionally). MacDonald, J. D.
I love you very dearly. Aiken, C. P.
"I play basketball." Person, W. T.
I Puritani. Palacio Valdes, A.

I, robot. Binder, E.
I rode a tornado. Stocker, J.
I see you never. Bradbury, R.
I seen 'em go. Ullman, J. R.
I shall not be moved. Stewart, O.
I, the unspeakable. Sheldon, W.
I, Tobit. Van Doren, M.
I took thee, Constance. Le Berthon, T.
I turn pearl-diver. Nordhoff, C. B.
I want to go home. Farrell, J. T.
I want to know why. Anderson, S.
I will not abandon! Marmur, J.
"I will send thee." Asch, S.
ICE HOCKEY. See Hockey
Ice ostrich. Coombs, C. I.
Ice palace. Fitzgerald, F. S. K.
ICE SKATING. See Skating
ICELAND
   Laxness, H. K. Icelandic pioneer
Icelandic pioneer. Laxness, H. K.
Icon on the wall. Goudge, E.
Iddings Clark. Goodman, P.
Idea of age. Taylor, E.
Ideal craftsman. De la Mare, W. J.
Ideal home. Powell, D.
IDEAL STATE. See Utopias
IDEALISM
   Hawthorne, N. Great stone face
   Lawrence, D. H. Things
Idealist. Del Rey, L.
The idealist. O'Donovan, M.
IDIOCY
   Bishop, L. Crazy Hymie and the nickel
   Wilson, A. Mummy to the rescue
     See also Feeble-minded; Insanity
IDIOTS. See Feeble-minded; Idiocy
Idle days on the Yan. Dunsany, E. J. M. D.P.
   18th baron
Idolater of Degas. Stern, J.
Idyll of Miss Sarah Brown. Runyon, D.
Idyll of Red Gulch. Harte, B.
Idyll through the looking-glass. Sitwell,
   Sir O. bart.
If a body. Carr, A. Z.
If God makes you pretty. Horwitz, J.
If he hollers let him holler. De Vries, P.
"If I forget thee, oh Earth. . ." Clarke, A. C.
If Lincoln had yielded. Waldron, W.
If not higher. Peretz, I. L.
If only it were yesterday. Rinehart, M. R.
If the shoe hurts. De Vries, P.
"If this goes on-" Heinlein, R. A.
If we could see. Meschi, E.
If you was a Molkin. Jenkins, W. F.
If you weel permit me. Vernam, G.
If youth knew, if age could. Collier, J.
Igongo elephants. Waldeck, T. J.
I'll be waiting. Chandler, R.
I'll cut your throat again, Kathleen. Brown, F.

I'll remember you. Summers, J. L.
I'll take the high road. Bonham, F.
ILLEGITIMACY
   Cooke, A. A. Another worry
   Davis, F. M. Five Alls
   Maupassant, G. de. Simon's papa
   O'Donovan, M. Lonely rock
   Rinehart, M. R. The scandal
   Waltari, M. T. Goldilocks
   Wharton, E. N. J. The old maid
ILLICIT DISTILLING. See Distilling,
   Illicit
ILLINOIS
Chicago
   Maugham, W. S. Fall of Edward Barnard
   Taylor, P. H. Dark walk
   Tucker, W. Street walker
ILLITERACY
   Maugham, W. S. The verger
   Porter, W. S. Schools and schools
   Sandy, S. Black lie
ILLNESS
   Aiken, C. P. Mr Arcularis
   Bottome, P. Pink medicine
   Hemingway, E. Day's wait
   Humphrey, W. In sickness and health
   Van Doren, M. The butterfly
   Verga, G. Home tragedy
     See also Invalids
The illumination. West, J.
The illusionaries. Russell, E. F.
ILLUSIONS. See Hallucinations and illu-
   sions
The illustrated man. Bradbury, R.
ILLUSTRATORS
   James, H. Real thing
I'm a fool. Anderson, S.
I'm in a hurry. Upson, W. H.
I'm really fine. Schulberg, S.
I'm scared. Finney, J.
Image of the Lost Soul. Munro, H. H.
IMAGINARY ANIMALS. See Animals,
   Imaginary
IMAGINARY CITIES
   De Quincey, T. Savannah-la-mar
Imaginary Jew. Berryman, J.
IMAGINARY KINGDOMS
   Doyle, Sir A. C. Maracot deep
   Dunsany, E. J. D. P. 18th baron. Sword
   of Welleran
IMAGINARY WARS AND BATTLES
   Wells, H. G. Dream of Armageddon
IMBECILES. See Feeble-minded; Idiocy
IMITATIONS. See Impersonations
Immensee. Storm, T.
IMMIGRANTS
   Francis, O. Ladies call on Mr Pussick
   Meyer, E. L. When the aliens left
   Schaefer, J. W. Hugo Kertchak, builder
     See also French in the United States;
   Germans in the United States; etc.
Immodest maiden. Marshall, B.
Immortal orange. Shneur, Z.
Immortal woman. Tate, A.

IMMORTALITY
Rocklynne, R. Backfire
Sharp, D. D. Eternal man
Simak, C. D. Second childhood
Unamuno y Jugo, M. de. Saint Manuel Bueno, martyr

IMMORTALITY, PHYSICAL
Pierce, J. A. Invariant
Porter, W. S. Door of unrest
Simak, C. D. Eternity lost
Simak, C. D. Second childhood
Imp of string. Van Doren, M.
Imp of the perverse. Poe, E. A.
Impacted man. Sheckley, R.

IMPERSONATIONS
Beerbohm, Sir M. Happy hypocrite
Beyle, M. H. Mina de Vanghel
Brod, M. Death is a passing weakness
Cockburn, C. Total recall
Collins, W. Lady of Glenwith Grange
Doyle, Sir A. C. Case of identity
Doyle, Sir A. C. Man with the twisted lip
Ekbergh, I. D. Lady's maid
Hale, E. E. My double, and how he undid me
Harrison, H. S. Miss Hinch
Harvey, W. F. Dark horses
Lewis, J. Wife of Martin Guerre
Locke, W. J. Adventure of the kind Mr Smith
Maugham, W. S. Lion's skin
Maugham, W. S. Wash-tub
Munro, H. H. Hounds of Fate
Munro, H. H. Lost sanjak
Munro, H. H. Schartz-Metterklume method
Munro, H. H. Touch of realism
Poe, E. A. Oblong box
Porter, W. S. Double-dyed deceiver
Porter, W. S. Duplicity of Hargraves
Porter, W. S. Lost on dress parade
Porter, W. S. Midsummer masquerade
Porter, W. S. Reformation of Calliope
Porter, W. S. Thimble, thimble
Porter, W. S. Transients in Arcadia
Porter, W. S. While the auto waits
Vickers, R. Double image
Wells, H. G. Late Mr Elvesham
Implode and peddle. Fyfe, H. B.
Impossible highway. Friend, O. J.
Impossible play. O'Rourke, F.

IMPOSTERS. See Impersonations

IMPRESSMENT
Melville, H. Billy Budd, foretopman

IMPROBABLE STORIES
Ashabranner, B. Genius of Strap Buckner
Calisher, H. Heartburn
Carmer, C. L. Mr Sims and Henry
Credle, E. Tall tale from the high hills
Li Fu-yen. Man who became a fish
Li Fu-yen. The tiger
Munro, H. H. "Ministers of Grace"
Munro, H. H. Seventh pullet
Munro, H. H. Tobermory
Poe, E. A. Loss of breath
Pratt, F. and De Camp, L. S. Tales from Gavagan's bar; 23 stories
Stockton, F. R. Widow's cruise

Impulse. Aiken, C. P.
Impulse. Russell, E. F.
In a backwoods town. Bergelson, D.
In a Bolshevist market-place. Yushkevich, S. S.
In a dry country. Lyle, D.
In a glass darkly. Sullivan, R.
"In a good cause—" Asimov, I.
In a grove. Akutagawa, R.
In a strange land. Maugham, W. S.
In accents of death! Farrell, J. T.
In another country. Hemingway, E.
In another image. Ashley, E. L.
In City Hall Square. Farrell, J. T.
In Cushing's saloon. Hendryx, J. B.
In dreams begin responsibilities. Schwartz, D.
In exchange for poverty. Cooke, A. A.
In exile. Chekhov, A. P.
In Greenwich there are many gravelled walks. Calisher, H.
In hiding. Shiras, W. H.
In Nazareth. Borden, M.
In Nazareth. Lagerlöf, S. O. L.
In northern waters. Williams, W. C.
In Odessa. Babel', I. E.
In pyjamas. Nordhoff, C. B. and Hall, J. N.
In quest of a solution. Doyle, Sir A. C.
In sickness and health. Humphrey, W.
In the absence of angels. Calisher, H.
In the abyss. Wells, H. G.
In the Avu observatory. Wells, H. G.
In the beginning. Gordimer, N.
In the borderland. Stockwell, J.
In the cards. Collier, J.
In the chair. Jackson, C. R.
In the days of our fathers. McClintic, W.
In the desert. Tennyson, H.
In the family bosom. Harris, G. W.
In the fields of Boaz. Fineman, I.
In the fog. Davis, R. H.
In the forest. De La Mare, W. J.
In the fourth ward. Benson, T.
In the French style. Shaw, I.
In the garden. Lincoln, V. E.
In the good old summer time. Miller, P. S.
In the moonlight. Maupassant, G. de
In the morning. Sansom, W.
In the name of the Great Jehovah and the Continental Congress. Allen, M. P.
In the patchwork quilt. Eggleston, M. W.
In the penal colony. Kafka, F.
In the prison. Eliot, G. pseud.
In the scarlet star. Williamson, J.
In the time of demonstrations. Hall, J. B.
In the train. O'Donovan, M.
In the twilight. Stegner, W. E.
In the year 2889. Verne, J.
In this sign. Bradbury, R.
In time of calamity. Newhouse, E.

In value deceived. Fyfe, H. B.
In what far country. Van Doren, M.
Incarnation of Krishna Mulvaney. Kipling, R.

INCAS
Wassermann, J. Gold of Caxamalca

INCENDIARISM. See Arson

Incident at Boiling Springs. Benefield, B.
Incident on a lake. Collier, J.
Inclán, Ramón del Valle. See Valle-Inclán, Ramón del

INCOME TAX
Seager, A. Second wedding

Incompatibility. Sheehan, P. A.
Inconstant star. Cousins, M.
Incubation. MacDonald, J. D.
Indecision. Forester, C. S.

INDEPENDENCE DAY. See Fourth of July celebrations

INDIA
Annixter, P. pseud. Brought to cover
Collier, J. Rope enough
Marshall, E. Love stories of India; 15 stories

Bengal
Munro, H. H. Comments of Moung Ka

British occupation, 1765-1947
Kipling, R. At the end of the passage
Kipling, R. Drums of the fore and aft
Kipling, R. Incarnation of Krishna Mulvaney
Kipling, R. Man who was
Kipling, R. Man who would be king
Kipling, R. Tomb of his ancestors
Kipling, R. Toomai of the elephants
Kipling, R. William the Conqueror
Kipling, R. Without benefit of clergy
Mukerji, D. G. Elephant adventure
Tagore, Sir R. Hungry stones

Native races
Porter, W. S. Diamond of Kali
Swinton, A. A brotherhood
Tagore, Sir R. Babus of Nayanjore

Religion
Tagore, R. The Cabuliwallah

Indian feather. Mabry, T. D.
Indian fighter. Thompson, H.

INDIAN ROPE TRICK
Collier, J. Rope enough

Indian summer. Caldwell, E.
Indian summer of Dry Valley Johnson. Porter, W. S.
Indian well. Clark, W. Van T.
Indian's Christmas gift. Eggleston, M. W.

INDIANS IN THE FIJI ISLANDS
Michener, J. A. Mynah birds

INDIANS OF BRAZIL. See Indians of South America

INDIANS OF CANADA. See Indians of North America—Canada

INDIANS OF CENTRAL AMERICA
Clifton, M. The conqueror

INDIANS OF GUATEMALA. See Indians of Central America

INDIANS OF MEXICO
Brenner, L. An artist grows up in Mexico; 7 stories
Steinbeck, J. Miracle of Tepayac

INDIANS OF NORTH AMERICA
Anderson, D. Forty years of firewood
Butterworth, H. My grandmother's grandmother's Christmas candle
Coatsworth, E. J. Race in the wilderness
Fenner, P. R. comp. Indians, Indians, Indians; 16 stories
Frazee, S. Great medicine
Harte, B. Dick Boyle's business card
Haycox, E. Scout detail
London, J. Strength of the strong
Schaefer, J. W. Out of the past
> *See also* names of individual Indian tribes or nations: e.g. Apache Indians; Crow Indians; Dakota Indians; etc.

Canada
Mowery, W. B. The scout
Perrault, E. G. Silver King

Captivities
Brick, J. The captives
Brown, W. C. Duel in Captive Valley
Gordon, C. The captive
Johnson, D. M. Flame on the frontier
Johnson, D. M. Journey to the fort
Johnson, D. M. Man called Horse
Peattie, M. R. Red Fox
Rees, G. Rod of God
Smith, J. Life among the Indians

Children
Stafford, J. Summer day

Education
Clark, W. Van T. The anonymous

Legends
Bear and the hunter's step-son
Coming of the white man
Trickster and the old witch

Mississippi
Faulkner, W. A justice
Faulkner, W. Red leaves

Mythology
> *See* Indians of North America— Religion and mythology

Religion and mythology
Johnson, D. M. Scars of honor
Johnson, D. M. The unbeliever
Johnson, D. M. Warrior's exile

Wars
Fox, N. A. Only the dead ride proudly
Johnson, D. M. Beyond the frontier

INDIANS OF SOUTH AMERICA
Bowles, P. F. Pastor Dowe at Tacaté
Burks, A. J. The captive

Captivities
Erskine, L. Y. Mystery of Mike

Indiscretions of Father Lawrence. Lieberman, R.

INDO-CHINA, FRENCH
Payne, P. S. R. Red mountain

The indomitable blue. Wolfert, I.

Indulgent husband. Colette, S. G.

INDUSTRIAL ACCIDENTS. See Accidents, Industrial

INDUSTRIALISTS. See Capitalists and financiers

Inexperienced ghost. Wells, H. G.

INFANTICIDE
Hunter, E. Small homicide
James, H. Author of Beltraffio
Maugham, W. S. The unconquered
Renard, J. A romance

INFANTS. See Children

Infernal Parliament. Munro, H. H.

INFIDELITY. See Marriage problems

Infidelity of Zenobia. Bunner, H. C.

Infinity zero. Wandrei, D.

Influence. Merochnik, M.

The infra-medians. Wright, S. P.

The infra-redioscope. Russell, B. A. W. R. 3d earl

Ingénue of the Sierras. Harte, B.

Ingraham, Joseph Holt, 1809-1866
The baptizing
Brentano, F. ed. The word lives on

Inheritance. Clarke, A. C.

INHERITANCE AND SUCCESSION
Caldwell, E. The windfall
Cobb, I. S. Boys will be boys
Collier, J. Incident on a lake
Coppard, A. E. Fifty pounds
Grau, S. A. Bright day
Harte, B. Mrs Skaggs's husbands
King, M. P. Chicken on the wind
Landa, M. J. Two legacies
Newhouse, E. Seventy thousand dollars
Platt, G. Very false alarm
Porter, W. S. One thousand dollars
Porter, W. S. Shocks of doom
Queen, E. pseud. Witch of Times Square
Shulman, M. Chance for adventure
Waugh, E. Period piece
Winslow, T. S. Angie Lee's fortune

Initiation. Conrad, J.

Initiation fee. Shallit, R.

Inland, western sea. Asch, N.

The inn. Maupassant, G. de

Inn was promise. Brookhouser, F.

Innis, Mary Emma (Quayle)
The bells
Pacey, D. ed. Book of Canadian stories

Innocence of Reginald. Munro, H. H.

Innocents. Hutchins, M. P. M.

Innocents of Broadway. Porter, W. S.

INNS. See Hotels, taverns, etc.

Inquest. Williams, W. C.

INQUISITION
Poe, E. A. Pit and the pendulum

INSANE. See Insanity

The insane. Williams, W. C.

INSANE HOSPITALS
Goss, J. M. Bird song
Heinlein, R. A. They
Waugh, E. Mr Loveday's little outing

INSANITY
Aiken, C. P. Bow down, Isaac!
Aiken, C. P. Silent snow, secret snow
Becker, S. D. Town mouse
Bellow, S. Sermon by Doctor Pep
Benson, T. Man from the tunnel
Bowles, P. F. You are not I
Brod, M. Death is a passing weakness
Brown, F. Come and go mad
Chekhov, A. P. Ward no. 6
Collier, J. Special delivery
Dostoevskiĭ, F. M. Faint heart
Farrell, J. T. A misunderstanding
Fitzgerald, F. S. K. Long way out
Harte, B. Mrs Skagg's husbands
Hauptmann, G. J. R. Flagman Thiel
Hergesheimer, J. Wild oranges
Huxley, A. L. Farcical history of Richard Greenow
Irving, W. Adventure of the German student
Jenkins, W. F. Strange case of John Kingman
Kuttner, H. De profundis
Kuttner, H. Dream's end
Leiber, F. Sanity
Lovecraft, H. P. Case of Charles Dexter Ward
Maupassant, G. de. Diary of a madman
Paget, V. Legend of Madame Krasinska
Peretz, I. L. Mad Talmudist
Poe, E. A. Fall of the house of Usher
Poe, E. A. System of Dr Tarr and Prof. Fether
Priestley, J. B. Grey ones
Salinger, J. D. Perfect day for bananafish
Sandoz, M. Y. On the verge; 4 stories
Sartre, J. P. The room
Schneider, R. Passing through Fieldsville
Steele, W. D. Bubbles
Steele, W. D. For they know not what they do
Steele, W. D. How beautiful with shoes
Still, J. Mrs Razor
Taylor, E. Sad garden
Temple, W. F. Counter-transference
Thompson, R. E. It's a nice day—Sunday
Waugh, E. Mr Loveday's little outing

The inscription. Munby, A. N. L.

Inscrutable man. Haycox, E.

INSECTS
Bretnor, R. Gnurrs come from voodvork out
Kafka, F. The metamorphosis
Melville, H. Apple-tree table
See also names of particular insects: Ants; Bees; Beetles; etc.

Inside earth. Anderson, P.

Insoluble problem. Chesterton, G. K.

INSOMNIA
Hemingway, E. Now I lay me
Jackson, C. R. Sleeper awakened
Schmitz, E. Generous wine

Inspector had a habit. Child, C. B.

Inspector's teeth. De Camp, L. S.

Instinct. Del Rey, L.

INSTRUCTION. See Education

INSULTS
Chekhov, A. P. Worse and worse

Intimacy. Sartre, J. P.
Into the pit. Mann, T.
Into the web. Newell, D. M.
Into thy hands. Asch, S.
Into thy hands. Del Rey, L.
INTOLERANCE. See Race problems; Toleration
INTOXICATION. See Alcoholism; Drunkards
Introducing Pete Collins. Hendryx, J. B.
The **invaders.** Campbell, J. W.
The **invaders.** Macauley, R.
INVALIDS
   Aiken, C. P. Mr Arcularis
   Betts, D. Serpents and doves
   Harte, B. Miggles
   James, H. Middle years
   Mansfield, K. Man without a temperament
     See also Illness
Invariant. Pierce, J. A.
Invasion. Long, F. B.
INVENTIONS
   Anderson, E. V. Wildy's secret revealer
   Dahl, R. Great automatic grammatisator
   Melville, H. Happy failure
   Stockton, F. R. Tale of negative gravity
INVENTORS
   Brace, G. W. Deep water man
   Freedman, D. Mendel Marantz—genius
   Keller, D. H. Service first
Investigations of a dog. Kafka, F.
Invisible boy. Bradbury, R.
Invisible collection. Zweig, S.
Invisible dove dancer of Strathpheen Island. Collier, J.
Invisible man. Chesterton, G. K.
Invisible prisoner. LeBlanc, M.
Invisible shepherd. Krige, U.
INVISIBILITY
   Bradbury, R. Invisible boy
   Brooks, W. R. Jimmy takes vanishing lessons
   London, J. Shadow and the flash
The **invitation.** Ellis, M. H.
Ionian cycle. Klass, P.
IONIAN ISLANDS
   Cicellis, K. Miracles of the Saint
IRAN. See Persia
IRELAND
   Collier, J. Invisible dove dancer of Strathpheen Island
   Corkery, D. The wager, and other stories; 16 stories
   Waugh, E. Bella Fleace gave a party
      18th century
   Edgeworth, M. Castle Rackrent
      19th century
   Benson, T. Not by bread alone
   London, J. Samuel
   O'Donovan, M. Orpheus and his lute
   Yeats, W. B. Red Hanrahan
      20th century
   Irwin, M. E. F. The collar

McLaverty, M. Game cock, and other stories; 12 stories
McNulty, J. Back where I had never been
O'Donovan, M. Majesty of the law
O'Donovan, M. More stories; 29 stories
O'Donovan, M. Traveller's samples; 14 stories
O'Donovan, M. Uprooted
O'Flaherty, L. The challenge
O'Hanlon, D. M. Life and death of a village
Walsh, M. Son of a tinker; 9 stories
      Clare
Collier, J. Lady on the grey
      County Kerry
Walsh, M. Quiet man
      Dublin
Farrell, J. T. Summer morning in Dublin in 1938
Joyce, J. Araby
Joyce, J. Ivy Day in the committee room
Joyce, J. Little cloud
      Farm life
   See Farm life—Ireland
      Folklore
   See Legends and folk tales—Ireland
Irina, Aleksander
   The Landrath
     Guerney, B. G. comp. New Russian stories
Irish, William, pseud. See Woolrich, Cornell
Irish and the Jews and everybody else. Ready, W. B.
IRISH IN ENGLAND
   Irwin, M. E. F. Courage
   O'Donovan, M. Darcy in the Land of Youth
   O'Donovan, M. Jerome
   O'Donovan, M. Lonely rock
   O'Donovan, M. The sentry
   O'Donovan, M. Unapproved route
IRISH IN INDIA
   Kipling, R. Incarnation of Krishna Mulvaney
Irish lad. Bendrodt, J. C.
IRON AND STEEL INDUSTRY
   Betts, D. Mark of distinction
Iron cross, first class. Schneider, G. W.
Iron maiden. Fitzgerald, B.
Iron moon. Elam, R. M.
Iron rose. Cunningham, J. M.
Iron shroud. Mudford, W.
Iron standard. Kuttner, H.
Irving, Cliff
   Buried alive
     Hathaway, B. and Sessions, J. A. eds. Writers for tomorrow. 2d ser.
Irving, Washington, 1783-1859
   Adalantado of the Seven Cities
     Cuff, R. P. ed. American short story survey
   Adventure of the German student
     Blodgett, H. W. ed. Story survey. 1953 ed.

Irving, Washington—*Continued*
The devil and Tom Walker
Eaton, H. T. ed. Short stories
Legend of Sleepy Hollow
Burrell, J. A. and Cerf, B. A. eds.
Anthology of famous American stories
Foerster, N. ed. American poetry and
prose. 1952 ed.
Short, R. W. and Sewall, R. B. eds.
Short stories for study. 1950 ed.
Rip Van Winkle
Burrell, J. A. and Cerf, B. A. eds.
Anthology of famous American stories
Cody, S. ed. Greatest stories and how
they were written
Day, A. G. ed. Greatest American short
stories
Foerster, N. ed. American poetry and
prose. 1952 ed.
Lamb, L. ed. Family book of best loved
short stories
Stout gentleman
Neider, C. ed. Great short stories from
the world's literature

Irving. Newhouse, E.

Irwin, Inez (Haynes) 1873-
Spring flight
First-prize stories, 1919-1954

Irwin, John M.
Pennies from heaven
Seventeen (Periodical) The Seventeen
reader

Irwin, Margaret Emma Faith
Bloodstock
Irwin, M. E. F. Bloodstock, and other
stories
The book
Davenport, B. ed. Tales to be told in
the dark
Irwin, M. E. F. Bloodstock, and other
stories
The collar
Irwin, M. E. F. Bloodstock, and other
stories
Country gentleman
Irwin, M. E. F. Bloodstock, and other
stories
Courage
Irwin, M. E. F. Bloodstock, and other
stories
The doctor
Irwin, M. E. F. Bloodstock, and other
stories
Earlier service
Irwin, M. E. F. Bloodstock, and other
stories
Magazine of fantasy and science fiction.
Best from Fantasy and science fiction;
2d ser.
Mistletoe
Irwin, M. E. F. Bloodstock, and other
stories
Mrs Oliver Cromwell
Irwin, M. E. F. Bloodstock, and other
stories
Monsieur seeks a wife
Irwin, M. E. F. Bloodstock, and other
stories
Where beauty lies
Irwin, M. E. F. Bloodstock, and other
stories

Is there nowhere else where we can meet?
Gordimer, N.

Isaacson, Bernice Kavinoky, 1914-
Last bed
American vanguard, 1952
The onlooker
American vanguard, 1950

Isherwood, Christopher, 1904-
The Nowaks
New writing (Perioidcal) Best stories
On Ruegen Island
Cory, D. W. pseud. comp. 21 variations
on a theme

Ish-Kishor, Sulamith
The Champ
Strang, R. M. and Roberts, R. M. eds.
Teen-age tales v 1

The island. Horwitz, J.

Island happy. Heatter, B.

Island in the sky. Wellman, M. W.

Island of five colors. Gardner, M.

Island of ice. Waltari, M. T.

Island of the blue macaws. Ullman, J. R.

Island of the fay. Poe, E. A.

ISLANDS
Bloomfield, H. The trap
Collier, J. Invisible dove dancer of Strath-
pheen Island
Etnier, E. J. The willow
Gardner, M. Island of five colors
Hearn, L. The storm
Irving, W. Adalantado of the Seven Cities
Rousseau, J. J. Isle of St Peter
See also Desert islands

Isle-Adam, Villiers de l'. See Villiers de
l'Isle-Adam, Jean Marie Mathias
Philippe Auguste, comte de

ISLE OF MAN. See Man, Isle of

Isle of St Peter. Rousseau, J. J.

Isle of voices. Stevenson, R. L.

Isolationist. Reynolds, M.

ISRAEL
Tennyson, H. Land of my fathers

It ain't always the breaks. Kaufman, W.

It had to be. Pinski, D.

It had to happen. Bro, M. H.

It happened like this. Caldwell, E.

It happened to me. Johnson, H.

It looks like justice. Cohn, E.

It never fails. Grimson, M. S.

It wasn't syzygy. Waldo, E. H.

ITALIAN ARISTOCRACY. See Aristocracy—Italy

ITALIANS IN FRANCE
Boyle, K. Effigy of war

ITALIANS IN THE UNITED STATES
Blue, E. Nothing overwhelms Giuseppe
Malamud, B. The prison
Pagano, J. Signor Santa
Porter, W. S. Philistine in Bohemia
Shaw, I. Triumph of justice

ITALY
Paget, V. Amour dure
Paget, V. Wedding chest

14th century
Boccaccio, G. Patient Griselda

20th century
Mann, T. Mario and the magician
Maugham, W. S. Salvatore
Montanelli, I. Hero returns
Tennyson, H. Home leave

Florence
Huxley, A. L. Young Archimedes
Maugham, W. S. Woman of fifty

Naples
Burns, J. H. Momma

Padua
Hawthorne, N. Rappaccini's daughter

Pompeii
Blackburn, E. R. Story of Pompeii

Rome (City)
Charteris, L. Rome: The Latin touch
Paget, V. Seeker of pagan perfection
Wharton, E. N. J. Roman fever

Rome (City)—Ancient
See Rome

Venice
James, H. Aspern papers
Mann, T. Death in Venice
Poe, E. A. The assignation

Itch to win. Verral, C. S.
It's a good life. Bixby, J.
It's a man's world. Foster, C. J.
It's a nice day—Sunday. Thompson, R. E.
"It's great to be back." Heinlein, R. A.
It's such a beautiful day. Asimov, I.
It's such a nice day—Sunday. Thompson, R. E.
'Ivanhoe'. Smith, L. P.
Ivanov, Vsevolod Viacheslavovich, 1895?-
The kid
    Guerney, B. G. comp. New Russian stories

IVY
Keller, D. H. Ivy war
Ivy Day in the committee room. Joyce, J.
Ivy war. Keller, D. H.
Ixion in heaven. Beaconsfield, B. D. 1st earl of
Izzard and the membrane. Miller, W. M.

J

Jabotinsky, Vladimir. See Zhabotĭnskiĭ, Vladimir Evgen'evich
Jack-of-all-trades. Agnon, S. J.
The jackal and the alligator. Frere, M. A. I.
The jackpot. McNulty, J.
Jackpot vs. Yellowstrike. Oblinger, M.
JACKASSES. See Asses and mules

Jackson, Charles Reginald, 1903-
Band concert
    Jackson, C. R. Sunnier side
Benighted savage
    Jackson, C. R. Sunnier side
Boy who ran away
    Jackson, C. R. Earthly creatures
The break
    Jackson, C. R. Earthly creatures
"By the sea"
    Jackson, C. R. Sunnier side
The cheat
    Jackson, C. R. Earthly creatures
How war came to Arcadia, N. Y.
    Jackson, C. R. Sunnier side
In the chair
    Jackson, C. R. Sunnier side
Money
    Jackson, C. R. Earthly creatures
Night visitor
    Jackson, C. R. Sunnier side
Old men and boys
    Jackson, C. R. Earthly creatures
The outlander
    Jackson, C. R. Earthly creatures
Palm Sunday
    Cory, D. W. pseud. comp. 21 variations on a theme
    Jackson, C. R. Sunnier side
Parting at morning
    Jackson, C. R. Earthly creatures
Rachel's summer
    Jackson, C. R. Sunnier side
Romeo
    Jackson, C. R. Earthly creatures
The sisters
    Jackson, C. R. Sunnier side
Sleeper awakened
    Jackson, C. R. Earthly creatures
Sophistication
    Jackson, C. R. Sunnier side
Sunday drive
    Jackson, C. R. Earthly creatures
Sunnier side
    Jackson, C. R. Sunnier side
Tenting tonight
    Jackson, C. R. Sunnier side

Jackson, Charles Tenney, 1874-
Buffalo wallow
    Best American short stories, 1953
Horse of Hurricane Reef
    Cuff, R. P. ed. American short story survey
Sea-horse of Grand Terre
    Dennis, W. ed. Palomino and other horses

Jackson, Clive
Swordsmen of Varnis
    Brown, F. and Reynolds, M. eds. Science-fiction carnival

Jackson, Dorothy V. S.
Gift of love
    McFarland, W. K. comp. Then it happened
    Seventeen (Periodical) Nineteen from Seventeen

Jackson, Margaret (Weymouth) 1895-
The hero
    Christ, H. I. and Shostak, J. eds. Short stories

Jackson, Margaret W.—*Continued*
South toward home
  Eaton, H. T. ed. Short stories
The stepmother
  Lass, A. H. and Horowitz, A. eds.
    Stories for youth
Jackson, Roberts Brock
Fly away home
  Best American short stories, 1953
Jackson, Shirley, 1920-
After you, my dear Alphonse
  Felheim, M.; Newman, F. B. and Stein-
    hoff, W. R. eds. Modern short stories
Charles
  Stauffer, R. M.; Cunningham, W. H. and
    Sullivan, C. J. eds. Adventures in
    modern literature
The lottery
  Heilman, R. B. ed. Modern short stories
Summer people
  Best American short stories, 1951
JACKSON, THOMAS JONATHAN, 1824-
  1863
Moody, M. H. Ghost of General Jackson
Jacobi, Carl, 1908-
Gentleman is an Epwa
  Derleth, A. W. ed. Worlds of tomorrow
La Prello paper
  Derleth, A. W. ed. Night's yawning peal
Tepondicon
  Derleth, A. W. ed. Far boundaries
White pinnacle
  Derleth, A. W. ed. Time to come
Jacobs, Joseph, 1854-1916
Golden arm
  Fenner, P. R. comp. Ghosts, ghosts,
    ghosts
The tail
  Fenner, P. R. comp. Fools and funny
    fellows
Jacobs, Sylvia
Pilot and the bushman
  Galaxy science fiction magazine. Galaxy
    reader of science fiction
Jacobs, William Wymark, 1863-1943
Monkey's paw
  Cerf, B. A. and Moriarty, H. C. eds.
    Anthology of famous British stories
  Corrington, H. ed. Week-end book of
    ghost stories
  Davenport, B. ed. Ghostly tales to be
    told
Jacobson, Lee, E. 1924-
Last Saturday
  Wolfe, D. M. ed. Which grain will grow
Jade goddess
  Lin, Y. ed. Famous Chinese short stories
Jade ring. Norling, M. E.
JAGUARS
Gill, T. Jungle war
JAI ALAI
Sylvester, R. Last tanto
Jakes, John W. 1932-
Machine
  Best science-fiction stories: 1953
Jam session at Abby's. Gregutt, H. C.
JAM SESSIONS. See Jazz music
Jam today. De Vries, P.

JAMAICA
Powell, F. Black flag
JAMES I, KING OF GREAT BRITAIN,
  1566-1625
Evans, T. M. Gentlemen of valor
James, Daniel Lewis
Moon of delirium
  Conklin, G. ed. Possible worlds of sci-
    ence fiction
James, Henry, 1843-1916
Altar of the dead
  Stegner, W. E.; Scowcroft, R. and
    Ilyin, B. eds. Writer's art
Aspern papers
  James, H. Selected fiction
  Neider, C. ed. Short novels of the
    masters
Author of Beltraffio
  Burrell, J. A. and Cerf, B. A. eds.
    Anthology of famous American stories
Beast in the jungle
  Gordon, C. and Tate, A. eds. House of
    fiction
  James, H. Selected fiction
  James, H. Selected short stories
Bench of desolation
  Lynskey, W. C. ed. Reading modern
    fiction
The birthplace
  James, H. Selected short stories
Bundle of letters
  James, H. Selected short stories
Crawford's consistency
  James, H. Eight uncollected tales
Daisy Miller
  James, H. Selected fiction
Death of the lion
  Foerster, N. ed. American poetry and
    prose. 1952 ed.
  James, H. Selected short stories
Four meetings
  Felheim, M.; Newman, F. B. and Stein-
    hoff, W. R. eds. Modern short stories
Gabrielle de Bergerac
  James, H. Eight uncollected tales
Ghostly rental
  James, H. Eight uncollected tales
Great good place
  Neider, C. ed. Great short stories from
    the world's literature
Jolly corner
  James, H. Selected fiction
  James, H. Selected short stories
The liar
  West, R. B. and Stallman, R. W. eds.
    Art of modern fiction
Madame de Mauves
  Ludwig, R. M. and Perry, M. B. eds.
    Nine short novels
Middle years
  Davis, R. G. ed. Ten modern masters
  James, H. Selected short stories
My friend Bingham
  James, H. Eight uncollected tales
Osborne's revenge
  James, H. Eight uncollected tales
Paste
  Blodgett, H. W. ed. Story survey. 1953
    ed.
  Davis, R. G. ed. Ten modern masters
A problem
  James, H. Eight uncollected tales

James, Henry—Continued
The pupil
Cory, D. W. pseud. comp. 21 variations
on a theme
James, H. Selected fiction
James, H. Selected short stories
Short, R. W. and Sewall, R. B. eds.
Short stories for study. 1950 ed.
Real thing
Burrell, J. A. and Cerf, B. A. eds. An-
thology of famous American stories
Foerster, N. ed. American poetry and
prose. 1952 ed.
James, H. Selected short stories
Lamb, L. ed. Family book of best loved
short stories
O'Faoláin, S. The short story
Story of a masterpiece
James, H. Eight uncollected tales
Story of a year
James, H. Eight uncollected tales
Tone of time
Millett, F. B. ed. Reading fiction
Tree of knowledge
Davis, R. G. ed. Ten modern masters
Turn of the screw
Schorer, M. ed. The story
Washington Square
James, H. Selected fiction

James, Marquis, 1891-
Stolen railroad train
Moskowitz, S. ed. Great railroad stories
of the world

James, Montague Rhodes, 1862-1936
Count Magnus
Davenport, B. ed. Ghostly tales to be
told
Lost hearts
Conklin, G. and Conklin, L. T. eds.
Supernatural reader
The mezzotint
Cerf, B. A. and Moriarty, H. C. eds.
Anthology of famous British stories

James, Will, 1892-1942
Best riding and roping
James, W. Will James' Book of cowboy
stories
Cattle rustlers
James, W. Will James' Book of cowboy
stories
Chapo—the faker
Dennis, W. ed. Palomino and other
horses
James, W. Will James' Book of cowboy
stories
For a horse
James, W. Will James' Book of cowboy
stories
For the sake of freedom
James, W. Will James' Book of cowboy
stories
His spurs
Fenner, P. R. comp. Cowboys, cowboys,
cowboys
Lone cowboy
Fenner, P. R. comp. Cowboys, cowboys,
cowboys
James, W. Will James' Book of cowboy
stories

Makings of a cowhorse
James, W. Will James' Book of cowboy
stories
Midnight
Fenner, P. R. comp. Cowboys, cowboys,
cowboys
Narrow escape
James, W. Will James' Book of cowboy
stories
On the dodge
James, W. Will James' Book of cowboy
stories
On the drift
James, W. Will James' Book of cowboy
stories
Once a cowboy
James, W. Will James' Book of cowboy
stories
Silver mounted
James, W. Will James' Book of cowboy
stories
Smoky, the range colt
James, W. Will James' Book of cowboy
stories
When in Rome—
James, W. Will James' Book of cowboy
stories
Winter months in a cow camp
James, W. Will James' Book of cowboy
stories

James A. Dukes. Willingham, C.

Jameson, Malcolm, 1891-1945
Admiral's inspection
Jameson, M. Bullard of the space patrol
Blind alley
Jenkins, W. F. ed. Great stories of sci-
ence fiction
Blind man's buff
Bleiler, E. F. and Dikty, T. E. eds.
Imagination unlimited
Blockade runner
Jameson, M. Bullard of the space patrol
Brimstone Bill
Jameson, M. Bullard of the space patrol
Bullard reflects
Jameson, M. Bullard of the space patrol
The bureaucrat
Jameson, M. Bullard of the space patrol
Lilies of life
Conklin, G. ed. Possible worlds of sci-
ence fiction
Orders
Jameson, M. Bullard of the space patrol
Pride
Merril, J. ed. Beyond human ken
White mutiny
Jameson, M. Bullard of the space patrol

Jane. Maugham, W. S.

Jane. Willingham, C.

Jane Dore—dear childe. Barker, A. L.

JANITORS
Sansom, W. Boiler room

JAPAN
Akutagawa, R. Rashomon, and other
stories; 6 stories
Grosskopf, E. K. Tea for Tamahara
Hearn, L. Boy who drew cats

Jarka. Elias, A.

Jarrell, Randall, 1914-
Gertrude and Sidney
Best American short stories, 1954

JAVA. See Dutch East Indies—Java

Jay Score. Russell, E. F.

Jaywalker. Rocklynne, R.

JAZZ MUSIC
De Vries, P. Jam today

JEALOUSY
Bowles, P. F. The echo
Porter, W. S. "Guilty party"
Rinehart, M. R. If only it were yesterday
Taylor, E. Hester Lilly
Van Doren, M. Fisk Fogle

Jealousy
Lin, Y. ed. Famous Chinese short stories

Jean Beicke. Williams, W. C.

Jeannette. Thériault, Y.

Jeannine. Charteris, L.

Jeep: the dog who came home. Little, G. W.

Jeeves and the song of songs. Wodehouse, P. G.

Jeff Peters as a personal magnet. Porter, W. S.

Jefferies, Richard, 1848-1887
Winds of heaven
Andrews, R. C. ed. My favorite stories of the great outdoors

Jelly-bean. Fitzgerald, F. S. K.

Jelly-fish. Keller, D. H.

Jenkin, Philip A. 1910-
Cool million
Story (Periodical) Story; no. 4

Jenkins, William Fitzgerald, 1896-
De profundis
Derleth, A. W. ed. Far boundaries
Jenkins, W. F. Sidewise in time, and other scientific adventures
Devil's henchman
Conklin, G. and Conklin, L. T. eds. Supernatural reader
Doomsday deferred
Best science fiction stories: 1950
Bleiler, E. F. and Dikty, T. E. eds. Science fiction omnibus: The best science fiction stories, 1949, 1950
First contact
Astounding science fiction (Periodical) Astounding science fiction anthology
Jensen, P. ed. Fireside book of flying stories
Sloane, W. M. ed. Stories for tomorrow
Fourth-dimensional demonstrator
Jenkins, W. F. Sidewise in time, and other scientific adventures
Gadget had a ghost
Year's best science fiction novels, 1953
Historical note
Astounding science fiction (Periodical) Astounding science fiction anthology
If you was a Molkin
Galaxy science fiction magazine. Galaxy reader of science fiction
The journey
Star science fiction stories [no. 1]
Keyhole
Heinlein, R. A. ed. Tomorrow, the stars
Life-work of Professor Muntz
Best science fiction stories: 1950
Bleiler, E. F. and Dikty, T. E. eds. Science fiction omnibus: the best science fiction stories, 1949, 1950

Little terror
Saturday evening post (Periodical) Saturday evening post stories, 1953
Logic named Joe
Brown, F. and Reynolds, M. eds. Science-fiction carnival
Jenkins, W. F. Sidewise in time, and other scientific adventures
Middle of the week after next
Best science-fiction stories: 1953
Conklin, G. ed. Science-fiction adventures in dimension
Nobody saw the ship
Conklin, G. ed. Big book of science fiction
Other now
Galaxy science fiction magazine. Galaxy reader of science fiction
Plague
Conklin, G. ed. Omnibus of science fiction
The plants
Greenberg, M. ed. Men against the stars
The power
Derleth, A. W. ed. The outer reaches
Jenkins, W. F. Sidewise in time, and other scientific adventures
Lesser, M. A. ed. Looking forward
Propagandist
Conklin, G. ed. Possible worlds of science fiction
Proxima centauri
Jenkins, W. F. Sidewise in time, and other scientific adventures
Search in the mist
Saturday evening post (Periodical) Saturday evening post stories, 1950
The sentimentalists
Year's best science fiction novels, 1954
Sidewise in time
Jenkins, W. F. Sidewise in time, and other scientific adventures
Strange case of John Kingman
Bleiler, E. F. and Dikty, T. E. eds. Science fiction omnibus: the best science fiction stories, 1949, 1950
Jenkins, W. F. ed. Great stories of science fiction
Symbiosis
Jenkins, W. F. ed. Great stories of science fiction
Things pass by
Margulies, L. and Friend, O. J. eds. Giant anthology of science fiction
This star shall be free
Conklin, G. ed. Invaders of earth
The wabbler
Merril, J. ed. Beyond human ken

Jenks, Almet, 1892-
No way down
Best American short stories, 1954

Jenny takes a holiday. Hayes, H. M.

Jepson, Selwyn, 1899-
God and the little cat
Joseph, M. ed. Best cat stories

JEREMIAH
Werfel, F. Jeremiah

Jeremy in the wind. Kneale, N.

Jeremy Rodock. Schaefer, J. W.

Jericho, Jericho, Jericho. Lytle, A. N.

Jerome. O'Donovan, M.
JEROME OF PRAGUE, d. 1415
　Blackburn, E. R. Jerome of Prague
Jerry. Meek, S. St P.
Jerry: the dog who refused to die. Little,
　G. W.
Jerry was a man. Heinlein, R. A.
Jersey, Guernsey, Alderney, Sark. Seager, A.
Jersey heifer. Love, P. H.
Jerusalem delivered. Zweig, A.
The jester. Klass, P.
JESTERS. See Fools and jesters
Jesting of Arlington Stringham. Munro,
　H. H.
Jesting pilot. Kuttner, H.
JESUITS
　O'Donovan, M. The miracle
JESUS CHRIST
　Austin, M. Green bough
　Eça de Queiroz, J. M. Woman taken in
　　adultery
　Gibran, K. Rafca, the bride of Cana
　Goudge, E. By the waters of Babylon
　Ingraham, J. H. The baptizing
　Lagerlöf, S. O. L. In Nazareth
　Marie, consort of Ferdinand I, King of
　　Rumania. What Vasile saw
　Oxenham, P. Of our meeting with Cousin
　　John
　Rosegger, P. Flight into Egypt
　Rosegger, P. Of love and joy
　Van Dyke, H. Lost boy

　　　　Crucifixion
　Asch, S. Into thy hands

　　　　Last Supper
　See Lord's Supper

　　　　Nativity
　Beauclerk, H. De V. The miracle of the
　　vineyard
　Broun, H. C. We, too, are bidden
　Oxenham, J. Their first meeting
　Van Dyke, H. Other Wise Man

Jesus complex. Mohler, C.
JET PROPULSION. See Rocket ships
Jetsam. Russell, J.
JEWELERS
　Dunsany, E. J. M. D. P. 18th baron. Dis-
　　tressing tale of Thangobrind the
　　jeweller
　Woolf, V. S. Duchess and the jeweller
JEWELRY
　James, H. Paste
　Maupassant, G. de. The jewels
　　See also Necklaces
The jewels. Maupassant, G. de
Jewels of Gwahlur. Howard, R. E.
Jewett, Sarah Orne, 1849-1909
　Courting of Sister Wisby
　　Burrell, J. A. and Cerf, B. A. eds. An-
　　　thology of famous American stories
　White heron
　　Barrows, H. ed. 15 stories
Jewish cat. Agnon, S. J.

JEWISH DIALECT STORIES. See Dia--
　lect stories—Jewish
JEWISH QUESTION. See Jews
JEWISH RITES AND CEREMONIES.
　See Jews—Rites and ceremonies
JEWS
　Aiken, C. P. The disciple
　Ausubel, N. ed. Treasury of Jewish humor;
　　82 stories
　Berryman, J. Imaginary Jew
　Cohn, E. Stories and fantasies from the
　　Jewish past; 10 stories
　Hecht, B. God is good to a Jew
　Heine, H. Tale of olden time
　Lincoln, V. E. Glass wall
　Ribalow, H. U. This land, these people;
　　24 stories
　Shaw, I. Act of faith
　Yushkevich, S. S. In a Bolshevist market-
　　place
　Zhabotïnskiĭ, V. E. Edmée

　　　　Persecutions
　Asch, S. Duty to live
　Asch, S. Kola Street
　Asch, S. Santification of the Name
　Cohn, E. Simhah of Worms
　Feuchtwanger, L. Mendel Hirsch
　Shapiro, L. White chalah
　Shneur, Z. Revenge
　Spiegel, I. Ghetto dog

　　　　Religion
　Glassman, B. Tarnished gold
　Goldman, A. Almost like dead
　Grade, C. My quarrel with Hersh Ras-
　　seyner
　Klein, A. The Minyan
　Reisin, A. Poor community
　Singer, I. J. Repentance
　　See also Rosh ha-Shanah; Yom Kippur

　　　　Rites and ceremonies
　Agnon, S. J. Sabbathai
　Bruggen, C. de H. van. Seder night
　Fleg, E. The adulteress
　Heine, H. Tale of olden time
　Ogus, A. D. Shofar blower of Lapinishok
　Perl, P. Man in Israel
　Rabinowitz, S. Passover guest
　Rugel, M. The flower
　Scheiner, F. Old man had four wives
　Weidman, J. The Kinnehorrah
Jew's beech tree. Droste-Hülshoff, A. E.
　Freiin von
JEWS IN AUSTRIA
　Katz, L. Gift of the emperor
　Werfel, F. V. Third commandment
JEWS IN CANADA
　Allan, T. Lies my father told me
JEWS IN ENGLAND
　Frankau, G. Outlier from his tribe
　Golding, L. Angels in Chayder
　Golding, L. Doomington wanderer
　Kersh, G. One way of getting a hundred
　　pounds
　Levy, A. Cohen of Trinity
　Maugham, W. S. Alien corn
　Rappoport, S. Moses Montefiore

Joe Smiley collects a reward. Hendryx, J. B.

Joe Smiley shows up on Halfaday. Hendryx, J. B.

Joe Terrace. Runyon, D.

JOHN THE BAPTIST, SAINT
Ingraham, J. H. The baptizing
Oxenham, J. Of our meeting with Cousin John

John Ferrier talks with the Prophet. Doyle, Sir A. C.

John Hitchcock. Farrell, J. T.

John the Indian and George Hopkins. Caldwell, E.

John the madman. Gibran, K.

John the revelator. La Farge, O.

John Thomas's cube. Leimert, J.

Johnnie Poothers. Odger, C.

Johnny Eames does well. Trollope, A.

Johnny One-Eye. Runyon, D.

Johnny Pye and the Fool-killer. Benét, S. V.

Johnny's old man. Farrell, J. T.

Johns, Veronica Parker, 1907-
Bezique of death
Mystery Writers of America, inc. Maiden murders
Homecoming
Queen, E. pseud. ed. Queen's awards: 7th ser.

Johnson, Cynthia. See Schwarz, Cynthia Johnson

Johnson, Dorothy Marie, 1905-
Beyond the frontier
Johnson, D. M. Indian country
Flame on the frontier
Argosy (Periodical) Argosy Book of adventure stories
Johnson, D. M. Indian country
Journey to the fort
Johnson, D. M. Indian country
Meredith, S. ed. Bar 3
Laugh in the face of danger
Johnson, D. M. Indian country
Man called Horse
Johnson, D. M. Indian country
Meredith, S. ed. Bar 1 roundup of best western stories
Man who shot Liberty Valance
Johnson, D. M. Indian country
Prairie kid
Johnson, D. M. Indian country
Scars of honor
Johnson, D. M. Indian country
The unbeliever
Johnson, D. M. Indian country
Meredith, S. ed. Bar 2
War shirt
Johnson, D. M. Indian country
Warrior's exile
Johnson, D. M. Indian country

Johnson, Harold
Baby sitter vs. Ronnie
Strang, R. M. and Roberts, R. M. eds. Teen-age tales v 1
It happened to me
Strang, R. M. and Roberts, R. M. eds. Teen-age tales v 1

Rocky
Strang, R. M. and Roberts, R. M. eds. Teen-age tales v2
She'll be sorry
Strang, R. M. and Roberts, R. M. eds. Teen-age tales v2

Johnson, Josephine Winslow, 1910-
Alexander to the park
Felheim, M.; Newman, F. B. and Steinhoff, W. R. eds. Modern short stories
Arcadia recalled
Blodgett, H. W. ed. Story survey. 1953 ed.
The author
Best American short stories, 1950
Mother's story
Best American short stories, 1951
Sorcerer's son
Abell, E. ed. American accent

Johnson, Margaret Sweet, 1893-
Rex of the Coast patrol
Harper, W. comp. Dog show

Johnson, Martha, pseud. See Lansing, Elisabeth Carleton (Hubbard)

Johnson, Owen McMahon, 1878-1952
Great pancake record
Burrell, J. A. and Cerf, B. A. eds. Anthology of famous American stories
Varmint tries dissipation
Fenner, P. R. comp. Fun! Fun! Fun!

Johnson, Robert Barbour
Far below
Moskowitz, S. comp. Editor's choice in science fiction

Johnson, Ruth
Cross buns for Friday
Ford, N. A. and Faggett, H. L. eds. Best short stories by Afro-American writers (1925-1950)

Johnson, William R. See Nemerov, H. jt. auth.

Johnson looked back. Burke, T.

Johnston, Northam F. 1921-
Absolutism
American vanguard, 1950
God and the angry men
American vanguard, 1952

Joining the Yankees. Graham, F.

Jo-Jo. Farrell, J. T.

Jojo. P'u Sung-ling

JOKES, PRACTICAL. See Humor—Practical jokes

Jolly. Thompson, T.

Jolly corner. James, H.

JONAH (BIBLICAL CHARACTER)
Melville, H. The sermon
Nathan, R. Testing of Jonah

Jonah curse. Wallace, J. F.

Jonathan Harrow. Greenfield, R.

Jones, Henry Bedford- See Bedford-Jones, Henry

Jones, James, 1921-
Two legs for the two of us
Esquire (Periodical) Girls from Esquire

JONES, JOHN PAUL, 1747-1792
Ellsberg, E. Battle in the moonlight

Jones, Louis Clark, 1908-
Spooks of the valley
Fenner, P. R. comp. Ghosts, ghosts, ghosts

Jones, Madison P. jr.
Dog days
Best American short stories, 1953

Jones, Neil R.
Hermit of Saturn's ring
Wollheim, D. A. comp. Flight into space

Jones, Raymond F. 1915-
Children's room
Jones, R. F. The toymaker
Deadly host
Jones, R. F. The toymaker
Farthest horizon
Norton, A. M. ed. Space pioneers
Sloane, W. M. ed. Stories for tomorrow
Forecast
Jones, R. F. The toymaker
Model shop
Jones, R. F. The toymaker
Noise level
Sloane, W. M. ed. Stories for tomorrow
Pete can fix it
Conklin, G. ed. Science-fiction adventures in dimension
Production test
Lesser, M. A. ed. Looking forward
Stone and a spear
Conklin, G. ed. Omnibus of science fiction
Tools of the trade
Sloane, W. M. ed. Space, space, space
The toymaker
Jones, R. F. The toymaker
Utility
Jones, R. F. The toymaker

Jones, Ruby S.
August tenth
Oberfirst, R. ed. 1952 anthology of best original short-shorts

Jon's world. Dick, P. K.

Jordan, Gladys
For the last time
Oberfirst, R. ed. 1952 anthology of best original short-shorts

Jorrocks, John, pseud. See Surtees, Robert Smith

JOSEPH, THE PATRIARCH
Mann, T. Into the pit

Josephine the singer; or, The Mouse Folk. Kafka, F.

JOSHUA (BIBLICAL CHARACTER)
Bradford, R. Strategem of Joshua

Joshua. Grau, S. A.

Josiah Crawley at the Palace. Trollope, A.

Josiah Crawley charged with theft. Trollope, A.

Josiah Willett. Schaefer, J. W.

Josie who took things. Strain, F. B.

JOURNALISM. See Journalists

JOURNALISTS
Aiken, C. P. Round by round
Bowen, E. Recent photograph
Brown, F. Night the world ended
Brier, H. M. Newspaper man

Carter, R. G. High-pressure stuff
Chalmers, B. The contest
Claudy, C. H. Helmet of Pluto
Clemens, S. L. Mr Skae's item
Clemens, S. L. My bloody massacre (I)
Coombs, C. I. Millie's big story
Coombs, C. I. Nose for news
Coppard, A. E. Fifty pounds
Davis, R. H. The deserter
Fletcher, V. Coda to a writer's conference
Gallico, P. W. McKabe
Goodman, J. T. "Trumpet" comes to Pickeye!
Grimson, M. S. Faith, hope and charity
Hillman, G. M. Copy girl
James, H. Death of the lion
Joyce, J. Little cloud
Kipling, R. Man who would be king
Kipling, R. Village that voted the earth was flat
Kirkland, J. Wall of fire
Munro, H. H. Secret sin of Septimus Brope
Munro, H. H. Yarkand manner
Poe, E. A. X-ing a paragrab
Porter, W. S. Calloway's code
Priestley, J. B. The statues
Schramm, W. L. My kingdom for Jones
Tarkington, B. Walterson
Taylor, S. W. Last voyage of the Unsinkable Sal
Ullman, J. M. Anything new on the strangler?
Verne, J. In the year 2889
Waddell, R. You'd better be right!
Wallace, R. Secret weapon of Joe Smith
Waltari, M. T. Before the twilight of the gods

JOURNALS. See Diaries (Stories in diary form)

The journey. Jenkins, W. F.

Journey for Wilbur. Schnabel, J. F.

Journey into smoke. Sansom, W.

Journey to the fort. Johnson, D. M.

Journeying through the milky way. Shapiro, L.

JOURNEYS. See Travel

JOVIANS. See Jupiter (Planet)

JOY AND SORROW
Berger, T. L. April is the cruelest month
James, H. Altar of the dead

Joy, joy, joy! Parker, J. R.

Joyce, James, 1882-1941
Araby
Neider, C. ed. Great short stories from the world's literature
Waite, H. O. and Atkinson, B. P. eds. Literature for our time
Clay
Lynskey, W. C. ed. Reading modern fiction
Short, R. W. and Sewall, R. B. eds. Short stories for study. 1950 ed.
Counterparts
West, R. B. and Stallman, R. W. eds. Art of modern fiction

Kafka, Franz, 1883-1924
  The burrow
    Kafka, F. Selected short stories
  Common confusion
    Kafka, F. Selected short stories
  Country doctor
    Kafka, F. Selected short stories
    Lange, V. ed. Great German short novels and stories
    Neider, C. ed. Great short stories from the world's literature
  A fratricide
    Kafka, F. Selected short stories
  Great wall of China
    Kafka, F. Selected short stories
  Hunger artist
    Heilman, R. B. ed. Modern short stories
    Kafka, F. Selected short stories
    Millett, F. B. ed. Reading fiction
    West, R. B. and Stallman, R. W. eds. Art of modern fiction
  Hunter Gracchus
    Gordon, C. and Tate, A. eds. House of fiction
    Kafka, F. Selected short stories
    Leftwich, J. ed. Yisröel. 1952 ed.
  In the penal colony
    Kafka, F. Selected short stories
  Investigations of a dog
    Kafka, F. Selected short stories
  Josephine the singer; or, The Mouse Folk
    Kafka, F. Selected short stories
  The judgment
    Felheim, M.; Newman, F. B. and Steinhoff, W. R. eds. Modern short stories
    Kafka, F. Selected short stories
  The metamorphosis
    Kafka, F. Selected short stories
    Ludwig, R M. and Perry, M. B. eds. Nine short novels
    Neider, C. ed. Short novels of the masters
    Pick, R. ed. German stories and tales
    Pratt, F. ed. World of wonder
  New advocate
    Kafka, F. Selected short stories
  Old manuscript
    Kafka, F. Selected short stories
    Same as: Old page
  Old page
    Lynskey, W. C. ed. Reading modern fiction
    Same as: Old manuscript
  Report to an academy
    Kafka, F. Selected short stories

Kagawa, Toyohiko, 1888-
  The last supper
    Brentano, F. ed. The word lives on

Kahanovich, Pinchas, 1884-
  From my estates
    Leftwich, J. ed. Yisröel. 1952 ed.

Kahler, Hugh MacNair, 1883-
  The buckpasser
    Shaw, H. and Bement, D. Reading the short story

Kahmann, Mable (Chesley) 1901-
  For the honor of XDY
    Story parade (Periodical) Adventure stories

Kahn, Bernard I.
  Command
    Norton, A. M. ed. Space service
  For the public
    Norton, A. M. ed. Space service
The **Kahn**. Wall, J. W.
Kaleidoscope. Bradbury, R.
Kalisman, Herbert H. 1920-
  The stray
    American vanguard, 1950
Kandel, Lenore, 1932-
  Boy with the innocent eyes
    American vanguard, 1953
Kane, Frank
  Slay upon delivery
    Mystery Writers of America, inc. Four-&-twenty bloodhounds
KANGAROOS
  Jenkins, W. F. Fourth-dimensional demonstrator
Kannitverstan. Hebel, J. P.
KANSAS
Farm life
  See Farm life—Kansas
Kantor, MacKinlay, 1904-
  Fabulous cabman
    Saturday evening post (Periodical) Saturday evening post stories, 1950
  Life in her hands
    Saturday evening post (Periodical) Saturday evening post stories, 1953
  Man who had no eyes
    Certner, S. and Henry, G. H. eds. Short stories for our times
  Papa Pierre's pipe
    This week magazine. This week's short-short stories
  That Greek dog
    Lass, A. H. and Horowitz, A. eds. Stories for youth
  Voice of Bugle Ann
    Andrews, R. C. ed. My favorite stories of the great outdoors
  Yea, he did fly
    Grayson, C. ed. Fourth round
Kaplan, Alvin Harold, 1904-
  Danger wears two faces
    Argosy (Periodical) Argosy Book of adventure stories
Kaplan, Ralph, 1917-
  The artist
    Best American short stories, 1950
  Night my brother came home
    Ribalow, H. U. ed. This land, these people
Karchmer, Sylvan, 1914-
  Bond
    Ribalow, H. U. ed. These your children
  Fistful of Alamo heroes
    Peery, W. W. ed. 21 Texas short stories
  "Hail, brother and farewell"
    Best American short stories, 1950
Kari the elephant. Mukerji, D. G.
Karmel, Ilona, 1925-
  Fru Holm
    Best American short stories, 1951
Karp, Deborah B. 1924-
  Carmi
    Ribalow, H. U. ed. These your children

Katherine the clown. Ekbergh, I. D.

Kathyanne and the piggy bank. Caldwell, E.

Katkov, Norman, 1918-
Charlie Baseball
Argosy (Periodical) Argosy Book of sports stories
Stop that fight!
Ribalow, H. U. ed. World's greatest boxing stories

Katrina. Parker, J. R.

Katti's Galapágos Christmas. Von Hagen, C. I. B.

Katz, Leo, 1892-
Gift of the emperor
Ausubel, N. ed. Treasury of Jewish humor
Technical expert
Ausubel, N. ed. Treasury of Jewish humor

Katz, Shlomo
Second Lieutenant, U.S.A. Res.
Ribalow, H. U. ed. These your children

Kaufman, Alvin, 1925-
Anchor me in mire
American vanguard, 1950

Kaufman, Anne, 1917-
First love
American vanguard, 1953

Kaufman, Wolfe
Cut yourself a slice of show
Kaufman, W. Call me Nate
Dames and ethics
Kaufman, W. Call me Nate
Diplomacy in Hollywood
Kaufman, W. Call me Nate
Dumas in Hollywood
Kaufman, W. Call me Nate
It ain't always the breaks
Kaufman, W. Call me Nate
Pity the poor producer
Kaufman, W. Call me Nate
Talking about writers
Kaufman, W. Call me Nate
That's picture business
Kaufman, W. Call me Nate
Three men on a nickel
Kaufman, W. Call me Nate
Wings of an angel
Kaufman, W. Call me Nate
You'll meet 'em all
Kaufman, W. Call me Nate

Kauffmann, Stanley, 1916-
Fulvous yellow
Cory, D. W. pseud. comp. 21 variations on a theme

Kaula, David
The huntress
Hathaway, B. and Sessions, J. A. eds. Writers for tomorrow. 2d ser.

Kay uses the evidence. Lansing, E. C. H.

Kaye-Smith, Sheila, 1887-1956
Day in a woman's life
Cerf, B. A. and Moriarty, H. C. eds. Anthology of famous British stories
The mockbeggar
Blodgett, H. W. ed. Story survey. 1953 ed.

Kazan. Curwood, J. O.

Keela, the outcast Indian maiden. Welty, E.

Keeler, Harry Stephen, 1890-
Hand of God
Mystery Writers of America, inc. 20 great tales of murder
Victim no. 5
Mystery Writers of America, inc. Maiden murders

Keene, Day
Great whirring of wings
Mystery Writers of America, inc. Maiden murders
Homicide House
Mystery Writers of America, inc. Crooks' tour
Remember the night
Best detective stories of the year—1950
"What so proudly we hail. . ."
Conklin, G. ed. Science-fiction adventures in dimension

Keep off the rail! Clements, C. J.

Keep your pity. Boyle, K.

Keeper of the dream. Beaumont, C.

Keeper of the faith. Sienkiewicz, H.

Keith, Earl, 1926-
Children's hour
American vanguard, 1953

Keith, Sam
Point of view
Hathaway, B. and Sessions, J. A. eds. Writers for tomorrow. 2d ser.
Siren of hope
Hathaway, B. and Sessions, J. A. eds. Writers for tomorrow. 2d ser.

Kelland, Clarence Budington, 1881-
Mark Tidd in the backwoods
American boy (Periodical) American boy anthology

Kelleam, Joseph E. 1913-
Rust
Greenberg, M. ed. Robot and the man

Keller, David Henry, 1880-
Biological experiment
Keller, D. H. Tales from Underwood
The bridle
Keller, D. H. Tales from Underwood
Creation unforgivable
Keller, D. H. Tales from Underwood
Dead woman
Keller, D. H. Tales from Underwood
The door
Keller, D. H. Tales from Underwood
The doorbell
Conklin, G. ed. Omnibus of science fiction
Keller, D. H. Tales from Underwood
Flying fool
Keller, D. H. Tales from Underwood
Free as the air
Keller, D. H. Tales from Underwood
God wheel
Keller, D. H. Tales from Underwood
Golden bough
Keller, D. H. Tales from Underwood
Ivy war
Keller, D. H. Tales from Underwood
Jelly-fish
Keller, D. H. Tales from Underwood
Literary corkscrew
Keller, D. H. Tales from Underwood
Margulies, L. and Friend, O. J. eds. From off this world

Kipling, Rudyard—*Continued*
Village that voted the earth was flat
Kipling, R. Maugham's choice of Kipling's best
William the conqueror
Kipling, R. Maugham's choice of Kipling's best
'Wireless'
Kipling, R. Maugham's choice of Kipling's best
Without benefit of clergy
Kipling, R. Maugham's choice of Kipling's best

Kirch, James A.
Murder for two
Best detective stories of the year—1950
Till death do us part
Best detective stories of the year—1953

KIRGHIZ
Ivanov, V. V. The kid

Kirk, Ralph G. 1881-
To him who waits
Cavanna, B. ed. Pick of the litter

Kirkland, Jack, 1901-
Wall of fire
Moskowitz, S. comp. Editor's choice in science fiction

Kirtland, Ann
Trial by fire
Strang, R. M. and Roberts, R. M. eds. Teen-age tales v2

Kishor, Sulamith Ish- See Ish-Kishor, Sulamith

Kismet and the nomad woman. Enders, G. B.

The kiss. Sansom, W.

Kiss for the Lieutenant. Gordon, A.

Kiss me again, stranger. Du Maurier, D.

Kiss of Kandahar. Blochman, L. G.

The kiss-off. Foran, J. P.

Kissing kind. Hine, A. B.

Kitchin, Clifford Henry Benn, 1895-
Chelsea cat
Asquith, Lady C. M. E. C. ed. Book of modern ghosts

The kite. Maugham, W. S.

KITES
Maugham, W. S. The kite

Kith of the Elf-folk. Dunsany, E. J. M. D. P. 18th baron

KITTENS. See Cats

Kittura Remsberg. Schaefer, J. W.

Kitty, kitty, kitty. Pudney, J.

Kjelgaard, Betty
Age of love
This week magazine. This week's short-short stories
Black horse
Furman, A. L. ed. Teen-age horse stories
Blood on the ice
Boys' life (Periodical) Boys' life adventure stories
Dog's dog
Furman, A. L. ed. Teen-age dog stories
Fifth friend
Fenner, P. R. comp. Indians, Indians, Indians

Red's education
Fenner, P. R. comp. Dogs, dogs, dogs
Wilderness road
Fenner, P. R. comp. Indians, Indians, Indians

Klass, Philip, 1920-
Alexander the bait
Conklin, G. ed. Omnibus of science fiction
Betelgeuse Bridge
Galaxy science fiction magazine. Galaxy reader of science fiction
Heinlein, R. A. ed. Tomorrow, the stars
Child's play
Astounding science fiction (Periodical) Astounding science fiction anthology
Pratt, F. ed. World of wonder
The deserter
Star science fiction stories [no. 1]
Firewater
Year's best science fiction novels, 1953
Generation of Noah
Best science fiction stories: 1952
House dutiful
Merril, J. ed. Beyond human ken
Ionian cycle
Greenberg, M. ed. Travelers of space
The jester
Conklin, G. ed. Science-fiction thinking machines
Null-P
Derleth, A. W. ed. Worlds of tomorrow
Venus and the seven sexes
Brown, F. and Reynolds, M. eds. Science-fiction carnival
Venus is a man's world
Galaxy science fiction magazine. Galaxy reader of science fiction
"Will you walk a little faster?"
Conklin, G. ed. Invaders of earth

Klein, Alexander, 1918-
The Minyan
Ribalow, H. U. ed. This land, these people

Klein, Jenny Machlowitz
Yisgadal
Ribalow, H. U. ed. This land, these people

Kleist, Heinrich von, 1777-1811
Beggar-woman of Locarno
Neider, C. ed. Great short stories from the world's literature
Earthquake in Chile
Lange, V. ed. Great German short novels and stories

KLEPTOMANIA
Munro, H. H. Seven cream jugs

Kline, Otis Adelbert, 1891?-1946
Stolen centuries
Moskowitz, S. comp. Editor's choice in science fiction

Klingsberg, Harry M.
Doowinkle, Attorney
Blaustein, A. P. ed. Fiction goes to court
Foolproof frame-up
Best detective stories of the year—1951

Kloepfer, Marguerite
Skeleton of Mr Nethersoul
Seventeen (Periodical) Nineteen from Seventeen

KLONDIKE
  Hendryx, J. B. Murder on Halfaday
    Creek; 30 stories
  London, J. Sun-Dog Trail

The **Klondiker.** Davis, A. L.

Knapp, Sally Elizabeth, 1918-
  Clipped wings
    American girl (Periodical) Favorite
    stories

Knapsack of salvation. Langewiesche-Brandt,
  W. E.

Kneale, Nigel
  Bini and Bettine
    Kneale, N. Tomato Cain, and other
    stories
  Calculation of N'bambwe
    Kneale, N. Tomato Cain, and other
    stories
  Chains
    Kneale, N. Tomato Cain, and other
    stories
  Clog dance for a dead farce
    Kneale, N. Tomato Cain, and other
    stories
  Curphey's follower
    Kneale, N. Tomato Cain, and other
    stories
  Enderby and the sleeping beauty
    Kneale, N. Tomato Cain, and other
    stories
  Essence of strawberry
    Kneale, N. Tomato Cain, and other
    stories
  The excursion
    Kneale, N. Tomato Cain, and other
    stories
  Flo
    Kneale, N. Tomato Cain, and other
    stories
  God and Daphne
    Kneale, N. Tomato Cain, and other
    stories
  Jeremy in the wind
    Kneale, N. Tomato Cain, and other
    stories
  Lotus for Jamie
    Kneale, N. Tomato Cain, and other
    stories
  Minuke
    Conklin, G. and Conklin, L. T. eds.
    Supernatural reader
    Kneale, N. Tomato Cain, and other
    stories
  Mrs Mancini
    Kneale, N. Tomato Cain, and other
    stories
  Nature study
    Kneale, N. Tomato Cain, and other
    stories
  "Oh, mirror, mirror"
    Kneale, N. Tomato Cain, and other
    stories
  Patter of tiny feet
    Kneale, N. Tomato Cain, and other
    stories
  Peg
    Kneale, N. Tomato Cain, and other
    stories
  The photograph
    Kneale, N. Tomato Cain, and other
    stories

  The pond
    Kneale, N. Tomato Cain, and other
    stories
  Putting away of Uncle Quaggin
    Kneale, N. Tomato Cain, and other
    stories
    Stauffer, R. M.; Cunningham, W. H. and
    Sullivan, C. J. eds. Adventures in
    modern literature
  Quiet Mr Evans
    Kneale, N. Tomato Cain, and other
    stories
  The stocking
    Kneale, N. Tomato Cain, and other
    stories
  Tarroo-ushtey
    Kneale, N. Tomato Cain, and other
    stories
  They're scared, Mr Bradlaugh
    Kneale, N. Tomato Cain, and other
    stories
  Tomato Cain
    Kneale, N. Tomato Cain, and other
    stories
  Tootie and the cat licenses
    Kneale, N. Tomato Cain, and other
    stories
  Who—me, signor?
    Kneale, N. Tomato Cain, and other
    stories
  Zachary Crebbin's angel
    Kneale, N. Tomato Cain, and other
    stories

Kneel to the rising sun. Caldwell, E.

The **knife.** Crane, S.

The **knife.** Gill, B.

Knife of the times. Williams, W. C.

Knife to cut the corn bread with. Caldwell, E.

Knight, Damon
  Ask me anything
    Galaxy science fiction magazine. Galaxy
    reader of science fiction
  Cabin boy
    Galaxy science fiction magazine. Galaxy
    reader of science fiction
  Catch that Martian
    Conklin, G. ed. Omnibus of science fic-
    tion
  Don't live in the past
    Galaxy science fiction magazine. Galaxy
    reader of science fiction
  Four in one
    Galaxy science fiction magazine. Second
    Galaxy reader of science fiction
  Not with a bang
    Conklin, G. ed. Big book of science
    fiction
  To serve man
    Best science fiction stories: 1951

Knight, Eric Mowbray, 1897-1943
  Flying Yorkshireman
    Jensen, P. ed. Fireside book of flying
    stories
  Lassie Come-Home
    Andrews, R. C. ed. My favorite stories
    of the great outdoors
    Bloch, M. ed. Favorite dog stories
    Harper, W. comp. Dog show

Knight, Norman L.
Crisis in Utopia
Greenberg, M. comp. Five science fiction novels

The **knight.** Bergengruen, W.

Knight-errant of the foothills. Harte, B.

Knight of the Cumberland. Fox, J.

The **knight** returns. Arico, V.

KNIGHTHOOD. See Knights and knighthood

KNIGHTS AND KNIGHTHOOD
Bergengruen, W. The knight
Bergengruen, W. Shining fools

Knipscheer, James M. W.
Start from scratch
Mystery Writers of America, inc. Four-&-twenty bloodhounds

Knister, Raymond, 1899-1932
The strawstack
Pacey, D. ed. Book of Canadian stories

Knock. Brown, F.

Knowles, John
Turn with the sun
Story (Periodical) Story; no. 4

Knowlton, Elizabeth
Petite première in the Mont Blanc Massif
Talbot, D. ed. Treasury of mountaineering stories

Knox, Joe
Courting of Miss Darlie Blanche
Knox, J. Little Benders
Curly maple
Knox, J. Little Benders
Death of Uncle Andy
Knox, J. Little Benders
How Brother Aaron was saved
Knox, J. Little Benders
Little Ben
Knox, J. Little Benders
Little Ben's railroad
Knox, J. Little Benders
Magic touch
Knox, J. Little Benders
Mamma and the pot of gold
Knox, J. Little Benders
Man in the chimney corner
Knox, J. Little Benders
Miss Dulcie and the strange baby
Knox, J. Little Benders
Miss Emma Grisby
Knox, J. Little Benders
Miss Whipple and the Creekers
Knox, J. Little Benders
Mr Caleb Westly and the stranger
Knox, J. Little Benders
Morning I went to buy the horseshoe
Knox, J. Little Benders
Night Mamma told a bald-faced lie
Knox, J. Little Benders
Pete
Knox, J. Little Benders
Uncle Sod's birthday social
Knox, J. Little Benders

Knox, Ronald Arbuthnott, 1888-
Ruth
Thinker's digest (Periodical) Spoiled priest, and other stories

Knute, the giant bullsnake. Rounds, G.

Kober, Arthur, 1900-
Always a bridesmaid
Kober, A. Bella, Bella kissed a fella
Bella's got a fella
Kober, A. Bella, Bella kissed a fella
Bronx oracle
Kober, A. Bella, Bella kissed a fella
Course of true love
Kober, A. Bella, Bella kissed a fella
Courtship deferred
Kober, A. Bella, Bella kissed a fella
He who woos and runs away
Kober, A. Bella, Bella kissed a fella
Letter from the Bronx
Ausubel, N. ed. Treasury of Jewish humor
Life with mother
Kober, A. Bella, Bella kissed a fella
Nobody can beat Freidkin's meats
Ribalow, H. U. ed. This land, these people
On (and off) the agenda
Kober, A. Bella, Bella kissed a fella
Other pebbles on the beach
Kober, A. Bella, Bella kissed a fella
Place in the sun
Kober, A. Bella, Bella kissed a fella
Return of the native
Kober, A. Bella, Bella kissed a fella
Suitor's white paper
Kober, A. Bella, Bella kissed a fella
Tête-à-tête
Kober, A. Bella, Bella kissed a fella
They shall inherit the earth
Kober, A. Bella, Bella kissed a fella
Time is out of joint
Kober, A. Bella, Bella kissed a fella

Kobold. Seager, A.

Kobrin, Leon, 1872-1946
Milchiger Synagogue and the blind preacher
Ausubel, N. ed. Treasury of Jewish humor
Soul that mice nibbled up
Ausubel, N. ed. Treasury of Jewish humor
Temptation of Reb Mottel
Ausubel, N. ed. Treasury of Jewish humor

Koestler, Arthur, 1905-
Apage Satanas
Burnett, W. ed. World's best

Kohn, Phyllis A. 1924-
Birthright
Wolfe, D. M. ed. Which grain will grow

Kola Road. Asch, S.

Kola Street. Asch, S.

Kolins, William F. 1926-
Years before anger
Wolfe, D. M. ed. Which grain will grow

Kompert, Leopold, 1822-1886
Silent woman
Leftwich, J. ed. Yisröel. 1952 ed.

Komroff, Manuel, 1890-
Alone the stranger passes
Brentano, F. ed. The word lives on
Death of Judas
Selden, R. ed. Ways of God and men

Komroff, Manuel—*Continued*
Light of the moon
Herzberg, M. J. comp. Treasure chest of
sport stories
Thousand-dollar bill
Certner, S. and Henry, G. H. eds. Short
stories for our times
Told in the stars
Brentano, F. ed. The word lives on
What is a miracle?
Lohan, R. and Lohan, M. eds. New
Christmas treasury

KONGO, BELGIAN. See Congo, Belgian

Kon-Tiki reaches the South Sea Islands.
Heyerdahl, T.

KOREAN WAR, 1950-1953
Burnet, D. Why did he leave me?
Chamberlain, W. Chaplain of Company C
Chase, F. General from the Pentagon
Landon, B. Advance party
Mauldin, W. H. Affair of the wayward
jeep
Sneider, V. J. A long way from home
Worden, W. L. Officers' girl

Kornbluth, Cyril M. 1923-
The adventurer
Pohl, F. ed. Assignment in tomorrow
Altar at midnight
Kornbluth, C. M. The explorers
Wollheim, D. A. ed. Prize science fiction
Dominoes
Star science fiction stories [no. 1]
Friend to man
Kornbluth, C. M. The explorers
Gomez
Kornbluth, C. M. The explorers
Goodly creatures
Kornbluth, C. M. The explorers
Marching morons
Best science fiction stories: 1952
The mindworm
Best science fiction stories: 1951
Kornbluth, C. M. The explorers
Only thing we learn
Conklin, G. ed. Big book of science
fiction
The remorseful
Star science fiction stories, no. 2
Rocket of 1955
Kornbluth, C. M. The explorers
Silly season
Heinlein, R. A. ed. Tomorrow, the stars
That share of glory
Kornbluth, C. M. The explorers
Norton, A. M. ed. Space service
Thirteen o'clock
Kornbluth, C. M. The explorers
With these hands
Kornbluth, C. M. The explorers

Kovner, B. pseud. See Adler, Jacob

Krambambuli. Ebner von Eschenbach, M.
Freifrau

Krepps, Robert Wilson, 1919-
Five years in the Marmalade
Best science fiction stories: 1950
Bleiler, E. F. and Dikty, T. E. eds.
Science fiction omnibus: the best sci-
ence fiction stories, 1949, 1950
See also Gold, H. L. jt. auth.

Krige, Uys, 1910-
Charcoal burners
Krige, U. The dream and the desert
Christmas box
Krige, U. The dream and the desert
The coffin
Krige, U. The dream and the desert
Death of the Zulu
Krige, U. The dream and the desert
The dream
Krige, U. The dream and the desert
Invisible shepherd
Krige, U. The dream and the desert
La Miseria
Krige, U. The dream and the desert
Two Daumiers
Krige, U. The dream and the desert

Krimsky, Josephine, 1930-
Andrew's father
American vanguard, 1952

Kristol, Irving, 1920-
Adam and I
Ribalow, H. U. ed. These your children

Kruse, Clifton B.
Dr Lu-Mie
Wollheim, D. A. comp. Every boy's
book of science-fiction

Kruse, John
Alone in shark waters
McFee, W. ed. Great sea stories of
modern times

KU KLUX KLAN (1915-date)
Berg, L. Nasty Kupperman and the Ku
Klux Klan

Kubilius, Walter, 1918-
Other side
Best science fiction stories: 1952

Kubilius, Walter, 1918- **and Pratt, Fletcher,**
1897-1956
Second chance
Sloane, W. M. ed. Space, space, space

Kuehn, Susan, 1926-
The hunt
Prize stories of 1950
The searchers
Best American short stories, 1952
Stanford short stories, 1951

Kulbak, Moishe, 1896-
Munie the bird dealer
Howe, I. and Greenberg, E. eds. Treas-
ury of Yiddish stories

Kummer, Frederic Arnold, 1873-1943
Forgiveness of Tenchu Taen
Greenberg, M. ed. Travelers of space

Kutner, Nanette
Do you remember Mary?
McFarland, W. K. comp. Then it hap-
pened

Kuttner, Henry, 1914-
Absalom
Heinlein, R. A. ed. Tomorrow, the stars
By these presents
Kuttner, H. Ahead of time
Camouflage
Kuttner, H. Ahead of time
Clash by night
Astounding science fiction (Periodical)
Astounding science fiction anthology

Kuttner, Henry—*Continued*

Compliments of the author
 Kuttner, H. Gnome there was, and other tales of science fiction and fantasy

The cure
 Kuttner, H. Gnome there was, and other tales of science fiction and fantasy

DP!
 Best science-fiction stories: 1954

De profundis
 Kuttner, H. Ahead of time

Deadlock
 Greenberg, M. ed. Robot and the man
 Kuttner, H. Ahead of time

Devil on Salvation Bluff
 Star science fiction stories, no. 3

Dream's end
 Crossen, K. F. ed. Future tense

Ego machine
 Brown, F. and Reynolds, M. eds. Science fiction carnival

Endowment policy
 Conklin, G. ed. Science-fiction adventures in dimension

Ex machina
 Bleiler, E. F. and Dikty, T. E. eds. Science fiction omnibus: the best science fiction stories, 1949, 1950
 Kuttner, H. Robots have no tails

Exit the professor
 Kuttner, H. Gnome there was, and other tales of science fiction and fantasy

Gallegher plus
 Kuttner, H. Robots have no tails

Ghost
 Kuttner, H. Ahead of time

Gnome there was
 Kuttner, H. Gnome there was, and other tales of science fiction and fantasy
 Merril, J. ed. Beyond human ken

Happy ending
 Bleiler, E. F. and Dikty, T. E. eds. Science fiction omnibus: the best science fiction stories, 1949, 1950

Hard-luck diggings
 Conklin, G. ed. Possible worlds of science fiction

Home is the hunter
 Kuttner, H. Ahead of time

Iron standard
 Greenberg, M. ed. Men against the stars

Jesting pilot
 Kuttner, H. Gnome there was, and other tales of science fiction and fantasy

King of thieves
 Lesser, M. A. ed. Looking forward

Line to tomorrow
 Derleth, A. W. ed. Worlds of tomorrow

Margin for error
 Conklin, G. ed. Big book of science fiction

Men of the ten books
 Best science fiction stories: 1952

Mimsy were the borogoves
 Kuttner, H. Gnome there was, and other tales of science fiction and fantasy

Noise
 Startling stories (Periodical) Best from Startling stories

Open secret
 Jenkins, W. F. ed. Great stories of science fiction

Or else
 Kuttner, H. Ahead of time

Pile of trouble
 Kuttner, H. Ahead of time

Private eye
 Best science fiction stories: 1950
 Bleiler, E. F. and Dikty, T. E. eds. Science fiction omnibus: the best science fiction stories, 1949, 1950

Proud robot
 Kuttner, H. Robots have no tails

Rain check
 Kuttner, H. Gnome there was, and other tales of science fiction and fantasy

See you later
 Kuttner, H. Gnome there was, and other tales of science fiction and fantasy

Shock
 Derleth, A. W. ed. The outer reaches
 Kuttner, H. Ahead of time

Sword of tomorrow
 Margulies, L. and Friend, O. J. eds. Giant anthology of science fiction

This is the house
 Kuttner, H. Gnome there was, and other tales of science fiction and fantasy

Time locker
 Kuttner, H. Robots have no tails

The Twonky
 Kuttner, H. Gnome there was, and other tales of science fiction and fantasy

Voice of the lobster
 Crossen, K. F. ed. Adventures in tomorrow

We kill people
 Lesser, M. A. ed. Looking forward

What you need
 Conklin, G. ed. Omnibus of science fiction
 Kuttner, H. Gnome there was, and other science fiction and fantasy

When the bough breaks
 Astounding science fiction (Periodical) Astounding science fiction anthology
 Derleth, A. W. ed. Beyond time & space

When the earth lived
 Margulies, L. and Friend, O. J. eds. From off this world

Winner lose all
 Conklin, G. ed. Omnibus of science fiction

World is mine
 Kuttner, H. Robots have no tails

Year day
 Kuttner, H. Ahead of time

Kuttner, Henry, 1914- and Moore, Catherine Lucile, 1911-

Wild surmise
 Star science fiction stories [no. 1]

KVASS. See Beer

Kyd, Thomas, pseud.

High court
 Queen, E. pseud, ed. The Queen's awards: 8th ser.

L

La Mère Sauvage. Maupassant, G. de
LABOR AND LABORING CLASSES
Bergelson, D. In a backwoods town
Labyrinth. Willman, P.
Lacework Kid. Runyon, D.
Lacy, Ed
Right thing
Ford, N. A. and Faggett, H. L. eds.
Best short stories by Afro-American
writers (1925-1950)
Lacy, March
Fighting finish
Ford, N. A. and Faggett, H. L. eds.
Best short stories by Afro-American
writers (1925-1950)
No fools, no fun
Ford, N. A. and Faggett, H. L. eds.
Best short stories by Afro-American
writers (1925-1950)
LADDERS
Sansom, W. Vertical ladder
Ladies call on Mr Pussick. Francis, O.
LADIES' MAIDS. See Servants—Maids
Lady. Buckingham, N.
The **lady.** Justice, D.
Lady and the dragon. Godfrey, P.
Lady and the tumblers. Constiner, M.
Lady higher up. Porter, W. S.
Lady-killer. Steele, W. D.
Lady of Glenwith Grange. Collins, W.
Lady of my own. Seide, M.
Lady of the sagas. O'Donovan, M.
Lady on the grey. Collier, J.
Lady, or the tiger? Stockton, F. R.
Lady over the wall. Van Doren, M.
Lady says murder. Fay, W.
Lady walks. Powell, J.
Lady's maid. Ekbergh, I. D.
Lady's maid's bell. Wharton, E. N. J.
La Farge, Christopher, 1897-1956
Motet for two voices
Greene, J. I. and Abell, E. eds. Stories
of sudden truth
La Farge, Oliver, 1901-
The bystander
Best detective stories of the year—1954
John the revelator
Magazine of fantasy and science fiction.
Best from Fantasy and science fiction,
1952
No, my darling daughter
This week magazine. This week's short-
short stories
Old century's river
Best American short stories, 1951
Prize stories of 1951
Old men's plans
Grayson, C. ed. Fourth round
Woman hunt no good
Queen, E. pseud. ed. Queen's awards:
6th ser.

Lagerkvist, Pär Fabian, 1891-
The adventure
Lagerkvist, P. F. Eternal smile, and
other stories
The basement
Lagerkvist, P. F. Eternal smile, and
other stories
Children's campaign
Lagerkvist, P. F. Eternal smile, and
other stories
Eternal smile
Lagerkvist, P. F. Eternal smile, and
other stories
Evil angel
Lagerkvist, P. F. Eternal smile, and
other stories
Experimental world
Lagerkvist, P. F. Eternal smile, and
other stories
Father and I
Lagerkvist, P. F. Eternal smile, and
other stories
God's little traveling salesman
Lagerkvist, P. F. Eternal smile, and
other stories
Guest of reality
Lagerkvist, P. F. Eternal smile, and
other stories
The hangman
Lagerkvist, P. F. Eternal smile, and
other stories
Hero's death
Lagerkvist, P. F. Eternal smile, and
other stories
Lift that went down into hell
Lagerkvist, P. F. Eternal smile, and
other stories
Marriage feast
Lagerkvist, P. F. Eternal smile, and
other stories
Masquerade of souls
Lagerkvist, P. F. Eternal smile, and
other stories
Myth of mankind
Lagerkvist, P. F. Eternal smile, and
other stories
Paradise
Lagerkvist, P. F. Eternal smile, and
other stories
Princess and all the kingdom
Lagerkvist, P. F. Eternal smile, and
other stories
Saviour John
Lagerkvist, P. F. Eternal smile, and
other stories
Venerated bones
Lagerkvist, P. F. Eternal smile, and
other stories
Wave of Osiris
Lagerkvist, P. F. Eternal smile, and
other stories
Lagerlöf, Selma Ottiliana Lovisa, 1858-1940
In Nazareth
Brentano, F. ed. The word lives on
The outlaws
Neider, C. ed. Great short stories from
the world's literature
The **lagoon.** Conrad, J.
Laidlaw, Clara
Little black boys
Thinker's digest (Periodical) Spoiled
priest, and other stories

Lake, Leonard M. See Rosmond, B. jt. auth.

The lake. Harvey, W. F.

LAKE TAHOE
Davis, S. P. Mystery of the Savage sump

The lamb. Cavanaugh, J. P.

Lamb and some slaughtering. Mowery, W. B.

Lamb chop for the little dog. Winslow, T. S.

Lamb to the slaughter. Dahl, R.

Lambert, Janet
Tall as the stars
American girl (Periodical) Favorite stories

Lamberton, Louise, 1901-
Sleet storm
Cooper, A. C. ed. Modern short stories

LAMBS. See Sheep

The lament. O'Flaherty, L.

Lamkin, Speed, 1927-
Comes a day
Best American short stories, 1950
Prize stories of 1950

L'Amour, Louis, 1908-
Gift of Cochise
Meredith, S. ed. Bar 3

Lamp at noon. Ross, S.

LAMPS
Peretz, I. L. Little Hanukkah lamp

Lamson, Ruth Rankin
Have a heart, lady!
Cavanna, B. ed. Pick of the litter

Land. Lewis, S.

Land ironclads. Wells, H. G.

Land of my fathers. Tennyson, H.

Land of No Shadow. Claudy, C. H.

Land of our enemies. Stuart, J.

Land rush. Haycox, E.

LAND SPECULATION
Garland, H. Under the lion's paw

LAND TENURE
Porter, W. S. Bexar scrip no. 2692
Porter, W. S. Georgia's ruling
Tolstoǐ, L. N. Graf. Three arshins of land

LAND TITLES. See Land tenure

Landa, Myer Jack, 1874-
Two legacies
Leftwich, J. ed. Yisröel. 1952 ed.

The landing. Leshinsky, T.

LANDLORD AND TENANT
Edgeworth, M. Castle Rackrent
Parker, J. R. The millennium

Landon, Margaret Dorothea (Mortenson) 1903-
Reconciliation
Brentano, F. ed. The word lives on

Landor's cottage. Poe, E. A.

The Landrath. Irina, A.

Landscape with figures. Sansom, W.

LANDSLIDES
Hawthorne, N. Ambitious guest

Lane, Carl Daniel, 1899-
River dragon
Fenner, P. R. comp. Indians, Indians, Indians

Lane, George C.
Ensign Carson, USCGR
Furman, A. L. ed. Teen-age sea stories

Lang, Allan Kim
Eel by the tail
Conklin, G. ed. Invaders of earth

Lang, Don
Elephant never forgets
Fenner, P. R. comp. Elephants, elephants, elephants
Tramp, the sheep dog
Harper, W. comp. Dog show

Langewiesche-Brandt, Wolfgang Ernst, 1907-
Knapsack of salvation
Jensen, P. ed. Fireside book of flying stories
Three secrets of human flight
Jensen, P. ed. Fireside book of flying stories

LANGUAGE AND LANGUAGES
Berryman, J. Berom
Heinlein, R. A. Gulf

Lanham, Edwin Moultrie, 1904-
Listen to me, boy
Argosy (Periodical) Argosy Book of sports stories

Lanning, George, 1925-
Old Turkey Neck
Best American short stories, 1951

Lansing, Elisabeth Carleton (Hubbard) 1911-
Kay uses the evidence
Furman, A. L. ed. Everygirls mystery stories
There's something about you
American girl (Periodical) Favorite stories
Touch of psychology
American girl (Periodical) On my honor

Laocoön complex. Furnas, J. C.

LAPLAND
Sjogren, E. Death in the pass

La Prello paper. Jacobi, C.

Laputa. Swift, J.

Larchmoor is not the world. Cassill, R. V.

Lardner, John, 1912-
Sudden attack of heartbreak
Dachs, D. ed. Treasury of sports humor

Lardner, Ring Wilmer, 1885-1933
Alibi Ike
Graber, R. S. ed. Baseball reader
Busher's letters home
Graber, R. S. ed. Baseball reader
Champion
Ribalow, H. U. ed. World's greatest boxing stories
Golden honeymoon
Burrell, J. A. and Cerf, B. A. eds. Anthology of famous American stories
Scribner treasury
Haircut
Best of the Best American short stories, 1915-1950
Day, A. G. ed. Greatest American short stories
Gordon, C. and Tate, A. eds. House of fiction
Queen, E. pseud. ed. Literature of crime
Scribner treasury
Harmony
Graber, R. S. ed. Baseball reader

Lardner, Ring W.—*Continued*
  Horseshoes
    Dachs, D. ed. Treasury of sports humor
    Graber, R. S. ed. Baseball reader
  Some like them cold
    Burrell, J. A. and Cerf, B. A. eds.
      Anthology of famous American stories
    Stegner, W. E.; Scowcroft, R. and Ilyin,
      B. eds. Writer's art
  There are smiles
    Blodgett, H. W. ed. Story survey. 1953
    ed.
  Zone of quiet
    Lynskey, W. C. ed. Reading modern
    fiction
Larkspur again: A lawn meet at Rosemount
  Grange. Surtees, R. S.
Larkspur hounds: A morning with a bag-
  man. Surtees, R. S.
Larsen, David
  Freeze-out
    Owen, F. ed. Teen-age winter sports
    stories
Lasker-Schüler, Else, 1876-
  Arthur Aronymus; my father's story
    Leftwich, J. ed. Yisröel. 1952 ed.
Lass with the delicate air. Bigland, E.
Lassie Come-Home. Knight, E. M.
Last accounting. O'Rourke, F.
Last American. Mitchell, J. A.
Last bed. Isaacson, B. K.
Last Christmas Puzo, M.
Last cigarette. Roper, W.
Last class. Daudet, A.
Last day. Lieberman, R.
Last day. Matheson, R.
Last day at the office. Reese, J. H.
Last day in the field. Gordon, C.
Last day of all. Stanley, F. G.
Last day of my life. Elston, A. V.
Last days of M.G.B. 1087. Monsarrat, N.
Last days of Shandakor. Brackett, L.
Last draw. Haycox, E.
Last enemy. Piper, H. B.
Last expedition of Baron Feuhbel-Feuhtze-
  nau. Sobol, A. M.
Last hope. Reisin, A.
Last husband. Humphrey, W.
Last king. Blackburn, E. R.
Last kopek. Frug, S. S.
Last leaf. Porter, W. S.
Last-Light Channel. Lindquist, W.
Last lobo. Annixter, P. pseud.
Last Martian. Brown, F.
Last monster. Anderson, P.
The **last** night. Barrie, Sir J. M. bart.
Last night of the world. Bradbury, R.
Last of Chéri. Colette, S. G.
Last of the belles. Fitzgerald, F. S. K.
Last of the grizzly bears. West, R. B.
Last of the troubadours. Porter, W. S.
Last out. O'Rourke, F.
Last pitch. O'Rourke, F.
Last race. Sylvester, H

Last Rebel yell. Tolbert, F. X.
Last refuge of a scoundrel. Howard, W.
Last Saturday. Jacobson, L. E.
Last séance. Christie, A. M.
Last shot. O'Rourke, F.
LAST SUPPER. See Lord's supper
Last supper. Gibran, K.
The **last** supper. Kagawa, T.
Last tanto. Sylvester, R.
Last terrestrials. Stapledon, W. O.
Last time around. O'Rourke, F.
Last time up. O'Rourke, F.
Last visit. Aiken, C. P.
Last voyage of the Unsinkable Sal. Taylor,
  S. W.
Last weapon. Sheckley, R.
Last woman. Gardner, T. S.
Last year. Mulhoffer, D. B.
The **latchkey.** Schweitzer, G.
Late afternoon of a faun. Brophy, B.
Late Mr Elvesham. Wells, H. G.
Late night final. Russell, E. F.
Later. Foster, M.
Later than you think. Leiber, F.
Latest sensation (II) Clemens, S. L.
Latham, Philip, pseud. See Richardson,
  Robert Shirley
LA TRÉMOILLE, LOUIS II, DUC DE,
  1460-1525
  Lernet-Holenia, A. M. Mona Lisa
Latter end. Loveridge, G.
Laugh in the desert. Prado, P.
Laugh in the face of danger. Johnson, D. M.
Laugh it off. Armstrong, C.
Laughing butcher. Brown, F.
Laughing man. Salinger, J. D.
Launcelot, Sir
  Malory, Sir T. Marvellous adventure of
  the sword
Laura. Munro, H. H.
Laurence, Bethel
  The call
    Best American short stories, 1952
Laurence, Margaret, 1926-
  Uncertain flowering
    Story (Periodical) Story; no. 4
Lauriston Gardens mystery. Doyle, Sir
  A. C.
Lavender, David Sievert, 1910-
  High victory
    Boys' life (Periodical) Boys' life Ad-
    venture stories
Lavin, Mary, 1912-
  Brother Boniface
    Gable, M. Sister, ed. Many-colored
    fleece
  Daggle-Tail
    Cavanna, B. ed. Pick of the litter
LAW AND LAWYERS
  Andrews, M. R. S. Counsel assigned
  Auchincloss, L. Great world and Timo-
  thy Colt
  Auchincloss, L. Legends of Henry
  Everett

LAW AND LAWYERS—*Continued*

Auchincloss, L. Maud

Blaustein, A. P. ed. Fiction goes to court; 17 stories

Chekhov, A. P. His first appearance

Chekhov, A. P. Perpetuum mobile

Chekhov, A. P. Saintly simplicity

Chekhov, A. P. Village Elder

Chekhov, A. P. Visit to friends

Chekhov, A. P. Worse and worse

Collier, J. Great possibilities

Harte, B. Colonel Starbottle for the plaintiff

Klass, P. Child's play

McNeil, S. Girl who wasn't wanted

Melville, H. Bartleby the scrivener

O'Donovan, M. Counsel for Œdipus

O'Donovan, M. Lady of the sagas

Pirandello, L. Reserved coffin

Porter, W. S. Emancipation of Billy

Porter, W. S. Hypotheses of failure

Salinger, J. D. Pretty mouth and green my eyes

Silone, I. Mr Aristotle

Verga, G. Don Licciu Papa

Weidman, J. Man inside

Law and order. Lowry, R. J.

Law and order. Porter, W. S.

Law and the profits. Cohen, O. R.

LAW CLERKS. See Law and lawyers

Lawlor, Harold

Silver highway

Conklin, G. and Conklin, L. T. eds. Supernatural reader

LAWN TENNIS. See Tennis

Lawrence, David Herbert, 1885-1930

Blind man

Blodgett, H. W. ed. Story survey. 1953 ed.

Captain's doll

West, R. B. and Stallman, R. W. eds. Art of modern fiction

The fox

Neider, C. ed. Short novels of the masters

Horse dealer's daughter

Schorer, M. ed. The story

Lovely lady

Heilman, R. B. ed. Modern short stories

Mother and daughter

Felheim, M.; Newman, F. B. and Steinhoff, W. R. eds. Modern short stories

Prussian officer

Cerf, B. A. and Moriarty, H. C. eds. Anthology of famous British stories

Cory, D. W. pseud. comp. 21 variations on a theme

Davis, R. G. ed. Ten modern masters

Rocking-horse winner

Davis, R. G. ed. Ten modern masters

Gordon, C. and Tate, A. eds. House of fiction

Ludwig, J. B. and Poirier, W. R. eds. Stories, British and American

Waite, H. O. and Atkinson, B. P. eds. Literature for our time

Shades of spring

Davis, R. G. ed. Ten modern masters

Shadow in the rose garden

Barrows, H. ed. 15 stories

Things

Ludwig, J. B. and Poirier, W. R. eds. Stories, British and American

Two blue birds

Neider, C. ed. Great short stories from the world's literature

Lawrence, Thomas Edward, 1888-1935

Blowing up a train

Moskowitz, S. ed. Great railroad stories of the world

Lawson, Edward

Ebony elephant

Ford, N. A. and Faggett, H. L. eds. Best short stories by Afro-American writers (1925-1950)

LAWSUITS. See Law and lawyers

LAWYERS. See Law and lawyers

Laxness, Halldor Kiljan, 1902-

Icelandic pioneer

Burnett, W. ed. World's best

Lay it down, Ziggy! Siegel, L.

Laziest man in Texas. Rogow, L.

LAZINESS

Fitzgerald, F. S. K. Jelly-bean

Leacock, Stephen, 1869-1944

Speculations of Jefferson Thorpe

Pacey, D. ed. Book of Canadian stories

Lead her like a pigeon. West, J.

Leader of the people. Steinbeck, J.

Leadington incident. Priestley, J. B.

Leaf thief. Saroyan, W.

Leander Frailey. Schaefer, J. W.

Leap for two lives. Whittemore, C. W.

Leap year. Grimson, M. S.

Learning's little tribute. Wilson, A.

Lebediger, Der. See Gutman, Chaim

Le Berthon, Ted

I took thee, Constance

Gable, M. Sister, ed. Many-colored fleece

Leblanc, Maurice, 1864-1941

Invisible prisoner

Stauffer, R. M.; Cunningham, W. H. and Sullivan, C. J. eds. Adventures in modern literature

The **lectern.** Munby, A. N. L.

LECTURERS. See Lectures and lecturing

LECTURES AND LECTURING

Pratt, F. and De Camp, L. S. When the night wind howls

Van Doren, M. Mrs Lancey

LECTURING. See Lectures and lecturing

Ledge on Bald Face. Roberts, Sir C. G. D.

Lee, Melicent (Humason) 1889-1943

Secret staircase

Story parade (Periodical) Adventure stories

Lee, Umphrey

Egg farm

Stanford short stories, 1952

Lee, Vernon, pseud. See Paget, Violet

Le Fanu, Joseph Sheridan, 1814-1873

Churchyard yew

Derleth, A. W. ed. Night's yawning peal

Room in the Dragon Volant

Connolly, C. ed. Great English short novels

Left-hand stuff. Gartner, J.
Left out on Lone Star Mountain. Harte, B.
The leg. Faulkner, W.
Leg man. Stewart, O.
LEGACIES. See Inheritance and succession
Legacy of Canyon John. Leighton, M. C.
Legal aid. O'Donovan, M.
LEGATIONS. See Diplomatic life
Legend of Madame Krasinska. Paget, V.
Legend of Rabbi Akiba. Cohn, E.
Legend of St Julian the Hospitaller. Flaubert, G.
Legend of Sleepy Hollow. Irving, W.
Legend of the first Christmas tree. Goudge, E.
Legend that walks like a man. Schulberg, B. W.
LEGENDS, JEWISH. See Legends and folk tales—Hebrew
LEGENDS AND FOLK TALES
Munro, H. H. Wolves of Cernogratz
Paget, V. Prince Alberic and the Snake Lady
Van Doren, M. The birds

China
Mrs White
T'uan Ch'engshih. Cinderella

France
Krige, U. Invisible shepherd

Germany
Hoffmann, E. T. A. History of Krakatuk
Keller, G. Little legend of the dance

Hebrew
Cohn, E. It looks like justice
Cohn, E. Legend of Rabbi Akiba
Cohn, E. Waters of Shiloah

Ireland
Corkery, D. Ploughing of the leaca

Japan
Akutagawa, R. The martyr

Negro
Harris, J. C. Wonderful Tar-Baby story

Norway
Bjørnson, B. How the mountain was clad

Portuguese
Krige, U. La Miseria

Russia
Tolstoĭ, L. N. Graf. Three hermits

South America
Finger, C. J. Na-Ha the fighter
Legends of Henry Everett. Auchincloss, L.
LEGISLATION
Kipling, R. Tods' amendment
Le Grand, pseud. See Henderson, Le Grand
Legs go first. Newhouse, E.
Lehmann, Rosamond, 1903-
    Red-haired Miss Daintreys
      New writing (Periodical) Best stories

Lehr, Wilson
    No competition
      Cory, D. W. pseud. comp. 21 variations on a theme
Leiber, Fritz, 1910-
    Appointment in tomorrow
      Best science fiction stories: 1952
    Bad day for sales
      Best science-fiction stories: 1954
      Galaxy science fiction magazine. Second Galaxy reader of science fiction
    Big holiday
      Best science-fiction stories: 1954
    Business of killing
      Conklin, G. ed. Science-fiction adventures in dimension
    Coming attraction
      Best science fiction stories: 1951
      Galaxy science fiction magazine. Galaxy reader of science fiction
    Destiny times three
      Greenberg, M. comp. Five science fiction novels
    Enchanted forest
      Derleth, A. W. ed. Worlds of tomorrow
    Foxholes of Mars
      Merril, J. ed. Beyond human ken
    Later than you think
      Derleth, A. W. ed. Far boundaries
    Moon is green
      Best science-fiction stories: 1953
    Night he cried
      Star science fiction stories [no. 1]
    Pail of air
      Galaxy science fiction magazine. Second Galaxy reader of science fiction
      Norton, A. M. ed. Space pioneers
    Poor superman
      Heinlein, R. A. ed. Tomorrow, the stars
    Sanity
      Conklin, G. ed. Big book of science fiction
    Ship sails at midnight
      Derleth, A. W. ed. The outer reaches
    Taboo
      Greenberg, M. ed. Journey to infinity
    Wanted—an enemy
      Derleth, A. W. ed. Beyond time & space
LEIF ERICSSON, fl. 1000
    Grimson, M. S. Leif goes west
Leif goes west. Grimson, M. S.
Leigh, Johanna, pseud. See Sayers, Dorothy Leigh
Leighton, Margaret (Carver) 1896-
    Legacy of Canyon John
      American girl (Periodical) Favorite stories
    Spruce Point mystery
      Furman, A. L. ed. Everygirls mystery stories
Leimert, John
    John Thomas's cube
      Conklin, G. ed. Omnibus of science fiction
Leiningen versus the ants. Stephenson, C.
Leinster, Murray, pseud. See Jenkins, William Fitzgerald
Leiper, Gudger Bart, 1921-
    The magnolias
      Prize stories of 1950

Lemelin, Roger, 1919-
Stations of the Cross
Weaver, R. and James, H. eds. Canadian short stories
Lemesurier inheritance. Christie, A. M.
Lena. Williams, W. C.
Lenore and the boys. Wright, H.
LEONARDO DA VINCI, 1452-1519
Lernet-Holenia, A. M. Mona Lisa
'Leopard' George. Lessing, D. M.
LEOPARDS
Balzac, H. de. Passion in the desert
Fletcher, I. White leopard
Leopard's spots. Runyon, D.
LEPERS. See Leprosy
LEPRECHAUNS
Pratt, F. and De Camp, L. S. All that glitters
The Leprechauns. Ready, W. B.
LEPROSY
Groseclose, E. E. The healing of the lepers
Kipling, R. Mark of the beast
White, H. C. Francis cures the leper
Lerner, Marvin, 1920?-
The brothers
Oberfirst, R. ed. 1954 anthology of best original short-stories
Lernet-Holenia, Alexander Maria, 1897-
Mona Lisa
Pick, R. ed. German stories and tales
Leshinsky, Tania
The landing
Story (Periodical) Story; no. 3
Leskov, Nikolaĭ Semenovich, 1831-1895
The Amazon
Rahv, P. ed. Great Russian short novels
Lesser, Milton A. 1928-
Black Eyes and the daily grind
Sloane, W. M. ed. Stories for tomorrow
Pen pal
Conklin, G. ed. Invaders of earth
Lessing, Bruno, pseud. See Block, Rudolph Edgar
Lessing, Doris May, 1919-
De Wets come to Kloof Grange
Lessing, D. M. This was the Old Chief's country
'Leopard' George
Lessing, D. M. This was the Old Chief's country
Little Tembi
Lessing, D. M. This was the Old Chief's country
No witchcraft for sale
Lessing, D. M. This was the Old Chief's country
The nuisance
Lessing, D. M. This was the Old Chief's country
Old Chief Mshlanga
Lessing, D. M. This was the Old Chief's country
Old John's place
Lessing, D. M. This was the Old Chief's country

Second hut
Lessing, D. M. This was the Old Chief's country
Sunrise on the veld
Lessing, D. M. This was the Old Chief's country
Winter in July
Lessing, D. M. This was the Old Chief's country
Lesson for Flying Goat. Verran, R.
Le Sueur, Meridel
Persephone
Swallow, A. ed. Anchor in the sea
The let-down. Dodson, D. B.
Let 'em eat cook. De Vries, P.
Let it rest. Patton, F. G.
Let me feel your pulse. Porter, W. S.
Let me go. Strong, L. A. G.
Let nothing you dismay. Sloane, W. M.
Let nothing you dismay. Wright, F. F.
Let the church roll on. Ford, N. A.
Let the wind blow. Vetter, M. M.
"Let there be light." Heinlein, R. A.
Let yourself go. Farwell, M. B.
Letitia, emeritus. Calisher, H.
The letter. Maugham, W. S.
The letter. Toland, S.
LETTER CARRIERS. See Postal service
Letter from the Bronx. Kober, A.
Letter in the cedarchest. Goyen, W.
Letter to a hostage. Saint Exupéry, A. de
Letter to a phoenix. Brown, F.
Letter to Ellen. Davis, C.
A letter to Klaus Brock. Bojer, J.
Letter to Mable. Streeter, E.
Letter to the Dean. Taber, G. B.
Letter to the editor. Hershman, M.
LETTER WRITERS
Silone, I. Mr Aristotle
LETTERS (STORIES IN LETTER FORM)
Aiken, C. P. I love you very dearly
Aldrich, T. B. Marjorie Daw
Bunner, H. C. Love-letters of Smith
Campbell, W. E. M. Personal letter
Chekhov, A. P. Vanka
Connolly, M. Natural causes
Elliott, G. P. The NRACP
Forester, C. S. Letters in evidence
James, H. Bundle of letters
Jenkins, W. F. The power
Kober, A. Letter from the Bronx
Lardner, R. W. Some like them cold
Milne, A. A. Rise and fall of Mortimer Scrivens
Munro, H. H. "Down pens"
Munro, H. H. Shock tactics
Paget, V. Dionea
Pasternak, B. L. Letters from Tula
Piper, H. B. Operation RSVP
Rabinowitz, S. Menachem-Mendel, fortune hunter
Upson, W. H. I'm in a hurry

LETTERS (STORIES IN LETTER FORM)—*Continued*
Waugh, E. Cruise
Whitehill, J. Day of the last rock fight
Winslow, T. S. Dear Sister Sadie
Wright, F. F. Declaration of independence

LETTERS, STORIES ABOUT
Collins, W. Stolen letter
McCarty, M. B. Your long black hair
Maugham, W. S. The letter
Poe, E. A. Purloined letter
Schnitzler, A. Death of a bachelor
Zangwill, I. The luftmensch

The **letters.** Swados, H.

Letters from Cairo. Miller, J. R.

Letters from Tula. Pasternak, B. L.

Letters in evidence. Forester, C. S.

Levelling with Elisha. Van Loan, C. E.

Lever, Charles James, 1806-1872
Con Cregan's legacy
Cerf, B. A. and Moriarty, H. C. eds. Anthology of famous British stories

Levin, Meyer, 1905-
After all I did for Israel
Ribalow, H. U. ed. These your children
Maurie finds his medium
Ribalow, H. U. ed. This land, these people

Levine, Samuel, 1907-
Gift for a birthday
American vanguard, 1952

Levine, Ted M.
Elaine's hope
Hathaway, B. and Sessions, J. A. eds. Writers for tomorrow. 2d ser.

LEVITATION. See Gravity

Levy, Amy, 1861-1889
Cohen of Trinity
Leftwich, J. ed. Yisröel. 1952 ed.

Lewis, Alun, 1915-1944
The raid
Barrows, H. ed. 15 stories
Ward 'O' 3 (b)
New writing (Periodical) Best stories

Lewis, Ethel G.
Portrait
Best American short stories, 1951

Lewis, Jack
Who's cribbing?
Startling stories (Periodical) Best from Startling stories

Lewis, Janet, 1899-
Wife of Martin Guerre
Swallow, A. ed. Anchor in the sea

Lewis, Morgan
Well of anger
Meredith, S. ed. Bar 1 roundup of best western stories

Lewis, Robert
Roman holiday
Herzberg, M. J. comp. Treasure chest of sport stories

Lewis, Sinclair, 1885-1951
An assemblage of husbands and wives
Burnett, W. ed. World's best
Land
Lamb, L. ed. Family book of best loved short stories

Stauffer, R. M.; Cunningham, W. H. and Sullivan, C. J. eds. Adventures in modern literature
Post-mortem murder
Queen, E. pseud. ed. Literature of crime
Willow walk
Grayson, C. ed. Fourth round
Young man Axelbrod
Thinker's digest (Periodical) Spoiled priest, and other stories

Lewis, Wyndham, 1886-
Bishop's fool
Lewis, W. Rotting Hill
Mr Patricks' toy shop
Lewis, W. Rotting Hill
My disciple
Lewis, W. Rotting Hill
My fellow traveller to Oxford
Lewis, W. Rotting Hill
Parents and horses
Lewis, W. Rotting Hill
Room without a telephone
Lewis, W. Rotting Hill
The rot
Lewis, W. Rotting Hill
Talking shop
Lewis, W. Rotting Hill
Time the tiger
Lewis, W. Rotting Hill

Lewisohn, Ludwig, 1882-1955
Holy Land
Leftwich, J. ed. Yisröel. 1952 ed.
Writ of divorcement
Ribalow, H. U. ed. This land, these people

LEXINGTON, KENTUCKY. See Kentucky—Lexington

Li, Guan-Yuen
My boy, my boy
Wolfe, D. M. ed. Which grain will grow

Li Fu-Yen, fl. 9th century
Lodging for the night
Lin, Y. ed. Famous Chinese short stories
Man who became a fish
Lin, Y. ed. Famous Chinese short stories
Matrimony Inn
Lin, Y. ed. Famous Chinese short stories
The tiger
Lin, Y. ed. Famous Chinese short stories

Li Kung-Tso, 770?-850?
Drunkard's dream
Lin, Y. ed. Famous Chinese short stories

Liang, Hsieh. See Hsieh, Liang

Liar! Asimov, I.

The **liar.** James, H.

LIARS
James, H. The liar
Munro, H. H. Defensive diamond

Lib. Farrell, J. T.

Liber amoris. Hazlitt, W.

LIBERTY
Benét, S. V. Freedom's a hard-bought **thing**

Limbo. Hallinan, N.
LIMBS, ARTIFICIAL. See Artificial limbs
LIME-KILNS
Hawthorne, N. Ethan Brand
Limitations of Pambé Serang. Kipling, R.
Limiting factor. Simak, C. D.
**LINCOLN, ABRAHAM, PRESIDENT
U.S.** 1809-1865
Andrews, M. R. S. Counsel assigned
Wellman, M. W. Tall Bram of Little
Pigeon
Lincoln, Victoria Endicott, 1904-
Death in the house
Lincoln, V. E. Wild honey
Glass wall
Best American short stories, 1950
In the garden
Lincoln, V. E. Wild honey
Lost in our wake, our archipelago
Lincoln, V. E. Wild honey
Lover's meeting
Lincoln, V. E. Wild honey
Make me real
Lincoln, V. E. Wild honey
Morning, a week before the crime
Lincoln, V. E. Wild honey
Morning wishes
Lincoln, V. E. Wild honey
No evidence
Lincoln, V. E. Wild honey
Now and again now
Lincoln, V. E. Wild honey
To live is to return
Lincoln, V. E. Wild honey
The understanding
Lincoln, V. E. Wild honey
Linda who daydreamed. Strain, F. B.
Lindquist, Willis
Last-Light Channel
Strang, R. M. and Roberts, R. M. eds
Teen-age tales **v** 1
Striving after the wind
Lantz, J. E. ed. Stories of Christian
living
Line to tomorrow. Kuttner, H.
LINOTYPE. See Printers and printing
Lion and the prey. Benson, T.
LION TAMERS. See Animals—Training
LIONS
Bottome, P. Caesar's wife's ear
Hemingway, E. Fable of the good lion
Hemingway, E. Short happy life of
Francis Macomber
Lions, harts, leaping does. Powers, J. F.
Lion's mouth. Marlowe, S.
Lion's skin. Maugham, W. S.
Lipman, Clayre, and Lipman, Michel
Dilemma of Grampa Dubois
Mystery Writers of America, inc.
Crooks' tour
My last book
Mystery Writers of America, inc. 20
great tales of murder
Walking corpse
Best detective stories of the year—1951
Lipman, Michel. See Lipman, C. jt. auth.
Lippincott, Joseph Wharton, 1887-
Wilderness champion
Harper, W. comp. Dog show

Lipsky, Eleazar, 1911-
Quality of mercy
Queen, E. pseud, ed. The Queen's
awards: 8th ser.
Stabbing in the streets
Best detective stories of the year—1953
Liqueur glass. Bottome, P.
LIQUEURS. See Wine and wine making
Liquid life. Hoar, R. S.
LIQUOR TRAFFIC
Grau, S. A. White girl, fine girl
LIQUORS
Pratt, F. and De Camp, L. S. Gin comes
in bottles
LISBON. See Portugal—Lisbon
Lispet, Lispett and Vaine. De La Mare,
W. J.
Listen. Dickson, G. R.
Listen to me, boy. Lanham, E. M.
Listening child. Seabright, I.
LITERARY CHARACTERS
Forster, E. M. Celestial omnibus
Literary corkscrew. Keller, D. H.
LITERARY CRITICS
Fletcher, V. Coda to a writers' conference
Gutman, C. No enemy of his
James, H. Death of the lion
**LITERARY FORGERIES AND MYSTI-
FICATIONS**
Dahl, R. Great automatic grammatisator
Munro, H. H. For the duration of the war
LITERARY LIFE
Maugham, W. S. Creative impulse
Literary love. Farrell, J. T.
Litten, Frederick Nelson, 1885-1951
Blackout over Cleveland
American boy (Periodical) American
boy Adventure stories
Tell it to the Marines
American boy (Periodical) American
boy Adventure stories
Winner's money
American boy (Periodical) American
boy anthology
Little, George Watson
Beau: the dog who served two masters
Little, G. W. True stories of heroic dogs
Bum: wearer of the Silver Shield
Little, G. W. True stories of heroic dogs
Cappy: the pride of Engine Company 65
Little, G. W. True stories of heroic dogs
Cooky: the heroic dog who wasn't brave
Little, G. W. True stories of heroic dogs
Dandy: the funny-looking dog
Little, G. W. True stories of heroic dogs
Duke: the gun-shy watchdog
Little, G. W. True stories of heroic dogs
Jeep: the dog who came home
Little, G. W. True stories of heroic dogs
Jerry: the dog who refused to die
Little, G. W. True stories of heroic dogs
Jim: a valiant Great Dane
Little, G. W. True stories of heroic dogs
Mutt: the mongrel who knew no fear
Little, G. W. True stories of heroic dogs
Pal: the dog who trained himself
Little, G. W. True stories of heroic dogs
Queenie: the gallant-hearted collie
Little, G. W. True stories of heroic dogs

Little, George W.—*Continued*
  Rusty: the brave dog who lost his bark
    Little, G. W. True stories of heroic dogs
  Smoky: who twice saved his master's life
    Little, G. W. True stories of heroic dogs
  Tom: the friend of all boys
    Little, G. W. True stories of heroic dogs
  Trixie: the dog who did her duty
    Little, G. W. True stories of heroic dogs
Little and unknown. Singmaster, E.
Little Anton. Bretnor, R.
Little apple hard to peel. Brown, F.
Little baseball world. Lowry, R. J. C.
Little Ben. Knox, J.
Little Ben's railroad. Knox, J.
LITTLE BIG HORN, BATTLE OF THE,
  1876
  Fox, N. A. Only the dead ride proudly
Little black boys. Laidlaw, C.
Little blond fellow. Farrell, J. T.
Little boy blues. Brookhouser, F.
Little Bubo. Willingham, C.
Little business with Saint Bernard. Lieber-
  man, R.
Little calf. Abramowitz, S. J.
Little cask. Maupassant, G. de
Little cloud. Joyce, J.
Little companion. Wilson, A.
Little creeps. Miller, W. M.
Little dreams of Mr Morgan. Willingham, C.
Little Eddie goes to town. Haywood, C.
Little ewe lamb. Myers, R. H.
Little farm. Bates, H. E.
Little fears. Sansom, W.
Little Flute. Shen, T.
Little general. Brenner, L.
Little genius. Rydberg, E.
"Little gentleman." Tarkington, B.
Little ghost. Ringwood, G. P.
Little girls. Hasley, L.
Little Goat. Taber, G. B.
Little guy. Crump, I.
Little Hanukkah lamp. Peretz, I. L.
Little hero. Dostoevskiĭ, F. M.
Little Herr Friedemann. Mann, T.
Little house at Croix-Rousse. Simenon, G.
A little journey. Bradbury, R.
Little legend of the dance. Keller, G.
Little local color. Porter, W. S.
Little lost robot. Asimov, I.
Little loves of Sister Helen. Lieberman, R.
Little memento. Collier, J.
Little Mohammed and Egypt's king. Drez-
  mal, G. I.
Little mother. O'Donovan, M.
Little mother up the Mörderberg. Wells,
  H. G.
Little old spy. Hughes, L.
Little Orvie's new dog Ralph. Tarkington, B.
Little Pharaoh. Coolidge, O. E.

Little photographer. Du Maurier, D.
Little Pinks. Runyon, D.
Little place. Van Doren, M.
Little red jungle. Siegel, B.
Little room. Sansom, W.
Little shoemakers. Singer, I. B.
Little sisters are such pests. Schweitzer, G.
"Little speck in garnered fruit." Porter,
  W. S.
Little talk about mobs. Porter, W. S.
Little Tembi. Lessing, D. M.
Little terror. Jenkins, W. F.
Little things like that. Vickers, R.
Little white cat. Baker, D. D.
Little white girl. Haardt, S. P.
Little white lye. Brown, F.
Littledale, Harold Alymer, 1927-
  Five parts of summer
    American vanguard, 1952
Live bait. Hershman, M.
Livesay, Dorothy, 1909-
  Glass house
    Best American short stories, 1951
Living machine. Keller, D. H.
Living torpedo. Yates, T.
Livvie. Welty, E.
Livvie is back. Welty, E.
Llewellyn, Richard
  Faith to be healed
    Brentano, F. ed. The word lives on
Lloyd, Bertha B.
  Forgotten greeting cards
    Oberfirst, R. ed. 1952 anthology of best
      original short-shorts
Lo! Faulkner, W.
The loan. Reisin, A.
LOANS
  Porter, W. S. Call loan
  Reisen, A. The loan
LOBBYING
  Porter, W. S. Hand that riles the world
Lobo, the king of Currumpaw. Seton, E. T.
LOBOS. See Wolves
Lock the doors, lock the windows. Cuevas, E.
Locke, Robert Donald
  Dark nuptial
    Startling stories (Periodical) Best from
      Startling stories
  Demotion
    Wollheim, D. A. ed. Prize science fic-
      tion
Locke, William John, 1803-1930
  Adventure of the kind Mr Smith
    Cerf, B. A. and Moriarty, H. C. eds.
      Anthology of famous British stories
  Wise men of Trehenna
    Thinker's digest (Periodical) Spoiled
      priest, and other stories
Locked out. Fyfe, H. B.
Locked room. Carr, J. D.
LOCKOUTS. See Strikes and lockouts
Locksmith of Philadelphia. Howe, J.
LOCKSMITHS
  Howe, J. Locksmith of Philadelphia

LOCUSTS
Gordimer, N. Soft voice of the serpent

The lodger. Chekhov, A. P.

Lodging for the night. Li Fu-yen

Lodging for the night. Stevenson, R. L.

LODGING HOUSES. See Boarding houses

LOG CABINS
Beck, W. Felix

Log of the "Evening Star." Noyes, A.

Log the man dead. Burdick, E. L.

LOGGERS. See Lumber industry

LOGGING. See Lumber industry

Logic named Joe. Jenkins, W. F.

Logic of empire. Heinlein, R. A.

Lomax pitching. Hillger, E. H.

London, Jack, 1876-1916
All-gold cañon
  Schramm, W. L. ed. Great short stories
At the rainbow's end
  London, J. Sun-Dog Trail and other
  stories
Brown Wolf
  London, J. Sun-Dog Trail and other
  stories
For love of a man
  Fenner, P. R. comp. Dogs, dogs, dogs
Love of life
  London, J. Sun-Dog Trail and other
  stories
Make westing
  London, J. Sun-Dog Trail and other
  stories
The Mexican
  Ribalow, H. U. ed. World's greatest
  boxing stories
Moon-face
  London, J. Sun-Dog Trail and other
  stories
Piece of steak
  Christ, H. I. and Shostak, J. eds. Short
  stories
  Ribalow, H. U. ed. World's greatest
  boxing stories
Raid on the oyster pirates
  London, J. Sun-Dog Trail and other
  stories
Samuel
  Fremantle, A. J. ed. Mothers
Scarlet plague
  Conklin, G. ed. Omnibus of science
  fiction
Shadow of the flash
  London, J. Sun-Dog Trail and other
  stories
Son of the sun
  London, J. Sun-Dog Trail and other
  stories
Strength of the strong
  London, J. Sun-Dog Trail and other
  stories
Sun-Dog Trail
  London, J. Sun-Dog Trail and other
  stories
That spot
  Bloch, M. ed. Favorite dog stories

To build a fire
  Andrews, R. C. ed. My favorite stories
  of the great outdoors
  Burrell, J. A. and Cerf, B. A. eds. An-
  thology of famous American stories
  London, J. Sun-Dog Trail and other
  stories
Too much gold
  London, J. Sun-Dog Trail and other
  stories

LONDON. See England—London

LONDON

Police
  See Police—London

London night's entertainment. Sharp, M.

Lone cowboy. James, W.

LONELINESS
Capote, T. Shut a final door
Horwitz, J. The roof
Prado, P. Laugh in the desert

Lonely day. Caldwell, E.

Lonely heart. Runyon, D.

Lonely lives. O'Faoláin, S.

Lonely poet. Gibran, K.

Lonely reef. Swenson, E. P.

Lonely rock. O'Donovan, M.

Lonesome place. Derleth, A. W.

Lonesome ride. Haycox, E.

Lonesome road. Porter, W. S.

Long, Amelia Reynolds, 1904-
Reverse phylogeny
  Conklin, G. ed. Science-fiction adven-
  tures in dimension

Long, E. Waldo
Green match
  Boys' life (Periodical) Boys' life Ad-
  venture stories

Long, Frank Belknap, 1903-
And someday to Mars
  Moskowitz, S. comp. Editor's choice
  in science fiction
Cones
  Conklin, G. ed. Possible worlds of
  science fiction
The critters
  Derleth, A. W. ed. The outer reaches
Great cold
  Derleth, A. W. ed. Worlds of tomorrow
Humpty Dumpty had a great fall
  Derleth, A. W. ed. Beyond time &
  space
Invasion
  Derleth, A. W. ed. Far boundaries
The Mercurian
  Wollheim, D. A. comp. Flight into space
Red Storm on Jupiter
  Wollheim, D. A. comp. Flight into space
To follow knowledge
  Conklin, G. ed. Science-fiction adven-
  tures in dimension
Two face
  Best science fiction stories: 1951

Long arm. Claudy, C. H.

Long dawn. Loomis, N.

Long hot day. Zelver, P. F.

Long in populous city pent. Schorer, M.

Long journey. Sitwell, Sir O. bart.

Long pike. Conner, R.

Long rain. Bradbury, R.

Long road. Harvey, W. F.

Long road to Ummera. O'Donovan, M.

Long shadow. Mowery, W. B.

Long-shot Porter, Person, W. T.

Long time ago. Benson, T.

Long view. Pratt, F.

Long watch. Heinlein, R. A.

Long way from home. Sneider, V. J.

Long way out. Fitzgerald, F. S. K.

Long winter. Drago, H. S.

Long year. Summers, J. L.

Longest day I live. Rath, I. E.

LONGEVITY
Binder, E. Conquest of life

Longstreet, Stephen, 1907-
No peace with the sea
Grayson, C. ed. Fourth round

Look after the strange girl. Priestley, J. B.

Look at the boats. McLaverty, M.

Look for the kid with the guts. O'Rourke, F.

Look of eagles. Foote, J. T.

Looking 'em over. Farrell, J. T.

LOOKING GLASSES. See Mirrors

Lookout. Boyd, J. jr.

Loomis, Noel M. 1905-
Long dawn
Conklin, G. ed. Big book of science fiction
Mustang trail to glory
Western Writers of America. Bad men and good
The twilighters
Meredith, S. ed. Bar 3

Loon laughs Macfarlan, A. A.

Loophole. Clarke, A. C.

Loose tiger. Annixter, P. pseud.

Lord, James
Boy who wrote 'no'
Horizon (Periodical) Golden Horizon

THE LORD. See God

Lord, Jonathan
The avenging
Meredith, S. ed. Bar 2

Lord, Mindret
Ransom note
Strang, R. M. and Roberts, R. M. eds. Teen-age tales v 1

Lord Mountdrago. Maugham, W. S.

Lord Oakhurst's curse. Porter, W. S.

Lord Scamperdale's finest day. Surtees, R. S.

LORD'S SUPPER
Gibran, K. Last supper
Greene, G. Hint of an explanation
Kagawa, T. The last supper

Loring, Selden M.
The eel-trap
Owen, F. ed. Teen-age victory parade

Loss of breath. Poe, E. A.

The lost. Boyle, K.

The lost. Cawley, C. C.

Lost blend. Porter, W. S.

Lost boy. Van Dyke, H.

Lost boy. Wolfe, T.

Lost cat. Ekbergh, I. D.

LOST CHILDREN. See Children, Lost

Lost decade. Fitzgerald, F. S. K.

LOST GENERATION. See Youth

Lost god. Russell, J.

Lost hearts. James, M. R.

Lost in our wake, our archipelago. Lincoln, V. E.

Lost in the barren lands. Mowat, F.

Lost legacy. Heinlein, R. A.

Lost memory. Phillips, P.

Lost on dress parade. Porter, W. S.

LOST PERSONS. See Disappearances

Lost Phoebe. Dreiser, T.

Lost room. O'Brien, F.-J.

Lost sanjak. Munro, H. H.

Lost school bus. Sandoz, M.

Lost soldier. Whitmore, S.

Lost trail. Macfarlan, A. A.

Lot. Moore, W.

Lott, Davis Newton, 1913-
Skipper played it safe
Argosy (Periodical) Book of adventure stories

LOTTERIES
Chekhov, A. P. 75,000
Jackson, S. The lottery
McNulty, J. The jackpot

The lottery. Jackson, S.

Lotus and the bottle. Porter, W. S.

Lotus eater. Maugham, W. S.

Lotus eaters. Weinbaum, S. G.

Lotus for Jamie. Kneale, N.

Lou Louder. Runyon, D.

Loud sing cuckoo. Weston, C.

LOUIS XII, KING OF FRANCE, 1462-1515
Lernet-Holenia, A. M. Mona Lisa

Louis. Munro, H. H.

Louise. Maugham, W. S.

Louise. Munro, H. H.

LOUISIANA

New Orleans
Cable, G. W. Madame Delphine
Colladay, M. M. Planetoid of doom

Love, Peggy Harding, 1920-
Jersey heifer
Prize stories of 1951

Love. Maupassant, G. de

Love affair. Whitmore, S.

Love affair in Paris. Farrell, J. T.

Love among the ruins. Waugh, E.

Love and betrayal. Andreev, L. N.

Love-bird. Sitwell, Sir O. bart.

Love comes to Miss Lucy. Quentin, P. pseud.

Love gift. Eggleston, M. W.

Love is a fallacy. Shulman, M.

Love-letters of Smith. Bunner, H. C.

Love lies bleeding. MacDonald, P.

Love me, love my car. Bretherton, V. R.

The love-nest. Pratt, F. and De Camp, L. S.

'Love-o'-women'. Kipling, R.

Love of life. London, J.

Love of two chemists. Shulman, M.

Love on toast. Willingham, C.

Love-philtre of Ikey Schoenstein. Porter, W. S.

LOVE POTIONS
Collier, J. The chaser

Love scene. Trollope, A.

Love smelled of vanilla. Upshaw, H.

Love song in a honky-tonk. Hawkins, J. and Hawkins, W.

Love story. Monig, C.

Love that is lost. Brookhouser, F.

Love, Tomi. Connolly, M.

Lovecraft, Howard Phillips, 1890-1937
Case of Charles Dexter Ward
Derleth, A. W. ed. Night's yawning peal
Color out of space
Conklin, G. ed. Omnibus of science fiction
From beyond
Derleth, A. W. ed. Worlds of tomorrow

Loved dead. Eddy, C. M. jr.

Lovely lady. Lawrence, D. H.

Lover, Samuel, 1797-1868
The gridiron
Cerf, B. A. and Moriarty, H. C. eds. Anthology of famous British stories

The lover. Bowen, E.

Lover and his lass. Rodgers, M. A.

Lover, when you're near me. Matheson, R.

Loveridge, George, 1904-
Latter end
Best American short stories, 1954

Lover's meeting. Lincoln, V. E.

Lovers' meeting. Sitwell, Sir O. bart.

Lovers of gain. Boyle, K.

Love's awakening. Maupassant, G. de

Low road go down. Kidd, H. L.

Low tide. Sitwell, Sir O. bart.

Low water. Household, G.

LOWER EAST SIDE. See New York (City)—East Side

Lower Mississippi is thicker than water. Parker, J. R.

Lowndes, Marion (Smith)
House of ocean born Mary
Fenner, P. R. comp. Ghosts, ghosts, ghosts

Lowndes, Robert W.
Highway
Lesser, M. A. ed. Looking forward
Pride in his holsters
Meredith, S. ed. Bar 1 roundup of best western stories

Lowrey, P. H.
Big Chlorinda, happy Chlorinda
Stanford short stories, 1950
Too young to have a gun
Prize stories, 1954

Lowry, Robert James Collas, 1919-
Be nice to Mr Campbell
Lowry, R. J. C. Happy New Year, kamerades!
Prize stories of 1950
Casualty
Lowry, R. J. C. Happy New Year, kamerades!
Day he got fired
Lowry, R. J. C. Happy New Year, kamerades!
Defense in University City
Lowry, R. J. C. Happy New Year, kamerades!
For girlhood and for love
Lowry, R. J. C. Happy New Year, kamerades!
Happy New Year, kamerades!
Lowry, R. J. C. Happy New Year, kamerades!
Law and order
Horizon (Periodical) Golden Horizon
Little baseball world
Lass, A. H. and Horowitz, A. eds. Stories for youth
Lowry, R. J. C. Happy New Year, kamerades!
Phistairus
Lowry, R. J. C. Happy New Year, kamerades!
Skyblue lady
Lowry, R. J. C. Happy New Year, kamerades!
The victim
Lowry, R. J. C. Happy New Year, kamerades!

LOYALTY
Critchell, L. S. Loyalty check

Loyalty check. Critchell, L. S.

Loyalty up and loyalty down. Auchincloss, L.

Lu Hsün, pseud. See Chou, Shu-jen

Lucas, Edward Verrall, 1868-1938
Anne's terrible good nature
Fenner, P. R. cmp. Giggle box

LUCERNE. See Switzerland—Lucerne

Lucerne: The loaded tourist. Charteris, L.

The Luceys. O'Donovan, M.

Lucian
True history
Derleth, A. W. ed. Beyond time & space

Lucian of Samosata. See Lucian

LUCK. See Chance

Luck. Steele, W. D.

Luck charm. Coolidge, O. E.

Luck of Ignatz. Del Rey, L.

Luck of Riley. Frazee, S.

Luck of Roaring Camp. Harte, B.

Lucky burglar. Maupassant, G. de

Lucky 'leven. Whitney, P. A.

Lucky Murdock. Van Doren, M.

Lucky star. Allard, P.

Lucky stick. Coombs, C. I.

The **luftmensch.** Zangwill, I.
Lukardis. Wassermann, J.
Luke Baldwin's vow. Callaghan, M. E.
Lukert, Edward P.
For military merit
Best Army short stories, 1950
Lull, Roderick, 1907?-
Choice of the litter
Cavanna, B. ed. Pick of the litter
Dog that sounded like a fire siren
This week magazine. This week's short-short stories
No room in her heart
Saturday evening post (Periodical) Saturday evening post stories, 1950
The **lull.** Munro, H. H.
Lull at Cassino. Berto, G.
Lulungomeena. Dickson, G. R.
LUMBER INDUSTRY
Galsworthy, J. Timber
LUMBERING. See Lumber industry
Lumber-room. Munro, H. H.
Lump of sugar. Queen, E. pseud.
Lumpkin, Grace
The treasure
Southern review. Anthology of stories from the Southern review
Lunar trap. Elam, R. M.
LUNATIC ASYLUMS. See Insane hospitals
Lunch. Bowen, E.
Lunch. Horwitz, J.
The **luncheon.** Maugham, W. S.
LUNCHEONS. See Dinners
LUNCHROOMS. See Restaurants, lunchrooms, etc.
Lure of perfume. Ekbergh, I. D.
LYING. See Liars; Truthfulness and falsehood
Lykin's sleigh-ride. Bergengruen, W.
Lyle, David
In a dry country
Hathaway, B. and Sessions, J. A. eds. Writers for tomorrow. 2d ser.
Open season
Hathaway, B. and Sessions, J. A. eds. Writers for tomorrow. 2d ser.
Lynch, John A. 1922-
Fields of wheat
Stanford short stories, 1950
LYNCHING
Alexander, D. And on the third day
Caldwell, E. Saturday afternoon
Deming, R. Hanging fire
Faulkner, W. Dry September
Thompson, C. H. Posse
See also Hanging; Murder stories
The **lynching.** Annixter, P. pseud.
Lyon, Katherine
Altar cloth
Neider, C. ed. Men of the high calling
Lytle, Andrew Nelson, 1902-
The guide
Gordon, C. and Tate, A. eds. House of fiction

Jericho, Jericho, Jericho
Southern review. Anthology of stories from the Southern review
Lytton, Edward George Earle Lytton Bulwer-Lyton, 1st baron, 1803-1873
House and the brain
Cerf, B. A. and Moriarty, H. C. eds. Anthology of famous British stories

M

M. Seguin's goat. Daudet, A.
"MCMLV." Tucker, W.
MWA murder. Arthur, R.
Mabel. Maugham, W. S.
Mabry, Thomas Dabney
Indian feather
First-prize stories, 1919-1954
Prize stories, 1954
MACARTHUR, MARY, 1930-1949
Kuttner, N. Do you remember Mary?
Macaulay, Rose
Whitewash
Asquith, Lady C. M. E. C. ed. Book of modern ghosts
Macauley, Robie, 1919-
The invaders
Prize stories of 1951
The wishbone
Best American short stories, 1951
MACAWS. See Parrots
McCall, Mary Caldwell, 1904-
Fraternity
Eaton, H. T. ed. Short stories
McCarthy, Mary Therese, 1912-
The blackguard
McCarthy, M. T. Cast a cold eye
C.Y.E.
McCarthy, M. T. Cast a cold eye
The cicerone
McCarthy, M. T. Cast a cold eye
"Cruel and barbarous treatment"
Southern review. Anthology of stories from the Southern review
Friend of the family
McCarthy, M. T. Cast a cold eye
Old men
McCarthy, M. T. Cast a cold eye
Unspoiled reaction
Felheim, M.; Newman, F. B. and Steinhoff, W. R. eds. Modern short stories
The weeds
McCarthy, M. T. Cast a cold eye
Yonder peasant, who is he?
McCarthy, M. T. Cast a cold eye
McCarthy hunts peace. Abdullah, A.
McCarty, Mary B.
Your long black hair
Oberfirst, R. ed. 1952 anthology of best original short-shorts
McCauley, Mary Claire
Li'l Reynard
Thinker's digest (Periodical) Spoiled priest, and other stories

McClintic, Winona
In the days of our fathers
Magazine of fantasy and science fiction.
Best from Fantasy and science fiction;
[1st ser]

McCloskey, Robert, 1914-
The doughnuts
Fenner, P. R. comp. Giggle box

McCloy, Helen
Chinoiserie
Mystery Writers of America, inc.
20 great tales of murder

McClure, Jane
Dark interlude
Queen, E. pseud. ed. Queen's awards:
7th ser.

McConnell, William, 1917-
The alien
Pacey, D. ed. Book of Canadian stories
Totem
Weaver, R. and James, H. eds. Cana-
dian short stories

McCormick, H. P. See Reynolds, J. M. jt.
auth.

McCourt, Edward A. 1907-
Dance for the devil
Saturday evening post (Periodical) Sat-
urday evening post stories, 1952
White mustang
Weaver, R. and James, H. eds. Cana-
dian short stories

McCoy, Esther
The cape
Best American short stories, 1950

McCoy, Horace, 1897-
They shoot horses, don't they?
Grayson, C. ed. Fourth round

McCullers, Carson (Smith) 1917-
Ballad of the sad café
McCullers, C. S. Ballad of the sad café
Domestic dilemma
Abell, E. ed. American accent
McCullers, C. S. Ballad of the sad café
The jockey
McCullers, C. S. Ballad of the sad café
Madame Zilensky and the King of Fin-
land
McCullers, C. S. Ballad of the sad café
The sojourner
McCullers, C. S. Ballad of the sad café
Prize stories of 1951
A tree. A rock. A cloud
McCullers, C. S. Ballad of the sad café
Wunderkind
McCullers, C. S. Ballad of the sad café

McDaniel, Ruel
Coroner de luxe
Blaustein, A. P. ed. Fiction goes to court

MacDonald, Dorothy
Child wore a pink sweater
Oberfirst, R. ed. 1954 anthology of best
original short-shorts

MacDonald, John Dann, 1916-
Common denominator
Galaxy science fiction magazine. Galaxy
reader of science fiction
Dance of a new world
Greenberg, M. ed. Journey to infinity

Death's eye view
Best detective stories of the year—1953
Flaw
Best science fiction stories: 1950
Bleiler, E. F. and Dikty, T. E. eds. Sci-
ence fiction omnibus: the best science
fiction stories, 1949, 1950
Game for blondes
Best science-fiction stories: 1953
Galaxy science fiction magazine. Second
Galaxy reader of science fiction
Homesick Buick
Queen, E. pseud. ed. Queen's awards:
5th ser.
I love you (occasionally)
This week magazine This week's short-
short stories
Incubation
Crossen, K. F. ed. Future tense
Mechanical answer
Greenberg, M. ed. Robot and the man
The miniature
Conklin, G. ed. Big book of science
fiction
Ring around the redhead
Conklin, G. ed. Science-fiction adven-
tures in dimension
Spectator sport
Conklin, G. ed. Omnibus of science fic-
tion
Susceptibility
Galaxy science fiction magazine. Galaxy
reader of science fiction

MacDonald, John Ross, pseud. See Miller,
Kenneth

MacDonald, Philip
Fingers of fear
MacDonald, P. Something to hide
Green-and-gold string
MacDonald, P. Something to hide
The hub
Magazine of fantasy and science fiction.
Best from Fantasy and science fiction;
[1st ser]
Love lies bleeding
MacDonald, P. Something to hide
Queen, E. pseud. ed. Queen's awards:
5th ser.
Malice domestic
MacDonald, P. Something to hide
Man out of the rain
Queen, E. pseud. ed. Ellery Queen's
awards: 9th ser.
Private—keep out
Pratt, F. ed. World of wonder
Something to hide
MacDonald, P. Something to hide
Wood-for-the-trees
MacDonald, P. Something to hide

MacDonald, Zillah Katherine
Shingle shack
Furman, A. L. ed. Everygirls mystery
stories
Standing into danger
Furman, A. L. ed. Everygirls mystery
stories

McDowell, Dorothy
Good-by, Debbie
Seventeen (Periodical) The Seventeen
reader

Macfarlan, Allan A.
Bullfrog hunt
  Macfarlan, A. A. Campfire adventure
  stories
Camp at Saint Adrien
  Macfarlan, A. A. Campfire adventure
  stories
Danger by candlelight
  Macfarlan, A. A. Campfire adventure
  stories
Loon laughs; mystery and adventure in
  Maine
  Macfarlan, A. A. Campfire adventure
  stories
Lost trail
  Macfarlan, A. A. Campfire adventure
  stories
Moose boy; adventures in the Canadian
  northwoods
  Macfarlan, A. A. Campfire adventure
  stories
Swift Foot the hunter
  Macfarlan, A. A. Campfire adventure
  stories
Tackle buster
  Macfarlan, A. A. Campfire adventure
  stories

MacFarlane, Wallace
Dead end
  Conklin, G. ed. Science-fiction thinking
  machines

McFee, William, 1881-
Reluctant hero
  McFee, W. ed. Great sea stories of
  modern times

McGarry and the television frame-up. Taylor, M.

McGarry joins the Easter parade. Taylor, M.

McGivern, William P.
Sound of murder
  Mystery writers of America, inc. Crooks'
  tour

Macgregor, James Murdoch
Hallucination orbit
  Galaxy science fiction magazine. Second Galaxy reader of science fiction
One in three hundred
  Best science-fiction stories: 1954

McGregor, R. J.
Perfect gentleman
  Startling stories (Periodical) Best from
  Startling stories

McGregor affair. Rowland, S.

Machen, Arthur, 1863-1947
Black seal
  Davenport, B. ed. Tales to be told in
  the dark
White people
  Davenport, B. ed. Tales to be told in
  the dark
White powder
  Davenport, B. ed. Ghostly tales to be
  told

The **machine.** Campbell, J. W.

Machine. Jakes, J. W.

Machine breaks down. Sitwell, Sir O. bart.

Machine stops. Forster, E. M.

MACHINERY AND MACHINISTS
Forster, E. M. Machine stops
Marshall, J. Old woman

MACHINISTS. See Machinery and machinists

McHugh, Vincent, 1904-
Alone Men
  Argosy (Periodical) Argosy Book of
  sea stories

McIlvaine's star. Derleth, A. W.

McIntosh, J. T. pseud. See Macgregor, James Murdoch

Mackintosh. Maugham, W. S.

McKabe. Gallico, P. W.

McKay, Margaret Curtis
Thirty trips to Washington
  American girl (Periodical) On my
  honor

McKelvey, Lynne, 1936-
The threshold
  McFarland, W. K. comp. Then it happened
  Seventeen (Periodical) Nineteen from
  Seventeen

McKelway, St Clair
Russian who wanted to be friends
  Saturday evening post (Periodical) Saturday evening post stories, 1951

McKenney, John
Skycaptain
  Creamer, J. B. comp. Twenty-two stories about horses and men

McKenney, Ruth, 1911-
Guinea pig
  Dachs, D. ed. Treasury of sports humor

McLaren, Floris Clark, 1904-
Date with Dora
  Weaver, R. and James, H. eds. Canadian short stories

MacLaren, Ian, pseud. See Watson, John

MacLaren-Ross, Julian
This mortal coil
  Horizon (Periodical) Golden Horizon

McLarn, Jack Clinton
Trackside grave
  Moskowitz, S. ed. Great railroad stories
  of the world
Yardmaster
  Moskowitz, S. ed. Great railroad stories
  of the world

McLaverty, Michael
Aunt Suzanne
  McLaverty, M. Game cock, and other
  stories
Father Christmas
  McLaverty, M. Game cock, and other
  stories
Game cock
  McLaverty, M. Game cock, and other
  stories
Look at the boats
  McLaverty, M. Game cock, and other
  stories
The mother
  McLaverty, M. Game cock, and other
  stories
Pigeons
  McLaverty, M. Game cock, and other
  stories
Poteen maker
  McLaverty, M. Game cock, and other
  stories

McLaverty, Michael—*Continued*
The prophet
McLaverty, M. Game cock, and other stories
Road to the shore
Gable, M. Sister, ed. Many-colored fleece
McLaverty, M. Game cock, and other stories
The schooner
McLaverty, M. Game cock, and other stories
White mare
McLaverty, M. Game cock, and other stories
Wild duck's nest
McLaverty, M. Game cock, and other stories

MacLean, Katherine
And be merry. . .
Conklin, G. ed. Omnibus of science fiction
Contagion
Best science fiction stories: 1951
Conklin, G. ed. Possible worlds of science fiction
Defense mechanism
Conklin, G. ed. Big book of science fiction
Merril, J. ed. Beyond the barriers of space and time
The fittest
Merril, J. ed. Beyond human ken
Pictures don't lie
Conklin, G. ed. Invaders of earth
Snowball effect
Galaxy science fiction magazine. Second Galaxy reader of science fiction

MacMahon, Bryan, 1909-
Corn was springing
Ludwig, J. B. and Poirier, W. R. eds. Stories, British and American
Sing, Milo, sing
Thinker's digest (Periodical) Spoiled priest, and other stories
Young Mari Li
Gable, M. Sister, ed. Many-colored fleece

MacManus, Seumas, 1869-
Apprentice thief
Fenner, P. R. comp. Fools and funny fellows

McMorrow, Thomas, 1886-
Mr Murphy of New York
Conklin, G. ed. Big book of science fiction

McNamara, Ed
Holohan's hoist
Story (Periodical) Story; no. 1

McNeil, Steve
Girl who wasn't wanted
Saturday evening post (Periodical) Saturday evening post stories, 1953

McNulty, John, 1895-1956
Back where I had never been
McNulty, J. Man gets around
Bellevue days
McNulty, J. Man gets around
Can't slip any drugs to sisters on Fifth Avenue
McNulty, J. Man gets around

The jackpot
McNulty, J. Man gets around
Mrs Carmody's store
McNulty, J. Man gets around
Müller with an umlaut
McNulty, J. Man gets around
Overlooked lady
McNulty, J. Man gets around
Slightly crocked
McNulty, J. Man gets around
Television helps, but not very much
McNulty, J. Man gets around
Third Avenue medicine
McNulty, J. Man gets around
Where the grass, they say, is blue
McNulty, J. Man gets around
Yellow-ball-in-the-side
McNulty, J. Man gets around

Mac's masterpiece. O'Donovan, M.

Mad house. Matheson, R.

Mad Island. Marmur, J.

Mad Lomasneys. O'Donovan, M.

Mad Talmudist. Peretz, I. L.

Mad woman. Maupassant, G. de

Madame Bo-Peep, of the ranches. Porter, W. S.

Madame D. Lien Pu

Madame Delphine. Cable, G. W.

Madame de Mauves. James, H.

Madame de Treymes. Wharton, E. N. J.

Madame Jean De Chantal. Heagney, H. J.

Madame Parisse. Maupassant, G. de

Madame Rose Hanie. Gibran, K.

Madame Tellier's excursion. Maupassant, G. de

Madame Zilensky and the King of Finland. McCullers, C. S.

Madden, Harry T.
Not what she pretended
Saturday evening post (Periodical) Saturday evening post stories, 1952

Made to measure. Bonner, P. H.

Made to measure. Gault, W. C.

Mlle de Scudéri. Hoffmann, E. T. A.

Mademoiselle Fifi. Maupassant, G. de

Madison Square Arabian night. Porter, W. S.

The madman. Frank, P.

MADNESS. See Insanity

Madness in the heart. Donahoe, E.

Maestro's magic wand. Schneider, G. W.

Maeterlinck, Maurice, 1862-1949
Massacre of the innocents
Neider, C. ed. Great short stories from the world's literature

MAGAZINES. See Periodicals

Maggie: a girl of the streets. Crane, S.

Maggie Winthrop. Doty, W. L.

MAGI
Broun, H. C. Frankincense and myrrh
Goudge, E. Well of the star
Komroff, M. Told in the stars
Van Dyke, H. Other Wise Man

MAGIC
Bergengruen, W. Ali Baba and the forty horse-power
Blish, J. Mistake inside
Collier, J. Rope enough
Coolidge, O. E. Black magician
Coolidge, O. E. Children of Set
Mann, T. Magic and the magician
Procter, M. No place for magic
Wells, H. G. Magic shop
See also Conjuring
Magic at midnight. Tippett, J. S.
Magic circle. O'Rourke, F.
Magic hour. Newhouse, E.
Magic night. Howland, R.
Magic shop. Wells, H. G.
Magic touch. Knox, J.
MAGICIANS. See Conjuring; Magic
MAGISTRATES. See Law and lawyers
Magnanimity contest. Bergengruen, W.
Magnes, William D.
The vise
Story (Periodical) Story; no. 1
Magnetism. Fitzgerald, F. S. K.
Magnificent merger. Chute, B. J.
The magnolias. Leiper, G. B.
Maguire, R. A.
Five wives of Fergus O'Malley
Story (Periodical) Story; no. 3
Mahoney, William B.
Wrong guy
Lass, A. H. and Horowitz, A. eds. Stories for youth
MAHOUTS
Kipling, R. Moti Guj—mutineer
The maiden. Stafford, J.
Maiden, maiden. Boyle, K.
MAIDS. See Servants—Maids
Maier, Howard
Red dog
Cavanna, B. ed. Pick of the litter
Collier's, the national weekly. Collier's best
World outside
Best American short stories, 1950
MAIL CARRIERS. See Postal service
MAIL ORDER BUSINESS
Milburn, G. Wish nook
Mail starts. Skelton, C. L.
Main currents of American thought. Shaw, I.
MAINE
Auchincloss, L. Finish, good lady
Auchincloss, L. Greg's peg
Etnier, E. J. The willow
19th century
Hale, E. E. My double, and how he undid me
Spofford, H. E. P. Circumstance
20th century
Rawlings, C. A. Flash of lightning
Majesty of the law. Ford, N. A.
Majesty of the law. O'Donovan, M.
Major and Mrs Fletcher. Newhouse, E.

Major Burl. Schaefer, J. W.
Major of Hussars. Bates, H. E.
Make me real. Lincoln, V. E.
Make westing. London, J.
Makes the whole world kin. Porter, W. S.
Making arrangements. Bowen, E.
Making of a minister. Barrie, Sir J. M. bart.
Making of a New Yorker. Porter, W. S.
Makings of a cowhorse. James, W.
Malacca cane. Vigny, A. V. comte de
Malachi's Cove. Trollope, A.
Maladjusted classroom. Nearing, H.
Malamud, Bernard, 1914-
The prison
Best American short stories, 1951
MALARIA
Verga, G. Malaria
Malaria. Verga, G.
Maloney's last stand. Young, S.
Man-taming woman. Fessier, M.
MALAYA
Conrad, J. The lagoon
Maugham, W. S. Book-bag
Maugham, W. S. Door of opportunity
Maugham, W. S. Footprints in the jungle
Nelson, E. D. P. The St George ball
Malcolmson, Anne (Burnett) 1910-
Blackbeard
Fenner, P. R. comp. Pirates, pirates, pirates
Pecos Bill
Fenner, P. R. comp. Cowboys, cowboys, cowboys
MALEDICTIONS. See Curses
Les malheurs des mannequins. Hutchins, M. P. M.
Malice afterthought. Grinnell, D. pseud.
Malice domestic. MacDonald, P.
MALLARDS. See Ducks
Mallea, Eduardo, 1903-
Heart's reason
De Onís, H. ed. Spanish stories and tales
Pillars of society
Burnett, W. ed. World's best
Malory, Sir Thomas, 15th century
Marvellous adventure of the sword
Cerf, B. A. and Moriarty, H. C. eds. Anthology of famous British stories
Maloy, Lois, 1902-
Swift Thunder of the prairie
Fenner, P. R. comp. Indians, Indians, Indians
Malraux, André, 1895-
The conquerors
Dupee, F. W. ed. Great French short novels
Maltz, Albert, 1908-
Man on a road
Best of the Best American short stories, 1915-1950
Happiest man on earth
First-prize stories, 1919-1954
Mama. Asch, S.
Mama and the pot of gold. Knox, J.

Mama's little girl. Caldwell, E.

Mammon and the archer. Porter, W. S.

MAN
Stapledon, W. O. Last terrestrials

MAN, ISLE OF
Kneale, M. Putting away of Uncle Quaggin
Sawyer, R. Fiddler, play fast, play faster

MAN, MECHANICAL. See Automata

MAN, PREHISTORIC
Annixter, P. pseud. First ally
Howard, R. E. Coming of Conan; 7 stories
Howard, R. E. King Conan; 5 stories
Howard, R. E. Sword of Conan; 4 stories
Loomis, N. Long dawn
Macfarlan, A. A. Swift Foot the hunter

The man. Bradbury, R.

Man about town. Porter, W. S.

Man alone at lunch. Aiken, C. P.

Man and boy. Steele, W. D.

Man and woman. Caldwell, E.

Man at Gantt's Place. Frazee, S.

Man at the gate. Taber, G. B.

Man called Horse. Johnson, D. M.

Man from Glasgow. Maugham, W. S.

Man from Mars. Miller, P. S.

Man from outside. Williamson, J.

Man from the south. Dahl, R.

Man from the tunnel. Benson, T.

Man greatly beloved. Milne, A. A.

Man higher up. Porter, W. S.

Man in gray. Weston, C. G.

Man in Israel. Perl, P.

Man in the chimney corner. Knox, J.

Man in the hard hat. Barker, S. O.

Man in moon. Norton, H. A.

Man in the moon. Reynolds, M.

Man in the moone. Godwin, F.

Man in the morgue. Arthur, R.

Man in the passage. Chesterton, G. K.

Man in the velvet hat. Prince, J. and Prince, H.

Man inside. Weidman, J.

Man-killer. Mowery, W. B.

Man needs a horse. Downing, J. H.

Man of character. Gallegos, R.

Man of destiny. Christopher, J.

Man of his own. Ford, C.

Man of the crowd. Poe, E. A.

Man of the house. O'Donovan, M.

Man on a road. Maltz, A.

Man on Stormrift Mountain. Strong, P. N.

Man out of the rain. MacDonald, P.

Man that corrupted Hadleyburg. Clemens, S. L.

Man who became a fish. Li Fu-yen

Man who collected Poe. Bloch, R.

Man who confessed. Packard, F. L.

Man who could work miracles. Wells, H. G.

Man who couldn't remember. Hendryx, J. B.

Man who drove Strindberg mad. Sitwell, Sir O. bart.

Man who evolved. Hamilton, E.

Man who flew into a rage. Grove, W.

Man who had been around. Wylie, P.

Man who had died a lot. Van Doren, M.

Man who had no eyes. Kantor, M.

Man who had no friends. Philips, J. P.

Man who hated people. Gallico, P. W.

Man who hated time. Canning, V.

Man who invented sin. O'Faoláin, S.

Man who liked ants. Charteris, L.

Man who looked like himself. Caldwell, E.

Man who married an ill-tempered wife. Juan Manuel, Infante of Castille

Man who missed the bus. Benson, S.

Man who rode the saucer. Holmes, K.

Man who saw through heaven. Steele, W. D.

Man who shot Liberty Valance. Johnson, D. M.

Man who slept through the end of the world. Nadir, I. M.

Man who sold himself. O'Rourke, F.

Man who sold rope to the gnoles. Seabright, I.

Man who sold the moon. Heinlein, R. A.

Man who was. Kipling, R.

Man who was loved. Stern, J.

Man who wasn't there. Todd, R.

Man who waved the flag. Green, H. G.

Man who would be king. Kipling, R.

Man who wouldn't break. Heyliger, W.

Man whose wishes came true. Forester, C. S.

Man with a conscience. Maugham, W. S.

Man with a family. Humphrey, W.

Man with a past. Haycox, E.

Man with English. Gold, H. L.

Man with the glass eye. Hendryx, J. B.

Man with the monocle. Doty, W. L.

Man with the phoney tin foot. Benson, T.

Man with the scar. Maugham, W. S.

Man with the sneer. Vickers, R.

Man with the strange head, Breuer, M. J.

Man with the twisted lip. Doyle, Sir A. C.

Man with two beards. Chesterton, G. K.

Man without a country. Hale, E. E.

Man without a temperament. Mansfield, K.

Man you couldn't kill. Sergíeev-Tsenskiĭ, S. N.

Mandel, George, 1920-
Beckoning sea
American vanguard, 1950

MANDRAKE
Ekbergh, I. D. Mysterious Chinese mandrake

Manger, Itzik, 1901-
Adventures of Hershel Summerwind
Howe, I. and Greenberg, E. eds. Treasury of Yiddish stories

Mango tree. Robinson, R. S.

MANHATTAN. See New York (City)—
Manhattan

Mania-head-in-the-clouds. Gronowicz, A.

MANIACS. See Insanity

MANICURISTS
Caldwell, E. We are looking at you, Agnes

MANIKINS (FASHION MODELS) See Models, Fashion (Persons)

Mann, Heinrich, 1871-1950
Three minute novel
Lange, V. ed. Great German short novels and stories

Mann, Thomas, 1875-1955
Death in Venice
Lange, V. ed. Great German short novels and stories
Neider, C. ed. Short novels of the masters
Pick, R. ed. German stories and tales
Disorder and early sorrow
Davis, R. G. ed. Ten modern masters
Gordon, C. and Tate, A. eds. House of fiction
Fight between Jappe and Do Escobar
Davis, R. G. ed. Ten modern masters
The hungry
Blodgett, H. W. ed. Story survey. 1953 ed.
Into the pit
Seldon, R. ed. Ways of God and men
Little Herr Friedemann
Davis, R. G. ed. Ten modern masters
West, R. B. and Stallman, R. W. eds. Art of modern fiction
Mario and the magician
Felheim, M.; Newman, F. B. and Steinhoff, W. R. eds. Modern short stories
Heilman, R. B. ed. Modern short stories
Lynskey, W. C. ed. Reading modern fiction
Short, R. W. and Sewall, R. B. eds. Short stories for study. 1950 ed.
Masters of Buddenbrooks
Burnett, W. ed. World's best
Railway accident
Schorer, M. ed. The story
Tonio Kröger
Ludwig, R. M. and Perry, M. B. eds. Nine short novels
Weary hour
Neider, C. ed. Great short stories from the world's literature

Manna. Galsworthy, J.

Manna. Phillips, P.

Manners of the age. Fyfe, H. B.

Mannikin talk. Mowery, W. B.

Manning, Laurence
Good-bye, Ilha!
Merril, J. ed. Beyond human ken

Mannix, Edward, 1928-
New Year for Juicy
American vanguard, 1953

Mannzen, Don
Aurora's Angus
Oberfirst, R. ed. 1954 anthology of best original short-shorts

Man's foes. Buck, P. S.

Man's game. Heinz, W. C.

Man's hand. Garrold, R. P.

Mansfield, Katherine, 1888-1923
At the bay
Stegner, W. E.; Scowcroft, R. and Ilyin, B. eds. Writer's art
Bliss
Heilman, R. B. ed. Modern short stories
Lynskey, W. C. ed. Reading modern fiction
Cup of tea
Bogorad, S. N. and Trevithick, J. eds. College miscellany
Shaw, H. and Bement, D. Reading the short story
Daughters of the late colonel
West, R. B. and Stallman, R. W. eds. Art of modern fiction
Dill pickle
Schramm, W. L. ed. Great short stories
Short, R. W. and Sewall, R. B. eds. Short stories for study. 1950 ed.
Doll's house
Lamb, L. ed. Family book of best loved short stories
Garden-party
Millett, F. B. ed. Reading fiction
Her first ball
Christ, H. I. and Shostak, J. eds. Short stories
Felheim, M.; Newman, F. B. and Steinhoff, W. R. Modern short stories
Life of Ma Parker
Cerf, B. A. and Moriarty, H. C. eds. Anthology of famous British stories
Stauffer, R. M.; Cunningham, W. H. and Sullivan, C. J. eds. Adventures in modern literature
Man without a temperament
Davis, R. G. ed. Ten modern masters
Pictures
Davis, R. G. ed. Ten modern masters
Taking the veil
Blodgett, H. W. ed. Story survey. 1953 ed.
Wind blows
Davis, R. G. ed. Ten modern masters

MANSLAUGHTER. See Assassination; Crime and criminals; Murder stories; Mystery and detective stories

Manuel, Juan. See Juan Manuel, Infante of Castille

Ms. found in a bottle. Poe, E. A.

Manuscript found in a vacuum. Hubbard, P. M.

Manuscript of a village doctor. France, A.

MANUSCRIPTS
James, H. Death of the lion

MANUSCRIPTS (PALIMPSESTS)
Pratt, F. and De Camp, L. S. Palimpsest of St Augustine

Many are called. Van Doren, M.

Many are the brave. Gardner, W. W.

MAPLE SUGAR
Bromfield, L. Sugar camp

Mappined life. Munro, H. H.

Maracot Deep. Doyle, Sir A. C.

MARATHON DANCES. See Dance marathons

MARBLE WORKERS. See Stone-cutters

March, William, pseud. See Campbell, William Edward March

Marche Militaire. Schneider, G. W.

Marching morons. Kornbluth, C. M.

MARCUS AURELIUS, EMPEROR OF ROME. See Aurelius Antoninus, Marcus, Emperor of Rome, 121-180

Marcus, Paul
Tip the green earth
This week magazine This week's short-short stories

Marcus, Pesach, 1896-
Higher and higher
Howe, I. and Greenberg, E. eds. Treasury of Yiddish stories

Margie passes. Shallit, J.

Margin for error. Kuttner, H.

Marguerite. Stein, G.

María Concepción. Porter, K. A.

Marie, Consort of Ferdinand I, King of Rumania, 1875-1938
What Vasile saw
Thinker's digest (Periodical) Spoiled priest, and other stories

MARIJUANA CIGARETTES. See Narcotics

Mario and the magician. Mann, T.

MARIONETTES. See Puppets and puppet plays

The marionettes. Porter, W. S.

Marionettes, inc. Bradbury, R.

Marjorie Daw. Aldrich, T. B.

Mark. Munro, H. H.

Mark of distinction. Betts, D.

Mark of the beast. Kipling, R.

Mark Robarts is adamant. Trollope, A.

Mark Robarts signs a bill. Trollope, A.

Mark Tidd in the backwoods. Kelland, C. B.

Mark Twain, pseud. See Clemens, Samuel Langhorne

Marker, Walter D.
Tree for two
Elmquist, R. M. ed. Fifty years to Christmas

Market Basing mystery. Christie, A. M.

Markewich, Robert, 1919-
Return to the Bronx
Ribalow, H. U. ed. This land, these people

Markfield, Wallace, 1926-
Ph.D.
Ribalow, H. U. ed. These your children

Markheim. Stevenson, R. L.

Marksman. Gault, W. C.

MARLOWE, CHRISTOPHER, 1564-1593
Bush, G. Great reckoning in a little room
Cabell, J. B. Porcelain cups

Marlowe, Stephen
Lion's mouth
Lesser, M. A. ed. Looking forward

Marmur, Jacland, 1901-
Below Cape Horn
American boy (Periodical) American boy Adventure stories

Bloodstained beach
Saturday evening post (Periodical) Saturday evening post stories, 1952
I will not abandon!
Saturday evening post (Periodical) Saturday evening post stories, 1953
Mad Island
This week magazine. This week's short-short stories
Proved by the sea
Bluebook (Periodical) Best sea stories from Bluebook

Marooned children. Carrighar, S.

Marotta, Giuseppe, 1902-
"Dear mother. . . "
Fremantle, A. J. ed. Mothers
Ungar, F. ed. To mother with love

Marquand, John Phillips, 1924-
Yoicks—and away
Burnett, W. ed. World's best
You can't do that
Stauffer, R. M.; Cunningham, W. H. and Sullivan, C. J. eds. Adventures in modern literature

Marquis, Don, 1878-1937
Blood will tell
Cavanna, B. ed. Pick of the litter
Country doctor
Fabricant, N. D. and Werner, H. eds. World's best doctor stories

Marquis and Miss Sally. Porter, W. S.

Marquis de Fumerol. Maupassant, G. de

MARRIAGE
Dostoevskiĭ, F. M. Christmas tree and a wedding
Li Fu-yen. Matrimony Inn
Waugh, A. Wed, my darling daughter

MARRIAGE, MIXED
Johnson, D. M. Flame on the frontier

MARRIAGE, PROMISE OF. See Betrothals

MARRIAGE BROKERS
Dworzan, H. L. Husband for Bluma
Wendroff, Z. Statistics
Wendroff, Z. Two pleasures

Marriage feast. Lagerkvist, P. F.

MARRIAGE OF CHILDREN. See Child marriage

Marriage of convenience. Maugham, W. S.

MARRIAGE PROBLEMS
Balzac, H. de. Other Diane
Bergelson, D. In a backwoods town
Beyle, M. H. Mina de Vanghel
Broch, H. Zerline, the old servant girl
Chekhov, A. P. Boa constrictor and rabbit
Chekhov, A. P. La Cigale
Chekhov, A. P. Out of sheer boredom
Cloete, S. Silence of Mr Prendegast
De Vries, P. Double or nothing
De Vries, P. How can I leave thee?
De Vries, P. You and who else?
Ekbergh, I. D. Matron in distress
Gilpatrick, E. Concrete experience
Greene, G. Basement room
Halladay, V. Once-beautiful Ellie
Harte, B. Bell-ringer of Angel's
Harte, B. Brown of Calaveras
Harte, B. Passage in the life of Mr John Oakhurst

MARRIAGE PROBLEMS—*Continued*

Hatch, E. Channel 10
Horwitz, J. The movers
Humphrey, W. Last husband
Huxley, A. Gioconda smile
Jackson, C. R. The outlander
Jordan, G. For the last time
Kaye-Smith, S. The mockbeggar
Kulbak, M. Munie the bird dealer
La Farge, C. Motet for two voices
Laurence, M. Uncertain flowering
Lawrence, D. H. Captain's doll
Lawrence, D. H. Two blue birds
Lincoln, V. E. The understanding
Mallea, E. Heart's reason
Mansfield, K. Bliss
Maugham, W. S. Back of beyond
Maugham, W. S. Casual affair
Maugham, W. S. Colonel's lady
Maugham, W. S. Creative impulse
Maugham, W. S. Flotsam and jetsam
Maugham, W. S. Footprints in the jungle
Maugham, W. S. Force of circumstance
Maugham, W. S. His Excellency
Maugham, W. S. The kite
Maugham, W. S. P. & O.
Maugham, W. S. Point of honour
Maugham, W. S. The promise
Maugham, W. S. Social sense
Maugham, W. S. Virtue
Maugham, W. S. Woman of fifty
Maupassant, G. de. The jewels
Murrie, P. New beau
O'Donovan, M. Counsel for Œdipus
O'Donovan, M. The frying-pan
O'Donovan, M. Lonely rock
O'Donovan, M. Unapproved route
Parker, D. R. Big blonde
Porter, K. A. Day's work
Saintsbury, E. B. Bread upon the waters
Salinger, J. D. Pretty mouth and green my eyes
Sandy, S. Black lie
Sansom, W. The windows
Schnitzler, A. Bachelor's death
Schulberg, B. W. All the town's talking
Shaw, I. The convert
Singer, I. B. Gimpel the fool
Somerville, A. W. Tale of the old main line
Stettner, S. Summer place
Stone, W. J. Retribution
Stuart, J. The storm
Tarkington, B. Uncertain Molly Collicut
Verga, G. Cavalleria rusticana
Waltari, M. T. Tie from Paris
Waugh, E. Period piece
Wechsberg, J. New York is full of girls
Wharton, E. N. J. The choice
White, A. Moment of truth
Winslow, T. S. Fur flies
Winslow, T. S. Obsession
Winslow, T. S. Technique
    See also Divorce; Husband and wife

Marriage that couldn't succeed. Richter, C.

Marry month of May. Porter, W. S.

MARS (PLANET)

Bellamy, E. Blindman's world
Brackett, L. Last days of Shandakor
Bradbury, R. Dwellers in silence
Bradbury, R. Fire balloons
Bradbury, R. Holiday

Bradbury, R. In this sign
Bradbury, R. Million-year picnic
Bradbury, R. One who waits
Bradbury, R. Other foot
Bradbury, R. Ylla
Carter, F. Ounce of prevention
Del Rey, L. "The years draw nigh"
Elam, R. M. Red sands
Fairman, P. W. Brothers beyond the void
Harris, J. B. Time to rest
Heard, G. B+M—planet 4
Kummer, F. A. Forgiveness of Tenchu Taen
Leiber, F. Foxholes of Mars
Leiber, F. Wanted—an enemy
Long, F. B. And someday to Mars
Serviss, G. P. Edison's conquest of Mars
Sheckley, R. Last weapon
Van Vogt, A. E. Enchanted village
Weinbaum, S. G. Martian odyssey
Weinbaum, S. G. Valley of dreams
White, W. A. P. Starbride
Williams, R. M. Red death of Mars
Williams, R. M. The seekers
Wolf, M. Homeland
    See also Martians

Mars is heaven. Bradbury, R.

Marseilles. See France—Marseilles

Marsh, Willard N. 1922-
Beachhead in Bohemia
    Best American short stories, 1953

Marshal and his secretary. Bergengruen, W.

Marshall, Bruce, 1899-
Immodest maiden
    Saturday evening post (Periodical) Saturday evening post stories, 1951

Marshall, Edison, 1894-
Benefit of clergy
    Marshall, E. Love stories of India
Beside the Shalimar
    Marshall, E. Love stories of India
Bird of Omen
    Marshall, E. Love stories of India
Bird of Paradise
    Marshall, E. Love stories of India
Cat that would not die
    Marshall, E. Love stories of India
Closed trophy room
    Marshall, E. Love stories of India
Detour to Calcutta
    Marshall, E. Love stories of India
Double cross
    Marshall, E. Love stories of India
Elephant remembers
    Andrews, R. C. ed. My favorite stories of the great outdoors
    Marshall, E. Love stories of India
Gentleman and the tiger
    Marshall, E. Love stories of India
Heart of Lily Long
    Marshall, E. Love stories of India
Heart of Little Shikara
    First-prize stories, 1919-1954
Masks off
    Marshall, E. Love stories of India
Matter of honor
    Marshall, E. Love stories of India
Pooja
    Marshall, E. Love stories of India
Upturned card
    Marshall, E. Love stories of India

Marshall, Elizabeth
Hill people
Best American short stories, 1953
Marshall, Joyce
Old woman
Weaver, R. and James, H. eds. Canadian short stories
Marshall, R. D.
Wrist watch and some ants
New writing (Periodical) Best stories
MARSHALS. See Sheriffs
MARSHES. See Swamps
Marsland, Anitra M.
Of shoes and ships
American girl (Periodical) On my honor
MARTENS
Reid, M. Battle of the marten and the porcupine
Martha Jean. Caldwell, E.
Martha's yesterdays. Cavanaugh, J. P.
Martian and the moron. Waldo, E. H.
Martian odyssey. Weinbaum, S. G.
MARTIANS
Bradbury, R. Concrete mixer
Brown, F. Last Martian
Brown, F. Mouse
Carr, R. S. Easter eggs
Carr, R. S. Those men from Mars
Curtis, B. Peculiar people
Grunert, K. Enemies in space
Jenkins, W. F. Nobody saw the ship
Knight, D. Catch that Martian
Long, F. B. Invasion
Miller, P. S. Man from Mars
Russell, E. F. Dear Devil
Stapledon, W. O. The Martians
Tucker, W. Gentlemen—the Queen!
Tucker, W. Job is ended
Tucker, W. Wayfaring strangers
Wells, H. G. Star begotten
White, W. A. P. The ambassadors
The Martians. Stapledon, W. O.
Martians and the Coys. Reynolds, M.
Martin, Charles Morris, 1891-
Horse drive
Fenner, P. R. comp. Cowboys, cowboys, cowboys
Martin, John
Adventure of Baron Munchausen
Fenner, P. R. comp. Fun! Fun! Fun!
Martin, Thomas H.
The switchboard
Best Army short stories, 1950
Martin, Violet Florence. See Somerville, E. A. O. jt. auth.
Martyr, Weston, 1885-
Sleeping draft
Cerf, B. A. and Moriarty, H. C. eds. Anthology of famous British stories
The martyr. Akutagawa, R.
The martyr. Farrell, J. T.
The martyr. Roth, C.
Martyrdom of the house. Comfort, A.
MARTYRS
Akutagawa, R. The martyr
The marvel. Smyth, E.

Marvellous adventure of the sword. Malory, Sir T.
Mary. Collier, J.
MARY, VIRGIN
Borden, M. In Nazareth
Güiraldes, R. Old ranch
Mary comes into money. Trollope, A.
Mary Lou's Christmas. Credle, E.
Mary, Mary, so contrary. Fillmore, P. H.
Mary O'Reilley. Farrell, J. T.
Mary with the high hand. Bennett, A.
MARYLAND

Georgetown
Tate, A. Immortal woman
Masculine principle. O'Donovan, M.
Masculine protest. O'Donovan, M.
Masefield, John, 1878-
Western islands
Cerf, B. A. and Moriarty, H. C. eds. Anthology of famous British stories
The mask. Chekhov, A. P.
Mask of Demeter. Pearson, M. and Corwin, C.
Masked angel. Charteris, L.
Masked monster. Gilpatric, G.
MASKS (FOR THE FACE)
Beerbohm, Sir M. Happy hypocrite
MASKS (PLAYS)
Hawthorne, N. Maypole of Merry Mount
Masks off. Marshall, E.
Mason, Grace (Sartwell) 1877-
First stone
Thinker's digest (Periodical) Spoiled priest, and other stories
Mason, Travis
Stood up
McFarland, W. K. comp. Then it happened
MASONRY (SECRET ORDER) See Freemasons
Masque of the Red Death. Poe, E. A.
Masquerade of souls. Lagerkvist, P. F.
MASQUERADES
Chekhov, A. P. The mask
Poe, E. A. Hop-Frog
Poe, E. A. Masque of the Red Death
MASQUES (PLAYS) See Masks (Plays)
MASS
Stafford, J. Between the porch and the altar
MASSACHUSETTS
Aiken, C. P. Last visit

18th century
Hawthorne, N. Wives of the dead

Boston—17th century
Hawthorne, N. Gray champion

Boston—20th century
Aiken, C. P. Night before prohibition

Concord
Thoreau, H. D. Winter at Walden

Nantucket
Strong, A. All on a winter's night

Massacre of the innocents. Maeterlinck, M.

Massacree! Brink, C. R.

MASSACRES
Maeterlinck, M. Massacre of the innocents
Verga, G. Liberty

Masses of men. Caldwell, E.

Master mind. Chute, B. J.

Master minds of Mars. Claudy, C. H.

Master of the inn. Herrick, R.

Master race. Ashby, R.

Master time. Still, J.

Masters of art. Porter, W. S.

Masters of Buddenbrooks. Mann, T.

Masterson. Maugham, W. S.

The **masterstroke.** Howard, W.

Masur, Harold Q. 1912-
Widow in waiting
Mystery Writers of America, inc.
Four-&-twenty bloodhounds

MATADORS. See Bullfighters and bull-
fighting

Match-maker. Munro, H. H.

MATCHMAKERS
Coolidge, O. E. Carpenter's daughter
Munro, H. H. Forbidden buzzards
Munro, H. H. The elk
See also Marriage brokers

Mateo Falcone. Mérimée, P.

Mathematical voodoo. Nearing, H.

MATHEMATICIANS
Jenkins, W. F. Sidewise in time

Mathematics of intelligence. Willingham, C.

Matheson, Richard, 1926-
Born of man and woman
Best science fiction stories: 1951
Matheson, R. Born of man and woman
Dance of the dead
Star science fiction stories, no. 3
Dear Diary
Matheson, R. Born of man and woman
Disappearing act
Matheson, R. Born of man and woman
Dress of white silk
Magazine of fantasy and science fiction.
Best from Fantasy and science fiction,
1952
Matheson, R. Born of man and woman
F—
Matheson, R. Born of man and woman
Full circle
Matheson, R. Born of man and woman
Last day
Best science-fiction stories: 1954
Lover, when you're near me
Best science-fiction stories: 1953
Galaxy science fiction magazine. Second
Galaxy reader of science fiction
Matheson, R. Born of man and woman
Mad house
Matheson, R. Born of man and woman
Return
Matheson, R. Born of man and woman
SRL ad
Brown, F. and Reynolds, M. eds. Sci-
ence-fiction carnival
Matheson, R. Born of man and woman

Shipshape home
Conklin, G. ed. Omnibus of science fic-
tion
Matheson, R. Born of man and woman
Third from the sun
Galaxy science fiction magazine. Galaxy
reader of science fiction
Matheson, R. Born of man and woman
Through channels
Matheson, R. Born of man and woman
To fit the crime
Matheson, R. Born of man and woman
The traveller
Matheson, R. Born of man and woman
The waker dreams
Galaxay science fiction magazine. Galaxy
reader of science fiction
The wedding
Matheson, R. Born of man and woman
Witch war
Best science fiction stories: 1952
Matheson, R. Born of man and woman

Mathews, Mack
Tough little Christmas story
Story (Periodical) Story; no. 4

Mating of a stamp collector. Thomason,
J. W.

Mating of Marjorie. Caldwell, E.

MATRIMONIAL AGENCIES. See Marriage brokers

Matrimony Inn. Li Fu-yen

Matron in distress. Ekbergh, I. D.

Matron of Ephesus. Petronius Arbiter

Matschat, Cecile (Hulse) See Del Rey, L.
jt. ed.

Matter of business. Maupassant, G. de

Matter of form. Gold, H. L.

Matter of honor. Marshall, E.

Matter of mean elevation. Porter, W. S.

Matter of seconds. Queen, E. pseud.

Matter of sentiment. Munro, H. H.

Matter of spelling. Stanley, J. B.

Matter of time. Lieberman, R.

Matter of vanity. Riter, F.

MATTERHORN
Mummery, A. F. The Matterhorn

The **Matterhorn.** Mummery, A. F.

Matthew and the lace curtain. Carroll, J. W.

Matthews, Ralph D.
Fisherman's luck
Ford, N. A. and Faggett, H. L. eds.
Best short stories by Afro-American
writers (1925-1950)

Maud. Auchincloss, L.

Maud Island. Caldwell, E.

Maugham, William Somerset, 1874-
Alien corn
Maugham, W. S. Complete short stories
v 1
Ant and the grasshopper
Maugham, W. S. Complete short stories
v2
Maugham, W. S. Encore
Appearance and reality
Maugham, W. S. Complete short stories
v2

Maugham, William S.—*Continued*

Man with a conscience
  Maugham, W. S. Complete short stories
    v2
Man with the scar
  Maugham, W. S. Complete short stories
    v2
Marriage of convenience
  Maugham, W. S. Complete short stories
    v2
Masterson
  Maugham, W. S. Complete short stories
    v2
Mayhew
  Maugham, W. S. Complete short stories
    v2
Mirage
  Maugham, W. S. Complete short stories
    v2
Miss King
  Maugham, W. S. Complete short stories
    v 1
Mr Harrington's washing
  Maugham, W. S. Complete short stories
    v 1
Mr Know-All
  Davis, R. G. ed. Ten modern masters
  Maugham, W. S. Complete short stories
    v2
  Maugham, W. S. Trio
The mother
  Maugham, W. S. Complete short stories
    v2
Neil MacAdam
  Maugham, W. S. Complete short stories
    v 1
Official position
  Maugham, W. S. Complete short stories
    v2
The outstation
  Lynskey, W. C. ed. Reading modern
    fiction
  Maugham, W. S. Complete short stories
    v 1
  Stauffer, R. M.; Cunningham, W. H.
    and Sullivan, C. J. eds. Adventures in
    modern literature
P. & O.
  Maugham, W. S. Complete short stories
    v 1
The poet
  Maugham, W. S. Complete short stories
    v2
Point of honour
  Maugham, W. S. Complete short stories
    v2
The pool
  Maugham, W. S. Complete short stories
    v 1
Portrait of a gentleman
  Maugham, W. S. Complete short stories
    v2
Princess September
  Maugham, W. S. Complete short stories
    v2
The promise
  Maugham, W. S. Complete short stories
    v2
Rain
  Gordon, C. and Tate, A. eds. House of
    fiction
  Maugham, W. S. Complete short stories
    v 1

Raw material
  Maugham, W. S. Complete short stories
    v2
Red
  Cerf, B. A. and Moriarty, H. C. eds.
    Anthology of famous British stories
  Maugham, W. S. Complete short stories
    v 1
Romantic young lady
  Maugham, W. S. Complete short stories
    v2
Round dozen
  Maugham, W. S. Complete short stories
    v 1
Salvatore
  Maugham, W. S. Complete short stories
    v2
Sanatorium
  Maugham, W. S. Complete short stories
    v2
  Maugham, W. S. Trio
Social sense
  Maugham, W. S. Complete short stories
    v2
Straight flush
  Maugham, W. S. Complete short stories
    v2
String of beads
  Maugham, W. S. Complete short stories
    v2
The taipan
  Maugham, W. S. Complete short stories
    v2
Three fat women of Antibes
  Maugham, W. S. Complete short stories
    v2
The traitor
  Maugham, W. S. Complete short stories
    v 1
The treasure
  Maugham, W. S. Complete short stories
    v2
The unconquered
  Maugham, W. S. Complete short stories
    v2
The verger
  Maugham, W. S. Complete short stories
    v2
  Maugham, W. S. Trio
Vessel of wrath
  Maugham, W. S. Complete short stories
    v 1
Virtue
  Maugham, W. S. Complete short stories
    v 1
Voice of the turtle
  Maugham, W. S. Complete short stories
    v2
Wash-tub
  Maugham, W. S. Complete short stories
    v2
Winter cruise
  Maugham, W. S. Complete short stories
    v2
  Maugham, W. S. Encore
Woman of fifty
  Maugham, W. S. Complete short stories
    v2
Yellow streak
  Maugham, W. S. Complete short stories
    v 1

Mauldin, William Henry, 1921-
  Affair of the wayward jeep
    Saturday evening post (Periodical) Sat-
      urday evening post stories, 1953

Maupassant, Guy de, 1850-1893
  At sea
    Geist, S. ed. French stories and tales
  Babette
    Maupassant, G. de. Selected tales
  Ball-of-fat
    Maupassant, G. de. Selected tales
    Same as: Ball-of-tallow; Boule de suif;
      Tallow-ball
  Clochette
    Maupassant, G. de. Selected tales
    Same as: Bellflower
  Costly outing
    Maupassant, G. de. Selected tales
  Country excursion
    Maupassant, G. de. Selected tales
  The devil
    Maupassant, G. de. Selected tales
  Diamond necklace
    Maupassant, G. de. Selected tales
  Diary of a madman
    Maupassant, G. de. Selected tales
    Same as: A madman
  The duel
    Maupassant, G. de. Selected tales
    Same as: A coward
  False gems
    Maupassant, G. de. Selected tales
    Same as: The jewels
  Family affair
    Maupassant, G. de. Selected tales
    Same as: Family life
  Farmer's wife
    Maupassant, G. de. Selected tales
    Same as: The farmer
  Fishing excursion
    Maupassant, G. de. Selected tales
    Same as: Fishing party
  The hand
    Queen, E. pseud. ed. Literature of crime
    Same as: The Englishman
  Happiness
    Barrows, H. ed. 15 stories
  Hautot, father and son
    O'Faoláin, S. The short story
    Same as: Hautot Senior & Hautot Junior
  Hautot Senior & Hautot Junior
    Maupassant, G. de. Selected tales
    Same as: Hautot, father and son
  The Horla
    Maupassant, G. de. Selected tales
  Humiliation
    Maupassant, G. de. Selected tales
    Same as: Rose
  In the moonlight
    Maupassant, G. de. Selected tales
    Same as: Claire de lune; Moonlight
  The inn
    Schramm, W. L. ed. Great short stories
    Talbot, D. ed. Treasury of mountaineer-
      ing stories
  The jewels
    Bogorad, S. N. and Trevithick, J. eds.
      College miscellany
    Davis, R. G. ed. Ten modern masters
    Same as: False gems
  Julie Romain
    Maupassant, G. de. Selected tales

  Little cask
    Maupassant, G. de. Selected tales
  Love
    Maupassant, G. de. Selected tales
    Schorer, M. ed. The story
  Love's awakening
    Maupassant, G. de. Selected tales
  Lucky burglar
    Maupassant, G. de. Selected tales
    Same as: The burglar
  Mad woman
    Maupassant, G. de. Selected tales
  Madame Parisse
    Maupassant, G. de. Selected tales
  Madame Tellier's excursion
    Maupassant, G. de. Selected tales
  Mademoiselle Fifi
    Maupassant, G. de. Selected tales
  Marquis de Fumerol
    Maupassant, G. de. Selected tales
  Matter of business
    Maupassant, G. de. Selected tales
  La Mère Sauvage
    West, R. B. and Stallman, R. W. eds.
      Art of modern fiction
    Same as: Mother Sauvage; Old Mother
      Sauvage
  Minuet
    Geist, S. ed. French stories and tales
    Same as: The dancers
  Moonlight
    Maupassant, G. de. Selected tales
    Same as: Claire de lune; In the moon-
      light
  Mother and son
    Ungar, F. ed. To mother with love
    Same as: Suspense
  My Uncle Sosthenes
    Maupassant, G. de. Selected tales
  The necklace
    Cody, S. ed. Greatest stories and how
      they were written
    Lamb, L. ed. Family book of best loved
      short stories
    Thinker's digest (Periodical) Spoiled
      priest, and other stories
  Normandy joke
    Maupassant, G. de. Selected tales
  Olive grove
    Maupassant, G. de. Selected tales
  One phase of love
    Maupassant, G. de. Selected tales
  Paul's mistress
    Cory, D. W. pseud. comp. 21 variations
      on a theme
  Piece of string
    Maupassant, G. de. Selected tales
    Same as: The string
  Saved
    Maupassant, G. de. Selected tales
  The signal
    Maupassant, G. de. Selected tales
    Same as: Playing with fire; The sign
  Simon's papa
    Maupassant, G. de. Selected tales
  The specter
    Maupassant, G. de. Selected tales
    Same as: The apparition; The spectre
  Story of a farm girl
    Gordon, C. and Tate, A. eds. House of
      fiction
    Maupassant, G. de. Selected tales

Maupassant, Guy de—*Continued*

The string
  Cody, S. ed. Greatest stories and how
    they were written
  Same as: Piece of string
That pig of a Morin
  Maupassant, G. de. Selected tales
  Same as: That pig, Morin
Toine
  Maupassant, G. de. Selected tales
Two friends
  Blodgett, H. W. ed. Story survey. 1953
    ed.
Two little soldiers
  Maupassant, G. de. Selected tales
  Same as: Little soldier
Ugly
  Maupassant, G. de. Selected tales
The umbrella
  Maupassant, G. de. Selected tales
A vagabond
  Maupassant, G. de. Selected tales
  Same as: The tramp
Vain beauty
  Maupassant, G. de. Selected tales
The vendetta
  Maupassant, G. de. Selected tales
  Same as: Semillante
Was it a dream?
  Maupassant, G. de. Selected tales
White wolf
  Maupassant, G. de. Selected tales

Mauriac, François, 1885-
Thérèse and the doctor
  Burnett, W. ed. World's best

Maurie finds his medium. Levin, M.

Maurois, André, 1885-
War against the moon
  Conklin, G. ed. Omnibus of science
    fiction

**Maxtone Graham, Joyce (Anstruther) 1901-
1953**
Cobbler, cobbler, mend my shoe
  Fenner, P. R. comp. Ghosts, ghosts,
    ghosts
Ugly sister
  Magazine of fantasy and science fiction.
    Best from Fantasy and science fiction;
    2d ser.

Maxwell, James A. 1912-
Fighter
  Prize stories, 1954

May, Julian
Dune roller
  Bleiler, E. F. and Dikty, T. E. eds.
    Imagination unlimited
  Sloane, W. M. ed. Stories for tomorrow

MAY DAY
Hawthorne, N. Maypole of Merry Mount

May Day. Fitzgerald, F. S. K.

May the Temple be restored! Opatoshu, J.

Maybe a queen. Runyon, D.

Maybe just a little one. Bretnor, R.

Mayhew. Maugham, W. S.

MAYORS
Kafka, F. Hunter Gracchus

Maypole of Merry Mount. Hawthorne, N.

Mayse, Arthur
Midnight Mike
  Saturday evening post (Periodical) Sat-
    urday evening post stories, 1953
Sea gypsy
  Saturday evening post (Periodical) Sat-
    urday evening post stories, 1951

Mazel tov. Weissenberg, I. M.

Me and Joe. Gannon, S. A.

Me and my brother. Sykes, C.

Meader, Stephen Warren, 1892-
Bat
  Fenner, P. R. comp. Pirates, pirates,
Capture of a brig
  Fenner, P. R. comp. Pirates, pirates,
    pirates
Crooked arm
  Fenner, P. R. comp. Crack of the bat
Three hundred innings
  Fenner, P. R. comp. Crack of the bat
Whaler 'round the Horn
  Fenner, P. R. comp. Stories of the sea

The meadow. Bradbury, R.

Meal for the poor. Spector, M.

Meal ticket. Schulberg, B. W.

Mechanical answer. MacDonald, J. D.

MECHANICAL MEN. See Automata

Medal for Becky. Erdman, L. G.

Meddlesome Jack. Caldwell, E.

Meddlin' Papa. Verner, C.

Medearis, Mary, 1916?-
Big Doc's girl
  McFarland, W. K. comp. Then it hap-
    pened

Mediators to the goatherd. Hinton, J.

MEDICAL LIFE. See Physicians

MEDICAL RESEARCH
Lerner, M. The brothers

MEDICAL STUDENTS. See Physicians

Medicine dancer. Brown, B.

MEDICINE MAN
Porter, W. S. Jeff Peters as a personal
    magnet

Medicine man. Caldwell, E.

**MEDICINES, PATENT, PROPRIE-
TARY, ETC.**
Caldwell, E. Medicine man
O'Donovan, M. Man of the house
Porter, W. S. Jeff Peters as a personal
    magnet
Porter, W. S. Makes the whole world kin
Porter, W. S. "Next to reading matter"

MEDUSA (LEGEND)
Moore, C. L. Shambleau

Meek, Sterner St Paul, 1894-
Dignity, a springer spaniel
  Harper, W. comp. Dog show
Jerry
  Harper, W. comp. Dog show

Meet the girls! Farrell, J. T.

Megelhoffer theory. Taylor, M.

Meigs, Cornelia Lynde, 1884-
Buffalo dance
  Fenner, P. R. comp. Indians, Indians,
    Indians
Ship's cat
  Story parade (Periodical) Adventure
    stories

Meihem in ce klasrum. Edwards, D.

Melancholy Dane. Runyon, D.

Melee of the Mages. Gallico, P. W.

Mellonta Tauta. Poe, E. A.

Melnick, Carol Renner
Bend down, indeed!
   Wolfe, D. M. ed. Which grain will grow

Melville, Herman, 1819-1891
Apple-tree table
   Melville, H. Selected writings
Bartleby
   Melville, H. Selected writings
   Same as: Bartleby the scrivener
Bartleby the scrivener
   Ludwig, J. B. and Poirier, W. R. eds.
     Stories, British and American
   Melville, H. Selected tales and poems
   Same as: Bartleby
The bell-tower
   Melville, H. Selected tales and poems
   Melville, H. Selected writings
Benito Cereno
   Foerster, N. ed. American poetry and
     prose. 1952 ed.
   Gordon, C. and Tate, A. eds. House of
     fiction
   Melville, H. Selected tales and poems
   Melville, H. Selected writings
   Neider, C. ed. Short novels of the
     masters
   West, R. B. and Stallman, R. W. eds.
     Art of modern fiction
Billy Budd, foretopman
   Burrell, J. A. and Cerf, B. A. eds. An-
     thology of famous American stories
   Melville, H. Selected tales and poems
   Melville, H. Selected writings
Cock-a-doodle-doo!
   Melville, H. Selected writings
The Encantadas; or, Enchanted Isles
   Melville, H. Selected tales and poems
   Melville, H. Selected writings
The fiddler
   Melville, H. Selected tales and poems
   Melville, H. Selected writings
Happy failure: A story of the River Hud-
   son
   Melville, H. Selected writings
I and my chimney
   Melville, H. Selected tales and poems
   Melville, H. Selected writings
Jimmy Rose
   Melville, H. Selected tales and poems
   Melville, H. Selected writings
Lightning-rod man
   Melville, H. Selected tales and poems
   Melville, H. Selected writings
Paradise of bachelors
   Melville, H. Selected tales and poems
   Melville, H. Selected writings
The piazza
   Melville, H. Selected writings
   Neider, C. ed. Great short stories from
     the world's literature
Poor man's pudding
   Melville, H. Selected writings
Rich man's crumbs
   Melville, H. Selected writings
The sermon
   Brentano, F. ed. The word lives on
Story of Toby
   Melville, H. Selected writings

Tartarus of maids
   Melville, H. Selected tales and poems
   Melville, H. Selected writings
Temple first
   Melville, H. Selected writings
Temple second
   Melville, H. Selected writings

The memento. Porter, W. S.

Memento. Thompson, T.

A memoir. Suckow, R.

Memoirs of a ghost. Stonier, G. W.

Memoirs of a yellow dog. Porter, W. S.

Memorandum. Caldwell, E.

Memorial Eve. Suckow, R.

Memorial synagogue. Goodman, P.

Memory. Waldo, E. H.

A memory. Welty, E.

Memory in white. Schulberg, B. W.

Memory machine. Dunsany, E. J. M. D. P.
   18th baron

Men against the stars. Wellman, M. W.

Men and babies. Prichard, R.

Men are different. Bloch, A.

Men at work. Greene, G.

Men from the boys. Wilson, E.

Men in the storm. Crane, S.

Men of the ten books. Kuttner, H.

Men running. Cozzens, J. G.

Men working. Beck, W.

Menachem-Mendel, fortune hunter. Rabinowitz, S.

Mendel and his wife. Farrell, J. T.

Mendel Hirsch. Feuchtwanger, L.

Mendel Marantz—genius. Freedman, D.

MENINGITIS
Beachcroft, T. O. The eyes

MENNONITES
Lincoln, V. E. Morning wishes

MENSERVANTS. See Servants—Menservants

MENTAL ILLNESS. See Insanity; Neurasthenia

MENTAL INSTITUTIONS. See Insane
hospitals

Mentiplay, Cedric R.
Mutiny below
   Argosy (Periodical) Argosy Book of
     sea stories

The Mentocrats. Newhouse, E.

Merchant of art. Brenner, L.

MERCHANTS
Caudill, R. Fern Barrie's new plans
Chekhov, A. P. Moscow hypocrites
Kuttner, H. What you need
Zangwill, I. Sabbath question in Sud-
   minster

Merchant's monument. Arico, V.

The Mercurian. Long, F. B.

MERCURY (PLANET)
Elam, R. M. Sol's little brother
Long, F. B. Cones
Long, F. B. The Mercurian

La Mère Sauvage. Maupassant, G. de

Meredith, George, 1828-1909
Case of General Ople and Lady Camper
Connolly, C. ed. Great English short
novels
Punishment of Shahpesh, the Persian, on
Khipil, the builder
Cerf, B. A. and Moriarty, H. C. eds.
Anthology of famous British stories

Mérimée, Prosper, 1803-1870
Mateo Falcone
Shaw, H. and Bement, D. Reading the
short story

The **mermaids.** Gibran, K.

Merochnik, Minnie, 1887-
Autumn leaves
Merochnik, M. Celeste, & other stories
Celeste
Merochnik, M. Celeste, & other stories
Influence
Merochnik, M. Celeste, & other stories
Prohibition
Merochnik, M. Celeste, & other stories
A saga
Merochnik, M. Celeste, & other stories

Merrick, Leonard, 1864-1939
Doll in the pink silk dress
Cerf, B. A. and Moriarty, H. C. eds.
Anthology of famous British stories

Merrie gentleman. Price, E. B.

Merril, Judith, 1923-
Barrier of dread
Greenberg, M. ed. Journey to infinity
Daughters of earth
Petrified planet
So proudly we hail
Star science fiction stories [no. 1]
Survival ship
Heinlein, R. A. ed. Tomorrow, the stars
That only a mother
Pratt, F. ed. World of wonder

Merriman, Henry Seton, pseud. See Scott,
Hugh Stowell

Merrittsville. Suckow, R.

Merry clouters. Farrell, J. T.

MERRY-GO-ROUNDS
Weissenberg, I. M. Father and the boys

Merry men. Stevenson, R. L.

Merson, Ben
The cross-up
Dachs, D. ed. Treasury of sports humor

Merwin, Sam, 1910-
Exiled from earth
Crossen, K. F. ed. Adventures in to-
morrow
Exit line
Conklin, G. ed. Possible worlds of sci-
ence fiction
Judas ram
Galaxy science fiction magazine. Galaxy
reader of science fiction

Meschi, Edward
If we could see
Ford, N. A. and Faggett, H. L. eds.
Best short stories by Afro-American
writers (1925-1950)

Mesdames Grantly and Proudie get together.
Trollope, A.

Mesmeric revelation. Poe, E. A.

MESMERISM. See Hypnotism

Message for Harold. Ullman, V.

Message for Uncle Billy. Brick, J.

Message that failed. Heimann, M.

Message to the Camel Corps. Miller, W. H.

The **messenger.** Sitwell, Sir O. bart.

MESSENGERS
Porter, W. S. By courier

MESSIAH
Frug, S. S. Last kopeck

METAMORPHOSIS
Kafka, F. The metamorphosis
Keller, D. H. The bridle
Mrs White
Smith, C. A. Metamorphosis of earth
Thackeray, W. M. Sultan stork
Tucker, W. My brother's wife
See also Supernatural phenomena

Metamorphosis. Kafka, F.

Metamorphosis of earth. Smith, C. A.

Metamorphosite. Russell, E. F.

Metcalfe, John, 1891-
Childish thing
Story (Periodical) Story; no. 2

Meteor. Harris, J. B.

Meteor. Powers, W. T.

Metzengerstein. Poe, E. A.

Metzker, Isaac, 1901-
To the new world
Howe, I. and Greenberg, E. eds. Treas-
ury of Yiddish stories

Mevorach, Jacob, 1915-
Telescope and the umbrella
American vanguard, 1952

Mewhu's jet. Sturgeon, T.

The **Mexican.** London, J.

MEXICAN BORDER
Brandon, W. Chiltipiquin
Porter, W. S. Caballero's way

MEXICANS IN ITALY
Maugham, W. S. Hairless Mexican

MEXICANS IN THE UNITED STATES
Bradbury, R. I see you never
Gilbertson, M. G. Christmas in Carthage
Hemingway, E. Gambler, the nun, and
the radio
Summers, J. L. Boy in the mirror

MEXICAN INDIANS. See Indians of
Mexico

MEXICO
Roper, W. Last cigarette

19th century
Porter, W. S. Matter of mean elevation

20th century
Azuela, M. Under dogs
Brenner, L. An artist grows up in Mex-
ico; 7 stories
Dresser, D. Big shot
Gordon, E. E. Value of the dollar
Hinton, J. Mediators to the goatherd
La Farge, O. Old century's river
Porter, K. A. Flowering Judas
Porter, K. A. María Concepción
Porter, W. S. Dicky

MEXICO—*Continued*

Presidents

Caldwell, E. Day the presidential candidate came to Ciudad Tamaulipas

Ranch life

See Ranch life—Mexico

Vera Cruz

Maugham, W. S. The bum

Meyer, Conrad Ferdinand, 1825-1898
Plautus in the convent
Lange, V. ed. Great German short novels and stories

Meyer, Ernest Louis, 1892-1952
When the aliens left
Lass, A. H. and Horowitz, A. eds. Stories for youth

Meyn, Marjorie. See Vetter, Marjorie (Meyn)

Meyouhas, Joseph
Noah the Prophet
Selden, R. ed. Ways of God and men

The **mezzotint.** James, M. R.

Miami-New York. Gellhorn, M. E.

MICE
Brown, F. Mouse
Brown, F. Star mouse
Collier, J. Steel cat
Hoffmann, E. T. A. History of Krakatuk
Kafka, F. Josephine the singer
Munro, H. H. The mouse

Michael Shayne as I know him. Dresser, D.

Michaëlis, Karin, 1872-1950
Teacher Jensen
Lohan, R. and Lohan, M. eds. New Christmas treasury

Michel, Ellison
Moon tide
Strang, R. M. and Roberts, R. M. eds. Teen-age tales v 1

Michener, James Albert, 1907-
The fossickers
Michener, J. A. Return to Paradise
The good life
Michener, J. A. Return to Paradise
The jungle
Michener, J. A. Return to Paradise
Milk run
Jensen, P. ed. Fireside book of flying stories
Mr Morgan
Michener, J. A. Return to Paradise
Mynah birds
Michener, J. A. Return to Paradise
Povenaa's daughter
Michener, J. A. Return to Paradise
The story
Michener, J. A. Return to Paradise
Until they sail
Michener, J. A. Return to Paradise

MICHIGAN
Macauley, R. The wishbone

Mickey. Weeks, E.

Microscopic giants. Ernst, P.

MICROSCOPE AND MICROSCOPY
O'Brien, F.-J. Diamond lens

Midas on a goatskin. Anderson, D.

MIDDLE AGE
Fielding, E. Fountain of youth
Taylor, E. Idea of age
Thompson, L. Grasshopper a burden
Waltari, M. T. Tie from Paris

Middle drawer. Calisher, H.

Middle of the week after next. Jenkins, W. F.

MIDDLE WEST
Beck, W. No continuing city

Farm life
See Farm life—Middle West

MIDDLE WESTERN DIALECT. See Dialect stories—Middle West

Middle years. James, H.

Middleton, Richard Barham, 1882-1911
Shepherd's boy
Magazine of fantasy and science fiction. Best from Fantasy and science fiction; 3d ser.

MIDGETS. See Dwarfs

Midnight. James, W.

Midnight blue. Collier, J.

Midnight in the stable. Goudge, E.

Midnight Mike. Mayse, A.

Midsummer knight's dream. Porter, W. S.

Midsummer masquerade. Porter, W. S.

Midsummer passion. Caldwell, E.

Midwinter guest. Caldwell, E.

Miers, Earl Schenck, 1910-
Bandy
Miers, E. S. The kid who beat the Dodgers, and other sports stories
The big splash
Miers, E. S. The kid who beat the Dodgers, and other sports stories
Black Bat
Miers, E. S. The kid who beat the Dodgers, and other sports stories
Christmas skis
Miers, E. S. The kid who beat the Dodgers, and other sports stories
Ghost runner
Miers, E. S. The kid who beat the Dodgers, and other sports stories
He who laughs last
Miers, E. S. The kid who beat the Dodgers, and other sports stories
Jimmy rides the seal herd
Miers, E. S. The kid who beat the Dodgers, and other sports stories
The kid who beat the Dodgers
Miers, E. S. The kid who beat the Dodgers, and other sports stories
No heroes wanted
Miers, E. S. The kid who beat the Dodgers, and other sports stories
Scrub cure
Miers, E. S. The kid who beat the Dodgers, and other sports stories
Skeedunk special
Miers, E. S. The kid who beat the Dodgers, and other sports stories
Weary Willie
Miers, E. S. The kid who beat the Dodgers, and other sports stories

Miggles. Harte, B.

Might of motherhood. Gorky, M.

Milburn, George, 1906-
The apostate
Heilman, R. B. ed. Modern short stories
Student in economics
Lass, A. H. and Horowitz, A. eds.
Stories for youth
Wish book
Southern review. Anthology of stories
from the Southern review

Milchiger Synagogue and the blind preacher.
Kobrin, L.

Miles, Mary K.
Sand fort
Stanford short stories, 1953

Miley Bennett. Schaefer, J. W.

MILITARY DESERTION. See Desertion,
Military

MILITARY LIFE. See Soldiers; also subdivision Army under various countries,
e.g. Great Britain—Army

MILITARY SERVICE, COMPULSORY
Coolidge, O. E. Judgment of the gods
Franzos, K. E. Saviour of the people

The milk pitcher. Brubaker, H.

Milk run. Michener, J. A.

MILL WORKERS. See Iron and steel industry

Millar, Bruce, 1925-
Chartered rowboat
American vanguard, 1952

Millar, Kenneth, 1915-
Find the woman
Mystery Writers of America, inc. Maid-
en murders
Wild goose chase
Queen, E. pseud. ed. Ellery Queen's
awards: 9th ser.

Millar, Margaret, 1915-
Couple next door
Queen, E. pseud. ed. Ellery Queen's
awards: 9th ser.

Millay, Edna St Vincent, 1892-1950
Murder in the Fishing Cat
Queen, E. pseud. ed. Literature of crime

The millennium. Parker, J. R.

Miller, Alice (Duer) 1874-1942
Plum pudding and mince pie
Lamb, L. ed. Family book of best loved
short stories

Miller, Arthur, 1915-
Monte Saint Angelo
Greene, J. I. and Abell, E. eds. Stories
of sudden truth
Prize stories of 1951
Ribalow, H. U. ed. These your children

Miller, Charlotte, 1917-
Westfield House
American vanguard, 1952

Miller, Clyde
Gentle season
Aswell, M. L. W. ed. New short novels

Miller, James Robbins, 1915-
Letters from Cairo
Collier's, the national weekly. Collier's
best

Miller, Jean (Dupont)
Somebody else, not me
American girl (Periodical) Favorite
stories

Miller, Mary Britton, 1883-
Ruth and Irma
Cory, D. W. pseud. comp. 21 variations
on a theme

Miller, Peter Schuyler, 1912-
Arrhenius horror
Miller, P. S. The Titan
As never was
Miller, P. S. The Titan
Forgotten
Miller, P. S. The Titan
Gleeps
Miller, P. S. The Titan
In the good old summer time
Miller, P. S. The Titan
Man from Mars
Margulies, L. and Friend, O. J. eds.
From off this world
Old Man Mulligan
Miller, P. S. The Titan
Spawn
Miller, P. S. The Titan
Status quondam
Healy, R. J. ed. New tales of space and
time
The Titan
Miller, P. S. The Titan
Trouble on Tantalus
Greenberg, M. ed. Travelers of space

Miller, Walter M. 1923-
Big hunger
Wollheim, D. A. ed. Prize science fic-
tion
Command performance
Best science-fiction stories: 1953
Galaxy science fiction magazine. Second
Galaxy reader of science fiction
Conditionally human
Year's best science fiction novels, 1953
Crucifixus Etiam
Best science-fiction stories: 1954
Dumb waiter
Conklin, G. ed. Science-fiction thinking
machines
Izzard and the membrane
Year's best science fiction novels, 1952
Little creeps
Lesser, M. A. ed. Looking forward
No moon for me
Sloane, W. M. ed. Space, space, space
Wolf pack
Merril, J. ed. Beyond the barriers of
space and time

Miller, Warren Hastings, 1876-
Message to the Camel Corps
American boy (Periodical) American
boy Adventure stories

MILLERS
Porter, W. S. Church with an overshot-
wheel
Stevenson, R. L. Will 'o the mill

Millie's big story. Coombs, C. I.

Millin, Sarah Gertrude (Liebson) 1889-
Why Adonis laughed
Leftwich, J. ed. Yisröel. 1952 ed.

MILLINERS
Bowen, E. Ann Lee's

MILLINERY. See Hats

Million-to-one chance. Vickers, R.

Million-year picnic. Bradbury, R.

Mr Pomponius Ego out with the Handley Cross. Surtees, R. S.

Mr Prohartchin. Dostoevskiĭ, F. M.

Mr Rabbi. Sandoz, M. Y. ·

Mr Shawn and Father Scott. Betts, D.

Mr Sherlock Holmes. Doyle, Sir A. C.

Mr Sims and Henry. Carmer, C. L.

Mr Skae's item. Clemens, S. L.

Mr Slope vanquished. Trollope, A.

Mr Smith kicks the bucket. Brown, F.

Mr Sponge's first day with the Flat Hat Hunt. Surtees, R. S.

Mr Sponge's first day with the Hanby. Surtees, R. S.

Mr Strenberry's tale. Priestley, J. B.

Mr Sweeney. Butler, M.

Mr Timothy and the model. Brookhouser, F.

Mr Tutt collects a bet. Train, A.

Mistletoe. Irwin, M. E. F.

Mistral. Faulkner, W.

Mrs Benson. Haycox, E.

Mrs Carmody's store. McNulty, J.

Mrs Crocker's mutiny. Benchley, N.

Mrs Golightly and the first convention. Wilson, E.

Mrs Ketting and Clark Gable. Chidester, A.

Mrs Kochinsky and the problem child. Osborne, M. H.

Mrs Lancey. Van Doren, M.

Mrs Mancini. Kneale, N.

Mrs Mandford's drawing-room. Brophy, B.

Mrs Manifold. Grendon, S.

Mrs Oliver Cromwell. Irwin, M. E. F.

Mrs Packletide's tiger. Munro, H. H.

Mrs Proudie goes too far. Trollope, A.

Mrs Proudie intervenes. Trollope, A.

Mrs Proudie vanquished. Trollope, A.

Mrs Razor. Still, J.

Mrs Ripley's trip. Garland, H.

Mrs Rivkin grapples with the drama. Rosenberg, E. C.

Mrs Skaggs's husbands. Harte, B.

Mrs Union Station. Welch, D.

Mrs Veal. Defoe, D.

Mrs Vincent. Bates, H. E.

Mrs Vogel and Ollie. Suckow, R.

Mrs White
Horizon (Periodical) Golden Horizon

Mrs Wilson's husband goes for a swim. Winslow, T. S.

Mrs Windermere. Bowen, E.

A misunderstanding. Farrell, J. T.

Mitchell, John Ames, 1845-1918
Last American
Derleth, A. W. ed. Far boundaries

Mitchell, Joseph, 1908-
Professor Sea Gull
Waite, H. O. and Atkinson, B. P. eds. Literature for our time

"Some bum might mistook me for a wrestler"
Dachs, D. ed. Treasury of sports humor

Mitchell, William Ormond, 1914-
Saint Sammy
Pacey, D. ed. Book of Canadian stories

Mitchison, Naomi Margaret (Haldane) 1897-
Take back your bay wreath
Cory, D. W. pseud. comp. 21 variations on a theme

Mitzie who was young for her age. Strain, F. B.

M'liss. Harte, B.

Mlle de Scudéri. Hoffmann, E. T. A.

Mock governor. Shulman, M.

The mockbeggar. Kaye-Smith, S.

Model of a judge. Samachson, J.

MODEL RAILROADS. See Railroads—Models

Model shop. Jones, R. F.

Modell, Jack
Day in the sun
American vanguard, 1950

Modell, Merriam, 1908-
Biggest doll in the house
Story (Periodical) Story; no. 3

MODELS, FASHION
Collier, J. Special delivery

MODELS, FASHION (PERSONS)
Farrell, J. T. American dream girl
Maugham, W. S. Appearance and reality

Modern rural sports. Porter, W. S.

Modest proposal. Stafford, J.

Modus operandi. Gilbert, M. F.

Moffett, George, 1920-
Life's old sweet dream
Burnett, W. and Burnett, H. S. eds. Sextet

MOHAMMEDANS
Graham, R. B. C. Faith

Mohler, Charles, 1913-
Jesus complex
Burnett, W. and Burnett, H. S. eds. Sextet

Moll, Elick, 1903-
Boy who went away
Saturday evening post (Periodical) Saturday evening post stories, 1951

Moller, Ernestine Carey (Gilbreth) 1908-
See Gilbreth, F. B. jt. auth.

Mollie. Bonner, P. H.

Molly Cotton-Tail. Caldwell, E.

Molnár, Ferenc, 1878-1952
Hussar who loved three Jews
Ausubel, N. ed. Treasury of Jewish humor

Mom in the spring. Yaffe, J.

Mom knows best. Yaffe, J.

Mom makes a bet. Yaffe, J.

Moment of judgment. Hersey, J. R.

Moment of truth. O'Rourke, F.

Moment of truth. White, A.

Moment of victory. Porter, W. S.

Moment without time. Rogers, J. T.

Momma. Burns, J. H.

Mona Lisa. Lernet-Holenia, A. M.

MONACO
Monte Carlo
Maugham, W. S. Facts of life
Monarch of Park Barren. Roberts, Sir
C. G. D.
Monarch the bum. Chamberlain, G. A.
MONASTERY LIFE. See Monasticism
and religious orders
**MONASTICISM AND RELIGIOUS OR-
DERS**
Daudet, A. Father Gaucher's elixir
See also Monks
Monchek, Barbara, 1924?-
Big bed
American vanguard, 1950
Monday come home. Rice, J. A.
Monday is better than Sunday. Gordimer,
N.
MONEY
Porter, W. S. Tale of a tainted tenner
Money. Jackson, C. R.
Money for jam. Guinness, A.
Money from the sky. Kelsey, A. G.
Money maze. Porter, W. S.
MONEY RAISING. See Fund raising
Money talks. Queen, E. pseud.
MONGOLIA
Vogau, B. A. Big heart
Monica's son. Augustine, Saint, Bp. of
Hippo
Monig, Christopher
Love story
Crossen, K. F. ed. Future tense
Monk. Faulkner, W.
Monkey business at Gibraltar. Gilpatric, G.
Monkey spirit. Poston, M. L.
MONKEYS
Gilbert, K. Jungle brothers
Munro, H. H. Remoulding of Groby
Lington
Monkey's paw. Jacobs, W. W.
MONKS
Daudet, A. Father Gaucher's elixir
Dinnis, E. M. The peacemaker
Dostoevskiĭ, F. M. Father Zossima's duel
France, A. Our Lady's juggler
Goudge, E. Canticle of the sun
Porter, W. S. Robe of peace
Monks revel at Winkton. Parker, J. R.
Monn, Albert
The award
Ford, N. A. and Faggett, H. L. eds.
Best short stories by Afro-American
writers (1925-1950)
Our country
Ford, N. A. and Faggett, H. L. eds.
Best short stories by Afro-American
writers (1925-1950)
MONOLOGS
Akutagawa, R. Kesa and Morito
Chekhov, A. P. On the harmful effects
of tobacco; first version
Chekhov, A. P. On the harmful effects
of tobacco; final version

Furman, L. Experience on the dress line
Lardner, R. W. Haircut
Wolfe, T. Only the dead know Brooklyn
Willingham, C. Eternal rectangle
MONOPOLIES
Neville, K. Franchise
Porter, W. S. Octopus marooned
Monroe, Lyle, pseud. See Heinlein, Robert
Anson
Monsarrat, Nicholas, 1910-
Last days of M.G.B. 1087
Saturday evening post (Periodical)
Saturday evening post stories, 1952
Monsieur Folantin. Huysmans, J. K.
Monsieur seeks a wife. Irwin, M. E. F.
M. Seguin's goat. Daudet, A.
The monster. Del Rey, L.
The monster. Van Vogt, A. E.
Monster of Blue-Hole Lake. Person, W. T.
MONSTERS
Anderson, P. The tinkler
Blackwood, A. The Wendigo
Bradbury, R. Beast from 20,000 fathoms
Bradbury, R. Fog horn
Broster, D. K. Crouching at the door
Del Rey, L. The monster
Doyle, Sir A. C. Horror of the heights
Ernst, P. Thing in the pond
Matheson, R. Born of man and woman
May, J. Dune roller
Merwin, S. Exit line
Peretz, I. L. The golem
Pratt, F. and Ruby, B. F. Thing in the
woods
Van Vogt, A. E. Vault of the beast
Wright, W. Washoe behemoth
See also Giants
The monsters. Sheckley, R.
MONT BLANC
Frison-Roche, R. Their kingdom
See also Alps, French
Montague, Charles Edward, 1867-1928
Action
Cerf, B. A. and Moriarty, H. C. eds.
Anthology of famous British stories
Greene, J. I. and Abell, E. eds. Stories
of sudden truth
Talbot, D. ed. Treasury of mountaineer-
ing stories
Montague, Margaret Prescott, 1878-
England to America
Cooper, A. C. ed. Modern short stories
First-prize stories, 1919-1954
MONTANA
Annixter, P. pseud. Last lobo
Johnson, D. M. Beyond the frontier
Johnson, D. M. Prairie kid
Montanelli, Indro, 1909-
Hero returns
This week magazine. This week's short-
short stories
MONTE CARLO. See Monaco—Monte
Carlo
Monte Saint Angelo. Miller, A.
Monte Verità. Du Maurier, D.

MONTEFIORE, SIR MOSES, 1784-1885
   Rappoport, S. Moses Montefiore
   Rappoport, S. Two great men
   Sforim, M. M. How the Czar fooled Montefiore

MONTEREY, CALIFORNIA. See California—Monterey

Montgomery the loyalest. Coblentz, C. C.

MONTREAL. See Canada—Montreal

Montross, Lois (Seyster) 1897-
   Day in New York
      Blodgett, H. W. ed. Story survey. 1953 ed.

Montross, Lynn, 1895-
   Nine ladies vs. fate
      Dachs, D. ed. Treasury of sports humor

Moodie, Sussannah (Strickland) 1803-1885
   Old Woodruff and his three wives
      Pacey, D. ed. Book of Canadian stories

Moody, Minnie (Hite) 1900-
   Ghost of General Jackson
      Jones, K. M. ed. New Confederate short stories

MOON
   Clarke, A. C. The sentinel
   Del Rey, L. Wings of night
   Elam, R. M. Lunar trap
   Ernst, P. "Nothing happens on the moon"
   Gallun, R. Z. Operation Pumice
   Godwin, F. Man in the moon
   Heinlein, R. A. Black pits of Luna
   Heinlein, R. A. Columbus was a dope
   Heinlein, R. A. Green hills of earth; 10 stories
   Heinlein, R. A. Man who sold the moon
   Kepler, J. Somnium
   Miller, W. M. No moon for me
   Norton, H. A. Man in the moon
   Phillips, A. M. Death of the moon
   Repton, H. From a private mad-house
   Reynolds, M. Man in the moon
   Robinson, F. M. Reluctant heroes
   Van Vogt, A. E. Defense
   Verne, J. Round the moon
      See also Science fiction

Moon artist. Keller, D. H.

Moon-face. London, J.

Moon is green. Leiber, F.

Moon lake. Welty, E.

Moon magic. Brenner, L.

Moon of delirium. James, D. L.

Moon tide. Michel, E.

Moonlight. Maupassant, G. de

Moonlight sonata. Woollcott, A.

Moonlit road. Bierce, A.

Moonscape. Waltari, M. T.

MOONSHINING. See Distilling, Illicit

Moonwalk. Fyfe, H. B.

Moore, Catherine Lucile, 1911-
   Black god's kiss
      Moore, C. L. Shambleau, and others
   Black god's shadow
      Moore, C. L. Shambleau, and others
   Black thirst
      Moore, C. L. Shambleau, and others
   The code
      Moore, C. L. Judgment night

Heir apparent
   Moore, C. L. Judgment night
Jirel meets magic
   Moore, C. L. Shambleau, and others
Judgment night
   Moore, C. L. Judgment night
No woman born
   Jenkins, W. F. ed. Great stories of science fiction
Paradise Street
   Moore, C. L. Judgment night
Promised land
   Moore, C. L. Judgment night
Scarlet dream
   Crossen, K. F. ed. Future tense
   Moore, C. L. Shambleau, and others
Shambleau
   Crossen, K. F. ed. Adventures in tomorrow
   Moore, C. L. Shambleau, and others
There shall be darkness
   Greenberg, M. ed. Journey to infinity
Tree of life
   Moore, C. L. Shambleau, and others
      See also Kuttner, H. jt. auth.

Moore, David E. 1923-
   Portrait
      American vanguard, 1953

Moore, George, 1852-1933
   Clerk's quest
      Cerf, B. A. and Moriarty, H. C. eds. Anthology of famous British stories

Moore, George M.
   Two for a ride
      Oberfirst, R. ed. 1954 anthology of best original short-shorts

Moore, Ina Skrifvars
   Family man
      Oberfirst, R. ed. 1952 anthology of best original short-shorts

Moore, John P.
   Beauty and the diamond ring
      Ford, N. A. and Faggett, H. L. eds. Best short stories by Afro-American writers (1925-1950)

Moore, Manning, 1914-
   Albert knows his place
      Wolfe, D. M. ed. Which grain will grow

Moore, Ward, 1903-
   Flying Dutchman
      Crossen, K. F. ed. Adventures in tomorrow
   Lot
      Best science-fiction stories: 1954
      Magazine of fantasy and science fiction. Best from Fantasy and science fiction; 3d ser.
   Peacebringer
      Conklin, G. ed. Big book of science fiction
   We the people
      Crossen, K. F. ed. Future tense

MOOSE
   Annixter, P. pseud. Kadiak
   Roberts, Sir C. G. D. Calling of the lop-horned bull
   Roberts, Sir C. G. D. Monarch of Park Barren

Moose boy. Macfarlan, A. A.

Morand, Paul, 1888-
Catalonian night
Dupee, F. W. ed. Great French short novels
Moravia, Alberto, pseud. See Pincherle, Alberto
More, Sir Thomas, 1478-1535
Utopia
Derleth, A. W. ed. Beyond time & space
More alarms at night. Thurber, J.
More like sisters. Winslow, T. S.
More than skin deep. Pratt, F. and De Camp, L. S.
Moreau, Louis, 1914-
The face
Southern review. Anthology of stories from the Southern review
Morehouse, Kathleen (Moore)
With the fog
Blodgett, H. W. ed. Story survey. 1953 ed.
Morella. Poe, E. A.
MORGAN, JOHN HUNT, 1825-1864
West, J. Battle of Finney's Ford
Morland, Nigel, 1905-
Flowers for an angel
Mystery writer's of America, inc. Crooks' tour
Queen, E. pseud. ed. Queen's awards: 6th ser.
Morley, Christopher Darlington, 1890-
The arrow
Burrell, J. A. and Cerf, B. A. eds. Anthology of American stories
Home again
Brentano, F. ed. The word lives on
Morlvera. Munro, H. H.
Morning, a week before the crime. Lincoln, V. E.
Morning I went to buy the horseshoe. Knox, J.
Morning star. Carr, R. S.
Morning star. Gonzalez, N. V. M.
Morning sun. Deasy, M.
Morning wishes. Lincoln, V. E.
Moroso, John Antonio, 1874-
Tierney meets a millionaire
American boy (Periodical) American boy anthology
MORPHINE, OVERDOSE OF
Porter, W. S. At arms with Morpheus
Morrill, George P.
One for O'Brien
Argosy (Periodical) Argosy Book of sea stories
Morris, Gouverneur, 1876-1947
Back there in the grass
Pratt, F. ed. World of wonder
Morrison, Arthur, 1863-1947
That brute Simmons
Cerf, B. A. and Moriarty, H. C. eds. Anthology of famous British stories
Morrison, Jack, 1922-
Harvest
Stanford short stories, 1952
Patchouly
Stanford short stories, 1951

Morrison, William, pseud. See Samachson, Joseph
Morrison, William Shepherd
The Sack
Heinlein, R. A. ed. Tomorrow, the stars
Morriss, Mack
Courtesy of the road
Collier's, the national weekly. Collier's best
MORTGAGES
Graham, M. C. Face of the poor
Mortimer. Van Doren, M.
MOSCOW. See Russia—Moscow
MOSCOW. UNIVERSITY
Chekhov, A. P. Good news
Moscow hypocrites. Chekhov, A. P.
Moseley, Howard, 1921-
Blood is a bright shadow
American vanguard, 1950
MOSES
Coolidge, O. E. First-born
Frischman, D. Sinai
Hurston, Z. N. Escape from Pharaoh
Hurston, Z. N. The tablets of the law
Moses Montefiore. Rappoport, S.
Mosquitoes of Arkansas. Weeks, R.
Most dangerous man in the world. Dunsany, E. J. M. D. P. 18th baron
Most unusual season. Temple, W. H.
Motet for two voices. La Farge, C.
Mother. Farmer, P. J.
A **mother.** Hedenstjerna, A. von
The **mother.** McLaverty, M.
The **mother.** Maugham, W. S.
The **mother.** Wiechert, E.
Mother and daughter. Lawrence, D. H.
Mother and son. Darwick, R.
Mother and son. Maupassant, G. de
Mother Earth. Asimov, I.
Mother of Angela Hogan. Norris, K. T.
MOTHERS
Baro, G. Angry lions, lazy lions
Betts, D. Very old are beautiful
Edginton, H. M. Purple and fine linen
Fisher, D. F. C. As ye sow—
Freeman, M. E. W. Revolt of "Mother"
Fremantle, A. J. ed. Mothers; 18 stories
Hale, N. No one my grief can tell
Harte, B. Prosper's "Old mother"
Horwitz, J. Old woman
Jackson, C. R. Parting at morning
McLaverty, M. The mother
Maupassant, G. de. La Mère Sauvage
Rugel, M. The flower
Taylor, E. "Taking mother out"
Ungar, F. ed. To mother with love; 18 stories
Winslow, T. S. Grandma
Yaffe, J. Mom in the spring

See also Grandmothers; Mothers and daughters; Mothers and sons; Mothers-in-law

MOTHERS AND DAUGHTERS
Albrizio, G. The bereft

MOTHERS AND DAUGHTERS—*Cont.*
  Auchincloss, L. Finish, good lady
  Barker, A. L. Domini
  Bowen, E. Coming home
  Cable, G. W. Madame Delphine
  Calisher, H. Middle drawer
  De Meyer, J. Boy crazy
  Johnson, J. W. Mother's story
  Karmel, I. Fru Holm
  La Farge, O. No, my darling daughter
  McDowell, D. Good-by, Debbie
  Reid, C. B. Yellow leaf
  Stewart, R. The promise
  Taber, G. B. Letter to the Dean
  Verga, G. Home tragedy
  Waugh, A. Wed, my darling daughter
  Winslow, T. S. More like sisters
MOTHERS AND SONS
  Auchincloss, L. Greg's peg
  Barrie, Sir J. M. bart. Making of a
    minister
  Beck, W. Verdict of innocence
  Beer, T. Tact
  Calisher, H. In Greenwich there are many
    gravelled walks
  Callaghan, M. All the years of her life
  Chidester, A. Mrs Ketting and Clark
    Gable
  Cicellis, K. Twisted branch
  Crane, S. George's mother
  Darwick, R. Mother and son
  De La Mare, W. J. Physic
  Froscher, W. Death in the family
  Gide, A. P. G. My mother
  Gordimer, N. Umbilical cord
  Hardy, T. Son's veto
  Heathcott, M. Neil's girl
  Keller, G. Regula Amrain and her young-
    est son
  Lawrence, D. H. Lovely lady
  Lull, R. No room in her heart
  Maugham, W. S. The mother
  Miller, A. D. Plum pudding and mince
    pie
  O'Donovan, M. Man of the house
  Taylor, E. Red-letter day
  Ungar, F. ed. To mother with love; 18
    stories
  Watson, J. His mother's sermon
  Waugh, E. Winner takes all
  Wells, H. G. Little mother up the
    Mörderberg
  Wright, J. E. Pay night
  Wyckoff, J. The door between
Mother's Christmas present. Eggleston,
  M. W.
MOTHERS-IN-LAW
  Harvey, W. F. Atmospherics
  Horwitz, J. The visitor
  O'Donovan, M. Sense of responsibility
  Seager, A. Sacrament
  Verga, G. She-wolf
Mother's letter. Balzac, H. de
Mother's meeting. Ready, W. B.
Mothers of the north. Roberts, Sir C. G. D.
Mother's story. Johnson, J. W.
Mother's tale. Agee, J.
MOTHS
  Kantor, M. Yea, he did fly
Moti Guj—mutineer. Kipling, R.

Motion of forgetfulness is slow. Eaton,
  C. E.
MOTION PICTURE ACTRESSES. See
  Moving picture actors and actresses
MOTION PICTURES. See Moving pic-
  tures
Motive goes round and round. Brown, F.
MOTOR BOATS. See Motorboats
MOTOR BUSES
  Asch, N. Inland, western sea
  Forster, E. M. Celestial omnibus
  Gill, B. Night bus to Atlanta
  Portor, L. S. Spendthrifts
  Sandoz, M. Lost school bus
  Spilo, R. Big Ed
MOTOR CARS. See Automobiles
MOTOR CYCLES. See Motorcycles
MOTORBOATS
  Douglas, J. S. Water broncs
  Sherman, H. M. Porky, the outboarder
  Vetter, M. M. Captain Kit
    See also Boats and boating
MOTORCYCLES
  Aiken, C. P. Pair of Vikings
  Jackson, R. B. Fly away home
  Rooney, F. Cyclists' raid
Mott, Frank Luther, 1886-
  Phantom flivver
    Saturday evening post (Periodical)
      Saturday evening post stories, 1950
MOUNT EVEREST. See Everest, Mount
The mountain. Ervine, St J. G.
MOUNTAIN CLIMBING. See Mountain-
  eering
MOUNTAIN GOATS. See Rocky Moun-
  tain goats
MOUNTAIN LIONS. See Pumas
Mountain madness. Hopkinson, H. T.
Mountain summer. Ballard, J. C.
Mountain victory. Faulkner, W.
**MOUNTAIN WHITES (SOUTHERN
  STATES)**
  Blackburn, E. R. Missed train
  Connell, E. S. I came from yonder moun-
    tain
  Fox, J. Knight of the Cumberland
  Harris, G. W. Sut Lovingood; 8 stories
  Morehouse, K. M. With the fog
  Porter, W. S. Blackjack bargainer
  Porter, W. S. Whirligig of life
  Smith, E. V. Prelude
  Still, J. Job's tears
  Still, J. Master time
  Strong, P. N. Man on Stormrift Mountain
  Stuart, J. Clearing in the sky & other sto-
    ries; 21 stories
    See also Dialect stories—Mountain
    Whites (Southern States)
The mountaineer. Tucker, W.
MOUNTAINEERING
  Du Maurier, D. Monte Verità
  Kaplan, A. H. Danger wears two faces
  Lavender, D. S. High victory
  Montague, C. E. Action
  Talbot, D. ed. Treasury of mountaineer-
    ing stories; 19 stories

Muir, John, 1838-1914
Adventure with a dog
Bloch, M. ed. Favorite dog stories
An adventure with a dog and a glacier
Andrews, R. C. ed. My favorite stories
of the great outdoors
Mujina. Hearn, L.
Mukerji, Dhan Gopal, 1890-1936
Elephant adventure
Fenner, P. R. comp. Elephants, ele-
phants, elephants
Kari the elephant
Fenner, P. R. comp. Elephants, ele-
phants, elephants
Mulatto flair. Spencer, G.
MULATTOES
Cable, G. W. Madame Delphine
Mule in the yard. Faulkner, W.
Mule tracks. Newton, D. B.
MULES. See Asses and mules
Mulhoffer, Dorothy Barrie
Last year
Hathaway, B. and Sessions, J. A. eds.
Writers for tomorrow. 2d ser.
Muller, Charles G.
Hat trick
Herzberg, M. J. comp. Treasure chest
of sport stories
Owen, F. ed. Teen-age winter sports
stories
Müller with an umlaut. McNulty, J.
Mummery, Albert Frederick, 1855-1895
The Matterhorn
Talbot, D. ed. Treasury of mountaineer-
ing stories
MUMMIES
Brod, M. Death is a passing weakness
Mummy to the rescue. Wilson, A.
Munby, Alan Noel Latimer
Alabaster hand
Munby, A. N. L. Alabaster hand, and
other ghost stories
Christmas game
Munby, A. N. L. Alabaster hand, and
other ghost stories
Devil's autograph
Munby, A. N. L. Alabaster hand, and
other ghost stories
Encounter in the mist
Munby, A. N. L. Alabaster hand, and
other ghost stories
Four-poster
Munby, A. N. L. Alabaster hand, and
other ghost stories
Herodes redivivus
Munby, A. N. L. Alabaster hand, and
other ghost stories
The inscription
Munby, A. N. L. Alabaster hand, and
other ghost stories
The lectern
Munby, A. N. L. Alabaster hand, and
other ghost stories
Negro's head
Munby, A. N. L. Alabaster hand, and
other ghost stories
Number seventy-nine
Munby, A. N. L. Alabaster hand, and
other ghost stories

Topley Place sale
Munby, A. N. L. Alabaster hand, and
other ghost stories
Tregannet book of hours
Munby, A. N. L. Alabaster hand, and
other ghost stories
Tudor chimney
Munby, A. N. L. Alabaster hand, and
other ghost stories
White sack
Munby, A. N. L. Alabaster hand, and
other ghost stories
MUNCHAUSEN
Adventure. See Martin, J. Adventure of
Baron Munchausen
MUNICIPAL EMPLOYEES. See Civil
service
Municipal report. Porter, W. S.
MUNICIPALITIES. See Cities and towns
Munie the bird dealer. Kilbak, M.
Munro, Hector Hugh, 1870-1916
Achievement of the cat
Munro, H. H. Short stories of Saki
Adrian
Munro, H. H. Short stories of Saki
The background
Munro, H. H. Short stories of Saki
The bag
Munro, H. H. Short stories of Saki
Bertie's Christmas Eve
Munro, H. H. Short stories of Saki
Birds on the western front
Munro, H. H. Short stories of Saki
Blind spot
Munro, H. H. Short stories of Saki
Blood-feud of Toad-Water
Munro, H. H. Short stories of Saki
Boar-pig
Munro, H. H. Short stories of Saki
Bread and Butter miss
Munro, H. H. Short stories of Saki
The Brogue
Munro, H. H. Short stories of Saki
The bull
Munro, H. H. Short stories of Saki
Byzantine omelette
Munro, H. H. Short stories of Saki
Canossa
Munro, H. H. Short stories of Saki
The Chaplet
Munro, H. H. Short stories of Saki
Clovis on parental responsibilities
Munro, H. H. Short stories of Saki
Clovis on the alleged romance of business
Munro, H. H. Short stories of Saki
The cobweb
Munro, H. H. Short stories of Saki
Comments of Moung Ka
Munro, H. H. Short stories of Saki
Cousin Teresa
Munro, H. H. Short stories of Saki
Cross currents
Munro, H. H. Short stories of Saki
Cupboard of the yesterdays
Munro, H. H. Short stories of Saki
Defensive diamond
Munro, H. H. Short stories of Saki
Disappearance of Crispina Umberleigh
Munro, H. H. Short stories of Saki
"Down pens"
Munro, H. H. Short stories of Saki
The dreamer
Munro, H. H. Short stories of Saki

Munro, Hector H.—*Continued*

Dusk
  Munro, H. H. Short stories of Saki
Easter egg
  Munro, H. H. Short stories of Saki
The elk
  Munro, H. H. Short stories of Saki
Esmé
  Munro, H. H. Short stories of Saki
Excepting Mrs Pentherby
  Munro, H. H. Short stories of Saki
Fate
  Munro, H. H. Short stories of Saki
Feast of Nemesis
  Munro, H. H. Short stories of Saki
Filboid Studge, the story of a mouse that
    helped
  Munro, H. H. Short stories of Saki
For the duration of the war
  Munro, H. H. Short stories of Saki
Forbidden buzzards
  Munro, H. H. Short stories of Saki
Forewarned
  Munro, H. H. Short stories of Saki
Fur
  Munro, H. H. Short stories of Saki
Gabriel-Ernest
  Conklin, G. and Conklin, L. T. eds.
    Supernatural reader
  Munro, H. H. Short stories of Saki
Gala programme
  Munro, H. H. Short stories of Saki
The guests
  Munro, H. H. Short stories of Saki
The hedgehog
  Munro, H. H. Short stories of Saki
The hen
  Munro, H. H. Short stories of Saki
Hermann the Irascible—A story of the
    Great Weep
  Munro, H. H. Short stories of Saki
Holiday task
  Munro, H. H. Short stories of Saki
Hounds of Fate
  Munro, H. H. Short stories of Saki
Hyacinth
  Munro, H. H. Short stories of Saki
Image of the Lost Soul
  Munro, H. H. Short stories of Saki
Infernal Parliament
  Munro, H. H. Short stories of Saki
Innocence of Reginald
  Munro, H. H. Short stories of Saki
The interlopers
  Munro, H. H. Short stories of Saki
Jesting of Arlington Stringham
  Munro, H. H. Short stories of Saki
Judkin of the parcels
  Munro, H. H. Short stories of Saki
Laura
  Munro, H. H. Short stories of Saki
Lost sanjak
  Munro, H. H. Short stories of Saki
Louis
  Munro, H. H. Short stories of Saki
Louise
  Munro, H. H. Short stories of Saki
The lull
  Munro, H. H. Short stories of Saki
Lumber-room
  Munro, H. H. Short stories of Saki
Mappined life
  Munro, H. H. Short stories of Saki

Mark
  Munro, H. H. Short stories of Saki
Match-maker
  Munro, H. H. Short stories of Saki
Matter of sentiment
  Munro, H. H. Short stories of Saki
"Ministers of Grace"
  Munro, H. H. Short stories of Saki
Mrs Packletides tiger
  Blodgett, H. W. ed. Story survey. 1953
    ed.
  Cerf, B. A. and Moriarty, H. C. eds.
    Anthology of famous British stories
  Dachs, D. ed. Treasury of sports humor
  Munro, H. H. Short stories of Saki
Morlvera
  Munro, H. H. Short stories of Saki
The mouse
  Munro, H. H. Short stories of Saki
Music on the hill
  Munro, H. H. Short stories of Saki
Name-day
  Munro, H. H. Short stories of Saki
Occasional garden
  Munro, H. H. Short stories of Saki
Old town of Pskoff
  Munro, H. H. Short stories of Saki
On approval
  Munro, H. H. Short stories of Saki
Open window
  Bogorad, S. N. and Trevithick, J. eds.
    College miscellany
  Carrington, H. ed. Week-end book of
    ghost stories
  Christ, H. I. and Shostak, J. eds. Short
    stories
  Davenport, B. ed. Tales to be told in
    the dark
  Munro, H. H. Short stories of Saki
  Shaw, H. and Bement, D. Reading the
    short story
The oversight
  Munro, H. H. Short stories of Saki
Peace of Mowsle Barton
  Munro, H. H. Short stories of Saki
Peace offering
  Munro, H. H. Short stories of Saki
The penance
  Munro, H. H. Short stories of Saki
Phantom luncheon
  Munro, H. H. Short stories of Saki
Philanthropist and the happy cat
  Munro, H. H. Short stories of Saki
Purple of the Balkan Kings
  Munro, H. H. Short stories of Saki
Quail seed
  Munro, H. H. Short stories of Saki
The quest
  Munro, H. H. Short stories of Saki
Quince tree
  Munro, H. H. Short stories of Saki
The Recessional
  Munro, H. H. Short stories of Saki
Reginald
  Munro, H. H. Short stories of Saki
Reginald at the Carlton
  Munro, H. H. Short stories of Saki
Reginald at the theatre
  Munro, H. H. Short stories of Saki
Reginald in Russia
  Munro, H. H. Short stories of Saki
Reginald on besetting sins
  Munro, H. H. Short stories of Saki

Munro, Hector H.—*Continued*

Reginald on Christmas presents
  Munro, H. H. Short stories of Saki
Reginald on house-parties
  Munro, H. H. Short stories of Saki
Reginald on tariffs
  Munro, H. H. Short stories of Saki
Reginald on the Academy
  Munro, H. H. Short stories of Saki
Reginald on worries
  Munro, H. H. Short stories of Saki
Reginald's choir treat
  Munro, H. H. Short stories of Saki
Reginald's Christmas revel
  Munro, H. H. Short stories of Saki
Reginald's drama
  Munro, H. H. Short stories of Saki
Reginald's peace poem
  Munro, H. H. Short stories of Saki
Reginald's Rubaiyat
  Munro, H. H. Short stories of Saki
Remoulding of Groby Lington
  Munro, H. H. Short stories of Saki
Reticence of Lady Anne
  Munro, H. H. Short stories of Saki
The romancers
  Munro, H. H. Short stories of Saki
Saint and the Goblin
  Munro, H. H. Short stories of Saki
Schartz-Metterklume method
  Munro, H. H. Short stories of Saki
Secret sin of Septimus Brope
  Munro, H. H. Short stories of Saki
Seven cream jugs
  Munro, H. H. Short stories of Saki
Seventh pullet
  Munro, H. H. Short stories of Saki
Sex that doesn't shop
  Munro, H. H. Short stories of Saki
She-wolf
  Munro, H. H. Short stories of Saki
The sheep
  Munro, H. H. Short stories of Saki
Shock tactics
  Munro, H. H. Short stories of Saki
Soul of Laploshka
  Munro, H. H. Short stories of Saki
Square egg
  Munro, H. H. Short stories of Saki
Sredni Vashtar
  Davenport, B. ed. Tales to be told in the dark
  Munro, H. H. Short stories of Saki
The stake
  Munro, H. H. Short stories of Saki
Stalled ox
  Munro, H. H. Short stories of Saki
Stampeding of Lady Bastable
  Munro, H. H. Short stories of Saki
Story of St Vespaluus
  Munro, H. H. Short stories of Saki
Story-teller
  Munro, H. H. Short stories of Saki
  Schramm, W. L. ed. Great short stories
The strategist
  Munro, H. H. Short stories of Saki
Talking-out of Tarrington
  Munro, H. H. Short stories of Saki
Tea
  Munro, H. H. Short stories of Saki
The threat
  Munro, H. H. Short stories of Saki

Tobermory
  Munro, H. H. Short stories of Saki
Touch of realism
  Munro, H. H. Short stories of Saki
Toys of peace
  Munro, H. H. Short stories of Saki
Treasure-ship
  Munro, H. H. Short stories of Saki
Unkindest blow
  Munro, H. H. Short stories of Saki
Unrest-cure
  Munro, H. H. Short stories of Saki
Way to the dairy
  Munro, H. H. Short stories of Saki
Wolves of Cernogratz
  Munro, H. H. Short stories of Saki
Wratislav
  Munro, H. H. Short stories of Saki
Yarkand manner
  Munro, H. H. Short stories of Saki
Young Turkish catastrophe
  Munro, H. H. Short stories of Saki

MURALS. See Paintings

The **murder.** Steinbeck, J.

Murder and the south wind. Rinehart, M. R.

Murder at City Hall. Carr, A. H. Z.

Murder at eleven. Milne, A. A.

Murder for two. Kirch, J. A.

Murder in the Fishing Cat. Millay, E. St V.

MURDER STORIES

Akutagawa, R. In a grove
Bergengruen, W. Concerning muskets
Blish, J. Beanstalk
Bradbury, R. Fruit at the bottom of the bowl
Brown, F. Voice behind him
Buckingham, N. Snake-eyes!!
Burke, T. Hands of Mr Ottermole
Clark, A. A. G. Amazing lady
Clemens, S. L. Latest sensation (II)
Cobb, I. S. Occurrence up a side street
Cockburn, C. Total recall
Collier, J. Another American tragedy
Collier, J. Back for Christmas
Collier, J. Midnight blue
Collier, J. Touch of nutmeg makes it
Collier, J. Wet Saturday
Connelly, M. C. Coroner's inquest
Dahl, R. Lamb to the slaughter
De La Mare, W. J. Ideal craftsman
De La Mare, W. J. Missing
Dickens, C. Captain Murderer
Ekbergh, I. D. Pink Ballerina
Ellin, S. Orderly world of Mr Appleby
Faulkner, W. Hand upon the waters
Faulkner, W. The hound
Faulkner, W. Tomorrow
Forester, C. S. Bower of roses
Gilmour, W. Danny Hagan's blind spot
Glaspell, S. Jury of her peers
Gordon, A. Alchemist's secret
Goyen, W. White rooster
Grau, S. A. Way of a man
Hall, J. B. Estate and trespass
Harvey, W. F. Vicar's web
Hauptmann, G. J. R. Flagman Thiel
Hawthorne, N. Mr Higginbotham's catastrophe
Hergesheimer, J. Wild oranges
Hume, S. T. Shake hands with a murderer
Huxley, A. L. Gioconda smile

Mystery. Claudy, C. H.

MYSTERY AND DETECTIVE STORIES

Best detective stories of the year—1950-1954; 61 stories
Blochman, L. G. Diagnosis: homicide; 8 stories
Bond, R. T. ed. Handbook for poisoners; 12 stories
Brown, F. Daymare
Brown, F. Mostly murder; 18 stories
Canning, V. The smuggler
Carr, J. D. Footprint in the sky
Charteris, L. Second Saint omnibus; 10 stories
Chesterton, G. K. Invisible man
Curtis, K. Drumbeaters Island
Davis, R. H. In the fog
Derleth, A. W. Memoirs of Solar Pons; 11 stories
Derleth, A. W. Three problems for Solar Pons; 3 stories
Furman, A. L. ed. Everygirls mystery stories; 10 stories
Futrelle, J. Problem of Cell 13
Green, A. K. The doctor, his wife, and the clock
Harrison, H. S. Miss Hinch
Kuttner, H. Private eye
MacDonald, P. Something to hide; 6 stories
Macfarlan, A. A. Loon laughs
Milne, A. A. Murder at eleven
Mystery Writers of America, inc. Butcher, baker, murder-maker; 20 stories
Mystery Writers of America, inc. Crooks' tour; 22 stories
Mystery Writers of America, inc. Maiden murders; 20 stories
Mystery Writers of America, inc. 20 great tales of murder; 19 stories
Peattie, D. C. and Peattie, L. R. Mystery in Four-and-a-Half Street
Queen, E. pseud. Murder without clues
Queen, E. pseud. ed. Queen's awards: 5th-9th ser; 76 stories
Queen, E. pseud. Queen's Bureau of Investigation; 18 stories
Queen, E. pseud. Sound of blackmail
Quentin, P. pseud. This looks like murder
Quentin, P. pseud. Town blonde, country blonde
White, W. A. P. ed. Four-&-twenty bloodhounds; 25 stories
Woolrich, C. Wait for me downstairs

Canada

Erskine, L. Y. Mystery at Moon Lake

England

Carr, J. D. The third bullet, and other stories; 7 stories
Chesterton, G. K. Father Brown omnibus; 51 stories
Chesterton, G. K. Hammer of God
Christie, A. M. Under dog, and other stories; 9 stories
Dickens, C. Hunted down
Doyle, Sir A. C. Adventure of the speckled band
Doyle, Sir A. C. Adventures of Sherlock Holmes; 50 stories
Doyle, Sir A. C. Book of Sherlock Holmes; 6 stories

Doyle, A. C. and Carr, J. D. Exploits of Sherlock Holmes; 12 stories
Dunsany, E. J. M. D. P. 18th baron. Two bottles of relish
Harvey, W. F. The lake
Harvey, W. F. Mishandled

France

LeBlanc, M. Invisible prisoner
Poe, E. A. Murders in the Rue Morgue
Poe, E. A. Mystery of Marie Roget
Poe, E. A. Purloined letter
Porter, W. S. Tracked to doom

United States

Gardner, E. S. Case of the irate witness
Poe, E. A. The gold-bug
Poe, E. A. "Thou art the man"
Porter, W. S. Adventures of Shamrock Jolnes
Porter, W. S. The sleuths
Porter, W. S. Theory and the hound
Porter, W. S. Tictocq
Queen, E. pseud. Calendar of crime; 12 stories
Rinehart, M. R. Burned chair
Rinehart, M. R. Frightened wife
Rinehart, M. R. Murder and the south wind
Stout, R. Triple jeopardy; 3 stories
Mystery at Moon Lake. Erskine, L. Y.
Mystery in Four-and-a-Half Street. Peattie, D. C. and Peattie, L. R.
Mystery of heroism. Crane, S.
Mystery of Kela Ouai. Canning, V.
Mystery of Marie Roget. Poe, E. A.
Mystery of Mike. Erskine, L. Y.
Mystery of the personal ad. Stribling, T. S.
Mystery of the Savage sump. Davis, S. P.
Mystery play. Verga, G.

MYSTICISM

Hesse, H. Within and without
Tolstoi, A. N. Graf. Fusty Devil
Myth of mankind. Lagerkvist, P. F.

MYTHICAL ANIMALS. See Animals, Mythical

MYTHOLOGY

Beaconsfield, B. D. 1st earl of. Ixion in heaven
See also Legends and folk tales

N

N.E.S.P.D.I.P. Parker, J. R.
N.R.A. for a dollar. Cooke, A. A.
The **NRACP.** Elliott, G. P.
Nadia Devereux. Eichrodt, J.
Nadir, Isaac Moishe, 1885-1943
Man who slept through the end of the world
Howe, I. and Greenberg, E. eds. Treasury of Yiddish stories
My first deposit
Ausubel, N. ed. Treasury of Jewish humor
My first love
Howe, I. and Greenberg, E. eds. Treasury of Yiddish stories

NEGROES—*Continued*

Boyd, J. Bloodhound
Boyd, J. Shiftless
Bradbury, R. Other feet
Buckingham, N. Death stalked the spring-stand!
Buckingham, N. Remember. . .
Caldwell, E. Big Buck
Caldwell, E. Blue Boy
Caldwell, E. Candy-Man Beechum
Caldwell, E. End of Christy Tucker
Caldwell, E. Kneel to the rising sun
Caldwell, E. Knife to cut corn bread with
Caldwell, E. Nine dollars' worth of mumble
Caldwell, E. People v. Abe Lathan, colored
Caldwell, E. Runaway
Conrad, J. The nigger of the Narcissus
Crane, S. The knife
Culver, M. Black water blues
Doughty, LeG. S. The firebird
Dreer, H. ed. American literature by Negro authors; 3 stories
Elliott, G. P. The NRACP
Faulkner, W. Dry September
Faulkner, W. That evening sun
Field, S. S. Good-by to Cap'm John
Foote, S. Ride out
Ford, N. A. and Faggett, H. L. eds. Best short stories by Afro-American writers; 40 stories
Gibbs, A. The test
Godchaux, E. Horn that called Bambine
Gordon, C. Her quaint honour
Grau, S. A. Black prince
Grau, S. A. Miss Yellow Eyes
Grau, S. A. Way of a man
Grau, S. A. White girl, fine girl
Haardt, S. P. Little white girl
Harris, J. C. Free Joe and the rest of the world
Howe, D. White kitten
Hughes, L. Laughing to keep from crying; 24 stories
Justice, D. The lady
Kidd, H. L. Low road go down
Laidlaw, C. Little black boys
Lincoln, V. E. In the garden
Melville, H. Benito Cereno
Noland, F. The whipping
Paul, L. No more trouble for Jedwick
Phillips, T. H. Shadow of an arm
Porter, W. S. Municipal report
Radford, M. Wm. Crane
Reynolds, M. and Brown, F. Dark interlude
Rice, A. C. H. Hoodooed
Sabin, E. L. Freedom
Schulberg, B. W. The one he called Winnie
Sellers, M. Something gay and foolish
Steele, W. F. Sooth
Taylor, P. H. What you hear from 'em?
Warren, R. P. Blackberry winter
Welty, E. Curtain of green
Welty, E. Keela, the outcast Indian maiden
Welty, E. Livvie
Welty, E. Livvie is back
Welty, E. Worn path

Willingham, C. Afternoon sun
Willingham, C. Excitement in Ergo
See also Slavery

Education
Calisher, H. Wreath for Miss Totten

NEGROES AS SERVANTS
Caldwell, E. The picture
Caldwell, E. Squire Dinwiddy
Faulkner, W. That evening sun
Johnson, J. W. The author
Lewis, E. G. Portrait
Steele, W. D. Can't cross Jordan by myself
Taylor, P. H. Bad dreams
Taylor, P. H. Cookie
Taylor, P. H. Wife of Nashville
See also Servants

Negro's head. Munby, A. N. L.

Neighbor Rosicky. Cather, W. S.

NEIGHBORS
Bojer, J. A letter to Klaus Brock
Canine, W. The clematis
Fitzgerald, F. S. K. Baby party
Gold, H. The witch
Grau, S. A. Girl with the flaxen hair
Munro, H. H. Blood-feud of Toad-Water
Rawlings, C. A. Flash of lightning

Neighbour Rosicky. Cather, W. S.

Neikirk, Mabel E.
Oscar on roller skates
Story parade (Periodical) Adventure stories
Oscar, the trained seal
Fenner, P. R. comp. Giggle box

Neil MacAdam. Maugham, W. S.

Ne'ilah in Gehenna. Peretz, I. L.

Neil's girl. Heathcott, M.

Neiman, Samuel, 1911-
Day papa died
American vanguard, 1950
Wine of one day
American vanguard, 1952

Neisloss, Myron, 1929-
The picnic
Wolfe, D. M. ed. Which grain will grow

Nelson, Alan, 1911-
Narapoia
Magazine of fantasy and science fiction. Best from Fantasy and science fiction; [1st] ser.

Nelson, Edna Deu Pree
St George ball
Story (Periodical) Story; no. 1

NELSON, HORATIO NELSON, VIS-COUNT, 1758-1805
Melville, H. Billy Budd, foretopman

Nemerov, Howard, and Johnson, William R.
Exchange of men
Greene, J. I. and Abell, E. eds. Stories of sudden truth

The nemesis. Stafford, J.

Nemesis and the candy man. Porter, W. S.

Ne-nu-ka. Davis, R.

Neo-Hebrew poet. Zangwill, I.

NEPHEWS
Collier, J. Green thoughts
See also Uncles

NEPTUNE (PLANET)
Harris, C. W. and Breuer, M. J. Baby on Neptune
NERVOUS BREAKDOWN. See Neurasthenia
Nesbit, Edith. See Bland, Edith (Nesbit)
Nests in a stone image. Goyen, W.
Net nemesis. Coombs, C. I.
Net profit. Spiller, B. L.
NETHERLANDS

Amsterdam
Charteris, L. Amsterdam: The angel's eye
NETHERLANDS INDIES. See Dutch East Indies
NEURASTHENIA
Ketcham, P. The mistake
Moore, D. E. Portrait
Priestley, J. B. The statues
Purcell, D. Rider of the avalanche
White, A. Moment of truth
NEUROSES
Cather, W. S. Paul's case
NEUROTICS. See Neuroses
NEVADA
Clark, W. Van T. Indian well
Clark, W. Van T. Wind and the snow of winter
NEVADA
19th century
Emrich, D. ed. Comstock bonanza; 21 stories
Ranch life
See Ranch life—Nevada
Washoe County
Browne, J. R. Peep at Washoe
Wright, W. Washoe behemoth
Never a dull moment. Taber, G. B.
Never anything that fades. Steele, W. D.
Never bet the devil your head. Poe, E. A.
Never come mourning. Winchell, P.
Never room with a couple. Hughes, L.
Never trust a lady. Canning, V.
Never trust a woman. Newhouse, E.
Never trust the obvious. Chute, V.
Never underestimate. . . Waldo, E. H.
Nevermore without end. Sansom, W.
Neville, Kris
Bettyann
Healy, R. J. ed. New tales of space and time
Sloane, W. M. ed. Stories for tomorrow
Cold war
Astounding science fiction (Periodical) Astounding science fiction anthology
Franchise
Sloane, W. M. ed. Stories for tomorrow
Hold back tomorrow
Bleiler, E. F. and Dikty, T. E. eds. Imagination unlimited
Old Man Henderson
Magazine of fantasy and science fiction. Best from Fantasy and science fiction; [1st] ser.
Underground movement
Merril, J. ed. Beyond human ken

New accelerator. Wells, H. G.
New advocate. Kafka, F.
New Atlantis. Bacon, F. viscount St Albans
New babes in old woods. Applegarth, M. T.
New beau. Murrie, P.
NEW BRUNSWICK. See Canada—New Brunswick
New cabin. Caldwell, E.
NEW CALEDONIA
Russell, J. Fourth man
New dress. Woolf, V. S.
NEW ENGLAND

17th century
Butterworth, H. My grandmother's grandmother's Christmas candle
Hawthorne, N. Endicott and the Red Cross
19th century
Jewett, S. O. Courting of Sister Wisby
NEW ENGLAND DIALECT. See Dialect stories—New England
NEW ENGLAND FARM LIFE. See Farm life—New England
New England nun. Freeman, M. E. W.
NEW FRANCE. See Canada
New girl. Van Doren, M.
NEW GUINEA
Cave, H. B. Peril of the river
Michener, J. A. The fossickers
Ullman, J. R. Am I blue?
New Guinea interlude. Valbor, K.
NEW HAMPSHIRE
Benét, S. V. Devil and Daniel Webster
Slosson, A. T. Fishin' Jimmy
New hat. Swinbank, G.
New house. Bowen, E.
New kid. Heyert, M.
NEW ORLEANS. See Louisiana—New Orleans
New police chief. Shneur, Z.
New reality. Harness, C. L.
New ritual. Seabright, I.
New shoes. Berry, J.
New suit. O'Flaherty, L.
New villa. Chekhov, A. P.
NEW YEAR
Bergengruen, W. Old Hussar
De Vries, P. Open house
Herbert, F. H. We were just having fun
Jackson, C. R. Boy who ran away
Mannix, E. New Year for Juicy
New Year for Juicy. Mannix, E.
New Year's Day. Newhouse, E.
NEW YEAR'S EVE. See New Year
New Year's Eve confession. Sudermann, H.
New York. Horwitz, J.
NEW YORK (CITY)
Johnson, R. B. Far below
19th century
Bunner, H. C. Story of a New York house
James, H. Washington Square

Not a soul will come along. Parsons, E.
Not blotted. Claudy, C. H.
Not by bread alone. Benson, T.
Not final! Asimov, I.
Not fit for children. Smith, E. E.
Not for psychologists. Sykes, C.
Not my story. Walsh, M.
Not only dead men. Van Vogt, A. E.
Not quite Martin. Wilson, L.
Not that kind of a deal. Brookhouser, F.
Not to be opened. Young, R. F.
Not what she pretended. Madden, H. T.
Not with a bang. Knight, D.
Not with our fathers. Rothberg, A. A.

NOTARIES
Clemens, S. L. Concerning notaries

NOTARY PUBLICS. See Notaries

Note on the literary life. Schulberg, B. W.

Notes from underground. Dostoevskiĭ, F. M.

Nothing can change it. Cooke, C.

Nothing ever breaks except the heart. Boyle, K.

Nothing happens in Brooklyn. Runyon, D.

"Nothing happens on the moon." Ernst, P.

Nothing new. O'Rourke, F.

Nothing overwhelms Giuseppe. Blue, E.

Nothing Sirius. Brown, F.

Nourse, Alan Edward
High threshold
Conklin, G. ed. Omnibus of science fiction
Nightmare brother
Sloane, W. M. ed. Space, space, space
Tiger by the tail
Conklin, G. ed. Science-fiction adventures in dimension
Galaxy science fiction magazine. Second Galaxy reader of science fiction

Novás Calvo, Lino, 1903-
Dark night of Ramón Yendía
De Onís, H. ed. Spanish stories and tales

Novelette. Barker, A. L.

NOVELISTS. See Authors

The novitiate. Howarth, J.

Now and again now. Lincoln, V. E.

Now I lay me. Hemingway, E.

Now there is peace. Sherman, R.

Now we are broke, my dear. Balchin, N.

The Nowaks. Isherwood, C.

Noyes, Alfred, 1880-
Log of the "Evening Star"
Cerf, B. A. and Moriarty, H. C. eds. Anthology of famous British stories
Uncle Hyacinth
Cooper, A. C. ed. Modern short stories

Nuhn, Ferner, 1903-
Ten
Blodgett, H. W. ed. Story survey. 1953 ed.

The nuisance. Lessing, D. M.

Null-P. Klass, P.

Number nine. Cartmill, C.

Number seventy-nine. Munby, A. N. L.

Number to remember. Stebel, S.

Nunc dimittis. Dahl, R.

NUNNERIES. See Convents

NUNS
Connolly, M. Big red house on Hope Street
Galsworthy, J. Salta pro nobis
Hemingway, E. Gambler, the nun, and the radio
Huxley, A. L. Nuns at luncheon
McLaverty, M. Road to the shore
MacMahon, B. Corn was springing
McNulty, J. Can't slip any drugs to sisters on Fifth Avenue
Pardo Bazán, E. condesa de. Sister Aparición
Roberts, E. M. Sacrifice of the maidens
Sansom, W. Little room

Nuns at luncheon. Huxley, A. L.

Nuns' holiday. Lieberman, R.

NUREMBERG. See Germany—Nuremberg

NURSES AND NURSING
Aiken, C. P. Bring! Bring!
Aiken, C. P. Night before prohibition
Bates, E. H. Time expired
Fitzgerald, F. S. K. Alcoholic case
Gordon, A. Old Ironpuss
Harvey, W. F. Account rendered
Harvey, W. F. Arm of Mrs Egan
Harvey, W. F. Atmospherics
Harvey, W. F. Chemist and druggist
Harvey, W. F. Dark horses
Harvey, W. F. Euphemia witchmaid
Harvey, W. F. Flying out of Mrs Barnard Hollis
Harvey, W. F. The lake
Harvey, W. F. No body
Harvey, W. F. Old masters
Harvey, W. F. Ripe for development
Keller, D. H. Psychophonic nurse
Lardner, R. W. Zone of quiet
Levine, T. M. Elaine's hope
Parker, D. R. Horsie
Scott, H. S. Sister
Ullman, J. R. Between you and I
Wilson, A. Mummy to the rescue

NUTS
Hoffmann, E. T. A. History of Krakatuk

Nuttose and protose. Nadir, I. M.

NYANJA (AFRICAN TRIBE)
Ullman, J. R. Am I blue?

Nye, Nelson Coral, 1907-
Homecoming
Western Writers of America. Holsters and heroes
Rock bottom
Western Writers of America. Bad men and good

NYGASSAS. See Nyanja (African tribe)

O

O city of broken dreams. Cheever, J.

O. Henry, pseud. See Porter, William Sydney

O. Henry Memorial awards. See First-prize stories, 1919-1954

O time in your flight. Cornier, V.

Oasis of gaiety. Taylor, E.

OBESITY. See Corpulence

OBJECTORS TO WAR. See Conscientious objectors

Oblinger, Michael
Jackpot vs. Yellowstrike
Dachs, D. ed. Treasury of sports humor

Oblong box. Poe, E. A.

O'Brien, Brian, 1898-
Pull, you lubbers!
Argosy (Periodical) Argosy Book of sea stories

O'Brien, Fitz-James, 1828-1862
Diamond lens
Burrell, J. A. and Cerf, B. A. eds. Anthology of famous American stories
Lost room
Conklin, G. and Conklin, L. T. eds. Supernatural reader

O'Brien, Jack. See O'Brien, John Sherman

O'Brien, John Sherman, 1898-1938
King and the Princess
Harper, W. comp. Dog show

OBSEQUIES. See Funeral rites and ceremonies

OBSERVATORIES, ASTRONOMICAL. See Astronomical observatories

Obsession. Winslow, T. S.

OBSTETRICS. See Childbirth

Obstinacy of Septimus Harding. Trollope, A.

Occasional garden. Munro, H. H.

Occurrence at Owl Creek bridge. Bierce, A.

Occurrence up a side street. Cobb, I. S.

OCEAN
Doyle, Sir A. C. Maracot Deep
Dunsany, E. J. M. D. P. 18th baron. Poltarnees, Beholder of Ocean
Elam, R. M. Project ocean floor
Knight, N. L. Crisis in Utopia

OCEAN TRAVEL
Aiken, C. P. Farewell! Farewell! Farewell!
Aiken, C. P. Mr Arcularis
Clark, W. Van T. Why don't you look where you're going
Dahl, R. Dip in the pool
De La Mare, W. J. Cape Race
De La Roche, M. Broken fan
Fitzgerald, F. S. K. Rough crossing
Maugham, W. S. Marriage of convenience
Maugham, W. S. Mr Know-All
Maugham, W. S. P. & O.
Maugham, W. S. Winter cruise
Michener, J. A. The jungle
Morley, C. D. The arrow
Poe, E. A. Oblong box
Tomlinson, H. M. The derelict
Wertenbaker, G. P. Ship that turned aside

OCEAN VOYAGES. See Ocean travel

Oceans are wide. Robinson, F. M.

O'Conaill, Domhnall
Lilacs out of the dead land
Burnett, W. and Burnett, H. S. eds. Sextet

O'Connell, Robert B.
You'll never mind
Hathaway, B. and Sessions, J. A. eds. Writers for tomorrow. 2d ser.

O'Connor, Flannery
Life you save may be your own
Prize stories, 1954

O'Connor, Frank, pseud. See O'Donovan, Michael

October and June. Porter, W. S.

OCTOGENARIANS. See Old age

OCTOPUS
Gordon, A. Sea devil
Hugo, V. M. comte. Combat with the octopus
White, R. Conflict is joined

Octopus marooned. Porter, W. S.

OCTOROONS. See Mulattoes

Odd chance. Haycox, E.

Odd old lady. Winslow, T. S.

Oddy and Id. Bester, A.

ODESSA. See Russia—Odessa

Odger, Charles
Johnnie Poothers
Joseph, M. ed. Best cat stories

O'Donnell, Lawrence, pseud. See Kuttner, Henry

O'Donnell, Mary (King). See King, Mary Paula

O'Donovan, Michael, 1903-
Babes in the wood
O'Donovan, M. Stories of Frank O'Connor [pseud]
Bridal night
O'Donovan, M. Stories of Frank O'Connor [pseud]
The cheapjack
O'Donovan, M. Stories of Frank O'Connor [pseud]
Christmas morning
O'Donovan, M. Stories of Frank O'Connor [pseud]
Counsel for Œdipus
O'Donovan, M. More stories by Frank O'Connor [pseud]
Custom of the country
O'Donovan, M. More stories by Frank O'Connor [pseud]
Darcy in the Land of Youth
O'Donovan, M. More stories by Frank O'Connor [pseud]
O'Donovan, M. Traveller's samples
Don Juan (Retired)
O'Donovan, M. More stories by Frank O'Connor [pseud]
Don Juan's temptation
O'Donovan, M. Stories of Frank O'Connor [pseud]
The drunkard
O'Donovan, M. Stories of Frank O'Connor [pseud]
O'Donovan, M. Traveller's samples
Eternal triangle
O'Donovan, M. More stories by Frank O'Connor [pseud]
Face of evil
O'Donovan, M. More stories by Frank O'Connor [pseud]

O'Donovan, Michael—_Continued_

Father and son
  O'Donovan, M. More stories by Frank O'Connor [pseud]
First confession
  Greene, J. I. and Abell, E. eds. Stories of sudden truth
  O'Donovan, M. Stories of Frank O'Connor [pseud]
  O'Donovan, M. Traveller's samples
First love
  O'Donovan, M. Stories of Frank O'Connor [pseud]
Freedom
  O'Donovan, M. Stories of Frank O'Connor [pseud]
Frying-pan
  O'Donovan, M. More stories by Frank O'Connor [pseud]
Guests of the nation
  Gordon, C. and Tate, A. eds. House of fiction
  O'Donovan, M. More stories by Frank O'Connor [pseud]
Holy door
  O'Donovan, M. Stories of Frank O'Connor [pseud]
House that Johnny built
  O'Donovan, M. Stories of Frank O'Connor [pseud]
The idealist
  O'Donovan, M. Stories of Frank O'Connor [pseud]
  O'Donovan, M. Traveller's samples
In the train
  O'Donovan, M. Stories of Frank O'Connor [pseud]
  O'Faoláin, S. The short story
Jerome
  O'Donovan, M. More stories by Frank O'Connor [pseud]
  O'Donovan, M. Traveller's samples
Judas
  Davis, R. G. ed. Ten modern masters
  O'Donovan, M. More stories by Frank O'Connor [pseud]
Lady of the sagas
  O'Donovan, M. More stories by Frank O'Connor [pseud]
  O'Donovan, M. Traveller's samples
Legal aid
  O'Donovan, M. Stories of Frank O'Connor [pseud]
  O'Donovan, M. Traveller's samples
Little mother
  O'Donovan, M. More stories by Frank O'Connor [pseud]
Lonely rock
  O'Donovan, M. More stories by Frank O'Connor [pseud]
Long road to Ummera
  O'Donovan, M. Stories of Frank O'Connor [pseud]
The Luceys
  O'Donovan, M. Stories of Frank O'Connor [pseud]
Mac's masterpiece
  Short, R. W. and Sewall, R. B. eds. Short stories for study. 1950 ed.
Mad Lomasneys
  O'Donovan, M. More stories by Frank O'Connor [pseud]

Majesty of the law
  Davis, R. G. ed. Ten modern masters
  O'Donovan, M. Stories of Frank O'Connor [pseud]
  Stauffer, R. M.; Cunningham, W. H. and Sullivan, C. J. eds. Adventures in modern literature
Man of the house
  O'Donovan, M. More stories by Frank O'Connor [pseud]
  O'Donovan, M. Traveller's samples
Masculine principle
  O'Donovan, M. Stories of Frank O'Connor [pseud]
  O'Donovan, M. Traveller's samples
Masculine protest
  O'Donovan, M. More stories by Frank O'Connor [pseud]
The miracle
  O'Donovan, M. More stories by Frank O'Connor [pseud]
The miser
  O'Donovan, M. Stories of Frank O'Connor [pseud]
My da
  O'Donovan, M. Stories of Frank O'Connor
My first Protestant
  O'Donovan, M. More stories by Frank O'Connor [pseud]
  O'Donovan, M. Traveller's samples
My Œdipus complex
  O'Donovan, M. Stories of Frank O'Connor [pseud]
News for the church
  O'Donovan, M. Stories of Frank O'Connor [pseud]
Old-age pensioners
  O'Donovan, M. Traveller's samples
Old faith
  O'Donovan, M. More stories by Frank O'Connor [pseud]
Old fellows
  O'Donovan, M. Stories of Frank O'Connor [pseud]
Orpheus and his lute
  O'Donovan, M. More stories by Frank O'Connor [pseud]
Peasants
  Lynskey, W. C. ed. Reading modern fiction
  O'Donovan, M. Stories of Frank O'Connor [pseud]
The pretender
  O'Donovan, M. Stories of Frank O'Connor [pseud]
A romantic
  O'Donovan, M. More stories by Frank O'Connor [pseud]
Sense of responsibility
  O'Donovan, M. More stories by Frank O'Connor [pseud]
The sentry
  O'Donovan, M. More stories by Frank O'Connor [pseud]
  O'Donovan, M. Traveller's samples
The shepherds
  O'Donovan, M. More stories by Frank O'Connor [pseud]
Song without words
  Gable, M. Sister, ed. Many-colored fleece
  O'Donovan, M. Stories of Frank O'Connor [pseud]

O'Hara, Mary, pseud. See Sture-Vasa, Mary
    (Alsop)
O'Higgins, Harvey Jerrold, 1876-1929
    Big Dan Reilly
        Burrell, J. A. and Cerf, B. A. eds. An-
            thology of famous American stories
    His mother
        Ungar, F. ed. To mother with love
OHIO
    Anderson, S. I'm a fool
    Anderson, S. Sophistication
    Bromfield, L. Sugar camp

            Frontier and pioneer life
        See Frontier and pioneer life—Ohio
OIL WELLS. See Petroleum
OJIBWAY INDIANS. See Chippewa In-
    dians
Okie. Blish, J.
Olaf the Magnificent. Sayres, W. C.
Olalla. Stevenson, R. L.
Old acquaintance. Collier, J.

Old acrobat and the ruined city. Putman, C.

OLD AGE
    Aldrich, B. S. Bid the tapers twinkle
    Aldrich, B. S. The dreams are real
    Anderson, E. V. Old Tom O'Grady of
        Shay Ranch
    Angoff, C. Alte Bobbe
    Ashley, E. L. Aunt Lil
    Auchincloss, L. Finish, good lady
    Baum, V. Old house
    Betts, D. End of Henry Fribble
    Betts, D. Serpents and doves
    Betts, D. Very old are beautiful
    Boyd, J. Old pines
    Burnet, D. Vision of Henry Whipple
    Calisher, H. Box of ginger
    Cather, W. S. Neighbor Rosicky
    Chekhov, A. P. Tædium vitæ
    Clark, W. Van T. Wind and the snow of
        winter
    Collier, J. Little memento
    Cooke, A. Christmas Eve
    De La Roche, M. Death of a centenarian
    Derleth, A. W. The telescope
    Dreiser, T. Lost Phoebe
    Elliott, H. S. Blue hat
    Ferber, E. Old man Minick
    Galsworthy, J. Ultima Thule
    Grimson, M. S. Eighty years old
    Hemingway, E. Clean, well-lighted place
    Hemingway, E. Old man at the bridge
    Humphrey, W. The Hardys
    Jameson, M. Blind alley
    Johnson, D. M. Laugh in the face of
        danger
    Kandel, L. Boy with the innocent eyes
    Karmel, I. Fru Holm
    Lardner, R. W. Golden honeymoon
    Munro, H. H. The cobweb
    Newhouse, E. Couple of old-timers
    Porter, K. A. Jilting of Granny Weather-
        all
    Praag, S. E. van. Weesperstraat
    Rosenfeld, J. Sick goose
    Schaefer, J. W. Old Anse
    Seager, A. Old man of the mountain
    Suckow, R. Some others and myself; 7
        stories

Tate, A. Immortal woman
Taylor, E. "Taking mother out"
Taylor, P. H. Their losses
Waugh, E. Bella Fleace gave a party
Welty, E. Old Mr Marblehall
Welty, E. Visit of charity
Welty, E. Worn path
West, J. Shivaree before breakfast
Old-age pensioners. O'Donovan, M.
Old Anse. Schaefer, J. W.
Old Calamity tries a bluff. Fishman, J. F.
Old century's river. La Farge, O.
Old Chief Mshlanga. Lessing, D. M.
Old crawdad. Wylie, P.
Old demon. Buck, P. S.
Old Doc Rivers. Williams, W. C.
Old Em's Kentucky home. Runyon, D.
Old faith. O'Donovan, M.
Old Faithful. Gallun, R. Z.
Old fellows. O'Donovan, M.
Old Gore. Stuart, J.
Old Hard. Beachcroft, T. O.
Old Hook 'n' Eye. Annixter, P. pseud.
Old house. Baum, V.
Old hunter. O'Flaherty, L.
Old Hussar. Bergengruen, W.
Old Ironpuss. Gordon, A.
Old John's place. Lessing, D. M.
OLD LADIES. See Old age
Old lady Mandle. Ferber, E.
Old maid. Balzac, H. de
Old maid. Wharton, E. N. J.
OLD MAIDS. See Spinsters
Old man. Du Maurier, D.
Old man. Faulkner, W.
Old man at the bridge. Hemingway, E.
Old man had four wives. Scheiner, F.
Old man Henderson. Neville, K.
Old man Isbell's wife. Davis, H. L.
Old man Minick. Ferber, E.
Old Man Mulligan. Miller, P. S.
Old man of the mountain. Seager, A.
Old man of the mountains. Gilbert, K.
Old man's bride. Byrd, S.
Old manuscript. Kafka, F.
Old masters. Harvey, W. F.
OLD MEN. See Old age
Old men. McCarthy, M. T.
Old men and boys. Jackson, C. R.
Old men's plans. La Farge, O.
Old Mr Marblehall. Welty, E.
Old mortality. Porter, K. A.
The old, old story. Street, J. H.
Old page. Kafka, F.
Old pal. Sullivan, R.
Old pastures. Foote, J. T.
Old people. Faulkner, W.
Old pines. Boyd, J.
Old ranch. Güiraldes, R.

Old Red. Gordon, C.

Old stock. Calisher, H.

Old time raid. Williams, W. C.

Old Tom O'Grady of Shay Ranch. Anderson, E. V.

Old town of Pskoff. Munro, H. H.

Old Turkey Neck. Lanning, G.

Old Well-Well. Grey, Z.

Old woman. Horwitz, J.

Old woman. Marshall, J.

Old woman. O'Flaherty, L.

Old Woodruff and his three wives. Moodie, S. S.

Old-world landowners. Gogol', N. V.

Olds, Helen (Diehl) 1895-
Susan steps out
Furman, A. L. ed. Everygirls career stories
Vic's Orr kid
Furman, A. L. ed. Everygirls career stories

Ole man Sanford. Foote, J. T.

The oleander. DeFord, M. A.

OLEANDERS
DeFord, M. A. The oleander

O'Leary, John T.
Protecting Mary
Oberfirst, R. ed. 1952 anthology of best original short-shorts

Olesha, Iurii Karlovich, 1899-
Envy
Rahv, P. ed. Great Russian short novels

Olive, Harry
Take it and like it
Argosy (Periodical) Argosy Book of sports stories

Olive grove. Maupassant, G. de

Oliver, Chad, 1928-
Ant and the eye
Sloane, W. M. ed. Stories for tomorrow
Any more at home like you?
Star science fiction stories, no. 3
Win the world
Lesser, M. A. ed. Looking forward

Ollivant, Alfred, 1874-1927
Shepherds' trophy
Fenner, P. R. comp. Dogs, dogs, dogs

Olsen, Bob
Four-dimensional roller-press
Wollheim, D. A. comp. Every boy's book of science-fiction

Olsen, Dolores (Birk) See Hitchens, Dolores (Birk)

Olyesha, Yuri. See Olesha, Iurii Karlovich

O'Meara, Walter
Bush medicine
O'Meara, W. Tales of the two borders
Child that walked at night
O'Meara, W. Tales of the two borders
Desert fire
O'Meara, W. Tales of the two borders
Lost child
O'Meara, W. Tales of the two borders
La Porcelaine Claire
O'Meara, W. Tales of the two borders

Red MacDonald
O'Meara, W. Tales of the two borders
To trouble the living
O'Meara, W. Tales of the two borders

On account of a hat. Rabinowitz, S.

On (and off) the agenda. Kober, A.

On approval. Munro, H. H.

On behalf of the management. Porter, W. S.

On Christmas Day. Eggleston, M. W.

On Christmas Eve. Eichelberger, R. K.

On Greenhow Hill. Kipling, R.

On guard. Waugh, E.

On lying awake at night. White, S. E.

On presenting arms. Bergengruen, W.

On Ruegen Island. Isherwood, C.

On skating. Skinner, C. O.

On stony ground. Sansom, W.

On the brink. Yaffe, J.

On the day of the crucifixion. Andreev, L. N.

On the dodge. James, W.

On the drift. James, W.

On the great alkali plain. Doyle, Sir A. C.

On the harmful effects of tobacco; first version. Chekhov, A. P.

On the harmful effects of tobacco; final version. Chekhov, A. P.

On the heights. Corkery, D.

On the road. Chekov, A. P.

On the road. Hughes, L.

On the roof of the world. Roberts, Sir C. G. D.

On the verge. Sandoz, M. Y.

On the way. Gorky, M.

On the way home. Hughes, L.

On trial. Hoffman, E.

O'Nan, Jill, pseud. See O'Nan, Mildred (Cook)

O'Nan, Mildred (Cook) 1906-
Table before me
Gable, M. Sister, ed. Many-colored fleece

Once a cowboy. James, W.

Once-beautiful Ellie. Halladay, V.

Once on a Sunday. Wylie, P.

Once on Christmas. Thompson, D.

Once upon a crime. Cohen, O. R.

Once upon a time. Parker, J. R.

Once upon a train. Rice, C. and Palmer, S.

One. De Vries, P.

One-armed John finds a corpse. Hendryx, J. B.

One-armed John voices a threat. Hendryx, J. B.

One autumn night. Gorky, M.

One dollar's worth. Porter, W. S.

One for O'Brien. Morrill, G. P.

One for the team. Regli, A. C.

One Friday morning. Hughes, L.

One grave too few. Asquith, Lady C. M. E. C.

One guy, one gal, one island. Holder, W.

One he called Winnie. Schulberg, B. W.

One hour of glory. Rinehart, M. R.

One in a million. Brown, G.

One in three hundred. McIntosh, J. T.

One leg too many. Alexander, W.

One man's meat. Chekhov, A. P.

One mile of ice. Garner, H.

One minute longer. Terhune, A. P

One missing. Cooke, A. A.

One more inning. O'Rourke, F.

One morning they'll hang him. Allingham, M.

One named Jesus. Buck, P. S.

One night. Portor, L. S.

One night in Bradford. Bentley, P. E.

One night in Coffin Creek. Thompson, T.

One of hers. Van Doren, M.

One of the chosen. Calisher, H.

One of the Garretsons. Van Doren, M.

One of the missing. Bierce, A.

One of three others. Suckow, R.

One ounce of common sense. O'Rourke, F.

One phase of love. Maupassant, G. de

One ride too many. Bonham, F.

One summer. Grau, S. A.

One summer afternoon. Dann, L.

One sunny afternoon. Sansom, W.

One thousand dollars. Porter, W. S.

One, two, three little Indians. Garner, H.

One way of getting a hundred pounds. Kersh, G.

One-way street. Willis, A. A.

One way to victory. Ford, N. A.

The one who waits. Bradbury, R.

The onlooker. Isaacson, B. K.

Only love me. Terr, I.

Only the dead know Brooklyn. Wolfe, T.

Only the dead ride proudly. Fox, N. A.

Only thing we learn. Kornbluth, C. M.

ONTARIO, CANADA. See Canada—Ontario

Opatoshu, Joseph, 1886-1954
Eternal wedding gown
  Howe, I. and Greenberg, E. eds. Treasury of Yiddish stories
Horse thief
  Leftwich, J. ed. Yisröel. 1952 ed.
May the Temple be restored!
  Howe, I. and Greenberg, E. eds. Treasury of Yiddish stories

Opatovsky, Joseph, pseud. See Opatoshu, Joseph

Open boat. Crane, S.

Open house. De Vries, P.

Open road. Farrell, J. T.

Open season. Lyle, D.

Open season. Summers, J. L.

Open secret. Kuttner, H.

Open, sesame! Grendon, S.

Open window. Munro, H. H.

Open winter. Davis, H. L.

Opening day with Mr Hardey's hounds. Surtees, R. S.

Opening day with the Duke of Tergiversation's hounds. Surtees, R. S.

Opening day with the Larkspur hounds. Surtees, R. S.

Opening doors. Shiras, W. H.

OPERA SINGERS. See Musicians—Singers

Operating instructions. Sheckley, R.

Operation pumice. Gallun, R. Z.

Operation RSVP. Piper, H. B.

OPERATIONS, SURGICAL. See Surgery

Opium eater. Keller, D. H.

OPIUM HABIT
Maugham, W. S. Mirage

OPIUM TRADE
Bowles, P. F. Señor Ong and Señor Ha

OPOSSUMS
Annixter, P. pseud. White possum

Or else. Kuttner, H.

Oracle of the dog. Chesterton, G. K.

ORANG-UTANS
Poe, E. A. Murders in the Rue Morgue

ORANGE
Shneur, Z. Immortal orange

Orange room. Stuart, L.

ORATORS
Saroyan, W. My cousin Dikran, the orator

Oratory contest. Farrell, J. T.

Orban twins. Bergengruen, W.

ORCHARDS
Fuchs, A. M. Among the trees

ORCHESTRA
Culver, M. Black water blues
Rice, C. Goodbye forever

ORCHIDS
Annixter, P. pseud. Orchids and crocodiles
Collier, J. Green thoughts
Wells, H. G. Strange orchid

Orchids and crocodiles. Annixter, P. pseud.

Ordeal in space. Heinlein, R. A.

Ordeal of Professor Klein. De Camp, L. S.

Orderly world of Mr Appleby. Ellin, S.

Orders. Jameson, M.

ORDERS, MONASTIC. See Monasticism and religious orders

Orders for Korea. Brown, M. F.

ORDNANCE
Aldrich, T. B. How we astonished the Rivermouthians
Bergengruen, W. Orban twins
    See also Arms and armor; Firearms

OREGON
Davis, H. L. Team bells woke me; 13 stories

O'Reilly, John, 1907?-
Sound of gunfire
  Meredith, S. ed. Bar 1 roundup of best western stories

O'Reilly, Tom
60 ways to lose a horse bet
  Dachs, D. ed. Treasury of sports humor

Oreste. Shultz, W. H.
ORGANISTS. See Musicians—Organists
The **orgy**: an idyll. De La Mare, W. J.
Ornitz, Samuel, 1890-
Yom Kipper fressers
Ausubel, N. ed. Treasury of Jewish
humor
O'Rourke, Frank, 1916-
Argument with death
O'Rourke, F. Ride west
Battle royal
O'Rourke, F. Ride west
Best position
O'Rourke, F. Greatest victory, and other
baseball stories
Cold water and cherry pie
O'Rourke, F. Ride west
Decision
O'Rourke, F. Greatest victory, and other
baseball stories
Delayed decision
O'Rourke, F. Greatest victory, and other
baseball stories
Easy going man
O'Rourke, F. Ride west
Flashing spikes
O'Rourke, F. Greatest victory, and other
baseball stories
Greatest victory
O'Rourke, F. Greatest victory, and other
baseball stories
Heavenly world series
O'Rourke, F. Heavenly world series,
and other baseball stories
Home game
O'Rourke, F. Greatest victory, and other
baseball stories
Impossible play
O'Rourke, F. Heavenly world series,
and other baseball stories
Last accounting
O'Rourke, F. Greatest victory, and other
baseball stories
Last out
O'Rourke, F. Greatest victory, and other
baseball stories
Last pitch
O'Rourke, F. Heavenly world series,
and other baseball stories
Last shot
Meredith, S. ed. Bar 2
O'Rourke, F. Ride west
Last time around
O'Rourke, F. Heavenly world series,
and other baseball stories
Last time up
O'Rourke, F. Greatest victory, and other
baseball stories
Look for the kid with the guts
O'Rourke, F. Heavenly world series,
and other baseball stories
Magic circle
O'Rourke, F. Heavenly world series,
and other baseball stories
Man who sold himself
O'Rourke, F. Ride west
Moment of truth
O'Rourke, F. Heavenly world series,
and other baseball stories
No color
O'Rourke, F. Heavenly world series,
and other baseball stories

Nothing new
O'Rourke, F. Greatest victory, and other
baseball stories
One more inning
O'Rourke, F. Greatest victory, and other
baseball stories
One ounce of common sense
O'Rourke, F. Heavenly world series,
and other baseball stories
Parade is ten minutes long
O'Rourke, F. Ride west
Right count
O'Rourke, F. Ride west
Twentieth game
O'Rourke, F. Greatest victory, and other
baseball stories
Violence at sundown
O'Rourke, F. Ride west
Whippletree
O'Rourke, F. Ride west
Widow's peak
O'Rourke, F. Ride west
ORPHANS
Ballard, J. C. Mountain summer
Benefield, B. Christmas Eve's Day
Norris, K. T. Mother of Angela Hogan
Paget, V. Dionea
Ringwood, G. P. Little ghost
Simak, C. D. Contraption
Taylor, E. Hester Lilly
See also Boys; Children; Girls
The **orphans.** Verga, G.
Orphans in uniform. Gilbreth, F. B. and
Carey, E. M. G.
Orpheus and his lute. O'Donovan, M.
Orwell, George, 1903-1950
Shooting an elephant
New writing (Periodical) Best stories
Osage Girl. Curry, P. S.
Osborne, Maybelle Hinton
Mrs Kochinsky and the problem child
Seventeen (Periodical) Nineteen from
Seventeen
Osborne, Robertson
Action on Azura
Greenberg, M. ed. Travelers of space
Same as: Contact, incorporated
Contact, incorporated
Conklin, G. ed. Big book of science fic-
tion
Same as: Action on Azura
Osborne's revenge. James, H.
Oscar on roller skates. Neikirk, M. E.
Oscar, the trained seal. Neikirk, M. E.
Ospina, Carlos Wyld. See Wyld Ospina,
Carlos
OSPREYS
Roberts, Sir C. G. D. Fishers of the air
OSTLERS. See Stablemen
Other Diane. Balzac, H. de
Other foot. Bradbury, R.
Other Margaret. Trilling, L.
Other now. Jenkins, W. F.
Other one. Colette, S. G.
Other pebbles on the beach. Kober, A.
Other people. Adler, W.
Other people's misfortune. Chekhov, A. P.

Other people's troubles. Chekhov, A. P.

The **other** place. Priestley, J. B.

Other river. Bowen, R. O.

Other side. Kubilius, W.

Other side of the hedge. Forster, E. M.

Other son. Pirandello, L.

Other tracks. Sell, W.

Other two. Wharton, E. N. J.

Other Wise Man. Van Dyke, H.

Other woman. Winslow, T. S.

OTTERS
Murphy, R. You've got to learn

Ounce of prevention. Carter, P.

Our advertisement brings a visitor. Doyle, Sir A. C.

Our country. Monn, A.

Our fair city. Heinlein, R. A.

Our father. Stern, J.

Our Felix. Rosenberg, E.

OUR LADY OF GUADALUPE. See Guadalupe, Our lady of

Our lady's juggler. France, A.

Our last day with the Handley Cross. Surtees, R. S.

Our vegetable love. Putnam, C.

Our white deer. Schulberg, B. W.

Oursler, Fulton, 1893-1952
Bargain in brimstone
Thinker's digest (Periodical) Spoiled priest, and other stories

Oursler, Will. See Oursler, William Charles

Oursler, William Charles, 1913-
Thread of life
Mystery Writers of America, inc. 20 great tales of murder

Out of Nazareth. Porter, W. S.

Out of sheer boredom. Chekhov, A. P.

Out of the night. Campbell, J. W.

Out of the past. Schaefer, J. W.

Out where the West begins. Newhouse, E.

Outcasts of Poker Flat. Harte, B.

OUTDOOR LIFE
Andrews, R. C. ed. My favorite stories of the great outdoors; 35 stories
Macfarlan, A. A. Moose boy
See also Camping

Outer limit. Doar, G.

OUTER SPACE, VISITS TO OR FROM.
See Interplanetary visitors; Interplanetary voyages

The **outlander.** Jackson, C. R.

The **outlaw.** Ross, S.

The **outlaw.** Smith, E. C.

Outlaw trail. Mowery, W. B.

OUTLAWS
Cheshire, G. Strangers in the evening
Foster, B. Outlaws are in town
Hendryx, J. B. Intrigue on Halfaday Creek; 28 stories
Hinton, J. Mediators to the goatherd
Johnson, D. M. Laugh in the face of danger
Lagerlöf, S. O. L. The outlaws

Loomis, N. M. The twilighters
Nye, N. C. Rock bottom
Porter, W. S. Caballero's way
Porter, W. S. Chaparral Christmas gift
Porter, W. S. Passing of Black Eagle
Roper, W. Last cigarette
Thompson, T. Silver saddle
Welty, E. Still moment
See also Brigands and robbers; Crime and Criminals

The **outlaws.** Lagerlöf, S. O. L.

Outlaws are in town. Foster, B.

Outlaw's boots. Thompson, T

An **outlier** from his tribe. Frankau, G.

The **outstation.** Maugham, W. S.

Oval portrait. Poe, E. A.

Over insurance. Collier, J.

Over the Green Mountains. Caldwell, E.

Over the line. Stevenson, C. L.

Over the mountain. Todd, R.

Over the top. Del Rey, L.

Over there. White, W.

The **overcoat.** Benson, S.

The **overcoat.** Gogol', N. V.

Overholser, Wayne D. 1906-
Patriarch of Gunsight Flat
Western Writers of America.. Holsters and heroes

OVERLAND JOURNEYS
Browne, J. R. Peep at Washoe
Chekhov, A. P. Across Siberia
La Farge, O. Old man's plans

Overlooked lady. McNulty, J.

The **oversight.** Munro, H. H.

Overthrow. Cartmill, C.

Overture De Vries, P.

Owner's interest. Dingle, A. E.

OXEN
Roberts, Sir C. G. D. Brothers of the yoke
Schaefer, J. W. Takes a real man . . .
See also Cattle

Oxenham, John, 1852-1941
Of our meeting with Cousin John
Brentano, F. ed. The word lives on
Their first meeting
Brentano, F. ed. The word lives on

OX-TEAMSTERS. See Teamsters

OYSTERS
London, J. Raid on the oyster pirates

Oyved, Moysheh. See Good, Edward

OZARK MOUNTAINS
Kantor, M. Life in her hands
Mowery, W. B. Tales of the Ozarks; 9 stories
See also Mountain whites (Southern States

P

P. & O. Maugham, W. S.

P.G. Christmas. Hertlein, R.

Ph.D. Markfield, W.

Pa sees again. Dixon, E. S.

PALESTINE—*Continued*

Bethlehem

Goudge, E. Son-of-David

Jerusalem

Hirshbein, P. Tears on stones

Stinetorf, L. A. Refugee village

Palimpsest of St Augustine. Pratt, F. and De Camp, L. S.

PALIMPSESTS. See Manuscripts (Palimpsests)

Palm Beach Santa Claus. Runyon, D.

Palm Island plane factory. Chichester, F. C.

Palm Springs. Charteris, L.

Palm Sunday. Jackson, C. R.

Palma, Ricardo, 1833-1919

Two cooing doves

De Onís, H. ed. Spanish stories and tales

Palmer, Stuart, 1905-

Jinx man

Best detective stories of the year—1953

Riddle of the Black Museum

Mystery Writers of America, inc. Butcher, baker, murder-maker

Riddle of the dangling pearl

Mystery Writers of America, inc. Maiden murders

Riddle of the snafu murder

Mystery Writers of America, inc. 20 great tales of murder

Riddle of the tired bullet

Mystery Writers of America, inc. Four-&-twenty bloodhounds

Where angels fear to tread

Best detective stories of the year—1952

See also Rice, C. jt. auth.

Palo. Saroyan, W.

Palomino. Murphy, B.

PAMPAS

Güiraldes, R. Old ranch

PAN (GOD)

Beauclerk, H. De V. Miracle of the vineyard

Munro, H. H. Music on the hill

PANCAKES. See Griddle cakes

Pangborn, Edgar

Angel's egg

Conklin, G. ed. Invaders of earth

Mrrrar!

Queen, E. pseud. ed. Queen's awards: 8th ser.

Pick-up for Olympus

Conklin, G. and Conklin, L. T. eds. Supernatural reader

Singing stick

Queen, E. pseud. ed. Queen's awards: 7th ser.

The **panther.** Norton, B.

PANTHERS. See Leopards; Pumas

Paolo Uccello. Schwob, M.

Papa Pierre's pipe. Kantor, M.

Papa's going bye-bye. Harwood, K.

Papashvily, George, 1895?- and Papashvily, Helen (Waite) 1906-

Getting quick rich

Fenner, P. R. comp. Fun! Fun! Fun!

Papashvily, Helen (Waite) See Papashvily, G. jt. auth.

PARABLES

Grimson, M. S. When Dan came home

Parachute warning. Carter, R. G.

PARACHUTES

Carter, R. G. Parachute warning

Parade is ten minutes long. O'Rourke, F.

Paradis, Marjorie (Bartholomew)

None but the fair

American girl (Periodical) Christmas all year 'round

Red wagon

American girl (Periodical) Christmas all year 'round

PARADISE. See Eden

Paradise. Lagerkvist, P. F.

Paradise. Simak, C. D.

Paradise of bachelors. Melville, H.

Paradise of thieves. Chesterton, G. K.

Paradise street. Moore, C. L.

Paradise II. Sheckley, R.

Paradox lost. Brown, F.

PARAPSYCHOLOGY. See Thought-transference

Parasite planet. Weinbaum, S. G.

The **parcel.** Zweig, A.

Parcel of land. Skinner, C. O.

Pardo Bazán, Emilia, condesa de, 1852-1921

Sister Aparición

De Onís, H. ed. Spanish stories and tales

The **pardon.** Rawlings, M. K.

Pardon my mistake. Pratt, F.

Pardoner's tale. Chaucer, G.

PARENT AND CHILD

Gordimer, N. The defeated

O'Donovan, M. Masculine protest

Schorer, M. What we don't know hurts us

See also Fathers and sons

Parents and horses. Lewis, W.

PARIS. See France—Paris

Paris scene: 1931. Farrell, J. T.

Paris: The covetous headsman. Charteris, L.

The **park.** Bates, H. E.

Parker, C. W.

Flimsy walls

Stanford short stories, 1950

Parker, Daniel Francis, 1893-

Passing of the first floor back

Dachs, D. ed. Treasury of sports humor

Parker, Dorothy (Rothschild) 1893-

Big blonde

Burrell, J. A. and Cerf, B. A. eds. Anthology of famous American stories

First-prize stories, 1919-1954

Horsie

Fabricant, N. D. and Werner, H. eds. World's best doctor stories

Parker, Sir Gilbert, bart. 1862-1932

The flood

Pacey, D. ed. Book of Canadian stories

Penglase, Flo
  Strange house
    Furman, A. L. ed. Everygirls mystery
    stories
Pennies from heaven. Irwin, J. M.
Pennsylvania Station. Faulkner, W.
PENSIONS (BOARDING HOUSES) See
  Boarding houses
Pentecost, Hugh, pseud. See Phillips, Jud-
  son Pentecost
Pentecost. Douglas, L. C.
PEONIES
  Parker, J. R. Hounds of spring
People of the black circle. Howard, R. E.
People v. Abe Lathan, colored. Caldwell,
  E.
People's choice. Caldwell, E.
Perchance to dream. Robineau, L.
Percy Grimm. Faulkner, W.
Peretz, Isaac Loeb, 1851-1915
  Bontsha the Silent
    Howe, I. and Greenberg, E. eds. Treas-
    ury of Yiddish stories
  Cabalists
    Howe, I. and Greenberg, E. eds. Treas-
    ury of Yiddish stories
  Dead town
    Howe, I. and Greenberg, E. eds. Treas-
    ury of Yiddish stories
  Devotion without end
    Howe, I. and Greenberg, E. eds. Treas-
    ury of Yiddish stories
  The golem
    Howe, I. and Greenberg, E. eds. Treas-
    ury of Yiddish stories
  If not higher
    Howe, I. and Greenberg, E. eds. Treas-
    ury of Yiddish stories
  Little Hanukkah lamp
    Ausubel, N. ed. Treasury of Jewish
    humor
  Mad Talmudist
    Howe, I. and Greenberg, E. eds. Treas-
    ury of Yiddish stories
  Miracle on the sea
    Leftwich, J. ed. Yisröel. 1952 ed.
  Ne'ilah in Gehenna
    Howe, I. and Greenberg, E. eds. Treas-
    ury of Yiddish stories
  Pious cat
    Ausubel, N. ed. Treasury of Jewish
    humor
  Rabbi Yochanan the warden
    Howe, I. and Greenberg, E. eds. Treas-
    ury of Yiddish stories
Perfect day for bananafish. Salinger, J. D.
Perfect gentleman. McGregor, R. J.
Perfect host. Waldo, E. H.
Perfect murder. Gold, H. L.
Perfect secretary. Brannon, W. T.
Perforce to dream. Harris, J. B.
Perfumed garden. Keller, D. H.
PERFUMERY
  Ekbergh, I. D. Lure of perfume
Peril of the blue world. Abernathy, R.
Peril of the river. Cave. H. B.
Period piece. Coupling, J. J. pseud.

Period piece. Waugh, E.
PERIODICALS
  Porter, W. S. "Rose of Dixie"
Perishing of the pendragons. Chesterton,
  G. K.
Perl, Philip
  Man in Israel
    Ribalow, H. U. ed. These your children
Perpetua puts one over. Kent, C. G.
Perpetual motion. De Camp, L. S.
Perpetuum mobile. Chekhov, A. P.
Perrault, Ernest G. 1922-
  Silver King
    Weaver, R. and James, H. eds. Cana-
    dian short stories
Perry, George Sessions, 1910-
  The fourflusher
    Peery, W. W. ed. 21 Texas short stories
PERSECUTION
  Téllez, H. Ashes for the wind
Persephone. Le Sueur, M.
PERSIA
          To 640 A.D.
  Meredith, G. Punishment of Shahpesh,
    the Persian, on Khipil, the builder
          640-date
  Wall, J. W. The Kahn
Person, William Thomas, 1900-
  Any way race
    Owen, F. ed. Teen-age victory parade
  "I play basketball"
    Owen, F. ed. Teen-age winter sports
    stories
  Long-shot Porter
    Owen, F. ed. Teen-age winter sports
    stories
  Monster of Blue-Hole Lake
    Owen, F. ed. Teen-age victory parade
  Pony Porter swing
    Owen, F. ed. Teen-age victory parade
  Poor retriever
    Furman, A. L. ed. Teen-age dog stories
  Won by a tail
    Owen, F. ed. Teen-age victory parade
PERSONAL FINANCE. See Budgets, Per-
  sonal
Personal letter. Campbell, W. E. M.
PERSONALITY, DISORDERS OF
  Goodman, P. Iddings Clark
  Maclaren-Ross, J. This mortal coil
Pertwee, Roland, 1885-
  Fish are such liars
    Cerf, B. A. and Moriarty, H. C. eds.
    Anthology of famous British stories
PERU
  Palma, R. Two cooing doves
          16th century
  Wassermann, J. Gold of Caxamalca
Peshkov, Alexis Maximovich. See Gorky,
  Maxim
The pest. Scott, W. R.
PESTILENCES. See Plagues
Pete. Knox, J.
Pete can fix it. Jones, R. F.

PETER, SAINT, APOSTLE
  Douglas, L. C. Pentecost
Peterkins' Christmas tree. Hale, L. P.
Peter's Christmas present. Eggleston, M. W.
Petersen, Eric Jens
  Who called you here?
    Eaton, H. T. ed. Short stories
Peterson, Charles Alden
  Dooley and the children's hour
    Seventeen (Periodical) Nineteen from
    Seventeen
Peterson, G. M.
  Sophomore forward
    Owen, F. ed. Teen-age winter sports
    stories
Petite première in the Mont Blanc Massif.
    Knowlton, E.
Petracca, Joseph
  Santa Lucia
    Gable, M. Sister, ed. Many-colored
    fleece
  Straight life
    Collier's, the national weekly. Collier's
    best
      See also Fenton, F. jt. auth.
Petrified man. Welty, E.
Petrified man (I-II) Clemens, S. L.
PETROLEUM
  Crowell, C. T. The stoic
  Sanford, W. M. Windfall
Petronius Arbiter, d. 66
  Matron of Ephesus
    Stegner, W. E.; Scowcroft, R. and
    Ilyin, B. eds. Writer's art
Petronius, Gaius. See Petronius Arbiter
Petrov, Vladimir, 1915-
  "Get a horse, comrade"
    This week magazine. This week's short
    short stories
Peyton, Green, pseud. See Wertenbaker,
    Green Peyton
Phalanstery of Theleme. Rabelais, F.
PHANTASIES. See Fantasies
Phantom cry-baby. Blochman, L. G.
Phantom flivver. Mott, F. L.
Phantom Hall. Anderson, E. V.
Phantom luncheon. Munro, H. H.
Phantom of the bridge. Ware, L.
PHANTOM SHIPS. See Ghost ships
PHARAOHS. See Kings and rulers
PHARMACISTS
  Bennett, S. Girls are so helpless
  Bloomgarden, S. Share of paradise
  Kipling, R. 'Wireless'
Pheasant hunter. Saroyan, W.
Phelps, Elizabeth Stuart. See Ward, Eliza-
    beth Stuart (Phelps)
Philanthropist and the happy cat. Munro,
    H. H.
PHILANTHROPISTS
  Porter, W. S. Chair of philanthromathe-
    matics
PHILANTHROPY. See Charity
PHILATELY. See Postage stamps

Philippa's fox-hunt. Somerville, E. A. O.
    and Martin, V. F.
Philistine in Bohemia. Porter, W. S.
Phillips, Alan, 1917-
  Presence in the grove
    Weaver, R. and James, H. eds. Ca-
    nadian short stories
Phillips, Alexander Moore, 1907-
  Death of the moon
    Wollheim, D. A. comp. Flight into
    space
Phillips, James Atlee, 1915-
  Fast break
    Argosy (Periodical) Argosy Book of
    sports stories
Philips, Judson Pentecost, 1903-
  Contradictory case
    Queen, E. pseud. ed. Queen's awards:
    6th ser.
  Man who had no friends
    Mystery Writers of America, inc. 20
    great tales of murder
  Room number twenty-three
    Mystery Writers of America, inc. Maid-
    en murders
Phillips, Peter, 1920-
  At no extra cost
    Best science fiction stories: 1952
  Counter charm
    Conklin, G. ed. Omnibus of science fic-
    tion
  Dreams are sacred
    Bleiler, E. F. and Dikty, T. E. eds.
    Imagination unlimited
  Field study
    Galaxy science fiction magazine. Gal-
    axy reader of science fiction
  Lost memory
    Galaxy science fiction magazine. Sec-
    ond Galaxy reader of science fiction
  Manna
    Conklin, G. ed. Big book of science fic-
    tion
  Plagiarist
    Crossen, K. F. Future tense
  She who laughs
    Pohl, F. ed. Assignment in tomorrow
  University
    Galaxy science fiction magazine. Sec-
    ond Galaxy reader of science fiction
  The warning
    Merril, J. ed. Beyond the barriers of
    space and time
Phillips, Thomas Hal, 1922-
  Shadow of an arm
    Prize stories of 1951
Phillpotts, Eden, 1862-
  "Hey diddle diddle, the cat..."
    Cerf, B. A. and Moriarty, H. C. eds.
    Anthology of famous British stories
Phistairus. Lowry, R. J. C.
Phoebe. Porter, W. S.
Phoenix. Smith, C. A.
Phoenix on the sword. Howard, R. E.
PHONOGRAPH
  Clark, W. Van T. Portable phonograph
  Wendroff, Z. The gramophone
Phonograph and the graft. Porter, W. S.
The photograph. Kneale, N.

PHOTOGRAPHERS
Bradbury, R. Sun and shadow
Olds, H. D. Vic's Orr Kid
Leighton, M. C. Legacy of Canyon John
PHOTOGRAPHY. See Photographers
PHRENOLOGY
O'Donovan, M. Jerome

Physic. De La Mare, W. J.

PHYSICAL IMMORTALITY. See Immortality, Physical

PHYSICIANS
Allen, H. Surgery at Aquila
Balzac, H. de. Atheist's mass
Beachcroft, T. O. The eyes
Bergengruen, W. Eye cure
Bergengruen, W. Sand doctor
Blochman, L. G. Brood of evil
Blochman, L. G. Diagnosis: homicide; 8 stories
Blochman, L. G. Kiss of Kandahar
Boyle, K. White horses of Vienna
Bunner, H. C. Infidelity of Zenobia
Campbell, W. E. M. Bill's eyes
Cheever, J. Season of divorce
Chekhov, A. P. Enemies
Chekhov, A. P. La Cigale
Chekhov, A. P. Perpetuum mobile
Chekhov, A. P. Unpleasant incident
Chekhov, A. P. An unpleasantness
Collier, J. De mortuis
Collins, W. Dead hand
Ekbergh, I. D. Strange story
Farrell, J. T. My friend the doctor
Fitzgerald, F. S. K. Family in the wind
France, A. Manuscript of a village doctor
Gordimer, N. In the beginning
Grimson, M. S. Will and a way
Hart, A. Doctor Mallory
Harvey, W. F. Arm of Mrs Egan
Harvey, W. F. Long road
Hawthorne, N. Rappaccini's daughter
Hecht, B. Double exposure
Hecht, B. Miracle of the fifteen murderers
Herrick, R. Master of the inn
Horwitz, J. Just love, love, sweet love
Irwin, M. E. F. The doctor
James, H. Middle years
Kafka, F. Country doctor
Kuttner, H. Dream's end
McCoy, E. The cape
Marquis, D. Country
Maugham, W. S. Happy man
Medearis, M. Big Doc's girl
Millar, M. Couple next door
O'Donovan, M. The miracle
Pearce, R. E. Touch of sun tan
Pirandello, L. The fly
Poe, E. A. Facts in the case of M. Valdemar
Porter, W. S. Let me feel your pulse
Porter, W. S. The marionettes
Pratt, F. and De Camp, L. S. Love-nest
Samachson, J. Country doctor
Sansom, W. Eye man
Schulberg, B. W. Road to recovery
Strong, L. A. G. White cottage
Turgenev, I. S. District doctor
Van Doren, M. Payments in full
Watson, J. Story of Dr MacLure
Weiss, E. Cardiac suture

West, J. Horace Chooney, M. D.
Williams, W. C. Use of force
Woody, R. L. J. Cue for Connie
Wright, S. F. The rat
Young, F. B. Busman's holiday
See also Surgery

PHYSICISTS
Porges, A. The rats

Physiology of fear. Forester, C. S.

Pi in the sky. Brown, F.

PIANISTS. See Musicians—Pianists

PIANO
Davis, S. P. Christmas carol

The **piazza.** Melville, H.

Pick-up for Olympus. Panghorn, E.

Picket lines of Marton Hevessy. Household, G.

Picking cotton. Caldwell, E.

Pickles and pearls. Hall, D.

PICKPOCKETS. See Crime and criminals; Thieves

Pickthall, Marjorie Lowry Christie, 1883-1922
Worker in sandalwood
Pacey, D. ed. Book of Canadian stories

The **picnic.** Neisloss, M.

The **picnic.** Pendergast, C.

Picnic of Mores the cat. Brentano, C. M.

PICNICS
Pendergast, C. The picnic
Welty, E. Asphodel

The **picture.** Caldwell, E.

Pictures. Mansfield, K.

Pictures don't lie. MacLean, K.

Pictures in the fire. Collier, J.

Piece of linoleum. Keller, D. H.

Piece of news. Welty, E.

Piece of pie. Runyon, D.

Piece of steak. London, J.

Piece of string. Maupassant, G. de

Pierce, John Alvin
Invariant
Astounding science fiction (Periodical)
Astounding science fiction anthology

Pierre. Brookhouser, F.

Pierrot, George F.
Sheriton turnabout
American boy (Periodical) American boy anthology

PIETY. See Religion

Piffingcap. Coppard, A. E.

Pig and whistle. Gissing, G.

Pig Wisps. Sandburg, C.

The **pigeon.** Gustafson, R.

Pigeon cree. Chaplin, S.

Pigeon from St Bartholomew's. Connolly, M.

PIGEONS
Asch, S. Kola Road
Collier, J. Invisible dove dancer of Strathpheen Island

PIGEONS—*Continued*
Gordimer, N. Kindest thing to do
Gustafson, R. The pigeon
Kalisman, H. H. The stray
McLaverty, M. Pigeons

Pigeons. McLaverty, M.

PIGS
Collier, J. Mary
Grimson, M. S. Won and lost
Still, J. Master time
Weeks, R. Arkansas

PILATE, PONTIUS, 1st century
France, A. Procurator of Judæa
Komroff, M. Told in the stars

Pile of trouble. Kuttner, H.

The **Pilgrim.** Powell, D.

Pillar to post. Harris, J. B.

Pillars of society. Mallea, E.

The **pillows.** St Clair, M.

Pilnick, Boris, pseud. See Vogau, Boris
Andreevich

Pilot and the bushman. Jacobs, S.

PILOTS, AIRPLANE. See Air pilots

Pimienta pancakes. Porter, W. S.

Pinch hitter. Cox, W. R.

Pincherle, Alberto, 1907-
Back to the sea
Horizon (Periodical) Golden Horizon

Pink and blue. Williams, W. C.

Pink ballerina. Ekbergh, I. D.

Pink medicine. Bottome, P.

Pink organdie. Albee, G. S.

Pinski, David, 1872-
And then he wept
Howe, I. and Greenberg, E. eds. Treasury of Yiddish stories
It had to be
Leftwich, J. ed. Yisröel. 1952 ed.

Pioneer city. Strachey, J.

PIONEER LIFE. See Frontier and pioneer
life

Pious cat. Peretz, I. L.

Piper, H. Beam, 1904-
He walked around the horses
Pratt, F. ed. World of wonder
Last enemy
Astounding science fiction (Periodical)
Astounding science fiction anthology
Operation RSVP
Pratt, F. ed. World of wonder
Uller uprising
Petrified planet

Piper pays. Ready, W. B.

PIPES, TOBACCO. See Tobacco pipes

PIRACY. See Pirates

Piracy preferred. Campbell, J. W.

Pirandello, Luigi, 1867-1936
The fly
Fabricant, N. D. and Werner, H. eds.
World's best doctor stories
Horse in the moon
Neider, C. ed. Great short stories from
the world's literature

House of agony
Blodgett, H. W. ed. Story survey.
1953 ed.
Other son
Ungar, F. ed. To mother with love
Reserved coffin
West, R. B. and Stallman, R. W. eds.
Art of modern fiction

Pirate and the gamecock. Bloomfield, H.

Pirate gold. Coppock, C.

Pirate island. Crump, I.

PIRATES
Allen, M. P. Two chests of treasure
Coppel, A. The peacemaker
Crump, I. Pirate island
Dunsany, E. J. M. D. P. 18th baron.
Story of land and sea
Fenner, P. R. comp. Pirates, pirates,
pirates; 14 stories
See also Sea stories

Pirates of Charles Town harbor. Holland,
R. S.

Pit and the pendulum. Poe, E. A.

Pit in the jungle. Cottrell, D. W.

Pittsburgh special. Doty, W. L.

Pity the poor producer. Kaufman, W.

PIUTE INDIANS. See Paiute Indians

PIZARRO, FRANCISCO, 1475?-1538
Wasserman, J. Gold of Caxamalca. 1952
ed.

Place in the sun. Kober, A.

Place of one's own. Sitwell, Sir O. bart.

Placet is a crazy place. Brown, F.

Plagiarist. Phillips, P.

PLAGUE
Dye, C. Syndrome Johnny
Feuchtwanger, L. Mendel Hirsch
Hofmannsthal, H. H. Edler von. Episode
in the life of the Marshal de Bassompierre
Jenkins, W. F. Plague
London, J. Scarlet plague
Poe, E. A. Masque of the Red Death
White, H. C. Watch in the night

Plague-cart before horse. Sitwell, Sir O.
bart.

The **plan.** Sulkin, S.

Plan goes wrong. Hendryx, J. B.

Planet passage. Wollheim, D. A.

PLANETARY ADVENTURES. See Interplanetary voyages

Planetoid of doom. Colladay, M. M.

PLANETS
Bloch, R. Fear planet
Jacobi, C. Tepondicon
Osborne, R. Contact, incorporated
See also names of individual planets,
e.g. Mars; Venus; etc.

The **plants.** Jenkins, W. F.

PLASTIC SURGERY. See Surgery, Plastic

Plato
Plato's Atlantis
Derleth, A. W. ed. Beyond time &
space

Plato's Atlantis. Plato

Platt, George, 1919-
　Play the field alone
　　Platt, G. Play the field alone, and
　　　other stories
　She shall have music
　　Platt, G. Play the field alone, and other
　　　stories
　Touchdown for Rex
　　Platt, G. Play the field alone, and other
　　　stories
　Very false alarm
　　Platt, G. Play the field alone, and other
　　　stories
Plattner story. Wells, H. G.
Plautus in the convent. Meyer, C. F.
Play the field alone. Platt, G.
PLAYGROUNDS
　Enright, E. Apple seed and apple thorn
PLAYING CARDS. See Cards
Playing even for Obadiah. Van Loan, C. E.
PLAYWRIGHTS. See Dramatists
Pleasant dreams. Robin, R.
Please come home, My Lady. Street, J. H.
Please, Mr Patron. Stock, G. A.
Pleasures of the table. Davies, R.
The plot. Saroyan, W.
Plot backfires. Hendryx, J. B.
Plot is hatched. Hendryx, J. B.
Ploughing of the Leaca. Corkery, D.
Plum duff. Van Dresser, P.
Plum pudding and mince pie. Miller, A. D.
Plumb, Beatrice, 1886-
　Good-willer
　　Elmquist, R. M. ed. Fifty years of
　　　Christmas
Plumbers. Claudy, C. H.
PLUTO (PLANET)
　Stone, L. F. Rape of the solar system
Plutonian drug. Smith, C. A.
Plutonian fire. Porter, W. S.
Plymouth Express. Christie, A. M.
PNEUMONIA
　Porter, W. S. Last leaf
POACHERS. See Poaching
POACHING
　Buckingham, N. Tight place
　Munro, H. H. The interlopers
Pod of a weed. Rosaire, F.
Poe, Edgar Allan, 1809-1849
　Angel of the odd
　　Poe, E. A. Poe's stories and poems
　The assignation
　　Poe, E. A. Tales. Dodd ed.
　Balloon-hoax
　　Jensen, P. ed. Fireside book of flying
　　　stories
　　Poe, E. A. Centenary Poe
　　Poe, E. A. The gold bug, and other
　　　tales and poems
　　Poe, E. A. Tales. Dodd ed.
　Berenice
　　Poe, E. A. Tales. Dodd ed.
　Black cat
　　Poe, E. A. Poe's stories and poems
　　Poe, E. A. Tales. Dodd ed.

Bon-Bon
　Poe, E. A. Tales. Dodd ed.
Cask of Amontillado
　Blodgett, H. W. ed. Story survey.
　　1953 ed.
　Bogorad, S. N. and Trevithick, J. eds.
　　College miscellany
　Day, A. G. ed. Greatest American short
　　stories
　Foerster, N. ed. American poetry and
　　prose. 1952 ed.
　Poe, E. A. Centenary Poe
　Poe, E. A. Poe's stories and poems
　Poe, E. A. Tales. Dodd ed.
Colloquy of Monos and Una
　Poe, E. A. Centenary Poe
　Poe, E. A. Tales. Dodd ed.
Conversation of Eiros and Charmion
　Kuebler, H. W. ed. Treasury of science
　　fiction classics
　Poe, E. A. Centenary Poe
　Poe, E. A. Tales. Dodd ed.
Descent into the maelström
　Poe, E. A. Centenary Poe
　Poe, E. A. The gold bug, and other
　　tales and poems
　Poe, E. A. Poe's stories and poems
　Poe, E. A. Tales. Dodd ed.
Devil in the belfry
　Poe, E. A. Tales. Dodd ed.
Domain of Arnheim
　Poe, E. A. Centenary Poe
　Poe, E. A. Tales. Dodd ed.
Le Duc de L'Omelette
　Poe, E. A. Centenary Poe
Eleonora
　Poe, E. A. Tales. Dodd ed.
The elk
　Poe, E. A. Tales. Dodd ed.
Facts in the case of M. Valdemar
　Fabricant, N. D. and Werner, H. eds.
　　World's best doctor stories
　Poe, E. A. Centenary Poe
　Poe, E. A. Tales. Dodd ed.
Fall of the House of Usher
　Foerster, N. ed. American poetry and
　　prose. 1952 ed.
　Gordon, C. and Tate, A. eds. House of
　　fiction
　Poe, E. A. Centenary Poe
　Poe, E. A. Poe's stories and poems
　Poe, E. A. Tales. Dodd ed.
Gold-bug
　Cody, S. ed. Greatest stories and how
　　they were written
　Lamb, L. ed. Family book of best loved
　　short stories
　Poe, E. A. Centenary Poe
　Poe, E. A. The gold bug, and other tales
　　and poems
　Poe, E. A. Poe's stories and poems
　Poe, E. A. Tales. Dodd ed.
Hop-Frog
　Poe, E. A. Tales. Dodd ed.
Imp of the perverse
　Neider, C. ed. Great short stories from
　　the world's literature
　Poe, E. A. Centenary Poe
　Poe, E. A. Tales. Dodd ed.
Island of the fay
　Poe, E. A. Tales. Dodd ed.
King Pest
　Poe, E. A. Tales. Dodd ed.

Poe, Edgar A.—*Continued*

Landor's cottage
Poe, E. A. Centenary Poe
Poe, E. A. Tales. Dodd ed.
Ligeia
Foerster, N. ed. American poetry and prose. 1952 ed.
Poe, E. A. Centenary Poe
Poe, E. A. Tales. Dodd ed.
Loss of breath
Poe, E. A. Tales. Dodd ed.
Man of the crowd
Poe, E. A. Tales. Dodd ed.
Ms. found in a bottle
Poe, E. A. Centenary Poe
Poe, E. A. The gold bug, and other tales and poems
Poe, E. A. Tales. Dodd ed.
Masque of the Red Death
Cuff, R. P. ed. American short story survey
Poe, E. A. Centenary Poe
Poe, E. A. The gold bug, and other tales and poems
Poe, E. A. Tales. Dodd ed.
Mellonta Tauta
Poe, E. A. Tales. Dodd ed.
Mesmeric revelation
Poe, E. A. Centenary Poe
Metzengerstein
Poe, E. A. Tales. Dodd ed.
Morella
Poe, E. A. Tales. Dodd ed.
Murders in the Rue Morgue
Burrell, J. A. and Cerf, B. A. eds. Anthology of famous American stories
Poe, E. A. Centenary Poe
Poe, E. A. Poe's stories and poems
Poe, E. A. Tales. Dodd ed.
Mystery of Marie Roget
Poe, E. A. Centenary Poe
Poe, E. A. Tales. Dodd ed.
Never bet the devil your head
Poe, E. A. Poe's stories and poems
Oblong box
Poe, E. A. Tales. Dodd ed.
Oval portrait
Poe, E. A. Tales. Dodd ed.
Pit and the pendulum
Burrell, J. A. and Cerf, B. A. eds. Anthology of famous American stories
Poe, E. A. Centenary Poe
Poe, E. A. The gold bug, and other tales and poems
Poe, E. A. Poe's stories and poems
Poe, E. A. Tales. Dodd ed.
Premature burial
Poe, E. A. Tales. Dodd ed.
Purloined letter
Burrell, J. A. and Cerf, B. A. eds. Anthology of famous American stories
Christ, H. I. and Shostak, J. eds. Short stories
Day, A. G. ed. Greatest American short stories
Foerster, N. ed. American poetry and prose. 1952 ed.
Poe, E. A. Centenary Poe
Poe, E. A. The gold bug, and other tales and poems
Poe, E. A. Poe's stories and poems
Poe, E. A. Tales. Dodd ed.

Shadow
Poe, E. A. Centenary Poe
Poe, E. A. Tales. Dodd ed.
Silence; a fable
Poe, E. A. Tales. Dodd ed.
The spectacles
Poe, E. A. Poe's stories and poems
Poe, E. A. Tales. Dodd ed.
The sphinx
Poe, E. A. Tales. Dodd ed.
System of Dr Tarr and Prof. Fether
Poe, E. A. Poe's stories and poems
Tale of the Ragged Mountains
Poe, E. A. The gold bug, and other tales and poems
Poe, E. A. Tales. Dodd ed.
Tell-tale heart
Poe, E. A. Centenary Poe
Poe, E. A. Tales. Dodd ed.
Schramm, W. L. ed. Great short stories
Three Sundays in a week
Poe, E. A. Poe's stories and poems
"Thou art the man"
Poe, E. A. Tales. Dodd ed.
Thousand-and-second tale of Scheherazade
Derleth, A. W. ed. Beyond time & space
Poe, E. A. Tales. Dodd ed.
Unparalleled adventure of one Hans Pfaall
Poe, E. A. Centenary Poe
William Wilson
Poe, E. A. Centenary Poe
Poe, E. A. Poe's stories and poems
Poe, E. A. Tales. Dodd ed.
X-ing a paragrab
Poe, E. A. Tales. Dodd ed.

About

Carr, J. D. Gentleman from Paris
The poet. Maugham, W. S.
Poet and the peasant. Porter, W. S.
Poet at home. Saroyan, W.
POETESSES. See Poets
POETRY
Heimann, M. Message that failed
Marsh, W. N. Beachhead in Bohemia
Munro, H. H. The Recessional
Munro, H. H. Reginald's peace poem
Munro, H. H. Reginald's Rubaiyat

POETS
Beck, W. Ask me no more
Brown, F. Greatest poem ever written
Carroll, J. W. At Mrs Farrelly's
Collier, J. Evening primrose
Collier, J. Possession of Angela Bradshaw
De La Mare, W. J. Willows
James, H. Aspern papers
Libin, S. Schlemihlov's works
Maugham, W. S. Colonel's lady
Maugham, W. S. The poet
Porter, W. S. Roads of destiny
Pratt, F. and De Camp, L. S. Gift of God
Taylor, C. L. The envelope
Wang Chu. Poets' club
Zangwill, I. Neo-Hebrew poet

Poets' club. Wang Chu

Poets' excursion. Gurnard, J.

POGROMS. See Jews—Persecution

Point of a pin. Chesterton, G. K.

Point of departure. Calisher, H.
Point of honour. Maugham, W. S.
Point of view. Keith, S.
Poirier, Normand R.
　Teletype machine
　　Hathaway, B. and Sessions, J. A. eds.
　　Writers for tomorrow. 2d ser.
Poison. Dahl, R.
POISONING
　Grosskopf, E. K. Tea for Tamahara
POISONOUS PLANTS
　Hawthorne, N. Rappaccini's daughter
POISONS
　Bond, R. T. ed. Handbook for poisoners;
　12 stories
　Queen, E. pseud. Three widows
POKER (GAME)
　Davis, S. P. Carson poker incident
　Erin, B. Quiet morning
　Maugham, W. S. Portrait of a gentleman
　Maugham, W. S. Straight flush
　Newhouse, E. Poker game
Poker game. Newhouse, E.
POLAND
1864-1918
　Asch, S. Kola Road
POLAR BEARS. See Bears
Polar night. Burke, N.
POLAR REGIONS. See Antarctic regions;
　Arctic regions
POLES IN ITALY
　Mann, T. Death in Venice
POLES IN THE UNITED STATES
　Farrell, J. T. Casual incident
POLICE
　Bruce, S. Farewell to crime
　Floherty, J. J. Duel at 70 miles an hour
　Frazee, S. Graveyard shift
　Snow, W. Fatal red hair
　Taylor, M. McGarry joins the Easter
　parade
Ireland
　O'Donovan, M. Majesty of the law
London
　Collins, W. Mr Policeman and the cook
New York (City)
　Porter, W. S. According to their lights
　Porter, W. S. After twenty years
　Porter, W. S. Clarion call
Russia
　Chekhov, A. P. Appropriate measures
　Shneur, Z. New police chief
United States
　Algren, N. Captain is impaled
　Brown, F. Death of Riley
　Lardner, R. W. There are smiles
　Porter, W. S. Badge of policeman O'Roon
　Porter, W. S. Cop and the anthem
　Taubes, F. Trouble on 98th Street
POLICEWOMEN. See Police
POLISH SOLDIERS. See Soldiers, Polish
Politeness. Brown, F.
POLITICAL CAMPAIGNS. See Politics
POLITICAL PRISONERS. See Prisoners,
　Political

POLITICIANS. See Politics
POLITICIANS, ENGLISH. See Politics
　—England
POLITICIANS, FRENCH. See Politics—
　France
POLITICS
　Johnson, D. M. Man who shot Liberty
　Valance
　Moore, W. We the people
　Stuart, J. Governor Warburton's right-
　hand man
Austria
　Boyle, K. White horses of Vienna
England
　Maugham, W. S. Lord Mountdrago
　Munro, H. H. Canossa
　Munro, H. H. Forewarned
　Munro, H. H. Infernal Parliament
　Munro, H. H. "Ministers of Grace"
　Priestley, J. B. Leadington incident
France
　Maugham, W. S. Appearance and reality
Ireland
　Joyce, J. Ivy Day in the committee room
Kentucky
　Fox, J. Knight of the Cumberland
New York (City)
　Horwitz, J. The campaign
　O'Higgins, H. J. Big Dan Reilly
Southern States
　Aswell, J. R. Shadow of evil
Texas
　Porter, W. S. Art and the bronco
United States
　Doty, W. L. Welcome home
　Porter, K. A. Day's work
Wisconsin
　Miner, H. Due process
POLITICS, CORRUPTION IN. See Cor-
　ruption (in politics)
Polka dot dress. Adler, W.
POLO
　Miers, E. S. Bandy
Polonaise. Hoffmann, E.
Poltarnees, Beholder of Ocean. Dunsany,
　E. J. M. D. P. 18th baron
POLYNESIANS
　Michener, J. A. Povenaa's daughter
Polzunkov. Dostoevskiĭ, F. M.
Pommery 1921. Seager, A.
POMPEII. See Italy—Pompeii
Pompey and some peaches. Sitwell, Sir O.
　bart
The pond. Kneale, N.
PONTIUS PILATE. See Pilate, Pontius
PONY EXPRESS
　Garthwaite, M. H. Riding the Pony Ex-
　press
　Skelton, C. L. Mail starts
Pony Porter swing. Person, W. T.
Pooja. Marshall, E.

POOL (GAME)
McNulty, J. Yellow-ball-in-the-side
See also Billiards
The **pool**. Maugham, W. S.
POOL HALLS. See Poolrooms
Pool of adventure. Gilbert, K.
Pool of narcissus. Calisher, H.
Pool of the black one. Howard, R. E.
Pooler, James, 1905-
Herself
Greene, J. I. and Abell, E. eds. Stories
of sudden truth
POOLROOMS
Stegner, W. E. Blue-winged teal
THE POOR. See Poverty
Poor black sheep. Cousins, M.
Poor community. Reisin, A.
Poor Cousin Evelyn. Yaffe, J.
Poor man's pudding. Melville, H.
Poor people. Horwitz, J.
Poor retriever. Person, W. T.
Poor rulc. Porter, W. S.
Poor superman. Leiber, F.
Pop's boy. Ashkenazy, I.
Porcelain cups. Cabell, J. B.

La **Porcelaine** Claire. O'Meara, W.

PORCUPINES
Gilbert, K. Pool of adventure
Reid, M. Battle of the marten and the
porcupine

Pore Perrie. Goyen, W.

Porges, Arthur, 1915-
The fly
Best science-fiction stories: 1953
Merril, J. ed. Beyond human ken
The rats
Best science fiction stories: 1952

Porky, the outboarder. Sherman, H. M.

PORT-AU-PRINCE. See Haiti—Port-au-
Prince

Portable phonograph. Clark, W. Van T.

Porte-cochere. Taylor, P. H.

Porter, Katherine Anne, 1894-
Day's work
Waite, H. O. and Atkinson, B. P. eds.
Literature for our time
Downward path to wisdom
Davis, C. B. ed. Eyes of boyhood
Flowering Judas
Heilman, R. B. ed. Modern short stories
Ludwig, J. B. and Poirer, W. R. eds.
Stories, British and American
Neider, C. ed. Great short stories from
the world's literature
West, R. B. and Stallman, R. W. eds.
Art of modern fiction
The grave
Peery, W. W. ed. 21 Texas short stories
Schorer, M. ed. The story
Jilting of Granny Weatherall
Fabricant, N. D. and Werner, H. eds.
World's best doctor stories
Gable, M. Sister, ed. Many-colored fleece
Schramm, W. L. ed. Great short stories

María Concepción
Burrell, J. A. and Cerf, B. A. eds. An-
thology of famous American stories
Foerster, N. ed. American poetry and
prose. 1952 ed.
Lynskey, W. C. ed. Reading modern
fiction
Noon wine
Ludwig, R. M. and Perry, M. B. eds.
Nine short novels
Old mortality
Gordon, C. and Tate, A. eds. House of
fiction
Southern review. Anthology of stories
from the Southern review
Pale horse, pale rider
Short, R. W. and Sewall, R. B. eds.
Short stories for study. 1950 ed.
That tree
Felheim, M.; Newman, F. B. and Stein-
hoff, W. R. eds. Modern short stories

Porter, William Sydney, 1862-1910
According to their lights
Porter, W. S. Complete works of O.
Henry
Adjustment of nature
Porter, W. S. Complete works of O.
Henry
The admiral
Porter, W. S. Complete works of O.
Henry
Adventures of Shamrock Jolnes
Porter, W. S. Complete works of O.
Henry
After twenty years
Porter, W. S. Complete works of O.
Henry
Porter, W. S. O. Henry's best stories
Afternoon miracle
Porter, W. S. Complete works of O.
Henry
Aristocracy versus hash
Porter, W. S. Complete works of O.
Henry
Art and the bronco
Peery, W. W. ed. 21 Texas stort stories
Porter, W. S. Complete works of
O. Henry
Assessor of success
Porter, W. S. Complete works of
O. Henry
At arms with Morpheus
Porter, W. S. Complete works of
O. Henry
Atavism of John Tom Little Bear
Porter, W. S. Complete works of
O. Henry
Babes in the jungle
Porter, W. S. Complete works of
O. Henry
Badge of policeman O'Roon
Porter, W. S. Complete works of
O. Henry
Best-seller
Porter, W. S. Complete works of
O. Henry
Between rounds
Porter, W. S. Complete works of
O. Henry
Bexar scrip no. 2692
Porter, W. S. Complete works of
O. Henry

Porter, William S.—*Continued*

Bird of Bagdad
  Porter, W. S. Complete works of O. Henry
Blackjack bargainer
  Burrell, J. A. and Cerf, B. A. eds. Anthology of famous American stories
  Porter, W. S. Complete works of O. Henry
Blind man's holiday
  Porter, W. S. Complete works of O. Henry
Brickdust row
  Porter, W. S. Complete works of O. Henry
Brief début of Tildy
  Porter, W. S. Complete works of O. Henry
Buried treasure
  Porter, W. S. Complete works of O. Henry
Buyer from Cactus City
  Porter, W. S. Complete works of O. Henry
By courier
  Porter, W. S. Complete works of O. Henry
Caballero's way
  Porter, W. S. Complete works of O. Henry
The cactus
  Porter, W. S. Complete works of O. Henry
Caliph and the cad
  Porter, W. S. Complete works of O. Henry
The caliph, cupid and the clock
  Porter, W. S. Complete works of O. Henry
Call loan
  Porter, W. S. Complete works of O. Henry
Call of the tame
  Porter, W. S. Complete works of O. Henry
Calloway's code
  Porter, W. S. Complete works of O. Henry
Caught
  Porter, W. S. Complete works of O. Henry
The chair of philanthromathematics
  Porter, W. S. Complete works of O. Henry
Champion of the weather
  Porter, W. S. Complete works of O. Henry
Chaparral Christmas gift
  Porter, W. S. Complete works of O. Henry
Chaparral prince
  Porter, W. S. Complete works of O. Henry
Cherchez la femme
  Porter, W. S. Complete works of O. Henry
Christmas by injunction
  Porter, W. S. Complete works of O. Henry
Church with an overshot-wheel
  Porter, W. S. Complete works of O. Henry

City of dreadful night
  Porter, W. S. Complete works of O. Henry
Clarion call
  Porter, W. S. Complete works of O. Henry
  Porter, W. S. O. Henry's best stories
Comedy in rubber
  Porter, W. S. Complete works of O. Henry
  Porter, W. S. O. Henry's best stories
Coming-out of Maggie
  Porter, W. S. Complete works of O. Henry
Complete life of John Hopkins
  Porter, W. S. Complete works of O. Henry
Compliments of the season
  Porter, W. S. Complete works of O. Henry
Confessions of a humorist
  Porter, W. S. Complete works of O. Henry
Conscience in art
  Porter, W. S. Complete works of O. Henry
Cop and the anthem
  Eaton, H. T. ed. Short stories
  Porter, W. S. Complete works of O. Henry
  Porter, W. S. O. Henry's best stories
Cosmopolite in a café
  Porter, W. S. Complete works of O. Henry
Count and the wedding guest
  Porter, W. S. Complete works of O. Henry
Country of elusion
  Porter, W. S. Complete works of O. Henry
Cupid à la carte
  Porter, W. S. Complete works of O. Henry
Cupid's exile number two
  Porter, W. S. Complete works of O. Henry
Day resurgent
  Porter, W. S. Complete works of O. Henry
Day we celebrate
  Porter, W. S. Complete works of O. Henry
Defeat of the city
  Porter, W. S. Complete works of O. Henry
Departmental case
  Porter, W. S. Complete works of O. Henry
Detective detector
  Porter, W. S. Complete works of O. Henry
Diamond of Kali
  Porter, W. S. Complete works of O. Henry
Dicky
  Porter, W. S. Complete works of O. Henry
Dinner at—
  Porter, W. S. Complete works of O. Henry
Discounters of money
  Porter, W. S. Complete works of O. Henry

Porter, William S.—*Continued*

Dog and the playlet
  Porter, W. S. Complete works of
  O. Henry
Door of unrest
  Porter, W. S. Complete works of
  O. Henry
A double-dyed deceiver
  Porter, W. S. Complete works of
  O. Henry
Dougherty's eye-opener
  Porter, W. S. Complete works of
  O. Henry
The dream
  Porter, W. S. Complete works of
  O. Henry
The duel
  Porter, W. S. Complete works of
  O. Henry
Duplicity of Hargraves
  Porter, W. S. Complete works of
  O. Henry
Easter of the soul
  Porter, W. S. Complete works of
  O. Henry
Elsie in New York
  Porter, W. S. Complete works of
  O. Henry
Emancipation of Billy
  Porter, W. S. Complete works of
  O. Henry
Enchanted kiss
  Porter, W. S. Complete works of
  O. Henry
Enchanted profile
  Porter, W. S. Complete works of
  O. Henry
Ethics of pig
  Porter, W. S. Complete works of
  O. Henry
Exact science of matrimony
  Porter, W. S. Complete works of
  O. Henry
Extradited from Bohemia
  Porter, W. S. Complete works of
  O. Henry
Ferry of unfulfilment
  Porter, W. S. Complete works of
  O. Henry
Fickle fortune; or, How Gladys hustled
  Porter, W. S. Complete works of
  O. Henry
Fifth wheel
  Porter, W. S. Complete works of
  O. Henry
Flag paramount
  Porter, W. S. Complete works of
  O. Henry
Fog in Santone
  Porter, W. S. Complete works of
  O. Henry
The fool-killer
  Porter, W. S. Complete works of
  O. Henry
Foreign policy of Company 99
  Porter, W. S. Complete works of
  O. Henry
Fourth in Salvador
  Porter, W. S. Complete works of
  O. Henry
"Fox-in-the-morning"
  Porter, W. S. Complete works of
  O. Henry

Friendly call
  Porter, W. S. Complete works of
  O. Henry
Friends in San Rosario
  Porter, W. S. Complete works of
  O. Henry
From the cabby's seat
  Porter, W. S. Complete works of
  O. Henry
From each according to his ability
  Porter, W. S. Complete works of
  O. Henry
Furnished room
  Burrell, J. A. and Cerf, B. A. eds. Anthology of famous American stories
  Porter, W. S. Complete works of
  O. Henry
  Porter, W. S. O. Henry's best stories
  Schramm, W. L. ed. Great short stories
Georgia's ruling
  Porter, W. S. Complete works of
  O. Henry
Ghost of a chance
  Porter, W. S. Complete works of
  O. Henry
Gift of the Magi
  Day, A. G. ed. Greatest American short stories
  Lamb, L. ed. Family book of best loved short stories
  Porter, W. S. Complete works of
  O. Henry
  Porter, W. S. O. Henry's best stories
"Girl"
  Porter, W. S. Complete works of
  O. Henry
  Porter, W. S. O. Henry's best stories
Girl and the graft
  Porter, W. S. Complete works of
  O. Henry
Girl and the habit
  Porter, W. S. Complete works of
  O. Henry
Gold that glittered
  Porter, W. S. Complete works of
  O. Henry
Greater Coney
  Porter, W. S. Complete works of
  O. Henry
Green door
  Porter, W. S. Complete works of
  O. Henry
Guardian of the accolade
  Porter, W. S. Complete works of
  O. Henry
"Guilty party"
  Porter, W. S. Complete works of
  O. Henry
Halberdier of the Little Rheinschloss
  Porter, W. S. Complete works of
  O. Henry
The hand that riles the world
  Porter, W. S. Complete works of
  O. Henry
Handbook of Hymen
  Porter, W. S. Complete works of
  O. Henry
The harbinger
  Porter, W. S. Complete works of
  O. Henry
Harlem tragedy
  Porter, W. S. Complete works of
  O. Henry

Porter, William S.—*Continued*

Missing chord
    Porter, W. S. Complete works of
    O. Henry

Modern rural sports
    Porter, W. S. Complete works of
    O. Henry

Moment of victory
    Porter, W. S. Complete works of
    O. Henry

Money maze
    Porter, W. S. Complete works of
    O. Henry

Municipal report
    Burrell, J. A. and Cerf, B. A. eds. Anthology of famous American stories
    Cuff, R. P. ed. American short story survey
    Porter, W. S. Complete works of
    O. Henry

Nemesis and the candy man
    Porter, W. S. Complete works of
    O. Henry

New York by camp fire light
    Porter, W. S. Complete works of
    O. Henry

Newspaper story
    Porter, W. S. Complete works of
    O. Henry

"Next to reading matter"
    Porter, W. S. Complete works of
    O. Henry

Night in new Arabia
    Porter, W. S. Complete works of
    O. Henry

No story
    Porter, W. S. Complete works of
    O. Henry

October in June
    Porter, W. S. Complete works of
    O. Henry

Octopus marooned
    Porter, W. S. Complete works of
    O. Henry

On behalf of the management
    Porter, W. S. Complete works of
    O. Henry

One dollar's worth
    Porter, W. S. Complete works of
    O. Henry

One thousand dollars
    Porter, W. S. Complete works of
    O. Henry
    Porter, W. S. O. Henry's best stories

Out of Nazareth
    Porter, W. S. Complete works of
    O. Henry

Passing of Black Eagle
    Porter, W. S. Complete works of
    O. Henry

Past one at Rooney's
    Porter, W. S. Complete works of
    O. Henry

The pendulum
    Porter, W. S. Complete works of
    O. Henry

Philistine in Bohemia
    Porter, W. S. Complete works of
    O. Henry

Phoebe
    Porter, W. S. Complete works of
    O. Henry

Phonograph and the graft
    Porter, W. S. Complete works of
    O. Henry

Pimienta pancakes
    Porter, W. S. Complete works of
    O. Henry

Plutonian fire
    Porter, W. S. Complete works of
    O. Henry

Poet and the peasant
    Porter, W. S. Complete works of
    O. Henry

Poor rule
    Porter, W. S. Complete works of
    O. Henry

Pride of the cities
    Porter, W. S. Complete works of
    O. Henry

Princess and the puma
    Porter, W. S. Complete works of
    O. Henry

Prisoner of Zembla
    Porter, W. S. Complete works of
    O. Henry

Proof of the pudding
    Porter, W. S. Complete works of
    O. Henry

Psyche and the pskyscraper
    Porter, W. S. Complete works of
    O. Henry

Purple dress
    Porter, W. S. Complete works of
    O. Henry

Queries and answers
    Porter, W. S. Complete works of
    O. Henry

Ramble in Aphasia
    Porter, W. S. Complete works of
    O. Henry

Ransom of Mack
    Porter, W. S. Complete works of
    O. Henry

Ransom of Red Chief
    Davis, C. B. ed. Eyes of boyhood
    Fenner, P. R. comp. Fun! Fun! Fun!
    Porter, W. S. Complete works of
    O. Henry
    Porter, W. S. O. Henry's best stories

The rathskeller and the rose
    Porter, W. S. Complete works of
    O. Henry

Red roses of Tonia
    Porter, W. S. Complete works of
    O. Henry

Reformation of Calliope
    Porter, W. S. Complete works of
    O. Henry

Remnants of the code
    Porter, W. S. Complete works of
    O. Henry

Renaissance at Charleroi
    Porter, W. S. Complete works of
    O. Henry

Retrieved reformation
    Porter, W. S. Complete works of
    O. Henry
    Porter, W. S. O. Henry's best stories

Roads of destiny
    Blodgett, H. W. ed. Story survey. 1953 ed.
    Porter, W. S. Complete works of
    O. Henry
    Pratt, F. ed. World of wonder

POULTRY
Dunsany, E. J. M. D. P. 18th baron. The hen
King, M. P. Chicken on the wind
Munro, H. H. Blood-feud of Toad-Water
See also Roosters

Pound of cure. Del Rey, L.

Povenaa's daughter. Michener, J. A.

POVERTY
Chekhov, A. P. A fragment
Crane, S. Experiment in misery
Crane, S. Men in the storm
Godchaux, E. Horn that called Bambine
Grinevskii, A. S. The ratcatcher
Heide, H. J. End of her rope
Krige, U. La Miseria
Melville, H. Poor man's pudding
Melville, H. Rich man's crumbs
Peretz, I. L. Bontsha the Silent
Pinski, D. And then he wept
Porter, W. S. Skylight room
Porter, W. S. Third ingredient
Reisen, A. Last hope
Reisen, A. Rich poor man
Swinbank, G. New hat
Verga, G. Black bread

Powder-white faces. Hughes, L.

Powell, Dawn, 1897-
Adam
Powell, D. Sunday, Monday and always
Artist's life
Powell, D. Sunday, Monday and always
Audition
Powell, D. Sunday, Monday and always
Blue hyacinths
Powell, D. Sunday, Monday and always
Cheerio
Powell, D. Sunday, Monday and always
The comeback
Powell, D. Sunday, Monday and always
Day after tomorrow
Powell, D. Sunday, Monday and always
Deenie
Powell, D. Sunday, Monday and always
Every day is ladies' day
Powell, D. Sunday, Monday and always
Feet on the ground
Powell, D. Sunday, Monday and always
The glads
Powell, D. Sunday, Monday and always
Grand march
Powell, D. Sunday, Monday and always
Here today, gone tomorrow
Powell, D. Sunday, Monday and always
Ideal home
Powell, D. Sunday, Monday and always
The Pilgrim
Powell, D. Sunday, Monday and always
The roof
Powell, D. Sunday, Monday and always
Such a pretty day
Powell, D. Sunday, Monday and always
You should have brought your mink
Powell, D. Sunday, Monday and always

Powell, Frances, 1935-
Black flag
Oberfirst, R. ed. 1954 anthology of best original short-stories

Powell, Jean
Lady walks
Stanford short stories, 1950

The **power**. Jenkins, W. F.

POWER BOATS. See Motorboats

Power of literature. Farrell, J. T.

Powerhouse. Bradbury, R.

Powerhouse. Welty, E.

Powers, Alfred
Hannibal's elephants
Fenner, P. R. comp. Elephants, elephants, elephants

Powers, James Farl, 1917-
Death of a favorite
Best American short stories, 1951
The forks
Heilman, R. B. ed. Modern short stories
He don't plant cotton
Lynskey, W. C. ed. Reading modern fiction
Lions, harts, leaping does
Gordon, C. and Tate, A. eds. House of fiction
Ludwig, J. B. and Poirier, W. R. eds. Stories, British and American
Prince of darkness
Best of the Best American short stories, 1915-1950
Thinker's digest (Periodical) Spoiled priest, and other stories
Valiant woman
Schorer, M. ed. The story

Powers, William T.
Meteor
Astounding science fiction (Periodical) Astounding science fiction anthology

Powys, Theodore Francis, 1875-1953
Christmas gift
Lohan, R. and Lohan, M. eds. New Christmas treasury

Praag, Siegfried Emanuel van, 1899-
Weesperstraat
Leftwich, J. ed. Yisröel. 1952 ed.

Practical joke. Farrell, J. T.

Practical joker. Simpson, M. E.

PRACTICAL JOKES. See Humor—Practical jokes

Prado, Pedro, 1894-
Laugh in the desert
Schramm, W. L. ed. Great short stories

Prairie kid. Johnson, D. M.

PRAIRIES
Garland, H. Under the lion's paw

Pratt, Fletcher, 1897-1956
Hormones
Star science fiction stories, no.2
Long view
Petrified planet
Official record
Pohl, F. ed. Assignment in tomorrow
Pardon my mistake
Derleth, A. W. ed. The outer reaches
Roger Bacon formula
Conklin, G. ed. Big book of science fiction
See also De Camp, L. S. jt. auth; Kubilius, W. jt. auth.

Price, Edith B.—*Continued*
Bobo and the Christmas spirit
American girl (Periodical) Christmas
all year 'round
Merrie gentlemen
American girl (Periodical) Christmas
all year 'round
Price on hide-rack. Balch, G.
Prichard, Roy
Men and babies
Oberfirst, R. ed. 1954 anthology of best
original short-shorts
Pride. Jameson, M.
PRIDE AND VANITY
Doty, W. L. College star
Doty, W. L. Man with the monocle
Winslow, T. S. Misses Grant
Pride in his holsters. Lowndes, R. W.
Pride of the cities. Porter, W. S.
Pride of Tony Colucci. Schulberg, B. W.
Priest and prophet at Bethel. Wilson, D. C.
Priest and the acolyte. Wilde, O.
Priest in the family. Kennedy, L.
Priestley, John Boynton, 1894-
Grey ones
Priestley, J. B. The other place, and
other stories of the same sort
Guest of honour
Priestley, J. B. The other place, and
other stories of the same sort
Leadington incident
Priestley, J. B. The other place, and
other stories of the same sort
Look after the strange girl
Priestley, J. B. The other place, and
other stories of the same sort
Mr Strenberry's tale
Kuebler, H. W. ed. Treasury of science
fiction classics
Priestley, J. B. The other place, and
other stories of the same sort
Night sequence
Priestley, J. B. The other place, and
other stories of the same sort
The other place
Priestley, J. B. The other place, and
and other stories of the same sort
The statues
Priestley, J. B. The other place, and
other stories of the same sort
Uncle Phil on TV
Priestley, J. B. The other place, and
other stories of the same sort
Primavera. Sitwell, Sir O. bart.
Priming the well. Caldwell, E.
Prince, Harold. See Prince, J. jt. auth.
Prince, Jerome, 1907- and **Prince, Harold**
Finger man
Mystery Writers of America, inc. Four-
&-twenty bloodhounds
Man in the velvet hat
Mystery Writers of America, inc. Mai-
den murders
Prince Alberic and the Snake Lady. Paget,
V.
Prince Godfrey frees mountain dwellers and
little shepherds from a savage were-
wolf and from witches. Gorska, H.

Prince of darkness. Powers, J. F.
PRINCES
Paget, V. Prince Alberic and the Snake
Lady
Princess and all the kingdom. Lagerkvist,
P. F.
Princess and the puma. Porter, W. S.
Princess September. Maugham, W. S.
Princess who couldn't say yes. Van Doren,
M.
PRINCESSES
Brophy, B. Crown princess
Coolidge, O. E. Luck charm
Street, J. L. Mr Bisbee's princess
Wilde, O. Birthday of the Infanta
PRINCETON UNIVERSITY
Boyd, J. Elms and Fair Oaks
Pringle. Barker, A. L.
PRINTERS AND PRINTING
Brown, F. Angelic angleworm
Brown, F. Etaoin Shrdlu
PRINTING. See Printers and printing
The **prism.** Van Doren, M.
The **prison.** Malamud, B.
PRISON SHIPS
Bedford-Jones, H. and Williams, L. B
Yellow Ship
The **prisoner.** Gordimer, N.
Prisoner of Zembla. Porter, W. S.
PRISONERS, CONDEMNED
Camus, A. Sentence of death
PRISONERS, POLITICAL
Bergengruen, W. Royal game
PRISONERS, RELEASED. See Ex-con-
victs
PRISONERS AND PRISONS
Benét, S. V. Blood of the martyrs
Brown, F. Cain
Eliot, G. pseud. In the prison
Maugham, W. S. Episode
Maugham, W. S. The kite
Maugham, W. S. Man with a conscience
Maugham, W. S. Official position
Michaëlis, K. Teacher Jensen
Munro, H. H. Lost sanjak
Poe, E. A. Pit and the pendulum
Schnabel, J. F. Journey for Wilbur
Steele, W. D. Renegade
Tucker, W. Exit
Van Doren, M. Episode at the Honeypot
Waugh, E. Love among the ruins

Italy

Mudford, W. Iron shroud

Russia

Dostoevskii, F. M. Peasant Marey
PRISONERS OF WAR
Blackburn, E. R. Sunrise
Downey, H. Crispin's way
Farrell, J. T. Digging our own graves
O'Donovan, M. Guests of the nation
Saint Exupéry, A. de. Letter to a hostage
Sansom, W. How Claeys died
Sartre, J. P. The wall

Pritchett, Victor Sawdon, 1900-
  The ape
    Heilman, R. B. ed. Modern short stories
  The sailor
    New writing (Periodical) Best stories
  Story of Don Juan
    Asquith, Lady C. E. C. ed. Book of
    modern ghosts
Private eye. Kuttner, H.
Private hell. Westbrock, J. T.
Private—keep out. MacDonald, P.
PRIVATE SECRETARIES. See Secretaries
PRIVATEERING
  Adams, J. D. Cap'n Ezra, privateer
  Hinternhoff, J. F. Mutineers be hanged
Privilege of the limits. Thompson, E. W.
Prize cargo. England, G. A.
Prize corn chowder. Haywood, C.
PRIZE FIGHTERS. See Boxing
PRIZE FIGHTING. See Boxing
PRIZES
  De La Roche, M. The celebration
Pro and con. Newhouse, E.
Pro arte. Seager, A.
A problem. James, H.
Problem for Emmy. Townes, R. S.
Problem of Cell 13. Futrelle, J.
Problem on Balak. Aycock, R. D.
Process. Van Vogt, A. E.
Procter, Maurice
  Fox in the Pennine Hills
    Mystery Writers of America, inc.
    Crooks' tour
  No place for magic
    Mystery Writers of America, inc.
    Butcher, baker, murder-maker
Procurator of Judæa. France, A.
PRODUCERS, THEATRICAL. See Theatrical producers
Production test. Jones, R. F.
The Professor. Farrell, J. T.
Professor. Hughes, L.
Professor Sea Gull. Mitchell, J.
PROFESSORS. See Teachers
Professor's teddy-bear. Waldo, E. H.
Prohibition. Merochnik, M.
Project ocean floor. Elam, R. M.
PROJECTILES
  Arico, V. The rebel
The promise. Maugham, W. S.
The promise. Stewart, R.
Promised land. Moore, C. L.
PROMISES
  Maugham, W. S. The promise
The promotion. Arico, V.
Proof. Stubbs, H. C.
Proof of the pudding. Porter, W. S.
Propagandist. Jenkins, W. F.
Property. Verga, G.

Propes, Arthur
  All that glitters
    Ford, N. A. and Faggett, H. L. eds.
    Best short stories by Afro-American
    writers (1925-1950)
PROPHECIES
  Alarcón, P. A. de. The prophecy
  Harvey, W. F. August heat
  Hawthorne, N. Great Stone Face
  Heinlein, R. A. Life-line
  Komroff, M. Told in the stars
  Munro, H. H. Peace offering
  Whitley, C. M. Destiny strikes back
The prophecy. Alarcón, P. A. de
The prophet. Appet, N.
The prophet. McLaverty, M.
A proposale. Ashford, D.
PROSPECTORS
  Brandon, W. Ghost lode
  Clark, W. Van T. Indian well
  Clark, W. Van T. Wind and the snow of
    winter
  Grey, Z. Tappan's burro
  London, J. All-gold cañon
  Purcell, D. Rider of the avalanche
  Rogow, L. Laziest man in Texas
  Schaefer, J. W. Something lost
Prosper's "old mother." Harte, B.
PROSTITUTES
  Brement, M. Youth
  Gold, I. Change of air
  Hemingway, E. Light of the world
  Jackson, C. R. Old men and boys
  Waltari, M. T. Goldilocks
Protected species. Fyfe, H. B.
Protecting Mary. O'Leary, J. T.
PROTECTION OF GAME. See Game
  protection
Protégée of Jack Hamlin's. Harte, B.
PROTESTANTISM
  O'Donovan, M. My first Protestant
Prothalamion. Sheehy, E.
Proud robot. Kuttner, H.
The Proudies entertain. Trollope, A.
Proust, Marcel, 1871-1922
  Filial sentiments of a parricide
    Neider, C. ed. Great short stories from
    the world's literature
Proved by the sea. Marmur, J.
Proverbial murder. Carr, J. D.
The provider. Guiney, L. I.
Prowler on the hill. Hole, L. E.
Proxima centauri. Jenkins, W. F.
Prudence by name. Schaefer, J. W.
Prudent man. Walsh, M.
Prussian officer. Lawrence, D. H.
PRUSSIANS. See Soldiers, German
Psyche and the pskyscraper. Porter, W. S.
Psychiatrist of one's own. Gellhorn, M. E.
PSYCHIATRISTS
  Collier, J. Interpretation of a dream
  Kuttner, H. Dream's end
  Kuttner, H. and Moore, C. L. Wild surmise

Pyle, Howard, 1853-1911
How the good gifts were used by two
Fenner, P. R. comp. Fools and funny
fellows
Tom Chist and his treasure box
Fenner, P. R. comp. Pirates, pirates,
pirates
Pyrénées-Orientales. See France, Provincial
and rural—Pyrénees-Orientales

Q

QUACKS AND QUACKERY
Caldwell, E. Medicine man
Phillips, P. Field study

QUADROONS. See Mulattoes
Quail for Mr Forester. Humphrey, W.
Quail seed. Munro, H. H.

QUAIL SHOOTING. See Hunting

QUAILS
Buckingham, N. Carry me back

QUAKERS. See Friends, Society of
Quality. Galsworthy, J.

Quality of mercy. Lipsky, E.

QUARRELING
Rabinowitz, S. Tit for tat
Scott, Sir W. Two drovers

QUARRIES AND QUARRYING
Van Doren, M. The quarry

The quarry. Van Doren, M.

Quarter section on Dullknife Creek. Haycox, E.

Quartet. De La Roche, M.

QUEBEC. See Canada—Quebec (Province).

Queen, Ellery, pseud.
Adventure of the Dauphin's doll
Queen, E. pseud. Calendar of crime
Adventure of the dead cat
Mystery Writers of America, inc. 20
great tales of murder
Queen, E. pseud. Calendar of crime
Adventure of the emperor's dice
Queen, E. pseud. Calendar of crime
Adventure of the fallen angel
Queen, E. pseud. Calendar of crime
Adventure of the Gettysburg bugle
Queen, E. pseud. Calendar of crime
Adventure of the ides of Michael Magoon
Queen, E. pseud. Calendar of crime
Adventure of the inner circle
Queen, E. pseud. Calendar of crime
Adventure of the medical finger
Queen, E. pseud. Calendar of crime
Adventure of the needle's eye
Queen, E. pseud. Calendar of crime
Adventure of the one-penny black
Mystery Writers of America, inc. Maid-
en murders
Adventure of the President's half disme
Queen, E. pseud. Calendar of crime
Adventure of the telltale bottle
Queen, E. pseud. Calendar of crime
Adventure of the three R's
Queen, E. pseud. Calendar of crime

Black ledger
Queen, E. pseud. Queen's Bureau of
Investigation
Child missing!
Queen, E. pseud. Queen's Bureau of
Investigation
Cold money
Queen, E. pseud. Queen's Bureau of
Investigation
Double your money
Queen, E. pseud. Queen's Bureau of
Investigation
Driver's seat
Queen, E. pseud. Queen's Bureau of
Investigation
Emperor's dice
Best detective stories of the year—1952
GI story
Queen, E. pseud. Queen's Bureau of
Investigation
Gambler's Club
Queen, E. pseud. Queen's Bureau of
Investigation
Gettysburg bugle
Mystery Writers of America, inc.
Butcher, baker, murder-maker
Ides of Michael Magoon
Mystery Writers of America, inc. Four-
&-twenty bloodhounds
Lump of sugar
Queen, E. pseud. Queen's Bureau of
Investigation
Matter of seconds
Queen, E. pseud. Queen's Bureau of
Investigation
Miser's gold
Queen, E. pseud. Queen's Bureau of
Investigation
Money talks
Queen, E. pseud. Queen's Bureau of
Investigation
Murder without clues
Best detective stories of the year—1951
This week magazine. This week's short-
short stories
"My queer Dean"
Best detective stories of the year—1954
Queen, E. pseud. Queen's Bureau of
Investigation
Myna birds
Queen, E. pseud. Queen's Bureau of
Investigation
Needle's eye
Mystery Writers of America, inc.
Crooks' tour
Question of honor
Queen, E. pseud. Queen's Bureau of
Investigation
Robber of Wrightsville
Queen, E. pseud. Queen's Bureau of
Investigation
Snowball in July
Queen, E. pseud. Queen's Bureau of
Investigation
Sound of blackmail
This week magazine. This week's short-
short stories
Three widows
Queen, E. pseud. Queen's Bureau of
Investigation
Witch of Times Square
Queen, E. pseud. Queen's Bureau of
Investigation

Queen of the Black Coast. Howard, R. E.
Queenie: the gallant-hearted collie. Little, G. W.
"Queer." Anderson, S.
Queer feet. Chesterton, G. K.
Queer kind of sorrow. Sullivan, R.
Queiroz, Eça de. See Eça de Queiroz, José Maria
Quentin, Patrick, pseud.
 All the way to the moon
  Queen, E. pseud. ed. Queen's awards: 6th ser.
 Boy's will
  Best detective stories of the year—1951
  Mystery Writers of America, inc.
 Crooks' tour
  Queen, E. pseud. ed. Queen's awards: 5th ser.
 Fat cat
  Joseph, M. ed. Best cat stories
 Girl overboard
  Mystery Writers of America, inc. Four- &-twenty bloodhounds
 Love comes to Miss Lucy
  Mystery Writers of America, inc. 20 great tales of murder
 This looks like murder
  This week magazine. This week's short-short stories
 Town blonde, country blonde
  This week magazine. This week's short-short stories
 Witness for the prosecution
  Mystery Writers of America, inc. Butcher, baker, murder-maker
Queries and answers. Porter, W. S.
The quest. Munro, H. H.
Quest for Saint Aquin. White, W. A. P.
Question of being businesslike. Yaffe, J.
Question of blood. Haycox, E.
Question of honor. Queen, E. pseud.
Quick one. Chesterton, G. K.
Quick shoots. Bonnaffon, A.
The quid pro quo. Danielson, R. E.
Quiet garden spot. Asch, S.
Quiet man. Walsh, M.
Quiet Mr Evans. Kneale, N.
Quiet morning. Erin, B.
Quiet one. Schuman, S.
A quiet wedding. Upson, W. H.
Quille, Dan de, pseud. See Wright, William
Quiller-Couch, Sir Arthur Thomas, 1863-1944
 Roll-call of the reef
  Cerf, B. A. and Moriarty, H. C. eds. Anthology of famous British stories
  Fenner, P. R. comp. Ghosts, ghosts, ghosts
Quince tree. Munro, H. H.
Quiroga, Horacio, 1879-1937
 The fatherland
  De Onís, H. ed. Spanish stories and tales
Quitandinha. Seager, A.

R

R.I.P. Trollope, A.
R. M. S. Titanic. Baldwin, H. W.
Rab and his friends. Brown, J.
Rabban Gamaliel. Cohn, E.
Rabbi and emperor. Cohn, E.
Rabbi and the siren. Spire, A.
Rabbi Itzik the fool. Steinberg, Y.
Rabbi Yochanan the warden. Peretz, I. L.
RABBIS
 Agnon, S. J. Story of the cantor
 Bergelson, D. In a backwoods town
 Bialik, H. N. Short Friday
 Bloch, J. R. Heresy of the water taps
 Cohn, E. Given years
 Cohn, E. Rabban Gamaliel
 Cohn, E. Rabbi and emperor
 Cohn, E. Remains of virtue
 Hamelin, Glückel of. A story
 Peretz, I. L. Cabalists
 Peretz, I. L. Devotion without end
 Peretz, I. L. If not higher
 Peretz, I. L. Rabbi Yochanan the warden
 Rabinowitz, S. Tit for tat
 Rappoport, S. Two great men
 Singer, I. J. Repentance
 Steinberg, Y. Rabbi Itzik the fool
 Werfel, F. V. Third commandment
 Zangwill, I. Neo-Hebrew poet
Rabbi's son. Babel', I. E.
RABBITS
 Caldwell, E. Molly-Cotton-Tail
 Cartmill, C. Number nine
 Seton, E. T. Raggylug
Rabchik, a Jewish dog. Rabinowitz, S.
Rabelais, Francois, 1490-1553?
 Phalanstery of Theleme
  Derleth, A. W. ed. Beyond time & space
RABIES. See Hydrophobia
Rabinowitz, Shalom, 1859-1916
 Dreyfus in Kasrilevke
  Howe, I. and Greenberg, E. eds. Treasury of Yiddish stories
 Eternal life
  Howe, I. and Greenberg, E. eds. Treasury of Yiddish stories
 Gy-ma-na-si-a
  Ausubel, N. ed. Treasury of Jewish humor
 Hodel
  Howe, I. and Greenberg, E. eds. Treasury of Yiddish stories
 Menachem-Mendel, fortune hunter
  Ausubel, N. ed. Treasury of Jewish humor
 My brother Eliyahu's drink
  Ausubel, N. ed. Treasury of Jewish humor
 On account of a hat
  Howe, I. and Greenberg, E. eds. Treasury of Yiddish stories
 Page from the Song of Songs
  Howe, I. and Greenberg, E. eds. Treasury of Yiddish stories
 The pair
  Howe, I. and Greenberg, E. eds. Treasury of Yiddish stories

Raine, William MacLeod, 1871-1954
Friend of Buck Hollister
    Western Writers of America. Bad men and good
Rainy day at Big Lost Creek. Stuart, J.
Rajah's Rock. Bonner, P. H.
Rakous, V. pseud. See Oesterreicher, A.
Ramble in Aphasia. Porter, W. S.
Rameau's nephew. Diderot, D.
Ramsay, Janet
Miracle at Eastpoint
    American girl (Periodical) Christmas all year 'round
Ramsey, Harmon B. 1907-
Mr Jones goes to Bethlehem
    Elmquist, R. M. ed. Fifty years to Christmas

RANCH LIFE
Brand, M. pseud. Dust storm
Cheshire, G. Bad year
Miers, E. S. Black Bat
    See also Cowboys

California
Steinbeck, J. The chrysanthemums
Steinbeck, J. The gift

Mexico
Bowles, P. F. At Paso Rojo

Nebraska
Jackson, C. T. Buffalo wallow

Nevada
Drago, H. S. Long winter

Oregon
Davis, H. L. Team bells woke me; 13 stories

Texas
Burtis, T. Rope and the bulldog
Porter, W. S. Hygeia at the Solito
Porter, W. S. Law and order
Porter, W. S. Madame Bo-Peep of the ranches
Porter, W. S. Missing chord
Rancher of the hills. Booker, A. E.
Rancher's horse. Bennett, R. H.
Randall, Kenneth Charles, 1898-
Wild hunter
    Fenner, P. R. comp. Dogs, dogs, dogs

Ramsom. Buck, P. S.

Ransom. Fyfe, H. B.

Ramsom note. Lord, M.

Ransom of Mack. Porter, W. S.

Ransom of Red Chief. Porter, W. S.

Ransom . . . $1,000,000. Runyon, D.

Rape of the lock. Pratt, F. and De Camp, L. S.

Rape of the solar system. Stone, L. F.

The **rapids.** Clark, W. Van T.

Rappaccini's daughter. Hawthorne, N.

Rappoport, Solomon, 1863-1920
Moses Montefiore
    Leftwich, J. ed. Yisröel. 1952 ed.

Two great men
    Ausubel, N. ed. Treasury of Jewish humor
Rashomon. Akutagawa, R.
Rasmussen, Gladys Fuller
Tea at Barnaby's
    Oberfirst, R. ed. 1952 anthology of best original short-shorts
The **rat.** Wright, S. F.
Rat race. De Courcy, D. and De Courcy, J.
Rat that could speak. Dickens, C.
The **ratcatcher.** Grinevskiĭ, A. S.
Rath, Ida Ellen, 1884-
Longest day I live
    Oberfirst, R. ed. 1954 anthology of best original short-shorts
The **rathskeller** and the rose. Porter, W. S.
RATS
De Courcy, D. and De Courcy, J. Rat race
Dickens, C. The rat that could speak
Muir, J. Pirate rat
Porges, A. The rats
The **rats.** Porges, A.
The **rattle.** Devin, B.
Rattlesnake Trail. Fitts, H. K.
Rattling good yarn. Milne, A. A.
Rattner, Joan, 1922-
Haitian incident
    American vanguard, 1953
Raw material. Maugham, W. S.
Rawlings, Charles A.
Boy who gave his dog away
    Saturday evening post (Periodical). Saturday evening post stories, 1952
Flash of lightning
    This week magazine. This week's short-short stories
Rawlings, Marjorie (Kinnan) 1896-1953
Benny and the bird-dogs
    Andrews, R. C. ed. My favorite stories of the great outdoors
Gal young un
    First-prize stories, 1919-1954
The pardon
    Blodgett, H. W. ed. Story survey. 1953 ed.
Rawson, Clayton, 1906-
Clues of the tattooed man & the broken legs
    Mystery Writers of America, inc. Four-&-twenty bloodhounds
Off the face of the earth
    Mystery Writers of America, inc. Butcher, baker, murder-maker
Ready, William B. 1914-
Angharad
    Ready, W. B. Great disciple, and other stories
Barring the weight
    Gable, M. Sister, ed. Many-colored fleece
    Ready, W. B. Great disciple, and other stories
Cattle raid on Cooley
    Ready, W. B. Great disciple, and other stories

Rees, Gilbert
Rod of God
Burnett, W. and Burnett, H. S. eds.
Sextet
Reese, John Henry
Cat-eyed woman
Saturday evening post (Periodical)
Saturday evening post stories, 1953
Desert orchid
Saturday evening post (Periodical)
Saturday evening post stories, 1952
Last day at the office
Saturday evening post (Periodical)
Saturday evening post stories, 1951
Rainmaker
Heinlein, R. A. ed. Tomorrow, the stars
Reeve, Joel
Doubles or nothing
Argosy (Periodical) Argosy Book of
sports stories
Referent. Bradbury, R.
Reformation of Calliope. Porter, W. S.
Refuge for tonight. Williams, R. M.
The **refugee.** Rice, J.
Refugee village. Stinetorf, L. A.
REFUGEES
Connolly, M. Seminary Hill
Forester, C. S. The unbelievable
Karo, D. B. Carmi
Kristol, I. Adam and I
Saint Exupéry, A. de. Letter to a hostage
Schulberg, D. W. Passport to nowhere
The **refugees.** Yaffe, J.
Regarding monuments. Grimson, M. S.
REGENERATION
Moore, C. L. No woman born
Porter, W. S. Higher abdication
Wyld Ospina, C. Honor of his house
Reginald. Munro, H. H.
Reginald at the Carlton. Munro, H. H.
Reginald at the theatre. Munro, H. H.
Reginald in Russia. Munro, H. H.
Reginald on besetting sins. Munro, H. H.
Reginald on Christmas presents. Munro,
H. H.
Reginald on house-parties. Munro, H. H.
Reginald on tariffs. Munro, H. H.
Reginald on the Academy. Munro, H. H.
Reginald on worries. Munro, H. H.
Reginald's choir treat. Munro, H. H.
Reginald's Christmas revel. Munro, H. H.
Reginald's drama. Munro, H. H.
Reginald's peace poem. Munro, H. H.
Reginald's Rubaiyat. Munro, H. H.
Regli, Adolph Casper, 1896-
One for the team
Furman, A. L. ed. Teen-age stories of
the diamond
Southpaw switch
Furman, A. L. ed. Teen-age stories of
the diamond
Trouble on the range
Fenner, P. R. comp. Cowboys, cowboys,
cowboys

Regula Amrain and her youngest son.
Keller, G.
Reid, Constance Bowman
Yellow leaf
Story (Periodical) Story; no. 4
Reid, Forrest, 1876-1947
Courage
Carrington, H. ed. Week-end book of
ghost stories
Reid, Mayne, 1818-1883
Battle of the marten and the porcupine
Andrews, R. C. ed. My favorite stories
of the great outdoors
Reid, Thomas Mayne. See Reid, Mayne
Reigate squires. Doyle, Sir A. C.
Rein, Harold E.
Days and nights
American vanguard, 1950
Reingelder and the German flag. Kipling, R.
Reisen, Abraham. See Reisin, Abraham
Reisin, Abraham, 1876-1953
Avrom the cobbler
Ausubel, N. ed. Treasury of Jewish
humor
Big succeh
Howe, I. and Greenberg, E. eds. Treas-
ury of Yiddish stories
Last hope
Ausubel, N. ed. Treasury of Jewish
humor
The loan
Ausubel, N. ed. Treasury of Jewish
humor
Poor community
Howe, I. and Greenberg, E. eds. Treas-
ury of Yiddish stories
The recluse
Howe, I. and Greenberg, E. eds. Treas-
ury of Yiddish stories
Rich poor man
Leftwich, J. ed. Yisröel. 1952 ed.
Tuition for the rebbe
Howe, I. and Greenberg, E. eds. Treas-
ury of Yiddish stories
Reiss, Isaac. See Nadir, Isaac Moishe
REJUVENATION
Bradbury, R. Hail and farewell
Derleth, A. W. McIlvaine's star
Hawthorne, N. Dr Heidegger's experiment
Jameson, M. Blind alley
Simak, C. D. Second childhood
Wright, S. F. The rat
RELATIVES. See Family life; also specific
relative, e.g. Aunts; Brothers; etc.
RELAY RACES. See Running
The **relic.** Annett, W. S.
Relic of the Vikings. Mowery, W. B.
RELIGION
Betts, D. Mr Shawn and Father Scott
Gally, J. W. Spirits
Harte, B. Bell-ringer of Angel's
Schaefer, J. W. Emmet Dutrow
RELIGIOUS BELIEF. See Faith
RELIGIOUS LIBERTY
Hawthorne, N. Endicott and the Red
Cross
Reluctant dragon. Grahame, K.

REUNIONS, FAMILY. See Family re-
unions
REVENGE
Clemens, S. L. Man that corrupted Had-
leyburg
Cohen, O. R. Law and the profits
Cross, J. A. Hunch that clicked
Haycox, E. Last draw
Keller, D. H. The doorbell
Kipling, R. Village that voted the earth
was flat
Maupassant, G. de. La Mère Sauvage
Munro, H. H. Feast of Nemesis
Munro, H. H. Lumber-room
Munro, H. H. The penance
O'Rourke, F. Last shot
Paget, V. Wedding chest
Poe, E. A. Cask of Amontillado
Poe, E. A. Hop-Frog
Porter, K. A. María Concepción
Porter, W. S. Last of the troubadours
Porter, W. S. One dollar's worth
Russell, B. A. W. R. 3d earl. Guardians
of Parnassus
Schaefer, J. W. Out of the past
Schnitzler, A. Bachelor's death
Shaw, I. Sailor off the Bremen
Van Doren, M. Mortimer
Vickers, R. Million-to-one chance
Revenge. Schneur, Z.
Revenue Charlie. Weeks, R.
REVERE, PAUL, 1735-1818
Benét, S. V. Tooth for Paul Revere
Reverend Father Gilhooley. Farrell, J. T.
Reverend John Smith prepares his sermon.
Crockett, S. R.
Reverend Mother and the foolish decision.
Lieberman, R.
REVERENDS. See Clergy
Reverse phylogeny. Long, A. R.
Revolt. Brenner, L.
Revolt of "Mother." Freeman, M. E. W.
Revolt of the pedestrians. Keller, D. H.
REVOLUTION, AMERICAN. See United
States—18th century—Revolution
The revolution. Newhouse, E.
Revolution racket. Charteris, L.
Revolutionary etude. Schneider, G. W.
REVOLUTIONS
Cicellis, K. Easy way
Novás Calvo, L. Dark night of Ramón
Yendía
O'Donovan, M. Eternal triangle
Porter, W. S. Caught
Porter, W. S. "Fox-in-the-morning"
Porter, W. S. Rouge et noir
Porter, W. S. Smith
Verga, G. Liberty
Reward of faith. Goudge, E.
Rex imperator. Wilson, A.
Rex of the Coast patrol. Johnson, M. S.
Rex v. Burnaby. Freeman, R. A.
Rey, Lester Del. See Del Rey, Lester

Reymont, Wladyslaw Stanislaw, 1868-1925
Twilight
Neider, C. ed. Great short stories from
the world's literature
Reynolds, Helen Mary Greenwood (Camp-
bell) 1884-
Adventure on Lone Gulch Trail
Story parade (Periodical) Adventure
stories
Reynolds, J. M. and McCormick, H. P.
Through Twelve-League Labyrinth
Bluebook (Periodical) Best sea stories
from Bluebook
Reynolds, Mack, 1918-
Business, as usual
Derleth, A. W. ed. Worlds of tomorrow
Discord makers
Conklin, G. ed. Invaders of earth
Isolationist
Conklin, G. ed. Big book of science
fiction
Man in the moon
Lesser, M. A. ed. Looking forward
Martians and the Coys
Brown, F. and Reynolds, M. eds. Sci-
ence-fiction carnival
Reynolds, Mack, 1918- and Brown, Fredric,
1906-
Dark interlude
Best science fiction stories: 1952
Galaxy science fiction magazine. Galaxy
reader of science fiction
Reynolds, Quentin James, 1902-
Glass of orange juice
Ribalow, H. U. ed. World's greatest
boxing stories
RHINE RIVER AND VALLEY
Charteris, L. The Rhine: The Rhine
maiden
The Rhine: The Rhine maiden. Charteris, L.
Rhodes, William Parle, 1902-
Women will out
Oberfirst, R. ed. 1954 anthology of best
original short-shorts
RHODES
Maugham, W. S. Human element
Rib steak. Anderson, E. V.
Rice, Alice Caldwell (Hegan) 1870-1942
Hoodooed
Summers, H. S. ed. Kentucky story
Theater party
Fenner, P. R. comp. Fun! Fun! Fun!
Rice, Craig, 1908-
Goodbye forever
Best detective stories of the year—1952
Rice, Craig, 1908- and Palmer, Stuart, 1905-
Cherchez la frame
Queen, E. pseud. ed. Queen's awards:
6th ser.
Once upon a train
Queen, E. pseud. ed. Queen's awards:
5th ser.
Rice, Jane
The refugee
Davenport, B. ed. Ghostly tales to be
told

Rice, John Andrew, 1888-
Monday come home
Collier's, the national weekly. Collier's best

Rich boy. Fitzgerald, F. S. K.

Rich man's crumbs. Melville, H.

RICH MEN. See Capitalists and financiers; Wealth

Rich, poor, and indifferent. Van Doren, M.

Rich poor man. Reisin, A.

Richards, Dick
Training Alice and Congo
Fenner, P. R. comp. Elephants, elephants, elephants

Richardson, Maurice Lane, 1907-
Way out in the continuum
Horizon (Periodical) Golden Horizon

Richardson, Robert Shirley, 1902-
Xi effect
Bleiler, E. F. and Dikty, T. E. eds. Imagination unlimited

A richer dust. Coward, N. P.

Richter, Conrad, 1890-
Doctor Hanray's second chance
Saturday evening post (Periodical) Saturday evening post stories, 1950
Marriage that couldn't succeed
Saturday evening post (Periodical) Saturday evening post stories, 1952
Sinister journey
Saturday evening post (Periodical) Saturday evening post stories, 1953

Rickenbacker, Edward Vernon, 1890-
The raft
McFee, W. ed. Great sea stories of modern times

The riddle. De La Mare, W.

Riddle of the Black Museum. Palmer, S.

Riddle of the dangling pearl. Palmer, S.

Riddle of the snafu murder. Palmer, S.

Riddle of the tired bullet. Palmer, S.

RIDDLES
Hamelin, Glückel of. A story
Porter, W. S. Bird of Bagdad

Ride a pale ghost into night and time. Clayton, J. B.

Ride 'im Chick Norris. Fleming, J. S.

Ride on the short dog. Still, J.

Ride out. Foote, S.

Ride the river. Haycox, E.

Rider of the avalanche. Purcell, D.

Rider on the pale horse. Eustis, H.

Riding. See Horsemanship

Riding the Pony Express. Garthwaite, M. H.

Rieseberg, Harry Earl
I dive for treasure
Fenner, P. R. comp. Stories of the sea

Rifleman's run. Brick, J.

Rig ship for diving. Bateman, A.

Right count. O'Rourke, F.

Right side. Collier, J.

Right thing. Lacy, E.

Right thing. Williams, W. C.

Rightful owner. Stuart, J.

RIGHTS OF WOMEN. See Woman—Rights of women

Rigmarole. Callaghan, M. E.

Rilke, Rainer Maria, 1875-1926
How old Timofei died singing
Lange, V. ed. Great German short novels and stories
Mirrored room
Fabricant, N. D. and Werner, H. eds. World's best doctor stories
The stranger
Neider, C. ed. Great short stories from the world's literature

Rinehart, Mary (Roberts) 1876-
Burned chair
Rinehart, M. R. Frightened wife, and other murder stories
Frightened wife
Rinehart, M. R. Frightened wife, and other murder stories
If only it were yesterday
Rinehart, M. R. Frightened wife, and other murder stories
Murder and the south wind
Rinehart, M. R. Frightened wife, and other murder stories
One hour of glory
Eaton, H. T. ed. Short stories
The scandal
Rinehart, M. R. Frightened wife, and other murder stories

Ring around the redhead. MacDonald, J. D.

RINGS
Norling, M. E. Jade ring

Ringstones. Wall, J. W.

Ringwood, Gwen (Pharis)
Little ghost
Weaver, R. and James, H. eds. Canadian short stories

RIOTS
Asch, S. Kola Street

Rip Van Winkle. Irving, W.

Ripe for development. Harvey, W. F.

Ripeness of the time. Fonger, H.

Rise and fall of Mortimer Scrivens. Milne, A. A.

Rise of Carthage. Williams, L.

Rise of Lorenzo Villari. Ferrone, J. R.

Ritchie, Lewis Anselm da Costa, 1886-
Some "Q" ships
McFee, W. ed. Great sea stories of modern times

Rite, Eva, pseud. See Anderson, Esther Victoria

Riter, Faye
Matter of vanity
Hathaway, B. and Sessions, J. A. eds. Writers for tomorrow. 2d ser.
Sense of destination
Hathaway, B. and Sessions, J. A. eds. Writers for tomorrow. 2d ser.

RITES AND CEREMONIES

Jews
See Jews—Rites and ceremonies

Rites of spring. Prevost, L. E.

Robinson, Frank M.—*Continued*
Oceans are wide
Year's best science fiction novels, 1954
Reluctant heroes
Galaxy science fiction magazine. Galaxy reader of science fiction
Santa Claus planet
Best science fiction stories: 1951
Robinson, Gertrude, 1876-
Winged feet
Fenner, P. R. comp. Indians, Indians, Indians
Robinson, Leonard Wallace, 1912-
Ruin of soul
Prize stories of 1950
Robinson, Rosanne Smith
Mango tree
Best American short stories, 1954
ROBOTS. See Automata
Robots return. Williams, R. M.
Roche, Mazo de la. See De La Roche, Mazo
Roche, Roger Frison- See Frison-Roche, Roger
Rochlin, R. J.
Storm winds
Creamer, J. B. comp. Twenty-two stories about horses and men
The **rock.** Yemtzen, V.
Rock bottom. Nye, N. C.
Rock crystal. Stifter, A.
Rock-of-the-mass. Corkery, D.
The **rocket.** Bradbury, R.
Rocket man. Bradbury, R.
Rocket of 1955. Kornbluth, C. M.
ROCKET SHIPS
Bradbury, R. Golden apples of the sun
Bradbury, R. The rocket
Coppel, A. The dreamer
Gallun, R. Z. Operation Pumice
Grendon, E. Trip one
Hallstead, W. F. Space Lane cadet
Jenkins, W. F. Proxima centauri
Matheson, R. Shipshape home
Russell, E. F. Jay Score
Verne, J. Round the moon
See also Space ships
Rocket to the sun. Van Dresser, P.
Rocketeers have shaggy ears. Bennett, K.
Rocking-horse winner. Lawrence, D. H.
Rocklynne, Ross
Backfire
Conklin, G. ed. Omnibus of science fiction
Jaywalker
Galaxy science fiction magazine. Galaxy reader of science fiction
Pressure
Bleiler, E. F. and Dikty, T. E. eds. Imagination unlimited
Winner take all
Derleth, A. W. ed. Time to come
Rocky. Johnson, H.
ROCKY MOUNTAIN GOATS
Gilbert, K. Old man of the mountains
White, S. E. Climbing for goats

ROCKY MOUNTAINS
White, S. E. Climbing for goats
Rod of God. Rees, G.
RODEOS
Miers, E. S. Black Bat
Schaefer, J. W. Harvey Kendall
Wood, K. Workaday cowboy
See also Cowboys
Rodgers, Mary Augusta
Lover and his lass
Lantz, J. E. ed. Stories of Christian living
Rodney. Nason, L. H.
Rodney has a relapse. Wodehouse, P. G.
Roger Bacon formula. Pratt, F.
Roger Malvin's burial. Hawthorne, N.
Rogers, Joel Townsley
Moment without time
Startling stories (Periodical) Best from Startling stories
Rogers, Kay
Experiment
Magazine of fantasy and science fiction. Best from Fantasy and science fiction; 3d ser.
Rogow, Lee
Laziest man in Texas
This week magazine. This week's short-short stories
That certain flavor
This week magazine. This week's short-short stories
Rogue ship. Van Vogt, A. E.
ROGUES AND VAGABONDS
Kipling, R. Man who would be king
Rogues in the house. Howard, R. E.
Rojas, Manuel
Glass of milk
Bachelor, J. M.; Henry, R. L. and Salisbury, R. eds. Current thinking and writing; 2d ser.
Rokefort, K. D. pseud. See Woodward, George B.
Roll-call of the reef. Quiller-Couch, Sir A. T.
Rolland, Kermit
Mr Carmody's safari
Joseph, M. ed. Best cat stories
Roman fever. Wharton, E. N. J.
Roman holiday. Lewis, R.
Roman remains. Blackwood, A.
ROMAN SOLDIERS. See Soldiers, Roman
A **romance.** Renard, J.
Romance lingers, adventure lives. Collier, J.
Romance of a busy broker. Porter, W. S.
The **romancers.** Munro, H. H.
A **romantic.** O'Donovan, M.
Romantic boy. Goudsmit, S.
Romantic interlude in the life of Willie Collins. Farrell, J. T.
Romantic young lady. Maugham, W. S.
Romantically inclined. Caldwell, E.

ROME
B.C. 510-30

Wilder, T. N. From a journal-letter of Julius Caesar

B.C. 30-476 A.D.

Blackburn, E. R. Before the burning of Rome

ROME (CITY) See Italy—Rome (City)

Rome: The Latin touch. Charteris, L.

Romeo. Jackson, C. R.

Romney. Barker, A. L.

Ronald leaves the academy. Tunis, J. R.

The roof. Horwitz, J.

The roof. Powell, D.

Roof sitter. Eisenberg, F.

The rookie. Dailey, J.

The room. Sartre, J. P.

Room in the Dragon Volant. Le Fanu, J. S.

Room in the world. Zugsmith, L.

Room number twenty-three. Phillips, J. P.

Room without a telephone. Lewis, W.

ROOMERS. See Boarding houses

ROOMING HOUSES. See Boarding houses

Rooney, Frank, 1913-
Cyclists' raid
Best American short stories, 1952
Prize stories of 1951

Roos, Kelley, pseud.
Two over par
Mystery Writers of America, inc. Four-&-twenty bloodhounds

ROOSTERS
Benson, T. White cock
Goyen, W. White rooster
McLaverty, M. Game cock
Melville, H. Cock-a-doodle-doo!
Stuart, J. The champion
See also Cock fighting; Poultry

The rope. Baudelaire, C. P.

Rope and the bulldog. Burtis, T.

Rope enough. Collier, J.

Roper, Winniford, 1890-
Last cigarette
Oberfirst, R. ed. 1954 anthology of best original short-shorts

ROPING
James, W. Best riding and roping

Rosaire, Forrest, 1902-
Pod of a weed
Lass, A. H. and Horowitz, A. eds. Stories for youth

Rose for Emily. Faulkner, W.

"Rose of Dixie." Porter, W. S.

Rosegger, Peter, 1843-1918
Flight into Egypt
Selden, R. ed. Ways of God and men
Of love and joy
Brentano, F. ed. The word lives on

Rosenberg, Edgar, 1925-
Happy one
Hathaway, B. and Sessions, J. A. eds. Writers for tomorrow. 2d ser.
Our Felix
Stanford short stories, 1953

Rosenberg, Ethel (Clifford) 1915-
Aunt Esther's galoshes
Ausubel, N. ed. Treasury of Jewish humor
Mrs Rivkin grapples with the drama
Ausubel, N. ed. Treasury of Jewish humor
Ribalow, H. U. ed. These your children
Uncle Julius and the BMT
Ausubel, N. ed. Treasury of Jewish humor

Rosenfeld, Jonah, 1882-1944
Competitors
Howe, I. and Greenberg, E. eds. Treasury of Yiddish stories
Return home
Leftwich, J ed. Yisröel. 1952 ed.
Sick goose
Howe, I. and Greenberg, E. eds. Treasury of Yiddish stories

Roses, ruses and romance. Porter, W. S.

ROSH HA-SHANA
Reisin, A. Poor community

Rosinback. Young, J. M.

Rosmond, Babette, 1917- and Lake, Leonard M.
Are you run-down, tired—
Conklin, G. and Conklin, L. T. eds. Supernatural reader

Ross, Alberta L.
Something special for Jane
Oberfirst, R. ed. 1954 anthology of best original short-shorts

Ross, James, 1911-
Zone of interior
Collier's, the national weekly. Collier's best

Ross, Julian Maclaren- See Maclaren-Ross, Julian

Ross, Leonard Q. pseud. See Rosten, Leo Calvin

Ross, Martin, pseud. See Martin, Violet Florence

Ross, Sinclair, 1908-
Lamp at noon
Pacey, D. ed. Book of Canadian stories
The outlaw
Weaver, R. and James, H. eds. Canadian short stories

Rossiter, H. D.
Allan Franklin
Hathaway, B. and Sessions, J. A. eds. Writers for tomorrow. 2d ser.
Black bile
Hathaway, B. and Sessions, J. A. eds. Writers for tomorrow. 2d ser.
How dear to my heart
Hathaway, B. and Sessions, J. A. eds. Writers for tomorrow. 2d ser.

Rosten, Leo Calvin, 1908-
Mr K*A*P*L*A*N the Magnificent
Ribalow, H U. ed. This land, these people

The rot. Lewis, W.

ROTARY INTERNATIONAL
Milburn, G. The apostate

Roth, Cecil, 1899-
The martyr
Leftwich, J. ed. Yisröel. 1952 ed.

Rothberg, Abraham Alan, 1922-
    Not with our fathers
        Best American short stories, 1950
        Ribalow, H. U. ed. These your childern
Rouge et noir. Porter, W. S
Rouge high. Hughes, L.
Rough crossing. Fitzgerald, F. S. K.
Rough green tree. Sullivan, R.
Round by round. Aiken, C. P.
Round dozen. Maugham, W. S.
ROUND TABLE. See Arthur, King
Round the circle. Porter, W. S.
Round the moon. Verne, J.
Round the world fliers. Williams, W. C.
Round trip. Sullivan, R.
The round up. Seredy, K.
Rounds, Glen, 1906-
    Knute, the giant bullsnake
        Fenner, P. R. ed. Fools and funny fel-
        lows
    Paul goes hunting
        Fenner, P. R. comp. Fun! Fun! Fun!
    Uncle Torwal and Whitey go to town
        Fenner, P. R. comp. Giggle box
    Whitey's first round-up
        Fenner, P. R. comp. Cowboys, cowboys,
        cowboys
Rousseau, Jean Jacques, 1712-1778
    Isle of St Peter
        Andrews, R. C. ed. My favorite stories
        of the great outdoors
ROWING
    Shattuck, R. Workout on the river
        See also Boat racing
Rowland, Sidney
    McGregor affair
        Mystery writers of America, inc. But-
        cher, baker, murder-maker
ROYAL CANADIAN MOUNTED PO-
    LICE. See Canada. Royal Canadian
    Mounted Police
Royal game. Bergengruen, W.
Rubaiyat of a Scotch highball. Porter, W. S.
RUBBER
    Maugham, W. S. Back of beyond
    Maugham, W. S. Flotsam and jetsam
RUBBER PLANTATIONS See Rubber
Rubber plant's story. Porter, W. S.
The rube. Grey, Z.
Rube and the racketeer. Mowery, W. B.
Ruby, B. F. See Pratt, F. jt. auth.
Rude awakening. Howard, W.
Rudnicki, Adolf, 1912-
    Ascent to heaven
        Rudnicki, A. Ascent to heaven
    Crystal stream
        Rudnicki, A. Ascent to heaven
    Dying man
        Rudnicki, A. Ascent to heaven
    Great Stefan Konecki
        Rudnicki, A. Ascent to heaven
Rudolph. Winslow, T. S.

Rugel, Miriam, 1911-
    The flower
        Abell, E. ed. American accent
        Prize stories, 1954
The Ruggleses go to the Christmas party.
    Wiggin, K. D. S.
RUGS, HOOKED
    Ross, A. L. Something special for Jane
Ruin of soul. Robinson, L. W.
Ruined by success. Nadir, I. M.
Rule of three. Waldo, E. H.
Ruler of men. Porter, W. S
RULERS. See Kings and rulers
The rulers. Van Vogt, A. E.
The Rull. Van Vogt, A. E.
Rum for dinner. Blochman, L. G.
The rumor. Caldwell, E.
Run for your life. Courtier, S. H.
Run, iron man. Herndon, B.
Runaround. Asimov, I.
Runaway. Caldwell, E.
The runaway. Zweig, S.
RUNAWAYS. See Hitchhikers
RUNAWAYS (CHILDREN)
    Crane, S. His new mittens
Runbeck, Margaret Lee, 1905-
    Dog for Miss Boo
        Cavanna, B. ed. Pick of the litter
RUNNERS. See Running
RUNNING
    Carter, R. G. Blue ribbon event
    Farrell, J. T. Fastest runner on Sixty-
        First Street
    Gartner, J. Jug Leg Kelley
    Miers, E. S. Ghost runner
    Miers, E. S. He who laughs last
    Person, W. T Any way race
    Strong, P. N. Anchor man
    Sylvester, H. Last race
    Tunis, J. R. Two-mile race
Running dark. Strong, P. N
Runyon, Damon, 1880-1946
    All horse players die broke
        Runyon, D. More guys and dolls
    Barbecue
        Runyon, D. More guys and dolls
    Baseball Hattie
        Graber, R. S. ed. Baseball reader
        Runyon, D. More guys and dolls
    Big Boy Blues
        Blodgett, H. W. ed. Story survey.
        1953 ed.
        Runyon, D. More guys and dolls
    Big shoulders
        Runyon, D. More guys and dolls
    Big umbrella
        Runyon, D. More guys and dolls
    Blonde mink
        Runyon, D. More guys and dolls
    Bred for battle
        Ribalow, H. U. ed. World's greatest
        boxing stories
    Broadway incident
        Runyon, D. More guys and dolls
    Burge McCall
        Runyon, D. More guys and dolls

Runyon, Damon—*Continued*
  Call on the President
    Runyon, D. More guys and dolls
  Cemetery bait
    Runyon, D. More guys and dolls
  Cleo
    Runyon, D. More guys and dolls
  Hold 'em Yale
    Herzberg, M. J. comp. Treasure chest
      of sport stories
  Idyll of Miss Sarah Brown
    Runyon, D. More guys and dolls
  Job for the Macarone
    Runyon, D. More guys and dolls
  Joe Terrace
    Runyon, D. More guys and dolls
  Johnny One-Eye
    Runyon, D. More guys and dolls
  Lacework Kid
    Runyon, D. More guys and dolls
  Leopard's spots
    Runyon, D. More guys and dolls
  Light in France
    Runyon, D. More guys and dolls
  Little Pinks
    Runyon, D. More guys and dolls
  Lonely heart
    Runyon, D. More guys and dolls
  Lou Louder
    Runyon, D. More guys and dolls
  Maybe a queen
    Runyon, D. More guys and dolls
  Melancholy Dane
    Runyon, D. More guys and dolls
  Neat strip
    Runyon, D. More guys and dolls
  Nothing happens in Brooklyn
    Runyon, D. More guys and dolls
  Old Em's Kentucky home
    Runyon, D. More guys and dolls
  Palm Beach Santa Claus
    Runyon, D. More guys and dolls
  Piece of pie
    Christ, H. I. and Shostak, J. eds. Short
      stories
    Runyon, D. More guys and dolls
  Ransom . . . $1,000,000
    Runyon, D. More guys and dolls
  Sense of humor
    Queen, E. pseud. ed. Literature of crime
  Situation wanted
    Runyon, D. More guys and dolls
  Snatching of Bookie Bob
    Dachs, D. ed. Treasury of sports humor
  So you won't talk
    Runyon, D. More guys and dolls
  Tight shoes
    Runyon, D. More guys and dolls
  Too much pep
    Runyon, D. More guys and dolls

Rupee. Willingham, C.

RURAL LIFE. See Farm life

Rus in urbe. Porter, W. S.

Rush hour. Benowitz, E.

Rush-hour romance. Crawford, E. and Dalmas, H.

Russell, Bertrand Arthur Willian Russell, 3d earl, 1872-
  Benefit of clergy
    Russell, B. A. W. R. 3d earl. Satan in
      the suburbs, and other stories

Corsican ordeal of Miss X
  Russell, B. A. W. R. 3d earl. Satan in
    the suburbs, and other stories
Guardians of Parnassus
  Russell, B. A. W. R. 3d earl. Satan in
    the suburbs, and other stories
The infra-redioscope
  Russell, B. A. W. R. 3d earl. Satan in
    the suburbs, and other stories
Satan in the suburbs
  Russell, B. A. W. R. 3d earl. Satan in
    the suburbs, and other stories

Russell, Eric Frank, 1905-
  And then there were none
    Sloane, W. M. ed. Stories for tomorrow
    Year's best science fiction novels, 1952
  Boomerang
    Conklin, G. ed. Science-fiction thinking
      machines
  Dear Devil
    Conklin, G. ed. Big book of science
      fiction
    Sloane, W. M. ed. Space, space, space
  Fast falls the eventide
    Best science-fiction stories: 1953
  Glass eye
    Merril, J. ed. Beyond human ken
  Hobbyist
    Astounding science fiction (Periodical)
      Astounding science fiction anthology
  I am nothing
    Best science-fiction stories: 1953
  The illusionaries
    Norton, A. M. ed. Space pioneers
  Impulse
    Conklin, G. ed. Invaders of earth
  Jay Score
    Heinlein, R. A. ed. Tomorrow, the stars
  Late night final
    Astounding science fiction (Periodical)
      Astounding science fiction anthology
  Metamorphosite
    Derleth, A. W. ed. Beachheads in space
    Greenberg, M. ed. Journey to infinity
  Muten
    Brown, F. and Reynolds, M. eds. Science-fiction carnival
  Test piece
    Conklin, G. ed. Omnibus of science
      fiction
  Timeless ones
    Wollheim, D. A. ed. Prize science fiction
  Ultima Thule
    Lesser, M. A. ed. Looking forward

Russell, John, 1885-
  Fourth man
    Day, A. G. ed. Greatest American short
      stories
  Jetsam
    Shaw, H. and Bement, D. Reading the
      short story
  Lost god
    Grayson, C. ed. Fourth round

RUSSIA
  Guerney, B. G. comp. New Russian stories; 16 stories
  Munro, H. H. Old town of Pskoff

To 1800

  Tynïanov, I. N. Second Lieutenant Likewise

SAILING VESSELS
Bloomfield, H. The trap
Hergesheimer, J. Wild oranges
Miers, E. S. Jimmy rides the seal herd

The **sailor.** Pritchett, V. S.

Sailor ashore. Hughes, L.

Sailor off the Bremen. Shaw, I.

Sailor! Sailor! Steele, W. D.

SAILORS. See Seamen

Sailor's pay. Carse, R.

Sailor's son. Williams, W. C.

St Clair, Margaret
Child of void
Conklin, G. ed. Invaders of earth
The gardener
Derleth, A. W. ed. Worlds of tomorrow
The pillows
Conklin, G. ed. Possible worlds of science fiction

Saint Exupéry, Antoine de, 1900-1944
Letter to a hostage
Neider, C. ed. Great short stories from the world's literature

SAINT ALBANS, VERMONT. See Vermont—Saint Albans

Saint and the Goblin. Munro, H. H.

Saint for Wessex. Bolton, I. M.

St Gabriel Zsbyski. Mowery, W. B.

Saint George. Sykes, C.

St George ball. Nelson, E. D. P.

Saint Joseph's ass. Verga, G.

Saint Manuel Bueno, martyr. Unamuno y Jugo, M. de

St Patrick's Day in the afternoon. Ready, W. B.

ST PETERSBURG. See Florida—St Petersburg

Saint Sammy. Mitchell, W. O.

Saintly simplicity. Chekhov, A. P.

SAINTS
Bowen, E. All saints
Flaubert, G. Legend of St Julian the Hospitaller
Munro, H. H. Saint and the Goblin
Unamuno y Jugo, M. de. Saint Manuel Bueno, Martyr

Saintsbury, Edward Bennett
Bread upon the waters
Oberfirst, R. ed. 1952 anthology of best original short-shorts

Saki, pseud. See Munro, Hector Hugh

Salad of Colonel Cray. Chesterton, G. K.

The **salesman.** Evans, T. M.

SALESMANSHIP. See Salesmen and salesmanship

Salesmanship. Chase, M. E.

SALESMEN AND SALESMANSHIP
Caldwell, E. Back on the road
Caldwell, E. Man who looked like himself
Chase, M. E. Salesmanship
De Vries, P. Through a glass darkly
Evans, T. M. The salesman
Herron, E. Hail fellow well met
Kafka, F. The metamorphosis

Kahler, H. M. The buckpasser
Porter, W. S. Lickpenny lover
Sansom, W. On stony ground
Upson, W. H. No rest for Botts; 12 stories
Welty, E. Death of a traveling salesman
Zevin, I. J. Pack of troubles for one cent

SALESWOMEN. See Salesmen and salesmanship

Salinger, Jerome David, 1919-
De Daumier-Smith's blue period
Salinger, J. D. Nine stories
Down at the dinghy
Salinger, J. D. Nine stories
For Esmé—with love and squalor
Prize stories of 1950
Salinger, J. D. Nine stories
Just before the war with the Eskimos
Salinger, J. D. Nine stories
Laughing man
Salinger, J. D. Nine stories
Perfect day for bananafish
Salinger, J. D. Nine stories
Pretty mouth and green my eyes
Burrell, J. A. and Cerf, B. A. eds. Anthology of famous American stories
Salinger, J. D. Nine stories
Teddy
Salinger, J. D. Nine stories
Uncle Wiggily in Connecticut
Salinger, J. D. Nine stories

Salisbury, Kathleen, pseud. See Morehouse, Kathleen (Moore)

Sally. Asimov, I.

Sally steps in. Cochran, R. G.

SALMON
Perrault, E. G. Silver King

SALOONS. See Hotels, taverns, etc.

Salt for the soul. Good, E.

Salt sea. Subercaseaux, B.

Salta pro nobis. Galsworthy, J.

SALVAGE
Munro, H. H. Treasure-ship

Salvage! Strong, P. N.

Salvation. Foote, J. T.

Salvatore. Maugham, W. S.

Salving of Pyack. Sullivan, A.

Sam and the dean. Foley, T.

Sam Hall. Anderson, P.

Sam Kravitz, that thief. Gold, M.

Sam Slick the clockmaker. Haliburton, T. C.

Samachson, Joseph, 1906-
Country doctor
Pohl, F. ed. Star science fiction stories
Model of a judge
Best science-fiction stories: 1954

SAMOA
Maugham, W. S. Mackintosh
Maugham, W. S. The pool
Maugham, W. S. Red

Pago Pago
Maugham, W. S. Rain

The **samovar.** Cournos, J.

Samuel. London, J.

Sanatorium. Maugham, W. S.

SANATORIUMS. See Hospitals and sanatoriums

Sanctification of the Name. Asch, S.

Sand. Singer, I. J.

Sand doctor. Bergengruen, W.

Sand fort. Miles, M. K.

Sandberg, Harold W. 1902-
Captain Kidder
Owen, F. ed. Teen-age winter sports stories
Kid from Shingle Creek
Owen, F. ed. Teen-age victory parade

Sandburg, Carl, 1878-
Huckabuck family and how they raised popcorn in Nebraska and quit and came back
Fenner, P. R. comp. Giggle box
Pig Wisps
Fenner, P. R. comp. Giggle box

The **sandman.** Hoffmann, E. T. A.

Sandoz, Mari, 1907-
Lost school bus
Saturday evening post (Periodical) Saturday evening post stories, 1951
Sit your saddle solid
Dennis, W. ed. Palomino and other horses

Sandoz, Maurice Yves, 1892-
Mr Rabbi
Sandoz, M. Y. On the verge
On the verge
Sandoz, M. Y. On the verge
The trap
Sandoz, M. Y. On the verge
The tsantsa
Sandoz, M. Y. On the verge

Sandy, Sue
Black lie
Oberfirst, R. ed. 1954 anthology of best original short-shorts

Sanford, Winifred Mahon, 1890-
Windfall
Peery, W. W. ed. 21 Texas short stories

Sangster, Margaret Elizabeth, 1894-
Beautiful tree
Elmquist, R. M. ed. Fifty years of Christmas
For this is Christmas Day
Lantz, J. E. ed. Stories of Christian living
What Christmas brought the stranger
Elmquist, R. M. ed. Fifty years of Christmas

Sanity. Leiber, F.

Sansom, William, 1912-
Afternoon
Sansom, W. South
Bank that broke the man at Monte Carlo
Sansom, W. South
Boiler room
Sansom, W. Something terrible, something lovely
Building alive
Sansom, W. Something terrible, something lovely
Cat up a tree
Joseph, M. ed. Best cat stories

The cliff
Sansom, W. Something terrible, something lovely
Crabfroth
Sansom, W. Something terrible, something lovely
Death of Baldy
Sansom, W. Passionate North
Displaced persons
Sansom, W. Something terrible, something lovely
Eye man
Sansom, W. Something terrible, something lovely
From the water junction
Sansom, W. Something terrible, something lovely
Girl on the bus
Sansom, W. Passionate North
Gliding gulls and going people
Sansom, W. Passionate North
Happy New Year
Sansom, W. Passionate North
How Claeys died
Barrows, H. ed. 15 stories
New writing (Periodical) Best stories
Sansom, W. Something terrible, something lovely
In the morning
Sansom, W. Something terrible, something lovely
Journey into smoke
Sansom, W. Something terrible, something lovely
The kiss
Sansom, W. Something terrible, something lovely
Landscape with figures
Sansom, W. South
Little fears
Sansom, W. Something terrible, something lovely
Little room
Sansom, W. Something terrible, something lovely
Miss Haines and the gondolier
Story (Periodical) Story; no. 2
My little robins
Sansom, W. South
My tree
Sansom, W. Something terrible, something lovely
Nevermore without end
Sansom, W. Passionate North
On stony ground
Ludwig, J. B. and Poirier, W. R. eds. Stories, British and American
One sunny afternoon
Sansom, W. Something terrible, something lovely
Pastorale
Sansom, W. South
Poseidon's daughter
Sansom, W. South
Saving grace
Sansom, W. Something terrible, something lovely
Small world
Sansom, W. Something terrible, something lovely
Something terrible, something lovely
Sansom, W. Something terrible, something lovely

Sansom, William—*Continued*
　Street song
　　Sansom, W. South
　Three dogs of Siena
　　Sansom, W. South
　Time and place
　　Sansom, W. Passionate North
　To Greenland, to Greenland
　　Sansom, W. Passionate North
　Tutti frutti
　　Sansom, W. South
　Various temptations
　　Sansom, W. Something terrible, some-
　　　thing lovely
　Vertical ladder
　　Sansom, W. Something terrible, some-
　　　thing lovely
　Waning moon
　　Sansom, W. Passionate North
　A wedding
　　Sansom, W. Passionate North
　The windows
　　Sansom, W. Something terrible, some-
　　　thing lovely
　World of glass
　　Sansom, W. Passionate North
SANTA CLAUS
　Aldrich, B. S. Another brought gifts
　Asimov, I. Christmas on Ganymede
　Cooke, A. Christmas Eve
　Cousins, M. Uncle Edgar and the re-
　　luctant saint
　McLaverty, M. Father Christmas
Santa Claus and the Tenth Avenue kid.
　Cousins, M.
Santa Claus planet. Robinson, F. M.
Santa Lucia. Petracca, J.
Santee, Ross, 1889-
　Fool about a horse
　　Dennis, W. ed. Palomino and other
　　　horses
Saphir, Moritz Gottlieb, 1795-1858
　A conquest
　　Ausubel, N. ed. Treasury of Jewish
　　　humor
　Gastronomy of the Jews
　　Ausubel, N. ed. Treasury of Jewish
　　　humor
Saratoga rain. Hughes, L.
"Sarban" pseud. See Wall, John W.
The **sardillion.** Enright, E.
Sargeson, Frank
　Great day
　　New writing (Periodical) Best stories
Saroyan, William, 1908-
　Ancient history and low hurdles
　　Lass, A. H. and Horowitz, A. eds.
　　　Stories for youth
　The Assyrian
　　Saroyan, W. The Assyrian, and other
　　　stories
　Be present at our table, Lord
　　Brentano, F. ed. The word lives on
　Cocktail party
　　Saroyan, W. The Assyrian, and other
　　　stories
　Cold day
　　Blodgett, H. W. ed. Story survey. 1953
　　ed.

Cornet players
　Saroyan, W. The Assyrian, and other
　　stories
Daring young man on the flying trapeze
　Burrell, J. A. and Cerf, B. A. eds. An-
　　thology of famous American stories
Fifty yard dash
　Dachs, D. ed. Treasury of sports humor
The foreigner
　Saroyan, W. The Assyrian, and other
　　stories
Leaf thief
　Saroyan, W. The Assyrian, and other
　　stories
Mr Mechano
　Waite, H. O. and Atkinson, B. P. eds.
　　Literature for our time
My cousin Dikran, the orator
　Greene, J. I. and Abell, E. eds. Stories
　　of sudden truth
Palo
　Best American short stories, 1952
Parsley garden
　Saroyan, W. The Assyrian, and other
　　stories
Pheasant hunter
　Saroyan, W. The Assyrian, and other
　　stories
The plot
　Saroyan, W. The Assyrian, and other
　　stories
Poet at home
　Saroyan, W. The Assyrian, and other
　　stories
Resurrection of a life
　Best of the Best American short sto-
　　ries, 1915-1950
Summer of the beautiful white horse
　Schramm, W. L. ed. Great short sto-
　　ries
Sunday zeppelin
　Felheim, M.; Newman, F. B. and Stein-
　　hoff, W. R. eds. Modern short stories
Theological student
　Saroyan, W. The Assyrian, and other
　　stories
Third day after Christmas
　Saroyan, W. The Assyrian, and other
　　stories
Train going
　Moskowitz, S. ed. Great railroad stories
　　of the world
Sarton, May, 1912-
　Return of Corporal Greene
　　Abell, E. ed. American accent
Sartre, Jean Paul, 1905-
　Childhood of a leader
　　Sartre, J. P. Intimacy, and other stories
　Erostratus
　　Sartre, J. P. Intimacy, and other stories
　Intimacy
　　Sartre, J. P. Intimacy, and other stories
　The room
　　Sartre, J. P. Intimacy, and other stories
　The wall
　　Neider, C. ed. Great short stories from
　　　the world's literature
　　Sartre, J. P. Intimacy, and other stories
　　West, R. B. and Stallman, R. W. eds.
　　　Art of modern fiction

Sass, Herbert Ravenel, 1884-
  Affair at St Albans
    Jones, K. M. ed. New Confederate short
      stories
  Grey eagle
    Andrews, R. C. ed. My favorite stories
      of the great outdoors
SATAN. See Devil
Satan. Gibran, K.
Satan in the suburbs. Russell, B. A. W. R.
  3d earl
Satan's best girl. Van Doren, M.
SATIRE
  Bradbury, R. The exiles
  Brandon, W. College queen
  Broun, H. C. Fifty-first dragon
  Clemens, S. L. Latest sensation (II)
  Clemens, S. L. My bloody massacre (I)
  Collier, J. Another American tragedy
  Collier, J. Fancies and goodnights; 50
    stories
  Collier, J. Frog prince
  Collier, J. Pictures in the fire
  Elliott, B. Battle of the S . . . S
  Harte, B. Bell-ringer of Angel's
  Hsieh Liang. Wolf of Chungshan
  Jenkins, W. F. Fourth-dimensional dem-
    onstrator
  Lucian. True history
  Maugham, W. S. Appearance and reality
  Maugham, W. S. Closed shop
  Maugham, W. S. The luncheon
  Maugham, W. S. Mabel
  Milne, A. A. The barrister
  Monig, C. Love story
  Moore, W. We the people
  Morley, C. D. Home again
  Munro, H. H. Short stories of Saki; 134
    stories
  Peacock, T. L. Nightmare Abbey
  Porter, W. S. Comedy in rubber
  Porter, W. S. Dinner at—
  Porter, W. S. Elsie in New York
  Porter, W. S. The sleuths
  Porter, W. S. Tracked to doom
  P'u Sung-ling. The bookworm
  Russell, B. A. W. R. 3d earl. Benefit of
    clergy
  Russell, B. A. W. R. 3d earl. Infraredio-
    scope
  Russell, E. F. And then there were none
  Tucker, W. Able to Zebra
  Walsh, M. Take your choice
  Wang Chu. Poets' club
  Waugh, E. Love among the ruins
  Wharton, E. N. J. Xingu
  Wicklein, J. F. Mr Moody
  Zozulya, E. D. Studio of Love-Your-Fel-
    lowman
Saturday afternoon. Caldwell, E.
Saturday nocturne. Sullivan, R.
SATURN (PLANET)
  James, D. L. Moon of delirium
  Jones, N. R. Hermit of Saturn's ring
Saucer of loneliness. Waldo, E. H.
Savannah-la-mar. De Quincey, T.
Savannah River payday. Caldwell, E.
Saved. Maupassant, G. de

Saved by the sale. Suhl, Y.
Saverio's secret. Werfel, F.
Saving grace. Sansom, W.
Saviour John. Lagerkvist, P. F.
Saviour of the people. Franzos, K. E.
Saw gang. Stegner, W. E.
Sawyer, Ruth, 1880-
  Deserted mine
    Hazeltine, A. I. comp. Selected stories
      for teen-agers
  Fiddler, play fast, play faster
    Fenner, P. R. comp. Ghosts, ghosts,
      ghosts
  The flea
    Fenner, P. R. comp. Fools and funny
      fellows
Say that Jimmy kissed me. Brookhouser, F.
Sayers, Dorothy Leigh, 1893-
  Suspicion
    Bond, R. T. ed. Handbook for poisoners
Sayres, William C.
  Olaf the Magnificent
    Story (Periodical) Story; no. 1
Scalawag pup. Mowery, W. B.
The scandal. Rinehart, M. R.
Scandal at Mulford Inn. Wilson, N. C.
Scandal detectives. Fitzgerald, F. S. K.
Scandal in Bohemia. Doyle, Sir A. C.
Scandal of Father Brown. Chesterton, G. K.
The scarab. Gallun, R. Z.
The scarecrow. Farrell, J. T.
Sacred. Bauer, G. V.
Scarlet citadel. Howard, R. E.
Scarlet dream. Moore, C. L.
Scarlet letter. Hawthorne, N.
Scarlet plague. London, J.
Scars. Waldo, E. H.
Scars of honor. Johnson, D. M.
SCENARIOS. See Moving pictures
Scene. De Vries, P.
Scent of sarsaparilla. Bradbury, R.
SCEPTICISM. See Skepticism
Schaefer, Jack Warner, 1907-
  Cat nipped
    Schaefer, J. W. The pioneers
  Cooter James
    Schaefer, J. W. Big range
  Elvie Burdette
    Schaefer, J. W. Big range
  Emmet Dutrow
    Meredith, S. ed. Bar 3
    Schaefer, J. W. Big range
  General Pingley
    Schaefer, J. W. Big range
  Harvey Kendall
    Schaefer, J. W. The pioneers
  Hugo Kertchak, builder
    Schaefer, J. W. The pioneers
  Jeremy Rodock
    Schaefer, J. W. Big range
  Josiah Willett
    Schaefer, J. W. Big range
  Kittura Remsberg
    Schaefer, J. W. Big range
  Leander Frailey
    Schaefer, J. W. The pioneers

Schaefer, Jack W.—*Continued*
Major Burl
  Schaefer, J. W. Big range
Miley Bennett
  Schaefer, J. W. Big range
My town
  Schaefer, J. W. The pioneers
Old Anse
  Schaefer, J. W. The pioneers
Out of the past
  Schaefer, J. W. The pioneers
Prudence by name
  Schaefer, J. W. The pioneers
Sergeant Houck
  Meredith, S. ed. Bar 1 roundup of best
    western stories
  Schaefer, J. W. Big range
Something lost
  Schaefer, J. W. The pioneers
Takes a real man. . .
  Schaefer, J. W. The pioneers
That Mark horse
  Schaefer, J. W. The pioneers

Schafhauser, Charles
Gleeb for earth
  Galaxy science fiction magazine. Second
    Galaxy reader of science fiction

Schedule. Walton, H.

Scheffrin, Gladys R. 1928-
When you blow on a dandelion
  Wolfe, D. M. ed. Which grain will
    grow

Scheiner, Frank
Old man had four wives
  Ribalow, H. U. ed. This land, these
    people

Schiller, Johann Christoph Friedrich von,
1759-1805
Sport of destiny
  Lange, V. ed. Great German short
    novels and stories

Schisgall, Oscar, 1901-
Eyes in the dark
  This week magazine. This week's short-
    short stories
"Take over, Bos'n!"
  This week magazine. This week's short-
    short stories

SCHIZOPHRENIA. See Insanity

Schlemihlov's work. Libin, S.

Schlichter, Etta W.
Big career
  Lantz, J. E. ed. Stories of Christian
    living

Schmidt, Carl F. 1923-
Ancestral voices
  Story (Periodical) Story; no. 4

Schmitt, Gladys, 1909-
David and Bathsheba
  Selden, R. ed. Ways of God and men

Schmitz, Ettore, 1861-1928
Generous wine
  Neider, C. ed. Great short stories from
    the world's literature

Schmitz, James H.
Caretaker
  Galaxy science fiction magazine. Second
    Galaxy reader of science fiction
End of the line
  Norton, A. M. ed. Space pioneers
Second night of summer
  Conklin, G. ed. Possible worlds of sci-
    ence fiction
We don't want any trouble
  Pohl, F. ed. Asignment in tomorrow
Witches of Karres
  Astounding science fiction (Periodical)
  Astounding science fiction anthology

Schnabel, James F.
Journey for Wilbur
  Best Army short stories, 1950

Schneider, George W. 1917-
Case of the southpaw spy
  Schneider, G. W. Clair de lune, and
    other stories
Clair de lune
  Schneider, G. W. Clair de lune, and
    other stories
Dove of God
  Schneider, G. W. Clair de lune, and
    other stories
For the want of a cigarette
  Schneider, G. W. Clair de lune, and
    other stories
Grandfather's tale
  Schneider, G. W. Clair de lune, and
    other stories
Iron cross, first class
  Schneider, G. W. Clair de lune, and
    other stories
Maestro's magic wand
  Schneider, G. W. Clair de lune, and
    other stories
Marche Militaire
  Schneider, G. W. Clair de lune, and
    other stories
No greater love
  Schneider, G. W. Clair de lune, and
    other stories
Render unto Caesar
  Schneider, G. W. Clair de lune, and
    other stories
Revolutionary etude
  Schneider, G. W. Clair de lune, and
    other stories
Shade of Omar
  Schneider, G. W. Clair de lune, and
    other stories
Sir Thomas
  Schneider, G. W. Clair de lune, and
    other stories
Star of Siam
  Schneider, G. W. Clair de lune, and
    other stories
What price genius
  Schneider, G. W. Clair de lune, and
    other stories
When titans meet
  Schneider, G. W. Clair de lune, and
    other stories

Schneider, Robert
Passing through Fieldsville
  Story (Periodical) Story; no. 2

Schneour, Salman. See Shneur, Zalman

Schneuer, Zalman. See Shneur, Zalman

Schnitzler, Arthur, 1862-1931
Bachelor's death
Pick, R. ed. German stories and tales
Same as: Death of a bachelor
Blind Geronimo and his brother
Blodgett, H. W. ed. Story survey. 1953 ed.
Death of a bachelor
Leftwich, J. ed. Yisröel. 1952 ed.
Same as: Bachelor's death
A farewell
Lange, V. ed. Great German short novels and stories

Schoenfeld, Bernard C.
Eagle and the cheetah
Story (Periodical) Story; no. 4

Schoenfeld, Howard
All of God's children got shoes
Queen, E. pseud. ed. Queen's awards: 8th ser.
Built up logically
Magazine of fantasy and science fiction. Best from Fantasy and science fiction, 1952
Tea pusher
Queen, E. pseud. ed. Queen's awards: 7th ser.

Scholz, Jackson Volney
Keystone feud
Fenner, P. R. comp. Crack of the bat
Furman, A. L. ed. Teen-age stories of the diamond

SCHOOL BUSES. See Motor buses

School for combat. Nordhoff, C. B. and Hall, J. N.

School life
Cassill, R. V. Larchmoor is not the world
Karchmer, S. "Hail, brother and farewell"
Kent, C. G. Perpetua puts one over
Lincoln, V. E. Glass wall

Canada
Reaney, J. C. The bully

England
Golding, L. Angels in Chayder
Hilton, J. The war years
Taylor, E. Hester Lilly

Germany
Mann, T. Masters of Buddenbrooks
Stafford, J. The nemesis
Zweig, S. Confusion of sentiment

Mexico
Brenner, L. Drunken lizard

Poland
Shapiro, L. Eating days

United States
Aldrich, B. S. Juno's swans
Auchincloss, L. Billy and the gargoyles
Brier, H. M. Yogi's dark horse
Calisher, H. Letitia, emeritus
Chute, B. J. Thank you Dr Russell
De Vries, P. Good boy
Doty, W. L. Parochial school
Erdman, L. G. Allen High's youth problem

Fitzgerald, F. S. K. Freshest boy
Goyen, W. Grasshopper's burden
Humphrey, W. Report cards
Johnson, O. M. Great pancake record
Johnson, O. M. Varmint tries dissipation
Knowles, J. Turn with the sun
O'Hara, J. Do you like it here?
Payne, L. V. Prelude
Saroyan, W. Ancient history and low hurdles
Stuart, J. Slipover sweater
Ullman, J. R. Visitation
White, M. To remember these things

SCHOOL PLAYS. See College and school drama

SCHOOL STORIES. See School life

SCHOOL TEACHERS. See Teachers

The schoolmistress. Chekhov, A. P.

SCHOOLS. See School life

Schools and schools. Porter, W. S.

The schooner. McLaverty, M.

Schorer, Mark, 1908-
Boy in the summer sun
Bogorad, S. N. and Trevithick, J. eds. College miscellany
Long in populous city pent
Cory, D. W. pseud. comp. 21 variations on a theme
What we don't know hurts us
Heilman, R. B. ed. Modern short stories

Schorr, Zygmunt
The appraisal
Ausubel, N. ed. Treasury of Jewish humor
Her rich American cousin
Ausubel, N. ed. Treasury of Jewish humor

Schramm, Wilbur Lang, 1907-
Horse that played third base for Brooklyn
Stauffer, R. M.; Cunningham, W. H. and Sullivan, C. J. eds. Adventures in modern literature
My kingdom for Jones
Creamer, J. B. comp. Twenty-two stories about horses and men
Dachs, D. ed. Treasury of sports humor

Schubert, Paul, 1899-
White Elk
This week magazine. This week's short-short stories

Schulberg, Budd Wilson, 1914-
All the town's talking
This week magazine This week's short-short stories
Breaking point
Esquire (Periodical) Girls from Esquire
Schulberg, B. W. Some faces in the crowd
Crowd pleaser
Ribalow, H. U. ed. World's greatest boxing stories
Schulberg, B. W. Some faces in the crowd
The dare
Schulberg, B. W. Some faces in the crowd
Enough
Schulberg, B. W. Some faces in the crowd

Schulberg, Budd W.—*Continued*
Ensign Weasel
  Schulberg, B. W. Some faces in the
    crowd
Face of Hollywood
  Schulberg, B. W. Some faces in the
    crowd
Foxhole in Washington
  Schulberg, B. W. Some faces in the
    crowd
Legend that walks like a man
  Schulberg, B. W. Some faces in the
    crowd
Meal ticket
  Schulberg, B. W. Some faces in the
    crowd
Memory in white
  Schulberg, B. W. Some faces in the
    crowd
My Christmas carol
  Burrell, J. A. and Cerf, B. A. eds. An-
    thology of famous American stories
  Schulberg, B. W. Some faces in the
    crowd
Note on the literary life
  Schulberg, B. W. Some faces in the
    crowd
One he called Winnie
  Schulberg, B. W. Some faces in the
    crowd
Our white deer
  Schulberg, B. W. Some faces in the
    crowd
Passport to nowhere
  Ribalow, H. U. ed. These your children
Pride of Tony Colucci
  Schulberg, B. W. Some faces in the
    crowd
Road to recovery
  Fabricant, N. D. and Werner, H. eds.
    World's best doctor stories
Short digest of a long novel
  Schulberg, B. W. Some faces in the
    crowd
Table at Ciro's
  Schulberg, B. W. Some faces in the
    crowd
Third nightcap, with historical footnotes
  Schulberg, B. W. Some faces in the
    crowd
Typical gesture of Colonel Duggan
  Schulberg, B. W. Some faces in the
    crowd
Your Arkansas traveler
  Schulberg, B. W. Some faces in the
    crowd

Schulberg, Stuart
I'm really fine
  Best American short stories, 1952

Schüler, Else Lasker- See Lasker-Schüler,
  Else

Schuman, Sylvie
Quiet one
  McFarland, W. K. comp. Then it hap-
    pened

Schuyler, William, 1912-
Back again
  Stanford short stories, 1953

Schwartz, Delmore, 1913-
Bitter farce
  Ribalow, H. U. ed. This land, these
    people

In dreams begin responsibilities
  Schorer, M. ed. The story
  Swallow, A. ed. Anchor in the sea
Schwartz, Max, 1919-
The victory
  Ribalow, H. U. ed. These your children
Schwartz, Richard H.
Good people of Milton
  Hathaway, B. and Sessions, J. A. eds.
    Writers for tomorrow. 2d ser.
Schwartz, Ruth A.
Shoes of bright green leather
  American vanguard, 1950
Schwartz-Metterklume method. Munro,
  H. H.
Schwarz, Cynthia Johnson, 1923-
After the hay-makin'
  American vanguard, 1952
Schwarz, Felix Conrad, 1906-
Serpent's tooth
  Oberfirst, R. ed. 1954 anthology of best
    original short-shorts
Schweitzer, Gertrude, 1909-
Because she was like me
  McFarland, W. K. comp. Then it hap-
    pened
Kid brother
  Strang, R. M. and Roberts, R. M. eds.
    Teen-age tales v2
The latchkey
  Stowe, A. comp. It's a date
Little sisters are such pests
  Lantz, J. E. ed. Stories of Christian
    living
Summer's end
  Lantz, J. E. ed. Stories of Christian
    living
Schwob, Marcel, 1867-1905
Crates
  Geist, S. ed. French stories and tales
Paolo Uccello
  Geist, S. ed. French stories and tales
SCIENCE FICTION
Asimov, I. I, robot; 9 stories
Astounding science fiction (Periodical)
  Astounding science fiction anthology;
    23 stories
Aycock, R. D. Unwelcome tenant
Best science fiction stories: 1950; 13 sto-
  ries
Best science fiction stories: 1951; 18 sto-
  ries
Best science fiction stories: 1952; 18 sto-
  ries
Best science-fiction stories: 1953; 15 sto-
  ries
Best science-fiction stories: 1954; 13 sto-
  ries
Bleiler, E. F. and Dikty, T. E. eds.
  Imagination unlimited; 13 stories
Bleiler, E. F. and Dikty, T. E. eds. Sci-
  ence fiction omnibus: the best science
  fiction stories, 1949, 1950; 25 stories
Bradbury, R. Illustrated man; 19 stories
Brown, F. Angels and spaceships; 17 sto-
  ries
Brown, F. Space on my hands; 9 sto-
  ries
Brown, F. and Reynolds, M. eds. Science-
  fiction carnival; 13 stories
Campbell, J. W. Black star passes; 3 sto-
  ries
Campbell, J. W. Cloak of Aesir; 7 sto-
  ries

SCIENCE FICTION—*Continued*

Wells, H. G. Man who could work miracles

Wollheim, D. A. comp. Every boy's book of science-fiction; 10 stories

Wollheim, D. A. comp. Flight into space; 12 stories

Wollheim, D. A. ed. Prize science fiction; 12 stories

Year's best science fiction novels, 1952; 5 stories

Year's best science fiction novels, 1953; 5 stories

Year's best science fiction novels, 1954; 5 stories

  See also Interplanetary visitors; Interplanetary voyages; Space ships; Future, Stories of the; Moon; Mars

Science of deduction. Doyle, Sir A. C.

Science teacher. Wiegand, W.

SCIENTIFIC EXPERIMENTS. See Experiments, Scientific

SCIENTIFIC STORIES. See Science fiction

SCIENTISTS

Barnard, L. G. Four men and a box

Benét, S. V. Blood of the martyrs

Forester, C. S. Physiology of fear

Jones, R. F. Stone and a spear

May, J. Dune roller

  See also Anthropologists; Biologists; Chemists; Zoologists; etc.

Scilken, Marjorie, 1923-

Oh joy, it's a boy

 American vanguard, 1953

The scoop. Farrell, J. T.

Score in the stands. Benchley, R. C.

The scorpion. Bowles, P. F.

SCOTCH DIALECT STORIES. See Dialect stories—Scotch

SCOTCH IN BORNEO

Maugham, W. S. Neil MacAdam

Maugham, W. S. Man from Glasgow

Skinner, C. L. Silent Scot

Tracy, D. Charity ward

Scotch settlement. Paterson, N.

SCOTLAND

19th century

Barrie, Sir J. M. bart. Courting of T'nowhead's Bell

Barrie, Sir J. M. bart. Farewell Miss Julie Logan

Scott, Sir W. Two drovers

Stevenson, R. L. Merry men

Strong, L. A. G. White cottage

Watson, J. Story of Dr MacLure

SCOTS. See Scotch

Scott, Duncan Campbell, 1862-1947

Paul Farlotte

 Pacey, D. ed. Book of Canadian stories

Scott, Hugh Stowell, 1862-1903

Sister

 Fabricant, N. D. and Werner, H. eds. World's best doctor stories

Scott, Virgil

Don't run, don't pass

 Argosy (Periodical) Argosy Book of sports stories

Scott, Sir Walter, 1771-1832

Two drovers

 Cerf, B. A. and Moriarty, H. C. eds. Anthology of famous British stories

Scott, William R. 1919?-

My father doesn't like me

 Strang, R. M. and Roberts, R. M. eds. Teen-age tales v2

The pest

 Collier's, the national weekly. Collier's best

SCOUNDRELS

Chekhov, A. P. Because of little apples

The scout. Mowery, W. B.

Scout detail. Haycox, E.

Scranton, Ruby R. pseud. See Jones, Ruby S.

Screaming skull. Crawford, F. M.

Screwball division. White, W. A. P.

SCRIBES. See Letter writers

SCRIVENERS. See Law and lawyers; Letter writers

Scrub cure. Miers, E. S.

SCULPTORS

Collier, J. Spring fever

Hameiri, A. Three Halutzot

Jade Goddess

James, H. Tree of knowledge

Winslow, T. S. Bronzes of Martel Greer

Zangwill, I. The luftmensch

Sculptors of life. West, W.

Scum of the earth. Cooke, A. A.

SEA. See Ocean

Sea afire. Floherty, J. J.

Sea anchor. Hill, M. Y.

SEA CAPTAINS. See Shipmasters

SEA DEVIL. See Octopus

Sea devil. Gordon, A.

Sea gypsy. Mayse, A.

Sea-horse of Grand Terre. Jackson, C. T.

Sea raiders. Wells, H. G.

SEA SCOUTS

Strong, P. N. Running dark

Sea serpent of Spoonville Beach. Helfer, H.

SEA-SERPENTS

Helfer, H. Sea serpent of Spoonville Beach

Jenkins, W. F. De profundis

SEA-SHORE

Mansfield, K. At the bay

SEA STORIES

Adams, B. M. The foreigner

Argosy (Periodical) Argosy Book of sea stories; 13 stories

Bluebook (Periodical) Best sea stories from Bluebook; 14 stories

Collins, W. 'Blow up with the brig!'

Connolly, J. B. The trawler

Conrad, J. Initiation

Conrad, J. Secret sharer

Conrad, J. Tales of land and sea; 12 stories

Conrad, J. Youth

Corkery, D. The awakening

Crane, S. Open boat

SEA STORIES—*Continued*
Dunsany, E. J. M. D. P. 18th baron.
Story of land and sea
Fenner, P. R. comp. Stories of the sea;
12 stories
Finger, C. J. Yankee captain in Patagonia
Forester, C. S. Mr Midshipman Horn-
blower; 10 stories
Furman, A. L. ed. Teen-age sea stories;
13 stories
Gilpatric, G. Last Glencannon omnibus;
10 stories
Lindquist, W. Last-Light Channel
London, J. Make westing
McFee, W. ed. Great sea stories of mod-
ern times; 12 stories
Martyr, W. Sleeping draft
Melville, H. Benito Cereno
Melville, H. Billy Budd, foretopman
Pease, H. Passengers for Panama
Poe, E. A. Ms. found in a bottle
Strong, P. N. Running dark
Subercaseaux, B. Salt sea
See also Mutiny; Seamen

SEA VOYAGES. See Ocean travel

Seabright, Idris, 1911-
Brightness falls from the air
Best science fiction stories: 1952
Hole in the moon
Magazine of fantasy and science fiction
Best from Fantasy and science fic-
tion; 2d ser.
Listening child
Magazine of fantasy and science fiction.
Best from Fantasy and science fiction;
[1st ser]
Man who sold rope to the gnoles
Merril, J. ed. Beyond human ken
Now ritual
Magazine of fantasy and science fiction.
Best from Fantasy and science fiction
3d ser.

SEAFARING LIFE. See Sea stories

Seager, Allan, 1906-
All problems are simple
Seager, A. Old man of the mountain,
and seventeen other stories
Bang on the head
Seager, A. Old man of the mountain,
and seventeen other stories
Berkshire comedy
Seager, A. Old man of the mountain,
and seventeen other stories
The conqueror
Seager, A. Old man of the mountain,
and seventeen other stories
Flight south
Seager, A. Old man of the mountain,
and seventeen other stories
Fugue for harmonicas
Seager, A. Old man of the mountain,
and seventeen other stories
Game chickens
Seager, A. Old man of the mountain,
and seventeen other stories
Jersey, Guernsey, Alderney, Sark
Seager, A. Old man of the mountain,
and seventeen other stories
Kobold
Seager, A. Old man of the mountain,
and seventeen other stories

No son, no gun, no streetcar
Seager, A. Old man of the mountain,
and seventeen other stories
Old man of the mountain
Seager, A. Old man of the mountain,
and seventeen other stories
Pommery 1921
Seager, A. Old man of the mountain,
and seventeen other stories
Pro arte
Seager, A. Old man of the mountain,
and seventeen other stories
Quitandinha
Seager, A. Old man of the mountain,
and seventeen other stories
Sacrament
Seager, A. Old man of the mountain,
and seventeen other stories
Second wedding
Cuff, R. P. ed. American short story
survey
The street
Seager, A. Old man of the mountain,
and seventeen other stories
This town and Salamanca
Seager, A. Old man of the mountain,
and seventeen other stories
Short, R. W. and Sewall, R. B. eds.
Short stories for study. 1950 ed.
The unicorn
Seager, A. Old man of the mountain,
and seventeen other stories

The seal. O'Flaherty, L.

Seal hunting. Stefánsson, V.

SEALING
England, G. A. Prize cargo

SEALS (ANIMALS)
Finger, C. J. Na-Ha the fighter
Niekirk, M. E. Oscar, the trained seal
Stefánsson, V. Seal hunting

SEAMEN
Argosy (Periodical) Argosy Book of sea
stories; 13 stories
Bowles, P. F. Fourth day out from Santa
Cruz
Carroll, J. W. At Mrs Farrelly's
Collins, W. 'Blow up with the brig!'
Crane, S. Open boat
Dingle, A. E. Owner's interest
Dunsany, E. J. M. D. P. 18th baron. Idle
days on the Yan
Dunsany, E. J. M. D. P. 18th baron.
Three sailors' gambit
England, G. A. Prize cargo
Gilpatric, G. Last Glencannon omnibus;
10 stories
Greene, F. S. Bunker Mouse
Kinau, R. Homesickness night
Maugham, W. S. Four Dutchmen
Melville, H. Billy Budd, foretopman
Schisgall, O. "Take over, bos'n!"

Search. Brown, F.

The search. Rabinowitz, S.

The search. Van Vogt, A. E.

The search. Woolley, R.

Search in the mist. Jenkins, W. F.

Search through the streets of the city.
Shaw, I.

The searchers. Kuehn, S.

Sharp, D. D.
  Eternal man
    Margulies, L. and Friend, O. J. eds.
      From off this world
Sharp, Margery, 1905-
  London night's entertainment
    Queen, E. pseud. ed. Literature of
      crime
  Winning sequence
    Dachs, D. ed. Treasury of sports humor
Sharp eyes. Burroughs, J.
SHARPSHOOTERS
  Brick, J. Rifleman's run
Shattered dream. Burnet, D.
Shattuck, Roger, 1923-
  Workout on the river
    Best American short stories, 1953
Shaw, Henrietta Otis
  Lighted candles
    American girl (Periodical) Christmas
      all year 'round
Shaw, Irwin, 1913-
  Act of faith
    Burrell, J. A. and Cerf, B. A. eds. An-
      thology of famous stories
    Ribalow, H. U. ed. This land, these
      people
  The convert
    Esquire (Periodical) Girls from Esquire
  Eighty-yard run
    Stegner, W. E.; Scowcroft, R. and Ilyin,
      B. eds. Writer's art
  Faith at sea
    Fabricant, N. D. and Werner, H. eds.
      World's best doctor stories
  In the French style
    Best American short sories, 1954
  Main currents of American thought
    Felheim, M.; Newman, F. B. and Stein-
      hoff, W. R. eds. Modern short stories
  Passion of Lance Corporal Hawkins
    Lynskey, W. C. ed. Reading modern
      fiction
  Return to Kansas City
    Ribalow, H. U. ed. World's greatest
      boxing stories
  Sailor off the Bremen
    Heilman, R. B. ed. Secret life of Walter
      Mitty
  Search through the streets of the city
    Best of the Best American short sto-
      ries, 1915-1950
  Triumph of justice
    Blaustein, A. P. ed. Fiction goes to
      court
  Walking wounded
    First-prize stories, 1919-1954
Shaw, Larry
  Simworthy's circus
    Brown, F. and Reynolds, M. eds. Sci-
      ence-fiction carnival
SHAWNEE INDIANS
  Kjelgaard, J. A. Wilderness road
She did not cry at all. Brookhouser, F.
She didn't like people. Cousins, M.
She made the big town! Brookhouser, F.
She never knew. Booker, S.
She shall have music. Platt, G.
She shall have music. Shulman, M.

She wanted a hero. Wylie, P.
She who laughs. Phillips, P.
She-wolf. Munro, H. H.
The she-wolf. Verga, G.
Shearing the wolf. Porter, W. S.
Sheckley, Robert, 1928-
  The altar
    Sheckley, R. Untouched by human
      hands
  Beside still waters
    Sheckley, R. Untouched by human
      hands
  Cost of living
    Sheckley, R. Untouched by human
      hands
  The demons
    Sheckley, R. Untouched by human
      hands
  Impacted man
    Sheckley, R. Untouched by human
      hands
  King's wishes
    Sheckley, R. Untouched by human
      hands
  Last weapon
    Star science fiction stories [no. 1]
  The monsters
    Sheckley, R. Untouched by human
      hands
  Odor of thought
    Star science fiction stories, no. 2
  Operating instructions
    Merril, J. ed. Beyond the barriers of
      space and time
  Paradise II
    Derleth, A. W. ed. Time to come
  Ritual
    Sheckley, R. Untouched by human
      hands
  Seventh victim
    Sheckley, R. Untouched by human
      hands
  Shape
    Sheckley, R. Untouched by human
      hands
  Specialist
    Galaxy science fiction magazine. Second
      Galaxy reader of science fiction
    Sheckley, R. Untouched by human
      hands
  Untouched by human hands
    Sheckley, R. Untouched by human
      hands
  Warm
    Galaxy science fiction magazine. Second
      Galaxy reader of science fiction
    Sheckley, R. Untouched by human
      hands
The shed. Evans, E. E.
Sheehan, David Vincent
  Get-away boy
    Strang, R. M. and Roberts, R. M. eds.
      Teen-age tales v 1
Sheehan, Patrick Augustine, 1852-1913
  Incompatibility
    Thinker's digest (Periodical) Spoiled
      priest, and other stories
  Spoiled priest
    Thinker's digest (Periodical) Spoiled
      priest, and other stories

Sheehy, Edward
    Prothalmion
        Gable, M. Sister, ed.   Many-colored
        fleece
Sheener. Williams, B. A.
SHEEP
    Davis, H. L. The homestead orchard
    Davis, H. L. The stubborn spearmen
    Warwick, J. Fire in the bush
The sheep. Munro, H. H.
SHEEP HERDERS. See Shepherds
SHEEP RAISING. See Sheep
Sheldon, Charles Monroe, 1857-1946
    Stolen Christmas
        Elmquist, R. M. ed. Fifty years of
        Christmas
Sheldon, Walt, 1917?-
    Chore for a spaceman
        Norton, A. M. ed. Space service
    I, the unspeakable
        Galaxy science fiction magazine. Galaxy
        reader of science fiction
The shell. Humphrey, W.
She'll be sorry. Johnson, H.
SHELL-FISH FISHERIES
    Hobbs, A. K. River pirates
Shell of sense. Dunbar, O. H.
Shelton, Jerry
    Culture
        Conklin, G. ed. Big book of science
        fiction
Shen, Tsung-wen, 1905-
    Little Flute
        Story (Periodical) Story; no. 1
The shepherd. Hyman, M.
SHEPHERDS
    Beachcroft, T. O. Erne from the coast
    Dunsany, E. J. M. D. P. 18th baron. East
        and West
    Gunnarson, G. Advent
    Krige, U. Invisible shepherd
    Oxenham, J. Their first meeting
    Porter, W. S. Roads of destiny
The shepherds. O'Donovan, M.
Shepherd's boy. Middleton, R. B.
Shepherds' trophy. Ollivant, A.
Sheppard, Jerome
    Black brassard
        Best Army short stories, 1950
Sheraton mirror. Derleth, A. W.
SHERIFFS
    Crane, S. Bride comes to Yellow Sky
    Cunningham, J. M. Tin star
    DeRosso, H. A. Bitter trail
    Perry, G. S. The fourflusher
    Raine, W. M. Friend of Buck Hollister
        See also Western stories
Sheriton turnabout. Pierrot, G. F.
Sherlock Holmes gives a demonstration.
    Doyle, Sir A. C.
Sherman, Dulcie
    Fifteen
        Wolfe, D. M. ed. Which grain will grow

Sherman, Harold Morrow, 1898-
    Fly chaser
        Fenner, P. R. comp. Crack of the bat
        Furman, A. L. ed. Teen-age stories of
        the diamond
    A hot dog on ice
        Furman, A. L. ed. Teen-age dog stories
    Porky, the outboarder
        Owen, F. ed. Teen-age victory parade
    Reeder, left defense
        American boy (Periodical) American boy
        anthology
    Wild pitch
        Furman, A. L. ed. Teen-age stories of
        the diamond
Sherman, Richard, 1906-
    Life of Riley
        Lass, A. H. and Horowitz, A. eds.
        Stories for youth
    Now there is peace
        Lass, A. H. and Horowitz, A. eds.
        Stories for youth
Sherred, T. L.
    E for effort
        Astounding science fiction (Periodical)
        Astounding science fiction anthology
        Conklin, G. ed. Big book of science fic-
        tion
Sherwood, Robert Emmet, 1896-1955
    "Extra! Extra!"
        Shaw, H. and Bement, D. eds. Reading
        the short story
Shiloh's waters. Davis, H. L.
Shingle shack. Macdonald, Z. K.
Shingles for the Lord. Faulkner, W.
Shining fools. Bergengruen, W.
Ship from nowhere. Chandler, A. B.
Ship of silence. Wetjen, A. R.
Ship sails at midnight. Leiber, F.
Ship that turned aside. Wertenbaker, G. P.
SHIPMASTERS
    Conrad, J. Secret sharer
    Marmur, J. I will not abandon!
    Marmur, J. Proved by the sea
    Martyr, W. Sleeping draft
    Patrick, J. Crowbar Captain
    Roberts, M. Captain of the "Ullswater"
    Strong, A. All on a winter's night
SHIPPING
    Marmur, J. I will not abandon!
SHIPS
    Fitzgerald, F. S. K. Rough crossing
    Van Doren, M. The birds
Ships. Porter, W. S.
SHIPS, ABANDONED
    Noyes, A. Log of the "Evening Star"
    Steele, W. D. Yellow cat
SHIPS, GHOST. See Ghost ships
Ship's cat. Meigs, C. L.
Shipshape home. Matheson, R.
Shipwreck of Crunch and Des. Wylie, P.
SHIPWRECKS AND CASTAWAYS
    Crane, S. Open boat
    Farley, W. The storm
    Hemingway, E. After the storm
    Holder, W. One guy, one gal, one island
    Lover, S. The gridiron

SHIPWRECKS & CASTAWAYS—*Cont.*

Marmur, J. Mad Island
Poe, E. A. Ms. found in a bottle
Quiller-Couch, Sir A. T. Roll-call of the reef
Schisgall, O. "Take over, bos'n!"

Shiras, Wilmar H. 1908-
In hiding
Bleiler, E. F. and Dikty, T. E. eds. Science fiction omnibus: the best science fiction stories, 1949, 1950
Jenkins, W. F. ed. Great stories of science fiction
Sloane, W. M. ed. Stories for tomorrow
Opening doors
Best science fiction stories: 1950
Bleiler, E. F. and Dikty, T. E. eds. Science fiction omnibus: the best science fiction stories, 1949, 1950

Shirley, Sylvia, 1919-
Slow journey
Prize stories of 1951

Shivaree before breakfast. West, J.

Shneour, Zalman. See Shneur, Zalman

Shneur, Zalman, 1887-
The girl
Howe, I. and Greenberg, E. eds. Treasury of Yiddish stories
Immortal orange
Ausubel, N. ed. Treasury of Jewish humor
Leftwich, J. ed. Yisröel. 1952 ed.
New police chief
Ausubel, N. ed. Treasury of Jewish humor
Revenge; extracts from a student's diary
Howe, I. and Greenberg, E. eds. Treasury of Yiddish stories

Shiftless. Boyd, J.

Shock. Kuttner, H.

Shock of doom. Porter, W. S.

Shock tactics. Munro, H. H.

Shock treatment. Stark, I.

SHOEMAKERS

Galsworthy, J. Quality
Maxtone Graham, J. A. Cobbler, cobbler, mend my shoe
Nexø, M. A. Birds of passage
Reisin, A. Avrom the cobbler
Singer, I. B. Little shoemakers
Van Doren, M. Little place

SHOE SHINERS. See Bootblacks

SHOES. See Boots and shoes

Shoes. Porter, W. S.

Shoes for breakfast. Treat, L.

Shoes of black green leather. See Schwartz, R. A. Shoes of bright green leather

Shoes of bright green leather. Schwartz, R. A.

SHOFAR. See Shophar

Shofar blower of Lapinishok. Ogus, A. D.

Sholokhov, Mikhail Aleksandrovich, 1905-
Civil War
Burnett, W. ed. World's best

SHOOTING

Bonner, P. H. The triumph
Saroyan, W. Pheasant hunter
Schaefer, J. W. My town
See also Hunting

The **shooting.** Caldwell, E.

Shooting an elephant. Orwell, G.

SHOPHAR

Ogus, A. D. Shofar blower of Lapinshok

SHOPKEEPERS. See Merchants

SHOPPING

De Vries, P. Household words
Munro, H. H. The dreamer
Munro, H. H. Sex that doesn't shop
Parker, J. R. Robes et modes

SHOPS, BEAUTY. See Beauty shops

Shore, Viola (Brothers) 1895-
'Bye, 'bye, Bluebeard
Queen, E. pseud. ed. Queen's awards: 6th ser.
Case of Karen Smith
Queen, E. pseud. ed. Queen's awards: 5th ser.

Shore for the sinking. Thompson, T.

Shores of Tripoli. Daniel, H.

Shorn lamb. Stafford, J.

Short digest of a long novel. Schulberg, B. W.

Short Friday. Bialik, H. N.

Short happy life of Francis Macomber. Hemingway, E.

Short space. Toole, K.

Short visit to Naples. Newhouse, E.

Shorty who wished he were taller. Strain, F. B.

SHOTGUNS. See Shooting

Shottle Bop. Waldo, E. H.

The **shout.** Graves, R.

Show window. Bradley, M. H.

SHOW WINDOWS

Blackburn, R. H. Clay dish

Shower of gold. Welty, E.

Shulman, Max, 1919-
Boy bites man
Shulman, M. The many loves of Dobie Gillis
Chance for adventure
This week magazine. This week's short-short stories
Everybody loves my baby
Shulman, M. The many loves of Dobie Gillis
Face is familiar but—
Shulman, M. The many loves of Dobie Gillis
King's English
Shulman, M. The many loves of Dobie Gillis
Love is a fallacy
Shulman, M. The many loves of Dobie Gillis
Love of two chemists
Shulman, M. The many loves of Dobie Gillis
Mock governor
Shulman, M. The many loves of Dobie Gillis

Shulman, Max—*Continued*
She shall have music
    Shulman, M. The many loves of Dobie
    Gillis
Sugar bowl
    Shulman, M. The many loves of Dobie
    Gillis
Unlucky winner
    Shulman, M. The many loves of Dobie
    Gillis
You think you got trouble?
    Shulman, M. The many loves of Dobie
    Gillis

Shultz, William Henry, 1913-
Oreste
    Best American short stories, 1953

Shut a final door. Capote, T.

Shute, Henry Augustus, 1856-1943
"Sequil"—or Things whitch aint finished
in the first
    Davis, C. B. ed. Eyes of boyhood

Shylock in Czernowitz. Franzos, K. E.

SIAM. See Thailand

SIBERIA
Chekhov, A. P. Across Siberia

SICILY
Verga, G. Little novels of Sicily; 12
stories

Sick bay to sea wall. White, R.

Sick child. Colette, S. G.

Sick goose Rosenfeld, J.

Sick horse. Caldwell, E.

Sidewise in time. Jenkins, W. F.

Siegel, Benjamin
Little red jungle
    Seventeen (Periodical) Nineteen from
    Seventeen

Siegel, Larry
Lay it down, Ziggy!
    Herzberg, M. J. comp. Treasure chest
    of sport stories

Sienkiewicz, Henryk, 1846-1916
Keeper of the faith
    Brentano, F. ed. The word lives on

SIERRA NEVADA MOUNTAINS
Breckenfeld, V. G. Touch of Arab

SIGHT
McKenney, J. Skycaptain
    See also Blind

SIGHTSEEING BUSES
Porter, W. S. Sisters of the golden rule
The **sign.** Dunsany, E. J. M. D. P. 18th
baron

Sign of the broken sword. Chesterton, G. K.

Sign of the four. Doyle, Sir A. C.

The **signal.** Maupassant, G. de

Signal man. Dickens, C.

SIGNAL MEN, RAILROAD. See Railroads—Employees

Signed with his seal. Undset, S.

Signor Santa. Pagano, J.

SIKSIKA INDIANS
Frazee, S. Great medicine

Silence. Poe, E. A.

Silence of Mr Prendegast. Cloete, S.

Silent Scot. Skinner, C. L.

Silent snow, secret snow. Aiken, C. P.

Silent wings. Coombs, C. I.

Silent woman. Kompert, L.

The **silken-swift.** Waldo, E. H.

Sillanpää, Frans Eemil, 1888-
Night of the harvest festival
    Burnett, W. ed. World's best

Silly season. Kornbluth, C. M.

Silone, Ignazio, 1900-
Mr Aristotle
    Neider, C. ed. Great short stories from
    the world's literature
Seed beneath the snow; excerpts
    Burnett, W. ed. World's best
The trap
    Blodgett, H. W. ed. Story survey.
    1953 ed.

Silver Blaze. Doyle, Sir A. C.

Silver cross. Doty, W. L.

Silver dollar. Thompson, T.

Silver King. Perrault, E. G.

SILVER MINES AND MINING
Davis, S. P. Mystery of the Savage sump
Hart, F. First Fourth in White Pine

Silver mounted. James, W.

Silver saddle. Thompson, T.

Silver spurs. Witham, E. C.

Silver sword. Ullman, J. R.

Silvers, Earl Reed, 1891-1948
Stars in the sky
    Certner, S. and Henry, G. H. eds. Short
    stories for our times

Silverspot: the story of a crow. Seton, E. T.

Simak, Clifford Donald, 1904-
Aesop
    Simak, C. D. City
The answers
    Sloane, W. M. ed. Stories for tomorrow
Asteroid of gold
    Wollheim, D. A. comp. Every boy's
    book of science-fiction
Beachhead
    Derleth, A. W. ed. Beachheads in space
Census
    Simak, C. D. City
City
    Simak, C. D. City
Contraption
    Star science fiction stories [no. 1]
Courtesy
    Sloane, W. M. ed. Space, space, space
Desertion
    Conklin, G. ed. Big book of science
    fiction
    Simak, C. D. City
Eternity lost
    Astounding science fiction (Periodical)
    Astounding science fiction anthology
    Best science fiction stories: 1950
    Bleiler, E. F. and Dikty, T. E. eds. Sci-
    ence fiction omnibus: the best science
    fiction stories, 1949, 1950
Good night, Mr James
    Derleth, A. W. ed. The outer reaches
    Galaxy science fiction magazine. Galaxy
    reader of science fiction

Simak, Clifford D.—*Continued*
Hobbies
Simak, C. D. City
Huddling place
Simak, C. D. City
Junkyard
Galaxy science fiction magazine. Second
Galaxy reader of science fiction
Limiting factor
Conklin, G. ed. Possible worlds of sci-
ence fiction
Paradise
Simak, C. D. City
Second childhood
Galaxy science fiction magazine. Galaxy
reader of science fiction
Sloane, W. M. ed. Stories for tomorrow
Simple way
Simak, C. D. City
Skirmish
Conklin, G. ed. Science-fiction thinking
machines

Simenon, Georges, 1903-
Château of missing men
Mystery Writers of America, inc.
Crooks' tour
Little house at Croix-Rousse
Mystery Writers of America, inc.
Maiden murders
Stan the killer
Mystery Writers of America, inc.
Butcher, baker, murder-maker

Simha of Worms. Cohn, E.

Simon's papa. Maupassant, G. de

Simple heart. Flaubert, G.

Simple way. Simak, C. D.

Simpson, Harriette Louisa. See Arnow,
Harriette Louisa (Simpson)

Simpson, Maud Edith, 1897-
Practical joker
Oberfirst, R. ed. 1954 anthology of best
original short-shorts

Simworthy's circus. Shaw, L.

SIN
Hawthorne, N. Minister's black veil
Sinclair, M. Where their fire is not
quenched

SIN, UNPARDONABLE
Hawthorne, N. Ethan Brand

Sinai. Frischman, D.

Sinclair, Jo, pseud. See Seid, Ruth

Sinclair, John L. 1902-
The killer and the pit
Western Writers of America. Holsters
and heroes

Sinclair, May, 1865?-1946
Nature of the evidence
Conklin, G. and Conklin, L. T. eds.
Supernatural reader
Where their fire is not quenched
Davenport, B. ed. Ghostly tales to be
told

Sing, Milo, sing. MacMahon, B.

SINGAPORE
Maugham, W. S. The letter

Singer, Israel Joshua, 1893-1944
Repentance
Howe, I. and Greenberg, E. eds. Treas-
ury of Yiddish stories
Sand
Howe, I. and Greenberg, E. eds. Treas-
ury of Yiddish stories
Singer, Isaac Bashevis, 1894-
Gimpel the fool
Howe, I. and Greenberg, E. eds. Treas-
ury of Yiddish stories
Little shoemakers
Howe, I. and Greenberg, E. eds. Treas-
ury of Yiddish stories

SINGERS. See Musicians—Singers

SINGING AND VOICE CULTURE
Fisher, D. F. C. As ye sow—

Singing stick. Pangborn, E.

Singmaster, Elsie, 1879-
Boy and a dog
Harper, W. comp. Dog show
Little and unknown
Brentano, F. ed. The word lives on

Sinister journey. Richter, C.

Sinister night. Chekhov, A. P.

SINN FEIN
Corkery, D. Unfinished symphony

Sins of Prince Saradine. Chesterton, G. K.

SIOUX INDIANS. See Dakota Indians

Sir Harry Scattercash's hounds: Mr Sponge
carries the horn. Surtees, R. S.

Sir Harry's hounds again: Mr Sponge and
Miss Lucy Glitters. Surtees, R. S.

Sir Louis dines out. Trollope, A.

Sir Rabbit. Welty, E.

Sir Thomas. Schneider, G. W.

Sire de Malétroit's door. Stevenson, R. L.

Siren of hope. Keith, S.

Sister. Humphrey, W.

Sister. Scott, H. S.

Sister Aparición. Pardo Bazán, E. condesa
de

Sister Innocent and the useful miracle.
Lieberman, R.

Sister superior. Wilson, A.

SISTERS
Curtis, M. Navy blue and bold
Davies, R. Resurrection
Davies, R. The sisters
Fleg, E. The adulteress
Gordimer, N. La vie Bohème
Horwitz, J. The burial
Horwitz, J. If God makes you pretty
Irwin, M. E. F. Where beauty lies
Johnson, D. M. Flame on the frontier
Lambert, J. Tall as the stars
Mansfield, K. Daughters of the late colo-
nel
Marshall, E. Hill people
O'Donovan, M. Little mother
O'Donovan, M. Mad Lomasneys
Schuman, S. Quiet one
Stern, G. B. Cinderella's sister
Welty, E. Why I live at the P.O.
Wharton, E. N. J. Bunner sisters

The **skit**. Chekhov, A. P.

SKULLS
Crawford, F. M. Screaming skull

Sky hook. Brier, H. M.

Sky line. Taylor, P. H.

Sky ride—a Tom Swift story. Appleton, V. pseud.

Skyblue lady. Lowry, R. J. C.

Skycaptain. McKenney, J.

Skylight Room. Porter, W. S.

SKYSCRAPERS
McMorrow, T. Mr Murphy of New York
Porter, W. S. Psyche and the pskyscraper

SLAUGHTERING AND SLAUGHTER-HOUSES
Still, J. Master time

SLAVE SHIPS
Melville, H. Benito Cereno
Sabin, E. L. Freedom

SLAVE TRADE
Melville, H. Benito Cereno

SLAVERY
Benét, S. V. Freedom's a hard-bought thing
Harris, J. C. Free Joe and the rest of the world

Egypt
Coolidge, O. E. The tree

Fugitive slaves
Faulkner, W. Was

Slay upon delivery. Kane, F.

Sleek sixteen. Curtis, M.

SLEEP
Nadir, I. M. Man who slept through the end of the world
See also Insomnia

SLEEP, PROLONGED
Cohn, E. Honi ha-Meaggel
Irving, W. Rip Van Winkle

SLEEP-WALKING. See Somnambulism

Sleeper awakened. Jackson, C. R.

Sleeping Beauty. Collier, J.

Sleeping draft. Martyr, W.

SLEEPLESSNESS. See Insomnia

Sleet storm. Lamberton, L.

SLEIGHT OF HAND. See Conjuring

Slesinger, Tess, 1905-1945
Missis Flinders
Gable, M. Sister, ed. Many-colored fleece

Sleuth-hound. Zoshchenko, M. M.

The **sleuths**. Porter, W. S.

Slice him down. Hughes, L.

Slightly crocked. McNulty, J.

Slipover sweater. Stuart, J.

Slipstream. Ford, C.

Slithering shadow. Howard, R. E.

Sloane, William Milligan, 1906-
Let nothing you dismay
Sloane, W. M. ed. Stories for tomorrow

Slosson, Annie (Trumbull) 1838-1926
Fishin' Jimmy
Scribner treasury

SLOT MACHINES. See Gambling

Slouch. Farrell, J. T.

Slow death. Caldwell, E.

Slow journey. Shirley, S.

Slowpoke. Paterson, R.

SLUM LIFE
Crane, S. Maggie: a girl of the streets

Small, Sidney Herschel, 1893-
Chinese dagger
Best detective stories of the year—1951
Stalking shadow
Best detective stories of the year—1950

Small day. Caldwell, E.

Small homicide. Hunter, E.

SMALL TOWN LIFE
Clemens, S. L. Man that corrupted Hadleyburg
Crowell, C. T. The stoic
Grau, S. A. Girl with the flaxen hair
Lord, J. Boy who wrote 'no'

Small world. Cousins, M.

Small world. Sansom, W.

SMALLPOX
Grimson, M. S. Story of Paula

Smell of smoke. Anderson, E. V.

The **smile**. Bradbury, R.

Smile box. Eggleston, M. W.

Smiling lady. Eggleston, M. W.

Smith, Clark Ashton, 1893-
Beyond the Singing Flame
Margulies, L. and Friend, O. J. eds. From off this world
City of Singing Flame
Margulies, L. and Friend, O. J. eds. From off this world
Metamorphosis of earth
Derleth, A. W. ed. Beachheads in space
Phoenix
Derleth, A. W. ed. Time to come
Plutonian drug
Derleth, A. W. ed. The outer reaches
Voyage to Sfanomoë
Derleth, A. W. ed. Beyond time & space

Smith, Edgar Valentine, 1875-1953
Prelude
First-prize stories, 1919-1954
McFarland, W. K. comp. Then it happened

Smith, Edmund Ware, 1900-
Underground episode
Certner, S. and Henry, G. H. eds. Short stories for our times

Smith, Edward Elmer, 1890-
Atlantis
Greenberg, M. ed. Journey to infinity

Smith, Eugene Cadwallader, 1877-
The outlaw
Fenner, P. R. comp. Elephants, elephants, elephants

Smith, Evelyn E. 1927-
Daxbr baxbr
Derleth, A. W. ed. Time to come
Not fit for children
Galaxy science fiction magazine. Second Galaxy reader of science fiction

Social sense. Maugham, W. S.

Social triangle. Porter, W. S.

SOCIAL WORKERS
Auchincloss, L. Edification of Marianne

SOCIALISM
Fisher, D. F. C. Drop in the bucket

Sociology in serge and straw. Porter, W. S.

SOCRATES
Alas, L. Cock of Socrates

Socrates. Christopher, J.

SOFAS
Anderson, E. V. Tapestry extravaganza

Soft-boiled. Stewart, O.

SOFT DRINKS. See Carbonated beverages

Soft voice of the serpent. Gordimer, N.

The sojourner. McCullers, C. S.

Solar plexus. Blish, J.

Solarite. Campbell, J. W.

The soldier. Dahl, R.

Soldier boy. Shaara, M.

Soldier of the realm. Ullman, J. R.

Soldier ran away. Boyle, K.

SOLDIERS
Bergengruen, W. On presenting arms
Hemingway, E. Way you'll never be
Ullman, J. R. Soldier of the realm

American
Arico, V. The promotion
Boyd, T. A. Responsibility
Boyle, K. Soldier ran away
Brookhouser, F. The inn was perfect
Brown, E. L. Hero
Downey, H. The hunters
Farrell, J. T. When boyhood dreams come true
Hume, S. T. Shake hands with a murderer
Landon, B. Advance party
Lowry, R. J. C. Casualty
Lowry, R. J. C. Happy New Year, kamerades!
Salinger, J. D. For Esmé—with love and squalor
Schaefer, J. W. Cat nipped
Shaw, I. Act of faith
Wasserman, N. A. Stars are black
Whitmore, S. Lost soldier
Winter, A. B. Party dress

British
Collier, J. Without benefit of Galsworthy
Downey, H. The hunters
Goldsmith, O. Disabled soldier
Kipling, R. Incarnation of Krishna Mulvaney
Kipling, R. 'Love-o'-women'
Kipling, R. Man who was
Kipling, R. On Greenhow Hill
O'Donovan, M. Guests of the nation
Shaw, I. Walking wounded
Taylor, E. Oasis of gaiety

Carthaginian
Powers, A. Hannibal's elephants

English
See Soldiers—British

Furloughs
Lowry, R. J. Law and order
Montague, M. P. England to America

German
Hebel, J. P. The hussar
Lawrence, D. H. Prussian officer

Hungarian
Bergengruen, W. Stabenhaüser

Polish
Gellhorn, M. E. Voyage forme la jeunesse

Roman
Powers, A. Hannibal's elephants

Russian
Shapiro, L. White chalah

SOLDIERS, DISABLED. See Cripples

Soliloquy at dinner. Hutchins, M. P. M.

Solipsist. Brown, F.

Solitaire. Stern, J.

Solitary Dogan. Ready, W. B.

Solitude. Unamuno y Jugo, M. de

Solitude. Williams, B. A.

SOLOMON, KING OF ISRAEL
Cohn, E. It looks like justice
Fleg, E. Solomon the King

Solomon the King. Fleg, E.

Sol's little brother. Elam, R. M.

Soman, Florence Jane
Your heart's out of order
Stowe, A. comp. It's a date

"Some bum might mistook me for a wrestler." Mitchell, J.

Some can't take it. Fowler, B. B.

Some heroes. Roark, E.

Some like them cold. Lardner, R. W.

Some of father's adventures. Gannett, R. S.

Some "Q" ships. Ritchie, L. A. da C.

Somebody else, not me. Miller, J. D.

Someone like you. Dahl, R.

Somerville, Andrew W. 1900-
Tale of the old main line
Moskowitz, S. ed. Great railroad stories of the world

Somerville, Edith Anna Œnone, 1861-1949, and Martin, Violet Florence, 1865-1915
Philippa's fox-hunt
Cerf, B. A. and Moriarty, H. C. eds. Anthology of famous British stories
Trinket's colt
Creamer, J. B. comp. Twenty-two stories about horses and men

Something for December eighth. Zelver, A.

Something gay and foolish. Sellars, M.

Something green. Brown, F.

Something in common. Hughes, L.

Something lost. Schaefer, J. W.

Something special for Jane. Ross, A. L.

Something terrible, something lovely. Sansom, W.

Something to hide. MacDonald, P.

Something wrong. Stern, J.

Sometimes a man needs a friend. Taber, G. B.

Sommerfield, John
Above the clouds
New writing (Periodical) Best stories

SOMNAMBULISM
Maclaren-Ross, J. This mortal coil

Somnium: or the astronomy of the moon. Kepler, J.

Son of a tinker. Walsh, M.

Son-of-David. Goudge, E.

Son of the sun. London, J.

Song and the sergeant. Porter, W. S.

Song of the flying fish. Chesterton, G. K.

Song of the pewee. Grendon, S.

Song without words. O'Donovan, M.

SONG WRITERS. See Musicians—Composers

SONG WRITING. See Music, Popular (Songs, etc.)—Writing and publishing

SONGS
Bates, H. E. Christmas song

SONS. See Fathers and sons; Mothers and sons

Son's veto. Hardy, T.

Sooth. Steele, W. D.

The soothsayer. Bennett, K.

Sophie Jackson. Winslow, T. S.

Sophistication. Anderson, S.

Sophistication. Jackson, C. R.

Sophomore forward. Peterson, G. M.

Sophy's Christmas dinner. Bunn, H. F.

Sorcerer's apprentice. O'Donovan, M.

Sorcerer's son. Johnson, J. W.

SORCERY. See Magic; Witchcraft

SORORITIES. See Greek letter societies

Sorority. Hogan, A.

SORROW. See Joy and sorrow

Sorrows of Captain Schreiber. Stern, R. G.

Sorrows of Young Werther. Goethe, J. W. von

SOTO, HERNANDO DE, 1500?-1542
Wassermann, J. Gold of Caxamalca

Soul of Laploshka. Munro, H. H.

Soul that mice nibbled up. Kobrin, L.

SOUND
Recording and reproducing
Dahl, R. Sound machine

The sound. Van Vogt, A. E.

Sound and fury. Porter, W. S.

Sound machine. Dahl, R.

Sound of blackmail. Queen, E. pseud.

Sound of gunfire. O'Reilly, J.

Sound of murder. McGivern, W. P.

Sound of thunder. Bradbury, R.

Sound of waiting. Calisher, H.

SOUND PRODUCTION BY ANIMALS
White, S. E. On lying awake at night

SOUPS
Heijermans, H. Shabbes-soup

Source of irritation. Aumonier, S.

Source seven. Gilbert, M. F.

Souse of the border. Gilpatric, G.

THE SOUTH. See Southern States

SOUTH AFRICA. See Africa, South

SOUTH AMERICAN INDIANS. See Indians of South America

SOUTH CAROLINA

Charleston

Holland, R. S. Pirates of Charles Town harbor
Steele, W. D. Can't cross Jordan by myself

Sullivan's Island

Poe, E. A. The gold-bug

SOUTH SEA ISLANDS
Crump, I. Pirate island
London, J. Son of the sun
Maugham, W. S. Red
Morris, G. Back there in the grass

South toward home. Jackson, M. W.

SOUTHERN DIALECT. See Dialect stories—Southern

SOUTHERN STATES
Clayton, J. B. Ride a pale ghost into night and time
Faulkner, W. The bear
Faulkner, W. Rose for Emily
Fitzgerald, F. S. K. Ice palace
Gordon, C. Forest of the South
Gordon, C. Old Red
Harris, G. W. Sut Lovingood; 8 stories
Humphrey, W. Fresh snow
King, M. P. Honey house
Lytle, A. N. Jericho, Jericho, Jericho
Mohler, C. Jesus complex
Moody, M. H. Ghost of General Jackson
Patton, F. G. Let it rest
Porter, K. A. Old mortality
Porter, W. S. Two renegades
Street, J. H. I am not a stranger
Tolbert, F. X. Last rebel yell
See also names of individual Southern states

SOUTHERNERS. See Southern States

Southpaw switch. Regli, A. C.

Souto Alabarce, Arturo
Coyote 13
De Onís, H. ed. Spanish stories and tales

Space. Buchan, J. 1st baron Tweedsmuir

SPACE AND TIME
Asimov, I. Red Queen's race
Blish, J. Mistake inside
Buchan, J. 1st baron Tweedsmuir. Space
Heinlein, R. A. Elsewhen
Jenkins, W. F. Sidewise in time
See also Time

Space jockey. Heinlein, R. A.

Space Lane cadet. Hallstead, W. F.

Space rating. Berryman, J.

SPACE SHIPS
Bradbury, R. Kaleidoscope
Carr, R. S. Morning star
Jameson, M. Bullard of the space partol; 7 stories
Jenkins, W. F. First contact

Spiegel, Isaiah, 1906-
Ghetto dog
Howe, I. and Greenberg, E. eds. Treasury of Yiddish stories

SPIES
Aumonier, S. Source of irritation
Maugham, W. S. Giulia Lazzari
Maugham, W. S. Hairless Mexican
Maugham, W. S. His Excellency
Maugham, W. S. Miss King
Maugham, W. S. Mr Harrington's washing
Maugham, W. S. The traitor
Noyes, A. Uncle Hyacinth
Silone, I. The trap

Spike. Bendrodt, J. C.

Spiller, Burton L.
Net profit
Dachs, D. ed. Treasury of sports humoi

Spilo, Robert, 1925?-
Big Ed
American vanguard, 1953

SPINSTERS
Anderson, S. Adventure
Ashley, E. L. Aunt Lil
Bowe, E. New house
Brush, K. I. Good Wednesday
De La Roche, M. Auntimay
Fisher, D. F. C. Drop in the bucket
Freeman, M. E. W. New England nun
Goyen, W. Her breath upon the windowpane
Mansfield, K. Daughters of the late colonel
Maugham, W. S. Vessel of wrath
Maugham, W. S. Winter cruise
Singmaster, E. Little and unknown
Sutro, A. Bread on the waters
Welty, E. Asphodel
Welty, E. Clytie
Wilson, A. Little companion
Winslow, T. S. Misses Grant

Spire, André, 1868-
Rabbi and the siren
Leftwich, J. ed. Yisröel. 1952 ed.

Spirit dope. Foote, J. T.

Spirits. Gally, J. W.

SPIRITUALISM
Ford, J. L. Spiritualist's tale
O'Brien, F.-J. Diamond lens

Spiritualist's tale. Ford, J. L.

SPITE. See Revenge

Splendid fellow. Bottome, P.

Split cherry tree. Stuart, J.

Split second. Du Maurier, D.

Spofford, Harriet Elizabeth (Prescott) 1835-1921
Circumstance
Cuff, R. P. ed. American short story survey

Spoiled cake. Renard, J.

Spoiled priest. Sheehan, P. A.

SPOILS SYSTEM. See Corruption (in politics)

Spooks of the valley. Jones, L. C.

Spooner. Farjeon, E.

SPOONERISMS
Queen, E. pseud. "My queer Dean!"

Sport of destiny. Schiller, J. C. F. von

Sporting blood. Wylie, P.

SPORTS
Argosy (Periodical) Argosy Book of sports stories; 20 stories
Chute, B. J. Teen-age sports parade; 11 stories
Coombs, C. L. Teen-age champion sports stories; 18 stories
Dachs, D. ed. Treasury of sports humor; 36 stories
Herzberg, M. J. comp. Treasure chest of sport stories; 19 stories
Newhouse, E. Bronze thing
Owen, F. ed. Teen-age victory parade; 13 stories
Owen, F. ed. Teen-age winter sports stories; 16 stories
See also Track athletics; and names of particular sports, e.g. Baseball, Golf; etc.

The sportsman. Bond, N. S.

Spot in history. Hall, J. B.

Spotted horses. Faulkner, W.

Sprague De Camp, Lyon. See De Camp, Lyon Sprague

Spring, Howard, 1889-
Sabre in the hand
Brentano, F. ed. The word lives on

SPRING
Porter, W. S. Easter of the soul

SPRING CLEANING. See House cleaning

Spring evening. Farrell, J. T.

Spring fever. Collier, J.

Spring fever. Davis, D. S.

Spring flight. Irwin, I. H.

Spring over Brooklyn. Gold, Z.

Springer, Sherwood
No Land of Nod
Startling stories (Periodical) Best from Startling stories

Springfield fox. Seton, E. T.

Springtime à la carte. Porter, W. S.

Spruce Point mystery. Leighton, M. C.

Spry old character. Taylor, E.

Spur piece. Barr, J. pseud.

Spurs for Antonia. Eyre, K. W.

Square egg. Munro, H. H.

Squaring the circle. Porter, W. S.

The squash. Bergelson, D.

Squaw fever. Gulick, G. C.

Squire Dinwiddy. Caldwell, E.

Squires, James Radcliffe. See Squires, Radcliffe

Squires, Radcliffe, 1917-
Baby buntings
Story (Periodical) Story; no. 2

Squirrel who was scared. Tracy, D.

SQUIRRELS
Tracy, D. Squirrel who was scared

Squirrels have bright eyes. Collier, J.

Squirt and the monkey. Stout, R.

Sredni Vashtar. Munro, H. H.

SRL ad. Matheson, R.

Stabbing in the streets. Lipsky, E.

Stabenhaüser. Bergengruen, W.

STABLEMEN
Collins, W. Dream-woman

Stacey Bell. Van Doren, M.

Stafford, Jean, 1915-
Between the porch and the altar
Stafford, J. Children are bored on Sunday
Bleeding heart
Stafford, J. Children are bored on Sunday
Children are bored on Sunday
Stafford, J. Children are bored on Sunday
Country love story
Prize stories of 1951
Stafford, J. Children are bored on Sunday
Echo and the nemesis
Stafford, J. Children are bored on Sunday
Healthiest girl in town
Best American short stories, 1952
Home front
Stafford, J. Children are bored on Sunday
Interior castle
Best of the Best American short stories, 1915-1950
Stafford, J. Children are bored on Sunday
The maiden
Stafford, J. Children are bored on Sunday
Modest proposal
Stafford, J. Children are bored on Sunday
The nemesis
Best American short stories, 1951
Ludwig, J. B. and Poirier, W. R. eds. Stories, British and American
A reunion
Swallow, A. ed. Anchor in the sea
Shorn lamb
Best American short stories, 1954
Prize stories, 1954
Summer day
Stafford, J. Children are bored on Sunday
Winter's tale
Aswell, M. L. W. ed. New short novels

STAGE-COACH LINES
Harte, B. Dick Boyle's business card
Harte, B. Ingénue of the Sierras
Harte, B. Miggles
Haycox, E. Stage to Lordsburg

STAGE LIFE. See Theater and stage life

Stage station. Haycox, E.

Stage to Lordsburg. Haycox, E.

Stage to Yuma. DeVries, M.

Staggered holiday. Sitwell, Sir O. bart.

STAGS. See Deer

Stair trick. Clingerman, M.

The **stake.** Munro, H. H.

Stalker & Co. Bonner, P. H.

Stalking shadow. Small, S. H.

Stalled ox. Munro, H. H.

Stallings, Laurence, 1894-
Vale of tears
Grayson, C. ed. Fourth round

Stampeding of Lady Bastable. Munro, H. H.

Stan the killer. Simenon, G.

Stancourt, Louis Joseph
Vacant cross
Thinker's digest (Periodical) Spoiled priest, and other stories

Stand-in. Wilson, B.

Stand to horse. Downey, F. D.

Standish, Burt L. pseud. See Patten, Gilbert

Standish, Robert, pseud. See Gerahty, Digby George

Stangland, A. G.
Ancient brain
Margulies, L. and Friend, O. J. eds. From off this world

Stanley, Dave, pseud. See Dachs, David

Stanley, Fay Grissom
Last day of all
Mystery Writers of America, inc. 20 great tales of murder

Stanley, John Berchman, 1910-
Matter of spelling
Boys' life (Periodical) Boys' life Adventure stories

Stanley who was adopted. Strain, F. B.

Stanton, Will
Barney
Magazine of fantasy and science fiction. Best from Fantasy and science fiction; [1st ser]
Town without a straight man
Queen, E. pseud. ed. Queen's awards: 8th ser.

Stapledon, Olaf. See Stapledon, William Olaf

Stapledon, William Olaf, 1886-
Flying men
Derleth, A. W. ed. Beyond time & space
Last terrestrials
Kuebler, H. W. ed. Treasury of science fiction classics
The Martians
Kuebler, H. W. ed. Treasury of science fiction classics

The **Star.** Keller, D. H.

The **star.** Wells, H. G.

Star begotten. Wells, H. G.

Star, Bright. Clifton, M.

Star buck. Kilcrin, I.

Star ducks. Brown, B.

Star dummy. White, W. A. P.

Star gypsies. Gresham, W. L.

Star light, star bright. Bester, A.

Star-linked. Fyfe, H. B.

Star mouse. Brown, F.

Star of Siam. Schneider, G. W.

Star producers. Charteris, L.

Star quality. Coward, N. P.

Starbride. White, W. A. P.

Stark, Irwin, 1912-
Shock treatment
Ribalow, H. U. ed. These your children

STARS
Brown, F. Pi in the sky
Derleth, A. W. McIlvaine's star
Porter, W. S. Phoebe

Stars are black. Wasserman, N.

Stars are the Styx. Waldo, E. H.

Stars in the sky. Silvers, E. R.

Start from scratch. Knipscheer, J. M. W.

Start in life. Kelly, R. G.

STARVATION
Saroyan, W. Daring young man on the flying trapeze

Starzl, R. F.
Hornets of space
Margulies, L. and Friend, O. J. eds. From off this world

STATE DEPARTMENT. See United States. State Department

State of mind. Aiken, C. P.

Statement of the case. Doyle, Sir A. C.

Stations of the Cross. Lemelin, R.

Statistics. Wendroff, Z.

STATUE OF LIBERTY, NEW YORK
Porter, W. S. Lady higher up

STATUES
Arico, V. Merchant's monument
Milton, M. E. Favor granted

The statues. Priestley, J. B.

Status quondam. Miller, P. S.

Steady like a rock. Bond, N. S.

STEALING. See Shoplifting; Theft; Thieves

Stebel, Sidney
Number to remember
Story (Periodical) Story; no. 3

Steel, Flora Annie (Webster) 1847-1929
Barber's clever wife
Fenner, P. R. comp. Fools and funny fellows

Steel brother. Dickson, G. R.

Steel cat. Collier, J.

STEEL WORKERS
Heyliger, W. Steelman's nerve

Steele, Flora Annie (Webster) See Steel, Flora Annie (Webster)

Steele, Wilbur Daniel, 1886-
Autumn bloom
Steele, W. D. Full cargo
Black road
Steele, W. D. Full cargo
Blue murder
Grayson, C. ed. Fourth round
Brother's keeper
Steele, W. D. Full cargo
Bubbles
First-prize stories, 1919-1954
By appointment
Steele, W. D. Full cargo
Can't cross Jordan by myself
First-prize stories, 1919-1954
Ching, Ching, Chinaman
Steele, W. D. Full cargo
Devil of a fellow
Steele, W. D. Full cargo
Fe-fi-fo-fum
Steele, W. D. Full cargo

For they know not what they do
Cuff, R. P. ed. American short story survey
Gray goose
Steele, W. D. Full cargo
How beautiful with shoes
Best of the Best American short stories, 1915-1950
Blodgett, H. W. ed. Story survey. 1953 ed.
Lady-killer
Queen, E. pseud. ed. Queen's awards: 5th ser.
Luck
Steele, W. D. Full cargo
Man and boy
Steele, W. D. Full cargo
Man who saw through heaven
Burrell, J. A. and Cerf, B. A. eds. Anthology of famous American stories
Never anything that fades
Steele, W. D. Full cargo
Renegade
Steele, W. D. Full cargo
Sailor! Sailor!
Steele, W. D. Full cargo
Six dollars
Steele, W. D. Full cargo
Sooth
Steele, W. D. Full cargo
The thinker
Steele, W. D. Full cargo
Two seconds
Steele, W. D. Full cargo
Way with women
Steele, W. D. Full cargo
Yellow cat
Shaw, H. and Bement, D. Reading the short story
Steele, W. D. Full cargo

Steelman's nerve. Heyliger, W.

STEEPLECHASING. See Horse racing

Stefánsson, Vilhjálmur, 1879-
Seal hunting
Andrews, R. C. ed. My favorite stories of the great outdoors

Stegner, Wallace Earle, 1909-
Balance his, swing yours
Stegner, W. E. Women on the wall
Berry patch
Stegner, W. E. Women on the wall
Beyond the glass mountain
Stegner, W. E. Women on the wall
Blue-winged teal
Abell, E. ed. American accent
First-prize stories, 1919-1954
Prize stories of 1950
Buglesong
Stegner, W. E. Women on the wall
Butcher bird
Stegner, W. E. Women on the wall
West, R. B. and Stallman, R. W. eds. Art of modern fiction
The Chink
Stegner, W. E. Women on the wall
Chip off the old block
Stegner, W. E. Women on the wall
The colt
Stegner, W. E. Women on the wall
Double corner
Stegner, W. E. Women on the wall

Stegner, Wallace E.—*Continued*
Goin' to town
  Stegner, W. E. Women on the wall
Hostage
  Stegner, W. E. Women on the wall
In the twilight
  Stegner, W. E. Women on the wall
Saw gang
  Stegner, W. E. Women on the wall
Sweetness of the twisted apples
  Stegner, W. E. Women on the wall
The traveler
  Best American short stories, 1952
Two rivers
  Stegner, W. E. Women on the wall
View from the balcony
  Stegner, W. E. Women on the wall
The volcano
  Stegner, W. E. Women on the wall
Women on the wall
  Best of the Best American short stories, 1915-1950
  Stegner, W. E. Women on the wall
  Stegner, W. E.; Scowcroft, R. and Ilyin, B. eds. Writer's art

Stein, Gertrude, 1874-1946
Bartholomew Arnold
  Stein, G. Mrs Reynolds, and five earlier novelettes
Brim Beauvais
  Stein, G. Mrs Reynolds, and five earlier novelettes
Good Anna
  Burrell, J. A. and Cerf, B. A. eds. Anthology of famous American stories
Hotel François Ier
  Stein, G. Mrs Reynolds, and five earlier novelettes
Marguerite
  Stein, G. Mrs Reynolds, and five earlier novelettes
What does she see when she shuts her eyes
  Stein, G. Mrs Reynolds, and five earlier novelettes

Stein, Mildred
First sad facts
  Wolfe, D. M. ed. Which grain will grow

Steinbeck, John, 1902-
The chrysanthemums
  Foerster, N. ed. American poetry and prose. 1952 ed.
The gift
  Stauffer, R. M.; Cunningham, W. H. and Sullivan, C. J. eds. Adventures in modern literature
Leader of the people
  Davis, C. B. ed. Eyes of boyhood
  Day, A. G. ed. Greatest American short stories
  Lamb, L. ed. Family book of best loved short stories
  Schramm, W. L. ed. Great short stories
  Shaw, H. and Bement, D. Reading the short story
  Short, R. W. and Sewall, R. B. eds. Short stories for study. 1950 ed.

Miracle of Tepayac
  Bachelor, J. M.; Henry, R. L. and Salisbury, R. eds. Current thinking and writing; 2d ser.
  Gable, M. Sister, ed. Many-colored fleece
  Grayson, C. ed. Fourth round
The murder
  Queen, E. pseud. ed. Literature of crime
Red pony
  Burrell, J. A. and Cerf, B. A. eds. Anthology of famous American stories
Snake of one's own
  Esquire (Periodical) Girls from Esquire

Steinberg, Yehudah, 1863-1908
Rabbi Itzik the fool
  Ausubel, N. ed. Treasury of Jewish humor
Reb Anshel the golden
  Ausubel, N. ed. Treasury of Jewish humor

Stendhal, De, pseud. See Beyle, Marie Henri

STENOGRAPHERS
  Winslow, T. S. Obsession

STEPBROTHERS
  Gaskell, E. C. S. Half-brothers

STEPFATHERS
  Kaufman, A. Anchor me in mire

Stephens, James, 1882-1950
The horses
  Blodgett, H. W. ed. Story survey. 1953 ed.
Three lovers who lost
  Cerf, B. A. and Moriarty, H. C. eds. Anthology of famous British stories
The threepenny-piece
  Magazine of fantasy and science fiction. Best from Fantasy and science fiction; [1st ser]

Stephenson, Carl, 1886-
Leiningen versus the ants
  Certner, S. and Henry, G. H. eds. Short stories for our times

Stephenson, Carol, pseud. See Isaacson, Bernice Kavinoky

The stepmother. Jackson, M. W.

STEPMOTHERS
  Jackson, M. W. The stepmother

Sterling, Stewart, pseud. See Winchell, Prentice

Stern, Daniel, 1928-
Conversation in Prague
  American vanguard, 1952

Stern, Gladys Browyn, 1890-
Cinderella's sister
  Leftwich, J. ed. Yisröel. 1952 ed.

Stern, James, 1904-
Broken leg
  Stern, J. Man who was loved
Face behind the bar
  Stern, J. Man who was loved
Idolater of Degas
  Stern, J. Man who was loved
Man who was loved
  Stern, J. Man who was loved
Next door to death
  New writing (Periodical) Best stories
  Stern, J. Man who was loved

Stern, James—*Continued*
Our father
Stern, J. Man who was loved
Solitaire
Stern, J. Man who was loved
Something wrong
Stern, J. Man who was loved
Travellers' tears
Stern, J. Man who was loved
Two men
Stern, J. Man who was loved
Under the beech tree
Stern, J. Man who was loved
Woman who was loved
Stern, J. Man who was loved

Stern, Richard G. 1928-
Present for Minna
This week magazine. This week's short-
short stories
Sorrows of Captain Schreiber
Prize stories, 1954

Stettner, Stella, 1923-
Costa Rican counterpoint
American vanguard, 1952
Summer place
American vanguard, 1953

Steve and Sarah and Cyril. Willingham, C.

Stevens, James, 1892-
Jerkline
Grayson, C. ed. Fourth round

Stevenson, C. Leigh
Over the line
Ford, N. A. and Faggett, H. L. eds.
Best short stories by Afro-American
writers (1925-1950)

Stevenson, Robert Louis, 1850-1894
Beach of Falesá
Stevenson, R. L. Strange case of Dr
Jekyll and Mr Hyde, and other stories
Body-snatcher
Stevenson, R. L. Strange case of Dr
Jekyll and Mr Hyde, and other stories
Bottle imp
Stevenson, R. L. Strange case of Dr
Jekyll and Mr Hyde, and other stories
Character of dogs
Andrews, R. C. ed. My favorite stories
of the great outdoors
Isle of voices
Stevenson, R. L. Strange case of Dr
Jekyll and Mr Hyde, and other stories
Lodging for the night
Blodgett, H. W. ed. Story survey.
1953 ed.
Cerf, B. A. and Moriarty, H. C. eds.
Anthology of famous British stories
Lamb, L. ed. Family book of best loved
short stories
Stevenson, R. L. Strange case of Dr
Jekyll and Mr Hyde, and other stories
Markheim
Neider, C. ed. Great short stories from
the world's literature
Queen, E. pseud. ed. Literature of crime
Stevenson, R. L. Strange case of Dr
Jekyll and Mr Hyde, and other stories
Merry men
Stevenson, R. L. Strange case of Dr
Jekyll and Mr Hyde, and other stories

Olalla
Stevenson, R. L. Strange case of Dr
Jekyll and Mr Hyde, and other stories
Pavilion on the links
Stevenson, R. L. Strange case of Dr
Jekyll and Mr Hyde, and other stories
Sire de Malétroit's door
Cerf, B. A. and Moriarty, H. C. eds.
Anthology of famous British stories
O'Faoláin, S. The short story
Stevenson, R. L. Strange case of Dr
Jekyll and Mr Hyde, and other stories
Strange case of Dr Jekyll and Mr Hyde
Stevenson, R. L. Strange case of Dr
Jekyll and Mr Hyde, and other stories
Thrawn Janet
Stevenson, R. L. Strange case of Dr
Jekyll and Mr Hyde, and other stories
Treasure of Franchard
Stevenson, R. L. Strange case of Dr
Jekyll and Mr Hyde, and other stories
Will o' the mill
Stevenson, R. L. Strange case of Dr
Jekyll and Mr Hyde, and other stories

STEWART, ALEXANDER TWINEY,
1803-1876
Benson, T. Bones of A. T. Stewart

Stewart, George Rippey, 1895-
Death of the glen
Bachelor, J. M.; Henry, R. L. and
Salisbury, R. eds. Current thinking
and writing; 2d ser.

Stewart, Ollie, 1906-
End of a dream
Ford, N. A. and Faggett, H. L. eds.
Best short stories by Afro-American
writers (1925-1950)
I shall not be moved
Ford, N. A. and Faggett, H. L. eds.
Best short stories by Afro-American
writers (1925-1950)
Leg man
Ford, N. A. and Faggett, H. L. eds.
Best short stories by Afro-American
writers (1925-1950)
No greater love
Ford, N. A. and Faggett, H. L. eds.
Best short stories by Afro-American
writers (1925-1950)
Soft-boiled
Ford, N. A. and Faggett, H. L. eds.
Best short stories by Afro-American
writers (1925-1950)

Stewart, Ramona, 1922-
The promise
Best American short stories, 1950

Stewart, Will, pseud. See Williamson, Jack

Stick up. French, F. C.

Stickit minister. Crockett, S. R.

Stifter, Adalbert, 1805-1868
Rock crystal
Pick, R. ed. German stories and tales
Talbot, D. ed. Treasury of mountaineer-
ing stories

Still, James, 1906-
Job's tears
Blodgett, H. W. ed. Story survey.
1953 ed.
Master time
Best American short stories, 1950
Mrs Razor
Summers, H. S. ed. Kentucky story

Story of a farm girl. Maupassant, G. de

Story of a masterpiece. James, H.

Story of a New York house. Bunner, H. C.

Story of a piebald horse. Hudson, W. H.

Story of a year. James, H.

Story of Dr MacLure. Watson, J.

Story of Don Juan. Pritchett, V. S.

Story of Krespel. Hoffmann, E. T. A.

Story of land and sea. Dunsany, E. J. M. D. P. 18th baron

Story of Mathias. Barker, A. L.

Story of my cats. Fabre, J. H. C.

Story of my death. Bosis, L. de

Story of Paula. Grimson, M. S.

Story of Pompeii. Blackburn, E. R.

Story of St Vespaluus. Munro, H. H.

Story of the bald-headed man. Doyle, Sir A. C.

Story of the cantor. Agnon, S. J.

Story of the days to come. Wells, H. G.

Story of the just Casper and the fair Annie. Brentano, C. M.

Story of the Saint Joseph's ass. Verga, G.

Story of the stone age. Wells, H. G.

Story of Toby. Melville, H.

Story of Webster. Wodehouse, P. G.

Story-teller. Munro, H. H.

STORY-TELLING
Munro, H. H. The story-teller
Parker, J. R. Once upon a time
Poe, E. A. Thousand-and-second tale of Scheherazade

STORY WITHIN A STORY
Clemens, S. L. Celebrated jumping frog of Calaveras County
Conrad, J. Heart of darkness
Davis, R. H. In the fog
Gally, J. W. Frozen truth
Grimson, M. S. Faith, hope and charity
Harvey, W. F. Vicar's web
Horwitz, J. Poor people
Jewett, S. O. Courting of Sister Wisby
Kipling, R. Incarnation of Krishna Mulvaney
Kipling, R. 'Love-o'-women'
Kipling, R. On Greenhow Hill
Lagerkvist, P. F. Eternal smile
Maugham, W. S. Red
Prado, P. Laugh in the desert
Pratt, F. and De Camp, L. S. Tales from Gavagan's bar; 23 stories
Priestley, J. B. The other place
Rabinowitz, S. Tit for tat
Salinger, J. D. Laughing man
Sansom, W. Crabfroth
Walsh, M. Thomasheen James and the dictation machine
West, R. B. Last of the grizzly bears

Stoumen, Louis Clyde
Blond dog
Story (Periodical) Story; no. 1

Stout, Rex, 1886-
The cop-killer
Stout, R. Triple jeopardy
Cop's gift
Mystery Writers of America, inc. Butcher, baker, murder-maker

Home to roost
Stout, R. Triple jeopardy
Squirt and the monkey
Stout, R. Triple jeopardy

Stout gentleman. Irving, W.

STOWAWAYS
Porter, W. S. Shamrock and the palm
Pratt, F. Pardon my mistake
Rocklynne, R. Jaywalker
Subercaseaux, B. Salt sea

Strachey, Julia
Pioneer city
New writing (Periodical) Best stories

Straight flush. Maugham, W. S.

Straight life. Petracca, J.

Strain, Frances (Bruce)
Babs and Phil who eloped
Strain, F. B. "But you don't understand"
Barney whose life was "all work and no play"
Strain, F. B. "But you don't understand"
Clumpy who was all arms and legs
Strain, F. B. "But you don't understand"
Cynthia who was afraid not to pet
Strain, F. B. "But you don't understand"
Jimmy who thought he "inherited bad blood"
Strain, F. B. "But you don't understand"
Josie who took things
Strain, F. B. "But you don't understand"
Linda who daydreamed
Strain, F. B. "But you don't understand"
Mitzie who was young for her age
Strain, F. B. "But you don't understand"
Pat who was afraid of boys
Strain, F. B. "But you don't understand"
Shorty who wished he were taller
Strain, F. B. "But you don't understand"
Stanley who was adopted
Strain, F. B. "But you don't understand"
Tommy who was overmanaged
Strain, F. B. "But you don't understand"

Strange bed. Lieber, W. M.

Strange case of Dr Jekyll and Mr Hyde. Stevenson, R. L.

Strange case of John Kingman. Jenkins, W. F.

Strange crime of John Boulnois. Chesterton, G. K.

Strange event at St Brendan's. Lieberman, R.

Strange girl. Van Doren, M.

Strange harvest. Wandrei, D.

Strange house. Penglase, F.

Strange little piper. Bennett, R.

Strange men. Elam, R. M.

Strange moonlight. Aiken, C. P.

Strange notion. Helfer, H.

Strange orchid. Wells, H. G.

Strange story. Ekbergh, I. D.

Strange story. Porter, W. S.

Strange story of Jonathan Small. Doyle, Sir A. C.

The stranger. Haycox, E.

The stranger. Hughes, R. A. W.

The stranger. Rilke, R. M.

Stranger arrives on Halfaday. Hendryx, J. B.

Stranger in the village. Gibbs, Sir P. H.

Strangers and pilgrims. De La Mare, W. J.

Strangers in the evening. Cheshire, G.

Stranger's note
  Lin, Y. ed. Famous Chinese short stories

Strasser, Sheila
  Case of the psychoanalyst
    Story (Periodical) Story; no. 2

Stratagem of Joshua. Bradford, R.

The strategist. Munro, H. H.

STRAWBERRIES
  Caldwell, E. Strawberry season

Strawberry season. Caldwell, E.

Strawberry window. Bradbury, R.

The strawstack. Knister, R.

The stray. Kalisman, H. H.

The stream. Young, E. H.

STREAM OF CONSCIOUSNESS
  Aiken, C. P. By my troth, Nerissa!
  Aiken, C. P. Field of flowers
  Aiken, C. P. Gehenna
  Aiken, C. P. Man alone at lunch
  Aiken, C. P. State of mind
  Bellow, S. Sermon by Doctor Pep
  Bruggen, C. de H. van. Seder night
  Cicellis, K. Turn of the tide
  Hale, N. No one my grief can tell
  Parker, G. Bright and morning
  Porter, K. A. Jilting of Granny Weatherall
  Porter, K. A. Pale horse, pale rider
  Sansom, W. The cliff
  Saroyan, W. Resurrection of a life
  Scilken, M. Oh joy, it's a boy
  Shattuck, R. Workout on the river
  Woolf, V. S. New dress

The streamliner. Van Doren, M.

Street, James Howell, 1903-1954
  I am not a stranger
    Jones, K. M. ed. New Confederate short stories
  The old, old story
    Brentano, F. ed. The word lives on
  Please come home, My Lady
    Cavanna, B. ed. Pick of the litter
    Furman, A. L. ed. Teen-age dog stories
  They know how
    Grayson, C. ed. Fourth round
  Weep no more, My Lady
    Bloch, M. ed. Favorite dog stories
    Certner, S. and Henry, G. H. eds. Short stories for our times
    Cooper, A. C. ed. Modern short stories
    Lass, A. H. and Horowitz, A. eds. Stories for youth

Street, Julian Leonard, 1879-1947
  Mr Bisbee's princess
    First-prize stories, 1919-1954

The street. Horwitz, J.

The street. Seager, A.

Street song. Sansom, W.

Street that got mislaid. Waddington, P.

Street walker. Tucker, W.

Streeter, Edward, 1891-
  Letter to Mable
    Fenner, P. R. comp. Fun! Fun! Fun!

Strength of Gideon. Dunbar, P. L.

Strength of the strong. London, J.

Stribling, Thomas Sigismund, 1881-
  Mystery of the personal ad
    Queen, E. pseud. ed. Queen's awards: 5th ser.

Strictly big league. Coombs, C. I.

Strictly business. Porter, W. S.

Strike of the Schnorrers. Spector, M.

STRIKES AND LOCKOUTS
  Munro, H. H. Byzantine omelette
  Munro, H. H. Unkindest blow

Strindberg, August, 1849-1912
  Autumn
    Blodgett, H. W. ed. Story survey. 1953 ed.

The string. Maupassant, G. de

String of beads. Maugham, W. S.

Striving after the wind. Lindquist, W.

Stroke of thirteen. De La Torre, L.

Strong, Austin, 1881-
  All on a winter's night
    Cooper, A. C. ed. Modern short stories

Strong, Joan, 1923-
  Hired man
    Best American short stories, 1950

Strong, Leonard Alfred George, 1896-
  Danse Macabre
    Asquith, Lady C. M. E. C. ed. Book of modern ghosts
  Let me go
    Carrington, H. ed. Week-end book of ghost stories
  White cottage
    Cerf, B. A. and Moriarty, H. C. eds. Anthology of famous British stories

Strong, Paschal Neilson, 1901-
  Anchor man
    Owen, F. ed. Teen-age victory parade
  Behind the plate
    Fenner, P. R. comp. Crack of the bat
  Man on Stormrift Mountain
    American boy (Periodical) American boy Adventure stories
  Running dark
    Furman, A. L. ed. Teen-age sea stories
  Salvage!
    Furman, A. L. ed. Teen-age sea stories
  Shantyboat pirate
    Furman, A. L. ed. Teen-age sea stories
  Terror of Buccaneer Bay
    Fenner, P. R. comp. Stories of the sea
  Trail of the whiffle-poof
    Boys' life (Periodical) Boys' life Adventure stories

The strudel. Horwitz, J.

Struggle for life. Aldrich, T. B.

Struther, Jan, pseud. See Maxtone Graham, Joyce (Anstruther)

Struttin' with some barbecue. Duke, O.

Stuart, Jesse, 1907-
  Anglo-Saxons of Auxierville
    Stuart, J. Clearing in the sky & other
    stories
  Battle with the bees
    Stuart, J. Clearing in the sky & other
    stories
  The champion
    Stuart, J. Clearing in the sky & other
    stories
  Clearing in the sky
    Stuart, J. Clearing in the sky & other
    stories
  Coming down the mountain
    Stuart, J. Clearing in the sky & other
    stories
  Competition at Slush Creek
    Stuart, J. Clearing in the sky & other
    stories
  Dawn of remembered spring
    Best of the Best American short stories,
    1915-1950
    Summers, H. S. ed. Kentucky story
  Evidence is high proof
    Stuart, J. Clearing in the sky & other
    stories
  Fight number twenty-five
    Lynskey, W. C. ed. Reading modern
    fiction
    Stuart, J. Clearing in the sky & other
    stories
  Governor Warburton's right-hand man
    Stuart, J. Clearing in the sky & other
    stories
  Horse-trading trembles
    Stuart, J. Clearing in the sky & other
    stories
  Hot-collared mule
    Stuart, J. Clearing in the sky & other
    stories
  Land of our enemies
    Stuart, J. Clearing in the sky & other
    stories
  No hero
    Stuart, J. Clearing in the sky & other
    stories
  No petty thief
    Stuart, J. Clearing in the sky & other
    stories
  Old Gore
    Stuart, J. Clearing in the sky & other
    stories
  Rainy day at Big Lost Creek
    Grayson, C. ed. Fourth round
  Red rats of Plum Fork
    Story (Periodical). Story; no. 3
  Rightful owner
    Lantz, J. E. ed. Stories of Christian
    living
  Road number one
    Stuart, J. Clearing in the sky & other
    stories
  Slipover sweater
    Stuart, J. Clearing in the sky & other
    stories
  Split cherry tree
    Certner, S. and Henry, G. H. eds. Short
    stories for our times
  The storm
    Stauffer, R. M.; Cunningham, W. H.
    and Sullivan, C. J. eds. Adventures
    in modern literature

  Testimony of trees
    Stuart, J. Clearing in the sky & other
    stories
  Thanksgiving hunter
    Hazeltine, A. I. comp. Selected stories
    for teen-agers
  Thirty-two votes before breakfast
    Stuart, J. Clearing in the sky & other
    stories
  To market, to market
    Stuart, J. Clearing in the sky & other
    stories
  When mountain men make peace
    Stuart, J. Clearing in the sky & other
    stories
  Woman in the house
    Southern review. Anthology of stories
    from the Southern review

Stuart, Lyle, 1922-
  Orange room
    American vanguard, 1952

Stubborn spearmen. Davis, H. L.

Stubbs, Harry Clement, 1922-
  Answer
    Conklin, G. ed. Science-fiction thinking
    machines
  Attitude
    Greenberg, M. ed. Travelers of space
  Cold front
    Greenberg, M. ed. Men against the stars
  Critical factor
    Star science fiction stories, no. 2
  Proof
    Conklin, G. ed. Possible worlds of sci-
    ence fiction

Student body. Wallace, F. L.

Student in economics. Milburn, G.

STUDENT LIFE. See School life

STUDENTS. See School life

Studio of Love-Your-Fellowman. Zozulya,
  E. D.

Studs. Farrell, J. T.

A **study** in scarlet. Doyle, Sir A. C.

Stuff of dreams. Boylston, H. D.

Stull, Paul
  Growing pains
    Oberfirst, R. ed. 1954 anthology of best
    original short-shorts

Sture-Vasa, Mary (Alsop) 1885-
  My friend Flicka
    Eaton, H. T. ed. Short stories

Sturgeon, Theodore, pseud. See Waldo,
  Edward Hamilton

Stutz and the tub. Whittemore, R.

Styron, William, 1925-
  Enormous window
    American vanguard, 1950

Subercaseaux, Benjamín, 1902-
  Salt sea
    De Onís, H. ed. Spanish stories and
    tales

Sublime vigil. Cuthberg, C. D.

SUBMARINE BOATS
  Bateman, A. Rig ship for diving
  Bateman, A. Submarine jitters
  Longstreet, S. No peace with the sea

SUBMARINE DIVING. See Diving, Submarine

Submarine jitters. Bateman, A.
Submarine plans. Christie, A. M.

SUBMARINE WARFARE
  Beach, E. L. Wahoo
  Lott, D. N. Skipper played it safe

SUBMARINES. See Submarine boats

Submissive wife. De La Roche, M.

Subterfuge. Bradbury, R.

Suburban frontiers. Young, R. F.

SUBURBAN LIFE
  De Vries, P. Life among the winesaps
  Humphrey, W. Last husband

Subway named Mobius. Deutsch, A. J.

SUBWAYS
  Adler, W. Other people
  Crawford, E. and Dalmas, H. Rush-hour
    romance
  Deutsch, A. J. Subway named Mobius
  Johnson, R. B. Far below

SUCCESS
  Maugham, W. S. The verger
  Verrinder, W. To a web begun

Success story. Barr, J. pseud.

Success story. Wodehouse, P. G.

SUCCESSION. See Inheritance and succession

**SUCCOTH (FEAST OF TABER-
  NACLES)** See Sukkoth

Such a pretty day. Powell, D.

Such darling dodos. Wilson, A.

Suckow, Ruth, 1892-
  Auntie Bissel
    Suckow, R. Some others and myself
  Elegy for Alma's Aunt Amy
    Suckow, R. Some others and myself
  Eltha
    Suckow, R. Some others and myself
  Eminence
    Lohan, R. and Lohan, M. eds. New
      Christmas treasury
  Golden wedding
    Blodgett, H. W. ed. Story survey.
      1953 ed.
  A memoir
    Suckow, R. Some others and myself
  Memorial Eve
    Suckow, R. Some others and myself
  Merrittsville
    Suckow, R. Some others and myself
  Mrs Vogel and Ollie
    Suckow, R. Some others and myself
  One of three others
    Suckow, R. Some others and myself

Sudden attack of heartbreak. Lardner, J.

Sudden heart. Barlow, T.

Sudermann, Hermann, 1857-1928
  New Year's Eve confession
    Blodgett, H. W. ed. Story survey.
      1953 ed.

Suffer the little children. Burnett, W.

SUFFERING
  Elliott, G. P. Faq'
  Gordon, C. W. The canyon flowers

"Sufficient." Ready, W. B.

SUFFRAGE. See Woman—Suffrage

Sugar bowl. Shulman, M.

Sugar camp. Bromfield, L.

Sugar for the horse. Bates, H. E.

Suhl, Yuri, 1908-
  Saved by the sale
    Ausubel, N. ed. Treasury of Jewish
      humor
  With the aid of the One Above
    Ausubel, N. ed. Treasury of Jewish
      humor
    Ribalow, H. U. ed. This land, these
      people

SUICIDE
  Benson, T. To-morrow is another day
  Caldwell, E. After-image
  Calisher, H. In Greenwich there are many
    gravelled walks
  Collier, J. Bird of prey
  Collier, J. Halfway to Hell
  Connolly, M. Natural causes
  Coppel, A. The exile
  Du Maurier, D. No motive
  Hunt, F. C. Egg from the sky
  Marcus, P. Higher and higher
  Maugham, W. S. The pool
  Maugham, W. S. Rain
  Pincherle, A. Back to the sea
  Rinehart, A. Mirrored room
  Seligsohn, I. J. The anchor

SUICIDE, ATTEMPTED. See Suicide

Suicide on skis. Findlay, D. K.

Suite homes and their romance. Porter, W. S.

Suitor's white paper. Kober, A.

SUKKOTH
  Landa, M. J. Two legacies
  Reisin, A. Big succeh
    See also Festivals

Sulkin, Sidney, 1918-
  The plan
    Ribalow, H. U. ed. These your children

Sullivan, Alan, 1868-
  Salving of Pyack
    Pacey, D. ed. Book of Canadian stories

Sullivan, Richard, 1908-
  Compline
    Sullivan, R. Fresh and open sky, and
      other stories
  The dispossessed
    Sullivan, R. Fresh and open sky, and
      other stories
  Dream of drums
    Sullivan, R. Fresh and open sky, and
      other stories
  Feathers
    Sullivan, R. Fresh and open sky, and
      other stories
  Fresh and open sky
    Sullivan, R. Fresh and open sky, and
      other stories
  Girl next door
    Sullivan, R. Fresh and open sky, and
      other stories
  Home fires
    Sullivan, R. Fresh and open sky, and
      other stories
  Honeymoon
    Sullivan, R. Fresh and open sky, and
      other stories
  In a glass darkly
    Sullivan, R. Fresh and open sky, and
      other stories

SUPERNATURAL PHENOMENA

Barrie, Sir J. M. bart. Farewell Miss Julie Logan
Bierce, A. Damned thing
Ch'en Hsüan-yu. Chienniang
De La Mare, W. J. The creatures
De La Mare, W. J. The vats
Du Maurier, D. Monte Verità
Ekbergh, I. D. Strange story
Finney, J. I'm scared
Forster, E. M. Celestial omnibus
Heinlein, R. A. Lost legacy
Hodgson, W. N. Noise in the night
Irving, W. Adalantado of the Seven Cities
Irwin, M. E. F. Earlier service
James, M. R. The mezzotint
Jenkins, W. F. Little terror
Le Fanu, J. S. Room in the Dragon Volant
Maupassant, G. de. The Horla
Munby, A. N. L. Alabaster hand, and other stories; 14 stories
Noyes, A. Log of the "Evening Star"
Priestley, J. B. Guest of honour
Priestley, J. B. Leadington incident
Priestley, J. B. Look after the strange girl
Priestley, J. B. Night sequence
Priestley, J. B. The other place
Priestley, J. B. Uncle Phil on TV
P'u Sung-ling. Cricket boy
Rescue at sea
Richter, C. Sinister journey
Stevenson, R. L. Isle of voices
Valle-Inclán, R. del. My sister Antonia
Wall, J. W. Ringstones
Wells, H. G. Stolen body

See also Ghosts; Witchcraft

SUPERSTITION

Cobb, I. S. Snake Doctor
Kipling, R. Tomb of his ancestors
Pratt, F. and De Camp, L. S. Eve of St John
Rice, A. C. H. Hoodooed

Supply and demand. Porter, W. S.

Suppressed edition. Curle, R.

Surface tension. Blish, J.

Surface tension of molten metal. Willingham, C.

Surfman number nine. Detzer, K. W.

SURGEONS. See Physicians; Surgery

SURGERY

Benét, S. V. End to dreams
Brown, J. Rab and his friends
Gold, H. L. Matter of form
Herrick, R. Master of the inn
Kuttner, H. Dream's end
Stafford, J. Interior castle
Walsh, M. The bonesetter
Weiss, E. Cardiac suture
Wells, H. G. Under the knife

SURGERY, PLASTIC

Alpert, H. The change

Surgery at Aquila. Allen, H.

SURGICAL OPERATIONS. See Surgery

SURPRISE ENDINGS

Lever, C. J. Con Cregan's legacy

The **surrender.** Hendryx, J. B.

Surtees, Robert Smith, 1803-1864

Afternoon hunt with the Tantivity hounds
Surtees, R. S. Hunting scenes
Another quiet bye with Mr Jorrocks
Surtees, R. S. Hunting scenes
Bye-day with Mr Jorrocks
Surtees, R. S. Hunting scenes
Cat and Custard-pot day with the Handley Cross
Surtees, R. S. Hunting scenes
Children's day with Mr Jovey Jessop's hounds
Surtees, R. S. Hunting scenes
Cub-hunting with Mr Neville's hounds
Surtees, R. S. Hunting scenes
Day in Hit-im-and-Hold-im-shire
Surtees, R. S. Hunting scenes
Day with Hard-and-Sharp hounds
Surtees, R. S. Hunting scenes
Great run with the F.H.H.
Surtees, R. S. Hunting scenes
Heavyside Hunt: The new Master's first day
Surtees, R. S. Hunting scenes
Heavyside Hunt again: The lady whipper-in
Surtees, R. S. Hunting scenes
Larkspur again: A lawn meet at Rosemount Grange
Surtees, R. S. Hunting scenes
Larkspur hounds: A morning with a bagman
Surtees, R. S. Hunting scenes
Lord Scamperdale's finest day
Surtees, R. S. Hunting scenes
Mr Pomponius Ego out with the Handley Cross
Surtees, R. S. Hunting scenes
Mr Sponge's first day with the Flat Hat Hunt
Surtees, R. S. Hunting scenes
Mr Sponge's first day with the Hanby
Surtees, R. S. Hunting scenes
Opening day with Mr Hardey's hounds
Surtees, R. S. Hunting scenes
Opening day with the Duke of Tergiversation's hounds
Surtees, R. S. Hunting scenes
Opening day with the Larkspur hounds
Surtees, R. S. Hunting scenes
Our last day with the Handley Cross
Surtees, R. S. Hunting scenes
Sir Harry Scattercash's hounds: Mr Sponge carries the horn
Surtees, R. S. Hunting scenes
Sir Harry's hounds again: Mr Sponge and Miss Lucy Glitters
Surtees, R. S. Hunting scenes
Two days with Mr Neville's hounds
Surtees, R. S. Hunting scenes
With Mr Jorrocks in Pinch-me-near Forest
Surtees, R. S. Hunting scenes
With the Hit-im-and-Hold-im-shire: The sham day
Surtees, R. S. Hunting scenes

SURVEYING

Stuart, J. Testimony of trees

Survival. Canzoneri, R.

Survival. Harris, J. B.

SURVIVAL (AFTER AIRPLANE AC-
CIDENTS, SHIPWRECKS, ETC)
Bloomfield, H. The trap
Carrighar, S. Marooned children
Kubilius, W. Other side
Mowat, F. Woman he left to die
Russell, J. Fourth man
Temple, W. F. Two shadows

Survival ship. Merril, J.

Susan steps out. Olds, H. D.

Susceptibility. MacDonald, J. D.

SUSPICION. See Skepticism

Suspicion. Sayers, D. L.

Sut and the Burns family. Harris, G. W.

Sut as a boy. Harris, G. W.

Sut meets the law. Harris, G. W.

Sut on the national scene. Harris, G. W.

Sut sets certain individuals right. Harris,
G. W.

Sut takes on the whole world. Harris,
G. W.

Sutro, Alfred, 1863-1933
Bread on the waters
Leftwich, J. ed. Yisröel. 1952 ed.

Sutton Place story. Cheever, J.

Svevo, Italo, pseud. See Schmitz, Ettore

Swados, Harvey B. 1920-
The letters
Best American short stories, 1952

SWALLOWS
De La Roche, M. Come fly with me

SWAMPS
Annixter, P. pseud. Dragon rider
Peattie, D. C. and Peattie, L. R. Weir-
wood marsh

Swan-moving. Taylor, E.

SWANS
Boyle, K. Bridegroom's body
Du Maurier, D. Old man
Taylor, E. Swan-moving

Swanson, Neil Harmon, 1896-
They kept the flag there
American boy (Periodical) American
boy Adventure stories

The swap. Heard, G.

Swaying elms. Blackburn, E. R.

SWEDEN
Lagerkvist, P. F. Guest of reality

SWEDES IN THE UNITED STATES
Caldwell, E. Country full of Swedes

Sweet girl graduate. Hutchins, M. P. M.

Sweetness of the twisted apples. Stegner,
W. E.

Swell-looking girl. Caldwell, E.

Swenson, Eric Pierson, 1918-
Lonely reef
Fenner, P. R. comp. Stories of the sea

Swift, Jonathan, 1667-1745
Laputa
Derleth, A. W. ed. Beyond time & space

Swift Foot the hunter. Macfarlan, A. A.

Swift Thunder of the prairies. Maloy, L.

SWIMMING
McKenney, R. Guinea pig
Maugham, W. S. Friend in need

Swinbank, Gene, 1884-
New hat
Oberfirst, R. ed. 1952 anthology of best
original short-shorts

SWINDLERS AND SWINDLING
Bergengruen, W. Eye cure
Charteris, L. Revolution racket
Cozzens, J. G. Clerical error
Curtis, K. The cameleers
Danielson, R. E. The quid pro quo
Dunsany, E. J. M. D. P. 18th baron.
Memory machine
Grimson, M. S. At the crossroads
Hecht, B. Swindler's luck
Hershman, M. Live bait
Porter, W. S. Conscience in art
Porter, W. S. Ethics of pig
Porter, W. S. Exact science of matri-
mony
Porter, W. S. Gold that glittered
Porter, W. S. Innocents of Broadway
Porter, W. S. Jeff Peters as a personal
magnet
Porter, W. S. Man higher up
Porter, W. S. Midsummer masquerade
Porter, W. S. Modern rural sports
Porter, W. S. On behalf of the manage-
ment
Porter, W. S. Poet and the peasant
Porter, W. S. Shearing the wolf
Porter, W. S. Tempered wind
Queen, E. pseud. Double your money

Swindler's luck. Hecht, B.

SWINDLING. See Swindlers and swindling

SWINE. See Pigs

Swinnerton, Frank Arthur, 1884-
The verdict
Queen, E. pseud. ed. Literature of
crime

Swinton, Allan
A brotherhood
American boy (Periodical) American
boy Anthology
Courage
American boy (Periodical) American
boy Adventure stories

SWISS ALPS. See Alps, Swiss

The switchboard. Martin, T. H.

Switzer, Robert
Death of a prize fighter
Prize stories of 1950
Ribalow, H. U. ed. World's greatest
boxing stories
No end to anything
Esquire (Periodical) Girls from Esquire

SWITZERLAND
Rousseau, J. J. Isle of St Peter
Welch, D. When I was thirteen

Lucerne
Charteris, L. Lucerne: The loaded tourist

Zurich
Jackson, C. R. Old men and boys

The sword. Betts, D.

Sword of tomorrow. Kuttner, H.

Sword of Welleran. Dunsany, E. J. M. D. P.
18th baron

Sword of Yung Lo. Walsh, M.

Takes a real man. . . Schaefer, J. W.

"Taking mother out." Taylor, E.

Taking the veil. Mansfield, K.

A **tale.** Hutchins, M. P. M.

A **tale.** Nahman Ben Simḥah, of Bratzlav

Tale of a chemist
  Derleth, A. W. ed. Far boundaries

Tale of a tainted tenner. Porter, W. S.

Tale of James Carabine. Byrne, D.

Tale of negative gravity. Stockton, F. R.

Tale of olden time. Heine, H.

Tale of Perez de Amorin. Zaferiou, S.

Tale of the old main line. Somerville, A. W.

Tale of the Ragged Mountains. Poe, E. A.

TALES. See Fables; Legends and folk
  tales

The **talisman.** De La Mare, W. J.

The **talisman.** Gordimer, N.

TALISMANS. See Charms

Talking about writers. Kaufman, W.

Talking-out of Tarrington. Munro, H. H.

Talking shop. Lewis, W.

Tall as the stars. Lambert, J.

Tall Bram of Little Pigeon. Wellman,
  M. W.

Tall hunter. Fast, H. M.

Tall men. Faulkner, W.

Tall one. Van Doren, M.

TALL STORIES. See Improbable stories

Tall story. Allingham, M.

Tall tale from the high hills. Credle, E.

TALL TALES. See Improbable stories

TAMERLANE, 1336-1405
  Gorky, M. Might of motherhood

Tangled hearts. Wodehouse, P. G.

Tanker man. Ward, M.

TANKS (MILITARY SCIENCE)
  Wells, H. G. Land ironclads

Tanner, Charles R.
  Angus MacAuliffe and the gowden tooch
    Conklin, G. and Conklin, L. T. eds.
    Supernatural reader

Tanzer, Ward
  My Tiare, good-bye
    Stanford short stories, 1951

Taper, Bernard, 1918-
  Kaddish
    Stanford short stories, 1953

TAPESTRY
  Anderson, E. V. Tapestry extravaganza

Tapestry extravaganza. Anderson, E. V.

Tappan's burro. Grey, Z.

Tarachow, Sidney. See Treat, L. jt. auth.

Tarkington, Booth, 1869-1946
  "Little gentleman"
    Burrell, J. A. and Cerf, B. A. eds. An-
    thology of famous American stories
  Little Orvie's new dog Ralph
    Furman, A. L. ed. Teen-age dog stories
  Rennie Peddigoe
    Tarkington, B. Three selected short
    novels

Uncertain Molly Collicut
    Tarkington, B. Three selected short
    novels
  Walterson
    Tarkington, B. Three selected short
    novels

Tarnished gold. Glassman, B.

Tarpon! Bell, V. M.

TARPON FISHING
  Bell, V. M. Tarpon

Tarroo-ushtey. Kneale, N.

TARTARS. See Tatars

Tartarus of maids. Melville, H.

Tashrak, pseud. See Zevin, Israel Joseph

Taste. Dahl, R.

Taste of command. Hail, S.

TATARS
  Chekhov, A. P. In exile

Tate, Allen, 1899-
  Immortal woman
    Summers, H. S. ed. Kentucky story

TATTOOING
  Bradbury, R. The illustrated man
  Dahl, R. Skin
  Friedman, B. H. As I am, you will be
  Munro, H. H. The background
  Porter, W. S. Double-dyed deceiver

Taubes, Frank
  Trouble on 98th Street
    Best detective stories of the year—1951

Tavern at Powell's Ferry. Haycox, E.

TAVERNS. See Hotels, taverns, etc.

TAX COLLECTORS. See Taxation

TAXATION
  Herbert, Sir A. P. Board of Inland Rev-
    enue v. Haddock

TAXES. See Taxation

TAXI DRIVERS. See Cab drivers

TAXICAB DRIVERS. See Cab drivers

TAXICABS
  Aiken, C. P. Hey, taxi!

Taylor, C. Lindsay
  The envelope
    Thinker's digest (Periodical) Spoiled
    priest, and other stories

Taylor, Elizabeth, 1912-
  Beginning of a story
    Taylor, E. Hester Lilly, and twelve
    short stories
  First death of her life
    Ludwig, J. B. and Poirier, W. R. eds.
    Stories, British and American
    Taylor, E. Hester Lilly, and twelve
    short stories
  Hester Lilly
    Taylor, E. Hester Lilly, and twelve
    short stories
  I live in a world of make-believe
    Taylor, E. Hester Lilly, and twelve
    short stories
  Idea of age
    Taylor, E. Hester Lilly, and twelve
    short stories
  Light of day
    Taylor, E. Hester Lilly, and twelve
    short stories

Technical error. Porter, W. S.
Technical expert. Katz, L.
Technical slip. Harris, J. B.
Technique. Winslow, T. S.
Teddy. Salinger, J. D.
TEEN-AGERS. See Adolescence
TEETH
Andreev, L. N. On the day of the cruci-
fixion
Poe, E. A. Berenice
Teething ring. Causey, J.
Telemachus, friend. Porter, W. S.
TELEPATHY. See Thought-transference
TELEPHONE OPERATORS. See Tele-
phone workers
TELEPHONE WORKERS
Ward, E. S. P. Chief operator
The telescope. Derleth, A. W.
Telescope and the umbrella. Mevorach, J.
TELETYPE
Poirier, N. R. Teletype machine
Teletype machine. Poirier, N. R.
TELEVISION
Carver, C. Twenty floors up
Grimson, M. S. When TV came to the
backwoods
Hatch, E. Channel 10
Priestley, J. B. Uncle Phil on TV
Schulberg, B. W. Your Arkansas traveler
Television helps, but not very much. Mc-
Nulty, J.
Tell it to the Marines! Litten, F. N.
Tell-tale heart. Poe, E. A.
Téllez, Hernando, 1908-
Ashes for the wind
De Onís, H. ed. Spanish stories and
tales
Temperate zone. Enright, E.
Tempered wind. Porter, W. S.
The tempest. Gibran, K.
Temple, Willard Henry, 1912-
Most unusual season
Dachs, D. ed. Treasury of sports hu-
mor
Record-breaker
Owen, F. ed. Teen-age winter sports
stories
Temple, William Frederick, 1914-
Counter-transference
Best sceince-fiction stories: 1953
Date to remember
Conklin, G. ed. Invaders of earth
Forget-me-not
Best science fiction stories: 1951
Two shadows
Best science fiction stories: 1952
Way of escape
Conklin, G. ed. Science-fiction adven-
tures in dimension
Temple first. Melville, H.
Temple second. Melville, H.
Temptation of Reb Mottel. Kobrin, L.
Ten. Nuhn, F.
TEN COMMANDMENTS. See Command-
ments, Ten

Ten thousand blueberry crates. Caldwell,
E.
Ten years on a desert island. Newhouse,
E.
TENANT. See Landlord and tenant
TENANT FARMING
Betts, D. Gentle insurrection
Caldwell, E. Kneel to the rising sun
Faulkner, W. Barn burning
Godchaux, E. Horn that called Bambine
Tender to the ship. Goldsmith, G.
TENEMENT HOUSES
Babikoff, V. Day of rest
Tenn, William, pseud. See Klass, Philip
TENNESSEE
Buckingham, N. Hallowed years
Taylor, P. H. Widows of Thornton; 8
stories
Farm life
See Farm life—Tennessee
Nashville
Porter, W. S. Municipal report
Taylor, P. H. Wife of Nashville
Tennessee's partner. Harte, B.
TENNIS
Chute, B. J. Double fault
Chute, B. J. Doubles or nothing
Chute, B. J. The winner
Coombs, C. I. Net nemesis
Maugham, W. S. Facts of life
Miers, E. S. Weary Willie
Reeve, J. Doubles or nothing
Taylor, M. Megelhoffer theory
TENNIS PLAYERS. See Tennis
Tennison, Jack, pseud. See Jackson, Charles
Tenney
Tennyson, Hallam, 1921-
Appendicitis
Tennyson, H. Wall of dust, and other
stories
Armistice
Tennyson, H. Wall of dust, and other
stories
Home leave
Tennyson, H. Wall of dust, and other
stories
In the desert
Tennyson, H. Wall of dust, and other
stories
Land of my fathers
Tennyson, H. Wall of dust, and other
stories
Wall of dust
Tennyson, H. Wall of dust, and other
stories
Tenth Street idyll. Parker, J. R.
Tenting tonight. Jackson, C. R.
Tepondicon. Jacobi, C.
Teresa. Charteris, L.
Terhune, Albert Payson, 1872-1942
Coming of Lad
Fenner, P. R. comp. Dogs, dogs, dogs
The "critter"
Bloch, M. ed. Favorite dog stories
Hero
Strang, R. M. and Roberts, R. M. eds.
Teen-age tales v 1

They weren't going to die. Boyle, K.

They're scared, Mr Bradlaugh. Kneale, N.

Thibaudeau, Colleen, 1925-
City underground
　　Weaver, R. and James, H. eds. Canadian short stories

The **thief.** Eggleston, M. W.

The **thief.** O'Donovan, M.

THIEVES
Aiken, C. P. Impulse
Bruce, S. Farewell to crime
Canning, V. Never trust a lady
Chaucer, G. Pardoner's tale
Cohen, O. R. Toot for a toot
Cooke, A. A. Scum of the earth
De Vries, P. If the shoe hurts
Doty, W. L. Mr Dee and the middleman
Doyle, Sir A. C. Blue carbuncle
Edginton, H. M. Purple and fine linen
Harte, B. Ingénue of the Sierras
Kobrin, L. Milchiger Synagogue and the blind preacher
Malamud, B. The prison
Moroso, J. A. Tierney meets a millionaire
Murdock, R. M. Stop, look, listen
Porter, W. S. Assessor of success
Porter, W. S. Clarion call
Porter, W. S. Makes the whole world kin
Porter, W. S. The marionettes
Porter, W. S. Retrieved reformation
Porter, W. S. Tommy's burglar
Rabinowitz, S. Passover guest
Reid, C. B. Yellow leaf
Stevenson, R. L. Lodging for the night
Stuart, J. No petty thief
Walsh, M. Thomasheen James goes to the dogs
　　　　See also Theft

Thimble, thimble. Porter, W. S.

Thing in the cellar. Keller, D. H.

Thing in the pond. Ernst, P.

Thing in the woods. Fletcher, P. and Ruby, B. F.

Thing in their hearts. Wolfe, E.

Thing of beauty. Lieberman, E.

Things. Lawrence, D. H.

Things in common. Pearce, J.

Things of distinction. Crossen, K. F.

Things pass by. Jenkins, W. F.

Things past. Sullivan, R.

Thing's the play. Porter, W. S.

The **thinker.** Steele, W. D.

THINKING MACHINES. See Automata

Third Avenue medicine. McNulty, J.

The **third** bullet. Carr, J. D.

Third commandment. Werfel, F. V.

Third day after Christmas. Saroyan, W.

Third from the sun. Matheson, R.

Third guest. Traven, B. pseud.

Third ingredient. Porter, W. S.

Third level. Finney, J.

Third nightcap, with historical footnotes. Schulberg, B. W.

Thirteen at table. Dunsany, E. J. M. D. P. 18th baron

Thirteen men. Bedford-Jones, H.

Thirteen o'clock. Kornbluth, C. M.

Thirty minutes to zero. Divine, A. D.

Thirty seconds—thirty days. Clarke, A. C.

Thirty trips to Washington. McKay, M. C.

Thirty-two votes before breakfast. Stuart, J.

This is the house. Kuttner, H.

This is the land. Bond, N. S.

This looks like murder. Quentin P. pseud.

This mortal coil. Maclaren-Ross, J.

This mortal coil. O'Donovan, M.

This star shall be free. Jenkins, W. F.

This time to-morrow. Coward, N. P.

This town and Salamanca. Seager, A.

This way out. Brown, F.

Thistledown. Aiken, C. P.

Thomas, David, pseud. See Furman, Abraham Loew

Thomas, Dylan, 1914-1953
Patricia, Edith, and Arnold
　　Barrows, H. ed. 15 stories

Thomas, Ruth
Crip, come home!
　　Bachelor, J. M.; Henry, R. L. and Salisbury, R. eds. Current thinking and writing; 2d ser.

Thomasheen James and the dictation machine. Walsh, M.

Thomasheen James goes to the dogs. Walsh, M.

Thomason, John William, 1893-1944
Mating of a stamp collector
　　Jones, K. M. ed. New Confederate short stories
Preacher goes to Texas
　　Neider, C. ed. Men of the high calling
　　Peery, W. W. ed. 21 Texas short stories

Thompson, C. Hall, 1923-
Posse
　　Meredith, S. ed. Bar 1 roundup of best western stories

Thompson, Dorothy, 1894-
Once on Christmas
　　Lohan, R. and Lohan, M. eds. New Christmas treasury

Thompson, Edward William, 1849-1924
Privilege of the limits
　　Pacey, D. ed. Book of Canadian stories

Thompson, Elizabeth
No meadow lark song
　　Stanford short stories, 1950

Thompson, Harlan
Cliff dance
　　Fenner, P. R. comp. Cowboys, cowboys, cowboys
Indian fighter
　　Furman, A. L. ed. Teen-age horse stories
Smoke arm
　　Furman, A. L. ed. Teen-age stories of the diamond

Thompson, Lorena
Grasshopper a burden
　　Oberfirst, R. ed. 1954 anthology of best original short-shorts

Thompson, Morton, 1907?-1953
My brother who talked with horses
　　Creamer, J. B. comp. Twenty-two stories about horses and men

Thompson, Robert Emmett, 1924-
It's a nice day—Sunday
  Prize stories of 1951
  Same as: It's such a nice day—Sunday
It's such a nice day—Sunday
  Stanford short stories, 1952
  Same as: It's a nice day—Sunday
Thompson, Thomas, 1913-
Burdick's last battle
  Thompson, T. They brought their guns
Chico and the badman
  Thompson, T. They brought their guns
Doctors of death
  Thompson, T. They brought their guns
Empty holster
  Thompson, T. They brought their guns
Gun job
  Thompson, T. They brought their guns
Jolly
  Southern review. Anthology of stories
  from the Southern review
Memento
  Thompson, T. They brought their guns
One night in Coffin Creek
  Thompson, T. They brought their guns
Outlaw's boots
  Thompson, T. They brought their guns
Passing of Poker Bill
  Thompson, T. They brought their guns
Settlin'-down feelin'
  Meredith, S. ed. Bar 3
Shadow of the butte
  Meredith, S. ed. Bar 2
Shore for the sinking
  Peery, W. W. ed. 21 Texas short
  stories
Silver dollar
  Thompson, T. They brought their guns
Silver saddle
  Western Writers of America. Bad men
  and good
Valley for Martha
  Thompson, T. They brought their guns
Thompson, Will, 1900?-1949
No one believed me
  Merril, J. ed. Beyond the barriers of
  space and time
Thoreau, Henry David, 1817-1862
Winter at Walden
  Andrews, R. C. ed. My favorite stories
  of the great outdoors
Thorne, Anthony, 1904-
Dark red chrysanthemum
  New writing (Periodical) Best stories
Thoroughbred. Brier, H. M.
Those men from Mars. Carr, R. S.
Those wily Americans. Frank, P.
"Thou art the man." Poe, E. A.
Thou good and faithful. Brunner, K. H.
Though dreamers die. Del Rey, L.
THOUGHT-TRANSFERENCE
Bates, H. Death of a sensitive
Bradbury, R. The veldt
Clifton, M. Star, Bright
Harvey, W. F. Flying out of Mrs Barnard Hollis
Heinlein, R. A. Lost legacy
MacLean, K. Defense mechanism
Matheson, R. Lover, when you're near me
Miller, W. M. Command performance
Shultz, W. H. Oreste
Tucker, W. Job is ended

Thousand-and-second tale of Scheherazade. Poe, E. A.
Thousand days for Mokhtar. Bowles, P. F.
Thousand-dollar bill. Komroff, M.
THRASHERS
Thomas, R. Crip, come home!
Thrawn Janet. Stevenson, R. L.
The thread. Sullivan, R.
Thread of life. Oursler, W. C.
The threat. Munro, H. H.
Three Annas. Chekhov, A. P.
Three arshins of land. Tolstoĭ, L. N. Graf
Three Bears Cottage. Collier, J.
Three buttonholes. Favicchio, J.
Three carpenters. Van Doren, M.
Three-day blow. Hemingway, E.
Three deaths. Tolstoĭ, L. N. Graf
Three dogs of Siena. Sansom, W.
Three dollars. Claudy, C. H.
Three dreams of Mr Findlater. Milne, A. A.
Three fat women of Antibes. Maugham, W. S.
Three friends. De La Mare, W. J.
Three gray men. Goudge, E.
Three Halutzot. Hemeiri, A.
Three hermits. Tolstoĭ, L. N. Graf
Three hours between planes. Fitzgerald, F. S. K.
Three hundred innings. Meader, S. W.
Three kings. Household, G.
Three links. Cooke, A. A.
Three lovers who lost. Stephens, J.
Three men on a nickel. Kaufman, W.
Three minute novel. Mann, H.
Three players of a summer game. Williams, T.
Three sailors' gambit. Dunsany, E. J. M. D. P. 18th baron
Three secrets of human flight. Langewiesche-Brandt, W. E.
Three Skeleton Key. Toudouze, G. G.
Three sneezes. Duvoisin, R. A.
Three strangers. Hardy, T.
Three-strips of flesh. Canaday, J. E.
Three Sundays in a week. Poe, E. A.
Three tools of death. Chesterton, G. K.
Three widows. Queen, E. pseud.
THREE WISE MEN. See Magi
The threepenny-piece. Stephens, J.
Threnody. White, W. A. P.
The threshold. McKelvey, L.
Through a glass darkly. De Vries, P.
Through channels. Matheson, R.
Through the purple cloud. Williamson, J.
Through Twelve-League Labyrinth. Reynolds, J. M. and McCormick, H. P.
Throwback. DeFord, M. A.
Thumbling and Sapling. Herzl, T.
Thunder and roses. Waldo, E. H.
Thunder and the wise guy. Hallstead, W. F.

Thunder Road. Gault, W. C.
Thundering Hurd. Aspinwall, M.
Thunderstorm. Caldwell, E.
Thurber, James, 1894-
　Catbird seat
　　Best of the Best American short stories,
　　　1915-1950
　　Grayson, C. ed. Fourth round
　　Queen, E. pseud. ed. Literature of crime
　　Schorer, M. ed. The story
　Greatest man in the world
　　Jensen, P. ed. Fireside book of flying
　　　stories
　More alarms at night
　　Burnett, W. ed. World's best
　Night the bed fell
　　Fenner, P. R. comp. Fun! Fun! Fun!
　Secret life of Walter Mitty
　　Burrell, J. A. and Cerf, B. A. eds. An-
　　　thology of famous American stories
　　Day, A. G. ed. Greatest American short
　　　stories
　　Heilman, R. B. ed. Modern short sto-
　　　ries
　　Shaw, H. and Bement, D. Reading the
　　　short story
　　Stauffer, R. M.; Cunningham, W. H. and
　　　Sullivan, C. J. eds. Adventures in
　　　modern literature
　　Waite, H. O. and Atkinson, B. P. eds.
　　　Literature for our time
　The whip-poor-will
　　Davenport, B. ed. Tales to be told in
　　　the dark
　You could look it up
　　Graber, R. S. ed. Baseball reader
THURSDAY ISLAND
　Maugham, W. S. French Joe
Thus I refute Beelzy. Collier, J.
Tictocq. Porter, W. S.
TIDAL WAVES
　Hearn, L. The storm
　Maugham, W. S. Yellow streak
The tide. Alabaster, M. E.
The tide. O'Flaherty, L.
Tie from Paris. Waltari, M. T.
Tierney meets a millionaire. Moroso, J. A.
The tiger. Li Fu-yen
Tiger by the tail. Nourse, A. E.
Tiger cat. Keller, D. H.
TIGERS
　Annixter, P. pseud. Loose tiger
　Bottome, P. Henry
　Li Fu-yen. The tiger
　Marshall, E. Heart of Little Shikara
　Munro, H. H. Mrs Packletide's tiger
Tight place. Buckingham, N.
Tight shoes. Runyon, D.
Till death do us part. Kirch, J. A.
Tillotson banquet. Huxley, A. L.
TIMBER. See Lumber industry
Timber. Galsworthy, J.
TIMBER WOLF. See Wolves
TIME
　Abernathy, R. Heritage
　Allen, G. Pausodyne
　Anderson, P. Flight to forever
　Bates, H. Alas, all thinking!

Bradbury, R. Scent of sarsaparilla
Clarke, A. C. All the time in the world
Conklin, G. ed. Science-fiction adventures
　in dimension; 23 stories
Dell, D. Biography project
Fenton, F. and Petracca, J. Tolliver's
　travels
Harris, J. B. The chronoclasm
Locke R. D. Demotion
Miller, P. S. Status quondam
Missing one's coach
Priestley, J. B. Look after the strange girl
Reynolds, M. and Brown, F. Dark inter-
　lude
Wells, H. G. New accelerator
White, W. A. P. Chronokinesis of Jona-
　than Hull
Time and place. Sansom, W.
TIME AND SPACE. See Space and time
Time expired. Bates, H. E.
Time for a change. Howard, Q. R.
Time for silence. Felder, D. F.
Time is out of joint. Kober, A.
Time is the traitor. Bester, A.
Time locker. Kuttner, H.
Time machine. Wells H. G.
TIME MACHINES
　Asimov, I. Red Queen's race
　Bradbury, R. Sound of thunder
　Harris, J. B. The chronoclasm
　Jenkins, W. F. Life-work of Professor
　　Muntz
　Kuttner, H. Shock
　Wells, H. G. Time machine
Time out. Newhouse, E.
Time the tiger. Lewis, W.
Time to rest. Harris, J. B.
TIME TRAVEL. See Time
TIME, TRAVELS IN
　Anderson, P. and Dickson G. Trespass
　Bradbury, R. Fox in the forest
Timeless ones. Russell, E. F.
Timperley, Rosemary
　Christmas meeting
　　Asquith, Lady C. M. E. C. ed. Book of
　　　modern ghosts
TIMUR. See Tamerlane
Tin star. Cunningham, J. M.
Ting-a-ling. Gray, D.
The tinkler. Anderson, P.
Tiny and the monster. Waldo, E. H.
Tip in time. Foote, J. T.
Tip the green earth. Marcus, P.
Tippett, James Sterling, 1885-
　Magic at midnight
　　Story parade (Periodical) Adventure
　　　stories
Tiptoe all the way. Kelly, R. G.
Tirol: The golden journey. Charteris, L.
Tit for tat. Rabinowitz, S.
The Titan. Miller, P. S.
To a web begun. Verrinder, W.
To be given to God. Forester, C. S.
To build a fire. London, J.
To entertain strangers. Claudy, C. H.

To fall asleep. Williams, W. C.

To fit the crime. Matheson, R.

To follow knowledge. Long, F. B.

To Greenland, to Greenland. Sansom, W.

To have and to lose. Galbraith, N. F.

To him who waits. Kirk, R. G.

To him who waits. Porter, W. S.

To live is to return. Lincoln, V. E.

To market, to market. Stuart, J.

To people a new world. Bond, N. S.

To punish the offender. Arico, V.

To remember these things. White, M.

To serve man. Knight, D.

To the limit. Haycox, E.

To the new world. Metzker, I.

To the ringing of bells. Lieberman, R.

To trouble the living. O'Meara, W.

TOADS. See Frogs; Horned toads

TOASTERS. See Household appliances

TOBACCO
Gordon, C. Her quaint honour
Mabry, T. D. Indian feather

TOBACCO INDUSTRY. See Tobacco

TOBACCO PIPES
Auerbach, B. Hansjorg and his pipe

Tobermory. Munro, H. H.

Tobias Gregson shows what he can do. Doyle, Sir A. C.

Tobin, Richard Lardner, 1910-
Act of God
Story (Periodical) Story; no. 1

Tobin's palm. Porter, W. S.

TOBOGGANING
Coombs, C. I. Brake happy

Today and today. De Vries, P.

Todd, Ruthven, 1914-
Man who wasn't there
Mystery Writers of America, inc. Crooks' tour
Over the mountain
Talbot, D. ed. Treasury of mountaineering stories

Tods' amendment. Kipling, R.

Toine. Maupassant, G. de

Toland, Stewart
The letter
McFarland, W. K. comp. Then it happened

Tolbert, Frank X. 1912-
Last Rebel yell
Jones, K. M. ed. New Confederate short stories

Told in the stars. Komroff, M.

TOLEDO. See Spain—Toledo

TOLERATION
Coffin, R. P. T. Seraph in the apple tree

Toll bridge. Haycox, E.

Tolliver's travels. Fenton, F. and Petracca, J.

Tolstoï, Alexseï Nikolaevich, Graf, 1882-1945
Fusty Devil
Guerney, B. G. comp. New Russian stories

Tolstoï, Alexis Nicholaievich. See Tolstoï, Aleksei Nikolaevich

Tolstoï, Alekseï Nikolaevich, Graf, 1882-1945
Death of Iván Ilých
Neider, C. ed. Short novels of the masters
Hadji Murad
Rahv, P. ed. Great Russian short novels
Three arshins of land
West, R. B. and Stallman, R. W. eds. Art of modern fiction
Three deaths
Gordon, C. and Tate, A. eds. House of fiction
Three hermits
Neider, C. ed. Great short stories from the world's literature
Neider, C. ed. Men of the high calling

Tolstoy, Leo Nikolaevich. See Tolstoï, Lev Nikolaevich, Graf

Tom Chist and his treasure box. Pyle, H.

Tom: the friend of all boys. Little, G. W.

Tomato Cain. Kneale, N.

Tomb of his ancestors. Kipling, R.

Tombling day. Bradbury, R.

Tomboy. Hodkin, R. E.

Tomlinson, Henry Major, 1873-
The derelict
Cerf, B. A. and Moriarty, H. C. eds. Anthology of famous British stories

Tommy who was overmanaged. Strain, F. B.

Tommy's burglar. Porter, W. S.

Tomorrow. Faulkner, W.

Tomorrow. Summers, J. L.

To-morrow is another day. Benson, T.

Tomorrow you're sentenced. Arico, V.

Tone of time. James, H.

Tongue of beast. Claudy, C. H.

Tonight will be different. Howland, R.

Tonio Kröger. Mann, T.

Tony Kytes, the arch-deceiver. Hardy, T.

Too big a dream. White, W.

Too close to nature. Chute, B. J.

Too good with a gun. Patten, L. B.

Too late for murder. Crossen, K. F.

Too many brides. Wilson, R.

Too many crooks. Heyliger, W.

Too much gold. London, J.

Too much horse. Butler, E. P.

Too much Hugo. Bosher, E. F.

Too much pep. Runyon, D.

Too young to have a gun. Lowrey, P. H.

Toole, Kathleen
Short space
Swallow, A. ed. Anchor in the sea

Tools of the trade. Jones, R. F.

Toomai of the elephants. Kipling, R.

Toot for a toot. Cohen, O. R.

TOOTH. See Teeth

The tooth. Dewey, G. G.

Tooth for Paul Revere. Benét, S. V.

Tooth, the whole tooth, and nothing but the tooth. Benchley, R. C.

TOOTHACHE. See Teeth

Tootie and the cat licenses. Kneale, N.

Toozee the puss. Ekbergh, I. D.

The top. Albee, G. S.

Top Hat goes to town. Taber, G. B.

Top man. Ullman, J. R.

Top secret. Grinnell, D.

Topley Place sale. Munby, A. N. L.

TOPOLOGY
Gardner, M. Island of five colors
Gardner, M. No-sided professor

Torch song. Cheever, J.

Tornado. Vaughn, G.

TORNADOES
Fitzgerald, F. S. K. Family in the wind
Vaughn, G. Tornado

TORONTO. See Canada—Toronto

Torrent damned. O'Donovan, M.

Torrid zone. Flora, F.

TORTURE
Poe, E. A. Pit and the pendulum

Total recall. Helvick, J. pseud.

Total stranger. Cozzens, J. G.

Totem. McConnell, W.

The touch. O'Flaherty, L.

Touch and go. De Vries, P.

Touch of Arab. Breckenfeld, V. G.

Touch of nutmeg makes it. Collier, J.

Touch of psychology. Lansing, E. C. H.

Touch of realism. Munro, H. H.

Touch of sun tan. Pearce, R. E.

Touchdown crazy. Fay, W.

Touchdown for Rex. Platt, G.

Touching wood. Sitwell, Sir O. bart.

Toudouze, George Gustave, 1877-
Three Skeleton Key
McFee, W. ed. Great sea stories of modern times

Tough little Christmas story. Mathews, M.

TOURIST TRADE
Annett, W. S. The relic
Goldsmith, G. Tender to the ship

Tourist trade. Tucker, W.

TOURISTS. See Tourist trade

Tournament star. Farrell, J. T.

TOURNAMENTS
Fox, J. Knight of the Cumberland

Tower of the Elephant. Howard, R. E.

Town blonde, country blonde. Quentin, P. pseud.

Town in eastern Oregon. Davis, H. L.

Town mouse. Becker, S. D.

Town wanted. Brown, F.

Town without a straight man. Stanton, W.

Townes, Robert Sherman
Problem for Emmy
Conklin, G. ed. Science-fiction thinking machines

TOWNS. See Cities and towns

The toymaker. Jones, R. F.

TOYS
Klass, P. Child's play
Munro, H. H. Toys of peace

Toys of peace. Munro, H. H.

TRACK ATHLETICS
Carter, R. G. Blue ribbon event
Chute, B. J. Magnificent merger
Chute, B. J. Red Pepper
Chute, B. J. Triple threat
Coombs, C. I. Varsity vaulter
Fessier, M. That's what happened to me
Person, W. T. Any way race
Saroyan, W. Fifty yard dash
Scott, W. R. My father doesn't like me
Strong, P. N. Anchor man
Verran, R. Lesson for Flying Goat
See also Running

Tracked to doom. Porter, W. S.

Trackside grave. McLarn, J. C.

Tractor hoarder. Upson, W. H.

TRACTORS
Upson, W. H. I'm in a hurry

Tracy, Don, 1905-
Charity ward
Saturday evening post (Periodical) Saturday evening post stories, 1950
Squirrel who was scared
Saturday evening post (Periodical) Saturday evening post stories, 1951
Strang, R. M. and Roberts, R. M. eds. Teen-age tales v 1

TRADE UNIONS
Williamson, J. Breakdown

Tradition of 1804. Hardy, T.

Tragedy at the Baths. Hughes, L.

Tragedy of Pondicherry Lodge. Doyle, Sir A. C.

Tragedy of two ambitions. Hardy, T.

Trail blazer. Gallun, R. Z.

Trail hand. Ernenwein, L. C.

Trail of the Sandhill Stag. Seton, E. T.

Trail of the whiffle-poof. Strong, P. N.

TRAILERS. See Automobiles—Trailers

The trailers. Roberts, Sir C. G. D.

Train, Arthur Cheney, 1875-1945
Dog Andrew
Blaustein, A. P. ed. Fiction goes to court
Mr Tutt collects a bet
Dachs, D. ed. Treasury of sports humor

Train from Rhodesia. Gordimer, N.

Train going. Saroyan, W.

TRAIN ROBBERS. See Brigands and robbers

TRAIN TRIPS. See Railroads—Travel

TRAINED NURSES. See Nurses and nursing

Training Alice and Congo. Richards, D.

TRAINING OF ANIMALS. See Animals—Training

Trainload of soldiers; excerpt from "Rufus M." Estes, E.

TRAINS, RAILROAD. See Railroads—Trains

The **traitor.** Hart, J. S.
The **traitor.** Maugham, W. S.
TRAITORS
  Maugham, W. S. The traitor
    See also Treason
Tramp, the sheep dog. Lang, D.
TRAMPS
  Chekhov, A. P. Drowning
  Huckabay, M. B. Ghost of Sam Bates
  Newhouse, E. Billy the Bastard
  Newhouse, E. The girl who had to get married
  Newhouse, E. Out where the West begins
  Nexø, M. A. Birds of passage
  O'Connor, F. Life you save may be your own
  Porter, W. S. The caliph, cupid and the clock
  Porter, W. S. Cop and the anthem
  Porter, W. S. Higher abdication
  Porter, W. S. Shocks of doom
  Warren, R. P. Blackberry winter
Transfer point. White, W. A. P.
TRANSFORMATION. See Metamorphosis
Transformation of Martin Burney. Porter, W. S.
Transience. Clarke, A. C.
Transients. Evans, T. M.
Transients in Arcadia. Porter, W. S.
TRANSMIGRATION
  Kipling, R. 'Finest story in the world'
  Poe, E. A. Ligeia
    See also Reincarnation
TRANSMUTATION. See Metamorphosis
The **trap.** Bloomfield, H.
The **trap.** Sandoz, M. Y.
The **trap.** Silone, I.
Trap is set. Hendryx, J. B.
TRAPPERS
  Edmonds, W. D. Judge
  Gulick, G. C. Rendezvous romance
  Gulick, G. C. Waters of Manitou
Trapper's mates. Williamson, H.
TRAVEL
  Chekhov, A. P. Across Siberia
  Collier, J. Incident on a lake
  Shulman, M. Chance for adventure
  Waugh, E. Cruise
    See also Ocean travel; Railroads—Travel
The **traveler.** Stegner, W.
TRAVELERS, COMMERCIAL. See Commercial travelers
TRAVELING SALESMEN. See Salesmen and salesmanship
The **traveller.** Crémieux, B.
The **traveller.** Matheson, R.
Traveller from the West and the traveller from the East. Warner, S. T.
Travellers' tears. Stern, J.
TRAVELS IN TIME. See Time, Travels in
Traven, B. pseud.
  Third guest
    Best American short stories, 1954

Travers, Pamela L. 1906-
  Ah Wong
    Bachelor, J. M.; Henry, R. L. and Salisbury, R. eds. Current thinking and writing; 2d ser.
TRAVESTIES. See Parodies
The **trawler.** Connolly, J. B.
TREASON
  Gellhorn, M. E. Honeyed peace
    See also Traitors
The **treasure.** Lumpkin, G.
The **treasure.** Maugham, W. S.
Treasure of Franchard. Stevenson, R. L.
Treasure of Tranicos. Howard, R. E.
Treasure-ship. Munro, H. H.
TREASURE-TROVE
  Allen, M. P. Two chests of treasure
  Calahan, H. A. Back to Treasure Island
  Coppock, C. Pirate gold
  Curtis, K. Cruises in the sun
  Delavigne, J. F. C. Up the garret stairs
  Dobie, J. F. Midas on a goatskin
  Munro, H. H. Treasure-ship
  Poe, E. A. The gold-bug
  Pyle, H. Tom Chist and the treasure box
  Queen, E. pseud. Needle's eye
  Wells, H. G. Mr Brisher's treasure
TREASURER
  Caldwell, E. The rumor
Treasures of the sea. Gordimer, N.
Treat, Lawrence, 1903-
  Shoes for breakfast
    Mystery Writers of America, inc. Maiden murders
Treat, Lawrence, 1903- and Tarachow, Sidney
  Wire brush
    Mystery writers of America, inc. Crooks' tour
The **tree.** Coolidge, O. E.
The **tree.** De La Mare, W. J.
A **tree.** A rock. A cloud. McCullers, C. S.
Tree for two. Marker, W. D.
Tree men of Potu. Holberg, L. baron
Tree of knowledge. James, H.
Tree of life. Moore, C. L.
Tree toad. Davis, R. H.
TREES
  Bjørnson, B. How the mountain was clad
  Cohn, E. Rebellious tree
  Coolidge, O. E. The tree
  De La Mare, W. S. The tree
  Holberg, L. baron. Tree men of Potu
  Kuttner, H. Hard-luck diggings
  Sansom, W. My tree
Tree's wife. Counselman, M. E.
Tregannet book of hours. Munby, A. N. L.
Tregarthen, John Coulson, 1854-1933
  Great run
    Andrews, R. C. ed. My favorite stories of the great outdoors
Trends. Asimov, I.
Trenton in thirty minutes. Felsen, G.
Très Jolie. Foote, J. T.

Trespass. Anderson, P. and Dickson, G.

The **trial**. Forster, E. M.

Trial by fire. Kirtland, A.

Trial of John Nobody. Carr, A. H. Z.

TRIALS
Algren, N. Captain is impaled
Benét, S. V. Devil and Daniel Webster
Bergengruen, W. Concerning muskets
Blish, J. Beanstalk
Carr, A. H. Z. Trial of John Nobody
Cobb, I. S. Boys will be boys
Connelly, M. C. Coroner's inquest
Davis, R. H. Wasted day
Duranty, W. The parrot
Faulkner, W. Tomorrow
Gally, J. W. Hualapi
Galsworthy, J. The juryman
Harte, B. Colonel Starbottle for the plaintiff
Harte, B. Tennessee's partner
Hurston, Z. N. Conscience of the court
Klingsberg, H. M. Doowinkle, Attorney
Lewis, J. Wife of Martin Guerre
Millar, K. Wild goose chase
Milne, A. A. The barrister
O'Donovan, M. Counsel for Œdipus
Post, M. D. Corpus delicti
Shaw, I. Triumph of justice
Swinnerton, F. A. The verdict
Train, A. C. Dog Andrew

India
Forster, E. M. The trial

Trials of a ballplayer's wife. Broun, H. C.

TRICKERY. See Hoaxes

Trickster and the old witch
Pacey, D. ed. Book of Canadian stories

Trigger tide. Guin, W.

Trilling, Lionel, 1905-
Of this time, of that place
Felheim, M.; Newman, F. B. and Steinhoff, W. R. eds. Modern short stories
Waite, H. O. and Atkinson, B. P. eds. Literature for our time
Other Margaret
Ludwig, J. B. and Poirier, W. R. eds. Stories, British and American
West, R. B. and Stallman, R. W. eds. Art of modern fiction

Trimmed lamp. Porter, W. S.

TRINITY COLLEGE. See Cambridge, England. University

Trinket's colt. Somerville, E. A. O. and Martin, V. F.

Trip one. Grendon, E.

Trip to Czardis. Cranberry, E. P.

Triple fugue. Sitwell, Sir O. bart.

Triple threat. Chute, B. J.

TRIPOLITAN WAR. See United States—19th century—Tripolitan War, 1801-1805

The **triumph**. Bonner, P. H.

Triumph of justice. Shaw, I.

Triumph with bells and laughter. Brookhouser, F.

Trivulzio and the King. Bergengruen, W.

Trixie: the dog who did her duty. Little, G. W.

Trollope, Anthony, 1815-1882
Bailiffs at Framley
Trollope, A. Bedside Barsetshire
Bartsetshire
Trollope, A. Bedside Barsetshire
Bartsetshire worthy—Archdeacon Grantly
Trollope, A. Bedside Barsetshire
Bishop sends his inhibition
Trollope, A. Bedside Barsetshire
Caleb Thumble returns to Barchester
Trollope, A. Bedside Barsetshire
Crosbie starts his honeymoon
Trollope, A. Bedside Barsetshire
Dr Fillgrave refuses a fee
Trollope, A. Bedside Barsetshire
The Duke entertains
Trollope, A. Bedside Barsetshire
Frank takes a brother's privilege
Trollope, A. Bedside Barsetshire
Grace Crawley and the Archdeacon
Trollope, A. Bedside Barsetshire
Johnny Eames does well
Trollope, A. Bedside Barsetshire
Josiah Crawley at the Palace
Trollope, A. Bedside Barsetshire
Josiah Crawley charged with theft
Trollope, A. Bedside Barsetshire
Love scene
Trollope, A. Bedside Barsetshire
Malachi's Cove
Cerf, B. A. and Moriarty, H. C. eds. Anthology of famous British stories
Mark Robarts is adamant
Trollope, A. Bedside Barsetshire
Mark Robarts signs a bill
Trollope, A. Bedside Barsetshire
Mary comes into money
Trollope, A. Bedside Barsetshire
Mesdames Grantly and Proudie get together
Trollope, A. Bedside Barsetshire
Mr Slope vanquished
Trollope, A. Bedside Barsetshire
Mrs Proudie goes too far
Trollope, A. Bedside Barsetshire
Mrs Proudie intervenes
Trollope, A. Bedside Barsetshire
Mrs Proudie vanquished
Trollope, A. Bedside Barsetshire
Obstinacy of Septimus Harding
Trollope, A. Bedside Barsetshire
The Proudies entertain
Trollope, A. Bedside Barsetshire
R.I.P.
Trollope, A. Bedside Barsetshire
Sir Louis dines out
Trollope, A. Bedside Barsetshire

Trouble in St Brendan's. Lieberman R.

Trouble on 98th Street. Taubes, F.

Trouble on Tantalus. Miller, P. S.

Trouble on the range. Regli, A. C.

Trouble with the angels. Hughes, L.

Trouble with the union. Harrington, D.

Troubled water. English, T.

TROUSERS
Caldwell, E. Corduroy pants

Trout widows. Ford, C.

TRUCK DRIVERS
Porter, W. S. Caliph and the cad

True history. Lucian

True lovers' knot. Sitwell, Sir O. bart.

True relation of the apparition of one Mrs Veal. Defoe, D.

The trumpet. De La Mare, W. J.

"Trumpet" comes to Pickeye! Goodman, J. T.

Trusting snakes. Arico, V.

TRUTH
Munro, H. H. Reginald on besetting sins

Truth about Pyecraft. Wells, H. G.

Truth about Sylvanus. Van Doren, M.

TRUTHFULNESS AND FALSEHOOD
Crane, S. The knife
Dickson, G. R. Lulungomeena
Gally, J. W. Frozen truth

Tryout. Barr, J. pseud.

The tsantsa. Sandoz, M. Y.

Tsung-Wen, Shen. See Shen, Tsung-wen

T'uan Ch'engshih, d. 863
Cinderella
Lin, Y. ed. Famous Chinese short stories

TUBERCULOSIS
Maugham, W. S. Sanatorium
Porter, W. S. Fog in Santone
Porter, W. S. Hygeia at the Solito
Waltari, M. T. Island of ice

Tucker, Bob, pseud. See Tucker, Wilson

Tucker, Louis
Cubic city
Margulies, L. and Friend, O. J. eds. From off this world

Tucker, Wilson, 1914-
Able to Zebra
Tucker, W. Science-fiction subtreasury
Exit
Moskowitz, S. comp. Editor's choice in science fiction
Tucker, W. Science-fiction subtreasury
Gentlemen—the Queen!
Tucker, W. Science-fiction subtreasury
Home is where the wreck is
Tucker, W. Science-fiction subtreasury
The job is ended
Tucker, W. Science-fiction subtreasury
The mountaineer
Tucker, W. Science-fiction subtreasury
My brother's wife
Tucker, W. Science-fiction subtreasury
"MCMLV"
Tucker, W. Science-fiction subtreasury
Street walker
Tucker, W. Science-fiction subtreasury
Tourist trade
Best science fiction stories: 1952
Heinlein, R. A. ed. Tomorrow, the stars
Wayfaring strangers
Tucker, W. Science-fiction subtreasury

Tudor chimney. Munby, A. N. L.

TUGBOATS
Strong, P. N. Salvage

Tuition for the rebbe. Reisin, A.

Tu Kwang-t'ing, 850-933
Curly-beard
Lin, Y. ed. Famous Chinese short stories

Tulip. De Vries, P.

Tunis, John Roberts, 1889-
Ronald leaves the academy
Hazeltine, A. I. comp. Selected stories for teen-agers
Two-mile race
Herzberg, M. J. comp. Treasure chest of sport stories
Unpredictable Dodgers
Fenner, P. R. comp. Crack of the bat

Tunkel, Joseph, 1881-1950
From what a Litvak makes a living
Ausubel, N. ed. Treasury of Jewish humor
The gift
Ausubel, N. ed. Treasury of Jewish humor
Glass of tea
Ausubel, N. ed. Treasury of Jewish humor

Tunkeler, Der. See Tunkel, Joseph

TUNNELS AND TUNNELING
Benson, T. Man from the tunnel
Maltz, A. Man on a road

Turgenev, Ivan Sergeevich, 1818-1883
Byézhin Meadow
Gordon, C. and Tate, A. eds. House of fiction
Same as: Bezhin Meadow; Byezhin Prairie
District doctor
Blodgett, H. W. ed. Story survey. 1953 ed.
Neider, C. ed. Great short stories from the world's literature
First love
Rahv, P. ed. Great Russian short novels

TURKEY
Constantinople
Bergengruen, W. Orban twins

Turkey-red. Wood, F. G.

TURKEYS
Buckingham, N. Comin' twenty-one

TURKISH BATHS. See Baths, Turkish

Turn and turn about. Holland, R. S.

Turn of the screw. James, H.

Turn of the tide. Cicellis, K.

Turn off the moon. Hause, M.

Turn with the sun. Knowles, J.

Turnabout. Faulkner, W.

Turner, Robert
The gunny
Meredith, S. ed. Bar 3

TURTLES
Keith, S. Point of view

Turtles played the hares. Stoakes, H. R.

TUTORS
James, H. The pupil
Wall, J. W. Ringstones

Tutti frutti. Sansom, W.

"Twa kings." De La Roche, M.

Twain, Mark, pseud. See Clemens, Samuel Langhorne

Twentieth floor. Van Doren, M.

Twentieth game. O'Rourke, F.

Twenty-five bucks. Farrell, J. T.

Twenty floors up. Carver, C.

Twenty-six and one. Gorky, M.

Twilight. Reymont, W. S.

Twilight of the wise. Hilton, J.

The twilighters. Loomis, N. M.

TWINS
Bergengruen, W. Orban twins
Collier, J. Season of mists
Cooke, A. A. Two peas in a pod
Lewis, S. Willow walk
Pratt, F. and De Camp, L. S. My brother's keeper
Walsh, M. Sword of Yung Lo
Wilson, H. L. Wrong twin

Twisted branch. Cicellis, K.

Two ages of man. Sunley, R.

Two anecdotes
Davenport, B. ed. Tales to be told in the dark

Two-bits of traffic C. Crump, I.

Two blue birds. Lawrence, D. H.

Two bottles of relish. Dunsany, E. J. M. D. P. 18th baron

Two brothers
Lohan, R. and Lohan, M. eds. New Christmas treasury

Two brothers. Farrell, J. T.

Two chests of treasure. Allen, M. P.

Two churches of 'Quawket. Bunner, H. C.

Two cooing doves. Palma, R.

Two Daumiers. Krige, U.

Two days with Mr Neville's hounds. Surtees, R. S.

Two drovers. Scott, Sir W.

Two face. Long, F. B.

Two-faced promise. Gulick, G. C.

Two for a ride. Moore, G. M.

Two for the show. Newcomb, E.

Two friends. Davies, R.

Two friends. Maupassant, G. de

Two great men. Rappaport, S.

Two in one. Chekhov, A. P.

Two infants. Gibran, K.

Two ladies in retirement. Taylor, P. H.

Two legacies. Landa, M. J.

Two legs for the two of us. Jones, J.

Two little Confederates. Page, T. N.

Two little soldiers. Maupassant, G. de

Two lovely beasts. O'Flaherty, L.

Two men. Stern, J.

Two men confer with Cuter Malone. Hendryx, J. B.

Two-mile race. Tunis, J. R.

Two miracles. Deledda, G.

Two Miss Koofers. Preston, B. B.

Two of a kind. Chekhov, A. P.

Two on trial. Nicola, H. B.

Two over par. Roos, K. pseud.

Two peas in a pod. Cooke, A. A.

Two pillars blight. Claudy, C. H.

Two pleasures. Wendroff, Z.

Two recalls. Porter, W. S.

Two renegades. Porter, W. S.

Two ringers. Foote, J. T.

Two rivers. Stegner, W. E.

Two seconds. Steele, W. D.

Two shadows. Temple, W. F.

Two sisters. Farrell, J. T.

Two soldiers. Faulkner, W.

Two strangers came to town. Dick, I. M.

Two Thanksgiving Day gentlemen. Porter, W. S.

Two were left. Cave, H. B.

Two wishes. Gibran, K.

Two wrongs. Fitzgerald, F. S. K.

The Twonky. Kuttner, H.

Tyger! Tyger! Carr, A. H. Z.

Tynîanov, Îurîî Nikolaevich, 1894-1943
Second Lieutenant Likewise
Guerney, B. G. comp. New Russian stories

Tynyanov, Yuri Nicholaievich. See Tynîanov, Îurîî Nikolaevich

Typhoon. Conrad, J.

Typical gesture of Colonel Duggan. Schulberg, B. W.

TYPISTS
Porter, W. S. Springtime à la carte

TYRANNY. See Despotism

TYROL
Charteris, L. Tirol: The golden journey

Tzagan. Wood, C.

Tzensky, Sergîeî Sergeev-. See Sergîeev-Tsenskiî, Sergîeî Nikolaevich

U

UCCELLO, PAOLO DI DONO, KNOWN AS, 1396?-1475
Schwob, M. Paolo Uccello

UGANDA. See Congo, Belgian—Uganda

Ugly. Maupassant, G. de

Ugly sister. Maxtone Graham, J. A.

Ugly weather. Verga, G.

UKRAINE. See Russia—Ukraine

Uller uprising. Piper, H. B.

Ullman, James M.
Anything new on the strangler?
Queen, E. pseud. ed. Ellery Queen's awards: 9th ser.

Ullman, James Ramsey, 1907-
Am I blue?
Ullman, J. R. Island of the blue macaws, and sixteen other stories
Between you and I
Ullman, J. R. Island of the blue macaws, and sixteen other stories
Chicken dinner
Ullman, J. R. Island of the blue macaws, and sixteen other stories
Deadly north face
Saturday evening post (Periodical) Saturday evening post stories, 1951

Unexpected reunion. Hebel, J. P.
UNFAITHFULNESS. See Marriage problems
Unfinished Christmas story. Porter, W. S.
UNFINISHED STORIES
Chekhov, A. P. De-compensation
Unfinished story. Porter, W. S.
Unfinished symphony. Corkery, D.
Unholy living and half dying. O'Faoláin, S.
Unholy three. Auchincloss, L.
Unholy trio. Hendryx, J. B.
The unicorn. Seager, A.
Unite and conquer. Waldo, E. H.
UNITED STATES

To 1776
Carter, R. G. Tea from the brigantine

18th century—Revolution
Brick, J. Rifleman's run
Erskine, L. Y. After school
Forbes, E. "Disperse, ye rebels!"
Hale, E. E. General Washington's pig
Skinner, C. L. Silent Scot

18th century—Revolution—Prisoners and Prisons
Brick, J. Rifleman's run

19th century—Tripolitan War, 1801-1805
Daniel, H. Shores of Tripoli

19th century—War of 1812
Swanson, N. H. They kept the flag there

19th century—Civil War
Allen, H. Surgery at Aquila
Bierce, A. Occurrence at Owl Creek bridge
Bierce, A. One of the missing
Boyd, J. Elms and Fair Oaks
Brick, J. Message for Uncle Billy
Clayton, J. B. Ride a pale ghost into night and time
Cozzens, J. G. Men running
Crane, S. Gray sleeve
Crane, S. Mystery of heroism
Danielson, R. E. Corporal Hardy
Dowdey, C. Bugles blow retreat
James, M. Stolen railroad train
Page, T. N. Burial of the guns
Page, T. N. Two little Confederates
Porter, W. S. Two renegades
Sass, H. R. Affair at St Albans
Street, J. H. They know how
Toland, S. The letter
Welty, E. The burning

19th century—Civil War—Prisoners and Prisons
Brick, J. Message for Uncle Billy

19th century—War of 1898
Crane, S. Episode of war

Army
Best Army short stories, 1950; 12 stories
Chase, F. General from the Pentagon
Cozzens, J. G. Men running
Haycox, E. Dispatch to the general

Haycox, E. Scout detail
Newhouse, E. Major and Mrs Fletcher
Newhouse, E. Position of the soldier
Newhouse, E. Time out
Porter, W. S. Moment of victory
Shaw, I. Act of faith
Tennyson, H. In the desert

Army—Recruiting, enlistment, etc.
Wilson, B. Stand-in

Army Air Forces
Gordon, A. Kiss for the Lieutenant

Coast Guard
Detzer, K. W. Surfman number nine

Naval Academy, Annapolis
White, R. Sick bay to sea wall

Navy
Auchincloss, L. Fall of a sparrow
Auchincloss, L. Loyalty up and loyalty down
Auchincloss, L. Wally
Burnet, D. Why did he leave me?
Faulkner, W. Turnabout
Hale, E. E. Man without a country
Heggen, T. Night watch
Schulberg, B. W. Ensign Weasel
White, R. An eye for an eye

State Department
Acheson, E. G. Big shot
UNIVERSE
Hamilton, E. Fessenden's worlds
Universe is not really expanding. Willingham, C.
University. Phillips, P.
UNIVERSITY OF MOSCOW. See Moscow. University
UNJUST ACCUSATION. See False accusation
Unkindest blow. Munro, H. H.
Unknown Chekhov. Chekhov, A. P.
Unknown quantity. Porter, W. S.
UNKNOWN SOLDIER
Dos Passos, J. R. Body of an American
Unlucky number. Coombs, C. I.
Unlucky winner. Shulman, M.
Unparalleled adventure of one Hans Pfaall. Poe, E. A.
UNPARDONABLE SIN. See Sin, Unpardonable
Unpleasant incident. Chekhov, A. P.
An unpleasantness. Chekhov, A. P.
Unpredictable Dodgers. Tunis, J. R.
Unprofitable servant. Porter, W. S.
Unquiet spirit. Coolidge, O. E.
Unready to wear. Vonnegut, K.
Unrest-cure. Munro, H. H.
The unsaid prayer. Van Paassen, P.
Unseen collection. Zweig, S.
Unspoiled reaction. McCarthy, M. T.
Untermeyer, Louis, 1885-
Donkey of God
Lohan, R. and Lohan, M. eds. New Christmas treasury

Until they sail. Michener, J. A.

Untimely toper. De Camp, L. S. and Pratt, F.

Untouched by human hands. Sheckley, R.

Unturned card. Marshall, E.

Unwanted one. Taber, G. B.

Unwelcome tenant. Aycock, R. D.

Up from the depths. Wodehouse, P. G.

Up in a balloon. Ekbergh, I. D.

Up the garret stairs. Delavigne, J. F. C.

Uprooted. O'Donovan, M.

Upshaw, Helen, 1928-
 The harvest
  American vanguard, 1950
 Love smelled of vanilla
  American vanguard, 1952

Upson, William Hazlett, 1891-
 Alexander Botts goes underground
  Upson, W. H. No rest for Botts
 Alexander Botts vs. the income tax
  Upson, W. H. No rest for Botts
 Botts and the brink of disaster
  Upson, W. H. No rest for Botts
 Botts and the jet-propelled tractor
  Upson, W. H. No rest for Botts
 Botts bogs down
  Upson, W. H. No rest for Botts
 Botts cleans out the parts department
  Upson, W. H. No rest for Botts
 Botts discovers uranium
  Upson, W. H. No rest for Botts
 Botts gets a new job
  Upson, W. H. No rest for Botts
 Botts makes magic
  Upson, W. H. No rest for Botts
 Expensive Mr Botts
  Upson, W. H. No rest for Botts
 Frank and honest
  Upson, W. H. No rest for Botts
 I'm in a hurry
  Cuff, R. P. ed. American short story
   survey
 A quiet wedding
  Dachs, D. ed. Treasury of sports humor
 Tractor hoarder
  Upson, W. H. No rest for Botts

Upturned face. Crane, S.

URANUS (PLANET)
 Bond, N. S. Day we celebrate
 Wollheim, D. A. Planet passage

Use of force. Williams, W. C.

USURERS. See Pawnbrokers

Utility. Jones, R. F.

Utopia. More, Sir T.

UTOPIAS
 Bacon, F. viscount St Albans. New Atlantis
 Blish, J. Okie
 Campanella, T. City of the sun
 Goldsmith, O. Asem
 More, Sir T. Utopia
 Richter, C. Sinister journey
 Russell, E. F. And then there were none

V

Vacancy in Westchester. Newhouse, E.

Vacant cross. Stancourt, L. J.

Vacation houses. See Summer resorts

VACATIONS
 Garland, H. Mrs Ripley's trip
 Hesse, H. Youth, beautiful youth
 Miller, C. Gentle season
 Young, E. H. The stream

VACCINATION
 Kipling, R. Tomb of his ancestors

A vagabond. Maupassant, G. de

VAGABONDS. See Tramps

VAGRANTS. See Tramps

Vain beauty. Maupassant, G. de

Valbor, Kirsten, 1919-
 New Guinea interlude
  American vanguard, 1952

Valdés, Armando Palacio. See Palacio
 Valdés, Armando

Vale of tears. Stallings, L.

Valiant lady. Bendrodt, J. C.

Valiant woman. Powers, J. F.

Valle-Inclán, Ramón del, 1870-1936
 My sister Antonia
  De Onís, H. ed. Spanish stories and
   tales

Valley for Martha. Thompson, T.

Valley of dreams. Weinbaum, S. G.

Valley of great wells. Van Doren, M.

Valley of spiders. Wells, H. G.

Valley of the beasts. Blackwood, A.

Value of the dollar. Gordon, E. E.

Vampire of the village. Chesterton, G. K.

Van Bruggen, Carry. See Bruggen, Carry
 (de Haan) van

Vance, Carol
 Captive heart
  Lantz, J. E. ed. Stories of Christian
   living

Vance, Jack, pseud. See Kuttner, Henry

Vandercook, John Womack, 1902-
 The challenge
  Queen, E. pseud. ed. Queen's awards:
   7th ser.
 Pretending makes it so
  Saturday evening post (Periodical)
   Saturday evening post stories, 1951

Van de Water, Frederic Franklyn, 1890-
 Eve enters
  Cavanna, B. ed. Pick of the litter

Van Doren, Mark, 1894-
 Bad corner
  Van Doren, M. Short stories
 Big enough for a horse
  Van Doren, M. Short stories
 Birdie, come back
  Van Doren, M. Short stories
 The birds
  Van Doren, M. Short stories
 Brown cap
  Van Doren, M. Nobody say a word,
   and other stories

Van Vogt, Alfred E.—*Continued*
  Second solution
    Van Vogt, A. E. Away and beyond
  Secret unattainable
    Van Vogt, A. E. Away and beyond
  The seesaw
    Derleth, A. W. ed. Beyond time & space
  The sound
    Van Vogt, A. E. Destination: universe!
  Vault of the beast
    Astounding science fiction (Periodical)
      Astounding science fiction anthology
    Van Vogt, A. E. Away and beyond
Variation on a theme. Collier, J.
Variations on a theme of rain. Barker, A. L.
VARIETY THEATERS. See Music halls
  (Variety theaters, cabarets, etc)
Various temptations. Sansom, W.
Varmint tries dissipation. Johnson, O. M.
Varsity vaulter. Coombs, C. I.
The **vats.** De La Mare, W. J.
Vaughn, Gertrude
  Tornado
    Oberfirst, R. ed. 1954 anthology of best
      original short-shorts
Vault of the beast. Van Vogt, A. E.
Vega. Cheever, J.
VEILS
  Hawthorne, N. Minister's black veil
The **veldt.** Bradbury, R.
Velia. Bonner, P. H.
The **vendetta.** Maupassant, G. de
Venerated bones. Lagerkvist, P. F.
VENEZUELA
  Hudson, W. H. Mysterious forest
VENGEANCE. See Revenge
VENICE. See Italy—Venice
VENTRILOQUISTS
  Collier, J. Spring fever
The **venturers.** Porter, W. S.
VENUS (PLANET)
  Bennett, K. Rocketeers have shaggy ears
  Bradbury, R. Long rain
  Brown, F. Politeness
  Carr, R. S. Morning star
  Elam, R. M. Venusway
  Jameson, M. Blind man's bluff
  Jameson, M. Lilies of life
  Kuttner, H. Clash by night
  Kuttner, H. Iron standard
  Lesser, M. Black Eyes and the daily grind
  Long, F. B. The critters
  MacLean, K. The fittest
  Moore, C. L. There shall be darkness
  Neville, K. Franchise
  Pratt, F. Roger Bacon formula
  Van Vogt, A. E. Can of paint
  Weinbaum, S. G. Lotus eaters
  Weinbaum, S. G. Parasite planet
The **Venus.** Williams, W. C.
Venus and the seven sexes. Klass, P.
Venus ascendant. Gellhorn, M. E.
Venus is a man's world. Klass, P.

VENUSIANS
  Crossen, K. P. Ambassadors from Venus
  Oliver, C. Win the world
  White, W. A. P. Nine-finger Jack
Venusway. Elam, R. M.
VERA CRUZ. See Mexico—Vera Cruz
Verbal transcription: 6 A.M. Williams, W. C.
The **verdict.** Swinnerton, F. A.
Verdict of innocence. Beck, W.
Verdun Belle. Woollcott, A.
Verga, Giovanni, 1840-1922
  Across the sea
    Verga, G. Little novels of Sicily
  Black bread
    Verga, G. Little novels of Sicily
  Cavalleria rusticana
    Verga, G. Cavalleria rusticana, and other
      narratives
  Don Licciu Papa
    Verga, G. Little novels of Sicily
  The gentry
    Verga, G. Little novels of Sicily
  His Reverence
    Verga, G. Cavalleria rusticana, and other
      narratives
    Verga, G. Little novels of Sicily
  Home tragedy
    Verga, G. Cavalleria rusticana, and other
      narratives
  Liberty
    Verga, G. Little novels of Sicily
  Malaria
    Verga, G. Little novels of Sicily
  Mystery play
    Verga, G. Cavalleria rusticana, and other
      narratives
    Verga, G. Little novels of Sicily
  The orphans
    Verga, G. Little novels of Sicily
  Property
    Verga, G. Cavalleria rusticana, and other
      narratives
    Verga, G. Little novels of Sicily
  Saint Joseph's ass
    Verga, G. Cavalleria rusticana, and
      other narratives
    Same as: Story of the Saint Joseph's ass
  The she-wolf
    Verga, G. Cavalleria rusticana, and
      other narratives
  So much for the King
    Verga, G. Little novels of Sicily
  Story of the Saint Joseph's ass
    Verga, G. Little novels of Sicily
    Same as: Saint Joseph's ass
  Ugly weather
    Verga, G. Cavalleria rusticana, and
      other narratives
The **verger.** Maugham, W. S.
VERGERS. See Sextons
Verlaine, Paul Marie, 1844-1896
  Charles Husson
    Cory, D. W. pseud. comp. 21 variations
      on a theme
VERMONT
  Fisher, D. F. C. Flint and fire
  Fisher, D. F. C. Witch doctor

VERMONT—*Continued*

Farm life

See Farm life—Vermont

Saint Albans

Sass, H. R. Affair at St Albans

Vernam, Glenn
If you weel permit me
Fenner, P. R. comp. Cowboys, cowboys, cowboys

Verne, Jules, 1828-1905
Dr Ox's experiment
Derleth, A. W. ed. Beyond time & space
In the year 2889
Conklin, G. ed. Big book of science fiction
Round the moon
Kuebler, H. W. ed. Treasury of science fiction classics

Verner, Clara, 1900-
Meddlin' Papa
Oberfirst, R. ed. 1954 anthology of best original short-shorts

Veronika. Storm, T.

Verotchka. Chekhov, A. P.

Verral, Charles Spain
Itch to win
Fenner, P. R. comp. Speed, speed, speed

Verran, Roger
Lesson for Flying Goat
Owen, F. ed. Teen-age winter sports stories

Verrinder, W.
To a web begun
Oberfirst, R. ed. 1952 anthology of best original short-shorts

Verse on the window. Boyd, J.

Vertical ladder. Sansom, W.

Very false alarm. Platt, G.

Very late spring. Caldwell, E.

Very mischief. Frost, L.

Very old are beautiful. Betts, D.

Very sharp for jagging. Clay, R.

Vessel of wrath. Maugham, W. S.

Veteran ballplayer. Wolfe, T.

VETERANS (CIVIL WAR)
Danielson, R. E. Corporal Hardy
Garland, H. Return of a private
See also Soldiers, American

VETERANS (EUROPEAN WAR, 1914-1918
Hemingway, E. In another country
Munro, H. H. Square egg
Nason, L. H. Rodney

VETERANS (IRELAND)
Walsh, M. Butcher to the Queen

VETERANS (WORLD WAR, 1939-1945)
Barker, A. L. Novelette
Beck, W. No continuing city
Galbraith, N. F. To have and to lose
Jones, J. Two legs for the two of us
Karchmer, S. "Hail, brother and farewell"
Purcell, D. Rider of the avalanche
Rothberg, A. A. Not with our fathers
Sarton, M. Return of Corporal Greene
Schwartz, R. H. Good people of Milton

VETERANS, DISABLED. See Cripples

Vetter, Marjorie (Meyn)
Captain Kit
American girl (Periodical) Favorite stories
Fool dog
American girl (Periodical) On my honor
Holiday house party
American girl (Periodical) Christmas all year 'round
Let the wind blow
American girl (Periodical) On my honor

VICARS. See Clergy

Vicar's web. Harvey, W. F.

Vickers, Roy
Double image
Queen, E. pseud. ed. Ellery Queen's awards: 9th ser.
Hair shirt
Queen, E. pseud. ed. Queen's awards: 6th ser.
Little things like that
Best detective stories of the year—1954
Man with the sneer
Best detective stories of the year—1952
Million-to-one chance
Best detective stories of the year—1950
Miss Paisley's cat
Queen, E. pseud. ed. Queen's awards: 8th ser.

Vic's Orr kid. Olds, H. D.

The **victim.** Lowry, R. J. C.

Victim no. 5. Keeler, H. S.

Victory. Faulkner, W.

Victory. Gregutt, H. C.

The **victory.** Schwartz, M.

Victory unintentional. Asimov, I.

La **vie** Bohème. Gordimer, N.

Vienna roast. Brecht, H. W.

View from the balcony. Stegner, W. E.

Vigny, Alfred Victor, comte de, 1797-1863
Malacca cane
Dupee, F. W. ed. Great French short novels

VIKINGS
Mowery, W. B. Relic of the Vikings

Village Elder. Chekhov, A. P.

Village that voted the earth was flat. Kipling, R.

Villain as a young boy. Barker, A. L.

Villiers de l'Isle-Adam, Jean Marie Mathias Philippe Auguste, comte de, 1838-1889
Desire to be a man
Geist, S. ed. French stories and tales

VILLON, FRANCOIS, b. 1431
Stevenson, R. L. Lodging for the night

Vineland's burning. Justice, D.

Vines, Howell, 1899-
Ginsing gatherers
Southern review. Anthology of stories from the Southern review

Vint. Chekhov, A. P.

Violence at sundown. O'Rourke, F.

Violent interlude. Haycox, E.

VIOLINISTS. See Musicians—Violinists

Vireo's song. Dunsing, D. M.

Virgin of the seven daggers. Paget, V.

Virginians are coming. Farrell, J. T.

Virtue. Maugham, W. S.

Virtuoso. Goldstone, H.

The **vise.** Magnes, W. D.

Vision. Corkery, D.

Vision of Henry Whipple. Burnet, D.

Vision of Mirzah. Addison, J.

VISIONS. See Dreams

Visit of charity. Welty, E.

Visit to a neighbor. Cicellis, K.

Visit to friends. Chekhov, A. P.

Visit to the fair. Williams, W. C.

Visitation. Ullman, J. R.

VISITING
  Betts, D. Sympathetic visitor
  Chekhov, A. P. Visit to friends
  Gellhorn, M. E. Week end at Grimsby
  Jackson, C. R. Parting at morning
  Rosenberg, E. C. Aunt Esther's galoshes
  Welty, E. Visit of charity

Visiting fire-eater. Wylie, P.

The **visitor.** Bowen, E.

The **visitor.** Bradbury, R.

The **visitor.** Caldwell, E.

The **visitor.** Horwitz, J.

VISITORS. See Guests

VISITORS, INTERPLANETARY. See
  Interplanetary visitors

The **vitagraphoscope.** Porter, W. S.

VOCATIONAL STORIES
  Furman, A. L. ed. Everygirls career stories; 12 stories

Vogau, Boris Andreevich, 1894-
  Big heart
    Guerney, B. G. comp. New Russian sto-
    ries

Voice behind him. Brown, F.

VOICE CULTURE. See Singing and voice
  culture

Voice of Bugle Ann. Kantor, M.

Voice of the city. Porter, W. S.

Voice of the lobster. Kuttner, H.

Voice of the turtle. Maugham, W. S.

The **voices.** Horwitz, J.

The **volcano.** Newhouse, E.

The **volcano.** Stegner, W. E.

VOLCANOES
  Ullman, J. R. Silver sword

Von Hagen, Christine Inez (Brown) 1912-
  Dueña for a day
    American girl (Periodical) Favorite sto-
    ries
  Katti's Galápagos Christmas
    American girl (Periodical) Christmas
    all year 'round

Von Hameln, Glückel. See Hameln, Glückel
  of

Vonnegut, Kurt, 1922-
  Big trip up yonder
    Pohl, F. ed. Assignment in tomorrow
  Report on the Barnhouse effect
    Heinlein, R. A. ed. Tomorrow, the stars
  Unready to wear
    Galaxy science fiction magazine. Second
    Galaxy reader of science fiction

VOODOOISM
  Maugham, W. S. Honolulu
  Maugham, W. S. P. & O.
  Nearing, H. The mathematical voodoo

Voorhees, Melvin B.
  Robe and the sword
    Best Army short stories, 1950

Voyage forme la jeunesse. Gellhorn, M. E.

Voyage that lasted six hundred years. Wilcox, D.

Voyage to Sfanomoë. Smith, C. A.

VOYAGES, OCEAN. See Ocean travel

Vries, Peter de. See De Vries, Peter

Vulfarts, M.
  Package tzoress
    Ausubel, N. ed. Treasury of Jewish
    humor

W

W. S. Hartley, L. P.

The **wabbler.** Jenkins, W. F.

Wacky afternoon. Newhouse, E.

Waddell, Richie
  You'd better be right!
    Strang, R. M. and Roberts, R. M. eds.
    Teen-age tales v2

Waddington, Patrick
  Street that got mislaid
    Weaver, R. and James, H. eds. Cana-
    dian short stories

The **wager.** Corkery, D.

WAGERS
  Betting Scotchman
  Chekhov, A. P. The bet
  Clemens, S. L. Celebrated jumping frog
    of Calaveras County
  Corkery, D. The wager
  Dahl, R. Man from the south
  Dahl, R. Taste
  Faulkner, W. Was
  Maugham, W. S. Mr Know-All
  Munro, H. H. Matter of sentiment
  O'Donovan, M. Don Juan (Retired)
  Poe, E. A. Never bet the Devil your head
  Pratt, F. and De Camp, L. S. Ancestral
    amethyst
  Runyon, D. Piece of pie

Wages of synergy. Waldo, E. H.

Wagstaff pearls. Eberhart, M. G.

Wahl, Betty
  Gingerbread
    Gable, M. Sister, ed. Many-colored fleece

Wahoo. Beach, E. L.

Wailing precipice. Bates, R.

WAILING WALL. See Palestine—Jerusalem—20th century

Wait for me. Summers, J. L.

Wait for me downstairs. Woolrich, C.

WAITERS. See Servants—Waiters

The wake. Hicks, M. A.

Wake of Patsy McLaughlin. Farrell, J. T.

Wakefield, Henry W.
Red Lodge
    Carrington, H. ed. Week-end book of ghost stories

Wakefield, Herbert Russell, 1889-
Gorge of the Churels
    Derleth, A. W. ed. Night's yawning peal

Wakefield. Hawthorne, N.

WAKEFULNESS. See Insomnia

Wakelee, Lee
Angela was eighteen
    Stowe, A. comp. It's a date

Waker dreams. Matheson, R.

WAKES. See Funeral rites and ceremonies

Waldeck, Theodore J. 1894-
Evil one
    Fenner, P. R. comp. Elephants, elephants, elephants
Igongo elephants
    Fenner, P. R. comp. Elephants, elephants, elephants

Walden, Amelia Elizabeth
So I'm home again
    American girl (Periodical) Favorite stories

Waldo, Edward Hamilton, 1918-
Bianca's hands
    Waldo, E. H. E pluribus unicorn
Cellmate
    Waldo, E. H. E pluribus unicorn
Chromium helmet
    Jenkins, W. F. ed. Great stories of science fiction
The clinic
    Star science fiction stories, no. 2
Completely automatic
    Conklin, G. ed. Possible worlds of science fiction
Die, Maestro, die!
    Waldo, E. H. E pluribus unicorn
Farewell to Eden
    Derleth, A. W. ed. The outer reaches
Fluffy
    Waldo, E. H. E pluribus unicorn
Golden egg
    Conklin, G. ed. Science-fiction thinking machines
The hurkle is a happy beast
    Best science fiction stories: 1950
    Bleiler, E. F. and Dikty, T. E. eds. Science fiction omnibus: the best science fiction stories, 1949-1950
It wasn't syzygy
    Waldo, E. H. E pluribus unicorn
Martian and the moron
    Derleth, A. W. ed. Worlds of tomorrow
Memory
    Crossen, K. F. ed. Adventures in tomorrow

Mewhu's jet
    Conklin, G. ed. Big book of science fiction
Minority report
    Derleth, A. W. ed. Beyond time & space
Mr Costello, hero
    Pohl, F. ed. Assignment in tomorrow
The music
    Waldo, E. H. E pluribus unicorn
Never underestimate. . .
    Conklin, G. ed. Omnibus of science fiction
Perfect host
    Merril, J. ed. Beyond human ken
Professor's teddy-bear
    Waldo, E. H. E pluribus unicorn
Rule of three
    Galaxy science fiction magazine. Galaxy reader of science fiction
Saucer of loneliness
    Galaxy science fiction magazine. Second Galaxy reader of science fiction
    Waldo, E. H. E pluribus unicorn
Scars
    Waldo, E. H. E pluribus unicorn
Sex opposite
    Waldo, E. H. E pluribus unicorn
Shottle Bop
    Conklin, G. and Conklin, L. T. eds. Supernatural reader
The silken-swift
    Waldo, E. H. E pluribus unicorn
Stars are the Styx
    Galaxy science fiction magazine. Galaxy reader of science fiction
Thunder and roses
    Astounding science fiction (Periodical) Astounding science fiction anthology
Tiny and the monster
    Conklin, G. ed. Invaders of earth
Unite and conquer
    Greenberg, M. ed. Journey to infinity
Wages of synergy
    Startling stories (Periodical) Best from Startling stories
Way of thinking
    Waldo, E. H. E pluribus unicorn
What dead men tell
    Bleiler, E. F. and Dikty, T. E. eds. Imagination unlimited
World well lost
    Waldo, E. H. E pluribus unicorn
Yesterday was Monday
    Conklin, G. ed. Science-fiction adventures in dimension

Waldron, D.
Evensong
    Best American short stories, 1952

Waldron, Webb, 1883-1945
If Lincoln had yielded
    Jones, K. M. ed. New Confederate short stories

WALES
Davies, R. Boy with a trumpet, and other selected short stories; 20 stories

Farm life
    See Farm life—Wales

Walk for me. Blackburn, E. R.

Walk in the dark. Clarke, A. C.

Walker, Augusta
Day of the cipher
Prize stories, 1954

Walker, David Harry, 1911-
Bait for a tiger
Saturday evening post (Periodical)
Saturday evening post stories, 1952

Walker, Turnley, 1913-
Wonderful automobile
Story (Periodical) Story; no. 1

WALKING
Bowen, E. Human habitation
Keller, D. H. Revolt of the pedestrians
Saroyan, W. Leaf thief
See also Hitchhikers

Walking corpse. Lipman, C. and Lipman, M.

Walking wounded. Shaw, I.

Wall, John W.
Calmahain
Wall, J. W. Ringstones, and other curious tales
Capra
Wall, J. W. Ringstones, and other curious tales
Christmas story
Wall, J. W. Ringstones, and other curious tales
The Khan
Wall, J. W. Ringstones, and other curious tales
Ringstones
Wall, J. W. Ringstones, and other curious tales

The **wall**. Sartre, J. P.

Wall around the world. Cogswell, T. R.

Wall of darkness. Clarke, A. C.

Wall of dust. Tennyson, H.

Wall of fire. Kirkland, J.

Wallace, F. L.
Student body
Galaxy science fiction magazine. Second Galaxy reader of science fiction

Wallace, John F.
Bound for the bottom
Argosy (Periodical) Argosy Book of sea stories
Jonah curse
Argosy (Periodical) Argosy Book of sea stories

Wallace, Robert
Secret weapon of Joe Smith
Prize stories, 1954

Wallace, W. J.
Dead run
Best detective stories of the year—1954

WALLS
Bradbury, R. Golden kite, the silver wind

Wally. Auchincloss, L.

Walnut hunt. Caldwell, E.

Walpole, Sir Hugh, 1885-1941
The life and death of a crisis
Brentano, F. ed. The word lives on
Mr Huffam
Lohan, R. and Lohan, M. eds. New Christmas treasury
Mr Oddy
Cerf, B. A. and Moriarty, H. C. eds. Anthology of famous British stories

WALRUSES
Roberts, Sir C. G. D. Mothers of the north

Walsh, Maurice, 1879-
The bonesetter
Walsh, M. Son of a tinker
Butcher to the queen
Walsh, M. Son of a tinker
Come back, my love
Saturday evening post (Periodical)
Saturday evening post stories, 1953
Walsh, M. Take your choice
A dialogue
Walsh, M. Son of a tinker
Heather wine
Walsh, M. Son of a tinker
Honest fisherman
Walsh, M. Take your choice
Mission sermon
Walsh, M. Son of a tinker
My fey lady
Walsh, M. Son of a tinker
Not my story
Walsh, M. Son of a tinker
Prudent man
Walsh, M. Son of a tinker
Quiet man
Walsh, M. Take your choice
Son of a tinker
Walsh, M. Son of a tinker
Sword of Yung Lo
Walsh, M. Take your choice
Take your choice
Walsh, M. Take your choice
Thomasheen James and the dictation machine
Walsh, M. Take your choice
Thomasheen James goes to the dogs
Walsh, M. Take your choice

Walsh, Thomas, 1908-
Blonde nurse
Mystery Writers of America, inc. Butcher, baker, murder-maker

Waltari, Mika Toimi, 1908-
Before the twilight of the gods
Waltari, M. T. Moonscape, and other stories
Goldilocks
Waltari, M. T. Moonscape, and other stories
Island of ice
Waltari, M. T. Moonscape, and other stories
Moonscape
Waltari, M. T. Moonscape, and other stories
Tie from Paris
Waltari, M. T. Moonscape, and other stories

Walterson. Tarkington, B.

Walton, Harry
Episode on Dhee Minor
Greenberg, M. ed. Travelers of space
Schedule
Greenberg, M. ed. Men against the stars

Wan Lee, the pagan. Harte, B.

Wanderer. Boyle, K.

The **wanderers.** Welty, E.

Wandering Gentile. Forester, C. S.

Watching baseball. Benchley, R. C.

The watchman. Van Doren, M.

WATCHMEN
O'Donovan, M. Eternal triangle
Van Doren, M. I, Tobit

Water broncs. Douglas, J. S.

Water bug. Coombs, C. I.

Water canteen. Arico, V.

Water ghost of Harrowby Hall. Bangs, J. K.

The water hen. O'Flaherty, L.

Water hole. Haycox, E.

Water is for washing. Heinlein, R. A.

WATERMELONS
Upshaw, H. The harvest

The waters of Bethesda. Bauer, F. A. M.

Waters of Manitou. Gulick, G. C.

Waters of Shiloah. Cohn, E.

WATERSPOUTS
Holland, R. S. Cobra's hood

Watkins, Richard Howells
Offshore
Bluebook (Periodical) Best sea stories from Bluebook

Watson, John, 1850-1907
His mother's sermon
Brentano, F. ed. The word lives on
Neider, C. ed. Men of the high calling
Story of Dr MacLure
Cerf, B. A. and Moriarty, H. C. eds. Anthology of famous British stories

Watson, John Cherry, 1909-
Benny and the Tar-Baby
Peery, W. W. ed. 21 Texas short stories

Waugh, Alec, 1898-
Wed, my darling daughter
This week magazine. This week's short-short stories

Waugh, Evelyn, 1903-
Bella Fleace gave a party
Cerf, B. A. and Moriarty, H. C. eds. Anthology of famous British stories
Waugh, E. Tactical exercise
Cruise
Waugh, E. Tactical exercise
Curse of the horse race
Waugh, E. Tactical exercise
Englishman's home
Waugh, E. Tactical exercise
Excursion in reality
Waugh, E. Tactical exercise
Love among the ruins
Waugh, E. Tactical exercise
Mr Loveday's little outing
Waugh, E. Tactical exercise
On guard
Waugh, E. Tactical exercise
Period piece
Waugh, E. Tactical exercise
Tactical exercise
Waugh, E. Tactical exercise
Winner takes all
Waugh, E. Tactical exercise
Work suspended
Waugh, E. Tactical exercise

Wave of Osiris. Lagerkvist, P. F.

The waveries. Brown, F.

WAX MUSEUMS. See Waxworks

The waxwork. Burrage, A. M.

WAXWORKS
Burrage, A. M. The waxwork

Way of a man. Grau, S. A.

Way of a traitor. Greenfield, R.

Way of all fish. Wylie, P.

Way of escape. Temple, W. F.

Way of thinking. Waldo, E. H.

Way out in the continuum. Richardson, M. L.

Way to the dairy. Munro, H. H.

Way with women. Steele, W. D.

Way you'll never be. Hemingway, E.

Wayfaring strangers. Tucker, W.

"We also walk dogs." Heinlein, R. A.

We are looking at you, Agnes. Caldwell, E.

We don't know. De Vries, P.

We don't want any trouble. Schmitz, J. H.

We kill people. Kuttner, H.

We the people. Moore, W.

We, too, are bidden. Broun, H. C.

We were just having fun. Herbert, F. H.

We won't be needing you, Al. Young, S.

WEALTH
Auchincloss, L. Finish, good lady
Balchin, N. Now we are broke, my dear
Fitzgerald, F. S. K. Diamond as big as the Ritz
Fitzgerald, F. S. K. Rich boy
Graham, M. C. Face of the poor
Porter, W. S. Mammon and the archer
Porter, W. S. Trimmed lamp
Steinberg, Y. Reb Anshel the golden
Zevin, I. J. Nogid's luck

Weaning of Laura Wade. Hayes, N.

The weapon. Brown, F.

WEAPONS. See Arms and armor

Weary hour. Mann, T.

Weary Willie. Miers, E. S.

WEATHER
Van Doren, M. Great deal of weather
Wollheim, D. A. Storm warning

Weaver, John Downing, 1912-
Second table
Collier's, the national weekly. Collier's best

Webb, Richard Wilson, and Wheeler, Hugh Callingham. See Quentin, Patrick, pseud.

Webber, Everett M.
Passage to Kentucky
Argosy (Periodical) Argosy Book of adventure stories

Weber, Lenora (Mattingly) 1895-
Christmas thaw
American girl (Periodical) Christmas all year 'round
American girl (Periodical) On my honor

WEBSTER, DANIEL, 1782-1852
Benét, S. V. Devil and Daniel Webster

Wechsberg, Joseph, 1907-
New York is full of girls
Esquire (Periodical) Girls from Esquire

Wed, my darling daughter. Waugh, A.

The **wedding.** Matheson, R.

The **wedding.** O'Flaherty, L.

Wedding. Sansom, W.

WEDDING ANNIVERSARIES
Aiken, C. P. The anniversary
Aldrich, B. S. Will the romance be the same?
Suckow, R. Golden wedding

Wedding at Cushing's Fort. Hendryx, J. B.

Wedding bells will ring so merrily. Farrell, J. T.

Wedding chest. Paget, V.

WEDDING CHESTS. See Hope chests

Wedding dance. Daguio, A. T.

Wedding ring. Van Dyke, H.

WEDDINGS
Babel', I. E. The King
Caldwell, E. Over the Green Mountains
Fitzgerald, F. S. K. Stories of F. Scott Fitzgerald
Schmitz, E. Generous wine
Schorr, Z. The appraisal
Spector, M. Meal for the poor
Spector, M. Strike of the Schnorrers

Sweden
Lagerkvist, P. F. Marriage feast

Wedekind, Frank, 1864-1918
Burning of Egliswyl
Lange, V. ed. Great German short novels and stories

The **weeds.** McCarthy, M. T.

Week end at Grimsby. Gellhorn, M. E.

Week of roses. Wesley, D.

Weekend at Grimsby. Gellhorn, M. E.

Weeks, Edward, 1898-
Mickey
Harper, W. comp. Dog show

Weeks, Jack
Summer's ending
Collier's, the national weekly. Collier's best

Weeks, Raymond, 1863-1954
Arkansas
Certner, S. and Henry, G. H. eds. Short stories for our times
Cooper, A. C. ed. Modern short stories
Brigands in Snuggletop Woods
Fenner, P. R. comp. Fun! Fun! Fun!
Mosquitoes of Arkansas
Fenner, P. R. comp. Fun! Fun! Fun!
Revenue Charlie
Fenner, P. R. comp. Fun! Fun! Fun!

Weep no more, My Lady. Street, J. H.

Weesperstraat. Praag, S. E. van

Weichert, Ernst
The mother
Fremantle, A. J. ed. Mothers

Weidman, Jerome, 1913-
The Kinnehórrah
Ribalow, H. U. ed. This land, these people
Man inside
This week magazine. This week's short-short stories

Weight of command. Haycox, E.

Weight of the sky. Sullivan, R.

Weinbaum, Stanley Grauman, 1902-1935
Lotus eaters
Derleth, A. W. ed. Beyond time & space
Martian odyssey
Margulies, L. and Friend, O. J. eds. From off this world
Parasite planet
Wollheim, D. A. comp. Flight into space
Valley of dreams
Margulies, L. and Friend, O. J. eds. From off this world

Weirwood marsh. Peattie, D. C. and Peattie, L. R.

Weiss, Ernst, 1884-1940
Cardiac suture
Pick, R. ed. German stories and tales

Weissenberg, Isaac Meier, 1881-1937
Father and the boys
Howe, I. and Greenberg, E. eds. Treasury of Yiddish stories
Mazel tov
Howe, I. and Greenberg, E. eds. Treasury of Yiddish stories

Welch, Denton
Judas tree
New writing (Periodical) Best stories
When I was thirteen
Cory, D. W. pseud. comp. 21 variations on a theme

Welch, Douglas, 1906-
Mrs Union Station
Moskowitz, S. ed. Great railroad stories of the world

Welcome home. Doty, W. L.

Welcome home, Hal! Aldrich, B. S.

We'll always have Christmas. Wuorio, E.-L.

Well, I'm blowed. Selver, P.

Well of angel. Lewis, M.

Well of the star. Goudge, E.

Well-oiled machine. Fyfe, H. B.

Well, that's that. Farrell, J. T.

Wellman, Manly Wade, 1905-
Desrick on Yandro
Magazine of fantasy and science fiction. Best from Fantasy and science fiction; 2d ser.
Dhoh
Derleth, A. W. ed. Night's yawning peal
Island in the sky
Margulies, L. and Friend, O. J. eds. Giant anthology of science fiction
Men against the stars
Greenberg, M. ed. Men against the stars
Tall Bram of Little Pigeon
Boys' life (Periodical) Boys' life Adventure stories
Vandy, Vandy
Magazine of fantasy and science fiction. Best from Fantasy and science fiction; 3d ser.
Where angels fear
Davenport, B. ed. Ghostly tales to be told

Wells, Herbert George, 1886-1946
Æpyornis Island
    Wells, H. G. 28 science fiction stories
Argonauts of the air
    Wells, H. G. 28 science fiction stories
Country of the blind
    Cerf, B. A. and Moriarty, H. C. eds.
      Anthology of famous British stories
    Stauffer, R. M.; Cunningham, W. H.
      and Sullivan, C. J. eds. Adventures
      in modern literature
    Wells, H. G. 28 science fiction stories
Crystal egg
    Wells, H. G. 28 science fiction stories
Dream of Armageddon
    Wells, H. G. 28 science fiction stories
Empire of the ants
    Wells, H. G. 28 science fiction stories
Filmer
    Wells, H. G. 28 science fiction stories
In the abyss
    Wells, H. G. 28 science fiction stories
In the Avu observatory
    Wells, H. G. 28 science fiction stories
Inexperienced ghost
    Christ, H. I. and Shostak, J. eds. Short
      stories
Land ironclads
    Wells, H. G. 28 science fiction stories
Late Mr Elvesham
    Wells, H. G. 28 science fiction stories
Little mother up the Mörderberg
    Talbot, D. ed. Treasury of mountain-
      eering stories
Magic shop
    Wells, H. G. 28 science fiction stories
Man who could work miracles
    Schramm, W. L. ed. Great short stories
    Wells, H. G. 28 science fiction stories
Mr Brisher's treasure
    Queen, E. pseud. ed. Literature of
      crime
Mr Britling writes until sunrise
    Brentano, F. ed. The word lives on
New accelerator
    Derleth, A. W. ed. Beyond time &
      space
    Wells, H. G. 28 science fiction stories
The Plattner story
    Wells, H. G. 28 science fiction stories
Remarkable case of Davidson's eyes
    Wells, H. G. 28 science fiction stories
Sea raiders
    Wells, H. G. 28 science fiction stories
The star
    Kuebler, H. W. ed. Treasury of science
      fiction classics
    Wells, H. G. 28 science fiction stories
Star begotten
    Wells, H. G. 28 science fiction stories
Stolen bacillus
    Wells, H. G. 28 science fiction stories
Stolen body
    Wells, H. G. 28 science fiction stories
Story of the days to come
    Wells, H. G. 28 science fiction stories
Story of the stone age
    Wells, H. G. 28 science fiction stories
Strange orchid
    Wells, H. G. 28 science fiction stories
Time machine
    Kuebler, H. W. ed. Treasury of science
      fiction classics

Truth about Pyecraft
    Wells, H. G. 28 science fiction stories
Under the knife
    Wells, H. G. 28 science fiction stories
Valley of spiders
    Wells, H. G. 28 science fiction stories

Wells, John, pseud. See Kaplan, Alvin
    Harold

WELLS
Van Doren, M. Valley of great wells

WELSH FARM LIFE. See Farm life—
    Wales

Welshimer, Helen, 1901-
Father comes home
    Elmquist, R. M. ed. Fifty years of
      Christmas

Welty, Eudora, 1909-
Asphodel
    Welty, E. Selected stories
At the landing
    Welty, E. Selected stories
The burning
    Davis, R. G. ed. Ten modern masters
    Prize stories of 1951
Clytie
    Welty, E. Selected stories
Curtain of green
    Best of the Best American short stories,
      1915-1950
    Welty, E. Selected stories
Death of a travelling salesman
    Schorer, M. ed. The story
    Waite, H. O. and Atkinson, B. P. eds.
      Literature for our time
    Welty, E. Selected stories
First love
    Lynskey, W. C. ed. Reading modern
      fiction
    Welty, E. Selected stories
Flowers for Marjorie
    Welty, E. Selected stories
The hitch-hikers
    Burrell, J. A. and Cerf, B. A. eds. An-
      thology of famous American stories
    Welty, E. Selected stories
June recital
    Welty, E. Golden apples
Keela, the Outcast Indian Maiden
    Ludwig, J. B. and Poirier, W. R. eds.
      Stories, British and American
    Welty, E. Selected stories
The key
    Welty, E. Selected stories
Lily Daw and the three ladies
    Welty, E. Selected stories
Livvie
    Welty, E. Selected stories
    Same as: Livvie is back
Livvie is back
    First-prize stories, 1919-1954
    Greene, J. L. and Abell, E. eds. Stories
      of sudden truth
    Same as: Livvie
A memory
    Ludwig, J. B. and Poirier, W. R. eds.
      Stories, British and American
    Welty, E. Selected stories
Moon Lake
    Welty, E. Golden apples
Music from Spain
    Welty, E. Golden apples

Welty, Eudora—*Continued*
Old Mr Marblehall
  Welty, E. Selected stories
Petrified man
  Davis, R. G. ed. Ten modern masters
  Millett, F. B. ed. Reading fiction
  Southern review. Anthology of stories
    from the Southern review
  Welty, E. Selected stories
Piece of news
  Welty, E. Selected stories
Powerhouse
  Welty, E. Selected stories
  West, R. B. and Stallman, R. W. eds.
    Art of modern fiction
Purple hat
  Welty, E. Selected stories
Shower of gold
  Felheim, M.; Newman, F. B. and Stein-
    hoff, W. R. eds. Modern short stories
  Welty, E. Golden apples
Sir Rabbit
  Welty, E. Golden apples
Still moment
  Welty, E. Selected stories
Visit of charity
  Welty, E. Selected stories
The wanderers
  Welty, E. Golden apples
The whistle
  Welty, E. Selected stories
Whole world knows
  Welty, E. Golden apples
Why I live at the P.O.
  Gordon, C. and Tate, A. eds. House of
    fiction
  Welty, E. Selected stories
Wide net
  First-prize stories, 1919-1954
  Welty, E. Selected stories
The winds
  Welty, E. Selected stories
Worn path
  Barrows, H. ed. 15 stories
  Davis, R. G. ed. Ten modern masters
  Heilman, R. B. ed. Modern short
    stories
  Welty, E. Selected stories
The **Wendigo**. Blackwood, A.
Wendroff, Zalman, 1879-
The gramophone
  Ausubel, N. ed. Treasury of Jewish
    humor
Statistics
  Ausubel, N. ed. Treasury of Jewish
    humor
Two pleasures
  Ausubel, N. ed. Treasury of Jewish
    humor

Wendrowsky, Zalman. See Wendroff, Zalman

Weren't you ever young! Summers, J. L.
WEREWOLVES. See Werwolves
Werfel, Franz V. 1890-1945
Jeremiah: the voice without and within
  Selden, R. ed. Ways of God and men
Saverio's secret
  Leftwich, J. ed. Yisröel. 1952 ed.
Third commandment
  Neider, C. ed. Men of the high calling
  Same as: Thou shalt not take the name
    of the Lord thy God in vain

Wertenbaker, Green Peyton, 1907-
Ship that turned aside
  Conklin, G. ed. Big book of science
    fiction
WERWOLVES
  Kipling, R. Mark of the beast
  Munro, H. H. Gabriel-Ernest
  Munro, H. H. She-wolf
  Rice, J. The refugee
  White, W. A. P. Compleat werewolf
Wesley, Donald, 1922-
Week of roses
  Best American short stories, 1953
West, Anne
Pulpit for Don
  Lantz, J. E. ed. Stories of Christian
    living
Wonder in Willow Hill
  Lantz, J. E. ed. Stories of Christian
    living
West, Cy
Smoke ball kid
  Owen, F. ed. Teen-age victory parade
West, Jessamyn
Battle of Finney's Ford
  Greene, J. I. and Abell, E. eds. Stories
    of sudden truth
Breach of promise
  Abell, E. ed. American accent
  Prize stories, 1954
Child's day
  Swallow, A. ed. Anchor in the sea
Homer and the lilies
  Thinker's digest (Periodical) Spoiled
    priest, and other stories
Horace Chooncy, M.D.
  Stegner, W. E.; Scowcroft, R. and Ilyin,
    B. eds. Writer's art
The illumination
  Brentano, F. ed. The word lives on
  Thinker's digest (Periodical) Spoiled
    priest, and other stories
Lead her like a pigeon
  Thinker's digest (Periodical) Spoiled
    priest, and other stories
Shivaree before breakfast
  Heilman, R. B. ed. Modern short
    stories
West, Michael Philip
Hector
  Derleth, A. W. ed. Night's yawning
    peal
West, Ray Benedict, 1908-
The ascent
  Talbot, D. ed. Treasury of mountain-
    eering stories
Last of the grizzly bears
  Best American short stories, 1951
West, Wallace
Sculptors of life
  Conklin, G. ed. Science-fiction thinking
    machines
THE WEST
  Harte, B. Bret Harte's stories of the old
    West; 11 stories
  Harte, B. Outcasts of Poker Flat
  Johnson, D. M. Indian country; 11 stories
  Schubert, P. White Elk
    See also Western stories

    Farm life
    See Farm life—The West

Westbrock, John T. 1918-
  Private hell
    American vanguard, 1950
Western islands. Masefield, J.
WESTERN STORIES
  Brand, M. pseud. Wine on the desert
  DeVries, M. Stage to Yuma
  Haycox, E. By rope and lead; 9 stories
  Haycox, E. Outlaw; 10 stories
  Haycox, E. Pioneer loves; 9 stories
  Haycox, E. Rough justice; 9 stories
  Hendryx, J. B. Intrigue on Halfaday
    Creek; 28 stories
  Hendryx, J. B. Murder on Halfaday
    Creek; 30 stories
  Meredith, S. ed. Bar 1 roundup of best
    western stories; 12 stories
  Meredith, S. ed. Bar 2; 12 stories
  Meredith, S. ed. Bar 3; 11 stories
  O'Rourke, F. Ride west; 11 stories
  Porter, W. S. Hearts and crosses
  Schaefer, J. W. Big range; 10 stories
  Thompson, T. They brought their guns;
    11 stories
  Western Writers of America. Bad men
    and good; 14 stories
  Western Writers of America. Holsters
    and heroes; 12 stories
      See also Cowboys; Ranch life

Westfield House. Miller, C.

Westmacott, Mary, pseud. See Christie,
  Agatha (Miller)

Weston, Christine (Goutiere) 1904-
  Forest of the night
    Best American short stories, 1953
  Loud sing cuckoo
    Best American short stories, 1952
  Man in gray
    Best American short stories, 1954
  Second pasture
    Collier's, the national weekly. Collier's
    best

Wet Saturday. Collier, J.

Wetjen, Albert Richard, 1900-1948
  Ship of silence
    Bluebook (Periodical) Best sea stories
    from Bluebook

Wexler, Jerry, 1917-
  I am Edgar
    Story (Periodical) Story; no. 2

Whaler 'round the Horn. Meader, S. W.
WHALES
  Davies, W. M. Battle with a whale
WHALING
  Carmer, C. L. Mr Sims and Henry
  Davies, W. M. Battle with a whale
  Marmur, J. Below Cape Horn
  Meader, S. W. Whaler 'round the Horn
      See also Sea stories
The wharf. De La Mare, W. J.

Wharton, Edith Newbold (Jones) 1862-
  1937
  After Holbein
    Wharton, E. N. J. Edith Wharton
    treasury
  Autre temps
    Wharton, E. N. J. Edith Wharton
    treasury

Bottle of Perrier
  Wharton, E. N. J. Edith Wharton
  treasury
Bunner sisters
  Wharton, E. N. J. Edith Wharton
  treasury
The choice
  Foerster, N. ed. American poetry and
  prose. 1952 ed.
Lady's maid's bell
  Wharton, E. N. J. Edith Wharton
  treasury
Madame de Treymes
  Scribner treasury
  Wharton, E. N. J. Edith Wharton
  treasury
Mission of Jane
  Burrell, J. A. and Cerf, B. A. eds. An-
  thology of famous American stories
Moving finger
  Wharton, E. N. J. Edith Wharton
  treasury
Old maid
  Wharton, E. N. J. Edith Wharton
  treasury
Other two
  Wharton, E. N. J. Edith Wharton
  treasury
Roman fever
  Wharton, E. N. J. Edith Wharton
  treasury
Xingu
  Wharton, E. N. J. Edith Wharton
  treasury
What Christmas brought the stranger.
  Sangster, M. E.
What dead men tell. Waldo, E. H.
What do hippos eat? Wilson, A.
What do you do? Newhouse, E.
What does she see when she shuts her eyes.
  eyes. Stein, G.
What happened to Alanna. Norris, K. T.
What have I done? Clifton, M.
What if. . . Asimov, I.
What is a miracle? Komroff, M.
What is rape? Willingham, C.
What John Rance had to tell. Doyle, Sir
  A. C.
What price genius. Schneider, G. W.
"What so proudly we hail. . ." Keene, D.
What thin partitions. Clifton, M. and Apos-
  tolides, A.
What time is it? Elam, R. M.
What Vasile saw. Marie, consort of Ferdi-
  nand I, King of Rumania
What we don't know hurts us. Schorer, M.
What you hear from 'em? Taylor, P. H.
What you need. Kuttner, H.
"What you want." Porter, W. S.
Whatever happened to Corporal Cuckoo?
  Pohl, F. ed.
What's in a corner. Horton, P.
What's in two names. Hutchins, M. P. M.
What's it like out there? Hamilton, E.
WHEAT
  Norris, F. Deal in wheat
Wheel of time. Arthur, R.

Wheeler, Hugh Callingham. See Quentin, Patrick, pseud.

When boyhood dreams come true. Farrell, J. T.

When Dan came home. Grimson, M. S.

When day is done. Cawley, C. C.

When I was thirteen. Welch, D.

"When in doubt—wash." Gallico, P. W.

When in Rome— James, W.

When mountain men make peace. Stuart, J.

When Riga was evacuated. Bergengruen, W.

When Santa helped. Eggleston, M. W.

When shadows fall. Hubbard, L. R.

When the aliens left. Meyer, E. L.

When the bough breaks. Kuttner, H.

When the earth lived. Kuttner, H.

When the green star waned. Dyalhis, N.

When the light gets green. Warren, R. P.

When the night wind howls. Pratt, F. and De Camp, L. S.

"When the season cometh round." Yaffe, J.

"When time who steals our years away!" Buckingham, N.

When titans meet. Schneider, G. W.

When TV came to the backwoods. Grimson, M. S.

When worlds collide. Balmer, E. and Wylie, P.

When you blow on a dandelion. Scheffrin, G. R.

Where angels fear. Wellman, M. W.

Where angels fear to tread. Palmer, S.

Where are your guns? Fast, H. M.

Where beauty lies. Irwin, M. E. F.

Where did yesterday go? Angoff, C.

Where early fa's the dew. Gilpatric, G.

Where falls not hail. Ready, W. B.

Where Teetee Wood lies cold and dead. Chapman, W.

Where the girls were different. Caldwell, E.

Where the grass, they say, is blue. McNulty, J.

Where their fire is not quenched. Sinclair, M.

"Where to, please?" Pratt, F. and De Camp, L. S.

While the auto waits. Porter, W. S.

WHIMSICAL STORIES. See Fantasies

Whinery, Marion. See Casey, Marian (Whinery)

The whip-poor-will. Thurber, J.

The whipping. Noland, F.

Whippletree. O'Rourke, F.

Whirligig of life. Porter, W. S.

WHIRLPOOLS
Poe, E. A. Descent into the maelström

The whistle. Doremus, J.

The whistle. Welty, E.

Whistle and the heroes. Wilner, H.

Whistler, Laurence, 1912-
Captain Dalgety returns
Asquith, Lady C. M. E. C. ed. Book of modern ghosts

Whistling Dick's Christmas stocking. Porter, W. S.

White, Antonia, 1901-
Moment of truth
Horizon (Periodical) Golden Horizon

White, Edward Lucas, 1866-1934
House of the nightmare
Davenport, B. ed. Ghostly tales to be told

White, Helen Constance, 1896-
Francis cures the leper
Thinker's digest (Periodical) Spoiled priest, and other stories
That mighty contact
Thinker's digest (Periodical) Spoiled priest, and other stories
Watch in the night
Thinker's digest (Periodical) Spoiled priest, and other stories

White, Leslie Turner, 1903-
Bayou bait
Argosy (Periodical) Argosy Book of sea stories

White, Milton
To remember these things
Lass, A. H. and Horowitz, A. eds. Stories for youth
Yellow turtleneck sweater
Seventeen (Periodical) Nineteen from Seventeen
Stanford short stories, 1950

White, Robb, 1909-
Conflict is joined
Boys' life (Periodical) Boys' life Adventure stories
Dog in the double bottoms
Furman, A. L. ed. Teen-age dog stories
An eye for an eye
Furman, A. L. ed. Teen-age sea stories
Pot Likker's first fox hunt
Fenner, P. R. comp. Dogs, dogs, dogs
Sick bay to sea wall
American boy (Periodical) American boy anthology

White, Stewart Edward, 1873-1946
Climbing for goats
Talbot, D. ed. Treasury of mountaineering stories
On lying awake at night
Andrews, R. C. ed. My favorite stories of the great outdoors

White, Will
Over there
Hathaway, B. and Sessions, J. A. eds. Writers for tomorrow. 2d ser.
Too big a dream
Hathaway, B. and Sessions, J. A. eds. Writers for tomorrow. 2d ser.

White, William Anthony Parker, 1911-
The ambassadors
Crossen, K. F. Future tense
Anomaly of the empty man
Mystery Writers of America, inc. Crooks' tour
Chronokinesis of Jonathan Hull
Jenkins, W. F. ed. Great stories of science fiction
Compleat werewolf
Merril, J. ed. Beyond human ken
Conquest
Star science fiction stories, no. 2

WIDOWERS
Betts, D. End of Henry Fribble
McNulty, J. Television helps, but not very much
Maugham, W. S. The dream
Verga, G. The orphans

WIDOWS
Aiken, C. P. Spider, spider
Benson, T. Bones of A. T. Stewart
Bowen, E. Requiescat
Breuer, B. Home is a place
Chastity
Chou, S. Benediction
Harte, B. Postmistress of Laurel Run
Horwitz, J. The roof
Kantor, M. Life in her hands
Lincoln, V. E. To live is to return
Maugham, W. S. The escape
Maugham, W. S. Jane
Queen, E. pseud. Three widows
Rasmussen, G. F. Tea at Barnaby's
Steele, W. D. Autumn bloom
Stockton, F. R. Widow's cruise
Taylor, P. H. Dark walk
Winslow, T. S. Lamb chop for the little dog

Widow's cruise. Stockton, F. R.

Widow's peak. O'Rourke, F.

Wiechert, Ernst
The mother
Ungar, F. ed. To mother with love

Wiegand, William, 1928-
Science teacher
Story (Periodical) Story; no. one

Wife of his youth. Chesnutt, C. W.

Wife of Martin Guerre. Lewis, J.

Wife of Nashville. Taylor, P. H.

Wiggin, Kate Douglas (Smith) 1856-1923
The Ruggleses go to the Christmas party
Fenner, P. R. comp. Giggle box

Wilbur, Richard, 1921-
Game of catch
Abell, E. ed. American accent
Prize stories, 1954

Wilby spirit. Willingham, C.

Wilcox, Don
Voyage that lasted six hundred years
Lesser, M. A. ed. Looking forward

WILD ANIMALS. See Animals

WILD BOARS. See Boars

WILD CATS. See Pumas

Wild duck's nest. McLaverty, M.

Wild flower. Babb, S.

Wild flowers. Caldwell, E.

Wild goat's kid. O'Flaherty, L.

Wild goose chase. Millar, K.

Wild hunter. Randall, K. C.

Wild Jack Rhett. Haycox, E.

Wild oranges. Hergesheimer, J.

Wild pitch. Sherman, H. M.

Wild surmise. Kuttner, H. and Moore, C. L.

Wild wet place. Van Doren, M.

WILDCATS. See Pumas

Wilde, Oscar, 1854-1900
Birthday of the Infanta
Cerf, B. A. and Moriarty, H. C. eds. Anthology of famous British stories
Priest and the acolyte
Cory, D. W. pseud. comp. 21 variations on a theme

Wilder, Thornton Niven, 1897-
From a journal-letter of Julius Caesar
Burnett, W. ed. World's best

WILDERNESS. See Outdoor life

The **wilderness.** Bradbury, R.

Wilderness champion. Lippincott, J. W.

Wilderness road. Kjelgaard, J.

Wildy's secret revealer. Anderson, E. V.

Wilkins, Mary E. See Freeman, Mary Eleanor (Wilkins)

Will and a way. Grimson, M. S.

Will o' the mill. Stevenson, R. L.

Will the romance be the same? Aldrich, B. S.

"Will you walk a little faster?" Klass, P.

Willard, Harriet W.
Just for you
American girl (Periodical) On my honor

Wm. Crane. Radford, M.

William Henry VanBuren. Hendryx, J. B.

William the conqueror. Kipling, R.

William Wilson. Poe, E. A.

Williams, Barbara
Hey wait for me
Seventeen (Periodical) Nineteen from Seventeen

Williams, Ben Ames, 1889-1953
Mine enemy's dog
Bloch, M. ed. Favorite dog stories
Sheener
Certner, S. and Henry, G. H. eds. Short stories for our times
Solitude
Grayson, C. ed. Fourth round
They grind exceeding small
Thinker's digest (Periodical) Spoiled priest, and other stories

Williams, Colleen
There will always be hope
Dreer, H. ed. American literature by Negro authors

Williams, Henry Lionel
Gold mine in the sky
Story parade (Periodical) Adventure stories

Williams, James Howard
Elephant intelligence
Fenner, P. R. comp. Elephants, elephants, elephants

Williams, L. B. See Bedford-Jones, H. jt. auth.

Williams, Lawrence, 1915-
Rise of Carthage
Collier's, the national weekly. Collier's best

Williams, Ralph
Emergency landing
Conklin, G. ed. Big book of science fiction

Williams, Ralph—*Continued*
Head hunters
Conklin, G. ed. Omnibus of science fiction
Sloane, W. M. ed. Stories for tomorrow

Williams, Robert E. 1926-
Feminine wiles
Oberfirst, R. ed. 1954 anthology of best original short-shorts

Williams, Robert Moore, 1907-
Castaway
Conklin, G. ed. Invaders of earth
Red death of Mars
Del Rey, L.; Matschat, C. H. and Carmer, C. L. eds. Year after tomorrow
Greenberg, M. ed. Men against the stars
Refuge for tonight
Best science fiction stories: 1950
Bleiler, E. F. and Dikty, T. E. eds. Science fiction omnibus: The best science fiction stories, 1949, 1950
Robots return
Greenberg, M. ed. Robot and the man
The seekers
Wollheim, D. A. comp. Flight into space

Williams, Roger, 1604?-1683
Hawthorne, N. Endicott and the Red Cross

Williams, Tennessee, 1914-
Resemblance between a violin case and a coffin
Best American short stories, 1951
Three players of a summer game
Best American short stories, 1953

Williams, William Carlos, 1883-
Above the river
Williams, W. C. Make light of it
The accident
Williams, W. C. Make light of it
Ancient gentility
Williams, W. C. Make light of it
At the front
Williams, W. C. Make light of it
The buffalos
Williams, W. C. Make light of it
Burden of loveliness
Williams, W. C. Make light of it
Cold world
Williams, W. C. Make light of it
Colored girls of Passenack—old and new
Williams, W. C. Make light of it
Comedy entombed: 1930
Williams, W. C. Make light of it
Country rain
Williams, W. C. Make light of it
Danse pseudomacabre
Williams, W. C. Make light of it
Dawn of another day
Williams, W. C. Make light of it
Descendant of kings
Williams, W. C. Make light of it
Difficult man
Williams, W. C. Make light of it
Face of stone
Williams, W. C. Make light of it
Final embarrassment
Williams, W. C. Make light of it

Four bottles of beer
Williams, W. C. Make light of it
Frankie the newspaperman
Williams, W. C. Make light of it
Girl with a pimply face
Williams, W. C. Make light of it
Good-natured slob
Williams, W. C. Make light of it
Good old days
Williams, W. C. Make light of it
Hands across the sea
Williams, W. C. Make light of it
In northern waters
Williams, W. C. Make light of it
Inquest
Williams, W. C. Make light of it
The insane
Williams, W. C. Make light of it
Jean Beicke
Williams, W. C. Make light of it
Knife of the times
Cory, D. W. pseud. comp. 21 variations on a theme
Williams, W. C. Make light of it
Lena
Williams, W. C. Make light of it
Life along the Passaic River
Williams, W. C. Make light of it
Lucky break
Williams, W. C. Make light of it
Mind and body
Williams, W. C. Make light of it
Night in June
Williams, W. C. Make light of it
No place for a woman
Williams, W. C. Make light of it
Old Doc Rivers
Williams, W. C. Make light of it
Old time raid
Williams, W. C. Make light of it
Pace that kills
Williams, W. C. Make light of it
Paid nurse
Williams, W. C. Make light of it
Pink and blue
Williams, W. C. Make light of it
Red head
Williams, W. C. Make light of it
Right thing
Williams, W. C. Make light of it
Round the world fliers
Williams, W. C. Make light of it
Sailor's son
Williams, W. C. Make light of it
Second marriage
Williams, W. C. Make light of it
To fall asleep
Williams, W. C. Make light of it
Under the greenwood tree
Williams, W. C. Make light of it
Use of force
Greene, J. I. and Abell, E. eds. Stories of sudden truth
Heilman, R. B. ed. Modern short stories
Schorer, M. ed. The story
Williams, W. C. Make light of it
The Venus
Williams, W. C. Make light of it
Verbal transcription: 6 A.M.
Williams, W. C. Make light of it
Visit to the fair
Williams, W. C. Make light of it

Williams, William C.—*Continued*

World's end
  Williams, W. C. Make light of it
The zoo
  Williams, W. C. Make light of it

Williamson, Henry, 1897-
Trapper's mates
  Cerf, B. A. and Moriarty, H. C. eds.
    Anthology of famous British stories

Williamson, Jack, 1908-
Breakdown
  Greenberg, M. ed. Journey to infinity
Crucible of power
  Greenberg, M. comp. Five science fiction novels
Guinevere for everybody
  Star science fiction stories, no. 3
Happiest creature
  Star science fiction stories, no. 2
Hindsight
  Astounding science fiction (Periodical)
    Astounding science fiction anthology
In the scarlet star
  Wollheim, D. A. comp. Every boy's book of science-fiction
Man from outside
  Derleth, A. W. ed. Beachheads in space
  Lesser, M. A. ed. Looking forward
Peddler's nose
  Pohl, F. ed. Assignment in tomorrow
Sun maker
  Margulies, L. and Friend, O. J. eds.
    Giant anthology of science fiction
Through the purple cloud
  Margulies, L. and Friend, O. J. eds.
    From off this world

Willie Collins. Farrell, J. T.

Willie craves action. Hendryx, J. B.

Willingham, Calder, 1922-
Afternoon sun
  Willingham, C. Gates of hell
Bird life
  Willingham, C. Gates of hell
Career of Augurt Nimrodtk
  Willingham, C. Gates of hell
Drop of pure liquid
  Willingham, C. Gates of hell
Eternal rectangle
  Willingham, C. Gates of hell
Eupepsia
  Willingham, C. Gates of hell
Excitement in Ergo
  Willingham, C. Gates of hell
Farewell, hon
  Willingham, C. Gates of hell
Guardian angel
  Willingham, C. Gates of hell
James A. Dukes
  Willingham, C. Gates of hell
Jane
  Willingham, C. Gates of hell
Little Bubo
  Willingham, C. Gates of hell
Little dreams of Mr Morgan
  Willingham, C. Gates of hell
Love on toast
  Willingham, C. Gates of hell
Mathematics of intelligence
  Willingham, C. Gates of hell
Pursuit of gloom
  Willingham, C. Gates of hell

Record of a man
  Willingham, C. Gates of hell
Rupee
  Willingham, C. Gates of hell
Secret journal
  Willingham, C. Gates of hell
Steve and Sarah and Cyril
  Willingham, C. Gates of hell
Sum of two angles
  Willingham, C. Gates of hell
Surface tension of molten metal
  Willingham, C. Gates of hell
Universe is not really expanding
  Willingham, C. Gates of hell
What is rape?
  Willingham, C. Gates of hell
Wilby spirit
  Willingham, C. Gates of hell

Willis, Anthony Armstrong, 1897-
One-way street
  Best detective stories of the year—1953

Willman, Paula
Labyrinth
  Wolfe, D. M. ed. Which grain will grow

The **willow.** Etnier, E. J.

Willow walk. Lewis, S.

Willows. De La Mare, W. J.

WILLS
Bennett, A. Mary with the high hand
Bernstein, H. Greatest funeral in the world
Collins, W. Mr Lepel and the housekeeper
Kneale, M. Putting away of Uncle Quaggin
Lever, C. J. Con Cregan's legacy
Parker, J. R. Estate of Alice V. Gregg

  See also Inheritance and succession

Wilner, Herbert
Whistle and the heroes
  Prize stories, 1954

Wilsey, Russell G. 1928-
For men only
  Wolfe, D. M. ed. Which grain will grow

Wilson, Angus, 1914?-
Christmas Day in the workhouse
  Wilson, A. Such darling dodos and other stories
Heart of elm
  Wilson, A. Such darling dodos and other stories
Learning's little tribute
  Wilson, A. Such darling dodos and other stories
Little companion
  Wilson, A. Such darling dodos and other stories
Mummy to the rescue
  Ludwig, J. B. and Poirier, W. R. eds.
    Stories, British and American
  Wilson, A. Such darling dodos and other stories
Necessity's child
  Wilson, A. Such darling dodos and other stories
Rex imperator
  Wilson, A. Such darling dodos and other stories

Wilson, Angus—*Continued*
Sister superior
Wilson, A. Such darling dodos and other stories
Such darling dodos
Wilson, A. Such darling dodos and other stories
What do hippos eat
Wilson, A. Such darling dodos and other stories

Wilson, Ben
Stand-in
Strang, R. M. and Roberts, R. M. eds. Teen-age tales v2

Wilson, Dorothy (Clarke) 1904-
Priest and prophet at Bethel
Brentano, F. ed. The word lives on

Wilson, Edward
Men from the boys
Stanford short stories, 1951

Wilson, Ethel, 1890-
Hurry, hurry!
Pacey, D. ed. Book of Canadian stories
Mrs Golightly and the first convention
Weaver, R. and James, H. eds. Canadian short stories

Wilson, Harry Leon, 1867-1939
Wrong twin
Davis, C. B. ed. Eyes of boyhood

Wilson, John Walter, 1920-
Grass grow again
Peery, W. W. ed. 21 Texas short stories

Wilson, Leon, 1913-
Not quite Martin
Fenner, P. R. comp. Ghosts, ghosts, ghosts

Wilson, Neill Compton, 1889-
Scandal at Mulford Inn
Saturday evening post (Periodical) Saturday evening post stories, 1952

Wilson, Richard
Back to Julie
Pohl, F. ed. Assignment in tomorrow
Friend of the family
Star science fiction stories, no. 2

Wilson, Robert McNair, 1882-
Cyprian bees
Bond, R. T. ed. Handbook for poisoners

Wilson, Ruth
Too many brides
Mystery Writers of America, inc. Maiden murders

Win the world. Oliver, C.

Wincelberg, Simon, 1924-
The conqueror
Best American short stories, 1953
Honeymoon
Story (Periodical) Story; no. 2

Winchell, Prentice, 1895-
Devil on wheels
Argosy (Periodical) Argosy Book of sports stories
Never come mourning
Mystery Writers of America, inc. Four-&-twenty bloodhounds

WIND. See Winds

Wind and the snow of winter. Clark, W. Van T.
Wind blows. Mansfield, K.
The **windfall**. Caldwell, E.
Windfall. Sanford, W. M.
WINDOW DRESSING. See Show windows
WINDOWS
Dunsany, E. J. M. D. P. 18th baron. Wonderful window
The **windows**. Sansom, W.
WINDS
Mansfield, K. Wind blows
The **winds**. Welty, E.
Winds of heaven. Jefferies, R.
WINE AND WINE MAKING
Daudet, A. Father Gaucher's elixir
De Vries, P. Life among the winesaps
Walsh, M. Heather wine
Wine of one day. Neiman, S.
Wine on the desert. Brand, M. pseud.
Wing walker. Gilpatric, G.
Winged feet. Robinson, G.
Wingless victory. Heard, G.
Wings. Clemens, S. L.
Wings of an angel. Kaufman, W.
Wings of night. Del Rey, L.

Winn, Josephine
Hungry sister
Abell, E. ed. American accent

The **winner**. Chute, B. J.
Winner lose all. Kuttner, H.
Winner take all. Rocklynne, R.
Winner takes all. Waugh, E.
Winner's money. Litten, F. N.
Winning pitcher. Worthington, J.
Winning sequence. Sharp, M.

Winslow, Anne (Goodwin)
Seasmiles
Prize stories of 1950

Winslow, Thyra (Samter) 1893-
The actress
Winslow, T. S. Sex without sentiment
Angie Lee's fortune
Winslow, T. S. Sex without sentiment
Bronzes of Martel Greer
Winslow, T. S. Sex without sentiment
Cycle of Manhattan
Burrell, J. A. and Cerf, B. A. eds. Anthology of famous American stories
Ribalow, H. U. ed. These your children
Dear Sister Sadie
Winslow, T. S. Sex without sentiment
Fur flies
Winslow, T. S. Sex without sentiment
Girls in black
Winslow, T. S. Sex without sentiment
Grandma
Leftwich, J. ed. Yisröel. 1952 ed.
Ungar, F. ed. To mother with love
Hotel dog
Winslow, T. S. Sex without sentiment

Winslow, Thyra S.—*Continued*
Interview
Winslow, T. S. Sex without sentiment
Lamb chop for the little dog
Winslow, T. S. Sex without sentiment
Misses Grant
Winslow, T. S. Sex without sentiment
Mrs Wilson's husband goes for a swim
Winslow, T. S. Sex without sentiment
More like sisters
Winslow, T. S. Sex without sentiment
Obsession
Winslow, T. S. Sex without sentiment
Odd old lady
Winslow, T. S. Sex without sentiment
Other woman
Winslow, T. S. Sex without sentiment
Rudolph
Winslow, T. S. Sex without sentiment
Sophie Jackson
Winslow, T. S. Sex without sentiment
Technique
Winslow, T. S. Sex without sentiment

Winston, Harry
Greater love
Ford, N. A. and Faggett, H. L. eds.
Best short stories by Afro-American
writers (1925-1950)
Life begins at forty
Ford, N. A. and Faggett, H. L. eds.
Best short stories by Afro-American
writers (1925-1950)

Winter, Arthur B.
Party dress
Oberfirst, R. ed. 1954 anthology of best
original short-shorts

Winter, J. A.
Expedition polychrome
Norton, A. M. ed. Space service

WINTER
Clark, W. Van T. Wind and the snow of
winter
Enright, E. Temperate zone
Thoreau, H. D. Winter at Walden

Winter at Walden. Thoreau, H. D.

Winter cruise. Maugham, W. S.

Winter detail. Denicoff, M.

Winter dreams. Fitzgerald, F. S. K.

Winter in July. Lessing, D. M.

Winter months in a cow camp. James, W.

Winter of his life. Patten, L. B.

Winterbotham, Russell Robert, 1904-
Fourth dynasty
Conklin, G. ed. Omnibus of science fic-
tion

Winters, Emmanuel, pseud. See Horowitz,
Emmanuel

Winters, Yvor, 1900-
Brink of darkness
Swallow, A. ed. Anchor in the sea

Winter's tale. Stafford, J.

Wire brush. Treat, L. and Tarachow, S.

'Wireless.' Kipling, R.

WISCONSIN
19th century
Garland, H. Return of a private

WISCONSIN POLITICS. See Politics—
Wisconsin

WISE MEN. See Magi

Wise men of Holmola. Bowman, J. C. and
Bianco, M. W.

Wise men of Trehenna. Locke, W. J.

The wish. Dahl, R.

Wish book. Milburn, G.

WISHES
Rossiter, H. D. How dear to my heart

The wishbone. Macauley, R.

Wister, Owen, 1860-1938
Journey in search of Christmas
Lohan, R. and Lohan, M. eds. New
Christmas treasury

WIT AND HUMOR. See Humor

The witch. Gold, H.

Witch doctor. Fisher, D. F. C.

WITCH DOCTORS. See Witchcraft

Witch of Ramoth. Van Doren, M.

Witch of Times Square. Queen, E. pseud.

Witch war. Matheson, R.

WITCHCRAFT
Barker, A. L. Jane Dore—dear childe
Bradbury, R. Invisible boy
Brenner, L. Moon magic
Brentano, C. M. Picnic of Mores the cat
Collier, J. Lady on the grey
Dunsany, E. J. M. D. P. 18th baron.
Widow Flynn's apple tree
Hawthorne, N. Young Goodman Brown
Irwin, M. E. F. Monsieur seeks a wife
Jenkins, W. F. The power
Keller, D. H. The bridle
Keller, D. H. Opium eater
King-Hall, S. By one, by two, and by
three
Munro, H. H. Peace of Mowsle Barton
Paget, V. Dionea
Pratt, F. and De Camp, L. S. Caveat
emptor

WITCHES. See Witchcraft

Witches' loaves. Porter, W. S.

Witches money. Collier, J.

Witches of Karres. Schmitz, J. H.

With an O X herd. Payne, S.

With his back to the wall. Roberts, Sir
C. G. D.

With men it's different. Newhouse, E.

With Mr Jorrocks in Pinch-me-near Forest.
Surtees, R. S.

With the aid of the One Above. Suhl, Y.

With the fog. Morehouse, K. M.

With the greatest of ease. Annixter, P.
pseud.

With the Hit-im-and-hold-im-shire: The
sham day. Surtees, R. S.

With these hands. Kornbluth, C. M.

Witham, E. C.
Silver spurs
Queen, E. pseud. ed. Queen's awards:
8th ser.

Witherow, James Milling, 1867-1934
The test
Thinker's digest (Periodical) Spoiled
priest, and other stories
Within and without. Hesse, H.
Without benefit of clergy. Kipling, R.
Without benefit of Galsworthy, Collier, J.
Witness for the prosecution. Quentin, P.
pseud.
WITNESSES
Chekhov, A. P. Women make trouble
Witnesses. Claudy, C. H.

WIVES. See Husband and wife

Wives of the dead. Hawthorne, N.

The **wizard.** Yakovlev, A. S.

Wodehouse, Pelham Grenville, 1881-
Birth of a salesman
Wodehouse, P. G. Nothing serious
Bramley is so bracing
Wodehouse, P. G. Nothing serious
Excelsior
Wodehouse, P. G. Nothing serious
Feet of clay
Wodehouse, P. G. Nothing serious
How's that, umpire
Wodehouse, P. G. Nothing serious
Jeeves and the song of songs
Cerf, B. A. and Moriarty, H. C. eds.
Anthology of famous British stories
Rodney has a relapse
Wodehouse, P. G. Nothing serious
Shadow passes
Wodehouse, P. G. Nothing serious
Story of Webster
Joseph, M. ed. Best cat stories
Success story
Wodehouse, P. G. Nothing serious
Tangled hearts
Wodehouse, P. G. Nothing serious
Up from the depths
Wodehouse, P. G. Nothing serious

Wohl, Sam
The bride
Ribalow, H. U. ed. These your children

Wolf, Mari
Homeland
Sloane, W. M. ed. Stories for tomorrow

The **wolf.** Newhouse, E.

Wolf of Chungshan. Hsieh Liang

Wolf pack. Miller, W. M.

Wolfe, Bernard, 1915-
Self portrait
Galaxy science fiction magazine. Second
Galaxy reader of science fiction
Greenberg, M. ed. Robot and the man

Wolfe, Elizabeth
Thing in their hearts
Stanford short stories, 1950

Wolfe, Thomas, 1900-1938
The far and the near
Moskowitz, S. ed. Great railroad stories
of the world
Lost boy
Stegner, W. E.; Scowcroft, R. and
Ilyin, B. eds. Writer's art
Waite, H. O. and Atkinson, B. P. eds.
Literature for our time

Only the dead know Brooklyn
Blodgett, H. W. ed. Story survey. 1953
ed.
Portrait of Bascom Hawke
Burrell, J. A. and Cerf, B. A. eds. An-
thology of famous American stories
Veteran ballplayer
Graber, R. S. ed. Baseball reader
World Series and a small town
Graber, R. S. ed. Baseball reader
About
Bradbury, R. Forever and the earth

Wolfert, Ira, 1908-
'Git or git got'
Jensen, P. ed. Fireside book of flying
stories
The indomitable blue
Best American short stories, 1952

Wolfson, Victor
Purification of Thelma Augenstern
Ribalow, H. U. ed. This land, these
people

Wollheim, Donald A.
Disguise
Sloane, W. M. ed. Stories for tomorrow
Planet passage
Wollheim, D. A. comp. Flight into
space
Storm warning
Conklin, G. ed. Invaders of earth

Wolson, Morton
The attacker
Best detective stories of the year—
1954

WOLVES
Annixter, P. pseud. Last lobo
Chekhov, A. P. Hydrophobia
Davis, H. L. The vanishing wolf
Gilbert, K. Old man of the mountains
Goodridge Roberts, T. White wolf
Hsieh Liang. Wolf of Chungshan
Kipling, R. Mowgli's brothers
Munro, H. H. Wolves of Cernogratz
Roberts, Sir C. G. D. With his back to
the wall
Seton, E. T. Lobo, the king of Cur-
rumpaw

Wolves of Cernogratz. Munro, H. H.

WOMAN

Relation to other women
Glaspell, S. Jury of her peers
Maugham, W. S. Romantic young lady
Maugham, W. S. Three fat women of
Antibes
Palma, R. Two cooing doves
Taylor, E. Hester Lilly
Welty, E. The winds
Winslow, T. S. Girls in black

Rights of women
Graham, R. B. C. Faith

Social and moral questions
De Ford, M. A. Throwback
Maugham, W. S. Rain

Suffrage
Munro, H. H. Gala programme
Munro, H. H. Hermann the Irascible
Munro, H. H. The threat
Munro, H. H. Young Turkish catastrophe

Woman from Twenty-One. Fitzgerald, F. S. K.

Woman he left to die. Mowat, F.

Woman hunt no good. La Farge, O.

Woman in love. Household, G.

Woman in the case. Chekhov, A. P.

Woman in the house. Caldwell, E.

Woman in the house. Stuart, J.

Woman of fifty. Maugham, W. S.

A woman of virtue. Field, R. L.

WOMAN SUFFRAGE. See Woman—Suffrage

Woman taken in adultery. Eça de Queiroz, J. M.

Woman who hated flowers. Sitwell, Sir O. bart.

Woman who was everybody. Calisher, H.

Woman who was loved. Stern, J.

Woman with a past. Fitzgerald, F. S. K.

The women. Sullivan, R.

WOMEN AS AUTHORS
Aiken, C. P. Your obituary, well written

WOMEN AS HUNTERS
Collier, J. Squirrels have bright eyes

WOMEN AS LAWYERS
Eichrodt, J. Nadia Devereux

WOMEN AS MURDERERS
Du Maurier, D. Kiss me again, stranger

WOMEN AS RANCHERS
Thompson, T. Shadow of the butte

WOMEN IN BUSINESS
Winslow, T. S. Girls in black

Women make trouble. Chekhov, A. P.

Women on the wall. Stegner, W. E.

WOMEN VOTERS. See Woman—Suffrage

Women will out. Rhodes, W. P.

WOMEN'S CLUBS
Wharton, E. N. J. Xingu

Won and lost. Grimson, M. S.

Won by a tail. Person, W. T.

Won by inches! Campbell, Sir M.

Wonder child. Shallit, J.

Wonder in Willow Hill. West, A.

Wonderful automobile. Walker, T.

Wonderful new machine. Hamsun, K.

Wonderful Tar-Baby story. Harris, J. C.

Wonderful window. Dunsany, E. J. M. D. P. 18th baron

Wood, Clement, 1888-1950
Tzagan
Denis, W. ed. Palomino and other horses

Wood, Frances (Gilchrist) 1859-1944
Turkey-red
Cooper, A. C. ed. Modern short stories

Wood, Kerry, 1907-
Workaday cowboy
Fenner, P. R. comp. Cowboys, cowboys, cowboys
Owen, F. ed. Teen-age victory parade

WOOD CARVING
Caldwell, E. Handy

Wood-for-the-trees. MacDonald, P.

Wood smoke. Chidester, A.

WOODCHOPPERS. See Woodcutters

WOODCUTTERS
Traven, B. pseud. Third guest
Van Doren, M. Tall one

Woods, William
Free man
Story (Periodical) Story; no. 4

Woodward, George B.
College marriage
Oberfirst, R. ed. 1952 anthology of best original short-shorts

Woody, Regina Llewellyn (Jones)
Cue for Connie
Furman, A. L. ed. Everygirls career stories
Second chance
American girl (Periodical) Favorite stories

Woolf, Virginia (Stephen) 1882-1941
Between the acts
Connolly, C. ed. Great English short novels
Duchess and the jeweller
Neider, C. ed. Great short stories from the world's literature
Kew Gardens
Felheim, M.; Newman, F. B. and Steinhoff, W. R. Modern short stories
New dress
Heilman, R. B. ed. Modern short stories

Woollcott, Alexander, 1887-1943
Moonlight sonata
Davenport, B. ed. Ghostly tales to be told
Verdun Belle
Cavanna, B. ed. Pick of the litter

Woolley, Rollo
The pupil
Horizon (Periodical) Golden Horizon
The search
New writing (Periodical) Best stories

Woolrich, Cornell, 1903-
Blue ribbon
Ribalow, H. U. ed. World's greatest boxing stories
Wait for me downstairs
Cuff, R. P. ed. American short story survey

Word for Coffey. De La Roche, M.

Worden, William L.
Officers' girl
Saturday evening post (Periodical) Saturday evening post stories, 1951

Words for John Willie. Higbee, A. R.

Work suspended. Waugh, E.

Workaday cowboy. Wood, K.

Worker in sandalwood. Pickthall, M. L. C.

Workout in the park. Farrell, J. T.

Workout on the river. Shattuck, R.

Works of God. Berto, G.

WORLD, END OF THE. See End of the world

World and the door. Porter, W. S.

World is mine. Kuttner, H.

World of glass. Sansom, W.

World of little doves. Davis, H. L.

World outside. Maier, H.

World Series and a small town. Wolfe, T.

World the children made. Bradbury, R.

WORLD WAR, 1939-1945
Karchmer, S. N. Fistful of Alamo heroes
Newhouse, E. I hope you'll understand
Newhouse, E. What do you do?
Saint Exupéry, A. de. Letter to a hostage

Aerial operations
Bates, H. E. Colonel Julian
Gallico, P. W. The bombardier
Newhouse, E. Short visit to Naples

Africa, North
Krige, U. Death of the Zulu
Krige, U. Two Daumiers

Children
Asch, S. Duty to live
Blue, E. Nothing overwhelms Giuseppe

Collaborationists
See Treason

Egypt
Shaw, I. Walking wounded

England
O'Donovan, M. Darcy in the Land of Youth
Van Paassen, P. The unsaid prayer

France
Boyle, K. Defeat
Boyle, K. They weren't going to die
Brookhouser, F. Triumph with bells and laughter
Downey, H. The hunters
Kantor, M. Papa Pierre's pipe
Macfarlan, A. A. Danger by candlelight
Maugham, W. S. The unconquered
Remarque, E. M. Darkness in Paris

Germany
Forester, C. S. The nightmare; 10 stories
Waltari, M. T. Before the twilight of the gods

Italy
Berto, G. Works of God and other stories; 4 stories
Krige, U. Charcoal burners
Ullman, J. R. Diversion

Jews
Schulberg, B. W. Enough

Medical and sanitary affairs
Krige, U. Christmas box
Ullman, J. R. Between you and I
Ullman, J. R. Presumed lost

Naval operations
Auchincloss, L. Fall of a sparrow
Eliot, G. F. Uncertain weapon

Naval operations—Submarine
Beach, E. L. Archerfish
Holmes, W. J. Action off Formosa
Taylor, S. W. Last voyage of the Unsinkable Sal
Yates, T. Living torpedo

Norway
Petersen, E. J. Who called you here?

Pacific Ocean
Arico, V. Water canteen
Heatter, B. Island happy

Poland
Gronowicz, A. Mania-head-in-the-clouds

Prisoners and prisons
Downey, H. Crispin's way
Krige, U. Charcoal burners

United States
Johnson, D. M. Scars of honor

WORLD WAR AMBULANCE DRIVERS. See World War, 1939-1945—Medical and sanitary affairs

World well lost. Waldo, E. H.

World without. Herbert, B.

WORLDS, NEW. See Future, Stories of the

World's end. Williams, W. C.

The worm. Keller, D. H.

WORMS
Keller, D. H. The worm

Worn path. Welty, E.

WORRY
Munro, H. H. Reginald on worries

Worse and worse. Chekhov, A. P.

Worst crime in the world. Chesterton, G. K.

Worthington, Jay
Box score battle
Furman, A. L. ed. Teen-age stories of the diamond
Winning pitcher
Furman, A. L. ed. Teen-age stories of the diamond

Worthington, Rex
Kind of scandal
Prize stories, 1954

The wounded. Putman, C.

WOUNDED IN BATTLE. See War—Casualties

Wratislav. Munro, H. H.

Wreath for Miss Totten. Calisher, H.

WRECKS, RAILROAD. See Railroad—Accidents

WRESTLING
Komroff, M. Light of the moon
Mitchell, J. "Some bum might mistook me for a wrestler"
Olive, H. Take it and like it
Upson, W. H. Quiet wedding

Wretched old capitalist. Hallack, C.

Wright, Frances (Fitzpatrick) 1897-
Best foot forward
American girl (Periodical) On my honor
Declaration of independence
American girl (Periodical) Favorite stories
Let nothing you dismay
American girl (Periodical) Christmas all year 'round
Miracles still happen
American girl (Periodical) Christmas all year 'round

Young, Francis Brett, 1884-1954
  Busman's holiday
    Cerf, B. A. and Moriarty, H. C. eds.
    Anthology of famous British stories
Young, James Martin
  Rosinback
    Collier's, the national weekly. Collier's
    best
Young, Roger Flint
  Not to be opened
    Best science fiction stories: 1951
  Suburban frontiers
    Conklin, G. ed. Science-fiction adventures in dimension
Young, Scott
  Dangerous ice
    Argosy (Periodical) Argosy Book of
    sports stories
  Maloney's last stand
    Argosy (Periodical) Argosy Book of
    sports stories
  We won't be needing you, Al
    Herzberg, M. J. comp. Treasure chest
    of sport stories
Young Archimedes. Huxley, A. L.
Young Goodman Brown. Hawthorne, N.
Young man Axelbrod. Lewis, S.
Young man from yesterday. Brookhouser, F.
Young man of his time. Putman, C.
Young Mari Li. MacMahon, B.
"The young ravens that call upon him."
    Roberts, Sir C. G. D.
Young Turkish catastrophe. Munro, H. H.
Your Arkansas traveler. Schulberg, B. W.
Your heart's out of order. Soman, F. J.
Your long black hair. McCarty, M. B.
Your obituary, well written. Aiken, C. P.
You're only young once. Sullivan, R.
YOUTH
  Anderson, S. Sophistication
  Elias, A. Jarka
  Fitzgerald, F. S. K. Jelly-bean
  Neville, K. Hold back tomorrow
  Payne, L. V. Prelude
  Strang, R. M. and Roberts, R. M. eds.
    Teen-age tales; 35 stories
  Waugh, A. Wed, my darling daughter
    See also Adolescence; Boys; Girls
Youth. Brement, M.
Youth. Conrad, J.
Youth, beautiful youth. Hesse, H.
YOUTH, ETERNAL. See Rejuvenation
Youth from Vienna. Collier, J.
You've got to learn. Murphy, R.
Yüan Chên. See Yuen Chin
Yuen Chin, 779-831
  Passion (or the Western room)
    Lin, Y. ed. Famous Chinese short stories
YUKON TERRITORY
  Hendryx, J. B. Intrigue on Halfaday
    Creek; 28 stories
  Hendryx, J. B. Murder on Halfaday
    Creek; 30 stories

London, J. All-gold cañon
London, J. At the rainbow's end
London, J. Love of life
London, J. To build a fire
Yule miracle. Terhune, A. P.
YUM KIPPUR. See Yom Kippur
Yushkevich, Semion Solomonovich, 1868-1927
  Algebra
    Guerney, B. G. comp. New Russian
    stories
  In a Bolshevist market-place
    Leftwich, J. ed. Yisröel. 1952 ed.
Yushkewitch, Simeon. See Yushkevich,
    Semion Solomonovich

Z

Zachary Crebbin's angel. Kneale, N.
Zaferiou, Socrates, 1925-
  Tale of Perez de Amorin
    American vanguard, 1952
Zaimis. Bendrodt, J. C.
Zamiatin, Eugene Ivanovich. See Zamîatin,
    Evgenii Ivanovich
Zamîatin, Evgenii Ivanovich, 1884-1937
  God
    Guerney, B. G. comp. New Russian
    stories
Zangwill, Israel, 1864-1926
  The luftmensch
    Ausubel, N. ed. Treasury of Jewish
    humor
  Neo-Hebrew poet
    Ausubel, N. ed. Treasury of Jewish
    humor
  Sabbath breaker
    Leftwich, J. ed. Yisröel. 1952 ed.
  Sabbath question in Sudminster
    Ausubel, N. ed. Treasury of Jewish
    humor
Zangwill, Louis, 1869-1938
  Prelude to a pint of bitter
    Leftwich, J. ed. Yisröel. 1952 ed.
Zara, Louis, 1910-
  The citizner
    Certner, S. and Henry, G. H. eds. Short
    stories for our times
  Resurgam
    Ribalow, H. U. ed. This land, these
    people
Zarapore beat. Blochman, L. G.
Zelver, Al
  Something for December eighth
    Stanford short stories, 1951
Zelver, Patricia Farrell, 1923-
  Long hot day
    Stanford short stories, 1950
Zeritsky's law. Griffith, A.
Zerline, the old servant girl. Broch, H.
Zero hour. Bradbury, R.
Zevin, Israel Joseph, 1872-
  Nogid's luck
    Ausubel, N. ed. Treasury of Jewish
    humor

Zevin, Israel J.—*Continued*
Pack of troubles for one cent
Ausubel, N. ed. Treasury of Jewish humor

Zhabotinskiĭ, Vladimir Evgen'evich, 1880-1940
Edmée
Leftwich, J. ed. Yisröel. 1952 ed.

ZIPPORAH (BIBLICAL CHARACTER)
Hazaz, C. Bridegroom of blood

Zola, Émile, 1840-1902
Captain Burle
Dupee, F. W. ed. Great French short novels
Julien
Geist, S. ed. French stories and tales

Zone of interior. Ross, J.

The zoo. Williams, W. C.

ZOOLOGICAL GARDENS
Richards, D. Training Alice and Congo

ZOOLOGISTS
Bloomgarden, S. Zoology

Zoology. Bloomgarden, S.

Zoshchenko, Mikhail Mikhaĭlovich, 1895-
The aristocrat
Stauffer, R. M.; Cunningham, W. H. and Sullivan, C. J. eds. Adventures in modern literature
Sleuth-hound
Guerney, B. G. comp. New Russian stories

Zostchenko, Mikhail. See Zoshchenko, Mikhail Mikhaĭlovich

Zozulya, Ephim Davidovich, 1891-
Studio of Love-Your-Fellowman
Guerney, B. G. comp. New Russian stories

Zugsmith, Leane, 1903-
Room in the world
Summers, H. S. ed. Kentucky story

ZULUS
Krige, U. Death of the Zulu

ZURICH. See Switzerland—Zurich

Zweig, Arnold, 1887-
Jerusalem delivered
Leftwich, J. ed. Yisröel. 1952 ed.
The parcel
Blodgett, H. W. ed. Story survey. 1953 ed.

Zweig, Stefan, 1881-1942
Confusion of sentiment
Cory, D. W. pseud. comp. 21 variations on a theme
Invisible collection
Schramm, W. L. ed. Great short stories
West, R. B. and Stallman, R. W. eds. Art of modern fiction
Same as: Unseen collection
The runaway
Stauffer, R. M.; Cunningham, W. H. and Sullivan, C. J. eds. Adventures in modern literature
Unseen collection
Leftwich, J. ed. Yisröel. 1952 ed.
Same as: Invisible collection

PART II

List of Collections Indexed

An author and title list of collections indexed, with their various editions.

Abell, Elizabeth, 1906-
(ed.) American accent; fourteen stories by authors associated with the Bread Loaf Writers' Conference; with a foreword by Theodore Morrison. Ballantine. 1954 193p
See also Greene, J. I. jt. ed.

Adventure stories, Boys' life. Boys' life (Periodical)

Adventure stories from Story parade. Story parade (Periodical)

Adventures in modern literature. Stauffer, R. M.; Cunningham, W. H. and Sullivan, C. J. eds.

Adventures in tomorrow. Crossen, K. F. ed.

Adventures of Sherlock Holmes. Doyle, Sir A. C.

Ahead of time. Kuttner, H.

Aiken, Conrad Potter, 1889-
Short stories. Duell 1950 416p

Akutagawa, Ryūnosuke, 1892-1927
Rashomon, and other stories; tr. by Takashi Kojima; introduction by Howard Hibbett, illus. by M. Kuwata. Liveright 1952 119p illus

Alabaster hand, and other ghost stories. Munby, A. N. L.

Aldrich, Bess (Streeter) 1881-
The Bess Streeter Aldrich reader. Appleton 1950 467p
Analyzed for short stories only

Aleichem, Sholom, pseud. See Rabinowitz, Shalom

American accent. Abell, E. ed.

American boy (Periodical)
American boy Adventure stories; selected by Cecile Matschat and Carl Carmer; illus. by Norman Guthrie Rudolph. Winston 1952 367p illus
American boy anthology; comp. by Franklin M. Reck; illus. by Clifford Geary. Crowell 1951 488p illus

American boy Adventure stories. American boy (Periodical)

American boy anthology. American boy (Periodical)

American dream girl. Farrell, J. T.

American girl (Periodical)
Christmas all year 'round; ed. by Marjorie Vetter; twenty-five Christmas stories. Abelard-Schuman 1952 320p
Favorite stories; selected and ed. by Marjorie Vetter and Ruth Baker Bowman. Nelson 1950 224p
On my honor; twenty stories from the American girl; selected and ed. by Marjorie Vetter. Longmans 1951 229p

American literature by Negro authors. Dreer, H. ed.

American short story survey. Cuff, R. P. ed.

American vanguard, 1950; ed. by Charles I. Glicksberg. . . ₁Pub. for the₁ New School for Social Research ₁by₁ Cambridge Pub. Co. 1950 314p

American vanguard, 1952; ed. by Don M. Wolfe. ₁Pub. for the₁ New School for Social Research ₁by₁ Greenberg 1952 325p
Analyzed for short stories only

American vanguard, 1953; ed. by Charles I. Glicksberg and Brom Weber. . . ₁Pub. for the₁ New School for Social Research ₁by₁ Dial Press 1953 314p
Analyzed for short stories only

Anchor in the sea. Swallow, A. ed.

Anderson, Esther Victoria, 1892-
Six tales for the family, by Eva Rite ₁pseud₁. Pageant Press 1951 71p

Anderson, Quentin
(ed.) James, H. Selected short stories

Andrews, Roy Chapman, 1884-
(ed.) My favorite stories of the great outdoors; nature lover's treasury; selected, and with an introduction. Greystone 1950 404p

Angels and spaceships. Brown, F.

Ann Lee's. Bowen, E. See Bowen, E. Early stories

Benson, Theodora, 1906-
Man from the tunnel, and other stories. Appleton 1950 271p

Bentley, Phyllis Eleanor, 1894-
Panorama; tales of West Riding. Macmillan 1952 287p

Bergengruen, Werner, 1892-
Last Captain of Horse; a portrait of chivalry. [Tr. from the German language edition by Eric Peters] Thames (N.Y.) 1953 303p
Analyzed for short stories only

Bernhard, Emil, pseud. See Cohn, Emil Bernhard

Berto, Giuseppe
Works of God, and other stories; tr. from the Italian by Angus Davidson. New Directions 1950 224p

The Bess Streeter Aldrich reader. Aldrich, B. S.

Best American short stories, 1950-1954; and the Yearbook of the American short story; ed. by Martha Foley, assisted by Joyce F. Hartman. Houghton 1950-54 5v

Best Army short stories, 1950. Rinehart 1950 243p

Best cat stories. Joseph, M. ed.

Best detective stories of the year— 1950-1954. Ed. by David C. Cooke. Dutton 1950-54 5v

Best from Fantasy and science fiction. Magazine of fantasy and science fiction

Best from Startling stories. Startling stories (Periodical)

Best of Bret Harte. Harte, B.

Best of Crunch and Des. Wylie, P.

Best of Hawthorne. Hawthorne, N.

Best of the Best American short stories, 1915-1950; ed. by Martha Foley. Houghton 1952 364p

Best science fiction stories: 1950-1954. Ed. by Everett F. Bleiler and T. E. Dikty. Fell 1950-54 5v (Fell's science fiction lib)

Best short stories by Afro-American writers (1925-1950) Ford, N. A. and Faggett, H. L. eds.

Best stories from New writing. New writing (Periodical)

Betts, Doris
Gentle insurrection, and other stories. Putnam 1954 274p

Beyond human ken. Merril, J.

Beyond infinity. Carr, R. S.

Beyond the barriers of space and time. Merril, J. ed.

Beyond time & space. Derleth, A. W. ed.

Big book of science fiction. Conklin, G. ed.

Big range. Schaefer, J. W.

Black prince, and other stories. Grau, S. A.

Black star passes. Campbell, J. W.

Blackburn, Ernest Richard, 1926-
The swaying elms, and other stories. Moody Press 1950 255p (Provident books)

Blaustein, Albert P. 1921-
(ed.) Fiction goes to court; favorite stories of lawyers and the law, selected by famous lawyers. Holt 1954 303p
Analyzed for short stories only

Bleiler, Everett Franklin, 1920-
(ed.) Best science fiction stories. See Best science fiction stories
(ed.) Year's best science fiction novels. See Year's best science fiction novels

Bleiler, Everett Franklin, 1920- and Dikty, Thaddeus Eugene
(ed.) Imagination unlimited; science-fiction and science. Farrar, Straus 1952 430p
(ed.) Science fiction omnibus: the best science fiction stories, 1949, 1950. Introduction by Melvin Korshak. Garden City Bks. 1952 2v in 1

Blessed are they. Baker, F.

Bloch, Marguerite
(ed.) Favorite dog stories; illus. by Robert Doremus. World Pub. 1950 250p illus

Blochman, Lawrence Goldtree, 1900-
Diagnosis: homicide; the casebook of Dr Coffee. Lippincott 1950 (Main line mysteries) 217p

Blodgett, Harold William, 1900-
(ed.) Story survey. Rev. ed. Lippincott 1953 825p

Bloodstock, and other stories. Irwin, M. E. F.

Bluebook (Periodical)
Best sea stories from Bluebook; ed. by Horace Vondys; with an introduction and notes by Donald Kennicott. McBride Co. 1954 359p

Bogorad, Samuel Nathaniel, 1917- and Trevithick, Jack, 1909-
(eds.) College miscellany; ed. with introductions. Rinehart 1952 621p
Analyzed for short stories only

Bond, Raymond Tostevin, 1893-
(ed.) Handbook for poisoners. . . Rinehart 1951 311p

Bonner, Paul Hyde, 1893-
Glorious mornings; stories of shooting and fishing. Scribner 1954 228p

Book of Canadian stories. Pacey, D. ed.

Book of cowboy stories, Will James'. James, W.

808.83
C79 Rac

Corkery, Daniel, 1878-
The wager, and other stories; illus. with wood engravings by Elizabeth Rivers. Devin-Adair 1950 192p illus

Cory, Donald Webster, pseud.
(comp.) 21 variations on a theme. Greenberg 1953 436p
Analyzed for short stories only

Courting of Susie Brown. Caldwell, E.

Cousins, Margaret, 1905-
Christmas gift. Doubleday 1952 219p

Coward, Noël Pierce, 1899-
Star quality; six stories by Noel Coward. Doubleday 1951 308p

Cowboys, cowboys, cowboys. Fenner, P. R. comp.

Coxe, George Harmon, 1901-
(ed.) Mystery Writers of America, inc. Butcher, baker, murder-maker

Crack of the bat. Fenner, P. R. comp.

808.83
C89 **Crane, Stephen,** 1871-1900
Stephen Crane; an omnibus; ed. with introduction and notes by Robert Wooster Stallman. Knopf 1952 703p front
Analyzed for short stories only

Creamer, Jack B.
(comp.) Twenty-two stories about horses and men; comp. with an introduction by Jack B. Creamer; with decorations by Ned King. Coward-McCann 1953 309p illus
Analyzed for short stories only

Crooks' tour. Mystery writers of America, inc.

Crossen, Kendall Foster, 1910-
(ed.) Adventures in tomorrow. Greenberg 1951 278p
(ed.) Future tense; new and old tales of science fiction. Greenberg 1952 364p

Crown princess & other stories. Brophy, B.

Cruises in the sun. Curtis, K.

Crump, Irving, 1887-
(ed.) Boys' life (Periodical) Boys' life Adventure stories

Crunch and Des, Best of. Wylie, P.

Cuff, Roger Penn, 1899-
(ed.) American short story survey. Stackpole Co. 1953 427p

Cunningham, William Hayes. See Stauffer, R. M. jt. auth.

Current thinking and writing; second series. Bachelor, J. M.; Henry, R. L. and Salisbury, R. eds.

Curtis, Kent
Cruises in the sun. Seymour 1950 287p illus

D

Dachs, David, 1922-
(ed.) Treasury of sports humor, ed. by Dave Stanley [pseud]; introduction by Ted Husing. Grosset 1946 487p illus

Dahl, Roald, 1916-
Someone like you. Knopf 1953 359p

Dannay, Frederic, 1905- **and Lee, Manfred Bennington,** 1905- See Queen, Ellery, pseud.

Davenport, Basil, 1905-
(ed.) Ghostly tales to be told; a collection of stories from the great masters, arranged for reading and telling aloud. Dodd 1950 317p
(ed.) Tales to be told in the dark; a selection of stories from the great authors, arranged for reading and telling aloud. Dodd 1953 335p

Davies, Rhys, 1903-
Boy with a trumpet, and other selected short stories; with an introduction by Bucklin Moon. Doubleday 1951 304p

Davis, Clyde Brion, 1894-
(ed.) Eyes of boyhood. Lippincott 1953 xxiii, 323p
Analyzed for short stories only

Davis, Harold Lenoir, 1896-
Team bells woke me, and other stories. Morrow 1953 300p

Davis, Robert Gorham, 1908-
(ed.) Ten modern masters; an anthology of the short story. Harcourt 1953 510p

Day, Arthur Grove, 1904-
(ed.) Greatest American short stories; twenty classics of our heritage. McGraw 1953 359p

De Camp, Lyon Sprague, 1907-
Continent makers, and other tales of the Viagens. Twayne 1953 272p
See also Pratt, F. jt. auth.

808.83
D33c **De La Mare, Walter John,** 1873-1956
Collected tales; chosen, and with an introduction, by Edward Wagenknecht. Knopf 1950 467p

De La Roche, Mazo, 1885-
Boy in the house, and other stories. Little 1952 244p

Delicate prey, and other stories. Bowles, P. F.

THESE →
IN
D 548 c

Egyptian adventures. Coolidge, O. E.

Eight uncollected tales. James, H.

Ekbergh, Ida Diana
Mysterious Chinese mandrake, and other stories. Pageant Press 1954 52p

Elam, Richard M.
Teen-age science fiction stories; introduction by Burr W. Leyson; illus. by Charles H. Geer. Lantern Press 1952 254p illus

Elephants, elephants, elephants. Fenner, P. R. comp.

Ellery Queen's awards. Queen, E. pseud. ed.

Elmquist, Ruth M.
(ed.) Fifty years of Christmas; an anthology of stories, poems and short pieces from the Christian herald; introduction by Daniel A. Poling. Rinehart 1951 300p
Analyzed for short stories only

Emrich, Duncan, 1908-
(ed.) Comstock bonanza; western Americana of J. Ross Browne ₁and others₁. . . Vanguard 1950 363p
Analyzed for short stories only

Encore. Maugham, W. S.

Encounters. Bowen, E. See Bowen, E. Early stories

Engle, Paul, 1908- and Martin, Hansford
(eds.) Prize stories 1954. See Prize stories 1954

Enormous radio, and other stories. Cheever, J.

Esquire (Periodical)
Girls from Esquire; introduction by Frederic A. Birmingham. Random House 1952 308p illus
Analyzed for short stories only

Eternal smile, and other stories. Lagerkvist, P. F.

Evans, Thomas M. 1881-
Gentlemen of valor, and other stories. Exposition 1951 221p

Every boy's book of science-fiction. Wollheim, D. A. comp.

Everygirls career stories. Furman, A. L. ed.

Everygirls mystery stories. Furman, A. L. ed.

Expedition to earth. Clarke, A. C.

Exploits of Sherlock Holmes. Doyle, A. C. and Carr, J. D.

The explorers. Kornbluth, C. M.

F

Fabricant, Noah Daniel, 1904- and Werner, Heinz, 1901-
(eds.) World's best doctor stories. Garden City Bks. 1951 276p

Faggett, Harry Lee, 1911- See Ford, N. A. jt. ed.

Family book of best loved short stories. Lamb, L. ed.

Famous Chinese short stories. Lin, Y.

Fancies and goodnights. Collier, J.

Far boundaries. Derleth, A. W. ed.

Far whistle, and other stories. Beck, W.

Farrell, James Thomas, 1904-
American dream girl. Vanguard 1950 302p
Further short stories. Sun Dial 1948 313p
At head of title: When boyhood dreams come true
Analyzed for short stories only
Short stories. Vanguard ₁1951, c1934₁ xxxvi, 534p
Published separately and entered in the main catalog under titles: Calico shoes; Guillotine party; Can all this grandeur perish?

Father Brown omnibus. Chesterton, G. K.

Faulkner, William, 1897-
Collected stories. Random House 1950 900p
Faulkner reader; selections from the works of William Faulkner. Random House 1954 682p
Analyzed for short stories only

Faulkner reader. Faulkner, W.

Favorite dog stories. Bloch, M. ed.

Favorite stories. American girl (Periodical)

808.83 **Felheim, Marvin, 1914- Newman,**
F 31 **Franklin B. and Steinhoff, William R.**
(eds.) Modern short stories. Oxford 1951 448p

j808.83 **Fenner, Phyllis Reid, 1899-**
F33c (comp.) Cowboys, cowboys, cowboys; stories of roundups & rodeos, branding & broncobusting. Illus. by Manning deV. Lee. Watts, F. 1950 287p illus
(comp.) Crack of the bat. Knopf 1952 160p
j808.83 (comp.) Dogs, dogs, dogs; stories
F33d of challengers and champions, heroes and hunters, warriors and workers; illus. by Manning deV. Lee. Watts, F. 1951 270p illus
(comp.) Elephants, elephants, elephants; stories of rogues and workers, tuskers and trekkers, jungle trails of circus tanbark; illus. by Manning deV. Lee. Watts, F. 1952 303p illus
(comp.) Fools and funny fellows; more "Time to laugh" tales; illus. by Henry C. Pitz. Knopf 1947 185p illus

Fenner, Phyllis R.—*Continued*
(comp.) Fun! Fun! Fun! Stories of fantasy and farce, mischief and mirth, whimsy and non-sense; illus. by Joseph J. Zabinski. Watts, F. 1953 283p illus

(comp.) Ghosts, ghosts, ghosts; stories of spooks and spirits, haunts and hobgoblins, were-wolves and will-o'-the-wisps. Illus. by Manning deV. Lee. Watts, F. 1952 281p illus

(comp.) Giggle box; pictures by William Steig. Knopf 1950 144p illus

(comp.) Indians, Indians, Indians; stories of tepees and tomahawks, wampum belts & war bonnets, peace pipes & papooses; illus. by Manning deV. Lee. Watts, F. 1950 287p illus

(comp.) Pirates, pirates, pirates; stories of cutlasses and corsairs, buried treasure and buccaneers, ships and swashbucklers. Illus. by Manning deV. Lee. Watts, F. 1951 287p illus

(comp.) Speed, speed, speed; stories of races and chases in hot rods and jets, trains and planes, submarines and speedboats; illus. by William Lohse. Watts F. 1954 246p illus
Analyzed for short stories only

(comp.) Stories of the sea; illus. by Kurt Werth. Knopf 1953 178p illus

(comp.) Yankee Doodle; stories of the brave and the free. Illus. by John Alan Maxwell. Knopf 1951 214p illus

Fiction goes to court. Blaustein, A. P. ed.

15 stories. Barrows, H.

Fifty years of Christmas. Elmquist, R. M. ed.

Fireside book of flying stories. Jensen, P. ed.

First-prize stories, 1919-1954; from the O. Henry Memorial awards; introduction by Harry Hansen. Hanover House 1954 495p

Fischer, Bruno, 1908-
(ed.) Mystery Writers of America, inc. Crooks' tour

Fitzgerald, Francis Scott Key, 1896-1940
Stories of F. Scott Fitzgerald; a selection of 28 stories; with an introduction by Malcolm Cowley. Scribner 1951 473p

Five science fiction novels. Greenberg, M. comp.

Flight into space. Wollheim, D. A. comp.

Flying Officer. See Bates, Herbert Ernest

Foerster, Norman
(ed.) Poetry and prose; shorter ed. prepared with supplementary notes by William Charvat. Houghton 1952 924p
Analyzed for short stories only

Foley, Martha
(ed.) Best American short stories. See Best American short stories
(ed.) Best of the Best American short stories

Foley, Martha, and Hartman, Joyce F.
(ed.) Best American short stories, 1953

Fools and funny fellows. Fenner, P. R. comp.

Foote, John Taintor, 1881-1950
Hoofbeats; the great horse stories. Appleton 1950 243p illus
Also available from Grosset

Ford, Nick Aaron, 1904- and **Faggett, Harry Lee,** 1911-
(eds.) Best short stories by Afro-American writers (1925-1950) Meador 1950 307p

Forester, Cecil Scott, 1899-
Mr Midshipman Hornblower. Little 1950 310p
The nightmare. Little 1954 242p

Four-&-twenty bloodhounds. Mystery Writers of America, inc.

Fourth round. Grayson, C.

Fremantle, Anne (Jackson) 1909-
(ed.) Mothers; a Catholic treasury of great stories; with 8 half-tone reproductions; ed. with an introduction. Daye [1951] 383p illus
Analyzed for short stories only

French stories and tales. Geist, S. ed.

Fresh and open sky, and other stories. Sullivan, R.

Friend, Oscar Jerome, 1897- See Margulies, L. jt. ed.

Frightened wife, and other murder stories. Rinehart, M. R.

From off this world. Margulies, L. and Friend, O. J. eds.

Full cargo. Steele, W. D.

Fun! Fun! Fun! Fenner, P. R. comp.

Furman, Abraham Loew, 1902-
(ed.) Everygirls career stories. Lantern Press 1954 221p illus
(ed.) Everygirls mystery stories; illus. by Albert L. Lake. Lantern Press 1954 222p illus
(ed.) Teen-age dog stories, ed. by David Thomas [pseud]; illus. by Richard N. Osborne. Grosset 1949 256p illus

Great French short novels. Dupee, F. W. ed.

Great German short novels and stories. Lange, V. ed.

Great railroad stories of the world. Moskowitz, S. ed.

Great Russian short novels. Rahv, P. ed.

Great sea stories of modern times. McFee, W. ed.

Great short stories. Neider, C. ed.

Great short stories. Schramm, W. L. ed.

Great short stories from the world's literature. Neider, C. ed.

Great stories of science fiction. Jenkins, W. F. ed.

Greatest American short stories. Day, A. G. ed.

Greatest stories and how they were written. Cody, S. ed.

Greatest victory, and other baseball stories. O'Rourke, F.

Green hills of earth. Heinlein, R. A.

Greenberg, Eliezer, 1896- See Howe, I. jt. ed.

Greenberg, Martin, 1918-
(comp.) Five science fiction novels. Gnome Press 1952 382p
(ed.) Journey to infinity; introduced by Fletcher Pratt. Gnome Press 1951 381p
(ed.) Men against the stars; introduced by Willy Ley. Gnome Press 1950 351p
(ed.) Robot and the man [by] John D. MacDonald [and others]. Gnome Press 1953 251p
(ed.) Travelers of space; introduced by Willy Ley; illus. by Edd Cartier. Gnome Press 1951 400p illus

Greene, Joseph Ingham, 1897- and Abell, Elizabeth, 1906-
(eds.) Stories of sudden truth. Ballantine 1953 255p

Grimson, Marie S.
At the crossroads, and other stories and sketches. Exposition 1953 125p

Guerney, Bernard Guilbert, 1894-
(comp.) New Russian stories; selected and tr. by Bernard Guilbert Guerney. New Directions 1953 240p

Guillotine party. Farrell, J. T. See Farrell, J. T. Short stories

H

Halliday, Bret, pseud. See Dresser, Davis

Hallowed years. Buckingham, N.

Handbook for poisoners. Bond, R. T. ed.

Happy New Year, kamerades! Lowry, R. J. C.

Harper, Wilhelmina, 1884-
(comp.) Dog show; a selection of favorite dog stories; with portraits of real dogs by Marie C. Nichols. Houghton 1950 182p illus
(ed.) Harte, B. Bret Harte's stories of the old West

Harris, George Washington, 1814-1869
Sut Lovingood; ed. with an introduction by Brom Weber. Grove 1954 262p

Harte, Bret, 1836-1902
Best of Bret Harte; selected by Wilhelmina Harper and Aimée M. Peters; illus. by Paul Brown. Houghton 1947 434p illus
Bret Harte's stories of the old West; selected by Wilhelmina Harper and Aimée M. Peters; illus. by Paul Brown. Wilcox & Follett 1940 322p illus
Analyzed for short stories only

Harvey, William Fryer, 1885-1937
Arm of Mrs Egan, and other strange stories. Dutton 1952 256p

Hathaway, Baxter, 1909- and Sessions, John A.
(eds.) Writers for tomorrow; 2d ser. A collection of fiction by writers of tomorrow for readers of today. Cornell Univ. Press 1952 227p

818
H39b
Hawthorne, Nathaniel, 1804-1864
Best of Hawthorne; ed. with introduction and notes, by Mark Van Doren. Ronald 1951 436p
Analyzed for short stories only

Haycox, Ernest, 1899-1950
By rope and lead. Little 1951 174p
Outlaw. Little 1953 179p
Pioneer loves. Little 1952 177p
Rough justice. Little 1950 177p

Hazeltine, Alice Isabel, 1878-
(comp.) Selected stories for teenagers; for pleasure and understanding. Abingdon 1952 240p illus
Analyzed for short stories only

Headley, Elizabeth (Cavanna) See Cavanna, Betty

Healy, Raymond J.
(ed.) New tales of space and time; introduction by Anthony Boucher [pseud]. Holt 1951 294p

Heaven is so high. Lieberman, R.

Heavenly world series, and other baseball stories. O'Rourke, F.

Heilman, Robert Bechtold, 1906-
(ed.) Modern short stories; a critical anthology. Harcourt 1950 438p

I

Kuebler, Harold W.
(ed.) Treasury of science fiction classics. Hanover House 1954 694p

Kuttner, Henry, 1914-
Ahead of time; ten stories of science fiction and fantasy. Ballantine 1953 177p
Gnome there was, and other tales of science fiction and fantasy, by Lewis Padgett [pseud]. Simon & Schuster 1950 276p
Robots have no tails [by] Lewis Padgett [pseud]. Gnome Press 1952 224p

L

Lagerkvist, Pär Fabian, 1891-
Eternal smile, and other stories; tr. by Alan Blair [and others]. Random House 1954 389p
Analyzed for short stories only

Lamb, Lawrence
(ed.) Family book of best loved short stories, ed. by Leland W. Lawrence [pseud]. Hanover House 1954 498p

Lange, Victor, 1908-
(ed.) Great German short novels and stories; ed. with an introduction by Victor Lange. Modern Lib. 1952 486p
Revision of the title originally ed. by B. A. Cerf, entered in the main catalog

Lantz, John Edward
(ed.) Stories of Christian living; foreword by Martha Foley. Assn. Press 1950 293p

Lass, Abraham Harold, 1907- and Horowitz, Arnold, 1913-
(eds.) Stories for youth. Harper 1950 374p

Last Captain of Horse. Bergengruen, W.

Last Glencannon omnibus. Gilpatric, G.

Last husband, and other stories. Humphrey, W.

Last refuge of a scoundrel, and other stories. Howard, W.

Laughing to keep from crying. Hughes, L.

Lawrence, Leland W. pseud. See Lamb, Lawrence

Lee Vernon, pseud. See Paget Violet

Leftwich, Joseph, 1892-
(ed.) Yisröel; the first Jewish omnibus. [Rev. ed.] Beechhurst Press 1952 723p

Lehmann, John, 1907-
(ed.) New writing (Periodical) Best stories

Leinster, Murray, pseud. See Jenkins, William Fitzgerald

Lesser, Milton, A. 1918-
(ed.) Looking forward; an anthology of science fiction. Beechhurst Press 1953 400p

Lessing, Doris May, 1919-
This was the Old Chief's country; stories. Crowell 1952 256p

Lewis, Wyndham, 1886-
Rotting Hill. Regnery 1952 265p

Lieberman, Rosalie
Heaven is so high. Bobbs 1950 283p

Lin, Yu-t'ang, 1895-
(ed.) Famous Chinese short stories; retold by Lin Yutang. Day 1952 299p

Lincoln, Victoria Endicott, 1904-
Wild honey; some pilgrims and vagrants going our way. Rinehart 1953 238p
Analyzed for short stories only

Literature for our time. Waite, H. O. and Atkinson, B. P. eds.

Literature of crime. Queen, E. pseud. ed.

Little, George Watson
True stories of heroic dogs; with an introduction by Mrs Albert Payson Terhune. Grosset 1951 256p illus

Little Benders. Knox, J.

Little novels of Sicily. Verga, G.

Lohan, Robert, 1889-1953, and Lohan, Maria
(eds.) New Christmas treasury; with more stories for reading aloud. Daye 1954 406p
Analyzed for short stories only

London, Jack, 1876-1916
Sun-Dog Trail and other stories. World Pub. 1951 251p

Looking forward. Lesser, M. A. ed.

Love is a pie. Hutchins, M. P. M.

Love stories of India. Marshall, E.

Lowry, Robert James Collas, 1919-
Happy New Year, kamerades! 11 stories. Drawings by the author. Doubleday 1954 256p illus
Analyzed for short stories only

Ludwig, Jack Barry, and Poirier, W. Richard
(eds.) Stories, British and American. Houghton 1953 505p
Analyzed for short stories only

Ludwig, Richard M. 1920- and Perry, Marvin B. 1918-
(eds.) Nine short novels. Heath 1952 li, 571p

Lynskey, Winifred C. 1905-
(ed.) Reading modern fiction; 30 stories with study aids. Scribner 1952 485p

M

McCarthy, Mary Therese, 1912-
Cast a cold eye. Harcourt 1950
212p

McCloy, Helen
(ed.) Mystery Writers of America, inc. 20 great tales of murder

McComas, J. Francis
(ed.) Best from Fantasy and science fiction; 2d ser.

McCullers, Carson (Smith) 1917-
Ballad of the sad café; the novels and stories of Carson McCullers. Houghton 1951 791p
Analyzed for short stories only

MacDonald, Philip
Something to hide. Doubleday 1952 220p

Macfarlan, Allan A.
Campfire adventure stories; illus. by Paulette Jumeau. Assn. Press 1952 225p illus

McFarland, Wilma K. 1890-
(comp.) Then it happened—stories of unforgettable moments. Watts, F. 1952 320p

McFee, William, 1881-
(ed.) Great sea stories of modern times; ed. with original material and an introduction. McBride Co 1953 346p

808.83
M16 *Rave*

McLaverty, Michael
Game cock; and other stories; with illus. by Sister Irena Uptegrove. Devin-Adair 1947 192p illus

McNulty, John, 1895-1956
Man gets around. Little 1951 280p

Magazine of fantasy and science fiction
Best from Fantasy and science fiction [1st]-3d ser. ed. by Anthony Boucher [pseud] and J. Francis McComas. Little 1952-1954 3v
2d ser. analyzed for short stories only

Maiden murders. Mystery Writers of America, inc.

Make light of it. Williams, W. C.

Man and beast. Bottome, P.

Man from the tunnel, and other stories. Benson, T.

Man gets around. McNulty, J.

Man who sold the moon. Heinlein, R. A.

Man who was loved. Stern, J.

Many are called. Newhouse, E.

Many-colored fleece. Gable, M. Sister, ed.

The many loves of Dobie Gillis. Shulman, M.

Margulies, Leo, 1900- and Friend, Oscar Jerome, 1897-
(eds.) From off this world. Gems of science fiction chosen from "Hall of Fame classics." Merlin 1949 430p
(eds.) Giant anthology of science fiction; 10 complete short novels. Merlin 1954 580p

Marshall, Edison, 1894-
Love stories of India. Farrar, Straus 1950 307p

Martin, Hansford
(ed.) Prize stories 1954. See Prize stories 1954

Matheson, Richard, 1926-
Born of man and woman; tales of science fiction and fantasy; introduction by Robert Bloch. Chamberlain Press 1954 252p

Matschat, Cecile (Hulse)
(ed.) American boy (Periodical) American boy Adventure stories

Maugham, William Somerset, 1874-
Complete short stories. Doubleday 1952 2v
Encore; original stories by W. Somerset Maugham; screenplays by T. E. B. Clarke, Arthur Macrae [and] Eric Ambler. Doubleday 1952 156p
Analyzed for short stories only
Trio; original stories by W. Somerset Maugham; screenplays by W. Somerset Maugham, R. C. Sherriff [and] Noel Langley. Doubleday 1950 156p
Analyzed for short stories only
(ed.) Kipling, R. Maugham's choice of Kipling's best

Maugham's choice of Kipling's best. Kipling, R.

Maupassant, Guy de, 1850-1893
Selected tales; ed. with an introduction by Saxe Commins; illus. by Adolf Dehn. Random House 1950 334p illus

Melville, Herman, 1819-1891
Selected tales and poems; ed. with an introduction by Richard Chase. Rinehart 1950 417p
Analyzed for short stories only
Selected writings. . . Random House 1952 903p
Analyzed for short stories only

Memoirs of Solar Pons. Derleth, A. W.

Men against the stars. Greenberg, M. ed.

Men of the high calling. Neider, C. ed.

Meredith, Scott, 1923-
  (ed.) Bar 1 roundup of best western stories; selected and with introductions, by Scott Meredith. Dutton 1952 256p
  (ed.) Bar 2; roundup of best western stories; selected and with introductions by Scott Meredith. Dutton 1953 256p
  (ed.) Bar 3; roundup of best western stories; selected and with introductions by Scott Meredith. Dutton 1954 223p

Merochnik, Minnie, 1887-
  Celeste & other stories. Storm 1950 247p

Merril, Judith, 1923-
  (ed.) Beyond human ken; twenty-one startling stories of science fiction and fantasy; with an introduction by Fletcher Pratt. Random House 1952 334p
  (ed.) Beyond the barriers of space and time; with an introduction by Theodore Sturgeon. Random House 1954 294p front

Michener, James Albert, 1907-
  Return to Paradise. Random House 1951 437p
    Analyzed for short stories only

Miers, Earl Schenck, 1910-
  The kid who beat the Dodgers, and other sports stories; illus. by Paul Galdone. World Pub. 1954 190p illus

Miller, Peter Schuyler, 1912-
  The Titan. Fantasy Press 1952 252p

Millett, Fred Benjamin, 1890-
  (ed.) Reading fiction; a method of analysis with selections for study. Harper 1950 269p
    Analyzed for short stories only

Milne, Alan Alexander, 1882-1956
  Table near the band. Dutton 1950 249p

Mines, Samuel
  (comp.) Startling stories (Periodical) Best from Startling stories

Miriam, Sister, 1886-
  (ed.) Thinker's digest (Periodical) Spoiled priest, and other stories

Mr Glencannon ignores the war. Gilpatric, G. See Gilpatric, G. Last Glencannon omnibus

Mr Midshipman Hornblower. Forester, C. S.

Mrs Reynolds, and five earlier novelettes. Stein, G.

Modern short stories. Cooper, A. C. ed.

Modern short stories. Felheim, M.; Newman, F. B. and Steinhoff, W. R. eds.

Modern short stories. Heilman, R. B. ed.

Moonscape, and other stories. Waltari, M. T.

Moore, Catherine Lucile, 1911-
  Judgment night; a selection of science fiction. Gnome Press 1952 344p
  Shambleau, and others. Gnome Press 1953 224p

More guys and dolls. Runyon, D.

More stories. O'Donovan, M.

Moskowitz, Samuel
  (comp.) Editor's choice in science fiction. McBride 1954 285p
  (ed.) Great railroad stories of the world; ed. with notes by Samuel Moskowitz; introduction by Freeman H. Hubbard. McBride Co. 1954 331p
    Analyzed for short stories only

Mostly murder. Brown, F.

Mothers. Fremantle, A. J. ed.

Mowery, William Byron, 1899-
  Sagas of the Mounted Police; illus. by Carl Kidwell. Bouregy 1953 256p illus
  Tales of the Ozarks; illus. by Mario Cooper. Bouregy 1954 253p illus

Munby, Alan Noel Latimer
  Alabaster hand, and other ghost stories. Macmillan 1950 192p

Munro, Hector Hugh, 1870-1916
  Short stories of Saki [pseud]; with an introduction by Christopher Morley. Modern Lib. 1951 718p (Modern lib. of the world's best bks)
    Analyzed for short stories only

Murder on Halfaday Creek. Hendryx, J. B.

My favorite stories of the great outdoors. Andrews, R. C. ed.

Mysterious Chinese mandrake, and other stories. Ekbergh, I. D.

Mystery Writers of America, inc.
  Butcher, baker, murder-maker, by members of the Mystery Writers of America; ed. and with an introduction by George Harmon Coxe. Knopf 1954 341p
  Crooks' tour, by members of the Mystery Writers of America; ed. by Bruno Fischer. Dodd 1953 301p
  Four-&-twenty bloodhounds. . . Ed. and with introductions by Anthony Boucher [pseud]. Simon & Schuster 1950 406p
  Maiden murders; introduction by John Dickson Carr. Harper 1952 302p

Mystery Writers of America, inc.
—*Continued*
20 great tales of murder, by experts of the Mystery Writers of America; ed. by Helen McCloy and Brett Halliday [pseud]. Preface by Baynard Kendrick. Random House 1951 336p
Analyzed for short stories only

N

808.83
N39

Neider, Charles, 1915-
(ed.) Great short stories from the world's literature. Rinehart 1950 502p
(ed.) Men of the high calling. Abingdon 1954 238p
(ed.) Short novels of the masters; ed. with an introduction. Rinehart 1948 643p

New Christmas treasury. Lohan, R. and Lohan, M. eds.

New Confederate short stories. Jones, K. M. ed.

New Russian stories. Guerney, B. G. comp.

New short novels. Aswell, M. L. W. ed.

New tales of space and time. Healy, R. J. ed.

New writing (Periodical)
Best stories; ed. by John Lehmann. Harcourt 1951 351p

Newhouse, Edward, 1911-
Many are called; forty-two short stories. Sloane 1951 384p

Newman, Franklin B. See Felheim, M. jt. ed.

The **nightmare.** Forester, C. S.

Night's yawning peal. Derleth, A. W. ed.

Nine short novels. Ludwig, R. M. and Perry, M. B. eds.

Nine stories. Salinger, J. D.

1954 anthology of best original short-shorts. Oberfirst, R. ed.

1952 anthology of best original short-shorts. Oberfirst, R. ed.

Nineteen from Seventeen. Seventeen (Periodical)

No but I saw the movie. De Vries, P.

No rest for Botts. Upson, W. H.

No trip like this, and other stories. Cawley, C. C.

Nobody say a word, and other stories. Van Doren, M.

Norton, Alice Mary
(ed.) Space pioneers; ed. with an introduction and notes by Andre Norton [pseud]. World Pub. 1954 294p

(ed.) Space service; ed. with an introduction and notes, by Andre Norton [pseud]. World Pub. 1953 277p

Nothing serious. Wodehouse, P. G.

Novelette; with other stories. Barker, A. L.

O

O. Henry, pseud. See Porter, William Sydney

O. Henry's best stories. Porter, W. S.

Oberfirst, Robert
(ed.) 1952 anthology of best original short-shorts. Humphries 1953 169p
(ed.) 1954 anthology of best original short-shorts; including Technique sells the short-short. Oberfirst Publications 1954 319p
Analyzed for short stories only

O'Connor, Frank, pseud. See O'Donovan, Michael

O'Donovan, Michael, 1903-
More stories by Frank O'Connor [pseud]. Knopf 1954 385p
808.83
O18
Stories of Frank O'Connor [pseud]. Knopf 1952 367p
Traveller's samples; stories and tales, by Frank O'Connor [pseud]. Knopf 1951 238p

Of men, dogs and horses. Bendrodt, J. C.

O'Faoláin, Séan, 1900-
808.3
O31
The short story. Devin-Adair 1951 370p
Analyzed for short stories only

O'Flaherty, Liam, 1897-
Two lovely beasts, and other stories; with illus. by John H. De Pol. Devin-Adair 1950 274p illus

Old man of the mountain, and seventeen other stories. Seager, A.

Old pines, and other stories. Boyd, J.

O'Meara, Walter
Tales of the two borders. Bobbs 1952 197p

Omnibus of science fiction. Conklin, G. ed.

On my honor. American girl (Periodical)

On the verge. Sandoz, M. Y.

Onís, Harriet de. See De Onís, Harriet

Open house. Parker, J. R.

Open season. Summers, J. L.

O'Rourke, Frank, 1916-
Greatest victory, and other baseball stories. Barnes, A.S. 1950 206p

O'Rourke, Frank—*Continued*
Heavenly world series, and other baseball stories. Barnes, A.S. 1952 192p
Ride west. Ballantine 1953 182p
The **other** place, and other stories of the same sort. Priestley, J. B.
The **outer** reaches. Derleth, A. W. ed.
Outlaw. Haycox, E.
Owen, Frank, 1893-
(ed.) Teen-age victory parade; illus. by William B. Ricketts. Lantern Press 1950 255p illus
Also available from Grosset
(ed.) Teen-age winter sports stories. Grosset 1949 256p

P

Pacey, Desmond, 1917-
(ed.) Book of Canadian stories; with an introduction and notes. ₁Rev. ed₁ Ryerson Press 1950 310p
Padgett, Lewis, pseud. See Kuttner, Henry
Paget, Violet, 1856-1935
Snake Lady, and other stories ₁by₁ Vernon Lee ₁pseud₁. Ed. and with an introduction by Horace Gregory. Grove 1954 288p
Palomino and other horses. Dennis, W.
Panorama. Bentley, P. E.
Parker, James Reid, 1909-
Open house; illus. by Leonard Shorthall. Doubleday 1951 219p illus
Passionate North. Sansom, W.
Paterson, Neil, 1915-
China run; a book of stories. Random House 1951 247p
Peery, William Wallace, 1910-
(ed.) 21 Texas short stories. Univ. of Tex. Press 1954 264p
Perry, Marvin B. See Ludwig, R. M. jt. ed.
Petrified planet; with an introduction by John Clark. Twayne 1952 263p
Pick, Robert, 1898-
(ed.) German stories and tales. Knopf 1954 371p
Pick of the litter. Cavanna, B. ed.
Pioneer loves. Haycox, E.
The **pioneers.** Schaefer, J. W.
Pirates, pirates, pirates. Fenner, P. R. comp.
Platt, George, 1919-
Play the field alone, and other stories. Vantage 1954 51p
Play the field alone, and other stories. Platt, G.

Poe, Edgar Allan, 1809-1849
Centenary Poe; tales, poems, criticism, marginalia and Eureka; ed. and with an introduction by Montagu Slater. McBride Co. 1950 559p
Analyzed for short stories only
The gold bug, and other tales and poems; illus. by Jacob Landau. Macmillan 1953 225p illus
Analyzed for short stories only
Poe's stories and poems; stories adapted by Ollie Depew; ed. by Herbert Spencer Robinson; illus. by Thomas G. Fraumeni. Globe Bk. 1951 257p illus
Analyzed for short stories only
Tales; with sixteen full-page illus. of the author, his family and environment and reproductions from previous editions together with an introductory biographical sketch and captions by Laura Benét. Dodd 1952 666p illus
Poe's stories and poems. Poe, E. A.
Poetry and prose. Foerster, N. ed.
Pohl, Frederik, 1919?-
(ed.) Assignment in tomorrow; an anthology; ed. and with an introduction by Frederik Pohl. Hanover House 1954 317p
(ed.) Star science fiction stories. See Star science fiction stories, no. 1-3
Poirier, W. Richard. See Ludwig, J. B. jt. ed.
Poor Cousin Evelyn. Yaffe, J.
Porter, William Sydney, 1862-1910
Complete works of O. Henry ₁pseud₁; foreword by Harry Hansen. Doubleday 1953 2v
Analyzed for short stories only
O. Henry's best stories; ed. by Lou P. Bunce. Globe Bk. 1953 297p
Possible worlds of science fiction. Conklin, G. ed.
Powell, Dawn, 1897-
Sunday, Monday and always. Houghton 1952 213p
Pratt, Fletcher, 1897-1956
(ed.) World of wonder; an introduction to imaginative literature; foreword by Edith Mirrielees. Twayne 1951 445p
Pratt, Fletcher, 1897-1956, **and De Camp,** Lyon Sprague, 1907-
Tales from Gavagan's bar; illus. by Inga. Twayne 1953 228p illus
Priestley, John Boynton, 1894-
The other place, and other stories of the same sort. Harper 1953 265p

Prize science fiction. Wollheim, D. A. ed.

Prize stories, 1919-1954. See First-prize stories, 1919-1954

Prize stories of 1950: the O. Henry awards; selected and ed. by Herschel Brickell. Doubleday 1950 325p

Prize stories of 1951: the O. Henry awards; selected and ed. by Herschel Brickell. Doubleday 1951 xxvi, 325p

No volumes issued for 1952-1953

Prize stories 1954: the O. Henry awards; selected and ed. by Paul Engle and Hansford Martin. Doubleday 1954 318p

Q

Queen, Ellery, pseud.
Calendar of crime. Little 1951 248p
(ed.) Literature of crime; stories by world-famous authors. Little 1950 405p
(ed.) Queen's awards: 5th-9th; the winners of the . . . annual detective short-story contest; sponsored by Ellery Queen's Mystery magazine. Little 1950-1954 5v
Ninth series has title: Ellery Queen's awards
Queen's Bureau of Investigation. Little 1954 228p

Queen's awards. Queen, E. pseud. ed.

Queen's Bureau of Investigation. Queen, E. pseud.

Quinn, Arthur Hobson, 1875-1944
(ed.) Wharton, E. N. J. Edith Wharton treasury

R

Rahv, Philip, 1908-
(ed.) Great Russian short novels; ed. with an introduction by Philip Rahv. Dial Press 1951 774p

Rashomon, and other stories. Akutagawa, R.

Reading fiction. Millett, F. B. ed.

Reading modern fiction. Lynskey, W. C. ed.

Reading the short story. Shaw, H. and Bement, D.

Ready, William B. 1914-
Great disciple, and other stories. Bruce Pub. 1951 158p

Reason for Ann, and other stories. Connolly, M.

Reck, Franklin Mering, 1896-
(comp.) American boy (Periodical) American boy Anthology

Red stocking, and other Christmas stories. Eggleston, M. W.

Return to Paradise. Michener, J. A.

Revolt in 2100. Heinlein, R. A.

Reward of faith. Goudge, E.

Rey, Lester del. See Del Rey, Lester

Reynolds, Mack, 1918- See Brown, F. jt. ed.

808.83
R48 *hue*
Ribalow, Harold Uriel, 1919-
(ed.) These your children; ed. with an introduction by Harold U. Ribalow. Beechhurst Press 1952 429p
(ed.) This land, these people ₍by Howard Fast and others₎ with an introduction by the editor. Beechhurst Press 1950 302p
(ed.) World's greatest boxing stories. Twayne 1952 309p

Ride west. O'Rourke, F.

Rinehart, Mary (Roberts) 1876-
Frightened wife, and other murder stories. Rinehart 1953 280p

Ringstones, and other curious tales. Wall, J. W.

Rite, Eva, pseud. See Anderson, Esther Victoria

Roberts, Sir Charles George Douglas, 1860-1943
Thirteen bears; chosen and ed. by Ethel Hume Bennett; illus. by John A. Hall. Ryerson Press 1947 254p illus

Roberts, Ralph Myron, 1915- See Strang, R. M. jt. ed.

Robot and the man. Greenberg, M. ed.

Robots have no tails. Kuttner, H.

Roche, Mazo de la. See De La Roche, Mazo

Romantic egoists. Auchincloss, L.

Rotting Hill. Lewis, W.

Rough justice. Haycox, E.

Rudnicki, Adolf, 1912-
Ascent to heaven; tr. by H. C. Stevens. Roy Pubs. 1951 204p illus

Runyon, Damon, 1880-1946
More guys and dolls; thirty-four of the best short stories by Damon Runyon, with an introduction by Clark Kinnaird. Garden City Bks. 1951 401p

Russell, Bertrand Arthur William Russell, 3d earl, 1872-
Satan in the suburbs, and other stories; illus. by Asgeir Scott. Simon & Schuster 1953 148p illus

S

Sagas of the Mounted Police. Mowery, W. B.

The Saint in Europe. Charteris, L.

Saki, pseud. See Munro, Hector Hugh

Salinger, Jerome David, 1919-
Nine stories. Little 1953 302p

Salisbury, Rachel. See Bachelor, J. M. jt. ed.

Sandoz, Maurice Yves, 1892-
On the verge; illus. by Salvador Dali. Doubleday 1950 127p illus 127p illus

Sansom, William, 1912-
Passionate North. Harcourt 1953 249p
Something terrible, something lovely. Harcourt 1954 231p
South; aspects and images from Corsica, Italy, and Southern France. Harcourt 1950 198p

"Sarban," pseud. See Wall, John W.

Saroyan, William, 1908-
The Assyrian, and other stories. Harcourt 1950 xxxix, 276p

Sartre, Jean Paul, 1905-
Intimacy, and other stories; tr. by Lloyd Alexander. New Directions 1948 270p

Satan in the suburbs, and other stories. Russell, B. A. W. R. 3d earl

Saturday evening post (Periodical)
Saturday evening post stories, 1950-1953 Random House 1950-53 4v

Saturday evening post stories, 1950-1953. Saturday evening post (Periodical)

Scandal of Father Brown. Chesterton, G. K. See Chesterton, G. K. Father Brown omnibus

Schaefer, Jack Warner, 1907-
Big range. Houghton 1953 203p
The pioneers. Houghton 1954 193p

Schneider, George W. 1917-
Clair de lune, and other stories. Vantage 1951 99p

Schorer, Mark, 1908-
(ed.) The story; a critical anthology. Prentice-Hall 1950 606p

Schramm, Wilbur Lang, 1907-
(ed.) Great short stories. Harcourt 1950 536p

Schulberg, Budd Wilson, 1914-
Some faces in the crowd; short stories. Random House 1953 308p

Science-fiction adventures in dimension. Conklin, G. ed.

Science-fiction carnival. Brown, F. and Reynolds, M. eds.

Science fiction omnibus: the best science fiction stories, 1949, 1950. Bleiler, E. F. and Dikty, T. E. eds.

Science-fiction subtreasury. Tucker, W.

Science-fiction thinking machines. Conklin, G. ed.

Scowcroft, Richard, 1916- See Stegner, W. E. jt. ed.

Scribner treasury; 22 classic tales, by Mary Raymond Shipman Andrews [and others] . . . introduction and notes by J. G. E. Hopkins. Scribner 1953 689p

Seager, Allan, 1906-
Old man of the mountain, and seventeen other stories. Simon & Schuster 1950 278p

Second Galaxy reader of science fiction. Galaxy science fiction magazine

Second Saint omnibus. Charteris, L.

Secret of Father Brown. Chesterton, G. K. See Chesterton, G. K. Father Brown omnibus

Selden, Ruth
(ed.) Ways of God and men; great stories from the Bible in world literature; ed. with an introduction. Daye 1950 403p

Selected fiction. James, H.

Selected short stories. James, H.

Selected short stories of Franz Kafka. Kafka, F.

Selected stories for teen-agers. Hazeltine, A. I. comp.

Selected tales and poems. Melville, H.

Selected writings. Melville, H.

Sessions, John A. See Hathaway, B. jt. ed.

Seton, Ernest Thompson, 1860-1946
Wild animals I have known; and 200 drawings by Ernest Seton Thompson. . . Scribner 1926 298p illus

Seventeen (Periodical)
Nineteen from Seventeen; stories from Seventeen magazine selected by Bryna Ivens. Lippincott 1952 239p
The Seventeen reader; stories and articles from Seventeen magazine; selected and ed. by Bryna Ivens. Lippincott 1951 310p illus
Analyzed for short stories only

The Seventeen reader. Seventeen (Periodical)

Sewall, Richard Benson. See Short, R. W. jt. ed.

Sex without sentiment. Winslow, T. S.

Sextet. Burnett, W. and Burnett, H. S. eds.

Shambleau, and others. Moore, C. L.

Shaw, Harry, 1905- and Bement, Douglas, 1898-1943
(eds.) Reading the short story. 2d ed. [by] Harry Shaw. Harper 1954 396p

She made the big town! And other stories. Brookhouser, F.

Steinhoff, William R. See Felheim, M. jt. ed.

Stephen Crane: an omnibus. Crane, S.

Stern, James, 1904-
Man who was loved. Harcourt 1951 234p

S 848 at

Stevenson, Robert Louis, 1850-1894
Strange case of Dr Jekyll and Mr Hyde, and other stories; illus. by W. Stein. Coward-McCann 1950 525p illus

Stewart, Beach, 1899-
(ed.) This week (Periodical) This week's short-short stories

Stories and fantasies from the Jewish past. Cohn, E.

Stories, British and American. Ludwig, J. B. and Poirier, W. R. eds.

Stories for discussion. Doty, W. L.

Stories for tomorrow. Sloane, W. M.

Stories for youth. Lass, A. H. and Horowitz, A. eds.

Stories of Christian living. Lantz, J. E. ed.

Stories of F. Scott Fitzgerald. Fitzgerald, F. S. K.

Stories of Frank O'Connor. O'Donovan, M.

Stories of sudden truth. Greene, J. I. and Abell, E. eds.

Stories of the sea. Fenner, P. R. comp.

Story (Periodical)
Story; the magazine of the short story in book form, number one-four; ed. by Whit Burnett and Hallie Burnett. McKay 1951-53 4v

The story. Schorer, M. ed.

Story; number one-four. Story (Periodical)

Story parade (Periodical)
Adventure stories from Story parade; outstanding stories of adventure. Winston 1950 314p

Story survey. Blodgett, H. W. ed.

Stout, Rex, 1886-
Triple jeopardy. Viking 1952 216p

Stowe, Aurelia
(comp.) It's a date; boy-girl stories for the teens; illus. by Eleanor Dart. Random House 1950 214p illus

Strain, Frances (Bruce)
"But you don't understand"; a dramatic series of teen-age predicaments. Appleton 1950 217p
Analyzed for short stories only

Strang, Ruth May, 1895- and Roberts, Ralph Myron, 1915-
(eds.) Teen-age tales. Heath 1954 2v illus
Analyzed for short stories only

Strange case of Dr Jekyll and Mr Hyde, and other stories. Stevenson, R. L.

Stuart, Jesse, 1907-
Clearing in the sky & other stories; woodcuts by Stanley Rice. McGraw 1950 262p illus

Sturgeon, Theodore, pseud. See Waldo, Edward Hamilton

Such darling dodos and other stories. Wilson, A.

Suckow, Ruth, 1892-
Some others and myself; seven stories and a memoir. Rinehart 1952 281p

Sullivan, Catherine J. See Stauffer, R. M. jt. ed.

808.83
S95fr

Sullivan, Richard, 1908-
Fresh and open sky, and other stories. Holt 1950 210p

Summers, Hollis Spurgeon, 1916-
(ed.) Kentucky story; a collection of short stories. Univ. of Ky. Press 1954 247p

Summers, James L. 1910-
Open season. Doubleday 1951 182p

Sun-Dog Trail and other stories. London, J.

Sunday, Monday and always. Powell, D.

Sunnier side. Jackson, C. R.

Supernatural reader. Conklin, G. and Conklin, L. T. eds.

Surtees, Robert Smith, 1803-1864
Hunting scenes; selected by Lionel Gough; with an introduction by Siegfried Sassoon. British Bk. Centre 1954 253p

Sut Lovingood. Harris, G. W.

Swallow, Alan, 1903-
(ed.) Anchor in the sea; an anthology of psychological fiction. Morrow 1947 255p

The swaying elms, and other stories. Blackburn, E. R.

The sword of Conan. Howard, R. E.

Sword of Welleran, and other tales of enchantment. Dunsany, E. J. M. D. P. 18th baron

Sykes, Christopher, 1907-
Character and situation; six short stories; introduction by Evelyn Waugh. Knopf 1950 240p

T

Taber, Gladys (Bagg) 1899-
When dogs meet people. Macrae Smith Co. 1952 237p illus

Table near the band. Milne, A. A.

Tactical exercise. Waugh, E.

Take your choice. Walsh, M.

Talbot, Daniel
(ed.) Treasury of mountaineering stories. Putnam 1954 337p

Welty, Eudora—*Continued*
Selected stories; containing all of A curtain of green, and other stories, and The wide net, and other stories; with an introduction by Katherine Anne Porter. Modern Lib. 1954 2v in 1

Werner, Heinz, 1901- See Fabricant, N. D. jt. ed.

West, Ray Benedict, 1908- **and Stallman, Robert Wooster,** 1911-
(eds.) Art of modern fiction. Rinehart 1949 652p
Analyzed for short stories only

Western Writers of America
Bad men and good; a roundup of western stories by members of the Western Writers of America; with a foreword by Luke Short ₁pseud₎. Dodd 1953 240p
Holsters and heroes; stories from the Western Writers of America; with a preface by Noel M. Loomis. Macmillan 1954 207p

Wharton, Edith Newbold (Jones) 1862-1937
Edith Wharton treasury; ed. and with an introduction by Arthur Hobson Quinn. Appleton 1950 xxxi, 581p
Analyzed for short stories only

When boyhood dreams come true. See Farrell, J. T. Further short stories

When dogs meet people. Taber, G. B.

Which grain will grow. Wolfe, D. M.

White, William Anthony Parker, 1911-
(ed.) Magazine of fantasy and science fiction. Best from Fantasy and science fiction
(ed.) Mystery Writers of America, inc. Four-&-twenty bloodhounds

White nights, and other stories. Dostoevskiĭ, F. M.

Widows of Thornton. Taylor, P. H.

Wild animals I have known. Seton, E. T.

Wild honey. Lincoln, V. E.

Will James' Book of cowboy stories. James, W.

Williams, William Carlos, 1883-
Make light of it; collected stories. Random House 1950 342p

Willingham, Calder, 1922-
Gates of hell. Vanguard 1951 190p

Wilson, Angus, 1914?-
Such darling dodos and other stories. Morrow 1950 187p

Winslow, Thyra Samter, 1893-
Sex without sentiment. Abelard-Schuman 1954 312p

Wisdom of Father Brown. Chesterton, G. K. See Chesterton, G. K. Father Brown omnibus

Wodehouse, Pelham Grenville, 1881-
Nothing serious. Doubleday 1951 222p

Wolf, Martin L.
(ed.) Gibran, K. Treasury of Kahlil Gibran

Wolfe, Don Marion, 1902-
(ed.) Which grain will grow; stories and sketches of childhood ₁by₎ Adler ₁and others₎. Cambridge Pub. Co. 1950 205p
Analyzed for short stories only
(ed.) American vanguard, 1952. See American vanguard, 1952

Wollheim, Donald A.
(comp.) Every boy's book of science-fiction; comp. and ed. by Donald A. Wollheim. Fell 1951 254p
(comp.) Flight into space; great science-fiction stories of interplanetary travel. Fell 1950 251p
(ed.) Prize science fiction; ed. with an introduction by Donald A. Wollheim. McBride Co. 1953 230p

Woman in the case, and other stories. Chekhov, A. P.

Women on the wall. Stegner, W. E.

The **word** lives on. Brentano, F. ed.

Works of God, and other stories. Berto, G.

World of wonder. Pratt, F. ed.

World's best. Burnett, W. ed.

World's best doctor stories. Fabricant, N. D. and Werner, H. eds.

World's greatest boxing stories. Ribalow, H. U. ed.

Worlds of tomorrow. Derleth, A. W. ed.

Writer's art. Stegner, W. E.; Scowcroft, R. and Ilyin, B. eds.

Writers for tomorrow. Hathaway, B. and Sessions, J. A.

Wylie, Philip, 1902-
Best of Crunch and Des. Rinehart 1954 404p
Three to be read. . . Rinehart 1951 312p

Y

Yaffe, James, 1927-
Poor Cousin Evelyn. Little 1951 269p

Yankee Doodle. Fenner, P. R. comp.

Year after tomorrow. Del Rey, L.; Matschat, C. H. and Carmer, C. L. eds.

Year's best science fiction novels, 1952-1954; ed. and with an introduction by Everett F. Bleiler and T. E. Dikty. Fell 1952-54 3v

Yisröel. Leftwich, J. ed.

Directory of Publishers

Abelard-Schuman. Abelard-Schuman, Inc, 404 4th Av, N.Y. 16

Abingdon. Abingdon Press, Hdqrs, 810 Broadway, Nashville 2, Tenn.

Am. Bk. American Book Company, 55 5th Av, N.Y. 3

Antioch Press, Yellow Springs, Ohio

Appleton. Appleton-Century-Crofts, Inc, 35 W 32d St, N.Y. 1

Arkham House, Sauk City, Wis.
Associated imprint: Mycroft & Moran

Assn. Press. Association Press (Nat. Council of Y.M.C.A's) 291 Broadway, N.Y. 7

Ballantine. Ballantine Books, Inc, 101 5th Av, N.Y. 3

Barnes, A.S. A. S. Barnes & Company, 232 Madison Av, N.Y. 16

Beechhurst Press. Beechhurst Press, Inc, 11 E 36th St, N.Y. 16

Bentley. Robert Bentley, Inc, 8 Ellery St, Cambridge 38, Mass.

Bobbs. The Bobbs-Merrill Company, Inc, 724-730 N Meridian St, Indianapolis 7

Bouregy. Bouregy & Curl, Inc, 22 E 60th St, N.Y. 22

British Bk. Centre. British Book Centre, Inc, 122 E 55th St, N.Y. 22

Bruce Pub. Bruce Publishing Company, 400 N Broadway, Milwaukee 1

Cambridge Pub. Co. Cambridge Publishing Company, 315 E 69th St, N.Y. 21

Chamberlain Press. The Chamberlain Press, Inc, P.O. Box 7713, Philadelphia

Citadel. Citadel Press, 222 4th Av, N.Y. 3

Cornell Univ. Press. Cornell University Press, 124 Roberts Pl, Cornell Heights, Ithaca, N.Y.

Coward McCann. Coward McCann, Inc, 210 Madison Av, N.Y. 16

Crowell. The Thomas Y. Crowell Company, 432 4th Av, N.Y. 16

Crown. Crown Publishers, 419 4th Av, N.Y. 16

Day. John Day Company, Inc, 210 Madison Av, N.Y. 16

Daye. Stephen Daye Press, Inc, N.Y. See Ungar

Devin-Adair. The Devin-Adair Company, 23-25 E 26th St, N.Y. 10

Dial Press. Dial Press, Inc, 461 4th Av, N.Y. 16

Dodd. Dodd, Mead & Company, Inc, 432 4th Av, N.Y. 16

Doubleday. Doubleday & Company, Inc, 575 Madison Av, N.Y. 22

Dover. Dover Publications, Inc, 920 Broadway, N.Y. 10

Duell. Duell, Sloan & Pearce, Inc, 124 E 30th St, N.Y. 16

Dutton. E. P. Dutton & Company, Inc, 300 4th Av, N.Y. 10

Exposition. The Exposition Press, Inc, 386 4th Av, N.Y. 16

Fantasy. Fantasy Publishing Company Inc, 8318-8320 Avalon Blvd, Los Angeles 3

Fantasy Press. Fantasy Press, Box 159, Reading, Pa.

Farrar, Straus. Farrar, Straus & Cudahy, Inc, 101 5th Av, N.Y. 3
Purchased Pellegrini & Cudahy

Fell. Frederick Fell, Inc, Inc, 386 4th Av, N.Y. 16

Follett. Follett Publishing Company, 1000 W Washington Blvd, Chicago 7

Funk. Funk & Wagnalls Company, 153 E 24th St, N.Y. 10

Garden City Bks. Garden City Books, 575 Madison Av, N.Y. 22
Also use imprint: Hanover House: Sun Dial

Globe Bk. Globe Book Company, Inc, 175 5th Av, N.Y. 10

Gnome Press. Gnome Press, 80 E 11th St, N.Y. 3

Greenberg. Greenberg Publisher, 201 E 57th St, N.Y. 22

Greystone. Greystone Corporation (Greystone Press) Publishers, 100 6th Av, N.Y. 13

Greystone Press. See Greystone

Grosset. Grosset & Dunlap, Inc, 1107 Broadway, N.Y. 10

Grove. Grove Press, 795 Broadway, N.Y. 3

Hanover House. See Garden City Bks.

Harcourt. Harcourt, Brace & Company, Inc, 383 Madison Av, N.Y. 17

Harper. Harper & Brothers (Pleiad Press Imprint) 49 E 33d St, N.Y. 16

Heath. D. C. Heath & Company, 285 Columbus Av, Boston 16

Heritage. Heritage Press, 595 Madison Av, N.Y. 22
Refer orders to Dial Press

Holt. Henry Holt & Company, Inc, 383 Madison Av, N.Y. 17

Houghton. Houghton Mifflin Company (Riverside Press, Cambridge) 2 Park St, Boston 7

House of Edinboro. House of Edinboro Publishers, 21 Edinboro St, Boston 11

Humphries. Bruce Humphries, Inc, Publishers, 48 Melrose St, Boston

Jewish Pub. The Jewish Publication Society of America, 222 N 15th St, Philadelphia 2

Kenedy. P. J. Kenedy & Son, 12 Barclay St, N.Y. 8

Knopf. Alfred A. Knopf, Inc, 501 Madison Av, N.Y. 22

La. State Univ. Press. Louisiana State University Press, University Station, Baton Rouge 3, La.

Lantern Press. Lantern Press, Inc, 257 4th Av, N.Y. 10

Lib. Pubs. Library Publishers, Inc, 8 W 40th St, N.Y. 18

Lippincott. J. B. Lippincott Company, 227-231 S 6th St, Philadelphia 5

Little. Little, Brown & Company, 34 Beacon St, Boston 6

Liveright. Liveright Publishing Corporation 386 4th Av, N.Y. 16

Longmans. Longmans, Green & Company, Inc, 55 5th Av, N.Y. 3

McBride. Medill McBride Company. See Crown

McBride Co. The McBride Company, Inc, 200 E 37th St, N.Y. 16

MacDonald & Co. MacDonald & Company (Publishers) Ltd, 16 Maddox St, London W 1

McGraw. McGraw-Hill Book Company, Inc, 330 W 42d St, N.Y. 36

McKay. David McKay Company, Inc, 55 5th Av, N.Y. 3

Macmillan. The Macmillan Company, 60 5th Av, N.Y. 11

McMullen. The Declan X McMullen Company, Inc, 839 Stewart Av, Garden City, N.Y.

Macrae Smith Co. Macrae Smith Company, Lewis Tower Bldg, 225 S 15th St, Philadelphia 2

Meador. Meador Publishing Company, 324 Newbury St, Boston 15

Merlin. Merlin Press, Inc, 250 W 57th St, N.Y. 19
Books distributed by Greenberg

Messner. Julian Messner, Inc, Publishers, 8 W 40th St, N.Y. 18

Modern Lib. Modern Library, Inc, 457 Madison Av, N.Y. 22

Moody Press. The Moody Press (The Moody Bible Institute of Chicago) 820 N LaSalle St, Chicago 10

Morrow. William Morrow & Company, Inc, 425 4th Av, N.Y. 16

Mycroft & Moran. See Arkham House

Nelson. Thomas Nelson & Sons, Copewood & Davis Sts, Camden, N.J.

New Directions, Norfolk, Conn.

Noonday. Noonday Press, 80 E 11th St, N.Y. 3

Oberfirst Pblns. Oberfirst Publications, Ocean City, N.J.

Oxford. Oxford University Press, 16-00 Pollitt Drive, Fair Lawn, N.J.

Oxford Bk. Co. Oxford Book Company, 222 4th Av, N.Y. 3

Pageant Press. Pageant Press, Inc, 130 W 42d St, N.Y. 36

Pamphlet Distributing. The William-Frederick Press Pamphlet Distributing Company, 313-315 W 35th St, N.Y. 1

Pellegrini & Cudahy. See Farrar, Straus

Prentice-Hall. Prentice-Hall, Inc, Route 9W, Englewood Cliffs, N.J.

Putnam. G. P. Putnam's Sons, 210 Madison Av, N.Y. 16

Random House. Random House, Inc, Promotion Dept, 457 Madison Av, N.Y. 22

Regnery. Henry Regnery Company, Publishers, 20 W Jackson Blvd, Chicago 4

Rinehart. Rinehart & Company, Inc, 232 Madison Av, N.Y. 16

Rodale. Rodale Books, Inc, 6th & Minor Sts, Emmaus, Pa.

Ronald. The Ronald Press Company, 15 E 26th St, N.Y. 10

Roy Pubs. Roy Publishers, 30 E 74th St, N.Y. 21

Rutgers Univ. Press. Rutgers University Press, New Brunswick, N.J.

Ryerson Press. Ryerson Press (United Church Publishing House) 299 Queen St, W. Toronto 2B

Scribner. Charles Scribner's Sons, 597-599 5th Av, N.Y. 17

Seymour. Ralph Fletcher Seymour, 410 S Michigan Av, Chicago 5

Shasta Pubs. 5525 S Blackstone, Chicago 37

Sheed. Sheed & Ward, Inc, 840 Broadway, N.Y. 3

Sherwin Cody Associates, Dobbs Ferry, N.Y.

Simon & Schuster. Simon & Schuster, Inc, 630 5th Av, N.Y. 20
Distribute Greystone Press Bks.

Sloane. William Sloane Associates, Inc, 425 4th Av, N.Y. 16

Stackpole Co. Stackpole Company, Telegraph Press Bldg, Cameron & Kelker, Harrisburg, Pa.

Stanford Univ. Press. Stanford University Press, Stanford, Calif.

Storm. Storm Publishers, Inc, 80 E 11th St, N.Y. 3

Sun Dial. Sun Dial Press, N.Y. See Garden City Bks.

Temple Pubs. Temple Publishers, McLachlen Bldg, 10th & G Sts, NW, Washington, D.C.

Thames (N.Y.) Thames & Hudson Publishers, Inc, 424 Madison Av, N.Y. 17
Refer orders to Vanguard

Twayne. Twayne Publishers, Inc, 31 Union Sq, W, N.Y. 3

Ungar. Freedrick Ungar Publishing Company, 105 E 24th St, N.Y. 10
Purchased Stephen Daye, Inc

Univ. of Kan. City Press. University of Kansas City Press, Kansas City 4, Mo.
Books distributed and also published jointly by Twayne

Univ. of Ky. Press. University of Kentucky Press, McVey Hall, Lexington 29, Ky.

Univ. of N.C. Press. University of North Carolina Press, Box 510, Chapel Hill, N.C.

Univ. of S.C. Press. University of South Carolina Press, Columbia 1, S.C.

Univ. of Tex. Press. University of Texas Press, Austin 12, Tex.

Vanguard. Vanguard Press, Inc, 424 Madison Av, N.Y. 17

Vantage. Vantage Press, Inc, 120 W 31st St, N.Y. 1

Viking. The Viking Press, Inc, 18 E 48th St, N.Y. 17

Wagner, J.F. Joseph F. Wagner, Inc, 53 Park Pl, N.Y. 7

Washburn. Ives Washburn, Inc, Publishers, 55 5th Av, N.Y. 3

Watts, F. Franklin Watts, Inc, 699 Madison Av, N.Y. 21

Westminster Press. Westminster Press, Witherspoon Bldg, Philadelphia 7

Wilcox & Follett. See Follett

William-Frederick Press. See Pamphlet Distributing

Winston. John C. Winston Company, 1006-1020 Arch St, Philadelphia 7

World Pub. The World Publishing Company, 2231 W 110th St, Cleveland 2

Wyn. A. A. Wyn, Inc, 23 W 47th St, N.Y. 36

Yale Univ. Press. Yale University Press, 143 Elm St, New Haven 7, Conn.